READING RESEARCH AT WORK

D1194858

READING RESEARCH AT WORK

Foundations of Effective Practice

edited by

KATHERINE A. DOUGHERTY STAHL
MICHAEL C. MCKENNA

Foreword by Lesley Mandel Morrow

THE GUILFORD PRESS
New York   London

© 2006 The Guilford Press
A Division of Guilford Publications, Inc.
72 Spring Street, New York, NY 10012
www.guilford.com

Printed in the United States of America

This book is printed on acid-free paper.

Last digit is print number: 9 8 7 6 5 4 3 2 1

Library of Congress Cataloging-in-Publication Data

Reading research at work : foundations of effective practice / edited by Katherine A.
Dougherty Stahl, Michael C. McKenna.
   p. cm.
  Includes bibliographical references and index.
  ISBN-10: 1-59385-299-1   ISBN-13: 978-1-59385-299-3 (trade paper)
  ISBN-10: 1-59385-300-9   ISBN-13: 978-1-59385-300-6 (trade cloth)
  1. Reading—Evaluation. 2. Reading—Code emphasis approaches. 3. Stahl, Steven A.
I. Stahl, Katherine A. Dougherty. II. McKenna, Michael C.
  LB1050.42.R434 2006
  372.48—dc22

                                               2005035082

About the Editors

Katherine A. Dougherty Stahl, EdD, is Assistant Professor in the Language and Literacy Division of the Department of Curriculum and Instruction at the University of Illinois at Urbana–Champaign. Her research interests focus on reading acquisition, including reading fluency and reading comprehension of novice readers. Dr. Stahl has taught in public elementary and middle school classrooms for over 25 years.

Michael C. McKenna, PhD, is Thomas G. Jewell Professor of Reading at the University of Virginia. He has authored, coauthored, or edited 15 books and more than 80 articles, chapters, and technical reports on a range of literacy topics. Dr. McKenna's research has been sponsored by the National Reading Research Center and the Center for the Improvement of Early Reading Achievement. He also serves on the editorial board of *Reading Research Quarterly*. Dr. McKenna's research interests include comprehension in content settings, reading attitudes, technology applications, and beginning reading.

Contributors

Original chapters only; authors of previously published papers are not included in this list.

Marilyn Jager Adams, PhD, Solilioquy Learning, Needham Heights, Massachusetts

Richard C. Anderson, EdD, Department of Educational Psychology, University of Illinois at Urbana–Champaign, Champaign, Illinois

Eurydice B. Bauer, PhD, Department of Curriculum and Instruction, University of Illinois at Urbana–Champaign, Champaign, Illinois

Isabel L. Beck, PhD, School of Education and Learning Research and Development Center, University of Pittsburgh, Pittsburgh, Pennsylvania

Linnea C. Ehri, PhD, Department of Educational Psychology, The Graduate Center, City University of New York, New York, New York

Janet S. Gaffney, PhD, Department of Special Education, University of Illinois at Urbana–Champaign, Champaign, Illinois

Georgia Earnest García, PhD, Department of Curriculum and Instruction, University of Illinois at Urbana–Champaign, Champaign, Illinois

James Hoffman, PhD, Department of Curriculum and Instruction, University of Texas, Austin, Texas

Melanie R. Kuhn, PhD, Graduate School of Education, Rutgers–The State University of New Jersey, New Brunswick, New Jersey

Marjorie Y. Lipson, PhD, Department of Education, University of Vermont, Burlington, Vermont

Michael C. McKenna, PhD, Department of Curriculum, Instruction, and Special Education, Curry School of Education, University of Virginia, Charlottesville, Virginia

Margaret G. McKeown, PhD, School of Education and Learning Research and Development Center, University of Pittsburgh, Pittsburgh, Pennsylvania

Bruce A. Murray, PhD, Department of Curriculum and Teaching, Auburn University, Auburn, Alabama

William Nagy, PhD, School of Education, Seattle Pacific University, Seattle, Washington

Jean Osborn, MEd, Bureau of Educational Research, University of Illinois at Urbana–Champaign, Champaign, Illinois

Scott G. Paris, PhD, School of Education, University of Michigan, Ann Arbor, Michigan

P. David Pearson, PhD, Graduate School of Education, University of California, Berkeley, California

Timothy Rasinski, PhD, Department of Teaching, Leadership, and Curriculum Studies, Kent State University, Kent, Ohio

Paula J. Schwanenflugel, PhD, Department of Educational Psychology, School of Education, University of Georgia, Athens, Georgia

Judith A. Scott, PhD, Department of Education, University of California, Santa Cruz, California

Cynthia Hynd Shanahan, EdD, Department of Curriculum and Instruction and Council on Teacher Education, University of Illinois at Chicago, Chicago, Illinois

Timothy Shanahan, PhD, Center for Literacy, University of Illinois at Chicago, Chicago, Illinois

Katherine A. Dougherty Stahl, EdD, Department of Curriculum and Instruction, University of Illinois at Urbana–Champaign, Champaign, Illinois

Keith E. Stanovich, PhD, Department of Human Development and Applied Psychology, University of Toronto, Toronto, Ontario, Canada

Paula J. Stanovich, PhD, Department of Special Education, Graduate School of Education, Portland State University, Portland, Oregon

Barbara M. Taylor, EdD, Department of Curriculum and Instruction and Minnesota Center for Reading Research, University of Minnesota, Minneapolis, Minnesota

Qiuying Wang, PhD, Department of Literacy Education, School of Teaching and Curriculum Leadership, Oklahoma State University, Stillwater, Oklahoma

Foreword

Steven Stahl was a husband, son, and father. He was a quiet man, a kind man, and a gentleman. Steve was an outstanding academic who died tragically at the peak of his career. In his short life he made important, lasting contributions to the field of literacy, advancing our profession immeasurably on many fronts. Yet he had so much more to give.

I am honored to write the foreword to this book, featuring some of the most important writings of Steven Stahl. I first knew Steve from reading his work and meeting him at conferences. I got to know him personally and had the valuable privilege of working with him professionally when he graciously invited me to be an investigator on his grant from the Interagency Educational Research Initiative (IERI) dealing with Fluency-Oriented Reading Instruction. The work was characteristically innovative. Also typical of Steve's undertakings are the important results and their consequent implications for practice.

The volume you are about to read creates a rich model for literacy instruction. Some of the most important pieces of work created by Steven Stahl and his vision for what works in classrooms to help children become better readers are included here. The volume presents Steve's broad perspective about how we learn to read. The five areas identified by the National Reading Panel report as those needed to become a competent reader are addressed. Steve had conducted investigations in each of these areas before the Panel issued its report, and his findings influenced the Panel's. He was characteristically ahead of his time in his thinking about the teaching of reading.

The editors of this volume, Katherine A. Dougherty Stahl, Steve's wife, and Michael C. McKenna, his close friend and colleague, have borrowed an interesting format from Keith E. Stanovich's *Progress in Understanding Reading: Scientific Foundations and New Frontiers* (2000). Each section of this book is situated around one or two articles written by Steven Stahl. One or more scholars in the field of literacy begin each section with a broad historical and theoretical context for what is to come. If the section deals with comprehension, for example, historical and theoretical contexts for that topic are provided first. The authors describe the evolution of knowledge in the domain being discussed. At this point a work by Steven Stahl is presented about the topic in question. The subsequent chapter in each section is written by one or more different authors with expertise in the topic and includes a discussion of Steve's research, other recent research in that area, the implications for instruction, and directions for future study. This format provides an interchange of ideas and perspectives that is both rich and rare. The format of the book reflects Steve's love for discussing intellectual issues about reading. He especially liked to talk about the controversies involved. The editors have selected a group of the best literacy academics in the country, all of whom worked with Steve during his career. Now they are participants again in a signal volume about his important work. The organization for the book makes it a current and a necessary read for those involved in literacy development. The book deals with history, theory, research, policy, and practice.

Part I deals with instructional trends prevalent in literacy instruction during the whole language era. In this section current issues are raised about the difficulties with some of the research dealing with the topic of whole language and how shifts begin to occur in reading instruction. The selections in this section make clear that Steve had the courage to confront difficult and controversial issues when it was unpopular to do so.

Part II explores early reading acquisition and the issues surrounding phonological awareness and phonics instruction. Steve seemed always to be at the cutting edge of reading instruction, and in many cases he led the way for the rest of us. A cursory check of the publication dates of the articles reprinted here reveals that he grasped important issues long before most others were thinking about them.

Part III deals with fluency. This is an area in which Steve has made an especially strong impact. Very little scientific research had been done in this area prior to the grant that Steve received from IERI. He was able to begin the grant, see it scale up to several states, and observe positive results for the treatment groups. As the results of this investigation are published, they will be a strong influence on instruction related to fluency, a long-neglected area of reading instruction in this country. Unfortunately, Steve will not be able to see this work to completion.

Vocabulary, another area that is often afforded too little emphasis considering its importance, is addressed in Part IV. The research study by Stahl and Fairbanks was probably Steve's earliest recognized contribution to the field of reading. It was and remains a landmark investigation. In 1986, Steve was working in an area to which few other scholars were attending, and now it is one of the five elements identified by the National Reading Panel as a predictor of reading success—yet another example of Steve's grasp and insight. Vocabulary research was a lifetime passion for Steve. Although he gained exemplary recognition for his work in phonics, he published a greater number of articles and book chapters on the topic of vocabulary. It is reassuring to see this body of work revisited and its impact appraised anew.

Part V includes an article that bridges the areas of comprehension and vocabulary. Steve and his colleagues had received an important grant in the area of comprehension only months before his death. In Chapters 19 and 26, this research is discussed. Although Steve's death prevented him from carrying out this project, his influence is evident.

Part VI, the last section in the book, deals with assessment, a topic that is tremendously difficult for all reading educators. What are appropriate types and uses of assessment to guide reading instruction? It was so like Steve to seek out the truly challenging questions, and his contributions to this area are substantive. The articles in this section exemplify his thinking on the subject, and he lived long enough to see an assessment text appear in print as well.

This book is rich with issues, instructively illuminated by Steve and by his colleagues—all of them outstanding contributors to the field of literacy. In each section, Steve's original work, used to anchor the commentary of others, appeared in the most prestigious journals in our field, including *Review of Educational Research, Pea-*

body Journal of Education, Journal of Educational Psychology, Reading Research Quarterly, and *Journal of Literacy Research*. His work always asked the most important questions. It always employed scientific and evidence-based research designs and analyses, and applied them impeccably. Most important, it always embraced the advancement of children's reading as its principal rationale.

Steve knew that reading was not a simple task but a process that required complex integration of multiple strategies. He wanted to find out about what works for children and what works for teachers in real classrooms. He was a realist, however, and appreciated that instructional approaches must be easy to implement in order to be sustainable. They cannot, he believed, greatly disrupt present routines if they are to become a part of those routines.

I feel fortunate that I had the opportunity to come to know Steve Stahl both as a person and as a professional. I learned a great deal about research design and analysis from him. It was a joy and a wonder to watch him solve problems that appeared insoluble. He made it seem easy by talking through the issues and evaluating alternatives.

Steve was the quintessential professor. A little absent-minded perhaps, his papers often scattered about, but he knew where everything was! A little "last minute" perhaps when it came to completing a task, but the task was always completed in an exemplary manner. His intelligence enabled him to gather all the pieces, big and small, related to an important research project and jigsaw them at the last moment into a brilliant piece of work.

Steve was presented with the William S. Gray Citation of Merit award for distinguished lifetime achievement in the field of literacy at the research awards banquet for the International Reading Association, held in Reno, Nevada, on Wednesday, May 5, 2004. I presided over the event as president of the IRA. His parents and daughter were at the banquet to receive the award, because Steve was too ill to travel. The next day we received the news that Steve had passed away early Thursday morning, May 6, 2004. At the closing session of the conference, I was able to honor Steve as we all stood for a moment of silent reflection to think in reverence about this kind gentleman who had contributed so much to the field of literacy. It is fitting that this volume permits those reflections to continue well into the future.

LESLEY MANDEL MORROW, PhD
Rutgers University

REFERENCE

Stanovich, K. E. (2000). *Progress in understanding reading: Scientific foundations and new frontiers.* New York: Guilford Press.

Preface

The bumper sticker read, "If you can read this, thank a teacher." But what does it mean? Does it mean that if you can mouth the words—/if/ /yü/ /keɪn/ /rid/ /this/ /thaŋk/ /eɪ/ /ticher/—you can read it? Or does it mean that if you can read this bumper sticker, a teacher taught you to do so and you should be grateful? Or does it mean that you understand the political and social implications of that bumper sticker—namely, that it was produced by a group who supports teachers; that it was probably put on the car by a teacher, who feels that teachers are underappreciated and that they should be more appreciated? The crazy thing is that you probably understood all of those meanings and did not have to think too seriously to come up with them. And, yes, for all of those different kinds of "reading," you probably should thank a teacher.

That we can simultaneously understand reading at all these levels—decoding the words, comprehending the message, and understanding the political and social context of the message—is fairly amazing. But it is no more amazing than any number of feats that the human body and mind can do. We do all this, and we do it without that much thought.

Where reading education gets in trouble is when we try to make things too simple. When we say that reading is only _____ (you can fill in the blank), then we get into trouble, because we are surely leaving something out. And when we leave something out, then children do not achieve as well as when we teach the "all" of reading. So that is the message of this book: to understand how to teach reading, we need to understand what it is, not just some of it, but all of it.

This passage was written by Steve as an introduction to a book that we planned to write together about reading instruction. Although Steve's illness prohibited the completion of any more than an introduction to that book, the collection of Steve's work has contributed to our understanding of each level of reading described in that passage. At all times, he was driven by the goal of assisting learners to become better readers. He consistently asked himself and other researchers, "How does this research help teachers help children become better readers?" As an instructor, he worked to ensure that teachers received access to the knowledge that makes "best practices" in the classroom possible. Overall, his contributions to research and practice have helped move the field of literacy education forward.

This collection is a celebration of Steve's work and the work of his colleagues and students. Although there are still many questions to be answered about reading instruction, we should never lose sight of all that we have learned. Steve's investigation of instructional trends (Stahl, 1998; Stahl & Miller, 1989), his meta-analyses (Ehri, Nunes, Stahl, & Willows, 2001; Ehri & Stahl, 2001; Stahl & Fairbanks, 1986), and his research syntheses (Kuhn & Stahl, 2003; Stahl, 1988, 1992) mark what we have learned as a field. His research interests were multifaceted, incorporating the five key domains selected as Reading First priorities: phonemic awareness, phonics, vocabulary, and, most recently, fluency and comprehension.

This volume consists of six parts. It begins with a look at instructional trends; the middle four sections then incorporate the five Reading First domains; and the volume concludes with a section on assessment. Steve's work in each area is used as a prototype or springboard for discussion by other researchers. Each part begins with an introductory chapter that provides a broad historical and theoretical context for that particular domain. The authors of the context-building chapters have long-standing records of research interests in their domain. These chapters describe the evolution of our knowledge in that domain. They also provide the theoretical background for the section. Next, there is a chapter that was written by Steve, usually in association with colleagues or students. The chapters that follow Steve's discuss the implications of his research and other recent research in that domain, emphasizing the authors' recent research. These chapters emphasize instructional implications as well as research implications.

This format is an adaptation based on Keith E. Stanovich's book *Progress in Understanding Reading: Scientific Foundations and New Frontiers* (2000). I am indebted to Keith for his organizational model. In addition, we received the chapter by Keith and Paula J. Stanovich early enough in the process to send it to other contributors who had questions about the appropriate voice for a text with this structure.

We wanted this book to be a tribute to the contributions made by Steve within the larger world of reading research. Steve worked in some capacity with all three large federally funded reading centers, the Center for the Study of Reading, the National Reading Research Center (principal investigator) and the Center for the Improvement of Early Reading Achievement (CIERA; co-director). The work he did during his career contributed to our body of knowledge about reading instruction, but more important, it reflected the work of a particular generation of reading research (1985–2005).

The sections are organized by theme, not chronologically. Chapters written by Steve were chosen based on two considerations: (1) their influence as indicated in the Social Sciences Citation Index and (2) contemporary relevance to the ongoing research in a particular domain. There were a few difficult choices. Steve's "P word" article was frequently reprinted and has been widely circulated among teachers (Stahl, 1992). And on a personal note, I fell in love with Steve upon reading it, long before we ever met. However, the selection chosen for this volume (Stahl, Duffy-Hester, & Stahl, 1998) discussed a wider range of specific phonics practices with explicit connections to research. This enabled Linnea C. Ehri (see Chapter 10) to make connections to the later findings by the National Reading Panel. It was also difficult to select a chapter on comprehension. Until Steve's recently renewed interest in comprehension, his comprehension work had been melded with vocabulary. The article by Stahl, Jacobson, Davis, and Davis (1989) was written fairly early in Steve's career. Contrasting this work with his final project (see Chapters 19 and 26), we are able to see a change in how he viewed comprehension and the ways that the field has changed as a result of the research during the intervening 17 years.

Education today is being strongly influenced by No Child Left Behind and Reading First. These policies call for teachers to use instructional procedures that are supported by scientific evidence. The definition and application of such evidence are controversial issues in academic and policy circles. These controversies result in confusion among teachers and are reflected in the pendulum shifts in instructional trends that we observe over time. Our volume opens with a discussion of these trends. Steve took an active role in investigating and reporting on these trends during his career (McKenna, Stahl, & Reinking, 1994; Stahl, 1998, 1999; Stahl, McKenna, & Pagnucco, 1994; Stahl & Miller, 1989). The Stahl and Miller meta-analysis provided scientific evidence that influenced the course of the whole-language debates of the early 1990s. Michael C. McKenna shared these interests with Steve and they collaborated on the "reading war" investigations of the mid-1990s. Mike provides the historical backdrop for Part I. Keith and Paula Stanovich eloquently address the political and practical impact of Stahl and Miller (1989) and conclude with the ways that policymakers and teachers can use converging evidence to promote and implement instructional practice that will benefit students. Timothy Shanahan uses Stahl (1998) as a springboard to discuss the current policies and political climate influencing reading instruction. He addresses the ways that No Child Left Behind and Reading First are influencing classroom practice and student achievement. Current policies are discussed within a broad historical and political context.

The accumulation of knowledge in the Reading First domains is addressed in the middle four sections of this book. Throughout his career, Steve conducted seminal research in all five domains. His interests over time tend to reflect our interests as a field. His dissertation and first published article examined the influence of vocabulary instruction on comprehension. During the 1980s, he extended this line of investigation and continued his work with struggling readers. In 1988 he took a temporary post at the University of Illinois at Urbana–Champaign, the site of the Center for the Study of Reading (CSR). The center produced many research projects that focused on comprehension (see Chapter 17). During that year Steve had an opportunity to develop influential relationships with David Pearson, Richard Anderson, and William Nagy. In Nagy, he found a friend and colleague who shared his passion for vocabulary. Nagy's knowledge of linguistics and vocabulary acquisition enhanced the work that Steve was doing with comprehension (see Chapter 14). Pearson and Anderson's work on schema theory and comprehension instruction changed Steve and our field. In addition, their leadership styles influenced Steve. Throughout his career, he tried to emulate the mentoring and collaborative atmosphere that he observed in his work during that year with Pearson (as dean of the College of Education) and Anderson (as director of CSR).

During this time period, CSR was the base for several other researchers who would profoundly influence reading research, instructional practice, and Steve (Scott, Rosenshine, Raphael, García, and Palincsar, to name just a few). It was also during this year that Steve worked with Fran Lehr and Jean Osborn to synthesize the empirical evidence reported in *Beginning to Read* (Adams, 1990) into a teacher-friendly summary. His interactions with Adams, Osborn, and Lehr, during the period of the whole language debates and the attention drawn to his findings from the Stahl and Miller (1989) meta-analysis, provoked his interest in phonics and phonemic awareness during the 1990s.

In 1990, Steve took a position in the Reading Education Department at the University of Georgia. Steve's student, Bruce A. Murray, shared Steve's interest in phonemic awareness and alphabetics. While Bruce was a student, they conducted the study that was reported in the *Journal of Educational Psychology* (see Chapter 7). As a field we learned a great deal about the role of phonemic awareness during the 1990s. In Chapter 8, Bruce reports what we have learned since the 1994 article, and he describes his most recent work, including his Test of Phoneme Identities and a three-step phoneme-direct model of instruction.

During the 1990s, we observed the pendulum swinging from the whole language movement to the phonics craze. Excessive amounts of instructional time were being spent engaging in phonics activities. This mania prompted Steve to write a series of articles, including the one on the "P word" (Stahl, 1992) and the article that is reprinted as Chapter 9. In 1999, Linnea Ehri invited Steve to participate in the phonics meta-analysis that was being conducted by the National Reading Panel Subgroup for Alphabetics. In Chapter 10, she summarizes those findings and their instructional implications. She also shares some of her most recent results from a longitudinal study at the Benchmark School (Ehri, Satlow, & Gaskins, 2004).

Steve spent a great deal of time in classrooms. While writing the papers about phonics instruction, he was observing in classrooms. He was also the director of the University of Georgia Reading Clinic. This enabled him to observe a wide range of tutoring sessions at least twice a week. Steve was an advocate of Chall's (1983) stage model. As a result, it became frustrating for him to see students who had mastered the alphabetic system continue to be drilled on letter–sound relationships or more obscure, irregular letter combinations while fluency with connected text was neglected. The work of both Adams (1990) and Stanovich (1986) had made it clear that it was important for developing readers to encounter volumes of text. Steve worried most about "Matthew effects" for struggling readers who were being cheated of opportunities for exposure to vast amounts of complex print. He turned to the work on automaticity by Samuels (1985) and classroom studies by Hoffman (1987) and Rasinski, Padak, Linek, and Sturtevant (1994) to develop a construct that would enable classroom teachers to deliberately foster reading fluency. Chapter 12 is a reprint of a recent article (Stahl & Heubach, 2005) that chronicles the development, earliest implementation, and research on Fluency-Oriented Reading Instruction (FORI). This research was conducted while Steve was a principal investigator for the National Reading Research Center.

At about this time, Jeanne Chall sent Steve a promising student from Harvard. Melanie R. Kuhn became Steve's advisee, friend, and colleague. Today, Melanie is a key member of the team carrying on the large-scale studies of FORI that have been funded by the Interagency Education Research Initiative. She and Paula J. Schwanenflugel share the most recent findings from the FORI studies and their instructional implications in Chapter 13.

Part IV of this volume was the first and easiest section to pull together. According to a count by Marilyn Jager Adams and Jean Osborn (see Chapter 6), Steve published more articles related to vocabulary than any other topic. It interested him from the beginning to the final days of his professional journey. According to the Social Science Citation Index, Stahl and Fairbanks (1986) is Steve's most frequently cited work. William Nagy and Judith A. Scott frame this piece within its historical context, sharing both theoretical and instructional implications. Margaret G. McKeown and Isabel L. Beck focus on the instructional implications of Stahl and Fairbanks, as well as a series of more recent studies (including their own recent work) that provide converging evidence on effective vocabulary instruction.

In 2000, Steve joined P. David Pearson as co-director of CIERA. CIERA was funded for 5 years and focused on early reading. Some of the products of CIERA were the series of studies on "schools that beat the odds" (Taylor, Pearson, Clark, & Walpole, 2000), teacher change (Birdyshaw, Pesko, Wixson, & Yochum, 2002), and policy studies (McDaniel, Sims, & Miskel, 2001; Valencia & Wixson, 2001). CIERA sponsored annual summer institutes to disseminate research to other academics, policymakers, and teachers. CIERA administrators and investigators organized a forum to discuss cutting-edge ideas and studies on reading comprehension assessment. They invited researchers from different fields (educational psychology, special education, curriculum and instruction, cognitive psychology) to participate. It resulted in the edited volume (Paris & Stahl, 2005) that is the source of Stahl and Hiebert (2005) reprinted here as Chapter 25. For Steve, CIERA was also the source of a community of colleagues whom he respected and enjoyed socially. As Steve's wife, I initially worried that the commitment to CIERA would be a strain on Steve's health. Instead, the collaborative community of researchers and the constant stream of ideas surrounding CIERA invigorated Steve and provided a purpose for living. As the days of CIERA funding were winding to a close, Steve's discussions with Barbara M. Taylor, P. David Pearson, and Georgia Earnest García resulted in a proposal for investigating comprehension instruction described in Chapter 19 and the comprehension assessment system described in Chapter 26.

I was a classroom teacher when I met Steve in 1996. During the 8 years I knew Steve, I was privileged to meet and get to know his colleagues. I have been amazed by the ability of these scholars to pursue multiple paths of interest simultaneously. Chapter 23 discusses the assessment model that Steve developed during his years as director of the University of Georgia Reading Clinic. These weekly experiences at the reading clinic enabled Steve to keep students as the focus of whatever other research he pursued. I believe it also helped him relate well to teachers in his research pursuits, lectures, and publications. He shared their successes, frustrations, and questions.

Steve was a generous mentor and scholar. He always viewed himself as a teacher and member of a research community. In his eyes, it was important to be generous because the value of his own work was contingent upon the collective knowledge accumulated by the larger research community. Steve enjoyed engaging in intellectual banter, either in print or in person, but he cherished his relationships with his colleagues and students. He was a man who found his own identity through his work. In this book, we take a look at two decades of progress in understanding reading processes and instruction through the eyes of Steven Stahl and his friends, who happened to be his colleagues and the brightest and best in the field.

KATHERINE A. DOUGHERTY STAHL

REFERENCES

Adams, M. J. (1990). *Beginning to read: Thinking and learning about print*. Cambridge, MA: The MIT Press.

Birdyshaw, D., Pesko, E., Wixson, K., & Yochum, N. (2002). From policy to practice: Using literacy standards in early reading instruction. In M. L. Kamil, J. B. Manning, & H. J. Walberg (Eds.), *Successful reading instruction* (pp. 75–99). Greenwich, CT: Information Age.

Chall, J. S. (1983). *Stages of reading development*. New York: McGraw-Hill.

Ehri, L., Nunes, S., Stahl, S., & Willows, D. (2001). Systematic phonics instruction helps students learn to read: Evidence from the National Reading Panel's meta-analysis. *Review of Educational Research, 71*, 393–447.

Ehri, L., Satlow, E., & Gaskins, I. (2004). *Word reading instruction: Graphophonemic analysis strengthens the keyword analogy method for struggling readers*. Manuscript submitted for publication.

Ehri, L., & Stahl, S. (2001). Beyond smoke and mirrors: Putting out the fire. *Phi Delta Kappan, 83*, 17–20.

Hoffman, J. (1987). Rethinking the role of oral reading. *Elementary School Journal, 87*, 367–373.

Kuhn, M. R., & Stahl, S. A. (2003). Fluency: A review of developmental and remedial practices. *Journal of Educational Psychology, 95*, 3–22.

McDaniel, J. E., Sims, C. H., & Miskel, C. G. (2001). The national reading policy arena: Policy actors and perceived influence. *Educational Policy, 15*, 92–114.

McKenna, M., Stahl, S., & Reinking, D. (1994). A critical commentary on research, politics, and whole language. *Journal of Reading Behavior, 26*, 211–233.

Paris, S. G., & Stahl, S. (2005). *Children's reading comprehension and assessment*. Mahwah, NJ: Erlbaum.

Rasinski, T. V., Padak, N., Linek, W., & Sturtevant, E. (1994). Effects of fluency development on urban second grade readers. *Journal of Educational Research, 87*, 158–165.

Samuels, S. J. (1985). Automaticity and repeated reading. In J. Osborn, P. T. Wilson, & R. C. Anderson (Eds.), *Reading education: Foundations for a literate America* (pp. 215–230). Lexington, MA: Lexington Books.

Stahl, S. A. (1988). Is there evidence to support matching reading styles and initial reading methods?: A reply to Carbo. *Phi Delta Kappan, 70*, 317–322.

Stahl, S. A. (1992). Saying the "P" word: Nine guidelines for effective phonics instruction. *The Reading Teacher, 45*, 618–625.

Stahl, S. A. (1998). Understanding shifts in reading and its instruction. *Peabody Journal of Education, 73*, 31–67.

Stahl, S. A. (1999). Why innovations come and go (and mostly go): The case of whole language. *Educational Researcher, 28*, 13–22.

Stahl, S. A., Duffy-Hester, A. M., & Stahl, K. A. D. (1998). Everything you wanted to know about phonics (but were afraid to ask). *Reading Research Quarterly, 33*, 338–355.

Stahl, S. A., & Fairbanks, M. M. (1986). The effects of vocabulary instruction: A model-based meta-analysis. *Review of Educational Research, 56*, 72–110.

Stahl, S. A., & Heubach, K. (2005). Fluency-Oriented Reading Instruction. *Journal of Literacy Research, 37*(1), 25–60.

Stahl, S. A., & Hiebert, E. H. (2005). The "word factors": A problem for reading comprehension assessments. In S. G. Paris & S. A. Stahl (Eds.), *Children's reading comprehension and assessment* (pp. 161–186). Mahwah, NJ: Erlbaum.

Stahl, S. A., Jacobson, M. G., Davis, C. E., & Davis, R. L. (1989). Prior knowledge and difficult vocabulary in the comprehension of unfamiliar text. *Reading Research Quarterly, 24*, 27–43.

Stahl, S. A., McKenna, M. C., & Pagnucco, J. (1994). The effects of whole language instruction: An update and reappraisal. *Educational Psychologist, 29*(4), 175–185.

Stahl, S. A., & Miller, P. D. (1989). Whole language and language experience approaches to beginning reading: A quantitative research synthesis. *Review of Educational Research, 59*, 87–116.

Stanovich, K. E. (1986). Matthew effects in reading: Some consequences of individual differences in the acquisition of literacy. *Reading Research Quarterly, 21*, 360–407.

Stanovich, K. E. (2000). *Progress in understanding reading: Scientific foundations and new frontiers.* New York: Guilford Press.

Taylor, B. M., Pearson, P. D., Clark, K., & Walpole, S. (2000). Effective schools and accomplished teachers: Lessons about primary grade reading instruction in low-income schools. *Elementary School Journal, 101*, 121–166.

Valencia, S. W., & Wixson, K. K. (2001). Inside English/language arts standards: What's in a grade? *Reading Research Quarterly, 36*, 202–217.

Acknowledgments

The chapters reprinted in this volume appear as they did in their original publications, edited only for the correction of typographical errors. Appreciation is expressed for permission to reprint the following works:

Chapter 2—S. A. Stahl and P. D. Miller. (1989). Whole Language and Language Experience Approaches to Beginning Reading: A Quantitative Research Synthesis. *Review of Educational Research, 59*(1), 87–116. Copyright 1989 by the American Educational Research Association.

Chapter 4—S. A. Stahl. (1998). Understanding Shifts in Reading and Its Instruction. *Peabody Journal of Education, 73*(3 & 4), 31–67. Copyright 1998 by Lawrence Erlbaum Associates, Inc.

Chapter 7—S. A. Stahl and B. A. Murray. (1994). Defining Phonological Awareness and Its Relationship to Early Reading. *Journal of Educational Psychology, 86*(2), 221–234. Copyright 1994 by the American Psychological Association.

Chapter 9—S. A. Stahl, A. M. Duffy-Hester, and K. A. D. Stahl. (1998). Everything You Wanted to Know about Phonics (but Were Afraid to Ask). *Reading Research Quarterly, 33*(3), 338–355. Copyright 1998 by the International Reading Association.

Chapter 12—S. A. Stahl and K. Heubach. (2005). Fluency-Oriented Reading Instruction. *Journal of Literacy Research, 37*(1), 25–60. Copyright 2005 by the National Reading Conference.

Chapter 15—S. A. Stahl and M. M. Fairbanks. (1986). The Effects of Vocabulary Instruction: A Model-Based Meta-Analysis. *Review of Educational Research, 56*(1), 72–110. Copyright 1986 by the American Educational Research Association.

Chapter 18—S. A. Stahl, M. G. Jacobson, C. E. Davis, and R. L. Davis. (1989). Prior Knowledge and Difficult Vocabulary in the Comprehension of Unfamiliar Text. *Reading Research Quarterly, 24*(1), 27–43. Copyright 1989 by the International Reading Association.

Chapter 20—S. A. Stahl, C. R. Hynd, B. K. Britton, M. M. McNish, and D. Bosquet. (1996). What Happens When Students Read Multiple Source Documents in History? *Reading Research Quarterly, 31*(4), 430–456. Copyright 1996 by the International Reading Association.

Chapter 23—S. A. Stahl, M. R. Kuhn, and J. M. Pickle. (1999). An Educational Model of Assessment and Targeted Instruction for Children with Reading Problems. In D. H. Evensen and P. B. Mosenthal (Eds.), *Advances in Reading/Language Research: Vol. 6. Reconsidering the Role of the Reading Clinic in a New Age of Literacy* (pp. 249–272). Copyright 1999 by Elsevier, Inc.

Chapter 25—S. A. Stahl and E. H. Hiebert. (2005). The "Word Factors": A Problem for Reading Comprehension Assessment. In S. G. Paris and S. A. Stahl (Eds.), *Children's Reading Comprehension and Assessment* (pp. 161–186). Copyright 2005 by Lawrence Erlbaum Associates, Inc.

Contents

READING RESEARCH AT WORK

I | INSTRUCTIONAL TRENDS

1

How Shall Research Inform Reading Instruction?

The Legacy of Steven A. Stahl

Michael C. McKenna

> Even though we all have prejudices, our allegiance to a set of rules that govern scientific inquiry forces us often to reject those prejudices and conclude that we were wrong.
>
> —Steven A. Stahl (1994, p. 127)

The contributions of Steven Stahl to reading research are largely inestimable at this writing, less than a year after his death on May 6, 2004. That they have been considerable, seminal, and broad is evident. A glance at the table of contents of this volume may surprise those who associate him with a single dimension of reading. To find that he was a principal contributor to all the dimensions identified as central to reading instruction by the National Reading Panel (National Institute of Child Health and Human Development, 2000), and that were in fact labeled the "five big ideas of reading" by Ed Kame'enui and his colleagues (reading.uoregon.edu/index.php), will come as a surprise to many. In an age of increasing specialization within the scholarly community, Steve found not only depth in each of these dimensions but the breadth to appreciate their interdependence. At his death he was planning a comprehensive integration of findings that it will be our misfortune to do without.

On another level, however, Steve's contribution extended beyond the painstaking accrual of knowledge that comes from the careful application of the scientific process. During the 1990s, he grew increasingly concerned over the ways in which research informs practice, and there is no more salient example than the controversy surrounding whole language. The two articles in this section are bookends to the whole language movement. The Stahl–Miller meta-analysis appeared in the initial phase of the movement and raised important questions about the efficacy of the approaches it embraced. The article on understanding shifts in reading, which appeared in the double issue of the *Peabody Journal of Education* that I coedited with Jack Miller, is retrospective in character, reflecting the sober change that befell its author over the intervening decade.

As the poet William Blake might have put it, these two articles represent Steve's journey from innocence to experience. By innocence, I mean the belief harbored by all disciplined researchers that findings arrived at with care will enter the scholarly arena, where they will inform discussion and subsequent inquiry. His first response to the vitriol occasioned by the meta-analysis was therefore one of astonishment. The epigraph to this chapter, though written after the firestorm had started, had long been his stance as a researcher and he assumed that all other researchers embraced it with him. The responses from whole language advocates persuaded him that a science of reading instruction had not yet been realized.

These responses were of three kinds. Some researchers, such as Ray Reutzel, pursued the high road (Reutzel & Hollingsworth, 1993). They conducted well-designed investigations of their own to test and refine the conclusions reached by Stahl and Miller. In so doing, they extended the scholarly dialogue on an impartial plane, allowing findings to fall where they may. Steve applauded their approach and recognized their results, including those that favored whole language.

A second response was to contest the findings on methodological, philosophical, and epistemological grounds. Although the meta-analysis was conducted impeccably, the individual studies it included could be faulted, the definition of whole language disputed, and the entire paradigm dismissed as incommensurable with the philosophy of whole language (e.g., Edelsky, 1990). After the appearance of Stahl–Miller, a group of whole language researchers at the University of Missouri, led by Dorothy Watson, convened to formulate a strategy for responding to it. I suspect that similar meetings occurred elsewhere, and that of all the strategies discussed, the option of accepting the findings was not entertained. This was because the movement was political in nature and the instructional methods it embraced were seen to be liberating. Findings related to reading acquisition missed the point that the real goal was social emancipation (see McKenna, Stahl, & Reinking, 1994; Stahl, 1994). Dick Allington (2002) has recently charged that federal reading initiatives, such as the National Reading Panel report, are a case of ideology trumping evidence. I can think of no phrase more apt to describe the obfuscation perpetrated by whole language advocates determined to devalue the findings of Stahl–Miller.

A third and decidedly unscientific response was to ignore the findings, pursuing instead a parallel scholarly discussion that provided its participants (and countless teachers) with an intentionally distorted perspective. Though kind and conciliatory to a fault, Steve could not countenance researchers who ignored or discounted evidence that refuted their claims. My colleagues and I once referred to this practice as "selective citation" (McKenna, Robinson, & Miller, 1990, p. 3), and the Stahl–Miller meta-analysis, still one of the most frequently referenced studies of the whole language era, went eerily uncited in many of the publications generated by the whole language community. When Diane Stephens (1991) wrote her review of research underlying whole language, Stahl–Miller was not mentioned, nor was any other conflicting evidence. Steve later referred to such cherry-picking as a "perversion of science" (Stahl, 1994, p. 127), in an uncharacteristically trenchant, though wholly merited, appraisal. "We can be partisan," he wrote, "indeed, how can we be otherwise? But we need to be seen as fair" (Stahl, 1994, p. 129).

His efforts to confront wrongheaded practice with research were not confined to whole language. While the prominence of that movement dwarfed the stature of his other battles, they nevertheless demonstrate that his tilt with whole language advocates was impersonal (despite *ad hominem* attacks on him), and that it extended to issues at the peripheries of the profession. For example, he challenged the research base grounding Helen Irlen's use of tinted overlays as a cure for "scotopic sensitivity syndrome." His exchange with Marie Carbo in *Phi Delta Kappan* (Stahl, 1988) challenged the evidence underlying the need to match children to instruction based on "reading styles." His objections were typically compelling, even unassailable, but they were insufficient to deter Carbo and others who have profited from the notion. Rita Dunn took up the same cudgel in an exchange of letters appearing in *Reading Today*, and the result was equally decisive. Behind the scenes, Steve and his colleagues admonished the International Reading Association not to accept advertising for reading styles workshops and materials. IRA refused, citing free speech and censorship concerns.

Steve's belief that instructional practice must be informed to the extent possible by research findings therefore extended to all aspects of reading. It predated whole language but was clearly sharpened by it, as was his recognition that resistance to unpopular findings can be motivated by ideology as well as proprietary interests.

However, with respect to the long-term picture of educational change, Steve contended that shifts have often occurred because of a research vacuum. That is, in the absence of evidence, practitioners must rely on personal experience, educated guesses, and instinct. In the latter half of the 20th century, the lack of evidence has been due to the fact that researchers rarely launch innovations; instead, they have come onto the scene after an innovation has been implemented. By the time their findings have rendered a judgment of effectiveness, the next fad has arrived.

In his *Peabody* article, Steve articulates this premise carefully, and, like his great mentor, Jeanne Chall, he attempts to discern changes that were causally connected to policy shifts. His reasoning runs roughly thus: The whole word approach that dominated instruction prior to 1965 gave way to calls for a stronger code emphasis. After a decade, children tended to become skilled decoders, but the need to enhance their comprehension was unmet. Comprehension became the principal focus of the late 1970s and early 1980s, but while comprehension tended to improve, new worries arose about children's motivation to read. The affective dimension became the rallying cry of whole language. Steve asserts that with each transition, the useful components of the previous era were largely discarded, so that a balanced program—one that includes effective word recognition instruction, sound fostering of comprehension strategies, and the development of an intrinsic motivation to read—has never taken root.

Because Steve was principally concerned with the interplay of research and practice, he does not revisit the early 20th century and before, a period when research evidence was too scant to influence instructional decision making. He was well aware, however, that the debate over the best methods of teaching reading goes back centuries. Adams (1990) recounts Horace Mann's objection to an emphasis on the alphabetic principle, which was the mainstay of the McGuffey Readers and competing materials. Letters, he claimed, are "bloodless, ghostly apparitions" (quoted in Adams, 1990, p. 22). A century earlier, Rousseau (1764/1979) leveled a high-profile attack on John Locke (conveniently dead at the time), who in the late 17th century had suggested that letter manipulatives (dice, in fact) be used to teach reading. Robinson, Baker, and Clegg (1998), in an article that immediately precedes Steve's in the *Peabody* themed double issue, trace the debate to the mid-17th century, when John

Amos Comenius (1657) took on the phonics-oriented educators of the day, calling the use of decoding strategies a "troublesome torture of wits" (quoted in Robinson et al., 1998, p. 18). Comenius was actually the first to use the term *whole language*, and while its modern-day proponents acknowledge that his definition differed from theirs, he is nevertheless claimed as an important forerunner of the movement (Goodman, 1989).

The entry of research into the fray over the past half century has provided advocates of all stripes with a wild card to play as they will. Had the Stahl–Miller meta-analysis unambiguously supported whole language methods, its proponents would have hailed it. The mixed results were cast as a flawed message from an untrustworthy messenger. In Steve there arose a consciousness of, and a resignation to, the fact that the results of studies conducted with rigor and objectivity will not be accepted by all, even when findings converge across multiple investigations. He found consolatory the faith that many educators would in fact permit their practice to be informed by such evidence. It was for their students' sake that he labored on.

In retrospect, it is now clear that Steve's role in the whole language debate was catalyst to a new tension. By the early 1990s, policymakers unschooled in the debate itself had grown increasingly impatient with the failure of public schools to solve the problem of low reading achievement. The National Assessment of Educational Progress (NAEP) was their primary indicator of U.S. literacy levels, and the stagnant means were and are appalling. A signal event occurred after the 1992 NAEP administration, as the government for the first time decided to release scores at the state level. The collective jaw of the reading community dropped when California appeared near the bottom of participating states and territories. California had embraced whole language early on and its poor NAEP performance could not be explained by demographics. Some have argued that the situation was in reality more complex, but the obvious inference was drawn by policymakers and educators alike. When I asked Steve if he planned another article on whole language, he replied that there was no need for one, that whole language had died of natural causes in California. Indeed, it had. It was a long, tortured death, to be sure, but the wound was mortal.

Policymakers reacted to the evidence they valued—scores on high-stakes tests. They came next to question how the community of reading researchers could be at loggerheads over how to proceed. Congress had already commissioned a synthesis of available evidence on beginning reading (Adams, 1990), only to find it attacked by whole language advocates and to see its author personally vilified. Steve elaborated these trends, further exposing the whole language position, in his writings between the meta-analysis and the *Peabody* article (McKenna, Stahl, & Reinking, 1994, 1995; Stahl, 1994; Stahl, McKenna, & Pagnucco, 1994). These writings helped profile a community in which research was contested rather than shared.

The result has been a continuing controversy over just where the seat of expertise resides, with the universities or with federal agencies. In 2002, Susan Neuman (personal communication), then Assistant Secretary of Education, hinted that Steve's writings, in conjunction with the exchange appearing in *Educational Researcher* (Edelsky, 1990; McKenna, Robinson, & Miller, 1990a, 1990b; see also Pressley, 2002), had fueled an internal debate within the department. The subsequent appointment of the National Reading Panel served not only to synthesize findings in multiple dimensions of reading but to set the criterion for what would count as research.

Peer-reviewed experimental and quasi-experimental studies were the new gold standard of reading research. These somewhat draconian limitations have rankled some researchers not formally aligned with whole language (see Allington, 2002).

However, I find two metaphors apt. One equates the federal government with parents who intervene in their children's squabbles. The other is *deus ex machina* (god from the machine). When the plot of an ancient play became hopelessly complicated, a god was sometimes lowered on a boom in the final scene to solve all the characters' problems through divine intervention.

Whether they be gods or devils, the National Reading Panelists and their associates within the National Institute of Child Health and Human Development and Reading First have framed a new reality for reading research. The work of Steve Stahl was instrumental in bringing about this change, which I unhesitatingly characterize as reform. Whether we embrace the new synthesis of evidence or continue with the Hegelian dialectic of successive antitheses that emerge in spite of evidence remains to be seen.

Steve (Stahl, 1994) observed that scholars in other disciplines tend to regard the internal debates in reading with amusement. While president of Harvard, Derek Bok commented that professors of education do not receive the respect to which they believe they are entitled because they lack an organized body of knowledge on which they all agree. Until we concur on what we know and on how we can add to that knowledge, our profession will continue to teeter and may eventually be toppled by those with the power to do so. I believe that Steve Stahl has nudged us away from this precipice through disciplined inquiry, reasoned interpretation, and fair-minded critical analysis. In his untimely passing we lose not only a friend and colleague but a powerful check on the excesses of what passes for research.

REFERENCES

Adams, M. J. (1990). *Beginning to read: Thinking and learning about print*. Cambridge, MA: MIT Press.

Allington, R. L. (2002). *Big Brother and the national reading curriculum: How ideology trumped evidenced*. Portsmouth, NH: Heinemann.

Chall, J. S. (1996). American reading achievement: Should we worry? *Research in the Teaching of English*, *30*, 303–310.

Comenius, J. A. (1979). *Orbis pictus*. Whitefish, MT: Kessinger. (Original work published 1657)

Edelsky, C. (1990). Whose agenda is this anyway? A response to McKenna, Robinson, and Miller. *Educational Researcher*, *19*(8), 7–11.

Goodman, Y. M. (1989). Roots of the whole language movement. *Elementary School Journal*, *90*, 113–127.

McKenna, M. C., Robinson, R. D., & Miller, J. W. (1990a). Whole language: A research agenda for the nineties. *Educational Researcher*, *19*(8), 3–6.

McKenna, M. C., Robinson, R. D., & Miller, J. W. (1990b). Whole language and the need for open inquiry: A rejoinder to Edelsky. *Educational Researcher*, *19*(8), 12–13.

McKenna, M. C., Stahl, S. A., & Reinking, D. (1994). Critical commentary on research, politics, and whole language. *Journal of Reading Behavior*, *26*, 211–233.

McKenna, M. C., Stahl, S. A., & Reinking, D. (1995). Rejoinder to Rasinski and Padak [Letter to the Editors]. *Journal of Reading Behavior*, *27*, 111–113.

National Institute of Child Health and Human Development. (2000). *Report of the National Reading Panel. Teaching children to read: An evidence-based assessment of the scientific research literature on reading and its implications for reading instruction* (NIH Publication No. 00-4769). Washington, DC: U.S. Government Printing Office. Available online at: www. nationalreadingpanel.org

Pressley, M. (2002). *Reading instruction that works: The case for balanced teaching* (2nd ed.). New York: Guilford Press.

Reutzel, D. R., & Hollingsworth, P. M. (1993). Effects of fluency training on second graders' reading comprehension. *Journal of Educational Research, 86,* 325–331.

Robinson, R. D., Baker, E., & Clegg, L. (1998). Literacy and the pendulum of change: Lessons for the 21st century. *Peabody Journal of Education, 73*(3&4), 15–30.

Rousseau, J.-J. (1979). *Emile, or On education* (A. Bloom, Trans.). New York: Basic Books. (Original work published 1764)

Stahl, S. A. (1988). Is there evidence to support matching reading styles and initial reading methods? A reply to Carbo. *Phi Delta Kappan, 70,* 317–322.

Stahl, S. A. (1994). Is whole language "The Real Thing"? Advertisements and research in the debate on whole language. In C. B. Smith (Ed.), *Whole language: The debate* (pp. 124–142). Bloomington, IN: ERIC Clearinghouse on Reading, English, and Communication.

Stahl, S. A., McKenna, M. C., & Pagnucco, J. R. (1994). The effects of whole language instruction: An update and a reappraisal. *Educational Psychologist, 29*(4), 175–185.

Stephens, D. (1991). *Research on whole language.* Katonah, NY: Richard C. Owen.

2 Whole Language and Language Experience Approaches for Beginning Reading

A Quantitative Research Synthesis

STEVEN A. STAHL

PATRICIA D. MILLER

For at least the better part of this century, there have been voices advocating that reading instruction begin in a natural manner, using the child's own language as a bridge to beginning reading instruction (see Hildreth, 1965). These approaches have been termed *activity approaches*, *informal approaches*, *language experience approaches*, or, most recently, *whole language approaches*. These terms represent an evolution of an idea, so that a whole language approach discussed today might be very different from an activity approach discussed by Wrightstone (1951), for example. They are also manifestations of a core approach to children's learning to read, namely, that the child's attention should be focused on the communicative function of written language rather than on its form (Goodman, 1986; Goodman & Goodman, 1979; Harste, 1985; Newman, 1985).

WHOLE LANGUAGE AND LANGUAGE EXPERIENCE

Proponents of whole language approaches emphasize it as a philosophy rather than a specific method (e.g., Altwerger, Edelsky, & Flores, 1987; Goodman, 1986; Newman, 1985), making it difficult to define for review purposes. These authors and others (e.g., Grundin, 1985; Weaver, 1988) have stressed the continuity between the whole language movement and the language experience approach used in the 1960s and 1970s.

An earlier version of this paper was presented at the annual meeting of the National Reading Conference. We would like to thank Patricia Hart, Richard C. Anderson, Peg Richek, Kathy Dulaney Barclay, and all of the anonymous reviewers of their comments and assistance.

There are several commonalities between the two approaches. First, both approaches stress the importance of children's own language productions as a bridge from oral to written language. Second, both approaches decry the use of skill sequences to organize instruction, as is done in most basal reading programs. Third, both approaches use children's literature, rather than basal readers, for instruction. It should be noted that basal readers also use children's literature in their texts, often the same stories. The basal reading programs "adapt" the stories with more or less fidelity to the original language. Whole language theorists such as Goodman (1986), for example, suggest that such adaptation distorts the predictability of the language, making the stories harder, rather than easier, to understand (see also Simons & Ammon, 1988). Fourth, both language experience and whole language approaches stress the importance of focusing on the meaningfulness of language and of not changing the focus to parts of nonmeaningful segments of language, such as individual sound–symbol relationships, unless that instruction is done within the context of a whole text. In other words, both language experience and whole language advocates do not recommend teaching words or individual sound–symbol relationships in isolation, but may teach them as needed to help students understand particular texts.

Although there is much in common between the earlier language experience approaches and current whole language approaches, there are some important differences. First, in language experience approaches, experience charts generated by children's dictation were used as the major part of instruction. In whole language approaches, such charts are recommended (see Goodman, 1986; Weaver, 1988), but more emphasis is placed on the reading of trade books, especially those with predictable patterns (see Bridge, Winograd, & Haley, 1983). In language experience approaches, trade books were also used extensively. They were read to groups of beginning readers who were encouraged to read them independently. It was the charts, however, rather than the trade books that received the most emphasis. Second, in whole language programs, greater emphasis is placed on children's own writing using invented spelling, rather than their dictated charts. Although language experience approaches stressed the interrelation of all four language processes (reading, writing, speaking, and listening), they recommended delaying writing until children had mastered a corpus of sight words (R. V. Allen, 1976; R. G. Stauffer, 1969); both Allen and Stauffer do, though, mention invented spelling. In whole language approaches, children are encouraged to write even before they can read words because of the belief that writing develops from scribbling to invented spelling to mature writing (e.g., Harste, 1985; Weaver, 1988).

The goal of both approaches is to bring children into literacy in a "natural" way, by bridging the gap between children's own language competencies and written language. Thus, written language should be seen as functional from the very beginning (R. V. Allen, 1976). Because it is functional, it is argued that children learn written language the way they do oral language, through exposure to a literate environment (Goodman & Goodman, 1979). In such an environment, children are led to realize that their language, and the ideas of others, can be written and thus read. R. V. Allen (1976) expressed this as follows: "What I can think about, I can talk about. What I can talk about, I can write. What I can write, I can read. I can read what I write and what other people can write for me to read" (p. 51).

These approaches are also based on the premise that speaking, listening, writing, and reading are interrelated and interdependent. Instruction in reading begins where children are, in terms of their ability to think with words, and it stimulates language development in all media of expression and reception, with the ultimate goal as reading the writings of others.

We see these approaches as being both part of a continuous evolution yet having some possibly important differences. Therefore, we will refer to the entire range of approaches as *whole language/language experience approaches*. If we are specifically referring to a study that uses one name or the other, we will use that label only.

STAGE MODELS OF READING DEVELOPMENT

Downing (1979) suggests three phases in the acquisition of reading skill: a *cognitive* phase in which the child becomes aware of the tasks needed to become a skilled performer, a *mastering* phase in which the skill is practiced until mastery is achieved, and an *automaticity* phase in which the learner practices until the skill can be performed without conscious attention.

Chall (1983b) has a similar stage model. In her initial stage, she suggests that prior to formal reading instruction, children need to develop skills prerequisite to learning to read. These skills and concepts have been investigated extensively under the framework of *emergent literacy* (see Teale, 1987; Teale & Sulzby, 1986). These include knowledge of their language, concepts about print, expectations about the nature of reading, and so forth. Researchers in this area have found similarities as well as differences in the functions that written language serves in different home environments and how children use written language across a variety of socioeconomic status (SES) groups. For example, some development of print awareness seems to be common across different cultures. They have also found vast differences in the quantity of exposure children get to written language, especially storybook reading. Adams (1990) estimates that some children may receive more than 1,000 hours of storybook reading by the time they begin formal reading instruction, whereas others may receive none. The informal interaction between parent and child during storybook reading may serve to familiarize the child with many of the conventions of print, such as where text begins on a page, directionality, punctuation, as well as the register of written language. Without such basic concepts, students may experience what Downing (1979) calls *cognitive confusion* when presented with text in formal reading instruction.

Whole language approaches may demonstrate the relations between written and spoken language in several ways. The process of directly translating oral language to experience charts may demonstrate the directionality of print, various print conventions, the concept of what a written word is, and some sound–symbol correspondences. The use of enlarged books may also approximate at school the types of interactions around print that take place in storybook reading. In these ways, whole language approaches might serve to clear up initial confusions about the functions of reading, of how written words relate to spoken words, and so forth (see McCormick & Mason, 1986).

Following this cognitive stage, according to the models of Downing (1979) and Chall (1983b), are stages concerned with mastery and automaticity. During the mastery stage, children learn to accurately decode print. Recent reviews have suggested that this is best accomplished through direct instruction of sound–symbol correspondences, rather than more indirect approaches (see Adams, 1990; Anderson, Hiebert, Scott, & Wilkinson, 1985; Chall, 1983a). In the automaticity stage, children learn to apply their decoding skills fluently and automatically. In this stage, children may benefit from reading large amounts of relatively easy, connected text, and through repeated readings of the same text (see Samuels, 1985).

It might be that whole language/language experience approaches may work best in the cognitive phase because they simulate the environment in which literate behaviors begin to emerge. They might not work as well during the mastering phase, because sound–symbol correspondence instruction in these approaches is unsystematic and indirect. In discussing whether whole language/language experience approaches are effective, it is important to examine what role they are intended to play, whether they are expected to provide this initial introduction to literacy or whether they are intended to provide systematic reading instruction. (The automaticity phase is beyond the scope of this review.)

REVIEWS OF LANGUAGE EXPERIENCE APPROACHES STUDIES

Hall (1972, 1977) summarized the results of 42 studies regarding the effects of language experience approaches. Her methodology was to report the significant and nonsignificant effects from each study as they were found. She concludes that there is evidence "to support that the overall reading achievement of students who receive language experience instruction is satisfactory, and, in some cases, it is superior to the achievement of children instructed by other approaches" (1977, p. 24). Although this claim is appropriately modest, it may overstate the effectiveness of language experience approaches. If two methods are approximately equal in their effects, both methods will produce some significantly higher scores than the other, by chance alone.

A partial synthesis of whole language/language experience approaches research was done by Grundin (1985) as part of his review of *Becoming a Nation of Readers* (Anderson et al., 1985). As part of their overall review of our knowledge of reading instruction, Anderson et al. suggested that the effects of language experience approaches have been indifferent, at least compared with conventional basal reading approaches. Grundin took issue with this conclusion. He argued that Anderson et al.'s conclusion was based only on one study, Bond and Dykstra's (1967) review of the Cooperative Research Program in First Grade, that this study was dated, and that the early language experience approaches were very different from modern whole language approaches.

Grundin (1985) did not cite any more recent research comparing whole language/language experience approaches and basal reader approaches that should have been considered by Anderson et al. Instead, Grundin reanalyzed the Bond and Dykstra (1967) data, totaling the average adjusted Stanford Achievement Test scores for each group, "ranking each approach according to how it compares to the overall mean of the study it is in" (p. 265), and comparing the average ranks for language experience/structure approaches, linguistic approaches, basal plus additional phonics, Initial Teaching Alphabet approaches, and basal-only approaches. Grundin interprets his reanalysis to show that whole language/language experience approaches were in fact the best performing of all five approaches.

We feel that Grundin's (1985) analysis was not the best approach to examine the Bond and Dykstra (1967) data. Bond and Dykstra's achievement test results were interval data, that is, they conveyed information both about the order of the effects and the magnitude of differences between the effects. By ranking, Grundin disregarded the information about magnitude and retained only the information about order, leading to possibly misleading conclusions. For example, it is possible to find sets of numbers whose average rank is identical but whose means are vastly different and to find sets in which the means are similar but the average ranks are markedly different. The average ranking procedure can both overestimate the importance of small differences and underestimate that of larger differences (the differences between 29 and 30 and between 30 and 70 both count as differences of one rank point). In addition, Grundin did not provide any information about variations between studies. Because the different studies varied from the means for each method, small differences between means may well be due to chance and may not represent a real difference in methods. Under the ranking method used by Grundin, small differences would be indistinguishable from larger, reliable differences.

Various methods of quantitative synthesis have been developed that might be more appropriate for analyzing the Bond and Dykstra (1967) data and other comparisons of whole language/language experience approaches with other forms of beginning reading instruction. This paper will attempt such a quantitative review of the effectiveness of these approaches to beginning reading, using two methods of quantitative synthesis, vote counting and meta-analysis, to evaluate our current knowledge of the effectiveness of whole language and language experience approaches to beginning reading and to suggest future research directions.

The synthesis will be directed toward four questions: (a) What are the overall effects of whole language/language experience approaches compared with the basal reading approach predominant at the time of the study? (b) Are these effects different at kindergarten (or at the child's first exposure to formal schooling) than in first grade? (c) Do whole language/language experience approaches have a differential effect on different aspects of reading (word recognition, decoding, reading comprehension, etc.)? and (d) Have whole language/language experience approaches grown more effective over time?

METHOD

Study Selection

We used several data sources to locate relevant studies. A study was deemed relevant if it compared an approach using a language experience or whole language approach as the majority or entirety of a beginning reading program to a basal or traditional approach. For the purposes of this review, we defined a whole language/language experience method as having the following characteristics, as best as we could determine:

1. The emphasis in the program was on using children's own language, either through experience charts or through their own writing using invented spelling, as a medium of instruction.
2. The lessons were child centered rather than teacher centered. In a whole lan-

guage/language experience classroom, it is assumed that children's competence will develop out of a need to use language to communicate better. In a basal classroom, skill sequences were used to sequence instruction.

3. An emphasis on trade books, rather than basals. This is not to say that basal reading programs were not used in any of the programs reviewed, but that they were used sparingly and were not the major emphasis.

4. Phonics lessons were not directly taught in isolation. Lessons in decoding were given as the need arose in the context of reading whole text.

Although this definition will probably not satisfy some (see Altwerger et al., 1987), it seemed to capture methods using the whole language philosophy as well as the earlier language experience studies. The studies reviewed as a whole represent a clear contrast with traditional basal reading programs. However, Slaughter (1988), who observed whole language and skills-oriented classes, found that whole language classes did include some direct skill instruction and skills classes contained some activities typical of whole language approaches. Her results suggest that the differences between whole language and other approaches may be a matter of emphasis, rather than mutually exclusive approaches.

We conducted computer searches of the ERIC and Dissertation Abstracts data bases using the descriptors "Language Experience" and "Whole Language." In addition, we checked references of obtained papers and bibliographies such as Crismore (1985), Hall (1977), and R. G. Stauffer (1976), checked conference programs, and wrote to major figures in the field. We found 46 studies in addition to the USOE first-grade studies. Only 15 of these provided enough information for the meta-analysis, resulting in 50 effect sizes for the non-USOE studies and an additional 71 effect sizes derived from the USOE first-grade studies, leaving a total of 121 separate effect sizes.

Several studies, mostly in the USOE group, were long-term follow-ups of children whose initial reading instruction used whole language/language experience approach procedures. These were included in both analyses. Although it could be argued that children observed in third grade should not be included with those observed in first grade, our review both with and without these studies found that studies might have exaggerated the effects of whole language/language experience approaches slightly because of the inclusion of more of R. G. Stauffer's (1976) results. As discussed below, because his program produced the strongest effects of the various language experience methods, it may have made whole language/language experience approaches appear slightly more effective than they would otherwise.

Because the purpose of the review was to get the broadest picture of the specific approach. There were clear differences between the language experience approaches espoused by R. G. Stauffer (1969) and R. V. Allen (1976), and, as noted above, differences between these and whole language programs, such as those described by Goodman (1986), Newman (1985), and Weaver (1988). Because few studies used observations to verify fidelity to the intended method, such limitations would be artificial. Some of the authors have used only language experience charts; others have used language experience in combination with other materials. Thus, included in our review are "pure" language experience approaches, language experience plus predictable books (Bridge et al., 1983; Ribowsky, 1985), language experience on computers (Educational Testing Service [ETS], 1984; Pickering & Pope, 1986), and so forth. Also, several of the studies used special populations including disadvantaged children (e.g., Brazziel & Terrell, 1962; Harris & Serwer, 1966), mildly retarded children (Woodcock, 1967), and so forth. When in doubt, we chose to include a study in order to avoid bias.

The review was limited, however, to instructional studies that compared the effects of a predominantly whole language or language experience program to a basal reading program. We did not include studies that compared students' reading of self-authored versus other authored materials (e.g., J. Allen, 1985) or studies that compared the number of words generated in experience stories to those used in basal texts (e.g., Gunderson & Shapiro, 1987), although these types of studies have also been used to support the efficacy of whole language/language experience approaches (see Hall, 1977). We also did not include studies that only examined the effects of tradebooks or predictable books (such as Bridge & Burton, 1982) or the effects of increased story reading on later reading achievement (Feitelson, Kita, & Goldstein, 1986; McCormick & Mason, 1986), although these also have been used to support whole language programs. Although Hall (1977) cites studies dating back to 1933, we limited our review to studies published after 1960 because of our uncertainty of the descriptions of the early whole language/language experience-prototype approaches.

Procedures

Two procedures were used to evaluate studies. First, a vote-counting procedure was used (Light & Pillemer, 1984). Each result was classified as either significantly favoring a whole language/language experience approach, significantly favoring the basal reader approach, or nonsignificant. Measures included not only standardized achievement tests but also attitude measures, miscue analysis, concepts about print, and so forth. Second, where available, results were translated into effect sizes (Glass, McGaw, & Smith, 1981; Light & Pillemer, 1984), using the following formula:

$$ES = \frac{\text{Mean}_{\text{whole language/language experience}} - \text{Mean}_{\text{basal}}}{SD_{\text{basal}}}$$

Where the standard deviation of the basal group was not available, the pooled standard deviation for the entire group (or the best approximation available) was used instead. Calculations were made using effect sizes in order to answer the four questions previously posed. In this analysis, a positive effect size means that the whole language/language experience group outperformed the basal reader group; a negative effect size suggests the opposite.

Because the majority of the effect sizes were obtained from the USOE Cooperative First Grade Studies, we have decided to present these separately from the non-USOE studies. For all analyses where this is appropriate, effect sizes will be presented for the group of USOE studies, the non-USOE studies, and the total. This will be done to avoid the problems of excessive reliance on one body of literature and to examine possible changes because the USOE studies were carried out more than 20 years ago.

RESULTS

Overall Effects

In the vote counting, overall, whole language/language experience approaches appear approximately equal to basal reader approaches in their effectiveness. Of the non-USOE studies, 26 comparisons favored whole language/language experience approaches, 16 favored basal reader approaches, and 58 did not find significant differences. For the USOE studies, 17 comparisons favored the whole language/language experience method, 6 favored the basal reading method, and 57 were nonsignificant. These include observations after first, second, third, and sixth grade. Thus, of 180 comparisons, 22% favored whole language/language experience programs, 12% favored basal reading programs, and 66% were nonsignificant. (Tables 2.1 and 2.2 report the studies used in the vote-counting analysis.)

If the two approaches were identical in their effects, conservatively one would expect about 5% of the differences to significantly favor one method and another 5% to favor the other by chance alone (Light & Pillemer, 1984). A chi-square test comparing the observed findings with this distribution found more significant differences than would have been expected by chance ($\chi^2 = 112.18$, $p < .0001$). Although the majority of the comparisons showed no differences between the two approaches, the number of significant differences suggests that this agglutination of findings may not represent one population, or that both whole language/language experience and basal reading programs may have different effects for different subsets of the studies.

The results of the meta-analysis confirm the general results of the vote counting. The mean of all 117 effect sizes was 0.09 ($SD = .61$). Effect sizes ranged from 1.91 to -1.46. A one-sample t test found that this was not significantly different from zero, suggesting that whole language/language experience approaches were not reliably different from basal reader approaches in their effects. (Tables 2.3 and 2.4 report the studies used in the meta-analysis.)

The results of both analyses suggest that the overall effects of whole language/language experience and basal reading programs are similar, but that the effects are not homogeneous. Because of the heterogeneity of the findings, the overall lack of differences between whole language/language experience and basal reading programs may obscure strong differences in certain subsets of the data.

Readiness versus Beginning Reading

When the vote-counting data were broken down by whether the whole language/language experience approach was used as a readiness program, preparatory for another beginning reading approach, or whether it was the beginning reading approach, an interesting pattern was found. For these readiness studies, 17 comparisons favor whole language/language experience approaches, 2 favor the basal, and 14 are nonsignificant, suggesting that whole language/language experience approaches are more effective in kindergarten. For first grade, the approaches are more equal. Of the non-USOE comparisons, 13 favor basal reader approaches, 43 are nonsignificant, and 9 favor whole language/language experience approaches. The effects of whole language/language experience programs on readiness and first-grade reading were significantly different ($\chi^2 = 14.45$, $p < .001$). Cramer's Phi, a measure of the strength of the association, was 0.39, suggesting a moderately strong relationship between the function of whole language/language experience instruction and its effectiveness. (Although the Bergemann, 1969, Brazziel & Terrell, 1962, and Hall, 1965, studies were conducted with first graders, this was the first exposure of these children to school. The use of language experience served the purpose of a readiness program for these children and their progress was partially measured using readiness tests. Therefore, we have chosen to include these studies with the studies using kindergarten children. We also classified Trachtenburg and Ferruggia's (1988) study with prefirst transition class children in the readiness group because their program was intended to prepare children for a first-grade reading program. The overall results would be similar no matter which way these are classified.)

For the meta-analysis, we were able to derive effect sizes only from five studies in the readiness group. Because of the small number of studies involved and the use of different measures (print concept measures as opposed to reading performance measures), no similar comparison was made using the meta-analysis data.

Two of the studies we reviewed spanned both grade levels. Both ETS (1984) and Phinney (cited in Weaver, 1988, pp. 213–215) found whole language/language experience approaches to significantly improve children's reading skills in kindergarten but not first grade. Phinney's study was an informal evaluation of the implementation of a whole language approach, whereas the ETS study used computers equipped with speech synthesis to implement a language experience program. These implementations may not be typical. They do mirror the trends found in the overall analysis.

Differential Effects

The second question addressed in this analysis was whether whole language/language experience approaches had different effects on different measures of reading achievement. For the USOE studies, the mean effect size for word recognition measures was 0.17, whereas that for comprehension measures was 0.09. These are both small effects and essentially similar to each other. For the non-USOE studies, the mean effect size for word recognition was 0.33 and for comprehension measures was $-.42$. These effects are both moderate, favoring whole language/language experience programs on the word recognition measures and favoring basal readers on comprehension. The difference between them is large, and statistically significant $[t(28) = 4.69, p < .005]$.

Older versus Newer Studies

Another analysis examined whether whole language/language experience approaches were becoming more effective over time, as implied by Grundin (1985). To answer this, we calculated a Pearson correlation between the year of publication of the study and the obtained effect size. To avoid the biasing effects of having many effect sizes at the same year, we excluded the USOE studies from this analysis and used only the non-USOE effect sizes. The obtained correlation was $-.14$ ($N = 50$), which was not statistically significant ($p > .05$).

Because the earlier analysis suggested that whole language/language experience programs function differently as a readiness program than they do as a beginning reading program, separate correlations were calculated for each data set. For the

TABLE 2.1. Vote Counting, Non-USOE Studies

Study	Grade	Word recognition	Decoding	Oral reading	Comprehension	Readiness	Letter names	Print concepts	Vocabulary
Readiness									
Brazziel & Terrell (1962)	a					LEA			
Bergemann (1969)	a			n.s.	n.s.	n.s.			
Bruckner, Morsillo, & Sample (1978)	K				LEA				LEA
ETS (1984)	K				LEA				
Guillemette (1979)	K	n.s.			n.s.				
Hall (1965)	a		n.s.		n.s.	n.s.			
O'Donnell & Raymond (1972)	K	LEA				LEA	n.s.		
Phinney (cited in Weaver, 1988)	K	n.s.				WL			
Pickering & Pope (1986)	K	n.s., LEA				LEA, n.s.			
Ribowsky (1985)	K		WL				WL	WL	
Stewart (1986)	K							WL	
Taylor, Blum, & Logsdon (1986)	K					n.s., WL		WL	
Trachtenburg & Ferruggia (1988)	Transition class			WL					WL
Walraven (1981)	K							BR, BR, LEA, n.s.	
Beginning reading									
Abt Associates (1977)									
Bank Street	3rd								BR
TEEM	3rd				BR				BR
Asphlund & Sunal (1976)	2nd	n.s.			n.s.				
Blachowitz et al. (1979)	1st		n.s.						
Bridge et al. (1983)	1st	LEA			BR				
Carrigan (1986)	1st				n.s.				
Crandall (1973)	1st				n.s.				
Dittus (1983)	1st		n.s.						
Duquette (1972)	1st	n.s.	n.s.		n.s.				n.s.

Study	Grade	2LEA			
ETS (1984)	2nd	n.s.			n.s.
Evans & Carr (1985)	1st			BR	
	1st			BR	
Ewoldt (1976)	3rd		n.s.	n.s.	
Farber & Putnam (1983)	1st			n.s.	
Fishman (1977)					
Experimental Program	1st			n.s.	
Allen's Program	1st			LEA	
Freeman & Freeman (1987)	1 s	n.s.		n.s.	
Fryburg (1972)	1st	BR	n.s.	BR	
Gallagher (1975)	1st	n.s.			
Harris et al. (1967b)	1st	n.s.		n.s.	
Hoffman (1977)	1st			n.s.	
Lamb (1971)	1st			n.s.	
Phinney (cited in Weaver, 1988)	1st		n.s.	n.s.	n.s.
Pollack & Brown (1980)	3rd		n.s.		
Powell et al. (1987)	1st			n.s.	
Ramig & Hall (1980)	1st		n.s.		
Sinatra (1984)	1st			WL	
Stallings (1975)				n.s.	
Bank Street	1st			BR	
TEEM	1st			BR	
M. A. Stauffer (1976)	1st	LEA	LEA	LEA	
Stice & Bertrand (1987)	1st		n.s.		
Stubbs (1983)	1st			n.s.	
Swanson (1981)	2nd			n.s.	
	1st			n.s.	
Tunmer & Nesdale (1985)	1st	BR		BR	
Woodcock (1967)	EMR	n.s.		n.s.	n.s.
		n.s.		n.s.	
				n.s.	

Note. LEA is used for programs specifically labeled *language experience*, WL for programs specifically labeled *whole language*, and BR is used for programs using the basal reading method.

[a] Subjects were first graders, but LEA was compared to a basal reading readiness programs rather than an initial reading program. See text.

TABLE 2.2. Vote Counting, USOE Studies

Study	Stanford Achievement Tests				Gilmore Oral Reading		Word Lists			Other	
	WR	Word study	Vocabulary	Paragraph meaning	Accuracy	Rate	Fry	Gates	Karlsen	NYS WR	NYS Comp
Observed after first grade											
Cleland[a]	LEA	LEA	LEA	LEA	n.s.	n.s.	LEA	LEA			
Hahn	n.s.	n.s.	n.s.	n.s.	n.s.	n.s.	n.s.	n.s.	n.s.	n.s.	n.s.
Kendrick	n.s.	n.s.	n.s.	n.s.	n.s.	n.s.	n.s.	n.s.	n.s.	n.s.	n.s.
Stauffer	LEA	n.s.	n.s.	n.s.	LEA	n.s.	LEA	LEA	LEA		
Harris	BR	BR	n.s.	BR	n.s.		LEA	n.s.			
Observed after second grade											
Pooled[b]	n.s.	n.s.	n.s.	n.s.	n.s.[c]	n.s.[c]	LEA[c]				
Pooled	n.s.	n.s.	n.s.	n.s.							
Pooled	n.s.	n.s.	n.s.	n.s.							
Harris et al. (1967b)	n.s.			n.s.	BR	BR	BR	n.s.			
Observed after third grade											
Harris et al. (1967b)			n.s.	n.s.	n.s.	n.s.					
Stauffer	n.s.	n.s.	n.s.	n.s.	LEA	LEA	LEA	LEA		n.s.	n.s.
Observed after sixth grade											
R. G. Stauffer (1976)			n.s.	n.s.	n.s.		LEA				

Notes. LEA = learning experience approach; BR = basal reading approach.

[a] The data in this table are derived from the following reports: Bond & Dykstra (1967), Cleland & Vilscek (1964), Dykstra (1968). Hahn (1966, 1967), Harris & Serwer (1966), Harris, Serwer, & Gold (1967a), Harris, Serwer, Gold, & Morrison (1967b), Kendrick & Bennett (1966, 1967), R. G. Stauffer (1966, 1976), Stauffer & Hammond (1967, 1969), Stauffer, Hammond, Oehlkers, & Houseman (1976), Vilscek & Cleland (1968), and Vilscek, Morgan, & Cleland (1966). We have used the convention adopted by Bond and Dykstra to refer to each project by a last name of one of its directors.

[b] Dykstra (1968) did not report individual effect sizes for the Cleland, Kendrick, and Stauffer projects continued into second grade. Because we could not obtain reports of all three projects, we reported the pooled means reported by Dykstra. Each pooled mean was counted three times in the analysis because it represented three separate studies.

[c] From R. G. Stauffer (1966).

TABLE 2.3. Effect Sizes Derived from Non-USOE Studies

Study	Grade	Word recognition	Decoding	Oral reading	Comprehension	Print concepts	Vocabulary	Letter recognition	Readiness
Readiness									
Bruckner et al. (1978)	K	0.03			0.70		0.62		
Guillemette (1979)	K	0.33			0.06				
Ribowsky (1985)	K		0.55			1.91			
Taylor et al. (1986)	K					0.38		0.51	
Walraven (1981)	K					−0.27			0.33
Beginning reading									
Abt Associates (1977)									
Bank Street	3rd				−0.06		−0.28		
TEEM	3rd				−0.34		−0.32		
Asphlund & Sunal (1976)	2nd	0.78							
Bridge et al. (1983)	1st	1.09			−1.46				
Carrigan (1986)	1st				−1.09				
Evans & Carr (1985)	1st				−0.85				
					−1.26				
					−0.29				
Ewoldt (1976)	3rd	0.13	−0.01		0.08				
Harris et al. (1967b)	1st	0.48		0.11	0.15		−0.11		
	2nd	0.08			0.19				
					−1.12				
Gallagher (1975)	1st	0.02			−0.49				
Lamb (1971)	1st	0.03			−0.18				
Stallings (1975)									
Bank Street	1st				−0.45				
TEEM	1st				−0.86				
Tunmer & Nesdale (1985)	1st		−1.17		−1.11				
			−0.91						
Woodcock (1967)	EMR	0.28			0.05		0.20		
		0.38			0.33				
					0.33				

21

TABLE 2.4. Effect Sizes Derived from USOE Studies

Study	Stanford Achievement Tests				Gilmore Oral Reading		Word lists			Other	
	WR	Word study	Vocabulary	Paragraph meaning	Accuracy	Rate	Fry	Gates	Karlsen	NYS WR	NYS Comp
				Observed after first grade							
Cleland[a]	0.50	0.36	0.45	0.41	0.07	0.13	0.24	0.36			
Hahn	0.25	0.13	0.16	0.13	-0.16	-0.08	0.12	-0.05	-0.03		
Kendrick	0.03	-0.10	-0.10	-0.26	0.39	-0.05	0.04	0.10	0.06		
Stauffer	0.33	0.03	0.14	0.21	0.64	-0.07		1.12	2.31		
Harris	-0.33	-0.34	-0.16	-0.43							
				Observed after second grade							
Pooled[b]	0.20	0.14	0.09	0.16	0.26[c]	0.03[c]					
Pooled	0.20	0.14	0.09	0.16							
Pooled	0.20	0.14	0.09	0.16							
Harris et al. (1967b)	0.18			0.45	-0.82	-2.50	-0.64	-0.29			
				Observed after third grade							
Harris et al. (1967b)			-0.09	-0.10	0.18	-0.05				-0.10	0.06
Stauffer		0.07	0.18	0.06	1.39	1.30	1.04	0.71			

[a] The date in this table are derived from the following reports: Bond & Dykstra (1967), Cleland & Volscek (1964), Dykstra (1968), Hahn (1966, 1967), Harris & Serwer (1966), Harris, Serwer, & Gold (1967a), Harris, Serwer, Gold, & Morrison (1967b), Kendrick & Bennett (1966, 1967), R. G. Stauffer (1966, 1976), Stauffer & Hammond (1967, 1969), Stauffer, Hammond, Oehlkers, & Houseman (1976), Vilscek & Cleland (1968), and Vilscek, Morgan, & Cleland (1966). We have used the convention adopted by Bond and Dykstra to refer to each project by a last name of one of its directors.

[b] Dykstra (1968) did not report individual effect sizes for the Cleland, Kendrick, and Stauffer projects continued into second grade. Because we could not obtain reports of all three projects, we reported the pooled means reported by Dykstra. Each pooled mean was counted three times in the analysis because it represented three separate studies.

[c] From R. G. Stauffer (1966).

readiness studies, the relationship between year of publication and effect size was moderate and positive (0.22) but was not significantly different from zero probably because of the small number of effect sizes ($N = 14$) used in the analysis. For the beginning reading studies, the effect was also moderate, $-.58$ ($N = 36$), which was statistically significant ($p < .001$). Because this correlation is negative, it suggests that between 1967 and 1986 there was a tendency for the whole language/language experience approaches used as beginning reading methods to be less effective in relation to basal reading approaches with later years of publication. This could be interpreted to mean that, as language experience approaches have evolved into whole language approaches, they have been associated with higher relative achievement in kindergarten and lower relative achievement in first grade.

Related were differences found between the USOE and non-USOE studies. The mean effect size derived from the USOE studies was small and positive (0.14). The mean effect size for the non-USOE studies, was near zero (.01). The average effect sizes for the USOE and non-USOE groups were significantly different from each other [$t(115) = 4.68$, $p < .001$], although both were small and neither was significantly different from zero. Therefore, the language experience treatments used in the USOE studies were more effective relative to the basals used at the time than that used in the non-USOE studies, confirming the trend for later studies to show lower effects for these approaches.

Disadvantaged and Lower SES Populations

It has been suggested by some (see Hall, 1972) that whole language/language experience approaches are especially suitable for disadvantaged or lower SES populations. To examine this, we looked separately at studies specifically examining these populations. We found 12 studies that specifically included those terms in the subject descriptions or were part of programs specifically set up for such populations, such as Project Follow Through. (We could not determine the SES of about a third of the studies we examined from the descriptions we had.) Of the three readiness studies that examined a lower SES population (Brazziel & Terrell, 1962; Hall, 1972; O'Donnell & Raymond, 1972) five comparisons favored whole language/language experience approaches, while five were nonsignificant. This is similar to that found in the overall analysis.

In the beginning reading group, of the nine studies that specifically examined lower SES groups (Abt Associates, 1977; Ewoldt, 1976; Fryburg, 1972; Gallagher, 1975; Harris, Serwer, & Gold, 1967a; Hoffman, 1977; Lamb, 1971; Powell, Needham, & Cochran, 1987; Stallings, 1975), 9 comparisons favored the basal reader approach and 15 were nonsignificant. None of the comparisons made with specifically lower SES populations at this level favored whole language/language experience approaches. In the overall analysis, the results were more equal. A contingency table analysis found significant differences between those beginning reading studies using specifically lower SES populations and the remainder of the studies ($\chi^2(2) = 17.78$, $p < .01$). Any conclusion should be tempered by the number of studies for which SES information was not available. It does appear, however, that whole language/language experience approaches do not have a particular advantage with lower SES populations. In fact, they may have less of an effect with this population than with more homogeneous or middle- or upper-class populations.

Standardized versus Naturalistic Measures

Some authors have suggested that children in basal reading programs are exposed to more testlike events in their instruction, biasing these measures toward programs with basic skills orientations (e.g., Harste, 1985; House, Glass, McLean, & Walker, 1978). It has been suggested, then, that more naturalistic measures should be used to measure more naturalistic programs. Such measures, such as oral reading miscue analysis and attitude measures, were included mostly in the vote-counting analysis because only one of these studies provided numerical data necessary to derive effect sizes.

The results from more naturalistic measures mirror those from the other measures. Four studies (Ewoldt, 1976; Pollack & Brown, 1980; Ramig & Hall, 1980; Stice & Bertrand, 1987) found no significant differences in the number of oral reading miscues produced by whole language/language experience trained and basal trained first graders (see also Blachowitz, McCarthy, & Ogle, 1979; Wilkinson & Brown, 1983). Ewoldt also found no differences between the groups on a qualitatively scored measure of retelling. On another naturalistic measure of comprehension—the number of predictions made after reading an open ended story—Farber and Putnam (1983) also failed to find significant differences between language experience trained first graders and basal trained first graders. Harris et al. (1967b) found that language experience trained students read more books than basal students when number of different books was the unit of analysis, but basal students read more pages in free reading.

The results of measures of children's attitudes toward reading are equally ambivalent. Some proponents of whole language/language experience approaches suggest that these approaches improve students' attitudes toward reading, whereas basal approaches deaden enthusiasm (e.g., Harste, 1985). The results of the vote counting found that whole language/language experience approaches had significant effects on attitude measures in 3 studies, whereas no significant difference was found in 11 studies. One difference favored the basal reader group.

The results of the naturalistic measures, therefore, mirror those derived from standardized tests. On both types of instruments, whole language/language experience approaches produce approximately the same levels of achievement and attitude toward reading.

Study Quality

Meta-analysis has been criticized by some (e.g., Slavin, 1986) for including all available studies, irrespective of quality. Slavin suggests a *best evidence* synthesis in excluding effect sizes from studies that did not meet rigorous criteria. Such a synthesis has its own problems because the criteria are necessarily post hoc, in that they are applied after the data are collected, no matter how logical they might seem. To examine study quality, we have chosen to present how each exclusionary criterion would affect the overall results.

Through an examination of the corpus of studies, we determined six criteria that characterized the best qualities of research in this area. They are as follows:

Treatment and control groups both are taught by more than one teacher. If only one teacher is assigned per group, then treatment and teacher factors are confounded.

Both programs should be at least in their second year of implementation. This is both to insure that teachers are comfortable using the programs and to dilute the high expectations that accompany any new program.

Treatment should last at least 6 months. We felt a better test of the effectiveness of a program was in how it fared over a relatively long term. Most of the studies were a full year in length.

Study should include observations in order to insure fidelity of treatment. Studies such as those of Chall and Feldmann (1966) suggest that how teachers identify their program may have little relation to what they are doing in the classroom. Studies in which a researcher observed instruction in the classroom were likely to have greater fidelity to the intended treatment.

Initial differences should be accounted for. This would usually involve covarying initial differences in readiness test scores or intelligence but might also include initial differences on criterion measures in a pretest–posttest gain score design.

Study should use traditional first graders. We excluded here studies that used as subjects Sikhs for whom English was a second language (Carrigan, 1986), educable mentally retarded children (Woodcock, 1967), and learning disabled children (Guillemette, 1979), but included those using disadvantaged populations (Ewoldt, 1976; Gallagher, 1975; Harris et al., 1967b; Lamb, 1971).

In addition, we included scores only from measures of reading, word recognition, oral reading, decoding, comprehension, or silent vocabulary given in kindergarten or first grade, and excluded measures of prereading skills or measures given a long-term follow-ups so that the studies would be more homogeneous.

Table 2.5 lists the exclusionary criteria, the studies each criterion includes, and the resulting effect size. Only two studies of the non-USOE group met all six criteria: Harris et al. (1967b) and Stallings (1975). The mean effect size from these studies was −.19, a small effect favoring the basal reading program. This would be the estimate from a best evidence synthesis. (The USOE studies, taken as a whole, met all of the

TABLE 2.5. Effects of Exclusionary Criteria on Meta-Analysis

Criterion	Studies meeting criterion	Effect size
More than one teacher	Carrigan (1986), Evans & Carr (1985), Harris et al. (1967b), Lamb (1971), Stallings (1975), Tunmer & Nesdale (1985), Woodcock (1967).	−.36
Second year or later	Carrigan, Evans & Carr, Stallings, Tunmer & Nesdale.	−.44
At least 6 months	Ribowsky (1985), Carrigan, Evans & Carr, Lamb, Stallings, Tunmer & Nesdale, Woodcock.	−.30
Observations for fidelity	Ribowsky, Bridge et al. (1983), Carrigan, Evans & Carr, Harris et al., Stallings.	−.34
Initial differences accounted for	Ribowsky, Asplund & Sunal (1976), Bridge et al., Carrigan, Evans & Carr, Gallagher (1975), Lamb, Stallings, Woodcock.	.08
Conventional students	Ribowsky, Asplund & Sunal (1976), Bridge et al., Evans & Carr, Harris et al., Gallagher, Lamb, Stallings, Tunmer & Nesdale.	−.30

above criteria except the second.) When the effect of applying each criterion was examined singly, for five of the six criteria, the resulting effect sizes were markedly lower than the overall effect size of 0.09 found for all studies. In addition, the correlation between the number of criteria each study met and its resulting effect size was −.41 ($p < .05$), also suggesting that as the study quality increased, the effect size tended to decrease or favor basal reading programs. This analysis thus suggests that the results of the overall meta-analysis might be an overestimation of the whole language/language experience methods' effects.

Outliers

Because massing of effect sizes can mask individual effective programs, separate descriptions will be made of outlier studies. An outlier study is one producing an effect size of ±1 standard unit from the mean of all studies. Examination of outliers allows one to test the trends found in the overall analysis, and to look at the characteristics of both very effective and very ineffective approaches.

The four outlier studies that showed strong effects for whole language/language experience showed similar trends. These studies found at least one effect size greater than +1 standard unit, or that the language experience or whole language group outperformed the basal control by a full standard deviation. Of these, three (Bridge et al., 1983; Ribowsky, 1985; Walraven, 1981) were concerned with the initial stages of reading, either in the beginning of first grade (Bridge et al.) or in kindergarten (Ribowsky; Walraven). These support the hypothesis that whole language programs are effective as an initial introduction to literacy.

The only other outlier showing a strong advantage for a whole language/language experience approach was the third-grade follow-up of Stauffer's (Stauffer & Hammond, 1969) USOE study. Unlike many of the USOE studies, Stauffer's second- and third-grade instruction was also especially adapted rather than conventional instruction. This large effect in third grade may be the culmination of Stauffer's overall curriculum, which included specially developed teaching techniques at the second- and third-grade levels as well rather than just the effects of a language experience approach. Stauffer's version of language experience, however, also produced consistently larger effects on first-grade measures than the versions used in other USOE projects. One possible reason for this will be discussed later.

Four studies found average effect sizes for whole language/language experience methods of −1.00 or less, or that an average student in the whole language/language experience group scored a full standard deviation below the average student in the basal group. All of these studies, Carrigan (1986), Evans and Carr (1985), Harris et al. (1967b), and Tunmer and Nesdale (1985), were evaluations of existing programs rather than deliberate manipulations in which an experimenter trained teachers to use a whole language/language experience approach and then evaluated the results of that instruction. The two other evaluation studies, the Follow Through evaluations by Abt Associates (1977) and Stallings (1975), also found basal reader programs to be superior to language experience approaches. (They also both found code emphasis approaches to be more effective than either a language experience approach or a basal approach.)

The results of a deliberate manipulation may be subject to an experimenter effect (Campbell & Stanley, 1966). In other words, the training or experimenter expectations may have biased the results in favor of the manipulated treatment when compared with a status quo, basal treatment. In some studies, the experimenter taught some of the experimental classes but not the basal control classes (e.g., Fishman, 1977; Ribowsky, 1985). Even when others do the teaching, they not only must be specially trained to be an effective whole language/language experience teacher but also must invest time, effort, and ingenuity preparing materials for their classes. Thus, the superiority of basal reader instruction on these evaluation studies suggests that the long-term effects of whole language/language experience might be lower than this meta-analysis found.

DISCUSSION

The results of the meta-analysis and vote-counting procedures appear to suggest that, overall, whole language/language experience approaches were approximately equal to basal reading approaches in their effects. This was found on both standardized and nonstandardized measures and on measures of both attitude and achievement. These results, however, were not consistent across all studies. Whole language/language experience approaches appear to be more effective when used in kindergarten or when used instead of a reading readiness program and seem to have had greater effects on measures of word recognition than on measures of comprehension in the more recent non-USOE studies. In addition, the studies that met more of our rigorous criteria for inclusion tended to favor basal reading programs over whole language/language experience programs. An analysis of outliers also confirms these general trends.

The finding that whole language/language experience programs appear more effective when used prior to a formal reading program fits well into the stage models of reading acquisition discussed earlier. Whole language approaches may approximate the kind of incidental learning about books that takes place in middle-class households (see Snow, 1983; Snow & Ninio, 1986) in which children are initiated to print through dialogue about its features. This learning may not take place in some households, especially where books are not present or literacy has a lower status (Chall & Snow, 1982). Although these print concepts are important, once they are mastered children may be ready for more systematic learning about the code of written language (see Chall, 1983b).

In the mastering phase, a more systematic approach to decoding than whole language approaches provide may be needed, at least for some children. It is possible to compare more systematic programs, such as those suggested by Adams (1990), Anderson et al. (1985) and Chall (1983a) as most effective in first-grade reading programs to language experience programs, at least in a limited manner. Bond and Dykstra (1967) included programs labeled "Phonic/Linguistic," which correspond most closely to Anderson et al.'s and Chall's (1983a) suggestions, in their analysis. Looking only at the results at the end of first grade, the three phonic/linguistic projects (Hayes, Tanyzer, and Wyatt) produced a mean effect size of 0.91 on the Stanford Word Reading subtest and 0.36 on the Stanford Paragraph Meaning subtest. The corresponding effects of the five whole language/language experience projects are 0.16 and 0.01. Thus, when compared with similar basal reading programs, phonic/linguistic programs used in first grade produced strikingly larger effects than language experience programs, suggesting that, in this mastering phase, the more systematic code-emphasis approaches were the more successful.

Many authors have argued that using a whole language or language experience approach precludes (or is an alternative to) teaching decoding systematically. This does not have to be the case. R. G. Stauffer's (1969) approach places the largest emphasis on word recognition in isolation, making extensive use of word banks and explicit teaching to bring word forms to the child's attention during reading of experience charts. Stauffer's program also produced larger effects in first grade than the other language experience programs in the USOE studies. This greater attention to word forms may have contributed to that success. Fishman (1977), similarly, integrated systematic attention to decoding into a language experience approach. This approach produced significantly higher reading comprehension achievement than either a language experience method based on R. V. Allen's (1976) work or a basal reader control.

Some authors have argued that students learn about the code through whole language approaches, through exposure to print, and through invented spelling (e.g., Goodman, 1986; Weaver, 1988). They argue that such an approach is preferable, that because it is integrated into the context of reading, students remain focused on comprehending whole texts. There is some evidence that children do learn decoding skills through such approaches (Gunderson & Shapiro, 1987), but such instruction is unavoidably less efficient for the specific purpose of learning sound–symbol relations than direct instruction. Less efficient approaches require more time for learning. Because lower SES and middle and upper SES students vary considerably in the amount of listening to storybooks and other conventional literacy directed behaviors in the home (see Adams, 1990, for review), this might explain why whole language/language experience approaches might be more effective as beginning reading programs with middle and upper SES populations. Such populations probably have learned more about the code through long-term exposure to print and the interactions around storybooks (see Snow, 1983). In other words, they have had more time to learn. Children who have not had as much exposure and the same types of interactions need direct instruction to catch up (see Chall, 1983a). Delpit (1988) suggests that more progressive approaches may simply give children the opportunity to show what they have learned, but systematic approaches teach letter sounds and other basic literacy concepts as new information children have not learned.

At least for some of the approaches studied, the effects found for whole language/language experience programs may have been related to the amount of reading done by the students. Harris and Serwer's (1966) formal observations of language experience and basal programs found that the children in their project's basal reading program spent more time on direct reading activities, such as reading connected text. Language experience pupils spent more time in indirect reading activities, such as talking about what they were going to write, talking about what they read, and so forth. They further found that the amount of time spent on direct reading activities was positively correlated with reading achievement while time spent on indirect activities tended to be negatively correlated. This second finding has been replicated by other researchers (e.g., Berliner, 1981).

It certainly would not be the intent of the proponents of whole language/language experience approaches that children spend less time reading. However, the philosophy that reading and speaking are equivalent aspects of a same general process seems to suggest that time spent on language, oral or written, would be equally profitable. If the goal is to improve reading skill, it does not appear to be the case. Evans and Carr (1985) found that gains in spoken language skills were negatively correlated to gains in reading skill, that is, the greater gains in oral language were associated with lower reading skills. Their interpretation was that children need *print-specific skills* for success in reading, and that children cannot benefit from their language skills unless they have a requisite amount of these print-specific skills. Therefore, spending more time on oral language development might not show an effect until children are able to identify a certain number of written words (see also Chall, 1983b). Curtis (1980), for example, found word recognition skill but not language comprehension skill to be related to reading comprehension in second grade, whereas both word recognition and language comprehension related strongly to reading comprehension in fifth grade.

Integrating Perspectives

Some authors (DeFord, 1985; Harste, 1985) have attempted to trichotomize the practice of reading, separating practices into phonics approaches, skills approaches, or whole language approaches. In this scheme, whole language approaches involve increased use of quality children's literature, writing, and insuring that all skills are applied in the context of reading, rather than treated as isolated exercises. These are virtues that should be a part of any reading program. It would be wrong to interpret the indifferent effects found for whole language/language experience programs at the first-grade level as supporting the banality of some basal reading stories, the excessive use of worksheets, or other aspects of the basal reading approach.

One goal of any reading instruction should be that children become efficient at constructing meaning from text. However, approaches that always emphasize the construction of meaning may not be the most effective in achieving their purpose in the end. It appears clear from the reviews of Adams (1990), Anderson et al. (1985), Chall (1983a, 1983b), and others, that children need to go through intermediate stages of mastering word recognition abilities to better develop the reading abilities necessary to read good quality literature with enjoyment and understanding. These intermediate stages appear to be better served with direct and systematic phonics instruction. On the other hand, it appears that even the most systematic phonics approaches work better as children get increased opportunities to read children's literature (Adams).

The research base seems to point to an amalgam of the three approaches. The trichomization has implied, however, that an acceptance of the virtues of one approach requires rejection of the other approaches. Quality phonics instruction need not be synonymous with excessive worksheets, nor must it exclude the use of quality literature. We have observed first-grade teachers who integrate direct instruction of phonics with a broad program using children's literature and individual writing. We have also observed teachers whose classes largely do round robin reading of the reader and worksheets on both phonics and comprehension skills. The first type of teacher seems ideal, and all too rare. The second type may create the impression that reading is drudgery to be avoided, and is all too common.

Limitations and Suggestions for Further Research

It is important to note some limitations of this review. First, we did not examine the effects of whole language/language experience approaches on writing. Individualized writing, possibly using invented spelling, could have positive effects on children's development of writing skills, irrespective of its effect on reading. Second, we limited our review to programs in the kindergarten or first-grade year. We do not intend for these results to apply to later grades, where the effects of whole language approaches might be quite different. The stage model of Chall (1983b) might suggest that increased amounts of more challenging reading and writing in reaction to that reading might have salutary effects in the later grades, after decoding becomes automatic and reading requires more information and reasoning skills. There is not enough research available, however, to evaluate the effects of whole language programs at these levels.

Third, because we limited our review to programs that predominantly used whole language/language experience approaches, these results may not apply when aspects of whole language/language experience approaches are used as supplements to other reading programs. Teachers report that language experience is often used in this way, but we have not found enough research examining the effectiveness of these approaches used in this role to draw conclusions. Swanson (1981) found nonsignificant correlations between the amount of language experience activities used in the first-grade classes she observed and reading achievement. The applicability of these results are limited, however, by the generally small amounts of language experience instruction she observed.

Last, many researchers interested in whole language approaches have used ethnographic methods. Typically, studies using these methods have painted an appealing picture of the whole language classroom, but, of course, studies of this type do not license conclusions about whether the approach is more or less effective than other approaches to teaching beginning reading.

The use of ethnographic research, however, may be premature. Such research is useful to get a participant's view of an effective instructional setting, or to contrast an effective setting with an ineffective one. Given the results reported here, one cannot establish that whole language classes are more effective than the status quo. Rather than more "Method A versus Method B" research comparing multicomponent packages, we suggest that future research be directed toward isolating effective components of beginning reading programs, regardless of philosophy. Evans and Carr (1985), Harris and Serwer (1966), and Stallings (1975) combined observations of the activities in whole language and basal oriented classrooms with overall evaluations of the effectiveness of the different approaches. They, however, used only general categories to characterize the activities they observed. Evans and Carr, for example, found that the amount of silent reading in both settings correlated significantly with overall achievement, whereas the amount of oral reading and word analysis activities did not. Without more information about the nature of these activities, these results are difficult to interpret. Does, for example, silent reading in trade books with "authentic" language have different effects than reading "basalese"? What are the effects of invented spelling specifically on decoding skill? Are they more effective than practice on worksheets? Such questions can best be answered through more fine-grained comparisons between classes. Ultimately, such comparisons are the only way to examine the contributions of the whole language movement to beginning reading instruction.

From the data reviewed, it appears that whole language approaches may have an important function early in the process of learning to read, but that as the child's needs shift, they become less effective. It could also be that the philosophy behind whole language/language experience approaches, that the function of reading is to communicate, needs to be learned by children early, but, once learned, children need to be able to decode written language fluently and automatically in order to be able to use reading for that purpose.

REFERENCES

Abt Associates. (1977). *Education as experimentation: A planned variation model. Vol. IV-B. Effects of follow through models.* Cambridge, MA: Author.

Adams, M. J. (1990). *Beginning to read: Thinking and learning about print.* Cambridge, MA: MIT Press.

Allen, J. (1985) Inferential comprehension: The effects of text source, decoding ability, and mode. *Reading Research Quarterly, 20*, 603–615.

Allen, R. V. (1976) *Language experiences in communication.* Boston: Houghton Mifflin.

Altwerger, B., Edelsky, C., & Flores, B. M. (1987). Whole language: What's new? *The Reading Teacher, 41*, 144–154.

Anderson, R. C., Hiebert, E., Scott, J., & Wilkinson, I. A. G. (1985). *Becoming a nation of readers.* Champaign, IL: Center for the Study of Reading and National Academy of Education.

Asphlund, B. B., & Sunal, C. S. (1976). *The effectiveness of the language experience approach as a supplement to a basal reader program.* (ERIC Document Reproduction Service No. ED 182 705)

Bergemann, V. E. (1969). *A modified language experience approach versus a basal approach to reading with first grade children.* Unpublished doctoral dissertation, University of Maryland, College Park.

Berliner, D. C. (1981). Academic learning time. In J. T. Guthrie (Ed.), *Comprehension and teaching: Research reviews* (pp. 203–226). Newark, DE: International Reading Association.

Blachowitz, C. L. F., McCarthy, L. B., & Ogle, D. M. (1979). Testing phonics: A look at children's response biases. *Illinois School Research and Development, 16*, 1–6.

Bond, G. L., & Dykstra, R. (1967). The cooperative research program in first grade reading instruction. *Reading Research Quarterly, 2*(4), 5–142.

Brazziel, W. F., & Terrell, M. (1962). For first graders: A good start in school. *The Elementary School Journal, 62*, 352–355.

Bridge, C. A., & Burton, B. (1982) Teaching sight vocabulary through patterned language materials. In J. A. Niles & L. A. Harris (Eds.), *New inquiries in reading research and instruction: Thirty-first yearbook of the National Reading Conference* (pp. 119–123). Washington, DC: National Reading Conference.

Bridge, C. A., Winograd, P. N., & Haley, D. (1983). Using predictable materials vs. preprimers to teach beginning sight words. *The Reading Teacher, 36*, 884–891.

Bruckner, J. H., Morsillo, C. M., & Sample, E. E. (1978). Supportive evidence for the language experience approach at the kindergarten level. *Graduate Student Association Journal, 1*, 15–29. (ERIC Document Reproduction Service No. ED 157 635)

Campbell, D. T., & Stanley, J. C. (1966). *Experimental and quasi-experimental designs for research.* Chicago: Rand McNally.

Carrigan, A. (1986, December). *Reading achievement of grade one students involved in language experience programs vs. basal reader programs.* Paper presented at the annual meeting of the National Reading Conference, Austin, TX.

Chall, J. S. (1983a). *Learning to read. The great debate* (2nd ed.). New York: McGraw-Hill.

Chall, J. S. (1983b). *Stages of reading development.* New York: McGraw-Hill.

Chall, J. S., & Feldmann, S. (1966). First grade reading: An analysis of the interactions of professed methods, teacher implementation, and child background. *The Reading Teacher, 19,* 569–575.

Chall, J. S., & Snow, C. E. (1982). *Families and literacy. A report to the National Institute of Education.* Cambridge, MA: Harvard Graduate School of Education.

Clay, M. (1985). *The early detection of reading disabilities* (3rd ed.). Portsmouth, NH: Heinemann.

Cleland, D. L., & Vilscek, E. (1964). *Comparison of the basal and the coordinated language experience approaches in first grade reading instruction.* (ERIC Document Reproduction Service No. ED 012 687)

Crandall, A. H. (1973). *A comparison of reading attitude and reading achievement among first graders in open concept and more formal classes.* Unpublished doctoral dissertation, University of Connecticut, Storrs.

Crismore, A. (1985). *Landscapes: A state-of-the-art assessment of reading comprehension research 1974–1984.* Bloomington: Language Education Department, Indiana University.

Curtis, M. E. (1980). Development of components of reading skill. *Journal of Educational Psychology, 72,* 656–669.

DeFord, D. (1985). Validating the construct of theoretical orientation in reading instruction. *Reading Research Quarterly, 20* 351–367.

Delpit, L. D. (1988). The silenced dialogue: Power and pedagogy in educating other people's children. *Harvard Educational Review, 58,* 280–298.

Dittus, C. H. (1983). *The influence of instructional approach, instruction/test overlap, and student behavior on reading achievement.* Unpublished doctoral dissertation, Rutgers, The State University of New Jersey.

Downing, J. (1979). *Reading and reasoning.* New York: Springer-Verlag.

Duquette, R. J. (1972). Barnette-Duquette study. *Childhood Education, 38,* 437–439.

Dykstra, R. (1968). Summary of the second-grade phase of the cooperative research program. *Reading Research Quarterly, 4,* 49–70.

Educational Testing Service. (1984). *The ETS evaluation of Writing to Read. Executive summary.* Princeton, NJ: Author.

Evans, M. A., & Carr, T. H. (1985). Cognitive abilities, conditions of learning, and the early development of reading skill. *Reading Research Quarterly, 20,* 327–349.

Ewoldt, C. (1976). *Miscue analysis of the reading of third grade Follow Through and non-Follow Through children in Wichita, Kansas.* Tuscon: Arizona Center for Educational Research and Development. (ERIC Document Reproduction Service No. ED 136 219)

Farber, F. D., & Putnam, L. P. (1983, October). *Convergent/divergent predictions of urban first graders.* Paper presented at the annual meeting of the College Reading Association, Atlanta, GA. (ERIC Document Reproduction Service No. ED 236 564)

Feitelson, D., Kita, B., & Goldstein, Z. (1986). Effects of listening to series stories on first graders' comprehension and use of language. *Research in the Teaching of English, 20,* 339–356.

Fishman, T. G. (1977). *A comparison of two different programs for implementing the language experience approach to beginning reading with a basic reader program and phonic supplement.* Unpublished doctoral dissertation, Boston University.

Freeman, R. H., & Freeman, G. G. (1987). Reading acquisition: A comparison of four approaches to reading instruction. *Reading Psychology, 8,* 257–272.

Fryburg, E. L. (1972). *The relations among English syntax, methods of instruction, and reading achievement of first grade disadvantaged black children.* Unpublished doctoral dissertation, New York University.

Gallagher, J. A. M. (1975). *Vocabulary retention of lower-class students in language experience and in basal text approaches to the teaching of reading.* Unpublished doctoral dissertation, University of South Carolina.

Glass, G. V, McGaw, B., & Smith, M. L. (1981). *Meta-analysis in social research.* Beverly Hills, CA: Sage.

Goodman, K. S. (1986). *What's whole in whole language.* Portsmouth, NH: Heinemann.

Goodman, Y., & Goodman, K. S. (1979). Learning to read is natural, In L. B. Resnick & P. A. Weaver (Eds.), *Theory and practice of early reading* (Vol. 1, pp. 137–154). Hillsdale, NJ: Erlbaum.

Grundin, H. (1985). A commission of selective readers: A critique of *Becoming a Nation of Readers. The Reading Teacher, 39,* 262–266.

Guillemette, M. (1979). *A study of the effectiveness of sight reading versus phonetic instruction for children with auditory learning disability.* (ERIC Document Reproduction Service No. ED 184 074)

Gunderson, L., & Shapiro, J. (1987). Some findings on whole language instruction. *Reading-Canada-Lecture, 5,* 22–26.

Hahn, H. T. (1966). Three approaches to beginning reading instruction—i.t.a., language arts, and basic readers. *The Reading Teacher, 19,* 590–594.

Hahn, H. T. (1967). Three approaches to beginning reading instruction—i.t.a., language arts, and basic readers—Extended into second grade. *The Reading Teacher, 20,* 711–715.

Hall, M. A. (1965). *The development and evaluation of a language experience approach to reading with first-grade culturally disadvantaged children.* Unpublished doctoral dissertation, University of Maryland.

Hall, M. A. (1972). *The language experience approach for the culturally disadvantaged.* Newark, DE: International Reading Association.

Hall, M. A. (1977). *The language experience approach for teaching reading. A research perspective.* Newark, DE: International Reading Association.

Harris, A. J., & Serwer, B. L. (1966). The CRAFT project: Instructional time in reading research. *Reading Research Quarterly, 2*(1), 27–56.

Harris, A. J., Serwer, B. L., & Gold, L. (1967a). Comparing reading approaches in first grade teaching with disadvantaged children—Extended into second grade. *The Reading Teacher, 20,* 698–703.

Harris, A. J., Serwer, B. L., Gold, L., & Morrison, C. (1967b). *A third progress report on the CRAFT project. Teaching reading to disadvantaged primary grade urban Negro children.* (ERIC Document Reproduction Service No. ED 015 841).

Harste, J. (1985). Becoming a nation of readers: Beyond risk. In J. Harste (Ed.), *Toward practical theory: A state of practice assessment of reading comprehension instruction.* Bloomington: Language Education Department, Indiana University.

Hildreth, G. H. (1965). Experience related reading for school beginners. *Elementary English, 42,* 280–297.

Hoffman, J. R. (1977). *An assessment of the language experience approach to beginning reading and additional teacher characteristics in eight summer migrant schools.* Unpublished doctoral dissertation, University of Colorado, Boulder.

House, E. R., Glass, G. V, McLean, L. D., & Walker, D. F. (1978). No simple answer: Critique of the Follow Through evaluation. *Harvard Educational Review, 48,* 128–160.

Kendrick, W. M., & Bennett, C. L. (1966). A comparative study of two first grade language arts programs. *Reading Research Quarterly, 2*(1), 83–118.

Kendrick, W. M., & Bennett, C. L. (1967). A comparative study of two first grade language arts programs—Extended into second grade. *The Reading Teacher, 20,* 747–755.

Knight, J. J. (1971). *A comparison of four different reading programs on children's expressed attitudes toward reading.* Unpublished doctoral dissertation, University of New Mexico.

Lamb, P. (1971). The language experience approach to teaching beginning reading to culturally disadvantaged pupils. (ERIC Document Reproduction Service No. ED 059 314)

Light, R. J., & Pillemer, D. B. (1984). *Summing up: The science of reviewing research.* Cambridge, MA: Harvard University Press.

McCormick, C. E., & Mason, J. M. (1986). Intervention procedures for increasing children's interest in and knowledge about reading. In E. Sulzby & W. Teale (Eds.), *Emergent literacy* (pp. 90–114). Norwood, NJ: Ablex.

Newman, J. M. (1985). *Whole language: Theory and use.* Portsmouth, NH: Heinemann.

O'Donnell, C. M., & Raymond, D. (1972). Developing reading readiness in the kindergarten. *Elementary English, 49,* 768–771.

Pickering, T., & Pope, S. (1986, October). *A study of computer assisted instruction vs. a traditional basal reader approach in kindergarten.* Paper presented at the annual meeting of the Mid-Western Educational Research Association, Chicago.

Pollack, J. F., & Brown, G. H. (1980, August). *Observing the effects of reading instruction.* Paper presented at the annual meeting of the World Congress on Reading, Manilla, The Philippines. (ERIC Document Reproduction Service No. ED 195 500)

Powell, D., Needham, R., & Cochran, K. (1987, December). *A comparison of Hispanic/Anglo, middle/low income, first and second graders' reading achievement: A pilot study.* Paper presented at the annual meeting of the National Reading Conference, St. Petersburg Beach, FL.

Ramig, C. J., & Hall, M. A. (1980). Reading strategies of first grade children taught by a language experience and a basal approach. *Reading World, 19,* 280–289.

Ribowsky, H. (1985). *The effects of a code emphasis and a whole language approach upon the emergent literacy of kindergarten children.* (ERIC Document Reproduction Service No. ED 269 720)

Samuels, S. J. (1985). Automaticity and repeated reading. In J. Osborn, P. T. Wilson, & R. C. Anderson (Eds.), *Reading education: Foundations for a literate America* (pp. 215–231). Lexington, MA: Lexington Books.

Simons, H. D., & Ammon, P. (1988). Primerese miscues. In J. E. Readence & R. S. Baldwin (Eds.), *Dialogues in literacy, 37th yearbook of the National Reading Conference* (pp. 115–121). Chicago, IL: National Reading Conference.

Sinatra, R. (1984, October). *How a holistic language arts curriculum influenced the reading and writing proficiency of kindergarten and primary grade children.* Paper presented at the annual meeting of the Eastern Regional Conference of the International Reading Association. (ERIC Document Reproduction Service No. ED 264 583)

Slaughter, H. B. (1988). Indirect and direct teaching in a whole language program. *The Reading Teacher, 42,* 30–34.

Slavin, R. (1986). Best-evidence synthesis: An alternative to meta-analytic and traditional reviews. *Educational Researcher, 15*(9), 5–11.

Snow, C. E. (1983). Language and literacy: Relationships during the preschool years. *Harvard Educational Review, 53,* 165–189.

Snow, C. E., & Ninio, A. (1986). The contracts of literacy: What children learn from learning to read books. In W. H. Teale & E. Sulzby (Eds.), *Emergent literacy. Writing and reading* (pp. 116–138). Norwood, NJ: Ablex.

Stallings, J. (1975). Implementation and child effects of teaching practices in follow through classrooms. *Monographs of the Society for Research in Child Development, 40*(7–8, Serial No. 163).

Stauffer, M. A. (1976). Comparative effects of language arts approach and basal reader approach to first grade reading achievement. In R. G. Stauffer (Ed.), *Action research in L.E.A. instructional procedures* (pp. 205–226). Newark: University of Delaware.

Stauffer, R. G. (1966). The effectiveness of language arts and basic reader approaches to first grade reading instruction. *The Reading Teacher, 20,* 18–24.

Stauffer, R. G. (1969). *Teaching reading as a thinking process.* New York: Harper & Row.

Stauffer, R. G. (1976). *Action research in L.E.A. instructional procedures.* Newark: University of Delaware.

Stauffer, R. G., & Hammond, W. D. (1967). The effectiveness of language arts and basic reader approaches to first grade reading instruction–Extended into second grade. *The Reading Teacher, 20,* 740–746.

Stauffer, R. G., & Hammond, W. D. (1969). The effectiveness of language arts and basic reader approaches to first grade reading instruction–Extended into third grade. *Reading Research Quarterly, 41,* 468–499.

Stauffer, R. G., Hammond, W. D., Oehlkers, W. J., & Houseman, A. (1976). The effectiveness of language arts and basic reader approaches to first grade reading instruction–Extended into sixth grade. In R. G. Stauffer (Ed.), *Action research in L.E.A. instructional procedures* (pp. 166–203). Newark: University of Delaware.

Stewart, J. P. (1986). *A study of kindergarten children's awareness of how they are learning to read: Home and school perspectives.* Unpublished doctoral dissertation, University of Illinois, Urbana.

Stice, C. F., & Bertrand, N. P. (1987, December). *The effects of a whole language program on the literacy development of at-risk children.* Paper presented at the annual meeting of the National Reading Conference, St. Petersburg Beach, FL.

Stubbs, C. A. (1983). *An investigation of the effect of structure of intellect training on academic achievement with low achieving primary students.* Unpublished doctoral dissertation, University of Tennessee.

Swanson, B. B. (1981). *The beginner's concepts about reading, attitudes, and reading achievement in relation to language environment.* Paper presented at the annual meeting of the University of South Carolina Conference of Educational Research, Columbia, SC. (ERIC Document Reproduction Service No. ED 209 637)

Taylor, N. E., Blum, I. H., & Logsdon, D. M. (1986). The development of written language awareness: Environmental aspects and program characteristics. *Reading Research Quarterly, 21,* 132–149.

Teale, W. H. (1987). Emergent literacy: Reading and writing development in early childhood. In *Annual yearbook of the National Reading Conference.* Chicago: National Reading Conference.

Teale, W. H., & Sulzby, E. (Eds.). (1986). *Emergent literacy: Writing and reading.* Norwood, NJ: Ablex.

Trachtenburg, P., & Ferruggia, A. (1988). Big books from little voices: Reaching high risk beginning readers. *The Reading Teacher, 42,* 284–289.

Tunmer, W. E., & Nesdale, A. R. (1985). Phonemic segmentation skill and beginning reading. *Journal of Educational Psychology, 77,* 417–427.

Vilscek, E., & Cleland, D. L. (1968). *Two approaches to reading instruction: Final report.* (ERIC Document Reproduction Service No. ED 022 647)

Vilscek, E., Morgan, L., & Cleland, D. (1966). Coordinating and integrating language arts instruction in first grade. *The Reading Teacher, 20,* 31–37.

Walraven, S. T. (1981). *The effect of linguistic awareness instruction on linguistic awareness concept development and reading attitudes of kindergarten children.* Unpublished doctoral dissertation, University of Georgia.

Weaver, C. (1988). *Reading process and practice.* Portsmouth, NH: Heinemann.

Wilkinson, I. A. G., & Brown, C. A. (1983). Oral reading strategies of year one children as a function of level of ability and methods of instruction. *Reading Psychology, 4,* 1–9.

Woodcock, R. W. (1967). The Peabody–Chicago–Detroit Reading Project–A report of the second year results. (ERIC Document Reproduction Service No. ED 017 413)

Wrightstone, J. W. (1951). Research related to experience records and basal readers. *The Reading Teacher, 5,* 5–6.

3

Fostering the Scientific Study of Reading Instruction by Example

KEITH E. STANOVICH
PAULA J. STANOVICH

The 1989 article in *Review of Educational Research (RER)* with Patricia Miller (reprinted as Chapter 2, this volume) is pure Steve Stahl. It is a wonderful example of how Steve's contributions influenced the field at multiple levels. Steve's body of research can be viewed as teaching the field of reading a meta-lesson: that progress can be made by careful practice of scientific methods and by the interpretation of results in a theoretically fair manner. Steve made an immense contribution toward moving the field in the direction of scientifically based practice, not by hectoring his colleagues (although he was certainly not reticent about commenting on the state of the field, see McKenna, Stahl, & Reinking, 1994; Stahl, 1998, 1999), but by leading by example—by demonstrating that knowledge can be won by the most honest and straightforward scientific methods.

The *RER* article demonstrates everything we mean when we talk about teaching by example. It is, of course, a meta-analysis carried out in the most meticulous way. But it is much more than a blizzard of effect sizes, correlations, and inferential tests (as such papers sometimes seem to be). Stahl and Miller are careful to set their meta-analysis within a theoretical context. This enables them to give the findings a much more nuanced interpretation than is often found in quantitative syntheses of this type.

There are two critical parts to the context that they set. The first part is no surprise. It concerns the reading wars, as they had played out through the early to mid-1980s—the debate about whole language and phonics as instructional approaches. However, the second part of the context of the *RER* paper plays an even more critical role. This part concerns the stage models of reading that had been influential throughout the 1980s (e.g., Chall, 1983; Downing, 1979)—models that certainly have undergone much refinement in the ensuing years but that nonetheless still make adequate first-pass models. These are the models that allow Stahl and Miller to draw their nuanced and highly contextualized conclusions.

In light of the increasingly vitriolic reading wars of the 1990s that followed the *RER* paper, it is instructive to consider the integrity and scientific steadiness of the conclusions that Stahl and Miller draw. Throughout the 1990s, debates about instructional approaches in early reading acquisition were often characterized (particularly in public, as opposed to scientific, outlets) by special pleading, *ad hominem* attack, ideology, and predetermined conclusions. Thus, in light of what we know about what transpired in the decade after the Stahl and Miller paper, consider not only the content but also the tone of their basic conclusions:

> The results of the meta-analysis and vote-counting procedures appear to suggest that, overall, whole language/language experience approaches were approximately equal to basal reading approaches in their effects. This was found on both standardized and nonstandardized measures and on measures of both attitude and achievement. These results, however, were not consistent across all studies. Whole language/language experience approaches appear to be more effective when used in kindergarten or when used instead of a reading readiness program and seem to have had greater effects on measures of word recognition than on measures of comprehension in the more recent non-USOE studies. In addition, the studies that met more of our rigorous criteria for inclusion tended to favor basal reading programs over the whole language/language experience programs. An analysis of outliers also confirms these general trends. (1989, p. 107)

These are the types of measured, data-based conclusions that could have healed our fractious field had those perpetuating the reading wars been at all influenced by evidence. Nevertheless, Steve updated these measured conclusions several years later (Stahl, McKenna, & Pagnucco, 1994) and continued to use both evidence and his deep historical understanding of reading instruction to provide valuable roadmaps through the minefields of the instructional debates of the 1990s (see McKenna et al., 1994; Stahl, 1998, 1999).

As we have mentioned, a striking scholarly feature of the Stahl and Miller paper is the degree to which they were careful to contextualize their meta-analysis so that it made a theoretical contribution to the field. Stage models of that period meshed well with the empirical conclusions that they derived: "whole language/language experience approaches may work best in the cognitive phase because they simulate the environment in which literate behaviors begin to emerge. They may not work as well during the mastering phase, because sound–symbol correspondence instruction in these approaches is unsystematic and indirect" (1989, p. 90). What the authors are referring to here is the tendency of whole language approaches to emphasize the "naturalness" of reading acquisition ("it is argued that children learn written language the way they do oral language, through exposure to a literate environment," p. 89). Thus, in this article, Stahl and Miller presaged what was to become one of the most well-acknowledged theoretical blunders of the whole language movement—the assumption that reading acquisition was a natural process (for an early example of the debate, compare Goodman & Goodman, 1979, with Gough & Hillinger, 1980). Stahl and Miller's article stands at a turning point in this debate. Historically, it perhaps represents just about the time when the tide was beginning to turn against this long-standing assumption of the whole language movement.

GETTING THE "NATURALNESS" ARGUMENT RIGHT

Let us examine an example of how the naturalness assumption was articulated in a book for parents published just a couple of years before the Stahl and Miller review:

Why do people create and learn written language? They need it! How do they learn it? The same way they learn oral language, by using it in authentic literacy events that meet their needs. Often children have trouble learning written language in school. It's not because it's harder than learning oral language, or learned differently. It's because we've made it hard by trying to make it easy. Frank Smith wrote an article called "12 Easy Ways to Make Learning to Read Hard." Every way was designed to make the task easy by breaking it up in small bits. But by isolating print from its functional use, by teaching skills out of context and focusing on written language as an end in itself, we made the task harder, impossible for some children. (Goodman, 1986, p. 24)

That was the argument in a book titled *What's Whole in Whole Language* (Goodman, 1986). The way that this passage equates written language learning with oral language learning illustrates a recurring theme in the whole language literature: that learning to read is just like learning to speak. However, as many cognitive psychologists have pointed out (see Byrne, 1998; Liberman, 1999; Perfetti, 1994; Rayner, Foorman, Perfetti, Pesetsky, & Seidenberg, 2001; Shankweiler, 1999), the use of the speech/reading analogy ignores the obvious facts that all communities of human beings have developed spoken languages but only a minority of these exist in written form; that speech is almost as old as the human species, but that written language is a recent cultural invention of only the last 3,000 or 4,000 years; and that virtually all children in normal environments develop speech easily, whereas most children require explicit tuition to learn to read and substantial numbers of children have difficulty even after intensive efforts on the part of teachers and parents. The argument of Liberman and Liberman (1990) is typical of scientific thinking on the oral/written language distinction:

Reflecting biological roots that run deep, speech employs a single, universal strategy for constructing utterances. . . . On the other hand, scripts, being artifacts, choose variably from a menu of strategies. . . . Speech is biologically primary in a way that reading and writing are not. Accordingly, we suppose that learning to speak is, by the very nature of the underlying process, much like learning to walk or to perceive visual depth and distance, while learning to read and write is more like learning to do arithmetic or to play checkers. (p. 55)

In a later paper, Liberman (1999) discusses the role of phonology in reading, why speech is easy and reading is hard, and why the model of language held by the extreme whole language advocates does not square with linguistic science. Stahl and Miller were on exactly the right track in their 1989 paper. Contrary to the "reading is natural" view, research since then has consistently supported the view that reading is *not* acquired naturally, in the same way as speech (Adams, 1990; Byrne, 1998; Ehri, Nunes, Stahl, & Willows, 2001; McCardle & Chhabra, 2004; Olson, 2002, 2004; Perfetti, 2003; Rayner et al., 2001; Share, 1995, 1999; Shaywitz, 2003).

ANALYTIC VERSUS HOLISTIC APPROACHES TO READING ACQUISITION

Another dimension Stahl and Miller use to contextualize the difference between whole language and basal approaches is the holistic versus analytic dimension. This, of course, is a classic issue in reading instruction debates: Do children best acquire reading skill in a holistic manner or through direct instruction that emphasizes analytic attention to language components (phonemes, words, etc.)? A consideration of this issue suggests why the positive effects of whole language in their meta-analysis did not extend to the later stages of reading mastery.

Research indicates that successful reading acquisition seems to require the development of an analytic processing stance toward words that is probably not the natural processing set adopted by most children (e.g., Byrne, 1998) and that some children have extreme difficulty in adopting such an analytic processing set. The latter group of children will, as a result, have considerable difficulty building up knowledge of subword spelling–sound correspondences—and such knowledge appears to be almost a necessary prerequisite of fluent reading.

We now have a wealth of evidence indicating what it is that makes the analytic processing set difficult for some children. Research indicates that some children have problems dealing with subword units of speech representations. Becoming aware of the segmental structure of language appears to be a prerequisite to rapid reading acquisition in an alphabetic orthography. Thus, it is not surprising that researchers have moved on to try to demonstrate the efficacy of training in phonological processing skills (Foorman, Francis, Fletcher, Schatschneider, & Mehta, 1998; Lovett, Barron, & Benson, 2003; Lovett et al., 1994; Torgesen, 2004, 2005; Vellutino et al., 1996). More important, this accumulating and convergent research explains the "washout" effect observed by Stahl and Miller. The whole language/language experience programs examined in the Stahl and Miller meta-analysis lacked precisely the instructional components that are now deemed necessary for an important subgroup of children. Training programs that help the subgroup of children who will struggle with initial reading acquisition invariably involve the segmentation of words, thus flying in the face of the frequent admonitions from whole language advocates not to fractionate language.

As the Stahl and Miller meta-analysis presaged, the admonition not to "break up" language is not very helpful to teachers faced with children who are struggling in reading. In contrast, the growing knowledge of the role of phonological processing that was advancing in leaps and bounds at around the same time as the Stahl–Miller meta-analysis held out great potential to help just those children who social justice advocates in the whole language community wanted to help (an irony that one of us has discussed elsewhere; see Stanovich, 2000). And, as will be amply demonstrated in the rest of this volume, Steve Stahl made monumental contributions to the understanding of phonological awareness and phonological processing in reading—contributions to understanding the construct of phonological awareness itself and contributions to the applied psychology of phonological training in reading acquisition (e.g., Ehri et al., 2001; Stahl, Duffy-Hester, & Stahl, 1998; Stahl & Murray, 1994).

GETTING THINGS RIGHT

When surveying one's own work from the distance of a decade or more it is possible to summarize one's reactions into the categories of things that still seem right and things that no longer seem right (as done in Stanovich, 2000). Applying this distinction to the Stahl and Miller paper with a decade and a half of hindsight, it is apparent that there is very little to put in the latter category. The conceptual stance, the conclusions, the caveats—all follow through pretty straightforwardly into contemporary work on the instructional psychology of reading. However, as we mentioned at the outset, perhaps what is most admirable about this paper and about Steve's ouevre as a whole is how much it shows—by the sheer force of its confidence in the scientific process—what our field could gain by adjudicating instructional disputes by reliance on evidence-based scholarly analysis.

The paper provides a beautiful example for teachers of how science builds conclusions cumulatively and by displaying what one of us has termed *connectivity* (Stanovich, 2004). The cumulativeness of science—and the reasons *why* it is cumulative—is one of the critical principles that we must communicate to teachers during their teacher preparation programs. Interestingly, in these times when many are concerned about teacher autonomy, there is nothing that has greater potential for making teachers autonomous scholars than a knowledge of the scientific process and the ability to evaluate scientific evidence—that is, to be independent evaluators of knowledge claims. Such skills provide not only the best protection against gurus and fads but other benefits as well. They provide teachers with tools to win intellectual battles with (often misinformed) principals, school boards, parents, school psychologists, and other ancillary supervisors and personnel who attempt to dictate teacher practice. For example, it is possible for teachers—in the most professional manner—to confront principals, learning disabilities specialists, and in-service gurus with the appropriate questions: "Has the evidence for this treatment been published in peer-reviewed scientific journals?" "If so, in what journals, so that I may provide the involved teachers with reprints of the studies?" "Have the studies that have been done on this treatment been more than case studies?" "Have they involved some type of control group?" "Is the proposed mechanism by which this treatment works consistent with the 30-year consensus in the voluminous literature on the determinants of reading disability?" "Have the results been replicated by independent researchers?" These are basic questions, and they can be used by informed teachers to great effect.

Conclusions in science do not derive from a single experiment but from the convergence of results from many different partially diagnostic studies. Of course, this is the lesson of the quantitative meta-analysis of the Stahl and Miller type (and, it should be noted, that such quantitative syntheses were much less prevalent in the 1980s than they are now). That is the scientific value of cumulativeness that is illustrated in the Stahl and Miller paper. However, because of the care they took in setting the meta-analysis within a theoretical context, their paper illustrates the principle of connectivity as well. In science, new theories and new practical applications *must make contact with existing convergent evidence*. A new theory or practical application in medicine, or engineering, or biology must make contact with previously established empirical facts; otherwise, scientists and practitioners are highly skeptical of it. Likewise, in the field of instructional applications, we need to keep the connectivity principle foregrounded in our thinking. This is the reason the introductory, theoretical context-setting section of the Stahl and Miller paper is so important. It establishes their commitment to the connectivity principle as a key context for the meta-analytic number crunching that follows.

MAINTAINING TEACHER AUTONOMY IN A SEA OF POLITICS

Both of us have written about the threats to teacher autonomy that are posed by the highly politicized nature of educational debates in North America (Stanovich, 1998, 2000; Stanovich & Stanovich, 1997, 2003). Our long-standing belief is that only through dedication to evidence-based practice will teachers maintain their autonomy. The ally and bulwark of teacher professionalism must be science.

Our argument has been that there are many epistemological commonalities between researchers and teachers and that these commonalities need to be emphasized because they can form the backbone of a new emphasis on teacher professionalism that will truly preserve teacher autonomy. A "what works" epistemology is a critical source of underlying unity in the worldviews of educators and researchers (Gersten, Chard, & Baker, 2000; Gersten & Dimino, 2001). Empiricism, broadly construed, is about watching the world, manipulating it when possible, observing outcomes, and trying to associate outcomes with features observed and with manipulations. This is of course what the best teachers do. And this is true despite the grain of truth in the oft-repeated cliche that "teaching is an art." As Berliner (1987) notes:

> No one I know denies the artistic component to teaching. I now think, however, that such artistry should be research based. I view medicine as an art, but I recognize that without its close ties to science it would be without success, status, or power in our society. Teaching, like medicine, is an art that also can be greatly enhanced by developing a close relationship to science. (p. 4)

In his review of the work of the Committee on the Prevention of Reading Difficulties for the National Research Council of the National Academy of Sciences (Snow, Burns, & Griffin, 1998), Pearson (1999) warned educators that resisting evaluation by hiding behind the "art of teaching" shibboleth will spawn threats to teacher autonomy. Teachers need creativity, but they also need to be able to show that they know what evidence is. They need to be able to show that they understand that they practice in a profession based in behavioral science that produces evidence relevant to deciding between teaching practices. While making it absolutely clear that he opposes legislative mandates, Pearson cautions:

> We have a professional responsibility to forge best practice out of the raw materials provided by our most current and most valid readings of research. . . . If professional groups wish to retain the privileges of teacher prerogative and choice that we value so dearly, then the price we must pay is constant attention to new knowledge as a vehicle for fine-tuning our individual and collective views of best practice. This is the path that other professions, such as medicine, have taken in order to maintain their professional prerogative, and we must take it, too. My fear is that if the professional groups in education fail to assume this responsibility squarely and openly, then we will find ourselves victims of the most onerous of legislative mandates. (p. 245)

Nothing embodies the "constant attention to new knowledge as a vehicle for fine-tuning our individual and collective views of best practice" that Pearson is talking about better than the life's work of Steven Stahl. In the paper that we have commented on and in many others in this volume (as well as many other papers that space precludes from this volume), Steve's work is a model for the field. Always data based but always looking for the practical import, Steve's papers are models for the scientist–practitioner. And this is equally as true for the scientist–practitioner in the first-grade classroom as it is for the university researcher.

It is easier to give strictures to one's colleagues than to live by them. Steve's scholarly career was not characterized by a disconnect in this respect. The Stahl and Miller article represents one of many examples whereby Steve practiced his principles of science and research-based practice. This is the reason that when he admonished the field, the advice had impact. At the end of a long summary of the state of reading instruction, Steve gave us the type of advice that we will sorely miss, but that echoes what his work exemplified:

> The politicization of recent years interferes with effective instruction because it hardens viewpoints and forces educators to adopt unreasonable tenets concerning instruction. One result of the movement is that teachers have a great many beliefs about reading instruction, some of which are tenable and some of which are not. As we approach the millennium, we need to step back, look at the evidence, and evaluate all our beliefs. (1998, p. 61)

ACKNOWLEDGMENTS

Preparation of this chapter was supported by a grant from the Social Sciences and Humanities Research Council of Canada and the Canada Research Chairs program.

REFERENCES

Adams, M. J. (1990). *Beginning to read: Thinking and learning about print*. Cambridge, MA: MIT Press.

Berliner, D. C. (1987). Knowledge is power: A talk to teachers about a revolution in the teaching profession. In D. C. Berliner & B. V. Rosenshine (Eds.), *Talks to teachers* (pp. 3–33). New York: Random House.

Byrne, B. (1998). *The foundation of literacy: The child's acquisition of the alphabetic principle*. Hove, UK: Psychology Press.

Chall, J. S. (1983). *Stages of reading development*. New York: McGraw-Hill.

Downing, J. (1979). *Reading and reasoning*. New York: Springer-Verlag.

Ehri, L. C., Nunes, S., Stahl, S., & Willows, D. (2001). Systematic phonics instruction helps students learn to read: Evidence from the National Reading Panel's meta-analysis. *Review of Educational Research, 71*, 393–447.

Foorman, B. R., Francis, D. J., Fletcher, J. M., Schatschneider, C., & Mehta, P. (1998). The role of instruction in learning to read: Preventing reading failure in at-risk children. *Journal of Educational Psychology, 90*, 37–55.

Gersten, R., Chard, D., & Baker, S. (2000). Factors enhancing sustained use of research-based instructional practices. *Journal of Learning Disabilities, 33*, 445–457.

Gersten, R., & Dimino, J. (2001). The realities of translating research into classroom practice. *Learning Disabilities: Research and Practice, 16*, 120–130.

Goodman, K. (1986). *What's whole in whole language?* Portsmouth, NH: Heinemann.

Goodman, Y., & Goodman, K. S. (1979). Learning to read is natural. In L. Resnick & A. Weaver (Eds.), *Theory and practice of early reading* (Vol. 1, pp. 137–154). Hillsdale, NJ: Erlbaum.

Gough, P. B., & Hillinger, M. L. (1980). Learning to read: An unnatural act. *Bulletin of the Orton Society*, *30*, 171–176.

Liberman, A. M. (1999). The reading researcher and the reading teacher need the right theory of speech. *Scientific Studies of Reading*, *3*, 95–111.

Liberman, I. Y., & Liberman, A. M. (1990). Whole language versus code emphasis: Underlying assumptions and their implications for reading instruction. *Annals of Dyslexia*, *40*, 51–77.

Lovett, M. W., Barron, R. W., & Benson, N. J. (2003). Effective remediation of word identification and decoding difficulties in school-age children with reading disabilities. In H. L. Swanson, K. R. Harris, & S. Graham (Eds.), *Handbook of learning disabilities* (pp. 273–292). New York: Guilford Press.

Lovett, M. W., Borden, S., DeLuca, T., Lacerenza, L., Benson, N., & Brackstone, D. (1994). Treating the core deficits of developmental dyslexia: Evidence of transfer of learning after phonologically- and strategy-based reading training programs. *Developmental Psychology*, *30*, 805–822.

McCardle, P., & Chhabra, V. (Eds.). (2004). *The voice of evidence in reading research*. Baltimore: Brookes.

McKenna, M., Stahl, S., & Reinking, D. (1994). A critical commentary on research, politics, and whole language. *Journal of Reading Behavior*, *26*, 211–233.

Olson, R. K. (2002). Dyslexia: Nature and nurture. *Dyslexia*, *8*, 143–159.

Olson, R. K. (2004). SSSR, environment, and genes. *Scientific Studies of Reading*, *8*, 111–124.

Pearson, P. D. (1999). A historically based review of preventing reading difficulties in young children. *Reading Research Quarterly*, *34*, 231–246.

Perfetti, C. A. (1994). Psycholinguistics and reading ability. In M. Gernsbacher (Ed.), *Handbook of psycholinguistics* (pp. 849–894). San Diego, CA: Academic Press.

Perfetti, C. A. (2003). The universal grammar of reading. *Scientific Studies of Reading*, *7*, 3–24.

Rayner, K., Foorman, B. R., Perfetti, C. A., Pesetsky, D., & Seidenberg, M. S. (2001). How psychological science informs the teaching of reading. *Psychological Science in the Public Interest*, *2*, 31–74.

Shankweiler, D. (1999). Words to meaning. *Scientific Studies of Reading*, *3*, 113–127.

Share, D. L. (1995). Phonological recoding and self-teaching: Sine qua non of reading acquisition. *Cognition*, *55*, 151–218.

Share, D. L. (1999). Phonological recoding and orthographic learning: A direct test of the self-teaching hypothesis. *Journal of Experimental Child Psychology*, *72*, 95–129.

Shaywitz, S. E. (2003). *Overcoming dyslexia: A new and complete science-based program for reading problems at any level*. New York: Knopf.

Snow, C. E., Burns, M. S., & Griffin, P. (Eds.). (1998). *Preventing reading difficulties in young children*. Washington, DC: National Academy Press.

Stahl, S. (1998). Understanding shifts in reading and its instruction. *Peabody Journal of Education*, *73*, 31–67.

Stahl, S. A. (1999). Why innovations come and go (and mostly go): The case of whole language. *Educational Researcher*, *28*, 13–22.

Stahl, S. A., Duffy-Hester, A. M., & Stahl, K. A. D. (1998). Everything you wanted to know about phonics (but were afraid to ask). *Reading Research Quarterly*, *33*, 338–355.

Stahl, S. A., McKenna, M. C., & Pagnucco, J. (1994). The effects of whole language instruction: An update and reappraisal. *Educational Psychologist*, *29*(4), 175–185.

Stahl, S. A., & Murray, B. (1994). Defining phonological awareness and its relationship to early reading. *Journal of Educational Psychology*, *86*, 221–234.

Stanovich, K. E. (1998). Twenty-five years of research on the reading process: The grand synthesis and what it means for our field. In T. Shanahan & F. Rodriguez-Brown (Eds.), *Forty-seventh yearbook of the National Reading Conference* (pp. 44-58). Chicago: National Reading Conference.

Stanovich, K. E. (2000). *Progress in understanding reading: Scientific foundations and new frontiers.* New York: Guilford Press.

Stanovich, K. E. (2004). *How to think straight about psychology* (7th ed.). Boston: Allyn & Bacon.

Stanovich, P. J., & Stanovich, K. E. (1997). Research into practice in special education. *Journal of Learning Disabilities, 30,* 477–481.

Stanovich, P. J., & Stanovich, K. E. (2003). *Using research and reason in education: How teachers can use scientifically-based research to make curricular and instructional decisions.* Washington, DC: U.S. Department of Education.

Torgesen, J. K. (2004). Lessons learned from research on interventions for students who have difficulty learning to read. In P. McCardle & V. Chhabra (Eds.), *The voice of evidence in reading research* (pp. 355–382). Baltimore: Brookes.

Torgesen, J. K. (2005). Recent discoveries on remedial interventions for children with dyslexia. In M. J. Snowling & C. Hulme (Eds.), *The science of reading: A handbook* (pp. 521–537). Malden, MA: Blackwell.

Vellutino, F. R., Scanlon, D. M., Sipay, E., Small, S., Pratt, A., Chen, R., et al. (1996). Cognitive profiles of difficult to remediate and readily remediated poor readers: Early intervention as a vehicle for distinguishing between cognitive and experiential as basic causes of specific reading disability. *Journal of Educational Psychology, 88,* 601–638.

4 Understanding Shifts in Reading and Its Instruction

STEVEN A. STAHL

Outside of education, people view the shifts and swings of instruction with bemusement, if they do not have school-age children, or with alarm, if they do. In reading, we have swung from a whole word methodology to phonics to direct instruction to whole language, with various stops along the way, over the course of my lifetime. These swings have had resultant swings of achievement (Chall, 1996a). Slavin (1989) suggested that the "pendulum swings" in education come from an idea being adopted before the research results are in. When the results of the program turn out to be disappointing, we quickly reject that program and move on to the next fad. This may have been the case with whole language, as the approach was widely adopted before adequate research was available. The research that was available suggested that whole language was as, or possibly less, effective than current instruction (Stahl & Miller, 1989).

Yet whole language spread like "wildfire" (Pearson, 1989). The 1992 National Assessment of Educational Progress (NAEP; Mullis, Campbell, & Farstrup, 1993) surveyed fourth-grade teachers nationwide and found that 42% reported a heavy emphasis on whole language and an additional 41% reported a moderate emphasis—that is, 83% of the total. For a movement that began in the late 1970s, this was explosive.

The swing is now away from doctrinaire whole language and toward "balance." In California, where the English Language Arts Framework for California Public Schools K–12 (1987) spurred the growth of literature-based instruction, this framework has been revised to stress balance in reading instruction, including instruction in decoding and comprehension strategies (*Report of the California Reading Task Force*, 1995). The California moves have been a result, in part, of their poor showing on the NAEP comparisons (Mullis et al., 1993). Teachers and administrators have been concerned about the poor reading achievement of children in whole language settings and are arguing for more phonics instruction in a "balanced reading program" (McIntyre & Pressley, 1996). The move toward balance has been echoed across the country.

In most cases, however, *balance* has meant adding phonics instruction to literature-based instruction. The result has been "Frankenclasses," with various components from various philosophical stances and instructional approaches stitched together with the loosest of sutures (Stahl, 1998). If we can understand the confluence of forces that led to the whole language revolution, we can come up with a better definition of what *balance* might entail. The purpose of this article is to propose a different understanding of what *reading* is and to use that understanding to propose a new sense of "balanced" reading instruction.

UNDERSTANDING SHIFTS IN READING INSTRUCTION

A Historical Perspective

Although the whole language movement would seem to have been a radical shift from previous instruction, its rise to prominence is partially a result of historical forces and partially a result of the political nature of whole language. These factors are discussed in turn.

Up to 1965

One can chart the changes in reading instruction by observing the changes in basal readers. Looking at Chall's (1996b) review, there were incremental changes in basal readers from the 1930s to the 1960s. By 1965, the dominant basal reader was published by Scott, Foresman, with Dick, Jane, Sally, and Spot. This program, and its competitors from other publishers, typically had a set of characters and stories about these characters. All stories were specially written about these characters, and no outside literature was used, at least not in the early grades. Although we typify these characters as white and middle class, by 1965, Scott, Foresman did include African American characters. They were perhaps only distinguishable from the others by the wash of brown tone on their skin, but they were definitely present.

Instructionally, these series used a whole word, meaning-emphasis approach. Although the stories are remembered with nostalgia and ridiculed as lacking content, there was a considerable effort, through teacher narration, to make these stories meaningful. Decoding skills were not taught until children had amassed a certain number of sight words. The number varied among series.

From 1965 to 1976

By 1976, Scott, Foresman was no longer dominant. Instead, the Ginn 720 program had become the market leader. In this program, there was still a set of series characters, but the settings were more diverse, representing more than the middle-class small town in which Dick and Jane lived. Although the stories were still written especially for the series, the vocabulary control had loosened considerably, making the stories more interesting and the language more "natural." In addition, some degree of phonics instruction was occurring earlier (see Popp, 1975). This took two forms. First, there was a greater degree of control of new vocabulary by emphasizing phonics patterns. Second, there was more instruction earlier, using an analytic phonics approach. If one were to place the two series next to one another, it would be clear that a major change had occurred.

This program shift can be viewed from the perspectives of the goals of the programs. From 1965 to 1976, there was a shift from an emphasis on acquiring a sight vocabulary to a greater emphasis on learning to decode words. This was spurred by the best seller, *Why Johnny Can't Read* (Flesch, 1955) and aided by the publication of *Learning to Read: The Great Debate* (3rd ed.) in 1967 (Chall, 1996b), a scholarly but readable review of research on teaching beginning reading. This shift was also aided by a general acceptance of the need for children to learn to decode words. Research tended to stress individual word decoding, as evidenced by the publication of *Language by Eye and by Ear* (Kavanagh & Mattingly, 1972), which contained several now-classic papers on single word decoding. Some of the first discussions of phoneme awareness were prominent in this collection. In addition, *Basic Studies in Reading* (Levin & Williams, 1970) was published during this time. This collection of papers attempted to bring insights from cognitive psychology and linguistics to reading.

From 1977 to 1986

Another major shift occurred a decade later. At this point, the Houghton Mifflin program had become the market leader. They published a series that not only did not contain continuing characters, but also contained a great deal of children's literature—in the words of the publishers, "literature that represents the finest authors past and present" (Houghton Mifflin, 1986, p. 3). Much of this literature was rewritten by reducing the vocabulary load by readability formulas and was arranged side by side with stories written especially for the program. Vocabulary control was still present but loosened considerably. There was more phonics instruction, but this instruction had largely shifted to the worksheets. A typical lesson might consist of a teacher's providing a brief introduction to a skill, what Durkin (1979) called "mentioning," followed by practice using worksheets. In a typical lesson, there was not only a phonics skill taught, but another phonics skill reviewed, a comprehension skill taught or reviewed, and another worksheet used to review the story. At that time, I was working for a school district, observing reading instruction, and noted that only 40% of the time allocated for reading instruction was used for "reading"—that is, the reading of connected text. The remaining 60% was spent on completing worksheets or doing supplemental work, like Weekly Readers. Gambrell, Wilson, and Gantt (1981) observed that average readers spent an average of 6 minutes per day reading connected text. Children with reading problems spent considerably less time actually reading—about 1 minute per day, on the average.

By the middle of the 1980s, there was an understanding that children could decode better but had difficulties comprehending. This was reflected, first, in the establishment in 1975 of a federally funded Center for the Study of Reading, whose mission was to study comprehension so that children could be better taught. The first wave of research from the Center was largely basic research, establishing principles of how one comprehends. It was not until the second wave that practical instructional approaches were developed. These were integrated into the basal readers of the late 1980s. The other major event was the publication of *Becoming a Nation of Readers* (Anderson, Hiebert, Wilkinson, & Scott, 1985). To date, this book has sold over 300,000 copies, more than any other book dealing with education.

The changes in basals due to the cognitive revolution began to be institutionalized by the 1989 revisions. These texts contained fewer skills, recast as strategies, but each strategy was taught more extensively, and practice was better integrated into story reading than in the 1986 basal readers. But the effects of this revolution were barely felt.

Whole Language Basals

By 1991, the advent of "whole language basals" had occurred (Hoffman et al., 1994). Conventional basal readers were restyled as "anthologies," containing unadapted literature, with little if any vocabulary control (see Hoffman et al., 1994). Lesson structures moved from the Directed Reading Activity (DRA), developed by Betts (1946) and used ever since, to different models of instruction, such as the shared reading model of Holdaway (1979). In the traditional DRA, a teacher might begin a story with a discussion of the new vocabulary the children would encounter and provide a purpose-setting statement, guide students' reading through the story with questions, and end with postreading questions and extension activities. In Holdaway's model, the teacher might begin with joint reading of the story, possibly with a big book, and opportunities for children to read the story independently or with a partner. This format constituted a radically different recasting of reading instruction. Instruction in skills, which predominated instructional time in the early 1980s, was often difficult to find in the 1991 basal reading programs, relegated to the back of the teacher's manual or integrated into suggestions for story reading.

By the late 1980s, however, there was a sense that we had dealt with comprehension adequately and had children who could comprehend but who were not motivated to read. Researchers at the National Reading Research Center (NRRC) conducted a nationwide survey of teachers in 1992 (O'Flahaven et al., 1992) and found that teachers' first priority was learning how to motivate students. The "engagement" perspective that motivated the research of the NRRC reflected this concern.

This shift to motivation as a primary goal was one of the impetuses for the whole language movement. Whole language programs promised that children would become motivated and engaged readers, by virtue of child-centered programs that stress student choice. As we discuss next, this promise has been, by and large, fulfilled by whole language programs. However, even though they tend to improve motivation, it has proved more difficult for whole language programs to lead children to more and more challenging texts. At the same time, children in such programs tend to see the need for more information about how text works than they are customarily afforded (which is, essentially, what decoding and comprehension strategy instruction delivers). Thus, the "return" to balanced reading instruction is in fact a return to a circumstance that has never occurred before—a concurrent emphasis on decoding, comprehension, and motivation.

Sorting Out the Alternatives

Each of the approaches in these basal reading programs was a solution to a different problem in reading. Each approach was developed originally to deal with a specific aspect of reading and extended to encompass the whole of reading instruction. In the process of extension, educators developed a view of reading rooted in their analysis of the original problem. Each of these views is limited and ultimately incomplete when advocates attempt to extrapolate it beyond the problem it was designed to solve.

Direct instruction approaches are rooted in task analyses of decoding, later extended to other aspects of reading (see Bereiter & Englemann, 1966). As such, they tended to view even the complex thought processes of comprehension as concatenations of subprocesses. From these models, the objective-based basal reading programs of the 1970s attempted to teach every skill that a student would need to read, with the assumption that, when students mastered enough skills, they would be accomplished readers. Reading matter, whether using a set of characters or using adapted literature, was used to reinforce the skills.

By the late 1980s, the focus had switched to teaching comprehension. The first basals were based on objective-based models, similar to the decoding models. With the cognitive revolution, these were recast as strategies, based on metacognitive models of strategy learning (e.g., Paris, Lipson, & Wixson, 1983). These models placed emphasis on explicit explanation of what a strategy was and why it was useful, as well as how to apply the strategy. The basals incorporated the new comprehension instructional procedures, such as story maps (Beck & McKeown, 1981) and semantic maps (Heimlich & Pittelman, 1986). Teachers taught fewer strategies, taught them more extensively, and made explicit how the strategy might be used in the reading of exposition and literature. In addition, teachers spent more time on activating background knowledge, from the influence of schema theory (Anderson & Pearson, 1984). The result was a more elaborated lesson, based on a cognitive view of comprehension. Even in first grade, where word recognition was traditionally stressed, lessons were comprehension oriented.

The activity-based model of learning in a whole language classroom harkens back to a number of sources, including the language experience movement in reading, as well as the work of educators in New Zealand, like Donald Holdaway, Marie Clay, and Sylvia Ashton-Warner. On the foundation of activity-based literacy education, they added influences from literary response theory and composition. From psychology, they drew on the developmental psychology of both Piaget and Vygotsky. This area is well reviewed by Y. M. Goodman (1989), who also draws on her personal history as a first-grade teacher. When whole language educators attempt to extend their model to upper grades (e.g., Pahl & Monson, 1992), they tend to view the processes of learning in the upper grades as analogous to those in the earlier grades.

Thus, both the objective-based basal readers of the 1970s and the whole language movement of the 1990s were rooted in different views of early literacy. The objective-based basals were rooted in a direct instruction model (Carnine, Silbert, & Kame'enui, 1996). based in a behavioral analysis of early reading competencies. In this view, children need to be taught a variety of subskills to succeed as readers. This view sees decoding as primary and uses instructional means found to be successful in teaching children to decode. The whole language movement of the 1990s, on the other hand, is rooted in a social activity model of early learning (Y. M. Goodman, 1989), in which children are seen as inherently active learners. In this model, motivation is seen as primary. If children are motivated to learn to read, they will learn to do so. The role of the teacher in such a classroom is to "lead from behind" (Newman, 1985) or to help children meet the goals that they have set for themselves.

In contrast, the basal reading programs of the 1980s were based on a model for teaching comprehension in the intermediate grades. This model was moved down to the primary grades, by the increased emphasis on background knowledge and the increased emphasis on teaching skills as strategies (G. G. Duffy & Roehler, 1987), although many of the skills remained the same. There were fewer skills, taught more in depth. In addition, the texts became more natural, with fewer adaptations, and had fewer words that fit a phonic pattern than in the previous decade. Comprehension was primary, with the assumption that other aspects of reading would follow if children could comprehend.

DEFINING READING

A Shift in Goals

What happened between 1965 and 1976, between 1977 and 1985, and between 1986 and 1991? These shifts were not random, but instead reflect shifts in the goals of reading instruction. Our discussions with teachers have led us to appreciate the need to juggle multiple goals in reading instruction. Teachers want their students to

- Appreciate good literature and be motivated to read.
- Be able to comprehend what they read and to learn from texts.
- Be able to read words accurately and automatically.

We have held these goals throughout. However, we shift among them, and it is these shifts that lead to changes in the philosophies behind reading programs. Further, these goals are interrelated. If one cannot decode a text fluently and automatically, then it is difficult to comprehend the text fully (Samuels, Schermer, & Reinking, 1992). If one cannot comprehend a text, it is difficult to appreciate it (Nell, 1988), and one is not motivated to read texts that are beyond one's comprehension.

These three goals for "reading" can be viewed as separable components of reading. For example, Gough and Tunmer (1986) argued that decoding and general language comprehension are separable components of reading comprehension. To further complicate matters, the type of reading that Gough and Tunmer talk about is what Rosenblatt (1985) called "efferent" reading, or reading to get information from text. One also needs to consider "aesthetic" reading, or affective responding to literature and expository prose, to get a complete picture of "reading." In the next section we outline a view of the nature of decoding, comprehension, and aesthetic reading and how these are developed.

Stages of the Development of Word Recognition

Readers seem to go through three stages (Chall, 1996c) as they develop efficient word recognition abilities. In the first stage, an *awareness* stage (my terminology), they develop a conceptual knowledge of the nature of written language and its relationship to speech. This involves learning how print functions and learning that it can tell stories, inform, direct, and so forth. This stage also involves learning the conventions of print, such as directionality, the fact that sentences begin with capital letters and end with periods, and the concept of what a "word" is in both written and spoken language. It involves learning about the form of print, including the letters of the alphabet. Children also learn, during this stage, that spoken words can be broken down into phonemes, a key insight for learning the relationships between letters and sounds (Stahl & Murray, 1994). Children who do not have phonological awareness tend to develop reading problems in first grade, problems that persist through their schooling. Juel (1988) found that children who were low in phonological awareness tended to end up in the lowest quartile of their class in fourth grade (see also Stanovich, 1986; Torgesen & Burgess, 1998). These four aspects of the written language/oral language relationship—functions, conventions, and form of print and awareness of phonemes—form the conceptual foundation on which reading knowledge is built (Labbo & Tealel, 1997). Children who lack any or all of these concepts have difficulty in learning to read, a difficulty that is magnified as they progress through the grades.

In the second stage, *accuracy*, children learn to accurately decode words. Children in this stage are "fixed" on the print, placing emphasis on accurate decoding of words. At this point, children's emphasis is on acquiring knowledge of words and of sound–symbol correspondences and applying that knowledge strategically to unlock simple texts. Ehri (1992) described children's growth in accurate word reading as going through several phases. At first, children use a visual cue to recognize words. Cues could be simple, such as the two "eyes" in look, or more complex. If children do not develop phonological awareness, as many children with reading problems do not, my observation is that they tend to use more and more complex visual cues to recognize words (Stahl, Kuhn, & Pickle, 1999). As children develop phonological awareness, they begin to use some partial sound information in the word, such as an initial or final sound (see Stahl & Murray, 1998). Ehri (1992) called this stage "phonetic cue reading." A child at this phase will rely on initial sounds. Knowledge of initial sounds can aid in fingerpointing (Ehri & Sweet, 1991), which can lead to more and more word knowledge (Clay, 1993). Efficient word recognition is dependent on more complete knowledge of sounds and symbols (M. J. Adams, 1990). In the cipher phase, children use all the letters and sounds to identify words. At this stage, children's reading can still be labored, relying on sounding out or other strategies such as using analogies (Cunningham, 1975–1976). It is important to note that the use of analogies is dependent on children's ability to do phonetic cue reading, or using initial sounds. Both Bruck and Treiman (1992) and Ehri and Robbins (1992) found that children needed to have some grapheme–phoneme knowledge to take advantage of analogy-based decoding strategies.

These phases are somewhat different for children's reading in context. Biemiller (1970) observed children learning to read in first grade. In the beginning of the year, children would substitute any word that made sense when reading a text, often substituting whole lines of text to maintain their momentum. This is roughly equivalent to Chall's (1996c) awareness stage, as children are not focusing on print to "read," but instead are focusing on the meaning of the text. At some point during the year, students would go through a no-response phase, apparently realizing that they did not know a word that matched what the print said. This realization requires an awareness of the alphabetic principle and some knowledge of the relationships between sounds and symbols. The last stage in Biemiller's observations was when children would substitute a word that not only made sense in the context but also shared letters with the text word. This would correspond to Ehri's phonetic cue reading and alphabetic phases. Children go through these phases differently, depending on the type of instruction that they have (see Barr, 1984), but all students seem to go through similar phases.

The accuracy stage is short lived and gives way to an automaticity stage. At this point, children begin to develop automatic word recognition skills so that the process of recognizing words is transparent and the reader can concentrate fully on the text (Samuels et al., 1992). Because humans have limited-capacity information processors that can only attend to a certain amount of information at any given time, devoting attention to word recognition would take cognitive resources away from processes needed to comprehend text. Slow word recognition thus interferes with comprehension.

The transition from accurate to automatic word recognition occurs over a number of years, conventionally from the end of first grade to the end of third grade. Following the model of M. J. Adams (1990), as children are exposed to more and more words and devote attention to their patterns, the children build up a network of relationships among letters. This network contains our knowledge of which letters typically appear with others. Thus, we know that *t* and *h* frequently occur together, as do *a* and *t* and thousands of other patterns. According to M. J. Adams, when one letter is recognized, it primes other letters in the network, with the strength of priming being related to the probability of the letters co-occurring. In other words, when *t* is recognized, its priming may spread to *h*, *a*, *n*, and many others, but not to letters such as *q* and *x*, which rarely co-occur with *t*. This principle accounts, in part, for the fact that orthographically regular nonwords are recognized nearly as well as real words in a variety of tasks, at least by proficient readers.

Exposure to more words of a particular pattern may hasten the development of automaticity. Juel and Roper-Schneider (1985) compared the word recognition skills of two groups of first graders, both taught with a synthetic phonics approach. One group read materials containing multiple instances of taught patterns from stories using a phonically controlled vocabulary. The other group read material from a conventional basal series, using a vocabulary controlled by word frequency. They found that the phonically controlled materials seemed to induce the earlier use of letter–sound relationships in recognizing words than did the other materials. Students in the conventional basal series seemed to rely on distinctive letter cues, such as *ight*, to identify words.

Matching Word Recognition Development with Instruction

This review suggests that development of automatic decoding skill occurs through a series of stages. For each stage, a different type of instruction is appropriate. For the awareness stage, it would seem that whole language approaches might be most effective in developing the conceptual base about reading instruction. The social interactions around a text, both student–teacher and student–student, mirror those found in households with a high literacy press (e.g., Snow & Ninio, 1986). In those households, parents and children read together, shifting their focus to different aspects of print as the need arises. Through these interactions, around Big Books or experience charts, children in whole language classes can develop a solid concept of the functions of print needed for formal reading instruction. Writing using invented spelling also seems to be a spur to the development of an understanding of many conditions of print, including spacing and directionality, as well as a beginning of knowledge of letter–sound relationships. Indeed, Stahl and Miller (1989) found that whole language approaches are significantly more effective in kindergarten than in first grade.

To build phoneme awareness, another essential precursor of success in reading that should be developed in kindergarten, whole language instruction may not be enough. Children will develop some awareness of phonemes through their attempts at invented spelling, as in a whole language classroom (Winsor, 1990), but some form of direct teaching might also be useful here. Successful programs for teaching phoneme awareness, such as those of Bradley and Bryant (1983) and Lundberg, Frost, and Peterson (1988), have been found to significantly improve students' reading skill 2 years later.

Many children make the transition from the awareness stage to accuracy and automaticity without any help. Durkin (1966) documented the growth of many "natural" readers who learned to read at home, without any formal instruction in phonics or in any other aspects of reading. Many others will make that transition in a whole language classroom by benefit of ample experiences with print. Others, including siblings of the children in Durkin's study, need some direct instruction to move forward in word recognition.

For those who need more instruction, it would seem that optimal approaches include those that (a) stress the importance of a strategy that gets children to attend to the order of letters in words and (b) give children ample practice reading phonically patterned words. These conditions would seem to be satisfied by a number of approaches, such as direct instruction, analogy-based approaches, spelling-based approaches, and embedded phonics approaches, as long as they provide equal emphasis on the analysis of words (Stahl, Duffy-Hester, & Stahl, 1998). Stahl, Duffy-Hester, and Stahl suggested that children construct knowledge of orthographic features in words. These constructions progress along the lines suggested by Ehri (1995), with progressively deeper analysis of words, both in reading and in spelling, and the development of more complex networks of knowledge about letters and how they fit together in words (M. J. Adams, 1990). For example, a person learns that *ck* never begins a word but often ends a word, that *v* rarely ends a word without an *e*, that *q* is rarely without *u*, that *t* is more likely to be followed by *h* or *r* than by *q* or *p*, and so forth (see Venezky, 1970). These conditional probabilities seem to aid efficient word recognition and are learned through exposure to words. Research, however, suggests that the organized exposure through a phonics program leads to more efficient word recognition than the unsystematic exposure found in many whole language classes (Chall, 1996b). Whole language teachers can, and often do, teach phonics (Church, 1996; Routman, 1996), often in a structured and organized manner (Dahl & Freppon, 1995; Freppon & Dahl, 1991), but embedded within a curriculum based on reading literature for authentic purposes (Stahl, Duffy-Hester, & Stahl, 1998).

Pointing out orthographic features and providing practice in reading words would seem to be antithetical to the insistence of whole language theorists that teachers keep focused on meaning and not break language into parts (e.g., Grundin, 1994). However, it is here that we have observed teachers who profess a whole language philosophy most often break with that philosophy. One teacher whom we interviewed said that although she believed in whole language, she felt her students, from homes without many literacy resources, needed direct instruction in phonics (Stahl, Osborn, Pearson, & Winsor, 1992).

To move from accuracy to automaticity, children need to read as much as possible. Such reading need not contain a vocabulary controlled by phonic elements. Instead, the children need to read material at an appropriate instructional level. This has been traditionally defined as a 95% to 99% accuracy rate (Wixson & Lipson, 1991), but there are some indications that children benefit from reading text with as low as a 90% accuracy rate in some circumstances (Clay, 1993). The instruction should stress increasing the volume of reading for children so that they will get an appropriate amount of practice, including using rereading of texts to develop fluency (Samuels et al., 1992; Stahl & Heubach, 2005). Hoffinan (1987; see also Reutzel & Hollingsworth, 1993) and Stahl and Heubach reported approaches that improve children's fluent and automatic reading. Stahl and Heubach's approach, similar to Hoffman's, is an attempt to use repeated readings in a regular classroom program to develop fluent and automatic word recognition in second graders. The program consists of three parts: (a) a home reading program in which students are encouraged to read 20 minutes per day at home, (b) a choice reading program in which students read materials of their own choosing (and usually near their instructional level) either alone or with a partner during the schoolday, and (c) a redesigned basal reading lesson. The redesigned basal reading lesson began with the teacher reading and discussing the basal story, including having the child read the story at home one or more times, depending on the child's needs; having the children read the story in partners; and responding to each story using a variety of means.

These lessons were given to all students in the class, using the second-grade basal reader. Because students in the class vary considerably in initial reading level, this material is well above the level of many children in the class and below the level of others. Because the classes were predominantly in schools serving lower socioeconomic status children, there were a great many children who had difficulty reading the material. However, over the 2 years that we collected data, children at all initial ability levels made roughly the same amount of progress—roughly 2 years' growth in instructional level on an informal reading inventory during the school year. In addition, all children who began reading at a primer level or higher could read at the second-grade level by the end of the year. Many of those reading below the primer level also were able to read second-grade material. In fact, of the 85 students in the first year, only 3 were still unable to read a second-grade passage by the end of the year. For the second year, the results were similar. All children but 2 who began the year reading at a primer level or higher (out of 105) could read the second-grade passage by the end of the year.

Thus, learning to recognize words may involve radically different instruction as children go through the grades. In the awareness stage, children may benefit from exposure to materials, in an activity-based classroom congruous with whole language principles, as long as adequate attention is paid to phonological awareness. In the accuracy phase, children need more direct instruction, but this instruction can be provided in a variety of classroom approaches. In the fluency stage, children need practice reading texts at an appropriate level, often using rereading.

Learning to Comprehend

The difficulties in learning to comprehend are rooted in the differences and similarities between oral and written language. Oral and written language share a common vocabulary, syntax, structure, and so forth. Children's syntactic development is nearly complete by the time they enter school (but see Chomsky, 1972), but children's vocabulary and general knowledge continue to grow. Growth in vocabulary is the most powerful predictor of growth in comprehension (Anderson & Freebody, 1981). Children learn new word meanings from a variety of sources, including listening to stories (e.g., Elley, 1989; Stahl, Richek, & Vandevier, 1991). The greatest growth in vocabulary while listening to stories is associated with teachers who stop and talk about words while reading (Dickinson & Smith, 1994). Certainly a program of reading to children should be part of a quality reading program. Later on, some amount of direct instruction in vocabulary seems to produce consistent achievement gains (Stahl & Fairbanks, 1986), although the majority of children's growth in vocabulary knowledge comes from reading widely (Stahl, 1998). Thus, an effective program to improve children's store of word meanings might include reading to children, especially but not only in the early grades, wide reading of a variety of challenging texts, and direct vocabulary teaching.

Children also need to gain knowledge about a variety of subjects, in literature, social studies, science, music, and art, to comprehend increasingly complex texts. Whether this growth in knowledge is done through a core knowledge approach (e.g., Hirsch, 1987) or through other means is beyond the scope of this article.

Skills and Strategies

Although teaching vocabulary and improving general knowledge are perhaps the major routes to improving comprehension, the majority of instructional time seems to be spent on teaching skills and strategies. Readers employ skills and strategies to act on their knowledge during reading. Following Paris et al. (1983), "skills" are cognitive processes that are executed automatically, without the reader's conscious attention or conscious choice. In contrast, "strategies" are deliberately chosen and applied to a situation in reading. Conventionally, a skill is a cognitive process that is executed without conscious attention. A strategy is executed deliberately, at least on some level, as when a reader chooses to make notes when studying or looks away from the text when reading to puzzle out an ambiguous sentence. As Paris et al. stated, "strategies are skills under consideration" (p. 295). A strategy might become a skill, as in sounding out words, which should lead to automatic recognition of words, or it might remain strategic, as in a study strategy like note taking.

When children learn to read, they use what they know about oral language to comprehend written language. The skills that children ordinarily use in oral language need minimal instruction to transfer to written language. For example, even young children can make inferences about familiar content (Paris & Lindauer, 1976). Inferencing is a natural part of language use, usually based on children's knowledge of the world (Anderson & Pearson, 1984). To get children to be better able to make inferences during reading may involve little more than encouraging them to do so. Teaching specific inferencing strategies may be unnecessary. Hansen (1981) found that increasing the percentage of inferential questions asked during a lesson was just as effective as a direct instruction inference training program in improving children's ability to answer inference questions. Similar results have been found with teaching children to use a story grammar in recalling stories, teaching children to get the meanings of unknown words from context, and teaching children sentence comprehension.

Oral and written language differ in several essential aspects. First, oral language makes assumptions about its audience that written language does not. Oral conversation assumes a shared knowledge base between speaker and listener so that much content can be implied. Written language cannot make use of that assumption because authors write for audiences unknown to them. Thus, written language tends to be autonomous, whereas oral language tends to be context bound (Olson, 1977). These differences in voice may create difficulties for some children, and teachers and texts attempt to make a transition between the context-bound oral language spoken by children and autonomous texts typical of school (C. D. Baker & Freebody, 1989). Learning about the school-like language of texts can also take place through exposure to storybooks and through parents or teachers reading aloud.

Second, there are strategies specifically used in comprehension of written texts that are not relied on in listening comprehension. Dole, Duffy, Roehler, and Pearson (1991) suggested four such strategies: determining importance, summarization, self-questioning, and comprehension monitoring. Pressley, Goodchild, Fleet, Zajchowski, and Evans (1989) suggested a more inclusive set of strategies to be taught. Dole et al. also suggested teaching children to make inferences, and Pressley et al. suggested teaching story grammars (both of which I feel are part of ordinary language comprehension and probably do not need to be taught directly). Both sets of authors suggested that these strategies be taught directly as part of a comprehension curriculum and cited research showing that such instruction leads to overall improvement in comprehension.

Traditional basal reading programs, such as the 1986 edition program from Houghton Mifflin, and direct instruction programs (e.g., G. L. Adams & Englemann, 1996) treat skills such as "getting the main idea" or "learning word meanings from context," which are part of students' general language behaviors and are used automatically in oral language comprehension, the same as strategies such as summarization, complex study approaches, and so forth, which are specific to written language and new to the student. Skills that students already use proficiently in their language comprehension may be best taught through minimal instruction, such as asking questions that require the skill (see Stahl, 1992, for review). The program of research by G. G. Duffy et al. (1986), involving having teachers transform the skills taught in objective-based basal reading programs into strategies, was not effective in raising student achievement (although students were better at articulating what they were doing during reading). Teaching a strategy, especially one that students do not use in any other context, may require more complex instruction.

Teaching Children to Comprehend

Two groups of instructional strategies have been used to teach children to comprehend text: explicit explanation and cognitive apprenticeships.

Explicit Explanation

Explicit explanation developed as an amalgam between the direct instruction technologies, rooted in behaviorism and task analyses of the reading process (Kame'enui, Simmons, Chard, & Dickson, 1997), and in the concepts of informed instruction and metacognition, as discussed by A. L. Brown, Campione, and Day (1981) and Paris et al. (1983). A number of studies have indicated that many students, especially younger and poorer readers, lack an awareness of the purposes of reading and of strategies used in reading and do not monitor their reading (see L. Baker & Brown, 1984, for review). Without the students' awareness of the purpose of a strategy, it was assumed to be unlikely that the students would transfer the use of that strategy from the instruction to their ordinary reading. Thus, explicit explanation approaches place a high priority on making students aware of the purpose of each strategy that educators teach. Students are explicitly told when the strategy is applicable, what types of texts or situations it works for, and when it does not work, and they are given checklists to determine that they have used the strategy correctly. Educators who use such approaches also believe that transfer will not occur unless it is explicitly trained. Therefore, explicit explanation approaches may begin with specially constructed materials but will include lessons in how the strategy can be used in ordinary reading. For example, Rinehart, Stahl, and Erickson (1986) began by teaching sixth graders to summarize short paragraphs, gradually lengthening the material used until the students were writing summaries from their social studies textbook. In the beginning of explicit explanation instruction, the responsibility for using a strategy lies largely with the teacher; by the end, the student is executing the strategy independently.

An example of an explicit explanation program is Raphael's work in teaching children to answer questions strategically using a Question–Answer Relationship taxonomy (e.g., Raphael & Wonnacott, 1985). In these lessons, students are taught about the relationships between questions and their answers. After an initial exposition of Raphael's taxonomy, students are shown a passage and given questions with their answers. As a class, they discuss the relationship between the question and the answer. In succeeding lessons, students had to answer questions given the relationship; provide the answer and the relationship; and finally generate their own questions, providing both answers and relationships. Thus, the students gradually assert "ownership" of the strategy.

Explicit explanation has been used to teach a wide variety of reading strategies, from using context to identify unknown words (G. G. Duffy et al., 1986) to making inferences during reading (Hansen & Pearson, 1983). It has also been used as a model for an entire school's curriculum, involving the explicit integration of strategies in all subject matter learning from the primary to the middle grades (I. W. Gaskins & Elliot, 1991).

There are some indications that, when teaching skills such as using context to identify words—skills that might have been mastered through children's oral language development—explicit explanation makes children better able to discuss what they are doing but does not directly improve their reading achievement (G. G. Duffy et al., 1986). G. G. Duffy et al. asserted that this greater awareness will eventually translate into higher achievement, but they did not present evidence that it does. Because skills are best performed automatically, without conscious application, it is not clear that explicit explanation would be useful. For strategies such as summarization, which are applied deliberately, such explicit explanation may be highly effective.

Cognitive Apprenticeship

Cognitive apprenticeship approaches attempt to set up a master–apprentice relationship between student and teacher. The teacher's role is to scaffold the learning, withdrawing support as students are able to proceed on their own. Just as an apprentice first watches the master as the master undertakes a skilled craft, so the student initially observes the teacher as the teacher models the processes of comprehension. Gradually, the teacher gives more and more responsibility to the student until it is the teacher who watches the student perform comprehension tasks.

Those who advocate the use of cognitive apprenticeships view reading as involving the orchestration of complex processes. Teaching those processes one by one inevitably distorts them, making it more difficult to integrate them into ordinary reading (J. S. Brown, Collins, & Duguid, 1989). In cognitive apprenticeships, texts are treated as wholes, using all appropriate strategies simultaneously. The task difficulty is lessened by the teacher's initially providing a great deal of scaffolding, gradually transferring control to the learner over the course of instruction. Teachers and students might read a text together, with the teacher providing as much support as necessary for the students to successfully work through the text. They might also argue that cognition is socially situated—that all cognitive acts take place within a social and cultural context and that the larger context can either support or impede cognitive activities, such as those involved in reading. This new view of cognition has been called "situated cognition" or "socially constructed knowledge" (J. S. Brown et al., 1989). From this view, researchers suggest that an apprenticeship model is more appropriate for teaching than the transmittal model of direct instruction. Through the process of interacting with the knowledgeable other, the students learn how an expert orchestrates the processes involved in comprehension (Garcia & Pearson, 1991). In cognitive apprenticeships, students and teacher work together to comprehend increasingly complex text.

The cognitive apprenticeship model places a great deal of emphasis on constructing the meaning of a text through social interactions and usually involves a reorganization of the basic organization of the class. Instead of a teacher-dominated class structure, cognitive apprenticeship models usually involve small groups working together. Cooperative learning (Stevens, Madden, Slavin, & Farnish, 1987), reciprocal teaching (Palinscar & Brown, 1984), collaborative problem solving (Palinscar, David, Winn, & Stevens, 1991), book clubs, and conversational discussion groups (McMahon, Raphael, Goatley, & Pardo, 1997; O'Flahaven, 1989) all use group dynamics to scaffold or support individual children's learning. For example, in reciprocal teaching, small groups of students work together with the teacher to read a text. Each person in the group takes turns being the "teacher." As the teacher, a child uses four teaching behaviors: questioning, summarizing, clarifying, and predicting. Unlike many of the training approaches discussed so far, reciprocal teaching usually takes place over a period of weeks or months, not a single class period. Initiation of reciprocal teaching might begin with direct instruction of the four teaching operations, followed by direct teacher modeling. In the early stages of reciprocal teaching, the teacher takes a dominant role, modeling the operations during his or her turn, and prompting students during theirs. Such prompts might include "What is the main idea of this paragraph?", "Could you make it into a question?", and so forth. Over time, the prompts become more general and less specific. Also, over time, students take over the groups, acting more and more like expert teachers.

By the artifice of having students act as teacher, reciprocal teaching requires that students externalize the operations of comprehension. Through this externalization, the teacher and other students are able to scaffold the development of each student's comprehension. The learning that occurs in conversational discussion groups, where groups of students respond to stories (O'Flahaven, 1989), or cooperative learning groups, which have been used for a great many learning situations (e.g., Stevens et al., 1987), involves similar scaffolding through group dynamic processes.

Another cognitive apprenticeship approach is Transactional Strategies Instruction (TSI; Pressley et al., 1992). In TSI, teachers embed strategy instruction into the reading of literature. TSI teaches a number of strategies simultaneously, modeling how to orchestrate strategies to construct meaning from text. The teacher's role in TSI is to scaffold students' learning and use of strategies in reading through modeling, questioning, and direct explanation. In SAIL (Bergman, 1992), students monitor their understanding by predicting, making visualizations, summarizing, "thinking aloud," or a combination of these items. Teachers can help students identify places in the text where these strategies might be most useful, comment on children's use of the strategies, and coach children, gradually withdrawing support to encourage student independence (Pearson & Gallagher, 1983).

There are a number of analyses of the effectiveness of cognitive apprenticeships. Rosenshine and Meister (1994) performed a meta-analysis of studies evaluating reciprocal teaching and found that it had moderate but significant effects on measures of comprehension. They also found that reciprocal teaching was most effective when it was combined with direct teaching of cognitive strategies. A. L. Brown and Palinscar (as cited in Prawat, 1991) compared reciprocal teaching to a peer-collaboration approach (which appears to be analogous to whole language but directed specifically toward science learning) and found that a peer-collaborative approach combined with text materials rewritten for conceptual coherence produced the highest quality of student discourse about science and evidence of higher-level thinking in writing samples. This line of research has been continued by A. L. Brown and her colleagues (A. L. Brown, 1992). A. L. Brown and Palinscar (as cited in Prawat, 1991) suggested that the original reciprocal teaching approach was successful in getting poor readers to focus on comprehension, but that its structure may not be necessary for accomplished readers to develop deeper understanding of content materials. R. Brown, Pressley, Van Meter, and Schuder (1996) found that second graders taught using TSI techniques showed evidence of greater strategy awareness and strategy use, greater acquisition of information from material read in reading groups, and superior performance on standardized reading tests than a control group by the end of the year.

The interactions among peers are used to develop not only strategic comprehension (Palincsar & Brown, 1984; Palincsar et al., 1991) but also critical thinking in reading (Commeyras, 1991) and literary response (O'Flahaven, 1989). In Vygotsky's model (see Wertsch, 1985), "higher-level thought" is a form of internal speech, a dialogue with oneself. This dialogue is modeled on dialogues that one can have with others. These groups, by discussing the text in sophisticated terms—strategically, critically, or with an emotional response—provide a model for the development of this internal speech.

In practice, cognitive apprenticeship models share a great many components with whole language instruction. First, they both treat the task of reading holistically, not breaking it down into subskills or teaching subskills in isolation. Second, they both stress the higher levels of thinking. If decoding or literal comprehension are dealt with, they are dealt with in the context of higher levels of comprehension, such as literary response or critical evaluation. Third, they both use social interaction as a model for desired comprehension behaviors, with both groups relying on Vygotsky for theoretical support.

The major difference between cognitive apprenticeships and whole language is philosophical—whole language theorists reject the master–apprentice metaphor. In some such apprenticeships, there is a great deal of teacher planning and control, at least initially. In reciprocal teaching, for example, the teacher begins clearly in control of the direction of the lesson, modeling what the teachers as experts feel are appropriate reading strategies. The teacher displays the strategies that the students are expected to learn. In whole language lessons, students direct the emphasis of the lesson from the beginning, with the teacher's role being to "lead from behind" (Newman, 1985). In whole language lessons, students learn strategies that they feel they will need to accomplish a desired literacy goal. Students may, for example, want to learn how to summarize because they have decided to learn about a particular topic and present that information to another. For this purpose, they may ask the teacher for hints on how to summarize. The teacher's role is to present interesting material to the students, to "invite" them to learn (again in Newman's, 1985, terminology). McIntyre and Pressley (1996) provided a number of examples of teachers who teach comprehension strategies explicitly within a whole language framework.

Nonetheless, it would seem that strategies can be taught best through the scaffolding provided by explicit explanation and cognitive apprenticeship approaches. Explicit explanation may be most effective when the strategy involved can be used singly. Two examples are Raphael's (Raphael & Wonnacott, 1985) program of teaching Question–Answer Relationships, discussed earlier, or teaching children to ask themselves questions while reading (e.g., Davey & McBride, 1986), a useful study strategy. However, it is difficult to think of more examples of discrete comprehension strategies. Instead, most comprehension strategies are orchestrated in the process of reading literature or learning from text. Such strategies as summarization, prediction, making visualizations, and so forth need to be contextualized into the act of reading. Cognitive apprenticeship approaches might be most effective for processes that work in orchestration with other processes, such as those taught in reciprocal teaching and transactional strategy instruction (R. Brown, et al., 1996; Palinscar & Brown, 1984; Rosenshine & Meister, 1994).

Responding to Literature and Motivation

Aesthetic Reading

We have been discussing what Rosenblatt (1985) called efferent reading. Efferent reading is centered on information to be acquired after reading from text, such as what is learned from a history text or from a set of directions. In contrast, aesthetic reading involves the reader's empathetic response to a work of art. Aesthetic reading is idiosyncratic, as the same text may activate different responses in each reader, given different life experiences and affective make-ups.

Response-oriented curricula based on reader-response theories (e.g., Purves, Rogers, & Soter, 1990) were developed for high school and college literature classes, as an alternative to the plot memorization found in many high school classes. Such a facts-only approach has been criticized rightly as dulling and as denying children the joy of literature. Response-oriented classes, in which students are encouraged to discuss their individual reactions to what they have read, are a bracing alternative. Galda and Guice (1997) described how response-oriented curricula might be transported to primary-grade classes.

Transporting a response-oriented approach to literature down to the early grades can create a new set of problems, however. First, texts used in the early grades are simpler than those which high school students are capable of reading. Although many of these texts are well written and evocative, many cannot bear the weight of individual response. Excessive response to a pleasant but not richly evocative text may be as numbing as excessive questioning on minute details. Second, responding to a work of literature presupposes that one can read the work. Nell (1988), in his work with avid readers, found that basic reading comprehension was a prerequisite for aesthetic reading. With able high school students, this presupposition is more likely to be valid than with children in the earlier grades. I have witnessed discussions in which children who do not appear to have understood what they have read fake their way through a discussion of what they like about the book.

Third, many of these discussions begin with a teacher reading a book to the children rather than the children reading on their own. In the whole language philosophy, reading is just one aspect of language, together with writing, speaking, and listening. Reading to children is one way of getting more complex works of literature to children, enriching their literary experiences. The effects of adult story reading are problematic, however. Meyer, Stahl, Wardrop, and Linn (1994), examining observational data in kindergarten and first grade, found that the amount of story reading to children had an effect on children's listening comprehension but had no effect on a variety of print reading measures. It was the amount of interaction by children with print, however, that had the strongest effects on children's reading skill. Just discussing a text that is heard may not improve children's ability to read other texts. Even if children read the text themselves, long discussions may take away time from more practice in reading. Harris and Serwer (1966) found that children in language-experience classes spent less time actually reading and more time discussing what they read than children in traditional classes. This discussion time was negatively correlated with their achievement. Some time spent on discussing what is read might be useful, but an excessive amount of time may displace other important interactions with text.

This is not to say that children should not be encouraged to respond aesthetically to texts in the early grades. Such responses are an integral part of understanding literary works, even simple works. I am arguing that such responses should not be the only way that texts are handled in classes, that some guidance through the text to ensure that children have comprehended the text should also be included. Such guidance might be withdrawn over the years as children become better comprehenders, but it seems to be necessary in the beginning.

Motivation

According to whole language theorists, exposure to quality literature in an environment that encourages aesthetic reading is inherently motivating. However, there is a research base supporting the effects of whole language instruction on motivation. A review of research on classroom structures that promote motivation for reading by Morrow and Tracey (1998) found that the following activities have been found to motivate learning:

1. Activities that promote choice of materials and experiences for learning.
2. Activities that challenge but can be accomplished.
3. Activities that give the learner responsibility and some control over the learning process, such as self-direction, selection, and pacing of learning activities and materials.
4. Activities that involve social collaboration with peers or adults.
5. Activities that are facilitated by teachers who model, guide, and scaffold information to be learned.
6. Activities that are meaningful and functional by using authentic materials and settings.
7. Activities with conceptual orientations that add interest to what is being learned.
8. Activities that offer time for practicing skills learned in settings that are independent of the teacher.
9. Activities and materials that are easily accessible.
10. Activities that offer the child a feeling of success.

As one can see, most of these conditions can be found in whole language classrooms, at least superficially. These are the positive conditions of whole language, which can be adopted reasonably easily. Turner (1995), whose research identified many of the activities discussed in Morrow and Tracey's review, found that children in classes that provided these conditions were more persistent in sticking to a task, controlled their attention better, and used more reading strategies.

Whole language programs do appear to improve student motivation but may do so at a cost to other aspects of achievement. Stahl, Suttles, and Pagnucco (1996) observed both traditional and whole language first-grade classes. They found that children in the whole language classes had little idea about who the best readers were in their class and were not aware of how they compared with others. Instead, both good and struggling readers believed that they were good readers. In the traditional classes, readers were aware of their standing, which may impair their motivation, but children in the traditional classes significantly outperformed those in the whole language classes.

BALANCED READING INSTRUCTION

To achieve these three goals of reading—automatic word recognition, comprehension, and motivation—one needs a balance in reading instruction between direct instruction of skills and whole language, using the strengths of both. This is not a call for a little of this and a little of that. Instead, the analysis of the reading process discussed previously suggests different programs at different grade levels, with adaptations to meet the needs of diverse learners within those grades.

Kindergarten

In kindergarten, the goals for decoding might be for children to develop a strong print concept, to learn the letters of the alphabet, and to develop phoneme awareness (M. J. Adams, 1990). For comprehension, one might want children to develop in their knowledge of language, including vocabulary, and their experience with science and social studies concepts developed through activity. For motivation, we would want to immerse children in a "garden of print" so that even children who lack exposure to print in their home will get exposure to quality children's literature. These conditions can all be met by a whole language classroom, with one possible exception. Teachers need to be aware of phoneme awareness and, if children need instruction in this area, be prepared to provide it. However, there is some evidence that many children can develop phoneme awareness through alphabet books (Murray, Stahl, & Ivey, 1996), through invented spelling (Tangel & Blachman, 1992), or through informal programs combining language experience and letter knowledge (Brennan & Ireson, 1997; Winsor, 1990). For other children, more formal training may be needed.

First Grade

It is only in first grade where instruction needs to amalgamate different reading approaches. An effective first-grade reading program, for example, might involve some systematic and direct instruction of decoding, with associated practice in decodable texts (Juel & Roper-Schneider, 1985). These can include some contrived texts, although not the "visual tongue twisters" (M. J. Adams, 1990) of the old linguistic series (e.g., Bloomfield & Barnhart, 1961). They also might include authentic literature chosen for repetition of taught patterns (Trachtenburg, 1990). Children also need a variety of interesting but easy texts, both for interest and for practice in reading a variety of materials. Some of these texts might be predictable, where the context supports word recognition, at least until the child develops more independent word recognitions strategies (Clay, 1993; Fountas & Pinnell, 1996). Predictable texts by themselves, however, may limit children's word learning (A. M. Duffy, McKenna, Stratton, & Stahl, 1996) unless the teacher draws specific attention to words in those texts (Johnson, 1995). Writing, using invented spelling, would also be useful for developing word knowledge (Clarke, 1989). As they invent spellings, children need to integrate their developing phoneme awareness with their knowledge of sound–symbol correspondences (Stahl & Murray, 1998).

Because first-grade children are focused on decoding in their text reading (Chall, 1996c), children's comprehension growth might best be accommodated by the teacher's reading aloud to the children. Studies have found that children can learn new vocabulary words from hearing stories (e.g., Elley, 1989). In addition, teachers can model more advanced comprehension strategies with read stories, as they are likely to have richer context than stories the child can read independently. This is not to say that comprehension should be ignored during children's reading.

Basic strategies such as recall (Koskinen, Gambrell, Kapinus, & Heathington, 1988) or story grammars (Beck & McKeown, 1981) can be profitably taught to children at this age. These strategies guide students' reading toward an understanding of the importance of information in texts.

An extensive teacher reading program would likely improve first graders' motivation toward reading, as would a daily period of choice reading (Morrow & Tracey, 1998). The program also should include open-ended tasks, such as free writing and responses to stories, as such tasks also improve motivation (Turner, 1995).

Thus, an effective first-grade program might involve elements associated with whole language (teacher reading aloud, invented spelling, free reading, extensive use of literature) as well as more direct instructional approaches (direct sound–symbol instruction, some use of decodable or even contrived texts). How these elements are managed might also depend on the needs of the children. Children who enter first grade with a limited literacy background may need more direct instruction to develop concepts that should have been learned through rich home experiences with literacy. Children with stronger literacy backgrounds may benefit from more time to choose their reading, with teacher support to read more and more complex materials.

Second Grade

In second grade, the goals for decoding shift, but those for comprehension and motivation remain constant. With a greater emphasis on fluency, children need to increase the volume of text read and may need to read the same text repeatedly to develop automaticity (e.g., Samuels et al., 1992). Approaches such as Fluency-Oriented Reading Instruction (Stahl & Heubach, 2005), Hoffman's (1987) Oral Recitation Lessons, and other approaches discussed earlier all seem to benefit struggling and normally achieving readers. Whatever approach is used, it is important that teachers continue to read to children to ensure exposure to more complex vocabulary and information as well as more complex story structures. At this grade, a teacher might begin interspersing chapter books with picture books to get children accustomed to understanding stories with extended plots. Teachers need to include a daily period of choice reading for motivation as well as practice in reading.

Third Grade Onward

By the end of third grade, decoding ceases to be an issue for most children, and instructional attention can shift to comprehension and motivation. An ideal third-grade program might be a cognitive apprenticeship program, with the teacher serving as a guide as children read literature and content texts of increasing levels of complexity. Following the model of Pearson and Gallagher (1983), a teacher should plan to introduce comprehension strategies such as summarizing, questioning, predicting, and deriving word meanings from context and gradually release control of these strategies to the students. This might involve a lesson structure such as reciprocal teaching or TSI or might involve comprehension strategies embedded within whole language classes. In addition, teachers need to teach more complex study and text reading strategies to prepare children for the work in middle and high school reading. This might be done through explicit explanation and guided practice.

Teachers should continue to read aloud to children (Stahl et al., 1991) but also should include daily vocabulary instruction. Such instruction does have a moderate effect on children's comprehension (Stahl & Fairbanks, 1986). General guidelines for that instruction might include teaching both definitional and contextual information about each word; involving the children in processing the meaning deeply by having them generate sentences, scenarios, and so forth about each word; and providing multiple exposures to each word in varied contexts (Stahl, 1998).

The use of open-ended tasks (Turner, 1995) seems appropriate in upper-level classes, where there might not be enough time during school to allocate time for choice reading (although choice reading should be encouraged at home). Open-ended tasks might include written responses to text, discussions in book clubs (McMahon et al., 1997), or projects that involve books read.

FINDING A MIDDLE GROUND

Matching what we know about effective approaches to meet the varied goals of a reading program at different stages would suggest different types of programs at different grade levels. Although instruction at all grade levels except first grade would strongly resemble whole language instruction, it would also include elements of traditional skill instruction. Some of the best programs today also are highly eclectic, drawing from many different instructional approaches. Two published examples, the classes that Cunningham, Hall, and Defee (1991) work with in North Carolina and the Benchmark School program (R. W. Gaskins, Gaskins, & Gaskins, 1992), incorporate teacher-directed instruction in decoding with process writing and reading self-selected literature. There are many other programs, heralded and unheralded, that follow a similar, eclectic course (see McIntyre & Pressley, 1996).

Teaching Skills, Strategies, and Phonics in Whole Language Classes

As I have noted throughout this article, the conditions of effective instruction can be met in whole language classes, and they often are. However, our observations (Stahl et al., 1991; Stahl et al., 1996) suggest that they are often not. For example, Stahl et al. (1996) found that (a) the level of materials used in whole language classes was considerably less challenging than the material used in the traditional classes we observed and (b) the level of challenge was strongly related to children's achievement.

Similarly, there was not much phonics instruction in the whole language classes we observed. Although whole language advocates discuss phonics extensively, even devoting entire books to the subject (K. S. Goodman, 1993), there is a perception that whole language and phonics are opposed to each other (e.g., Collins, 1997). The difference between whole language advocates and others is not whether phonics should be taught—they both agree that it should be—but in *how* phonics should be taught. Whole language advocates decry the use of worksheets, as in the objective-oriented basal readers of the 1970s and 1980s, and suggest that phonics instruction be embedded in the reading of literature. As both Routman (1996) and Church (1996) recommended in their recent books, teaching phonics within a whole language context is both necessary and difficult. Routman began a chapter in her latest book as follows:

> It would be irresponsible and inexcusable not to teach phonics. Yet the media are having a field day getting the word out that many of us ignore phonics in the teaching of reading. It just isn't so. Some of us may not be doing as good a job as we need to be doing, but I don't know a knowledgeable teacher who doesn't teach phonics. (p. 91)

I know teachers who don't; they may not be knowledgeable, but they use the whole language movement as a justification for their not teaching phonics. When I first read this, I thought she (and others) were merely backpedaling. Now I am convinced that the whole language folks are sincere that they were talking about teaching phonics from the beginning. But the type of phonics instruction they were advocating was difficult. First, it involved "kidwatching," or close analysis of children's writing and invented spelling, and observation of children's miscues during reading. This involves a teacher's knowing (and carrying around in his or her head) a scope and sequence of phonics skills and a knowledge of where every child is in relation to that scope and sequence. It involved targeting instruction to a child's level so that a child gets instruction in short *a*, for example, when she or he is ready for it, not at a point in the year when the guidebook says it should be taught. This involves some fairly expert teaching, and quite frankly, I have not yet seen a teacher pull it off in a whole class. Where such instruction occurs is in Reading Recovery™ (Clay, 1993), which uses one-on-one tutoring to deliver instruction with highly trained teachers. A good Reading Recovery teacher chooses texts that match each child's needs based on a daily individual diagnostic evaluation and provides instructional support to meet those needs, all in a fast-paced lesson (Stahl et al., 1999). It may be possible to provide similar instruction in a classroom setting (see Fountas & Pinnell, 1996, for a suggestion) or in small-group settings (Hiebert, 1994; Taylor, Short, & Shearer, 1990), but these lessons involve significant divergences from the principles of whole language.

The result of these two types of messages—some easy to do in the classroom and some difficult to do—is that teachers chose to do what is easy and did not do what is difficult. This is not laziness. Many teachers simply were not prepared, through coursework, through inservice, and so forth, to teach phonics or any other reading skill off the top of their heads. The message of this instruction was not laid out well either. To convince teachers that they should embrace whole language, advocates stressed the aspects that were easy to do and soft-pedaled the difficult aspects of teaching in this approach.

The stressing of what is easy to do in whole language and soft-pedaling the difficulty of maintaining instruction is a political technique. It is more attractive to masses of teachers to think that children will learn on their own than it is to know the difficulties of closely monitoring the learning of 25 children and providing appropriate on-the-spot instruction to those children. But teaching children to read involves challenging them, prodding them, forcing them to deal with increasingly difficult texts. Traditionally, this has been done by progress through a basal reader with increasingly difficult reading selections. Children were led to more difficult material through word recognition instruction, prereading preparation, and the support of the directed reading activity. Leaving children to choose books may mean that children will choose books that are too easy to provide the challenge they need for their own growth (Stahl et al., 1996).

Politics and Eclecticism

The use of explicit political techniques both fueled the growth of the whole language movement, discussed at the beginning of this article, and may retard the movement toward the greater eclecticism that is needed for more effective instruction. Whole language has used the techniques of political and advertising campaigns to grow (McKenna, Stahl, & Reinking, 1994; Stahl, 1994). One technique is the use of language. Whole language advocates, either deliberately or through common communication, use certain catch phrases to describe whole language and other phrases to describe those who oppose it. Whole language is "natural," "authentic," "child centered," and "empowering." This, of course, has built-in implications that what is not whole language is "artificial," "inauthentic," "anti-children," and "disempowering," or "deskilling." Further, opponents of whole language are for "skill and drill," "rote learning," "recitation," and so forth. The use of propagandist terms is a political technique, one which has not been employed in a pedagogical debate. Some have used stronger terms. I have been called a "word fetishist" and a "phonicator" (Grundin, 1994), but in recent years this rhetoric has cooled.

The use of catch phrases to describe both oneself and one's opponents, reminds me of a manual for political campaigns sent out by GOPAC, Newt Gingrich's Political Action Committee. Page (1990) discussed GOPAC's pamphlet, *Language: A Key Mechanism of Control*, which tells how to win elections by grabbing the good words for your side and hurling invectives at your opponents. In this manual, GOPAC recommended that Republican candidates monitor the language that they were using, stressing that they were for "opportunity," "lower taxes," "equal treatment," "pro-life" and so forth, and that their opponents were "anti-opportunity," were "tax-and-spend liberals," favored "preferences based on race," were "pro-abortion," and so forth. This use of language by the Republicans was successful in leading to the Republican revolution of 1994, but the polarization made it impossible for them to govern, at least at the present time.

Although I do not believe that the use of polarizing language by whole language advocates is as organized and deliberate as that by the followers of Gingrich, the polarization has had the same effect. Because the claims of whole language have fallen short of the reality, there is little common ground to effect a middle ground. In fact, that middle ground has been explicitly rejected by whole language advocates. Newman and Church (1990), for example, stated that one cannot "just do a little bit of whole language and leave everything else untouched" (p. 26). K. S. Goodman (1992) stated this more clearly:

> Eclecticism, taking useful bits and pieces from here and there, is probably the best policy for teachers who don't have a well-articulated belief system and knowledge base. They can put together activities that work for them without integrating it all or being overly concerned with inconsistencies. Whole language teachers are beyond eclecticism. (p. 361)

Deegan (1995) was even more direct. In a response to an article suggesting that elements of whole language and direct instruction can be mixed, she stated:

Toward the end of her article, Spiegel pursues her final rationale that "the reality of the world of schooling is that teachers *will* draw what works best for them from both worlds (i.e., the world of whole language and the world of direct instruction) (p. 43). It is this statement that reveals her hand and proves her position to be antithetical to the fundamental principles of whole language. Essentially, a "what works" argument represents a position hostile to theory. On the contrary, the challenge of whole language is to constantly assess practice by referring to theory; anything less is simply not whole language. *"What works" can never be a justification for practice. Though it may be construed as both plausible and neat, it is concomitantly wrong* [italics added]. (p. 692)

Whole language basically sees itself as a political movement, with a goal of transforming society through the transformation of schools. Deegan (1995), at least, seems to view literacy instruction as a means of achieving larger societal goals and achievement in reading and writing to be secondary to those larger goals. Shannon (as cited in Deegan, 1995), for example, stated that whole language "has human emancipation as its goal" (p. 690). Deegan expanded this to propose these two principles of "a moral and ethical pedagogy: The purpose of education in a democratic society is human emancipation, and the means of such an education must be likewise emancipatory and respectful of human voice and agency" (p. 690). This is heady stuff for an approach to teaching reading, and indeed, most advocates see whole language as much more than just a way of improving literacy. In whole language parlance, the empowerment of students in the classroom is to serve as a model for empowerment of people in society.

The high ideals of the whole language movement might explain the animosity that its proponents have toward those who have questioned it or those who work from a different paradigm. K. S. Goodman (1993) devoted a chapter to the politics of phonics, arguing that the right wing is "using phonics as a means of furthering their political agendas, as a means of frightening and politicizing especially rural and working class parents" (p. 99). He cited the U.S. Senate Republican Policy Committee document, *Illiteracy: An Incurable Disease or Education Malpractice?*, which supports a "phonics-first" curriculum, as evidence that whole language needs to be defended against those forces of reaction that threaten not only whole language but the interests of children in general.

What is needed is precisely the eclecticism condemned by K. S. Goodman (1989, 1992), Deegan (1995), Newman and Church (1990), Shannon (1994), and others. For rather than approaching reading through a consistent philosophical stance, be it whole language or some other stance, an effective teacher of reading has to understand how reading develops, in all of its manifestations. This involves a deeper understanding of the development of automatic word recognition, comprehension, and motivation and appreciation and a skill in weaving these various goals into a coherent program.

The politization of recent years interferes with effective instruction because it hardens viewpoints and forces educators to adopt unreasonable tenets concerning instruction. One result of the movement is that teachers have a great many beliefs about reading instruction, some of which are tenable and some of which are not. As we approach the millennium, we need to step back, look at the evidence, and evaluate all our beliefs about reading instruction.

REFERENCES

Adams, G. L., & Englemann, S. (1996). *Research on direct instruction: 25 years beyond DISTAR.* Seattle, WA: Educational Achievement Systems.

Adams, M. J. (1990). *Beginning to read: Thinking and learning about print.* Cambridge, MA: MIT Press.

Anderson, R. C., & Freebody, P. (1981). Vocabulary knowledge. In J. T. Guthrie (Ed.), *Comprehension and teaching: Research reviews* (pp. 77–117). Newark, DE: International Reading Association.

Anderson, R. C., Hiebert, E. F., Wilkinson, I. A. G., & Scott, J. (1985). *Becoming a nation of readers.* Champaign, IL: National Academy of Education and Center for the Study of Reading.

Anderson, R. C., & Pearson, P. D. (1984). A schema-theoretic view of basic processes in reading. In P. D. Pearson (Ed.), *Handbook of reading research* (Vol. 1, pp. 255–292). White Plains, NY: Longman.

Baker, C. D., & Freebody, P. (1989). *Children's first school books.* Oxford, UK: Blackwell.

Baker, L., & Brown, A. L. (1984). Metacognitive skills and reading. In P. D. Pearson (Ed.), *Handbook of reading research* (Vol. 1, pp. 353–394). White Plains, NY: Longman.

Barr, R. (1984). Beginning reading instruction, from debate to reformation. In P. D. Pearson, R. Barr, M. L. Kamil, & P. Mosenthal (Eds.), *Handbook of reading research* (Vol. 1, pp. 545–582). White Plains, NY: Longman.

Beck, I. L., & McKeown, M. G. (1981). Developing questions that promote comprehension: The story map. *Language Arts, 58,* 913–918.

Bereiter, C., & Englemann, S. (1966). *Teaching disadvantaged children in the preschool.* Englewood Cliffs, NJ: Prentice-Hall.

Bergman, J. (1992). The SAIL program. *The Reading Teacher, 45,* 601–608.

Betts, E. A. (1946). *Foundations of reading instruction.* New York: American Books.

Biemiller, A. (1970). The development of the use of graphic and contextual information as children learn to read. *Reading Research Quarterly, 6,* 75–96.

Bloomfield, L., & Barnhart, C. (1961). *Let's read: A linguistic approach.* Detroit, MI: Wayne State University Press.

Bradley, L., & Bryant, P. E. (1983). Categorizing sounds and learning to read—A causal connection. *Nature, 301,* 419–421.

Brennan, F., & Ireson, J. (1997). Training phonological awareness: A study to evaluate the effects of a program of metalinguistic games in kindergarten. *Reading and Writing: An Interdisciplinary Journal, 9,* 241–263.

Brown, A. L. (Chair). (1992, April). *Learning and thinking in a community of learners.* Symposium presented at the annual meeting of the American Educational Research Association, San Francisco.

Brown, A. L., Campione, J. C., & Day, J. D. (1981). Learning to learn: On training students to learn from texts. *Educational Researcher, 10*(2), 14–21.

Brown, J. S., Collins, A., & Duguid, P. (1989). Situated cognition and the culture of learning. *Educational Researcher, 18*(1), 32–42.

Brown, R., Pressley, M., Van Meter, P., & Schuder, T. (1996). A quasi-experimental validation of transactional strategies instruction with low-achieving second grade readers. *Journal of Educational Psychology, 88,* 18–37.

Bruck, M., & Treiman, R. (1992). Learning to pronounce words: The limitations of analogies. *Reading Research Quarterly, 27,* 374–388.

Carnine, D., Silbert, J., & Kame'enui, E. (1996). *Direct instruction reading* (2nd ed.). Columbus, OH: Merrill.

Chall, J. S. (1996a). American reading achievement: Should we worry? *Research in the Teaching of English, 30,* 303–310.

Chall, J. S. (1996b). *Learning to read: The great debate* (3rd ed.). New York: McGraw-Hill.

Chall, J. S. (1996c). *Stages of reading development* (2nd ed.). Fort Worth, TX: Harcourt Brace.

Chomsky, C. (1972). Stages in language development and reading exposure. *Harvard Educational Review, 42,* 1–33.

Church, S. M. (1996). *The future of whole language: Reconstruction or self-destruction.* Portsmouth, NH: Heinemann.

Clarke, L. K. (1989). Encouraging invented spelling in first graders' writing: Effects on learning to spell and read. *Research in the Teaching of English, 22,* 281–309.

Clay, M. M. (1993). *Reading Recovery: A guidebook for teachers in training.* Portsmouth, NH: Heinemann.

Collins, J. (1997, October 27). How Johnny should read. *Time, 150*(17), 78–81.

Commeyras, M. (1991). *Dialogical-thinking reading lessons: Promoting critical thinking among "learning disabled" students.* Unpublished doctoral dissertation, University of Illinois at Champaign–Urbana.

Cunningham, P. M. (1975–1976). Investigating a synthesized theory of mediated word identification. *Reading Research Quarterly, 11,* 127–143.

Cunningham, P. M., Hall, D. P., & Defee, M. (1991). Non-ability grouped, multilevel instruction: A year in a first grade classroom. *The Reading Teacher, 44,* 566–571.

Dahl, K. L., & Freppon, P. A. (1995). A comparison of inner-city children's interpretations of reading and writing instruction in the early grades in skills-based and whole language classrooms. *Reading Research Quarterly, 30,* 50–74.

Davey, B., & McBride, S. (1986). Effects of question-generation training on reading comprehension. *Journal of Educational Psychology, 78,* 256–262.

Deegan, D. H. (1995). The necessity of debate: A comment on commentaries. *The Reading Teacher, 48,* 688–695.

Dickinson, D. K., & Smith, M. W. (1994). Long-term effects of preschool teachers' book readings on low-income children's vocabulary and story comprehension. *Reading Research Quarterly, 29,* 104–122.

Dole, J. A., Duffy, G. G., Roehler, L. R., & Pearson, P. D. (1991). Moving from the old to the new: Research on reading comprehension instruction. *Review of Educational Research, 61,* 239–264.

Duffy, A. M., McKenna, M., Stratton, B., & Stahl, S. A. (1996, December). *Tales of Mrs. Wishy-Washy: The effects of predictable books on learning to recognize words.* Paper presented at the annual meeting of the National Reading Conference, Charleston, SC.

Duffy, G. G., & Roehler, L. R. (1987). Teaching skills as strategies. *The Reading Teacher, 40,* 414–419.

Duffy, G. G., Roehler, L. R., Meloth, M., Vavrus, L., Book, C., Putnam, J., & Wesselman, R. (1986). The relationship between explicit verbal explanation during reading skill instruction and student awareness and achievement: A study of reading teacher effects. *Reading Research Quarterly, 21,* 237–252.

Durkin, D. (1966). *Children who read early.* New York: Teacher's College Press.

Durkin, D. (1979). What classroom observations reveal about reading comprehension instruction. *Reading Research Quarterly, 14,* 481–533.

Ehri, L. C. (1992). Reconceptualizing the development of sight word reading and its relationship to recoding. In P. Gough, L. C. Ehri, & R. Treiman (Eds.), *Reading acquisition* (pp. 107–143). Hillsdale, NJ: Erlbaum.

Ehri, L. C. (1995). Phases of development in learning to read words by sight. *Journal of Research in Reading, 18,* 116–125.

Ehri, L. C., & Robbins, C. (1992). Beginners need some decoding skill to read words by analogy. *Reading Research Quarterly, 27,* 12–26.

Ehri, L. C., & Sweet, J. (1991). Fingerpoint-reading of memorized text: What enables beginners to process the print. *Reading Research Quarterly, 26,* 442–462.

Elley, W. B. (1989). Vocabulary acquisition from listening to stories. *Reading Research Quarterly,* *24,* 174–187.

English language arts framework for California Public Schools K–12. (1987). Sacramento: California Department of Education.

Flesch, R. (1955). *Why Johnny can't read.* New York: Harper & Row.

Fountas, I. C., & Pinnell, G. S. (1996). *Guided reading: Good first teaching for all children.* Portsmouth, NH: Heinemann.

Freppon, P. A., & Dahl, K. L. (1991). Learning about phonics in a whole language classroom. *Language Arts, 68,* 190–197.

Galda, L., & Guice, S. (1997). Response-based reading instruction in the elementary grades. In S. A. Stahl & D. A. Hayes (Eds.), *Instructional models in reading* (pp. 311–330). Mahwah, NJ: Erlbaum.

Gambrell, L. B., Wilson, R. M., & Gantt, W. N. (1981). Classroom observations of task-attending behaviors of good and poor readers. *Journal of Educational Research, 74,* 400–404.

Garcia, G., & Pearson, P. D. (1991). Modifying reading instruction to maximize its effectiveness of "all" students. In M. S. Knapp & P. M. Shields (Eds.), *Better schooling for children of poverty: Alternatives to conventional wisdom* (pp. 31–60). Berkeley, CA: McCutchan.

Gaskins, I. W., & Elliot, T. (1991). *Implementing cognitive strategy training across the school: The Benchmark manual for teachers.* Cambridge, MA: Brookline.

Gaskins, R. W., Gaskins, I. W., & Gaskins, J. (1992). Using what you know to figure out what you don't know: An analogy approach to decoding. *Reading and Writing Quarterly: Overcoming Learning Difficulties, 8,* 197–221.

Goodman, K. S. (1989). Whole language is whole: A response to Heymsfeld. *Educational Leaders, 46*(6), 69–70.

Goodman, K. S. (1992). Why whole language is today's agenda in education. *Language Arts, 69,* 354–363.

Goodman, K. S. (1993). *Phonics phacts.* Portsmouth, NH: Heinemann.

Goodman, Y. M. (1989). Roots of the whole-language movement. *Elementary School Journal, 90,* 113–127.

Gough, P. B., & Tunmer, W. E. (1986). Decoding, reading, and reading disability. *Remedial Special Education, 7,* 6–10.

Grundin, H. (1994). Whole language. In F. Lehr & J. Osborn (Eds.), *Reading, language, and literacy: Instruction for the twenty-first century* (pp. 77–88). Hillsdale, NJ: Erlbaum.

Hansen, J. (1981). The effects of inferences training and practice on young children's reading comprehension. *Reading Research Quarterly, 16,* 391–417.

Hansen, J., & Pearson, P. D. (1983). An instructional study: Improving the inferential comprehension of fourth grade good and poor readers. *Journal of Educational Psychology, 75,* 821–829.

Harris, A. J., & Serwer, B. L. (1966). The CRAFT project: Instructional time in reading research. *Reading Research Quarterly, 2,* 27–57.

Heimlich, J. E., & Pittelman, S. D. (1986). *Semantic mapping: Classroom applications.* Newark, DE: International Reading Association.

Hiebert, E. H. (1994). A small group literacy intervention with Chapter 1 students. In E. H. Hiebert & B. M. Taylor (Eds.), *Getting reading right from the start* (pp. 85–106). Boston: Allyn & Bacon.

Hirsch, E. D. (1987). *Cultural literacy.* Boston: Houghton Mifflin.

Hoffman, J. (1987). Rethinking the role of oral reading. *Elementary School Journal, 87,* 367–373.

Hoffman, J. V., McCarthey, S. J., Abbott, J., Christian, C., Corman, L., Curry, C., et al. (1994). So what's new in the new basals? A focus on first grade. *Journal of Reading Behavior, 26,* 47–73.

Holdaway, D. (1979). *The foundations of literacy.* Sydney: Ashton-Scholastic.

Houghton Mifflin. (1986). *Trumpets teacher's guide.* Boston: Author.

Johnson, F. R. (1995, December). *Learning to read with predictable text: What kinds of words do beginning readers remember?* Paper presented at the annual meeting of the National Reading Conference, New Orleans, LA.

Juel, C. (1988). Learning to read and write: A longitudinal study of fifty-four children from first through fourth grade. *Journal of Educational Psychology, 80,* 437–447.

Juel, C., & Roper-Schneider, D. (1985). The influence of basal readers on first grade reading. *Reading Research Quarterly, 20,* 134–152.

Kame'enui, E. J., Simmons, D. C., Chard, D., & Dickson, S. (1997). Direct instruction reading. In S. A. Stahl & D. A. Hayes (Eds.), *Instructional models in reading* (pp. 59–84). Mahwah, NJ: Erlbaum.

Kavanagh, J., & Mattingly, I. (Eds.). (1972). *Language by eye and by ear.* Cambridge, MA: MIT Press.

Koskinen, P. S., Gambrell, L. B., Kapinus, B. A., & Heathington, B. S. (1988). Retelling: A strategy for enhancing students' reading comprehension. *The Reading Teacher, 41,* 892–896.

Labbo, L. D., & Teale, W. (1997). Emergent literacy as an instructional model. In S. A. Stahl & D. A. Hayes (Eds.), *Instructional models in reading* (pp. 249–281). Mahwah, NJ: Erlbaum.

Levin, H., & Williams, J. (1970). *Basic studies in reading.* New York: Basic Books.

Lundberg, I., Frost, J., & Peterson, O.-P. (1988). Effects of an extensive program for stimulating phonological awareness in preschool children. *Reading Research Quarterly, 23,* 263–284.

McIntyre, E., & Pressley, M. (1996). *Balanced instruction: Strategies and skills in whole language.* Norwood, MA: Christopher-Gordon.

McKenna, M. C., Stahl, S. A., & Reinking, D. (1994). A critical commentary on research, politics, and whole language. *Journal of Reading Behavior, 26,* 211–233.

McMahon, S. I., Raphael, T. E., Goatley, V. J., & Pardo, L. S. (1997). *The book club connection.* Newark, DE: International Reading Association.

Meyer, L. A., Stahl, S. A., Wardrop, J. L., & Linn, R. L. (1994). The effects of reading storybooks aloud to children. *Journal of Educational Research, 88,* 69–85.

Morrow, L. M., & Tracey, D. (1998). Motivating contexts for young children's literacy development: Implications for word recognition development. In J. Metsala & L. Ehri (Eds.), *Word recognition in beginning literacy* (pp. 341–356). Mahwah, NJ: Erlbaum.

Mullis, I. V. S. Campbell, F. R., & Farstrup, A. E. (1993). *NAEP 1992 reading report card for the nation and the states.* Washington, DC: U.S. Department of Education, Office of Educational Research and Development.

Murray, B. A., Stahl, S. A., & Ivey, M. G. (1996). Developing phoneme awareness through alphabet books. *Reading and Writing: An Interdisciplinary Journal, 8,* 307–322.

Nell, V. (1988). *Lost in a book: The psychology of reading for pleasure.* New Haven, CT: Yale University Press.

Newman, J. (1985). *Whole language.* Portsmouth, NH: Heinemann.

Newman, J. M., & Church, S. M. (1990). Commentary: Myths of whole language. *The Reading Teacher, 44,* 20–27.

O'Flahaven, J. O. (1989). *Second graders' social, intellectual, and affective development in varied group discussions about narrative texts: An exploration of participation structures.* Unpublished doctoral dissertation, University of Illinois at Urbana–Champaign.

O'Flahaven, J., Gambrell, L. B., Guthrie, J., Stahl, S. A., Baumann, J. F., & Alvermann, D. A. (1992). Poll results guide activities of research center. *Reading Today, 10*(1), 12.

Olson, D. R. (1977). From utterance text: The bias of language in speech and writing. *Harvard Educational Review, 47,* 257–281.

Page, C. (1990, September 19). Talk like a Newt with the Gingrich diatribe dictionary. *Chicago Tribune,* p. 19.

Pahl, M. M., & Monson, R. J. (1992). In search of whole language: Transforming curriculum and instruction. *Journal of Reading, 35*, 518–525.

Palincsar, A. S., & Brown, A. L. (1984). Reciprocal teaching of comprehension-fostering and comprehension-monitoring activities. *Cognition and Instruction, 1*, 117–175.

Palincsar, A. S., David, Y. M., Winn, J. A., & Stevens, D. D. (1991). Examining the context of strategy instruction. *Remedial and Special Education, 12*(3), 43–53,

Paris, S. G., & Lindauer, B. K. (1976). The role of inference in children's comprehension and memory. *Cognitive Psychology, 8*, 217–227.

Paris, S. G., Lipson, M. Y., & Wixson, K. K. (1983). Becoming a strategic reader. *Contemporary Educational Psychology, 8*, 293–316.

Pearson, P. D. (1989). Reading the whole language movement. *Elementary School Journal, 90*, 231–241.

Pearson, P. D., & Gallagher, M. C. (1983). The instruction of reading comprehension. *Contemporary Educational Psychology, 8*, 317–344.

Popp, H. M. (1975). Current practices in the teaching of beginning reading. In J. B. Carroll & J. S. Chall (Eds.), *Toward a literate society* (pp. 101–146). New York: McGraw-Hill.

Prawat, R. S. (1991). The value of ideas: The immersion approach to the development of thinking. *Educational Researcher, 20*(2), 3–10.

Pressley, M., El-Dinary, P. B., Gaskins, I., Schuder, T., Bergman, J. L., Almasi, J., & Brown, R. (1992). Beyond direct explanation: Transactional instruction of reading comprehension strategies. *Elementary School Journal, 92*, 513–555.

Pressley, M., Goodchild, F., Fleet, J., Zajchowski, R., & Evans, E. D. (1989). The challenges of classroom strategy instruction. *Elementary School Journal, 89*, 301–342.

Purves, A. C., Rogers, T., & Soter, A. 0. (1990). *How porcupines make love II: Teaching a response-centered literature curriculum*. White Plains, NY: Longman.

Raphael, T. E., & Wonnocott, C. A. (1985). Heightening fourth-grade students' sensitivity to sources of information for answering comprehension questions. *Reading Research Quarterly, 20*(3), 282–296.

Report of the California Reading Task Force. (1995). Sacramento: California Department of Education.

Reutzel, D. R., & Hollingsworth, P. M. (1993). Effects of fluency training on second graders' reading comprehension. *Journal of Educational Research, 86*, 325–331.

Rinehart, S. D., Stahl, S. A., & Erickson, L. G. (1986). Some effects of summarization training on reading and studying. *Reading Research Quarterly, 21*(4), 422–438.

Rosenblatt, L. M. (1985). The transactional theory of the literary work: Implications for research. In C. R. Cooper (Ed.), *Researching response to literature and the teaching of literature: Points of departure* (pp. 33–53). Norwood, NJ: Ablex.

Rosenshine, B., & Meister, C. (1994). Reciprocal teaching: A review of the research. *Review of Educational Research, 64*, 479–530.

Routman, R. (1996). *Literacy at the crossroads*. Portsmouth, NH: Heinemann.

Samuels, S. J., Schermer, N., & Reinking, D. (1992). Reading fluency: Techniques for making decoding automatic. In S. J. Samuels & A. E. Farstrup (Eds.), *What research says about reading instruction* (2nd ed., pp. 124–144). Newark, DE: International Reading Association.

Shannon, P. (1994). "People who live in glass houses. . . . " In C. Smith (Ed.), *Whole language: The debate* (pp. 81–100). Bloomington, IN: ERIC/EdInfo Press.

Slavin, R. E. (1989). PET and the pendulum: Faddism in education and how to stop it. *Phi Delta Kappan, 70*, 752–775.

Show, C. E., & Ninio, A. (1986). The contracts of literacy: What children learn from learning to read books. In W. H. Teale & E. Sulzby (Eds.), *Emergent literacy: Writing and reading* (pp. 116–138). Norwood, NJ: Ablex.

Stahl, S. A. (1992). *The state of the art of reading instruction in the USA* (JIEP Research Report No. 197). Paris: International Institute for Educational Planning.

Stahl, S. A. (1994). Is whole language "The Real Thing"? Advertisements and research in the debate on whole language. In C. B. Smith (Ed.), *Whole language: The debate* (pp. 124–142). Bloomington, IN: ERIC and Edinfo Press.

Stahl, S. A. (1998). Four questions about vocabulary knowledge and reading and some answers. In C. Hynd (Ed.), *Learning from text across conceptual domains* (pp. 74–94). Mahwah, NJ: Erlbaum.

Stahl, S. A., Duffy-Hester, A. M., & Stahl, K. A. D. (1998). Everything you wanted to know about phonics (but were afraid to ask). *Reading Research Quarterly, 33*(3), 338–355.

Stahl, S. A., & Fairbanks, M. M. (1986). The effects of vocabulary instruction: A model-based meta-analysis. *Review of Educational Research, 56*(1), 72–110.

Stahl, S. A., & Heubach, K. (2005). Fluency-Oriented Reading Instruction. *Journal of Literacy Research, 37*, 25–60.

Stahl, S. A., Kuhn, M. R., & Pickle, J. M. (1999). An educational model of assessment and targeted instruction for children with reading problems. In D. H. Evensen & P. B. Mosenthal (Eds.), *Advances in reading/language research* (Vol. 6, pp. 249–272). Stamford, CT: JAI.

Stahl, S. A., & Miller, P. D. (1989). Whole language and language experience approaches for beginning reading: A quantitative research synthesis. *Review of Educational Research, 59*(1), 87–116.

Stahl, S. A., & Murray, B. A. (1994). Defining phonological awareness and its relationship to early reading. *Journal of Educational Psychology, 86*, 221–234.

Stahl, S. A., & Murray, B. A. (1998). Issues involved in defining phonological awareness and its relationship to early reading. In J. Metsala & L. C. Ehri (Eds.), *Word recognition in beginning literacy* (pp. 65–88). Mahwah, NJ: Erlbaum.

Stahl, S. A., Osborn, J., Pearson, P. D., & Winsor, P. (1992). *The effects of beginning reading instruction: Six teachers in six classrooms.* Unpublished manuscript, University of Illinois at Urbana–Champaign.

Stahl, S. A., Richek, M. G., & Vandevier, R. (1991). Learning word meanings through listening: A sixth grade replication. In J. Zutell & S. McCormick (Eds.), *Learning factors/teaching factors: Issues in literacy research. Fortieth yearbook of the National Reading Conference* (pp. 185–192). Chicago: National Reading Conference.

Stahl, S. A., Suttles, C. V., & Pagnucco, J. R. (1996). The effects of traditional and process literacy instruction on first graders' reading and writing achievement and orientation toward reading. *Journal of Educational Research, 89*, 131–144.

Stanovich, K. E. (1986). Matthew effects in reading: Some consequences of individual differences in the acquisition of literacy. *Reading Research Quarterly, 21*, 360–407.

Stevens, R. J., Madden, N. A., Slavin, R. E., & Famish, A. M. (1987). Cooperative Integrated Reading and Composition: Two field experiments. *Reading Research Quarterly, 22*, 433–454.

Tangel, D. M., & Blachman, B. A. (1992). Effect of phoneme awareness instruction on kindergarten children's invented spellings. *Journal of Reading Behavior, 24*, 233–262.

Taylor, B. M., Short, R., & Shearer, B. (1990, December). *Early intervention in reading: Prevention of reading failure by first grade classroom teachers.* Paper presented at the annual meeting, National Reading Conference, Miami, FL.

Torgesen, J., & Burgess, S. R. (1998). Consistency of reading-related phonological processes throughout early childhood. In J. Metsala & L. Ehri (Eds.), *Word recognition in beginning literacy* (pp. 161–188). Mahwah, NJ: Erlbaum.

Trachtenburg, P. (1990). Using children's literature to enhance phonics instruction. *The Reading Teacher, 43*, 648–653.

Turner, J. C. (1995). The influence of classroom contexts on young children's motivation for literacy. *Reading Research Quarterly, 30*, 410–441.

Venezky, R. L. (1970). *The structure of English orthography.* The Hague, The Netherlands: Mouton.

Wertsch, J. V. (1985). *Vygotsky and the social formation of mind.* Cambridge, MA: Harvard University Press.

Winsor, P. (1990). *Phonemic awareness development and beginning reading: At-risk children in programs of integrated language arts instruction.* Unpublished doctoral dissertation, University of Illinois at Urbana–Champaign.

Wixson, K. K., & Lipson, M. Y. (1991). *Reading disability.* New York: HarperCollins.

5 | The Shift from Polarization in Reading

Relying on Research Rather Than Compromise

Timothy Shanahan

I knew Steven Stahl as a brilliantly intense man with deep and abiding commitments to literacy research and education. Steve possessed a rich array of gifts: a quick and supple mind, fearlessness in the face of adversity, and generosity of spirit, to name a few. He believed the world could be a better place and that the choices we made mattered. Truth be told, he was also capable of obstinacy, and he could be woefully wrong-headed—displays of which we traded regularly in our many disagreements over the years. Like all of Steve's friends, I miss him considerably, but for me, it is those contentious differences of opinion (the ones our wives miscalled "fights" and tried to quell) that I miss. Much was learned by me when either of us pointed out the errors of the other's ways. It wasn't that there was no mutual admiration along the way—complimentary moments far outweighed any debates we had, but it was the differences that sharpened our minds and added to our understanding.

It is in that context that I react to Steve Stahl's (1998) article "Understanding Shifts in Reading and Its Instruction" (reprinted as Chapter 4, this volume). This is a valuable historical document; one that reveals Steve to be a far better historian than prognosticator, and a better scholar than political gamesman. He wrote this article near the peak of the divisive unpleasantness that came to be known in the popular press as the "reading wars" (Collins, 1997; Lemann, 1997), and his article reveals both profound concerns for healing the divide and a lack of awareness of the impending historical forces already at work to shift the pendulum to a newer place—a place not contemplated then by Steve (and certainly not by me, or anyone else, perhaps).

What I will do here, despite my yen to scrabble with Steve over many of the smaller points in "Understanding Shifts," will be to provide a sketch of the ensuing policy changes that took place, providing both an analysis of where we are and why we have ended up here. It doesn't take a deep reading of "Understanding Shifts" to discern Steve to be someone marked by the bitter polarization of reading education and the research community; he hoped to quell the acrimony and find common ground on which to unify the field. Progress, or more properly, learning—not winning the argument—were his goals; though Steve was certainly a phonics partisan. Like Steve, I seek light rather than heat, and hope that in some small way this brief essay will serve as a timely reminder to those who "burn with the truth" that it is dangerous to play with matches.

STEVE'S AGENDA

Steve's distress is palpable in this article, and it is not surprising that, as an active and committed scholar, he would be as sensitive as a tuning fork to the conceptual and methodological differences then dividing the field. He was evidently less attuned to the problems those divisions were posing for the larger educational and political communities, or to the historical forces that the debates were letting loose, but we'll get to that. First, let's consider what Steve was trying to do and why it, ultimately, failed.

Steve—and others (e.g., McIntyre & Pressley, 1996; Pearson, 1996)—sought a rapprochement between those in the whole language community and those who favored more traditional forms of instruction. "Understanding Shifts" includes an accurate chronology of the rapidity with which whole language became the major force in reading education; he doesn't show how this happened. Though whole language has been described as a "grassroots movement" nourished by the desires of progressive teachers (Goodman, 1989)—a description Steve's essay seems to have accepted—in fact, both its remarkable impetus as well as the seeds of its eventual demise were much due to the fact that it was a political movement that was often in conflict with the views and concerns of classroom teachers and parents. Whole language became popular, in part, by winning over the educational bureaucracies of states that had the most centralized educational authority and through this political influence were able to impose the tenets of whole language on teachers and publishers—and, most important, on children.

California, like many western states, long has had a tradition of centralized purchasing of textbooks. State bureaucrats allow schools to choose from a small number of the programs available on the market. This contrasts with so-called open territory states, such as Illinois or New York, where local school districts make purchasing decisions themselves, with minimal state influence. By the mid-1980s, California was no longer just selecting among what was on the market. It is such a significant part of the textbook market (about 10%) that it can make specific demands on publishers, specifying designs that must be adhered to in order to even compete to participate in the California market.

Whole language advocates convinced then–Commissioner of Education, Bill Honig, to "deskill" early reading instruction—or, more accurately, to so thoroughly emphasize nonskilled aspects of beginning reading that instruction in phonics and skills were all but lost. Commissioner Honig then used state textbook purchasing policy to shape reading instruction in that direction—despite the availability of the kind of persuasive research alluded to in Steve's article, concerning the dubious impact of whole language approaches on student achievement. These whole language–influenced policies translated into a ban on the use of state money to purchase spelling books (whole language proponents opposed spellers) and the adoption of the

English language arts framework noted by Steve. The state imposed policies that required publishers to use children's literary trade books as the basis of reading instruction at all levels, precluding the use of texts written specifically for the teaching of reading. Many teachers, parents, and children were charmed by the beauty and literary quality of the new books, while others were simply dismayed at instructional materials that were suddenly too difficult for young children to read independently (for studies on the consequences of these policies on beginning reading books and student learning, see Foorman, Francis, Davidson, Harm, & Griffin, 2004; Hiebert, 1999; Hoffman, Sailors, & Patterson, 2002).

This top-down reform in the guise of a grassroots movement received its next great push a short time later by the state of Texas, another centralized textbook purchaser. Texas, too, put out reading textbook specifications that moved textbooks even further in the directions already established by California, bringing about what can only be described as the greatest shift of reading instructional methods to take place in the United States during the 20th century (Hoffman et al., 1994).

The rapidly waxing influence of whole language was rivaled only by its eventual rapid waning. In the early 1990s, as Steve notes, the impact of the whole language emphasis was starting to be felt in national and state achievement statistics. Chall (1996) documented how increases in reading skills instruction had been accompanied by sizable gains in reading achievement for African American children, and how nearly two decades of such gains were vitiated by the whole language pendulum swing. California bureaucrats, who had touted their "whole language reforms" widely and proudly, now became aware of appallingly low levels of reading achievement in their state—lower than in states that had not adopted such radical instructional reforms.

At that point, the pendulum swing reversed—as Steve describes—but this did not happen without a painful and ugly fight (the "reading wars"), to which Steve's article was an attempt to bring to a meaningful peace. Whole language advocates who had used state bureaucrats to cajole teachers into accepting whole language instructional tenets were now upset that higher political forces were being appealed to by their opponents (Taylor, 1998). School teachers and principals ultimately must answer to the state educational bureaucracy, but state bureaucrats answer to elected officials (governors and state legislators), and it was to those political forces to whom the whole language opposition appealed.

Steve was not alone at the time in trying to find peace. Others put forth their own agendas of "balanced literacy" toward the same purpose: to recoup peace in the educational community by trying to "balance" the best each side could offer. Steve claimed whole language was primarily about motivation, and in this article he speculated that adopting motivation as one of our educational goals would be a way of bringing everybody to the table. I doubt very much that, had other important historical events not intervened soon after the publication of Steve's article, his argument would have been sustained. Whole language, like any movement, was complex, and it would be a mistake to assume such a diverse movement was impelled by—or could be satisfied by the accomplishment of—a single simple goal.

Whole language advocates were part of a larger and older progressive movement in education and they had a wide range of complex purposes, including the improvement of literacy and social justice, and, in due course, a reworking of the power relations of society. The idea that folks impelled by such powerful and overarching goals could be satisfied by a greater focus on children's literature within the traditional elementary curriculum is not compelling.

WHAT CHANGED?

Eventually, the decibel level of this debate—both because of its recourse to public political forces and because of its impact on children and the nation's educational well-being—attracted public attention and public response. The most immediate changes were in those states that had done the most to move whole language forward; they reversed position, and then required textbook publishers to sell materials that stressed skills instruction above all. Because California and Texas together comprise about 20% of the nation's textbook market, these changes were quickly felt almost everywhere.

However, if that was all that happened one could sit back and wait for the next swing of this pendulum—sort of like observing changing fashion dictates for skirt lengths or tie widths. But more than that happened—much more; and it was these next changes that Steve, and the rest of us, failed to contemplate. Both whole language advocates and their opponents had vociferously contended research supported their positions, and it was these kinds of claims and counterclaims that have resulted in what may turn out to be a permanent change in the reading education climate: a true *pax literatus*, rather than just another mundane truce.

In 1997, as a direct result of the conflicting claims about educational research findings and their meaning, the U.S. Congress requested that a study be conducted into the research on reading. This study, the first of its kind ever required in education, was to make a public determination of what the research had to say about the effectiveness of various approaches to teaching reading. This determination was to be made by a panel of scientists, without financial interest in the outcomes, and they were to do so not by reaching some kind of political compromise or consensus but through a public, objective, rule-based approach to reviewing the research.

The National Reading Panel (NRP) was appointed to conduct that analysis and in 2000 it reported its findings to the U.S. Senate. The findings themselves were not particularly remarkable: instruction in phonemic awareness, phonics, vocabulary, oral reading fluency, and reading comprehension strategies were all found to provide children a clear learning advantage, as did professional development for their teachers. By the time the NRP report was issued (National Institute of Child Health and Human Development [NICHD], 2000), the worst of the "reading wars" were receding, and the findings were consistent with already available consensus reports (Snow, Burns, & Griffin, 1998) and, as a result, were considered to be rather tepid by some (Pressley, 2002).

However, the importance of these findings was twofold. Although this report had been issued during President Bill Clinton's administration, it was embraced by a newly elected President George W. Bush when he took office. He made it the cornerstone of federal literacy policy, and Congress followed suit by appropriating $5 billion to help schools implement these research findings throughout the nation. Many states and local districts made changes to follow these findings as well, and despite some consternation about various provisions in No Child Left Behind (NCLB), Reading First (the reading education portion of NCLB) has garnered great support within the educational community.

Greater than any of the changes to reading instruction, however, was the shift in how educational policy was established in this case. By requiring that reading policy and practice accord with research findings, the government created not just a way to quell this particular argument or "war" but a way to maintain the peace long into the future.

Steve had sought a political compromise with whole language. But his attempts, and those of others, at balance and compromise, no matter how clever or well intended, could only give temporary respite; if someone were to let down his guard or there was any shift of political power, educational requirements and instructional choices would be expected to start swinging once again. Political compromise is a sound way to settle political disputes, but not substantive ones. The most important line in Steve's essay was the one in which he incisively and quietly—far too quietly for my taste—noted the real importance of these pendulum swings: "These swings have had resultant swings of achievement" (Stahl, 1998, p. 31). Steve was, I think, correct in that assessment, and given that, notions of political compromise make little sense.

Think of it in terms of other, substantive issues facing professional fields. Medical experts passionately disagree on best courses of action, but when evidence finally coalesces around the benefits of a particular approach to the patients' well-being, the experts close ranks pretty quickly, adopting that as the new standard of care. Research findings and agreed-on standards of evidence for interpreting those findings in the end are better ways to determine how to move forward; even better than trying to accomplish some political balance among opposing forces or compromises among divergent views.

The effectiveness of various breast cancer screening routines has, for example, been a matter of disagreement. Some contend frequent screenings are needed to detect quick-growing cancers, with others countering that such approaches lead to too many false positives and that current screening techniques fail to reveal the quickest-growing varieties of cancer. That is the kind of determination that most of us would prefer the physicians decided on the basis of research evidence as opposed to a political compromise: "Okay, since you want screenings every 6 months, and I say once every two years is enough, let's do them annually. That way everybody's view is included." Everybody, but the patient.

The NRP report and the public policies that have ensued are a rejection of the kind of compromise Steve sought during those contentious days of the late 1990s. A case in point as to how this may work in the future is evident specifically in the issues of motivation that Steve raised in the "Understanding Shifts" essay.

WHERE ARE WE NOW?

Steve asserted that whole language advocates were putting forth a new goal, a goal of motivation. That, according to Steve, is why the whole language agenda was so taken up with issues such as choice and quality of literature. (One way to think of this, perhaps, is whole language advocates were very concerned about how children perceived their current experiences, while traditionalists were more concerned about the long-term implications of instruction, what was learned, how well prepared children were for the future.)

The NRP looked at one aspect of this issue: how to encourage children to read (NICHD, 2000). That is, NRP sought evidence that showed that encouraging students to read led to changes in how much students read and, as a result of such increases, how well they read. Although the NRP was painstaking in its efforts to identify published research studies on this topic—searching both the PsycInfo and ERIC databases for studies of a wide array of motivational approaches such as sustained silent reading, DEAR (drop everything and read), Accelerated Reader, and incentive programs, few studies were found, and none were found on the more ambitious whole language efforts to create reading communities. Furthermore, none of these studies showed that these approaches to encouraging reading led to any increases in how much children read, and few of these studies reported any convincing advantages due to the procedures; a very different picture than the ones that emerged from looking at instruction in phonemic awareness, phonics, oral reading fluency, vocabulary, and reading comprehension strategies.

A similar imbalance of result is evident in Steve's effort to combine traditionalist and whole language goals. The word recognition and comprehension strategy outcomes described by Steve are supported, in his article, with a rich array of research citations, showing the clear advantages of these approaches. (His summaries on these issues are less thorough than those provided by NRP—or than he provided in other reviews that he published along the way, but the direction is the same: lots of solid evidence showing that kids benefit from such teaching.) But then look at the pages he devotes to motivation. In trying to make the political case for combining motivation with the other goals, Steve's usually outstanding scholarship fails—that is, he, too, evidently could not find studies that supported this kind of teaching and relied heavily on correlational studies, theories, and claims alone, very different from the evidentiary base underlying the goals of decoding and comprehension.

The approach adopted by the NRP (NICHD, 2000) was to put forth findings when there were copious amounts of solid evidentiary support for an approach to teaching, and to call for more research when such evidence wasn't available. Rather than seeking to placate those who advocate for such instructional approaches through some kind of compromise, the NRP determined that not enough was yet known to support such instruction and called on researchers and researcher funders to carry out work in that area.

Reading First reflects this approach. The federal government is providing funding for programmatic efforts that match with the findings of NRP, and only allows Reading First funds to be expended in those ways. Although it is certainly *possible* that motivation should be accorded the same status as other more cognitive variables, it will not achieve this status, in terms of federal funding, until there is sufficient research evidence supporting its inclusion. That is, until we have solid, reliable evidence showing that there are instructional approaches that improve motivation in ways that matter, federal funds cannot be used to implement such teaching.

This new evidence-based approach to literacy policy insulates it from the kind of political manipulation that was evident in the state reading policymaking efforts of the 1980s and 1990s. Those unhappy with the scope of the current policy cannot overturn it simply by capturing the loyalty of a bureaucrat here or a politician there. They must develop a solid body of research evidence showing that a particular approach provides a learning benefit to children. Moreover, the current federal commitment to particular approaches can be rolled back, but only through the accumulation of counterevidence that successfully shows that the NRP findings were incorrect in some important way.

Where Steve sought compromise, historical forces instead implemented a dynamic mechanism that could avoid these kinds of disputes in the future. Where Steve, for the sake of peace, was willing to embrace the varied goals and approaches of a variety of powerbrokers, historical forces put in place a set of standards of evidence that must be met before these varied goals and approaches can hold equal sway. It is not the kind of peace that Steve envisioned, but it is one that goes even farther than he dared hope in protecting the education of children.

REFERENCES

Chall, J. S. (1996). American reading achievement: Should we worry? *Research in the Teaching of English, 30*, 303–310.

Collins, J. (1997, October 27). How Johnny should read. *Time, 150*(17), 78–81.

Foorman, B. R., Francis, D. J., Davidson, K. C., Harm, M. W., & Griffin, J. (2004). Variability in text features in six grade 1 basal reading programs. *Scientific Studies of Reading, 8*, 167–197.

Goodman, Y. M. (1989). Roots of the whole-language movement. *Elementary School Journal, 90*, 113–127.

Hiebert, E. H. (1999). Text matters in learning to read. *The Reading Teacher, 52*, 552–569.

Hoffman, J. V., McCarthey, S. J., Abbott, J., Christian, C., Corman, L., Curry, C., et al. (1994). So what's new in the new basals? A focus on first grade. *Journal of Reading Behavior, 26*, 47–73.

Hoffman, J. V., Sailors, M., & Patterson, E. U. (2002). Decodable texts for beginning reading instruction: The year 2000 basals. *Journal of Literacy Research, 34*, 269–298.

Lemann, N. (1997). The reading wars. *Atlantic Monthly, 280*(5), 128–134.

McIntyre, E., & Pressley, M. (Eds.). (1996). *Balanced instruction: Strategies and skills in whole language*. Norwood, MA: Christopher-Gordon.

National Institute of Child Health and Human Development. (2000). *Report of the National Reading Panel. Teaching children to read: An evidence-based assessment of the scientific research literature on reading and its implications for reading instruction: Reports of the subgroups* (NIH Publication No. 00-4754). Washington, DC: U.S. Government Printing Office. Available online at: www.nichd.nih.gov/publications/nrp/report.htm

Pearson, P. D. (1996). Reclaiming the center. In M. Graves, P. van den Broek, & B. M. Taylor (Eds.), *The first R: Every child's right to read* (pp. 259–274). New York: Teachers College Press.

Pressley, M. (2002). What I have learned until now about research methods in reading education. *Yearbook of the National Reading Conference, 51*, 33–44.

Snow, C. E., Burns, M. S., & Griffin, P. (Eds.). (1998). *Preventing reading difficulties in young children*. Washington, DC: National Academies Press.

Stahl, S. A. (1998). Understanding shifts in reading and its instruction. *Peabody Journal of Education, 73*(3 & 4), 31–67.

Taylor, D. (1998). *Beginning to read and the spin doctors of science*. Urbana, IL: National Council of Teachers of English.

II | READING ACQUISITION

6 Phonics and Phonemic Awareness

MARILYN JAGER ADAMS
JEAN OSBORN

The two papers by Steven Stahl in this section, "Defining Phonological Awareness and Its Relationship to Early Reading" and "Everything You Wanted to Know about Phonics (but Were Afraid to Ask)" appeared in 1994 and 1998 (reprinted as Chapters 7 and 9, this volume, respectively). The two papers contributed to Stahl's reputation as a reading researcher concerned with components of beginning reading instruction. The first paper describes his and Bruce Murray's research about young children's phonemic awareness. But Stahl was not only a conductor of studies about aspects of beginning reading, he was an explainer. The second paper, which appeared in *Reading Research Quarterly*, is an attempt to explain many aspects of a then hot topic, phonics. In the paper, he and his coauthors, Ann Duffy-Hester and Katherine Dougherty Stahl, present an overview of beliefs about phonics, a description of some principles of good phonics instruction, a description of specific approaches to phonics instruction, and a summary of research evidence of the effectiveness (or lack of evidence) of these approaches.

Among the remarkable qualities of Steven Stahl's work on reading is its range. This book began with a paper examining the efficacy of whole language and language experience approaches for emergent readers. Later sections of the book address his work on fluency, vocabulary, comprehension, and assessment. This section includes papers on two of the most critical and controversial aspects of reading acquisition: phonemic awareness and phonics.

Perhaps because Stahl had begun his education sojourn as a special education teacher, or perhaps it was because his graduate mentor was Jeanne Chall—whatever the reason, he remained an outspoken proponent of alphabetic basics throughout his career. To understand the intent—and courage—of the articles in this section, one must consider the reading climate in which they were written.

Across most of the 20th century, academic psychology was dominated by learning theory. Within this framework, the print was the stimulus, and the vocalization, the response. The key to teaching lay in presenting and exercising stimulus–response pairings until they were learned. Thus, reading and writing instruction were seen as straightforward tasks—except for one hugely disruptive controversy: What were the most productive stimulus–response pairs for the beginner? Were they written and spoken forms of whole words? Or were they letters and sounds?

The words-first group held that instruction on letter–sound principles was too slow, too tedious, too abstract, too unreliable, and too far removed from the meaningful layers of language to be appropriate for beginning readers. The words-first group argued that given a little more maturity and a basic foundation in actual reading, children would be more interested in analyzing spellings and sounds. Plus, with a basic inventory of words under their belt, the students would have examples for generalizing: Having learned, for example, *book*, as a sight word, it would be available as an anchor for observing that the letter *b* represents /b/ in general. Thus, the words-first group argued that children should begin reading with sight words, introduced through flashcards and through simple texts with lots of wordwise repetition. Phonics should be introduced gradually and as needed in contexts of reading and otherwise in service of spelling instruction, which was generally begun with the "language arts" program in grade 2. Because the words-first approach was endorsed by William S. Gray (e.g., 1948), surely the most prominent reading expert of the era and lead author of the very popular Scott, Foresman ("Dick and Jane") reading program, it held great sway.

To the claim that phonics was too complex and too abstract for young children, the phonics-first group responded that instruction must therefore be structured and presented such that it was neither. By carefully ordering the introduction of letters and sounds, they repeatedly demonstrated that one could create a curriculum that progressed manageably in complexity and that permitted meaningful reading and writing at least as quickly as might be achieved through flashcards. The difference, claimed the phonics-first people, was that the strategy of presenting phonics "little and late" was too risky. Too many children failed to grasp the point and developed serious reading delay. That structured phonics lessons were but invariably core to the successful remediation of such students was in itself strong argument that reading should be firmly and transparently anchored on the alphabetic principle from the start. Because the phonics-first approach was strongly represented by educators who had devoted themselves to children who had experienced (e.g., Monroe, 1932; Orton, 1937; and followers) or were expected to experience difficulty in learning to read (e.g., Montessori, 1916/1964), it held great sway.

For contemporary audiences, it is worth underscoring that both sides in this debate agreed that phonics was useful. Both sides agreed that without grasp of the alphabetic principle, students lacked means for generalizing their lessons and for successfully recognizing and spelling new words on their own. The question was not whether phonics should be learned, but when and how. Nevertheless, this was the phonics debate of the era. It stretched roughly from 1920 through the 1960s, and it was at least as heated and divisive as any in history.

Jeanne Chall's (1967/1983) effort to contribute to this debate was a voluntary undertaking. The field was torn apart by this debate and progress in any other aspect of reading was paralyzed: Could not this endless debate be usefully informed through research? Chall visited classrooms, interviewed experts, analyzed instructional materials, and carefully reviewed and synthesized the then-existing research on beginning reading. The conclusions were clear. Yes, she concluded, ensuring that beginners knew their ABCs—a highly controversial issue at the time—was vital. And yes, she concluded, teaching beginners phonics was wholly worthwhile. Most jarringly, however, it was where phonics was taught systematically and explicitly that Chall found its advantages to be strongest, broadest, and most enduring, resulting in higher word recognition, vocabulary, and reading comprehension across the primary grades. Chall's book, *Learning to Read: The Great Debate*, is properly heralded as a landmark in the field of reading education. Nevertheless, many were angered by it, and Jeanne Chall was marginalized by the center of the profession for the rest of her life.

From 1978 to 1982, Steven Stahl worked toward his doctoral degree in reading at the Harvard Graduate School of Education. Jeanne Chall was his graduate advisor. Chall required all of her students to spend time in the Harvard Reading Laboratory tutoring struggling readers. Steven became supervisor of the laboratory. While at Harvard, Steven also provided research assistance to Chall on a number of projects including, significantly, her 1983 revision of *The Great Debate*. He was also among the few students whom Chall invited to coauthor papers with her (Chall & Stahl, 1982, 1983, 1985a, 1985b, 1988). A shrewd judge of both scholarship and character, Chall was fussy about whom she would and would not accept as a student, but Steve was one of her favorites. She was very fond of him and him, of her. Chall saved her pennies in a coffee can for Steven's son, Max. Steve proudly sported the t-shirt that Chall's graduate students made for her retirement party, her famous refrain, "Where's the evidence?" emblazoned across his chest. It was Steven who wrote Chall's memorial piece in *The Educational Researcher* (2000), and it was Steven who most recently chaired the Jeanne Chall Fellowship Committee of the International Reading Association. And Steven forever honored the lessons that Jeanne Chall had taught him.

In the 1970s, in the wake of Chall's (1967/1983) book, the basal reading publishers began to accord more careful support to alphabetic basics (Popp, 1975). But the reform was short-lived. Very soon there erupted a broader and more virulent attack on phonics, anchored on misguided application of cognitive psychology's principle of top-down processes (e.g., Smith, 1973). With the ascendance of neoromantic views of child-as-learner, the goodness of teaching itself was denigrated. Meanwhile, postmodern philosophies cast the very asking of what works as impolitic at best (e.g., Edelsky, 1990; Marshall & Peters, 1994). The question was no longer when and how phonics should be taught, it was whether it should be taught at all.

The decade in which these two papers by Steven Stahl appeared (1991–2000) was a period of great controversy about beginning reading instruction. There were many arguments among people proposing varying theories about the nature of reading and the varying instructional practices that reflected these theories. The arguments sometimes centered on theory and sometimes centered on practice, but they almost always focused on beginning reading, both theory and instruction. The arguments were frequently intense and often rancorous. Sometimes the resulting attacks were very personal. These sometimes colorful arguments took place not only in the offices and classrooms of academic institutions and between the covers of professional journals, but also (often even more colorfully) at the regional and national meetings of professional organizations. In many of these meetings the arguments among the academics were picked up by school reading teachers attending the sessions, often resulting in even more rancorous exchanges, many mixed messages, and a lot confusion. Added to this scene were people from many walks of life who had developed strong opinions about the nature of reading instruction and who often offered a great deal of advice. These people often testified about reading instruction at meetings of local school boards and at state boards of education.

In the midst of all this controversy, and related to it, another topic of great concern emerged in the educational community: the many students who were not learning to read well enough to cope with the demands of school. Concerns about these students were voiced by parents, educators, researchers, and interested citizens. Soon this group of people included state and national legislators. Reading instruction thus became a political issue as well as an educational issue. One of the results of this interest was a renewed interest in research about beginning reading. This interest provided the impetus for a decade of reports about reading and each of these reports was supported at least in part by the U.S. Department of Education. These reports represent an attempt to compile scientifically based research in a form that would help guide effective reading instruction in the classrooms of U.S. schools.

Becoming a Nation of Readers, published in 1985, became one of the best-selling books about reading ever published. By the year 2000, over 300,000 copies had been purchased by elementary school teachers, local and state school administrators, teachers of preservice reading courses, and in-service staff development programs. Funded by the U.S. Department of Education and developed at the Center for the Study of Reading at the University of Illinois, *Becoming a Nation of Readers* was written to provide research-based information to professors, teachers, parents, and other interested people. Its intent was to resolve some of the arguments about reading instruction and, in particular, to help teachers gain knowledge of and insight about reading practices that would help them provide effective instruction for all of the students in their classrooms, particularly those children who were experiencing difficulty in learning to read. One young scholar who was especially interested in this report was Steven Stahl, who had recently become an associate professor at nearby Western Illinois University.

In the 1990s three more, federally sponsored reports followed: *Beginning to Read, Thinking and Learning about Print* (Adams, 1990), *Preventing Reading Difficulties in Young Children* (National Research Council, 1998), and *The Report of the National Reading Panel: Teaching Children to Read* (National Institute of Child Health and Human Development, 2000). With the exception of *Beginning to Read*, each of these reports (and including *Becoming a Nation of Readers*) was the result of the deliberations of a committee. Each of the reports covered many aspects of the nature of reading, and of the need for reading instruction to take account of all these aspects. As well, however, each report firmly emphasized the importance of deliberate teaching of alphabetic basics and phonics in programs of beginning reading instruction.

Of all the reports, *Beginning to Read, Thinking and Learning about Print* provided the most detailed review of the cognitive science of reading. Such research richly documented not only that the intended lessons of phonics are invaluable to young readers but also why and how that was so. And more, research showed that ready, working knowledge of spelling patterns and their relations to speech patterns were essential not only to spelling and word recognition but also to oral reading fluency, vocabulary growth, and comprehension capacity. Conversely, it explained how word recognition and spelling growth are reciprocally influenced not just by students' phonological awareness and orthographic knowledge but also by their language, vocabulary, background knowledge, and metacognitive habits.

Beginning to Read also brought the budding construct of phonemic awareness to the forefront. Phonemic awareness is the *insight* that every spoken word can be conceived as a sequence of those little speech sounds represented by the letters. It is this insight on which the logic and learnability of an alphabetic script depends. Like the traditional words-first curriculum, the phonemic awareness approach depends on top-down processing. Unlike the traditional words-first curriculum, the top-down processing that matters is not of the visual configurations of the printed words but, instead, of the children's understanding of how the writing system works coupled with their own oral knowledge of the word in focus. Like the traditional phonics-first curriculum, the phonemic awareness approach depends on direct instruction. Unlike the traditional phonics-first approach, the lessons delivered through direct instruction are intended not as targets of memorization in and of themselves but, instead, as *examples* that the children are expected to transfer and extend to their own reading and writing through their own thought. Also like the traditional phonics-first curriculum, the phonemic awareness approach is systematic. Unlike the traditional phonics-first curriculum, however, the objective of this systematicity is to ensure that the children have each layer—each family—of conventions in command before each new layer is added. Thus, for oral language, instruction progresses in order of psychological accessibility—from rhythm and rhyme to syllables to long vowels then short to initial then final then blended consonants, and so on. For written language, instruction progresses in order of complexity—from simple consonants and simple short vowels to consonant blends to long vowel markers to syllabification, and so on. In other words, and in contrast to either of the traditional approaches, the phonemic awareness approach is intended to promote growth in word recognition and spelling not through flashcards or drill and skill but through thinking, understanding, and doing. As now so overly documented by research, the key to the learnability of phonics and spelling, as for every other dimension of the literacy challenge, is understanding. Unfortunately, too many of those who hoped to hear "phonics" would not hear this distinction even as too many of those who refused to hear "phonics" could not hear it. And so the fight continues, ever at the expense of the teachers and the children.

Steven voluntarily read and critiqued each chapter of *Beginning to Read* as it was written. Throughout and over and over, he expressed genuine delight at the experimental craft, empirical discoveries, and theoretical mullings of the researchers in its pages. Afterwards, he was one of the trio who transformed the book into a digestable version for teachers (Stahl, Lehr, & Osborn, 1990).

Steven Stahl was a scholar's scholar. He loved to learn through reading. But, whether in the classroom or through research, he loved also to roll up his sleeves and see how to understand better by working with children. The study of phonemic awareness that he conducted with Bruce Murray (Stahl & Murray, 1994) is a quintessential example: The tasks were drawn from the classroom inventory, the analyses straightforward, and the conclusion direct: "Yup, phonemic awareness really makes the difference."

In complement, Steven invested extraordinary effort in finding ways to interpret and present research information in ways that would resonate with his colleagues in the classroom. Thus, in his essay with Duffy-Hester and Dougherty Stahl (1998), he seeks not just to inform but to embrace and encourage the teachers for whom he is writing.

Steve Stahl was an outspoken proponent of phonics throughout his career, gentle and unflinching regardless of the slings and arrows. His curriculum vita includes more than 21 publications on beginning reading, specifically about phonics and phonemic awareness. Yet, he consistently applied his interests and energy to other dimensions of education—to name just a few, instructional models, content area learning, in-classroom discussion—and especially to other dimensions of reading. A rough compilation of Stahl's published work on reading (sometimes as the sole author, many times with colleagues) over the roughly 20 years of his career reveals 30 titles on vocabulary, 11 on reading comprehension, and 9 on issues related to special education. In the mid-1990s he turned his focus to the development of reading fluency, publishing 11 titles on that topic. In addition, he published 18 chapters and journal articles that are specifically addressed to teachers and that seek to explain interrelated aspects of reading instruction. The written record that Steven Stahl leaves behind confirms that he honored the many aspects of reading and that he was both a researcher and an explainer. Both his research and his explanations will be missed.

REFERENCES

Adams, M. J. (1990). *Beginning to read, thinking and learning about print*. Cambridge, MA: MIT Press.

Chall, J. S. (1983). *Learning to read: The great debate*. New York: McGraw-Hill. (Original work published 1967)

Chall, J. S., & Stahl, S. A. (1982). Reading. In H. Mitzel (Ed.), *Encyclopedia of educational research* (5th ed.). New York: American Educational Research Association/Free Press.

Chall, J. S., & Stahl, S. A. (1983). Reading. In *Funk and Wagnalls New Encyclopedia*. New York: Funk and Wagnalls. (Revised, 1989; reprinted in *Microsoft Encarta*, Redmond, WA: Microsoft)

Chall, J. S., & Stahl, S. A. (1985a). Initial reading methods. In T. Husen & T. N. Postlethwaite (Eds.), *International encyclopedia of education* (pp. 4211–4213). Oxford, UK: Pergamon Press.

Chall, J. S., & Stahl, S. A. (1985b). Reading comprehension research in the past decade: Implications for educational publishing. *Book Research Quarterly, 1*(1), 95–102.

Chall, J. S., & Stahl, S. A. (1988). Reading. In E. Barnouw (Ed.), *International encyclopedia of communications*. Philadelphia: Annenberg School of Communications and Oxford University Press.

Edelsky, C. (1990). Whose agenda is this anyway? A response to McKenna, Robinson, and Miller. *Educational Researcher, 19*(8), 7–11.

Gray, W. S. (1948). *On their own in reading*. Chicago: Scott, Foresman.

Marshall, J., & Peters, M. (1994). Post-modernism and education. In T. Husen & T. N. Postlethwaite (Eds.), *International encyclopedia of education* (pp. 4639–4642). Oxford, UK: Pergamon Press.

Monroe, M. (1932). *Children who cannot read*. Chicago: University of Chicago Press.

Montessori, M. (1964). *The Montessori method*. New York: Schocken Books. (Original work published 1916)

National Institute of Child Health and Human Development. (2000). *Report of the National Reading Panel. Teaching children to read: An evidence-based assessment of the scientific research literature on reading and its implications for reading instruction* (NIH Publication No. 00-4769). Washington, DC: U.S. Government Printing Office.

National Research Council. (1998). *Preventing reading difficulties in young children*. Washington, DC: National Academies Press.

Orton, S. T. (1937). *Reading, writing, and speech problems in children*. New York: Norton.

Popp, H. J. (1975). Current practices in the teaching of beginning reading. In J. B. Carroll & J. S. Chall (Eds.), *Toward a literate society* (pp. 101–146). New York: McGraw-Hill.

Smith, F. (1973). *Psycholinguistics and reading*. New York: Holt, Rinehart & Winston.

Stahl, S. A. (2000). Jeanne S. Chall (1921–1999): An appreciation. *Educational Researcher, 29*(5), 41–43.

Stahl, S. A, Duffy-Hester, A. M., & Dougherty Stahl, K. A. (1998). Everything you wanted to know about phonics (but were afraid to ask). *Reading Research Quarterly, 33*(3), 338–355.

Stahl, S. A., Lehr, F., & Osborn, J. (1990). *Beginning to read: Thinking and learning about print by Marilyn Jager Adams. A summary*. Champaign: Center for the Study of Reading, University of Illinois.

Stahl, S. A., & Murray, B. A. (1994). Defining phonological awareness and its relationship to early reading. *Journal of Educational Psychology, 86*(2), 221–234.

7 | Defining Phonological Awareness and Its Relationship to Early Reading

STEVEN A. STAHL
BRUCE A. MURRAY

The relationship between phonological awareness[1] and early reading has been well established since the 1970s (see Adams, 1990, for a review). Phonological awareness is an awareness of sounds in spoken (not written) words that is revealed by such abilities as rhyming, matching initial consonants, and counting the number of phonemes in spoken words. These tasks are difficult for some children because spoken words do not have identifiable segments that correspond to phonemes; for example, the word *dog* consists of one physical speech sound. In alphabetic languages, however, letters usually represent phonemes, and to learn about the correspondences between letters and phonemes, the child has to be aware of the phonemes in spoken words.

Evidence for the importance of phonological awareness comes from a number of sources. First, correlational studies have shown strong concurrent and predictive relations between phonemic awareness and success in reading (e.g., Liberman, Shankweiler, Fischer, & Carter, 1974; Mann, 1984). In one study (Juel, 1988) it was found that first graders who had difficulty with phonological awareness tasks such as blending sounds together to make words, segmenting words into sounds, and manipulating initial and final consonants typically remained in the bottom quarter of their class in reading 4 years later. Another study (MacLean, Bryant, & Bradley, 1987) found that children's knowledge of nursery rhymes at age 3 years strongly predicted their later development of more abstract phonological knowledge and, more important, their early reading ability.

At least some ability to distinguish phonological elements smaller than syllables seems to be necessary to make use of an alphabetic orthography (Gough, Juel, & Griffith, 1992). Preliterate measures of phonological awareness predict achievement in beginning reading more accurately than do many common correlates of school achievement, including IQ scores, age, and measures of socioeconomic status (Share, Jorm, Maclean, & Matthews, 1984). Longitudinal studies locate the development of metalinguistic phonological skills prior to the onset of reading (Wagner & Torgesen, 1987). Successful efforts to train phonological awareness have led to significant achievement differences in reading acquisition (e.g., Ball & Blachman, 1991; Bradley & Bryant, 1983; Lundberg, Frost, & Petersen, 1988; Wallach & Wallach, 1979; Williams, 1979); these are differences that have far-reaching consequences in leveraging reading performance (Stanovich, 1986).

Although the general relationships between phonological awareness and early reading are well established, there are two distinct questions that need to be answered: How should one measure phonological awareness? and How much phonological awareness is needed to learn to read? The first question relates to the nature of phonological awareness and how it grows; the second relates to reading and the phonological features of which a child must be aware to be able to learn to read.

DEFINING PHONOLOGICAL AWARENESS

Phonological awareness has been measured, and consequently defined, by many different tasks. Tasks designed to assess the construct range from recognition of rhyme (Does *fish* rhyme with *dish*?) and sound-to-word matching (Does *fish* begin with /f/?) to isolating single sounds from words (What is the first sound in *fish*?), blending (What does /f-i-sh/ say?), deleting phonemes (Say *fish* without /f/), and other even more complex manipulations, such as children's secret languages (Mann, 1991; Savin, 1972). Because these diverse tasks vary in difficulty, children may be rated as high in awareness on one measure and as low in awareness on another. Without an agreed on means of operationalizing phonological awareness, progress in understanding and applying the construct will be limited (Adams, 1990, Lewkowicz, 1980). For example, to determine whether phonological awareness is a cause or a consequence of reading acquisition requires agreement on the ways in which phonological awareness is to be defined and measured.

In a synthesis of the literature on reading acquisition, Adams (1990) theorized that the tasks used to measure phonological awareness fall into five levels of difficulty. The most primitive level, according to Adams, consists of having an ear for the sounds of words, which is revealed by the ability to remember familiar rhymes (see Maclean et al., 1987). A second level consists of the ability to recognize and sort patterns of rhyme and alliteration in words, which requires more focused attention to sound components; this ability is revealed in oddity tasks (see Bradley & Bryant, 1983). A third level requires familiarity both with the idea that syllables can be divided into phonemes and with the sounds of isolated phonemes; this level is indicated by blending tasks (see Perfetti, Beck, Bell, & Hughes, 1987) and by syllable-splitting tasks, for example, isolating initial phonemes (see Share et al., 1984; Wallach & Wallach, 1979). A fourth level of difficulty is encountered in tasks that require full segmentation of component phonemes (e.g., tapping tests; see Liberman et al., 1974). Most difficult of all are tasks that require children to add, delete, or otherwise move phonemes and to regenerate the resultant word of pseudoword (e.g., Rosner, 1974).

Yopp (1988) attempted to empirically resolve the problem of operationalizing phonological awareness. She administered 10 different measures of phonological awareness to a group of kindergartners to determine the reliability and relative difficulty of each measure and to assess task validity through correlation with a pseudoword decoding task. Yopp also carried out a factor analysis, in which she found two skills that influence test performance: a simple phonemic awareness factor (observed in segmentation, blending, sound isolation, and phoneme counting tests) and a compound phonemic awareness factor, observed in tasks that require holding a sound in memory while performing additional operations.

Although Yopp (1988) seems to demonstrate two clearly different levels of phonological awareness, she noted that there are problems with the tasks commonly used to assess the construct. Items vary greatly both between and within measures on the same type of task. For example, some blending tasks use nonsense words, some real words; some have more short consonant–vowel–consonant (CVC) words, others contain more words with consonant blends. One important source of variability not controlled in Yopp's tasks is linguistic level (Treiman, 1992). Syllables seem to break most readily between the onset (any beginning consonants) and the rime (the vowel and any final consonants). The rime may be further divisible into the vowel nucleus and the coda, or any final consonants. For example, most people find it easier to divide *stamp* into /st/ and /amp/ than into other dichotomous parts. This tendency is illustrated by the unintended slips people construct when they blend the onset of one word with the rime of another. Treiman simulated this by asking adults to combine *frail* and *slat* into one new word. Most (62%) said "frat," which moved the onset of the first word onto the rime of the second. Very few said "frait" ("freight"). Treiman's research demonstrates the salience of onset and rime units within the syllable. Accordingly, it is more difficult to delete the initial phoneme in *trick* than it is in *tick*, because the former involves breaking up the blended phonemes within an onset, and the latter only requires separating the onset from the rime. Because Yopp used or adapted extant tasks of phonological awareness, it was not possible to directly compare performance on items constructed to be equivalent in linguistic complexity.

As part of this project, we reexamined the items on Yopp's (1988) measures[2] by assigning a weight for each level of linguistic complexity tapped: *recognition of a rhyme* (1), *manipulating onset and rime* (2), *manipulating vowel and coda* (3), *manipulating phonemes within a cluster onset* (4), and *manipulating phonemes within a cluster coda* (5). We rated each item on linguistic complexity and averaged these ratings as a measure of task difficulty. When we correlated task difficulty with the mean score obtained by Yopp's participants on each task (see Yopp, 1988, Table 3), we found a .95 correlation between our *post hoc* measure of task difficulty and the levels of difficulty obtained by Yopp. This suggested that linguistic complexity may be an important factor in phonological awareness. It also suggested that Yopp's measures may have confounded linguistic complexity and task.

RELATIONS BETWEEN PHONOLOGICAL AWARENESS AND EARLY READING

As stated earlier, the correlations between phonological awareness and beginning reading are robust and much replicated. However, a second problem in this literature is the difficulty of establishing to what degree phonological awareness is either a cause or a result of success in beginning reading.

Correlational Studies

Early theorists suggested that children's ability to reflect on sounds in spoken words was necessary for them to learn to map letter sounds onto speech sounds (Liberman et al., 1974). Because the sounds in a spoken word are blended together to form a single acoustic unit, the individual sounds in a word are not readily apparent. It has been suggested that children who do not reflect on sounds in words and who cannot segment a spoken word into its component sounds are prone to have difficulty in learning to read (Liberman et al., 1974; Savin, 1972; Stanovich, 1986). Evidence for this view comes from a number of correlational studies involving phonological awareness and beginning reading, in which both concurrent correlations (see Adams, 1990, for a review) and predictive correlations (e.g., Maclean et al., 1987; Perfetti et al., 1987) have been found.

Other researchers, such as Adams (1990), have suggested that children learn about English orthography through both a familiarity with letter shapes and an awareness of phonemes in spoken words. The research reviewed by Adams suggests that letter knowledge and phonological awareness are the strongest predictors of children's success in reading. For example, Lomax and McGee (1987) used a LISREL analysis to test a model of reading acquisition with 3- to 6-year-olds. Lomax and McGee examined five clusters of factors associated with beginning reading and found a developmental sequence progressing from Concepts About Print, to Graphic Awareness, Phonemic Awareness, Grapheme–Phoneme Correspondence, and Word Reading. The Concepts About Print factor was also associated with the Grapheme–Phoneme Correspondence factor. In the Lomax and McGee model, Concepts About Print included measures of knowledge of the functions of print, technical language of print, and literacy behavior. Phoneme Awareness was assessed by three measures, one involving determining whether a pair of words consisted of the same word repeated twice or two different words and two involving the isolation of initial and final consonants. These isolation measures assess what Yopp (1988) calls simple phoneme awareness. Lomax and McGee did not include more difficult phonological awareness tasks, such as those requiring blending or deletion of phonemes.

Training Studies

Further evidence that phonological awareness underlies beginning reading skill comes from training studies. Bradley and Bryant (1983) taught prereaders either to sort words by common sounds or to sort words and to spell these sounds with letters, and they found that the combination program had impressive effects on children's reading acquisition, with the combination group reading a full 9 months ahead of the Hawthorne control and 12.5 months ahead of the no-treatment control group by the end of second grade. The effects for the phonological training group alone were less impressive and were not statistically significant. Because the combination group received both phonological awareness training and letter name training, it seems that phonological awareness training is strongly facilitated by training in spelling (see also Byrne & Fielding-Barnsley, 1993; Wagner & Rashotte, 1993).

Other researchers have found that phonological awareness training has a significant effect on early reading without the concurrent use of letter training. For example, Lundberg et al. (1988) administered Danish kindergartners 8 months of phonological awareness training that specifically excluded letter–sound instruction. They found that their training led not only to gains in phonological awareness but also to significant effects on spelling in grades 1 and 2 and on reading achievement in grade 2.

Reciprocal Causation

Others have argued that phonological awareness is a result rather than a cause of learning to read. Morais, Bertelson, Cary, and Alegria (1986) found that illiterate adults were significantly inferior to a matched group of newly literate adults on a phonemic segmentation task. The finding that otherwise intelligent, illiterate adults do not develop phonological skill suggests that it is not a naturally developing ability. That newly literate adults do have this ability suggests to Morais et al. that the ability to reflect on spoken words comes after rather than before learning to read. Ehri and Wilce (1986) found that children who already could read responded differently than did children who could not read, and they appeared to use their knowledge of letters in words in several phoneme awareness tasks that involved identifying whether the first syllable of words containing an alveolar flap (Ca*d*illac) ended with a /t/ or /d/ (*cat* or *cad*).

It may be that certain levels of phonological awareness, as measured either by different tasks or by different levels of linguistic complexity, precede learning to read, whereas more advanced levels may result from learning to read. Adams (1990) suggests that the tapping test (Liberman et al., 1974), which requires children to tap out the number of phonemes that a word contains, may be influenced by children's reading ability, rather than the other way around. The demands of tapping out the number of phonemes in a word may put an unreasonable load on short-term memory unless the word is mediated by its spelling.

Ehri (1992) has suggested that the relation between phonological awareness and early reading is one of reciprocal causation, where a certain amount of ability to reflect on spoken words is necessary (but probably not sufficient) to understand the alphabetic system and thus to acquire a slight vocabulary. Expansion of a child's sight vocabulary, in turn, requires increasing reflection on spoken words, thus improving children's awareness of phonemes. Having a sight vocabulary also mediates many of the tasks used in phonological awareness, as suggested by Adams (1990). This notion of reciprocal causation suggests that the strong correlations between phonological awareness measures and measures of reading skill mask two different causal patterns.

Our purpose in this study was to examine, first, the relative importance of linguistic complexity and task differences in measuring phonological awareness, and, second, the relationship of phonological awareness to early reading skill with these perspectives.

METHOD

Participants

Participants were 113 kindergarten and first-grade children (52 kindergartners and 61 first graders). Approximately half of these children attended a Catholic school in a small city in the southeastern United States. The remainder attended a public school in the same city. Nearly all the parochial students were white. In the public school, approximately one-half of the students were African American. In the parochial school, the students were largely from middle- and upper-middle-class backgrounds; in the public school, there was a wider range of socioeconomic status. In both samples, girls and boys were evenly represented. (These subjects also participated in a related study by Stahl & Murray, 1993.)

Measures

Tests of Phonological Awareness

Our intent was to overcome the confounding factor of linguistic level by constructing a our own phonological awareness test. We began with four tasks commonly used in phonological awareness studies: blending, isolation, segmentation, and deletion. Real-word items were found for each task at each of four levels of linguistic complexity: analyzing onsets and rimes, analyzing vowels and codas within rimes, analyzing phonemes composing cluster onsets, and analyzing phonemes composing cluster codas. These items were designed to be parallel in the use of continuant and stop consonants.

Fourteen tests of five items each (see Figure 7.1) were constructed so that the items represented the four tasks—phoneme blending, isolation, segmentation, and deletion—at four levels of linguistic complexity (onset–rime, vowel–coda, cluster onset, and cluster coda). The tests are shown in Appendix 7.1. Blending required the child to synthesize segmented phonemes to recognize a word. Phoneme isolation

	Blending	Segmentation	Phoneme Isolation	Deletion
Onset–Rime	CVC Words	CVC Words (Onset–Rime Score)	CVC Words (Beginning)	CVC Words (Beginning)
Vowel–Coda		CVC Words (Total Segmentation Score)	CVC Words (Final)	CVC Words (Final)
Cluster Onset	CCVC Words	CCVC Words	CCVC Words	CCVC Words
Cluster Coda	CCVC Words	CCVC Words	CCVC Words	CCVC Words

FIGURE 7.1. Item composition of tests of phonemic awareness by task and linguistic level. C = consonant. V = vowel.

required the child to say the first or last sound of a spoken word. Deletion required the child to remove sounds from the beginning or end of one word and to form another word, such as saying *face* without /f/. Segmentation required pronouncing all phonemes of a word. We derived an extra score from the CVC word segmentation task. Children's scores were based on whether they segmented the onset from the rime and whether they made a complete segmentation of the word. For example, a child who segmented *move* as /m-uv/ got credit when this item was counted for segmentation of an onset from a rime but not when it was counted for a complete segmentation. These two scores were used to create different composite scores in the linguistic complexity analysis, described below, but only the complete segmentation score was used in the segmentation task score.

We did not use a measure of blending just the onset with the rime because our pilot testing indicated that this was at ceiling for participants similar in ability to our participants. The CVC blending test was used to assess both onset–rime blending and rime–coda blending on the basis of the assumption that to blend three phonemes of a word together requires both abilities. However, the onset–rime and rime–coda scores are not completely independent.

In addition, the cluster onset score also requires the ability to manipulate the remainder of the word, not just the onset. The cluster rime score has the same limitation. As discussed later, virtually no children were successful at manipulating the cluster onset when they were not successful at manipulating a simple onset. The rime results, also discussed below, are somewhat more complex, possibly because of the nature of the cluster rimes.

We created two sets of scores from these tests, which allowed us to compare tasks (the columns on Figure 7.1) and levels of linguistic complexity (the rows on Figure 7.1). This enabled us both to ensure that the various subtests were not confounded by the different levels of linguistic complexity and to examine the effects of linguistic complexity and task differences separately. The resulting 70-item measure has a Cronbach's alpha of .96, which indicates that it is highly reliable.

Written Language Measures

For alphabet knowledge, we used the letter recognition test taken from Clay (1993). This consists of a list of 54 letters (upper and lower case, as well as alternative forms of *a* and *g*). Score was the number of letters correctly identified by name.

As a reading measure, we used a commercially published informal reading inventory (Johns, 1991). This test consists of a series of graded word lists and graded passages. The word lists were used to find an appropriate level of passage for oral reading. We derived a number of different scores from this measure—the number of words read correctly, the instructional level on the word list, and the instructional level achieved on the passages.

To speed up administration, we asked children to retell the information in the passage that they read rather than to answer questions about the passage. Children were considered to have passed the passage if they could read it with 95% accuracy and with a retelling judged as adequate. The retelling was used only to ensure that children were reading for meaning, not as a measure of comprehension.

We also gave a measure of the child's ability to read common logos, such as McDonald's. We presented a set of logos to each child, and later in the testing, we asked them to identify the words from these logos typed in plain letters. These data were reported elsewhere (Stahl & Murray, 1993) and are not discussed here, except to say that presenting the logo task as one of the first tasks was useful in making children feel comfortable and in establishing rapport.

Finally, we gave a spelling measure designed to capture children's emerging knowledge of words (Tangel & Blachman, 1992). This measure consisted of five words (*lap, sick, elephant, pretty, train*) that were dictated to the students with example sentences. Students were told to spell each word the best that they could and that "we know you may not know exactly how to spell the word since you didn't study it." This measure was scored following the guidelines of Tangel and Blachman on a 7-point scale ranging from *random strings of letters* (0) through increasingly sophisticated invented spellings, to *the conventional spellings* (6). Tangel and Blachman found interrater agreement to be .93.

Memory Measure

To examine the role that differences in working memory might play in both phonological awareness and the relationship of phonological awareness and word recognition to spelling abilities, we administered the Digit Span subtest of the Wechsler Intelligence Scale for Children–Revised (WISC-R; Wechsler, 1974). Raw scores were used in the analysis.

Procedure

We tested each child individually outside his or her classroom. Prior to the session, each teacher introduced us to the class. We spent between 30 and 40 minutes with each child. We first introduced ourselves by name and explained that we were interested in how children learn to read and that we wanted to find out how children learn to read by asking them to do some reading and listening. After the introduction, we asked children to identify logos, administered the phonological awareness measures (blending first, then phoneme isolation, segmentation, and deletion), had them identify the words taken from the logos out of context, administered the informal reading inventory, and administered the digit span test. After the testing, the child was invited to pick a gift from a bag of rings and trinkets. Children were administered the spelling test in small groups at a later time. Because we reached the end of the school year, only 85 of the 113 children were able to take the spelling test, due to interruptions such as field trips and assemblies.

RESULTS

Defining Phonological Awareness

Relative Difficulty

First, we examined the relative frequencies of students' scores on the various tasks and at the various levels of linguistic complexity. As shown in Tables 7.1 and 7.2, phoneme isolation was the easiest task, followed by blending, deletion, and segmentation. This was similar to Yopp's (1988) finding for similar tasks. Using a repeated

TABLE 7.1. Means for the Phonological Awareness Measures

Analysis	M	SD
Task		
Phoneme isolation	4.02	1.08
Phoneme blending	2.69	1.62
Phoneme deletion	2.44	1.42
Phonological segmentation	2.02	1.34
Linguistic complexity		
Onsets and rimes	3.72	1.35
Vowels and codas	3.36	1.08
Cluster onsets	2.00	1.45
Cluster codas	2.28	1.43

Note. On all subsets, maximum score = 5. $N = 113$.

measures analysis of variance (ANOVA) with Bonferroni t tests for the six pairwise comparisons (familywise $\alpha = .05$), we found that when the scores were calculated by task, phoneme isolation was by far the easiest of the tasks, followed by blending, deletion, and segmentation, $F(3, 451) = 146.55$; $p < .01$, $MS_e = .70$. All these differences were significantly different from each other (all p's $< .001$), except the difference between blending and deletion performance (where $p = .011$).

Analyzing the data by linguistic complexity (see Table 7.1) by using an analysis similar to that described above, we found that the easiest linguistic level was analyzing onsets and rimes, followed by analyzing vowels and codas, followed by analyzing cluster codas, followed by analyzing cluster onsets, $F(3, 451) = 201.32$, $p < .01$, $MS_e = .38$. These differences were all significantly different from each other (all p's $< .001$).

TABLE 7.2. Subtest Means and Standard Deviations

Subtest	M	SD
Phoneme isolation		
CVC (initial)	4.70	0.91
CVC (final)	4.13	1.45
CCVC (initial)	3.62	1.74
CVCC (final)	3.64	1.73
Blending		
CVC words	3.41	1.59
CCVC words	2.23	1.85
CVCC words	2.44	1.85
Deletion		
CVC (initial)	3.20	1.96
CVC (final)	2.94	1.91
CCVC (initial)	1.27	1.54
CVCC (final)	2.36	1.72
Segmentation		
CVC (onset–rime)	3.57	1.95
CVC (complete)	2.95	1.95
CCVC	0.89	1.47
CVCC	0.69	1.25

Note. All subtests have a maximum score of 5. $N = 113$. C = consonant; V = vowel.

Children tended to treat certain blends, such as *st* and *pl*, as units, removing *st* from *state* when asked for the first sound. We found that 714 of the 1,168 errors that the children (61%) made on items requiring manipulation of cluster onsets or codas on the isolation, segmentation, and deletion subtests involved the child treating the blend as a whole. (We did not include data from blending here because it is unclear whether failure to blend was due to a difference in conception or memory.)

Nasal blends (in our study, *nk*, *nd*, and *mp*) and liquid blends (in our study, *ld*), which tend to be found in rimes, seemed to be easier for the children to break up. Many of the children tended to either stretch the nasal or drop the nasal as part of their dialect. Treiman (1984) suggested that postvocalic consonants differ in sonority, which determines how closely they adhere to the vowel. In her analysis, liquids (/l/ or /r/) tended to adhere more closely to the vowel than did nasals (/m/ or /n/), which in turn adhered more closely than did obstruents (stops and fricatives such as /s/, /t/, or /p/). In our study, we used sets of clusters consistently across tasks, which allowed us to replicate Treiman's findings with younger participants. Across the tasks of isolation, deletion, and segmentation (in blending, the examiner makes the separation), we found that postvocalic clusters containing a liquid were easier to separate (*M* = .50, *SD* = .29) than were those containing nasals (*M* = .46, *SD* = .26), which in turn were easier to separate than those containing obstruents (*M* = .37, *SD* = .30). By using a repeated measures ANOVA, we found these differences to be statistically significant, $F(2, 224) = 14.65$, $p < .001$, $MS_e = .03$. Using paired *t* tests we found the difference between a liquid and a nasal to be significant, $t(112) = 2.21$, $p = .029$. The difference between a nasal and an obstruent was also significant, $t(112) = 3.45$, $p < .001$. An alternative explanation for these differences, at least for some of the participants, is that many of the children tended to drop the final consonant as part of a Southern dialect (*sand*, for example, might be pronounced as /sæn/; this was especially true for the African American children). As examiners, we were not sure whether some children were actually deleting the /d/ or /t/ deliberately or whether they were repeating the word in their dialect.

Factor Analysis

In contrast to Yopp's (1988) study, we found that a single factor best described our data, whether we analyzed the data by scores, tasks, or levels of linguistic complexity. When the 15 individual subtest scores were analyzed, with a criterion of accepting a factor if its eigenvalue was greater than 1, three factors were generated. However, the first factor had an eigenvalue of 7.45, which accounted for 49.7% of the variance, and all but four of the subtests had substantial (greater than .40) loadings on that factor. The other two factors were smaller in magnitude (eigenvalues of 1.41 and 1.16). The two most difficult subtests (segmentation of cluster codas and cluster blends) loaded on the second factor, and the two easiest subtests (isolation of simple onsets and codas) loaded on the third. These last two factors seem to reflect restricted variance, rather than separate underlying constructs. When tasks were used for analysis, the scores for the four tasks across all levels of linguistic analysis were used as variables. In this analysis, a single factor accounted for 72.6% of the common variance (eigenvalue = 2.91). When levels of linguistic analysis were used, the scores at the various levels, summed across the tasks, were used in the analysis. Here, one factor accounted for 81.7% of the common variance (eigenvalue = 3.32). (For both analyses,

TABLE 7.3. Factor Loadings Resulting from Two Analyses

Analysis	Loading
Task	
Phoneme isolation	.74
Phoneme deletion	.89
Blending	.90
Segmentation	.87
% of variance	72.60
Linguistic complexity	
Onsets and rimes	.93
Vowel-codas	.80
Cluster onsets	.94
Complex rimes	.93
% of variance	81.70

we forced a two-factor solution and attempted various rotations. In all cases, the first factor was more pronounced.) These sets of loadings are shown in Table 7.3.

With these two sets of loadings, it appears that both ways of defining phonological awareness, through tasks and through levels of linguistic complexity, yield a single common factor. (Yopp, 1988, also found one large factor [eigenvalue = 5.86, which accounted for 58.6% of the variance] and one much smaller factor [eigenvalue = .95, which accounted for 9.5% of the variance].) A comparison of the two loadings however, suggests that the notion of levels of linguistic complexity accounts for somewhat more variance in a common factor. Therefore, it appears that linguistic complexity across tasks is a better way of defining phonological awareness. Our further analysis suggests that this may be a fruitful way of looking at the relations between phonological awareness and reading.

Phonological Awareness and Reading

Ordinarily one might show a relationship between two sets of variables with either multiple regression analysis or path analysis. In our case, the distributions of nearly all of the variables were skewed in one way or another. For example, nearly all of our participants knew most or all of the letters of the alphabet. Similar ceiling effects were found on the ability to manipulate onsets and rimes and to manipulate vowels and codas. Floor effects were found on the word recognition measures, because a number of subjects could not read any words at all. These abnormal distributions made interpretation of correlations or regression equations problematic.

To analyze the relationships between variables, we reverted to a more elemental logical analysis. We assumed that some level of phonological awareness is necessary for children to be able to recognize words. Such awareness is certainly not sufficient, because there are any number of factors that affect children's word reading ability. We speculated that if factor A is necessary but not sufficient for factor B, then if A was not found, then B would also not be found. Our basic form of analysis was to graph two variables of interest, using scattergrams to examine the number of cases that did not conform to this pattern. We then used McNemar's test (Siegel, 1956) to test for statistical significance. For example, Figure 7.2 shows the relationship between the number of letters identified (out of 54) and the ability to manipulate onsets and rimes. The two lines represent the means for the letter recognition measure and a criterion of 70% for passage on the onset–rime scale. (The choice of these dividing marks is arbitrary. We assumed that a child who could pass 70% of the onset–rime items across the various tasks had mastered onset–rime manipulation, but 80% correct could have just as easily indicated mastery.) Although the cutting lines are arbitrary, the scattergrams show that any reasonable placement of dividing lines would not essentially change the results.

As shown in Figure 7.2, there were a large number of children who could both identify 45 or more letters and split an onset from a rime, and there were a smaller number who could do neither. There were also 24 children who could identify letters but who could not split an onset from a rime. Only one child exceeded our criterion for onset–rime manipulation but did not know at least 45 letters χ^2 (1, $N = 25$) =

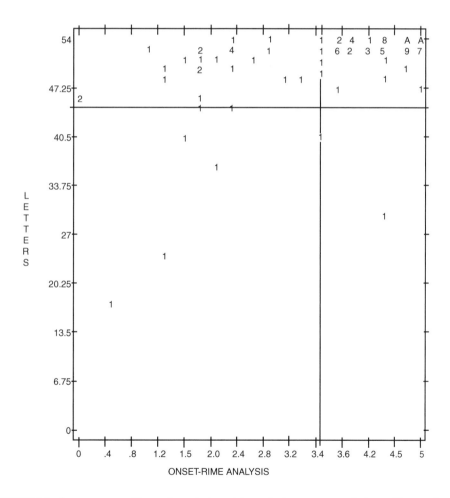

FIGURE 7.2. Scattergram of letter knowledge with analyzing onsets and rimes. Numerals represent the number of children who scored at that coordinate, and the letter *A* represents 10 children.

21.16, $p < .001$. This suggests that knowledge of letter names may provide children with a foundation for learning to manipulate onsets and rimes (see Murray, Stahl, & Ivey, 1993).

As shown in Figure 7.3, the ability to separate an onset from a rime seems, in turn, to aid children with word recognition. In this scattergram, we examined the relationship between separation of an onset from a rime and word recognition χ^2 (1, $N = 26$) = 18.62, $p < .001$. We put a reference line at 20 for the word recognition task, which represents a preprimer level on the Basic Reading Inventory (Johns, 1991). As can be seen, there were children who were proficient at both tasks and children who were proficient at neither. There were 24 children who were above average at manipulating onsets and rimes who could not read words at the preprimer level, but there were only two children who could read a reasonable number of words but who had difficulty analyzing words into onsets and rimes. This suggests that awareness of onsets and rimes may be necessary for children to read words.

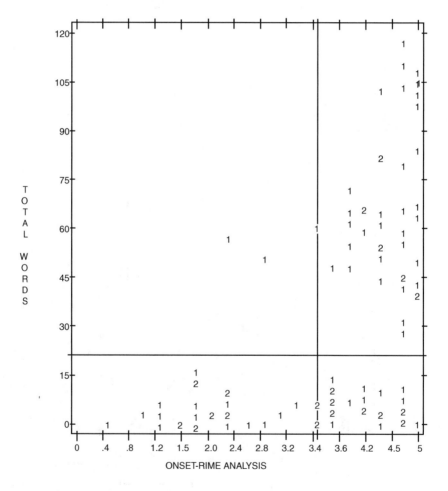

FIGURE 7.3. Scattergram of word recognition with onset–rime analysis. Numerals represent the number of children who scored at that coordinate.

In contrast, as shown in Figure 7.4, 29 children had a word recognition level above the preprimer level but had difficulty breaking rimes into vowels and codas, while 8 children could break rimes into vowels and codas but had word recognition skill below a preprimer level. In this analysis, 25.7% of the total sample could recognize words above the preprimer level but could not break a rime into a vowel and a coda, and 7% of the total sample could break up a rime but could not read words above the preprimer level. In Figure 7.3, there were only two children (1.8% of the total sample) who could recognize words above the preprimer level but could not analyze a word into an onset and a rime. This suggests that the ability to recognize words might aid the analysis of rimes into vowels and codas, rather than vice versa. Although the relation between the ability to break up a rime and word recognition is still statistically significant (with McNemar's test) χ^2 (1, $N = 37$) = 11.92, $p < .001$, this relation is not as clear as the relation between splitting an onset from a rime and word recognition.

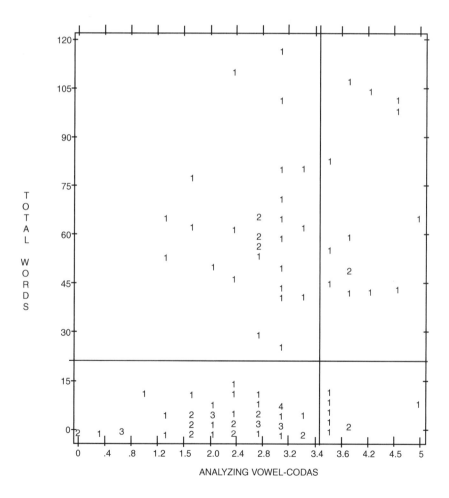

FIGURE 7.4. Scattergram of word recognition with analyzing vowel and codas. Numerals represent the number of children who scored at that coordinate.

Task Differences and Reading

In a similar analysis with the tasks, we found that only one of the four tasks showed a similar relationship with reading. Phoneme isolation, the easiest of the four tasks, appeared to distinguish children who could read from children who were unable to pass the criterion on the preprimer list. As shown in Figure 7.5, of the 20 children who scored below 3.5 on the phoneme isolation task, 18 (90%) were unable to pass the criterion on the preprimer list. Of the 81 who scored at or above 3.5 on the phoneme isolation task, only 39 (48%) were unable to pass the criterion on the preprimer list χ^2 (1, N = 38) = 30.42, p < .001. Of these 39, 32 were kindergartners who may not have received instruction.

In the tasks that involved the manipulation of sounds in consonant blends such as *st* or *dr*, children often treated the blend as a single unit. Thus, when asked to give the first sound of *plain*, children would commonly say /pl/, or when asked to say

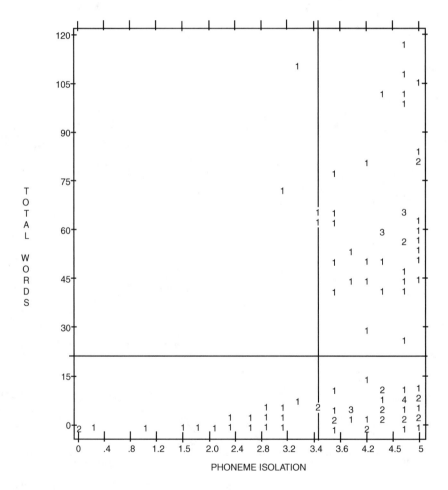

FIGURE 7.5. Scattergram of word recognition with phoneme isolation. Numerals represent the number of children who scored at that coordinate.

flight without the /f/, they would say /ait/. These were usually children who were reading at about a first-grade level. They tended to treat the blend as if it were a single unit and to delete it as any onset. Although linguists view the /pl/ as a blend, it may not matter whether children treat it as such. Children can learn that *pl* represents /pl/ in a way that is distinct from the knowledge that *p* represents /p/ and *l* represents /l/. Children can use that knowledge functionally to decode words that begin with *pl*. (Of course, just because the children did not break up blends does not mean that they could not do it. Because as Treiman, 1992, argued, segmenting a word between onset and rime is more natural, it may be that these children are choosing to break words there, even if they could break up a cluster onset or coda, if encouraged to do so.)

Phonological Awareness and Spelling

Replicating the findings of previous studies, we found strong correlations between phonological awareness and spelling ability. For example, the correlation between onset–rime awareness and spelling ability was .63 ($p < .01$), and other correlations were of similar strength. The correlations do not tell the entire story. An early phonemic spelling (Bear & Barone, 1989), such as LESTR for LAP, in which the first sound is correctly represented but the rest of the sounds are not, seems to require the ability to separate an onset from a rime. However, only one child who spelled at this level was able to reach mastery on the onset–rime separation tasks. The remainder did quite poorly on the onset–rime tasks. Using a scattergram for analysis (see Figure 7.6), one can see that most children who passed the onset–rime criteria were considerably better spellers, who scored an average of 3 for each word. The score of 3 involves representing two or more of the consonants correctly and having some vowel (Tangel & Blachman, 1992). This suggests that the spelling task is an easier measure of phonological awareness than are the oral phonological awareness measures (as suggested by Treiman, 1991). The scattergram for the relation between spelling and analysis of rimes into vowels and codas was similar, except that most of the children who passed the criterion had a score of 4 or higher, thus indicating a more sophisticated spelling ability.

One explanation is that invented spelling, at least for children who know letter names, minimizes the need for memory, compared with oral phonological awareness tasks. When deleting a phoneme, for example, one needs to keep the word in memory, mentally remove a phoneme, and reconstitute the word. When spelling, one can put down a letter and then concentrate on successive letters. To test this hypothesis, we computed a regression analysis using spelling score as the dependent variable. In a hierarchical regression equation, digit span did not account for any additional variance in spelling ability after that accounted for by the phonological awareness measures entered as a block. In contrast, when word recognition was made the dependent variable in a similar analysis, digit span accounted for a small but significant additional percent of variance (2.5%) in word recognition scores after phonological awareness was entered. This supports the hypothesis that spelling is less demanding of memory, because short-term memory would be implicated in sounding out words that could not be recognized immediately. Invented spelling seems to minimize the demands on short-term memory because the written letters serve as a memory aid. In

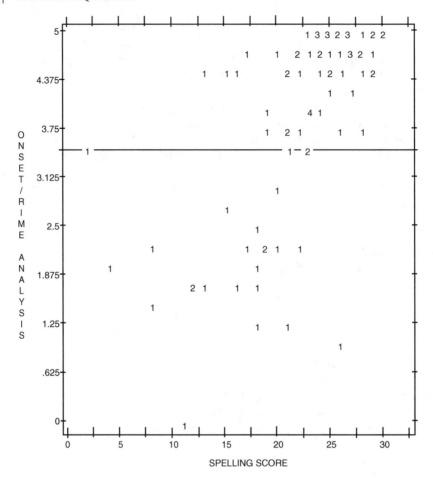

FIGURE 7.6. Scattergram of spelling with onset–rime analysis. Numerals represent the number of children who scored at that coordinate.

contrast, learning conventional spellings involves memory for which of these spellings is the one that is accepted, because there can be several plausible invented spellings for a given word.

DISCUSSION

In this study we addressed two issues in the relation between phonological awareness and reading: What is the best way of conceptualizing (and measuring) phonological awareness for the purpose of examining the relation with beginning reading? and Which abilities involved in phonological awareness are coincident with reading ability?

Comparing the different conceptualizations of phoneme awareness using a measure not confounded by linguistic level or task difficulty, we found that a single factor best described the data, whether analyzed by score, task, or level of linguistic complexity. Through our examination of the distributions of the data, we believe that the notion of levels of linguistic complexity (better than differences between tasks) describes the construct of phonological awareness.

As to the amount of phoneme awareness necessary for reading, it appears that the ability to manipulate onsets and rimes within syllables relates most strongly to reading, once an adequate level of letter recognition is achieved. The ability to isolate a phoneme from either the beginning or the end of a word, the easiest of the phonological awareness abilities, also seems to be crucial to reading, because nearly all children who could not adequately perform this task also had not achieved a preprimer instructional level.

Combining these results with those from the analysis by linguistic complexity, we can speculate on a series of necessary but not sufficient conditions among the variables examined. Knowledge of letter names might enable children to manipulate onsets and rimes, which, in turn, would enable basic word recognition. Basic word recognition might enable more complex forms of phonological awareness, as suggested by Barron (1991).

One scenario might be that children first learn letter names, perhaps through hearing alphabet books read aloud or by singing the alphabet song (see Adams, 1990), and then they learn to match individual letters with their names. As a part of teaching the letter names, sound values are taught. For example, a child might read an alphabet book in which letters are paired with pictures of animals containing their names. The parent or teacher who taught the letter names might also include beginning sound instruction with the letter name instruction. Alternatively because most consonants contain the phonemes most commonly associated with them in their names, learning a letter name helps children identify its sound value. Either way, learning the letter names seems to be necessary but not sufficient for children to mentally separate an onset from a rime. Similar results were reported by Griffith and Klesius (1992), who used cross-lagged correlations as well as scattergrams.

Children may, in turn, use initial consonant knowledge to gain some word knowledge, as suggested by Ehri (1992). In Ehri's model of the acquisition of word recognition, phonetic cue reading was described as a stage in which the developing reader uses initial or final consonant information to help identify words. This is an intermediate stage between visual cue reading, in which the child makes arbitrary associations among the visual features of the word and its meaning, and phonological recoding, in which the child makes full use of sound–symbol correspondences. Ehri and Sweet (1991), for example, found that some degree of phonological awareness seems to be needed for a child to identify words through finger pointing to memorized text. In both Figure 7.3 and 7.5 we suggest that the isolation of initial or final phonemes may be a precursor to developing a rudimentary sight vocabulary. As children acquire more and more words, they become more sensitive to the structure of written words. This sensitivity leads them to greater sensitivity to the phonological structure of words, thus enabling them to analyze rimes, as seen in Figure 7.4. This greater sensitivity to the phonological structure of words may, in turn, enable more generalizable decoding skill, such as the ability to decode words not previously seen. This "cipher reading" (Gough et al., 1992), often measured by pseudoword decoding tasks, is the hallmark of children who read well. Because we did not administer such tasks as part of this study, we can only speculate about these relations.

It is the nature of phoneme awareness that makes it difficult to measure. On the one hand, it is an insight. As such, it is a new and relatively permanent way of thinking about language. On the other hand, we see phoneme awareness as developing, possibly through the early grades, with children gaining greater and greater sophistication in manipulating sounds in spoken words. In our analysis, the awareness that words can be broken into onsets and rimes leads to an awareness that rimes can be decomposed into peaks and codas and that cluster onsets and cluster codas can be thought of as individual phonemes. As children's reflections on spoken words become more complex, ordinarily with the aid of learning to read in an alphabetic cipher (cf. Perfetti et al., 1987), this series of insights looks like a continuously developing ability.

The development of cipher knowledge may also be a series of insights, one of which appears to be the insight that spoken words can be broken down into at least onsets and rimes. This insight allows children to develop the understanding that letters in written words stand for sounds in spoken words (namely, the alphabetic principle.) More refined understanding of the alphabetic principle also continues to develop. Further development of phoneme awareness, especially awareness of sounds in cluster onsets and cluster codas, may aid in spelling development (Treiman, 1991) or in more sophisticated knowledge of sound–symbol relations.

The analysis of blends, either in the onset or in the rime, seems to be relatively unrelated to reading ability, because many children in our sample who could read well for their grade could not analyze blends adequately. Many of these children treated blends as wholes, for example, providing /fl/ as the first sound of *flood*. The notion that the sound of *fl* is /fl/ may be all that is needed to read words containing that blend. The knowledge that the sound /fl/ can be broken down into the sounds /f/ and /l/ may not be needed for beginning reading. Stanovich (1992), however, suggests that complete segmentation ability can facilitate reading development.

The relations between spelling and phonological awareness are complex. Because invented spelling is more concrete and minimizes reliance on memory, it seems that invented spelling is an easier task than that posed by the oral phonological awareness measures used here, and it might be more sensitive to the subtle knowledge of phonological segments.

The instrument and conceptualizations that we used are not without their limitations. We did not provide an onset–rime blending task, because pilot testing suggested that such a task was too easy for similar participants. Instead, we assumed that the CVC blending task requires onset–rime blending and thus was included with that score. We included such a measure in another study (Murray et al., 1993), in which we used younger children.

In designing our instrument, we consciously used a task hierarchy. The cluster onset and cluster coda measures all required analysis not only of the target segment but also of the rest of the word. In fact, no child could split a cluster who could not analyze the rest of the word, as we expected. The label, however, may be misleading.

Because this study is not experimental, it would be premature to impute causal relations. To establish causality, one needs training or closer and longitudinal observation of how children develop letter name knowledge, phonological awareness, and knowledge of written words. The paths found in this data, however, seem to be logical and may lead to well-defined programs of teaching children to be aware of phonemes in words and to use that knowledge in reading.

APPENDIX 7.1. TESTS OF PHONEMIC AWARENESS

Administration: For each subtest, give feedback only for practice words. Use additional examples if necessary. When the idea is clear, discontinue feedback and continue with test items.

I. Blending.

Instructions: I'm going to say some words in a secret code, spreading out the sounds until they come out one at a time. Guess what word I'm saying. For example, if I say h-a-m, you say *ham*. (For each item, pronounce the segments with as little additional vowel as possible.)

Practice words: f-un; k-ing; s-o-me; p-u-t; s-e-n-d.

1. Vowel–coda   m-a-p t-e-n s-e-t d-i-d sh-ee-p
2. Cluster onset   f-l-a-t c-r-a-ck s-p-a-ce p-l-ai-n s-t-e-p
3. Cluster coda   f-i-n-d p-i-n-k c-a-m-p w-i-l-d l-a-s-t

II. Isolation.

Instructions: This time I want you to listen for just one sound in a word. Tell me the sound you hear at the beginning of each word I say. For example, if I say *fix*, you say /f/.

Practice words: no (/n/); ship (/sh/); time (/t/); hot (/h/); jump (/j/)

1. Onset–rime   food (/f/) came (/k/) side (/s/) pad (/p/) seal (/s/)
2. Cluster onset   flood (/f/) cross (/k/) speak (/s/) please (/p/) state (/s/)

Instructions: Now I want you to listen and tell me the sound at the very end of each word I say. For example, if I say *watch*, you say /ch/.

Practice words: off (/f/); fish (/sh/); egg (/g/)

3. Vowel–coda   room (/m/) not (/t/) gas (/s/) sled (/d/) cross (/s/)
4. Cluster coda   sand (/d/) junk (/k/) limp (/p/) build (/d/) best (/t/)

III. Segmentation.

Instructions: Do you remember when I said the words in a secret code and you guessed what word I was saying? This time I want you to say the word in a secret code. I'll say a word, and you spread out all the sounds in the word. For example, if I say *sheep*, you say /sh-ee-p/.

Practice words: me; fish; can; sand; ash

1. Onset–rime and vowel–coda   m o v e t i m e s i c k d o n e s o u p
2. Cluster onset   f l o a t c r e a m s p e e d p l a c e s t i c k
3. Cluster coda   s e n d t h i n k r a m p s o l d t o a s t

IV. Deletion.

Instructions: I wonder if you could take a sound away from a word and make a whole new word. For example, say *meat*. Now say it again, but don't say /m/. (For each item, use this form: Say [word]. Now say it again, but don't say [phoneme].)

Practice words: make (ache); learn (earn)

1. Onset–rime   face (ace) kin (in) sat (at) page (age) sand (and)
2. Cluster onset   flight (light) crash (rash) spot (pot) plug (lug) stone (tone)

Instructions: Now listen for the sound at the end.

Practice words: keep (key); pail (pay)

3. Vowel–coda   lime (lie) might (my) race (ray) need (knee) rice (rye)
4. Cluster coda   tend (ten) sink (sing) bump (bum) hold (hole) paste (pace)

NOTES

1. We used the term *phonological awareness* rather than *phoneme awareness* because in many cases we are referring to units larger than a single phoneme.
2. We thank Hallie Yopp for kindly allowing us to use her measures.

REFERENCES

Adams, M. J. (1990). *Beginning to read: Thinking and learning about print.* Cambridge, MA: MIT Press.

Ball, E. W., & Blachman, B. A. (1991). Does phoneme segmentation training in kindergarten make a difference in early word recognition and developmental spelling? *Reading Research Quarterly, 26*, 49–66.

Barron, R. W. (1991). Proto-literacy, literacy, and the acquisition of phonological awareness. *Learning and Individual Differences, 3*, 225–242.

Bear, D., & Barone, D. (1989). Using children's spellings to group for word study and directed reading in the primary classroom. *Reading Psychology, 10*, 275–292.

Bradley, L., & Bryant, P. E. (1983). Categorizing sounds and learning to read—A causal connection. *Nature, 301*, 419–421.

Byrne, B., & Fielding-Barnsley, R. (1993). Evaluation of a program to teach phonemic awareness to young children: A 1-year follow-up. *Journal of Educational Psychology, 85*, 104–111.

Clay, M. M. (1993). *An observation survey of early literacy achievement.* Portsmouth, NH: Heinemann.

Ehri, L. C. (1992). Reconceptualizing the development of sight word reading and its relationship to recoding. In P. B. Gough, L. C. Ehri, & R. Treiman (Eds.), *Reading acquisition* (pp. 107–144). Hillsdale, NJ: Erlbaum.

Ehri, L. C., & Sweet, J. (1991). Fingerpoint-reading of memorized text: What enables beginners to process the print? *Reading Research Quarterly, 26*, 442–462.

Ehri, L. C., & Wilce, L. S. (1986). The influence of spellings on speech: Are alveolar flaps /d/ or /t/? In J. D. B. Yaden & S. Templeton (Ed.), *Metalinguistic awareness and beginning literacy* (pp. 101–114). Portsmouth, NH: Heinemann.

Gough, P. B., Juel, C., & Griffith, P. L. (1992). Reading, spelling, and the orthographic cipher. In P. B. Gough, L. C. Ehri, & R. Treiman (Eds.), *Reading acquisition* (pp. 35–48). Hillsdale, NJ: Erlbaum.

Griffith, P. L., & Klesius, J. P. (1992, December). *Kindergarten children's understanding of the alphabetic principle.* Paper presented at the annual meeting of the National Reading Conference, San Antonio, TX.

Johns, J. (1991). *Basic Reading Inventory.* Dubuque, IA: Kendall–Hunt.

Juel, C. (1988). Learning to read and write: A longitudinal study of fifty-four children from first through fourth grade. *Journal of Educational Psychology, 80*, 437–447.

Lewkowicz, N. A. (1980). Phonemic awareness training: What to teach and how to teach it. *Journal of Educational Psychology, 72*, 686–700.

Liberman, I. Y., Shankweiler, D., Fischer, F. W., & Carter, B. (1974). Reading and the awareness of linguistic segments. *Journal of Experimental Child Psychology, 18*, 201–212.

Lomax, R. G., & McGee, L. M. (1987). Young children's concepts about print and reading: Toward a model of reading acquisition. *Reading Research Quarterly, 22*, 237–256.

Lundberg, I., Frost, J., & Petersen, O.-P. (1988). Effects of an extensive program for stimulating phonological awareness in preschool children. *Reading Research Quarterly, 23*, 263–284.

Maclean, M., Bryant, P., & Bradley, L. (1987). Rhymes, nursery rhymes, and reading in early childhood. *Merrill-Palmer Quarterly, 33*, 255–281.

Mann, V. A. (1984). Longitudinal prediction and prevention of early reading difficulty. *Annals of Dyslexia, 34*, 115–136.

Mann, V. A. (1991). Phonological awareness and early reading ability: One perspective. In D. J. Sawyer & B. J. Fox (Eds.), *Phonological awareness in reading: The evolution of current perspectives.* New York: Springer-Verlag.

Morais, J., Bertelson, P., Cary, L., & Alegria, J. (1986). Literacy training and speech segmentation. *Cognition, 7*, 323–331.

Murray, B. A., Stahl, S. A., & Ivey, M. G. (1993, December). *Developing phonological awareness through alphabet books.* Paper presented at the annual meeting of the National Reading Conference, Charleston, SC.

Perfetti, C. A., Beck, I. L., Bell, L. C., & Hughes, C. (1987). Phonemic knowledge and learning to read are reciprocal: A longitudinal study of first grade children. *Merrill-Palmer Quarterly, 33*, 283–319.

Rosner, J. (1974). Auditory analysis training with prereaders. *The Reading Teacher, 27*, 379–384.

Savin, H. B. (1972). What the child knows about speech when he starts to learn to read. In J. Kavanagh & I. Mattingly (Eds.), *Language by eye and by ear* (pp. 319–326). Cambridge, MA: MIT Press.

Share, D. L., Jorm, A. F., Maclean, R., & Matthews, R. (1984). Sources of individual differences in reading acquisition. *Journal of Educational Psychology, 76*, 1309–1324.

Siegel, S. (1956). *Non-parametric statistics for the behavioral sciences.* New York: McGraw-Hill.

Stahl, S. A., & Murray, B. A. (1993). Environmental print, phonemic awareness, letter recognition, and word recognition. In D. J. Leu & C. K. Kinzer (Eds.), *Examining central issues in literacy research, theory and practice: 42nd yearbook of the National Reading Conference* (pp. 227–233). Chicago: National Reading Conference.

Stanovich, K. E. (1986). Matthew effects in reading: Some consequences of individual differences in the acquisition of literacy. *Reading Research Quarterly, 21*, 360–407.

Stanovich, K. E. (1992). Speculations on the causes and consequences of individual differences in early reading acquisition. In P. B. Gough, L. C. Ehri, & R. Treiman (Eds.), *Reading acquisition* (pp. 307–342). Hillsdale, NJ: Erlbaum.

Tangel, D. M., & Blachman, B. (1992, April). *Effect of phoneme awareness training on the invented spelling of kindergarten and first grade children and on the standard spelling of first and second grade children.* Paper presented at the annual meeting of the National Reading Conference, San Antonio, TX.

Treiman, R. (1984). On the status of final consonant clusters in English syllables. *Journal of Verbal Learning and Verbal Behavior, 23*, 343–356.

Treiman, R. (1991). Children's spelling errors on syllable–initial consonant clusters. *Journal of Educational Psychology, 83*, 346–360.

Treiman, R. (1992). The role of intrasyllabic units in learning to read and spell. In P. B. Gough, L. C. Ehri, & R. Treiman (Eds.), *Reading acquisition* (pp. 65–106). Hillsdale, NJ: Erlbaum.

Wagner, R. K., & Rashotte, C. A. (1993, April). *Does phonological awareness training really work? A meta-analysis.* Paper presented at the annual meeting of the American Educational Research Association, Atlanta, GA.

Wagner, R. K., & Torgesen, J. K. (1987). The nature of phonological processing and its causal role in the acquisition of reading skills. *Psychological Bulletin, 101*, 192–212.

Wallach, M. A., & Wallach, L. (1979). Helping disadvantaged children learn to read by teaching them phoneme identification skills. In L. B. Resnick & P. A. Weaver (Eds.), *Theory and practice of early reading* (pp. 197–216). Hillsdale, NJ: Erlbaum.

Wechsler, D. (1974). *Wechsler Intelligence Scale for Children–Revised.* New York: Psychological Corporation.

Williams, J. (1979). The ABDs of reading: A program for the learning disabled. In L. B. Resnick & P. A. Weaver (Eds.), *Theory and practice of early reading* (Vol. 3, pp. 179–196). Hillsdale, NJ: Erlbaum.

Yopp, H. K. (1988). The validity and reliability of phonemic awareness tests. *Reading Research Quarterly, 23*, 159–177.

8 Hunting the Elusive Phoneme

A Phoneme-Direct Model
for Learning Phoneme Awareness

BRUCE A. MURRAY

The discovery of the nature and enabling importance of phoneme awareness has been called the single greatest breakthrough in reading pedagogy in this century (California Department of Education, 1996). When Steve Stahl and I wrote the previous article (Stahl & Murray, 1994; reprinted as Chapter 7, this volume) over a decade ago, the field of reading education was just beginning to accommodate to the far-reaching promise of this discovery.

That accommodation remains incomplete. Phoneme awareness has entered the mainstream of our educational discourse, publicized in government reports (National Reading Panel, 2000), promoted by popular methods books (Adams, Foorman, Lundberg, & Beeler, 1998), incorporated into basal readers, presented in packaged teaching materials, taught with educational software, even required by law in some states. Yet basic confusions about the nature of phoneme awareness persist, limiting the effectiveness of instruction. For this reason, the questions we addressed in our 1994 article—how to measure phonological awareness and how much phoneme awareness is needed to learn to read—remain unresolved, at least in educational practice, in 2006.

Definitions of important terms such as *phonological awareness* emerge from the interplay of theory and experimental data as we better understand the phenomena we are attempting to define (Stanovich, 2004). The term *phonological* refers to the structure of the spoken word and includes syllables, rimes, and other subword parts as well as phonemes. *Awareness* suggests a general sensitivity to speech units or mechanical skill in manipulating them. Combining these two ideas, Adams (1990) proposed that children descend through levels of linguistic awareness:

> Linguistic mediation of visual communication evolved gradually in both time and levels of abstraction—first words, then syllables, then phonemes. Interestingly, the ease and order with which cultures have become aware of these levels of abstraction in history and exploited them as units of writing is mirrored in the ease and order with which children become aware of them developmentally. (p. 294)

In bringing Adams's important book to a wide audience of reading professionals, Steve Stahl had an important role in promulgating the idea of linguistic levels to explain children's acquisition of phonological awareness (Stahl, Osborn, & Lehr, 1990).

I call this idea of gaining phoneme awareness by progressing downward through levels of linguistic complexity the *depth-chart model* (Figure 8.1). Children first recognize larger, more obvious units such as messages, words, and syllables and gradually come to notice smaller, less obvious, more abstract, temporally briefer units such as onsets, rimes, and phonemes. This model does explain certain phenomena. For example, the step down from words to syllables has the character of an insight. Once a beginner gets the idea of listening for the loud beats in words, syllables are quite easy to detect in most words. Segmenting onsets and rimes, too, appears to be a generalizable strategy of breaking the syllable just before the loud vowel (Treiman, 1985). Phonemes in onsets tend to be more accessible than phonemes in consonant clusters, and more generally, the linguistic complexity of a phoneme awareness task explains task difficulty better than differences across tasks (Stahl & Murray, 1994). However, the depth-chart model fails to explain other phenomena. For example, syllables are often more salient than words. How many words are there in *alright/all right*? It is easy to hear two loud beats, but counting one or two words depends on knowing about the spacing of the printed words, a result of learning to read.

In our final collaboration (Stahl & Murray, 1998), Steve and I were beginning to question "mechanical notions of phonological awareness." The manipulations of blending and segmentation, though central in decoding and spelling words, cannot be understood as mechanical actions, given the nature of a phoneme. Isabelle Liberman (Liberman & Liberman, 1992) explained phonemes as fluid vocal gestures, continuous movements of the tongue, lips, and vocal apparatus that are coarticulated as we produce a spoken word (the popular term *sound* better fits a spoken syllable). Vocal gestures are not physically distinct; no matter how slowly we stretch the pronunciation of a word, we find no clear demarcation between one phoneme and the next. Phonemes are coarticulated (i.e., they morph together), making subtle changes in neighboring phonemes. For example, compare your mouth position in preparing to say *dive*, and then *drive*. With *drive*, your lips and tongue are positioned to say /r/

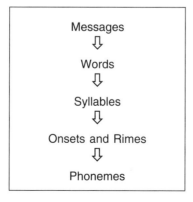

FIGURE 8.1. The depth-chart model of phonological awareness.

even before you pronounce /d/. Another problem in recognizing phonemes is that we pronounce them at the extraordinary speed of 10–20 phonemes per second. The speech stream is fraught with rapids.

The task of detecting phonemes might be likened to the difficulty of learning the components of the fluid act of pitching a baseball. The windup, kick, stride, and follow-through compose a rapid, continuous motion of delivering the baseball. Without specific instruction in the features of these component movements, it is hard to see how simply observing a pitcher could reveal their separate identities.

The depth-chart model suggests that descending to a finer-grained level of phonological sensitivity unlocks all units at that level, as with the insights about syllables. But some phonemes are more salient than others. For example, the phoneme /f/ involves a visible contact of the upper teeth on the lower lip, but /ng/ is "hidden" far back in the mouth. There is some evidence that continuant phonemes such as /s/ are easier to recognize than stops such as /d/ because children can stretch them to sample their sound and kinesthetic feeling (Marsh & Mineo, 1977; Skjelfjord, 1976). Contrary to the depth-chart model, the evidence of phoneme salience suggests that awareness requires knowledge of the individual identities of phonemes.

Attaining phoneme awareness in the depth-chart model presents a quandary that Byrne and Fielding-Barnsley (1990) called "an essential asymmetry between identity and segmentation" (p. 806). Identity—recognition of phoneme invariance across words—entails segmentation, the ability to parse words into phonemes. However, children can mechanically break words into phoneme segments without recognizing the identity of phonemes across words (Byrne & Fielding-Barnsley, 1990). Lewkowicz (1980) explained segmentation as a search for familiar elements in the stretched pronunciation of a word. The vocal gestures unique to phonemes, along with their accompanying sounds, become familiar elements recycled across words; these gestures come to acquire identities (from the Latin *idem*, meaning "same") when their sameness comes to be recognized across different words (Stahl & Murray, 1998).

Suppose we ask a child to detect the three phonemes in *cup*, which to the ear presents a single syllabic sound. How do you recognize the vocal gestures /k/, /u/, and /p/ without learning the articulatory features of each phoneme? We wouldn't expect children to learn letters by abstracting them out of printed words. We wouldn't expect adult learners to recognize species of tropical fish, edible wild plants, or songbirds without instruction in the salient features of each variety. We learn about fish, plants, birds, letters, and phonemes one by one.

Byrne and Fielding-Barnsley (Byrne, 1992, 1998; Byrne & Fielding-Barnsley, 1989, 1990, 1991, 1993a, 1993b, 1995; Byrne, Fielding-Barnsley, & Ashley, 2000) theorize that phoneme identity is the phoneme awareness skill basic to decoding. In an early study, Byrne and Fielding-Barnsley (1990) taught one group of 4-year-olds to recognize four phonemes across different words, and they taught a second group to segment the same words into onset and rime. They asked both groups to decode beginning letters to distinguish rhyming words (e.g., is MET *met* or *set*?), which Ehri (1990) calls phonetic cue reading. Learning phoneme identities enabled success on the simple decoding task, and identity knowledge transferred to decoding the initial letters with *untaught* phonemes. However, some children who learned segmentation using words with the four taught phonemes also learned phoneme identities and demonstrated transfer to reading. No direct comparisons were made between groups.

Byrne and Fielding-Barnsley (1991) enlisted 96 preschool 5-year-olds in a 3-month experiment. Experimental participants were taught the identities of six phonemes in 12 half-hour weekly sessions, a total of 6 hours of instruction. Control children were taught to classify words by meaning, using the same materials with the same teacher for an equal amount of time. Posttests showed that the experimental group acquired greater phoneme awareness and were better able to transfer their knowledge to successfully negotiate the phonetic-cue-reading task. In annual follow-ups (Byrne, 1992, 1998; Byrne & Fielding-Barnsley, 1993a, 1995; Byrne et al., 2000) the phoneme identity group continued to show an advantage in reading words, persisting even 6 years after the experiment.

Under Steve Stahl's guidance, I replicated the Byrne and Fielding-Barnsley (1990) study, which suggested the superiority of identity knowledge over segmentation skill, with a larger group of 48 kindergartners (Murray, 1998). Children in the identity group worked with a limited set of eight phonemes. They learned meaningful names for the phonemes, stretched alliterative tongue twisters, explored articulation, and practiced finding the phonemes in spoken words. Children in the manipulations group worked at similar activities aimed at teaching blending and segmentation skill rather than identity knowledge. They worked with unrestricted phonemes in words from rhyming verses rather than alliterations, stretched and isolated beginning and final phonemes, and practiced segmenting and blending words. A third group listened to read-alouds and composed language experience stories. The manipulations group demonstrated better segmentation and blending skill than the identity group. However, children in the identity group were better able to transfer their identity knowledge to phonetic cue reading, the initial step into decoding words.

From a meta-analysis of phoneme-awareness training studies to examine the elements of the most successful studies (Murray, 1995), I formulated a three-step phoneme-direct model for acquiring phoneme awareness (see Figure 8.2). Working with a limited set of phonemes one by one, rather than trying to segment words into whatever phonemes they contain, allows beginners to focus on the articulatory properties that distinguish each phoneme. Establishing multiple access routes in memory makes a phoneme familiar. Identifying the phoneme in its natural habitat—the spoken word—establishes the basic level of phoneme awareness needed for decoding (i.e., the ability to recognize phonemes in spoken-word contexts).

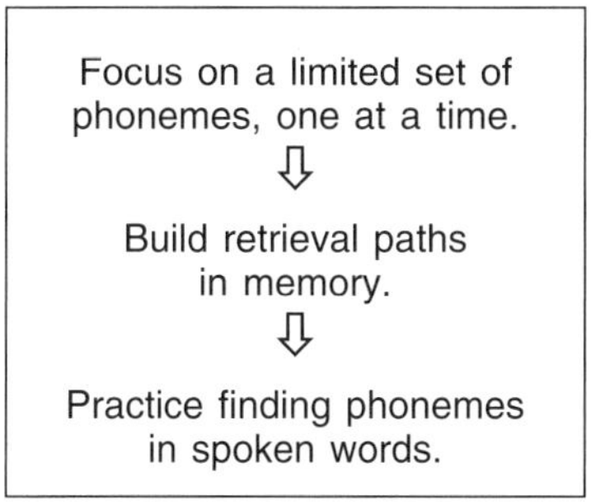

Focus on a limited set of
phonemes, one at a time.
⇩
Build retrieval paths
in memory.
⇩
Practice finding phonemes
in spoken words.

FIGURE 8.2. The phoneme-direct model of acquiring phoneme awareness.

The Test of Phoneme Identities (TPI; Murray, Smith, & Murray, 2000) is a simple, 10-minute test to assess this defining level of phoneme awareness in pre-alphabetic children. Most phoneme awareness tests sample phoneme manipulation skills that come as a result of learning to read and spell words (Stahl & Murray, 1994). I designed the TPI as a straightforward measure of children's ability to locate phonemes in spoken words. The TPI takes the form of a "repeating game" in which children are asked to repeat a sentence, articulate an isolated phoneme, and then decide which of two words has that phoneme. For instance, "Say: 'This is a nice night.' Now say /s/. Do you hear /s/ in *nice* or *night*?" In a dynamic assessment of teaching phonetic cue reading to kindergartners, the TPI proved more sensitive than the Yopp–Singer Segmentation Test (Yopp, 1995) and the Test of Phonological Awareness (Torgesen & Bryant, 1994) in predicting alphabetic insight with pre-alphabetic readers.

TEACHING CHILDREN TO SPOT THE ELUSIVE PHONEME

Researchers have carried out many teaching studies to improve children's phoneme awareness and make them more successful in learning to read (for a recent review, see Ehri et al., 2001). Not all phoneme awareness training has been equally effective. The phoneme-direct model of acquiring phoneme awareness suggests that effective phoneme awareness programs have three crucial components. First, they focus on individual phonemes, one at a time. Second, they make each phoneme memorable. Third, they provide practice finding the phoneme in spoken words.

Focus on Individual Phonemes

Most programs to teach children to recognize phonemes are based on the depth-chart model of phoneme awareness as a generalized skill in phoneme manipulations. Accordingly, they work on segmenting and blending *any* word into *whatever* phonemes it contains. Trying to teach all the phonemes at once militates against learning any phoneme in particular. If novice readers need identity knowledge of each phoneme they will use in reading and spelling words, then phoneme awareness instruction must deal with phonemes one by one. However, this does not mean children must be taught every phoneme explicitly. Research has demonstrated that learning the identities of a few carefully chosen phonemes in spoken word contexts makes it easy to recognize other phonemes (Byrne, 1998).

Make the Phoneme Memorable

Remembering requires retrieval paths from the new experience to previous experiences, thus connecting new concepts with prior knowledge. With beginners, we can make phonemes memorable by introducing connections with letters, meaningful names, pictures, and gestures. For example, a teacher might say, "Here's a quiet sound teachers use: /sh/," teach the classic finger-to-the-lips gesture invoking quiet, show students that the phoneme /sh/ is written with two letters, *sh*, and post an illustration of a shushing librarian. This brief introduction initiates several retrieval paths. First, the letter or digraph becomes a visual symbol of phoneme, making it easier to remember. Research has demonstrated that connecting phonemes with letters helps beginners remember phonemes (Ehri et al., 2001; Hohn & Ehri, 1983). Most letter names (e.g., *L*) feature the principal phoneme prominently, and thus likely serve to remind novice readers of the vocal gesture. By helping the novice reader "see" a phoneme, the letter or digraph serves as a lifelong referent in written words. Second, a meaningful name (e.g., /l/ is a "lightsaber") relates the phoneme to a familiar experience. The name can be illustrated with an image that evokes a similar sound (see Figure 8.3). Third, a phoneme gesture (e.g., raising a lightsaber for /l/) makes an entertaining activity as well as a ready phoneme reminder. Whether children are in the classroom or at home, a phoneme gesture is literally always at their fingertips.

The crucial concept to communicate to children is that a phoneme is the same mouth move, despite minor variations, repeated across different words; this is the concept of phoneme identity. One good way to demonstrate phoneme identity is to have students learn an alliteration that features the target phoneme at the beginning of several words. Wallach and Wallach (1976) composed a clever set of alliterative "tongue twisters" for a phoneme awareness teaching experiment (e.g., "Nobody was nice to Nancy's neighbor Nick, but he was never nasty"). Teachers may devise shorter alliterations for young children, such as "Many mice make music." Alliterations with vowels can be difficult to compose. Teachers should not give in to the temptation to choose example words with the vowel in the interior, where it requires phoneme awareness to identify. If phoneme awareness is the goal, it should not be presumed by practice activities. Once children can repeat an alliteration, have them stretch out the target phoneme as they recite. Wallach and Wallach found it helpful for children to break the phoneme away from each word to experience it in isolation (e.g., M-any m-ice m-ake m-usic). This allows them to sample the kinesthetic sensations of the phoneme as they work with it in word contexts.

A good alphabet book offers a ready source of alliterations. For example, *Dr. Seuss's ABC* (Geisel, 1963) answers the question, "What begins with *U*?" by citing "Uncle Ubb's umbrella and his underwear, too." The traditional way of presenting phonemes (e.g., "*M* is for moon") presumes that children already have sufficient phoneme awareness to recognize that /m/ is one of the vocal gestures in *moon*; it pre-

FIGURE 8.3. Lightsaber illustrating the phoneme /l/.

sumes what we are trying to teach. In addition, many alphabet books are designed to teach vocabulary or showcase an illustrator's work rather than to help young children identify the phonemes represented by letters. For purposes of phoneme awareness instruction, children need alphabet books with multiple examples of familiar words.

In two experiments using alphabet books to teach phoneme awareness (Brabham, Murray, & Hudson, 2001; Murray, Stahl, & Ivey, 1996), we have picked up a couple of insights. First, children learn phonemes better when teachers make letter–phoneme connections explicit. We used *Dr. Seuss's ABC* (Geisel, 1963) to contrast a phoneme emphasis with the usual meaning emphasis with which teachers explain the vocabulary of alphabet books (Brabham et al., 2001). In the phoneme emphasis, teachers said, for example, "*F* tells your mouth to say /f/. Watch my mouth: Ffffour. Fffeathers." Next, they read the text on the page: "Big *F*, little *f*, what begins with *f*? Four fluffy feathers on a Fiffer-feffer-feff." Then teachers asked children questions such as, "When you see this letter, what's your mouth move? What's a word with /f/?" Children made the best gains in phoneme awareness when teachers emphasized phonemes in this way, provided that they practiced with books on tape or with an adult reader. When they practiced with an animated computer program, the music and animations proved so distracting that children apparently lost their focus on phonemes.

The other insight teachers drove home to us in both experiments is that alphabet books read straight through are terribly boring. Children like books that tell stories, especially stories with problems or goals worked out during the course of the plot. Moreover, alphabet books violate the instructional principle of presenting phonemes one at a time. For these reasons, it is probably better to read alphabet books a page at a time, working only with pages featuring a single target phoneme and its example words, rather than straining children's patience and overwhelming their learning capacity by reading the whole book at once.

Phoneme awareness is one realm in which discovery learning can be effective because most children already know how to produce phonemes—they simply lack conscious awareness of phoneme identities. Teachers can ask children to be "scientists" and figure out how a phoneme is made. For example, the teacher might say, "Today we are studying the gong phoneme, /ng/. Say *sing*, and stretch out the ending. Now pretend you're teaching me how to talk. How do you say /ng/?" In exploring their articulation, they feel the position of their tongues, find out where air is coming out, and discover the kinesthetics of the sound they are producing. This focuses attention on the essential features of the phoneme. Lindamood and Lindamood (1998) have developed creative teaching materials focusing on identifying phonemes as vocal gestures in words. In a recent phoneme awareness teaching experiment, Castiglioni-Spalten and Ehri (2003) gave children mouth pictures to arrange in Elkonin boxes to represent the phoneme sequence in words and helped children study articulation with mirrors. This articulatory instruction enhanced word learning for novice readers.

Find the Phoneme in Spoken Words

Children are not really aware of phonemes until they recognize them in their natural habitat, spoken words. It takes no phoneme awareness to recite a correspondence such as "*U* says uh." Children demonstrate phoneme awareness when they can tell you that /u/ is in *thumb*, but not in *hand*. The TPI (Murray et al., 2000) assesses phoneme awareness in this way.

Once children recognize a grapheme as a phoneme symbol, teachers should encourage them to write daily with invented spellings. We have good evidence (Clarke, 1988) that inventing spellings improves both spelling and word identification in young children who have not achieved phoneme awareness. The likely mechanism is that inventing spellings provides effective practice identifying phonemes. Children gain familiarity with phonemes as they stretch pronunciations, spot phonemes, and symbolize them with letters. As a practical matter, the teacher who would encourage invented spelling must evade children's requests for standard spellings until they develop phoneme awareness. Teachers can help students stretch out a spoken word to identify phonemes to be recorded with letters.

Teacher-effectiveness research has found that modeling is a critical ingredient of good teaching (Rosenshine, 1995). Teachers model when they work problems for students and dramatize the steps in solving the problems aloud. To model phoneme awareness, the teacher stretches words, talks about the clue that reveals the target phoneme, and decides aloud whether or not the phoneme is there. For example, the teacher might say, "I'm going to hunt for the hummingbird sound, /m/, in the word *pump*. I'll know it's there if my lips come together and hum. Pu-u-u-mmmp. P u-u-u-mmm . . . There! In the middle, my lips came together and I hummed. That was /m/. Hummingbird /m/ *is* in *pump*."

The easiest place to find a phoneme is in the onset, the salient beginning (Stahl & Murray, 1994). Teachers can have children listen for a target phoneme and respond in a memorable way. For example, a teacher could say, "Listen for /m/, the hummingbird sound. Make hummingbird wings with your fingers to show me when you hear /m/. Do you hear /m/ in *mop*? *Rake*? *Motor*?" Later have them search elsewhere in the word (e.g., for /m/ in *broom*, *dump*, or *nut*). Using words related in meaning challenges children's focus on phonemes as well as meaning. For example, the teacher could ask, "Do you hear /m/ in *boy* or *man*? In *more* or *less*? In *sun* or *moon*?" Using related words requires children to make a metalinguistic shift from the meanings of words to their spoken forms.

Blending is a crucial phoneme manipulation for decoding written words. Blending builds on phoneme identity by combining identified phonemes into a phonological structure close enough to a spoken word to identify the word. In teaching children to blend phonemes into words, it is important to remember that effective phoneme awareness instruction addresses one phoneme at a time. Most blending practice programs expect children to deal with a variety of phonemes they have never learned to identify, and to blend these odd sounds, not yet recognized as phonemes, into words. Effective programs for teaching phoneme awareness begin by blending only the target phoneme to the chunks of spoken words.

Surprisingly, we have evidence that blending a new phoneme to the end of a word is easier than blending it to the beginning (Brabham, Murray, & Villaume, 2002). Eldredge (2005) recommends a blending procedure involving body and coda segments to minimize phoneme distortion. The body comprises any initial consonants with the vowel, and the coda includes any consonants that follow the vowel. For example, the word *thick* could be segmented into /thi/ (the body) and /k/ (the coda). We found children were more successful with body–coda blending than with onset–rime blending. The likely reason is that body–coda blending joins the syllable at its "stickiest" point, after the vowel, rather than at its most fragile point, before the vowel. Body–coda chunks are ideal for initial blending practice, for example, "What am I saying: *roo-m*? *Crea-m*? *Sli-me*?" To respond, children need only join a familiar vocal gesture, made memorable by phoneme awareness instruction, to a spoken word chunk at the linguistically "stickiest" spot in the syllable to identify a word. When they have achieved this milestone, children can move on to the slightly more difficult task of onset–rime blending, assembling (e.g., *m-oon* and *m-ess*). Our research team is currently testing the effectiveness of this procedure experimentally in teaching full alphabetic decoding.

Application to Reading

Cunningham (1990) demonstrated that children taught the purposes of phoneme awareness and how to apply phoneme awareness in reading words derive greater benefits from phoneme awareness instruction than children who learn phoneme awareness skills without application training. The most basic level of decoding is using beginning letters to distinguish rhyming words, which Ehri terms partial-alphabetic decoding (Ehri, 1998). For example, a beginner who has learned the identity of the phoneme /l/ and its letter *L* should be able to determine that the printed word LIKE is *like* and not *bike*. Teaching children to apply phoneme identity knowledge requires explicit explanation, modeling how to solve example words, scaffolding when children are not sure how to proceed, and helping children correct misidentified words. As in all good phoneme awareness instruction, application to reading focuses on only one new phoneme (and its letter representation) at a time. However, a review of phonemes learned in the past allows an expanding stock of phonemes for partial-alphabetic decoding, and children can generalize lessons learned from a few phonemes to quickly acquire new phonemes with minimal instruction (Byrne & Fielding-Barnsley, 1989).

The letterbox lesson (Murray & Lesniak, 1999) provides explicit instruction in phoneme awareness and alphabetic mapping. Each lesson introduces one new correspondence. First, the teacher reviews the phoneme, reintroducing its name and gesture, and giving practice stretching an alliterative tongue twister. Then the teacher models how to spell example words with letter manipulatives in Elkonin "letterboxes," revealing the number of phonemes to spell, and shows how to read words using vowel-first, body–coda blending. Next, the student spells a series of simple example words, graduating to four-, five-, or six-phoneme words. The teacher guides children's phoneme exploration and helps them identify each word's complete phoneme sequence and standard spelling. After spelling all the example words, the student reads them, thus transferring letter–phoneme connections from spelling to reading.

CONCLUSIONS ABOUT HUNTING THE ELUSIVE PHONEME

Discoveries about phoneme awareness are revolutionizing instruction in beginning reading. However, in their zeal for leading children into this vital ability, teachers have sometimes encouraged games and phoneme manipulations that have little direct transfer to learning to read. The phoneme awareness children need to read is knowledge of phoneme identities sufficient to recognize phonemes in their natural habitat, the spoken word (Byrne & Fielding-Barnsley, 1990; Murray, 1998). To teach phoneme awareness for maximum reading transfer, the literature on phoneme awareness instruction suggests we focus on one phoneme at a time, make it memorable, and give students practice finding that phoneme in spoken words.

The evidence of doubled effect sizes when letters are used in phoneme awareness training (Ehri et al., 2001) shows there is no absolute line between phoneme awareness and phonics; the difference is primarily a matter of emphasis. In a phoneme awareness lesson, the letter or digraph acts as a symbol for the phoneme, making the phoneme easier to remember. The emphasis in a phoneme awareness lesson is on making the vocal gesture so familiar that it is easy to find in spoken words. A phonics lesson, on the other hand, emphasizes using the correspondences between letters and phonemes to decode written words.

There is one other important difference: Most phoneme awareness lessons, certainly those typical of kindergarten, focus on consonants. Though a few phonics lessons teach digraphs, most focus on vowels. This has an important practical implication: Children rarely need phonics lessons on consonants. For children familiar with phonemes, consonants already signal phonemes, and they are already using initial consonants to decode boundary letters in printed words. However, they seldom know what to do with vowels. Phonics lessons provide instruction in using complete alphabetic mapping, including the elusive vowels, to decode written words.

In early kindergarten, teachers should introduce phonemes with a variety of developmentally appropriate activities. Children should work primarily with consonants, make their mouth moves familiar and memorable, and practice finding each new phoneme in spoken words. Hunting down an elusive phoneme in a spoken word is the heart of phoneme awareness.

In late kindergarten, in first grade, and with older poor readers, teachers should review phonemes to introduce phonics lessons. With a foundation in phoneme awareness, children should recognize consonant phonemes and use consonants in partial-alphabetic decoding. But many of them lack the vowels to complete the alphabetic mappings in spellings to read and remember printed words. Short vowels—the first vowels taught in phonics—tend to be among the most difficult phonemes to spot in spoken words. Thus, a phoneme awareness review is an excellent introduction to a phonics lesson teaching novice readers to use vowels to decode and spell written words.

Much of our understanding of phoneme awareness owes to the pioneering explorations, experiments, and syntheses of Steve Stahl. Beyond the many contributions reviewed here, Steve was a gifted communicator who could translate the arcane language of research into practical advice for teachers. His research agenda was broad, his knowledge of the reading research literature encyclopedic. A generation of teachers is better informed about the science of reading education through his influence, and countless children who will never know the name of Steven A. Stahl will learn to read earlier and more easily through his influence.

REFERENCES

Adams, M. J. (1990). *Beginning to read: Thinking and learning about print.* Cambridge, MA: MIT Press.

Adams, M. J., Foorman, B. R., Lundberg, I., & Beeler, T. (1998). *Phonemic awareness in young children: A classroom curriculum.* Baltimore: Brookes.

Brabham, E. G., Murray, B. A., & Hudson, S. (2001). *Developing phoneme awareness, letter knowledge, and vocabulary through interactive reading aloud and multimedia interactions with alphabet books.* Paper presented at the National Reading Conference, San Antonio, TX.

Brabham, E. G., Murray, B. A., & Villaume, S. K. (2002). *Effects of three segmentation options on ease of blending for pre-alphabetic and partial alphabetic readers.* Paper presented at the National Reading Conference, Miami, FL.

Byrne, B. (1992). Longitudinal data on the relations of word–reading strategies to comprehension, reading time, and phonemic awareness. *Reading Research Quarterly, 27,* 140–151.

Byrne, B. (1998). *The foundation of literacy: The child's acquisition of the alphabetic principle.* Hove, UK: Psychology Press.

Byrne, B., & Fielding-Barnsley, R. (1989). Phonemic awareness and letter knowledge in the child's acquisition of the alphabetic principle. *Journal of Educational Psychology, 81,* 313–321.

Byrne, B., & Fielding-Barnsley, R. (1990). Acquiring the alphabetic principle: A case for teaching recognition of phoneme identity. *Journal of Educational Psychology, 82,* 805–812.

Byrne, B., & Fielding-Barnsley, R. (1991). Evaluation of a program to teach phonemic awareness to young children. *Journal of Educational Psychology, 83,* 451–455.

Byrne, B., & Fielding-Barnsley, R. (1993a). Evaluation of a program to teach phonemic awareness to young children: A 1-year follow-up. *Journal of Educational Psychology, 85,* 104–111.

Byrne, B., & Fielding-Barnsley, R. (1993b). Recognition of phoneme invariance by beginning readers: Confounding effects of global similarity. *Reading and Writing: An Interdisciplinary Journal, 5,* 315–324.

Byrne, B., & Fielding-Barnsley, R. (1995). Evaluation of a program to teach phonemic awareness to young children: A 2- and 3-year follow-up and a new preschool trial. *Journal of Educational Psychology, 87,* 488–503.

Byrne, B., Fielding-Barnsley, R., & Ashley, L. (2000). Effects of preschool phoneme identity training after six years: Outcome level distinguished from rate of response. *Journal of Educational Psychology, 92,* 659–667.

California Department of Education. (1996). *Teaching reading: A balanced, comprehensive approach to teaching reading in prekindergarten through grade three.* Sacramento, CA: CDE Press.

Castiglioni-Spalten, M. L., & Ehri, L. C. (2003). Phonemic awareness instruction: Contribution of articulatory segmentation to novice beginners' reading and spelling. *Scientific Studies of Reading, 7,* 25–52.

Clarke, L. K. (1988). Invented versus traditional spelling in first graders' writings: Effects on learning to spell and read. *Research in the Teaching of English, 22,* 281–309.

Cunningham, A. E. (1990). Explicit versus implicit instruction in phonemic awareness. *Journal of Experimental Child Psychology, 50,* 429–444.

Ehri, L. C. (1990). Development of the ability to read words. In R. Barr, M. L. Kamil, P. Mosenthal, & P. D. Pearson (Eds.), *Handbook of reading research* (Vol. 2, pp. 383–417). New York: Longman.

Ehri, L. C. (1998). Grapheme–phoneme knowledge is essential for learning to read words in English. In J. L. Metsala & L. C. Ehri (Eds.), *Word recognition in beginning literacy* (pp. 3–40). Mahwah, NJ: Erlbaum.

Ehri, L. C., Nunes, S. R., Willows, D. M., Schuster, B. V., Yaghoub-Zadeh, Z., & Shanahan, T. (2001). Phonemic awareness instruction helps children learn to read: Evidence from the National Reading Panel's meta-analysis. *Reading Research Quarterly, 36,* 250–287.

Eldredge, J. L. (2005). *Teach decoding: Why and how.* Upper Saddle River, NJ: Pearson.

Geisel, T. S. (1963). *Dr. Seuss's ABC.* New York: Random House.

Hohn, W. E., & Ehri, L. C. (1983). Do alphabet letters help prereaders acquire phonemic segmentation skill? *Journal of Educational Psychology, 75,* 752–762.

Lewkowicz, N. K. (1980). Phonemic awareness training: What to teach and how to teach it. *Journal of Educational Psychology, 72*, 686–700.

Liberman, I. Y., & Liberman, A. M. (1992). Whole language versus code emphasis: Underlying assumptions and their implications for reading instruction. In P. B. Gough, L. C. Ehri, & R. Treiman (Eds.), *Reading acquisition* (pp. 343–366). Hillsdale, NJ: Erlbaum.

Lindamood, P. C., & Lindamood, P. (1998). *The Lindamood phoneme sequencing program for reading, spelling, and speech: The LIPS program* (Clinical, 3rd ed.). Austin, TX: Pro-Ed.

Marsh, G., & Mineo, R. J. (1977). Training preschool children to recognize phonemes in words. *Journal of Educational Psychology, 69*, 748–753.

Murray, B. A. (1995). *A meta-analysis of phoneme awareness teaching studies.* Paper presented at the American Education Research Association, San Francisco.

Murray, B. A. (1998). Gaining alphabetic insight: Is phoneme manipulation skill or identity knowledge causal? *Journal of Educational Psychology, 90*, 461–475.

Murray, B. A., & Lesniak, T. (1999). The letterbox lesson: A hands-on approach for teaching decoding. *The Reading Teacher, 52*, 644–650.

Murray, B. A., Smith, K. A., & Murray, G. G. (2000). The Test of Phoneme Identities: Predicting alphabetic insight in prealphabetic readers. *Journal of Literacy Research, 32*, 421–447.

Murray, B. A., Stahl, S. A., & Ivey, M. G. (1996). Developing phoneme awareness through alphabet books. *Reading and Writing: An Interdisciplinary Journal, 8*, 307–322.

Rosenshine, B. (1995). Advances in research on education. *Journal of Educational Research, 88*, 262–268.

Skjelfjord, V. (1976). Teaching children to segment spoken words as an aid in learning to read. *Journal of Learning Disabilities, 9*, 297–306.

Stahl, S. A., & Murray, B. A. (1994). Defining phonological awareness and its relationship to early reading. *Journal of Educational Psychology, 86*, 221–234.

Stahl, S. A., & Murray, B. A. (1998). Issues involved in defining phonological awareness and its relation to early reading. In J. L. Metsala & L. C. Ehri (Eds.), *Word recognition in beginning literacy* (pp. 65–88). Mahwah, NJ: Erlbaum.

Stahl, S. A., Osborn, J., & Lehr, F. (1990). *Beginning to read: Thinking and learning about print, A summary.* Champaign: University of Illinois, Center for the Study of Reading.

Stanovich, K. E. (2004). *How to think straight about psychology* (7th ed.). Boston: Allyn & Bacon.

Torgesen, J. K., & Bryant, B. R. (1994). *Test of Phonological Awareness.* Austin, TX: Pro-Ed.

Treiman, R. (1985). Onsets and rimes as units of spoken syllables: Evidence from children. *Journal of Experimental Child Psychology, 39*, 161–181.

Wallach, M. A., & Wallach, L. (1976). *Teaching all children to read.* Chicago: University of Chicago Press.

Yopp, H. K. (1995). A test for assessing phonemic awareness in young children. *The Reading Teacher, 49*, 20–29.

9

Everything You Wanted to Know about Phonics (but Were Afraid to Ask)

STEVEN A. STAHL
ANN M. DUFFY-HESTER
KATHERINE A. DOUGHERTY STAHL

It is difficult to talk about phonics. Regie Routman (1996) used to say that "phonics is a lot like sex. Everyone is doing it behind closed doors, but no one is talking about it" (p. 91). This has changed. People are talking about it, mostly in confusion about how to do it (phonics, that is). This is true in the media (e.g., Collins, 1997; Levine, 1994) as well as among teachers we talk to. In California, a bellwether state in education, a new report from the California Task Force on Reading (California Department of Education, 1995) recommended that "every school and district must organize and implement a comprehensive and balanced reading program that is research-based and combines skill development with literature and language-rich activities," and asserted that "the heart of a powerful reading program is the relationship between explicit, systematic skills instruction and literature, language and comprehension. While skills alone are insufficient to develop good readers, no reader can become proficient without those foundational skills" (p. 3).

There is a consensus of belief that good reading instruction includes some attention to decoding. Whole language advocates such as Church (1996) and Routman (1996) devoted chapters of their recent books to teaching phonics, and Goodman (1993) wrote a book devoted entirely to phonics. These whole language advocates argued that whole language teachers should be teaching phonics and that decoding instruction had always been part of whole language teaching. To quote Routman again:

> It would be irresponsible and inexcusable not to teach phonics. Yet the media are having a field day getting the word out that many of us ignore phonics in the teaching of reading. It just isn't so. Some of us may not be doing as good a job as we need to be doing, but I don't know a knowledgeable teacher who doesn't teach phonics. (1996, p. 91)

Results of a recent U.S. national survey of elementary school teachers indicated that 99% of K–2 teachers consider phonics instruction to be essential (67%) or important (32%) (Baumann, Hoffman, Moon, & Duffy-Hester, 1998).

BELIEFS AND PHONICS

A lot of people are talking about phonics but in different ways. How people talk about phonics depends on their belief systems about reading in general. Different people have different beliefs about how reading should be defined (DeFord, 1985; Stahl, 1997), which might affect how they think about phonics instruction. Some people believe that if one can recognize all of the words in a text quickly and accurately, one will be able to understand and appreciate that text. Therefore, the primary task in teaching reading for people who hold this belief is to teach students how to recognize words (e.g., Gough & Hillinger, 1980). Others believe that reading should begin with interpretations of whole texts, and that phonics should be used only to support the reader's need to get meaning from text (e.g., Goodman, 1993). It is not difficult to see how these different belief systems might lead to different forms of phonics instruction.

The whole language movement helped to change the way we talk about phonics. This movement exploded onto the educational scene, rapidly changing basic beliefs about education (Pearson, 1989) and basal reading programs (Hoffman et al., 1994), as well as views on reading and reading instruction, and focusing on uses of written language for communication and on individual responses to literature and exposition (e.g., Goodman, 1986). Whole language advocates generally include phonics (or graphophonemics) as one of the cuing systems used in identifying words. Their model of reading is partially based on Goodman (1976) who suggested that readers use three cuing systems—graphophonemic, syntactic, and semantic—to identify words as they encounter them in meaningful text.

Goodman based his model on his work with miscue analysis (e.g., Goodman & Goodman, 1977), or the analysis of oral reading miscues that readers make during reading. Whole language teachers have advocated teaching children about letter–sound correspondences, but *only as an aid to a child's ongoing process of getting meaning from a text or producing a text*, and *only as needed*. In some instructional programs based on the whole language philosophy, the teacher does not teach from a predetermined scope and sequence but instead gives children the information they need to understand texts.

Although the issue should never have been whole language versus phonics but instead issues of how best to teach children to decode, the polarizing rhetoric used by some on the whole language movement seems to have convinced people that whole language and phonics are opposed to each other (McKenna, Stahl, & Reinking, 1994; Moorman, Blanton, & McLaughlin, 1994). Many teachers adopting a whole language philosophy perceived that they should never teach words in isolation, should provide phonics instruction only when students demonstrate the need for this instruction, and should never use unauthentic literature, such as books chosen for spelling patterns, in instruction. Although these rules are often violated by knowledgeable whole language teachers (see McIntyre & Pressley, 1996; Mills,

O'Keefe, & Stephens, 1992; Pressley, Rankin, & Yakoi, 1996), they were nonetheless somehow communicated to many others.

These (mis)perceptions of whole language teaching resulted in confusion for many whole language teachers. Further, when some teachers (or their administrators) perceived a need for phonics instruction, they added on a program unrelated to their regular, literature-based program. These *Frankenclasses* were stitched together, with neither part of the curriculum informing the other. Such a curriculum may be no more desirable than the omission of phonics instruction.

In this article, we will review basic principles underlying word learning and phonics instruction. These principles are applicable in many primary-grade classrooms. Next, we will discuss approaches to teaching phonics. Finally, we will draw some tentative conclusions on how an integrated language arts program that includes phonics instruction may look in first-grade classrooms.

UNDERSTANDING PHONICS INSTRUCTION

When evaluating phonics instruction, we can rely on a research base going back to the 1920s for some empirical principles, but we also need to rely on some common sense. Research tells us that an early and systematic emphasis on teaching children to decode words leads to better achievement than a later or more haphazard approach (Adams, 1990; Chall, 1989, 1996). Further, being able to decode words is necessary for children to become independent word learners and thus to be able to develop as readers without teacher assistance (Share, 1995). This much seems clear. But such instruction can occur in a variety of settings, including traditional classes and whole language classes (Church, 1994; Dahl & Freppon, 1995; Mills et al., 1992). What is important is that phonics instruction is done well. Research (and common sense) suggest the following principles of good phonics instruction.

Good Phonics Instruction Should Develop the Alphabetic Principle

The key to learning to decode words is the principle that letters can represent sounds. Many languages such as Chinese use logographs, or stylized pictures, to represent meanings. Others use symbols to represent whole syllables. English, like many other languages, uses letters to represent individual sounds in words. Although English is not entirely regular—that is, there is not always a one-to-one correspondence between letters and sounds—understanding that letters do have a relationship with the sounds in words is a hallmark of successful beginning readers (Adams, 1990).

At its most basic level, the *alphabetic principle* is the notion that letters in words may stand for specific sounds. Initially, children developing this principle understand that words have initial sounds. As this awareness develops, children learn more about letters and sounds, analyzing each word fully, and including more complex orthographic elements such as consonant blends (*bl*, *st*, *nd*), consonant digraphs (*th*, *sh*, *ch*, and *wh*), vowel digraphs (*ea*, *oa*, *oo*), diphthongs (*aw*, *au*,*ou*, *ow*), and phonograms (*ight* and *ough*).

One can observe children's growth in knowledge of the alphabetic principle through both their reading and invented spelling. Ehri (1992) described children's growth in accurate word reading as going through three stages. At first, children use a visual cue to recognize words. Cues can be simple, such as the two eyes in *look*, or more complex. This is a *prealphabetic* stage (Ehri, 1995), since children are not using letters and sounds but are instead using the look of each word.

As children develop phonological awareness, they begin to use some partial sound information in the word, such as an initial or final sound (see Stahl & Murray, 1998). Ehri (1995) called this stage *phonetic cue reading*. In this stage, a child might substitute a word that begins with the same letter, such as *bird* for *bear*, when reading words in text or in lists.

As children learn more words, phonetic cue reading becomes less efficient, and children analyze the word more deeply. In the *cipher* or *full alphabetic* stage (Ehri, 1995), children use all the letters and sounds. At this stage, children's reading can still be labored, relying on sounding out or other, less efficient strategies. With greater practice, children will develop automatic word recognition so that they do not have to think about the words in a text and can concentrate fully on the meaning of the text (Chall, 1996; Ehri, 1995).

Another way of observing children's growth of the alphabetic principle is to look at their invented spellings. Children go through a similar set of stages in how they invent spellings for words (see Bear & Barone, 1989; Gillet & Temple, 1990; Zutell & Rasinski, 1989). Initially, a child may spell a word by drawing a picture or scribbling something that looks like writing (Harste, Burke, & Woodward, 1982). As children learn that words need letters, they may use random letters to represent a word. Gillet and Temple (1990) called this the *prephonemic* stage. At this point, the writers themselves are the only ones who can read what they have written.

As children begin to think about sounds in words, their spelling may represent only one sound in a word, usually an initial sound, and occasionally a final sound. Sometimes they represent a word with a single letter, or pair of letters, but often they represent a word with the correct initial letter followed by some random letters. For example, one child in our reading clinic wrote *fish* with an initial *f* and continued by adding an additional six letters, stating that "words that begin with *f* have a lot of letters in them."

As children analyze words further, they go to a *letter name* stage, where they use the names of letters to represent sounds. Here they represent at least all of the consonants in a word, often not using vowels. For example, they might spell *girl* as GRL or *ten* as TN. Gillet and Temple (1990) called the next stage *transitional*. In this stage, children use vowels, and the words they write resemble the actual word, like DRAGUN for *dragon*. However, children in this stage may not always use conventional spellings.

Good Phonics Instruction Should Develop Phonological Awareness

The key to the development of the alphabetic principle, word recognition, and invented spelling is phonological awareness. Phonological awareness is one of the most important concepts to arise out of the past 20 years of research in reading (Stanovich, 1991). Phoneme awareness is the awareness of sounds in *spoken* words. As words are spoken, most sounds cannot be said by themselves. For example, the spoken word /cat/ has one continuous sound and is not pronounced "kuh-a-tuh."

Children ordinarily concentrate on the meaning and do not think of the sounds in the word. But, since letters represent sounds, a child must learn to think of words as having *both* meaning and sound in order to understand the alphabetic principle (Stahl & Murray, 1998).

As children grow in their recognition of words, from nonalphabetic to phonetic cues to full alphabetic reading, and as they grow in their invented spelling from prealphabetic to early phonemic to letter name and transitional spelling, they are also growing in their ability to analyze spoken words. In the beginning, children are able to analyze the initial sound in words, since this sound can be perceived easily when they say a word (see Stahl & Murray, 1994, 1998). As they analyze more of the word, often by stretching a word out, they are able to include more letters in their word recognition and spelling. They also develop a sense of phoneme identity (Byrne & Fielding-Barnsley, 1991; Murray, 1995), or an understanding that the /s/ in *sun* is the same sound as the /s/ in *bus*.

Many tasks have been used to teach children to become aware of sounds in spoken words. Among these tasks are:

- *Rhyming*, either by recognizing rhymes or rhyme production,
- *Word-to-word matching tasks*, which involve having a child determine whether a series of words begins or ends the same, or which word in a group is the odd man out (e.g., determining which word does not belong in a group of words such as *man*, *move*, and *pit*),
- *Sound-to-word matching tasks*, which involve having a child determine whether a particular sound can be found in a word (e.g., determining whether there is an /m/ in *man*),
- *Initial (or final) sounds*, in which the child gives the first (or last) sound in a spoken word (e.g., the first sound in *fish*),
- *Segmentation*, which involves breaking a word up into sounds, a very difficult task for children to do orally. This task usually requires some sort of concrete aid such as Elkonin boxes (Clay, 1993; Elkonin, 1973) or boxes set up like this ☐☐☐ in which a child puts a counter or letter in the box when he or she hears a new sound in a word, wooden blocks (Calfee, Lindamood, & Lindamood, 1973), or letters (Hohn & Ehri, 1983),
- *Blending*, the flip side of segmentation, which involves putting spoken sounds together into a word (e.g., recognizing that /k/a/t/ is *cat*), and
- *Deletion and manipulation*, in which a child is told to mentally remove a portion of a word to make another word (e.g., the child is asked to say *coat*, and then to say it again without the /k/). In more complex manipulation tasks, children are asked to remove a phonemic segment and put it elsewhere in the word to make a new word, or to perform other complex manipulations, such as in Pig Latin.

A good phonics program should contain at least one of these tasks. Although phoneme awareness is often conceived as manipulating *spoken* words, often this awareness is taught as an introduction to teaching letter sounds. Thus, a program that begins by having a child listen to a word and say the first sound as a way of introducing a letter sound is giving some attention to phoneme awareness, but probably not enough to help a child with difficulty in this area.

There are other ways of developing phoneme awareness that should be part of a beginning reading program. One way is to read alphabet books to children. We found that 4-year-old children who were read one alphabet book per day significantly improved in their awareness of phonemes (Murray, Stahl, & Ivey, 1996). To understand why *b* is for *bear*, for example, the child needs to understand that the first sound of *bear* is /b/ (Yaden, Smolkin, & MacGillivray, 1993). This understanding is the beginning of phonological awareness.

Another way to develop this awareness is to encourage children to use invented spellings, because children need to think about sounds in words and usually do some form of segmentation in order to invent a spelling. Tangel and Blachman (1992) found that phonemic awareness training increased children's growth in invented spelling. It would make equal sense that practice in invented spelling would similarly increase phonological awareness.

How much attention to phoneme awareness is necessary depends on the child. A child with a history of reading problems may need a variety of activities and many repetitions. Other children may not need as much.

Good Phonics Instruction Should Provide a Thorough Grounding in the Letters

The other part of learning letter–sound relationships is learning the forms of letters. Efficient word recognition is dependent on children's thorough familiarity with letters. They should not have to think, for example, that the letter *t* is the one with the up and down line and the cross thingy. Instead, children should recognize *t* immediately. Adams (1990) suggested that children need to recognize the forms of the letters automatically, without conscious effort, to be able to recognize words fluently.

There is some uncertainty about whether knowing the names of letters is absolutely necessary. On one hand, children can learn to recognize words without knowing the names of letters, and some reading programs do not require that children learn the names of the letters (Adams, 1990). On the other hand, knowing the names of letters is one of the best predictors of success in reading (Chall, 1996). Knowing the names of letters also helps children talk about letters. All in all, it is preferable to teach the names of letters, although children can begin to learn to read without knowing *all* the names of the letters. Thus, children should be reading and listening to connected texts before they know, and as they are learning, the names of all the letters of the alphabet.

Children often learn the names of letters first through an alphabet song. As many parents can attest, memorizing the song often leads to confusion, most notably the notion that there is a letter called "elemenope." But nearly all children recover from that confusion and eventually learn to identify the letters individually. Some programs begin with the alphabet song and teach the letters in order. Other programs begin with letters with easily pronounced sounds such as *m*, *n*, and *s* and proceed to teach the consonants, then the vowels. We know of no research to determine the best order for introducing letters. When teaching the alphabet, a good phonics program will make sure that children can identify both capital and lowercase letters individually, in any order.

Good Phonics Instruction Should Not Teach Rules, Need Not Use Worksheets, Should Not Dominate Instruction, and Does Not Have to Be Boring

There are a number of misconceptions about phonics instruction. Although traditional phonics instruction did teach rules, used worksheets, and was, frankly, often boring, it does not have to be.

Clymer (1963, 1996) reviewed commonly taught phonics rules and compared them to the words that primary children were likely to encounter in their reading. He found that commonly taught rules were rarely applicable to any more than 75% of the words children encounter in their reading. For example, the rule *when two vowels go walking, the first one does the talking*, is applicable to about 45% of words children encounter. The rule applies for the words *boat*, *fail* and *meet*, but does not apply for *does, would,* or *bread*. The lack of applicability does not mean that teachers should never state a rule. Often a rule is useful for clarifying the aspect of the word that is under study. But it does mean that students should not be required to memorize rules, nor should a teacher give students words and have them tell which phonics rule applies. Further, as Adams (1990) pointed out, vowel sounds are more consistent in phonograms. This research suggests that vowels might be taught through phonograms, at least as part of an effective phonics program.

What seems to work in phonics instruction is direct teacher instruction, not practice on worksheets. Two observational studies by Haynes and Jenkins (1986) and Leinhardt, Zigmond, and Cooley (1981) found that the amount of time students spent on worksheets did not relate to gains in reading achievement. This may be because completing worksheets takes students' time away from reading stories or content material, and because instructional aspects of worksheets are often poorly designed (Osborn, 1984). What appeared to be most relevant was time spent reading connected text (Leinhardt et al., 1981).

In the 1970s and 1980s, much instructional time was devoted to having students complete workbooks. A typical lesson might consist of a teacher providing a brief introduction to a skill, what Durkin (1978–1979) called *mentioning*, followed by student practice using worksheets. In a typical lesson there was not only a phonics skill taught, but another phonics skill reviewed, a comprehension skill taught or reviewed, and another worksheet used to review the story. At that time, one of the authors was working for a school district as an observer of reading instruction and noted that only 40% of the time allocated for reading instruction was used for reading connected text. The additional 60% was spent on doing worksheets or supplemental work, such as *Weekly Reader*. Gambrell, Wilson, and Gantt (1981) observed that average readers spent about 6 minutes per day reading connected text. Children with reading problems spent considerably less, about 1 minute per day on average.

Currently, children spend considerably more time reading connected texts. This is as it should be. Effective phonics instruction should not take a great deal of classroom time. Programs such as those of Eldredge and Butterfield (1986; Eldredge, 1995) and the Benchmark School Word Identification program (Gaskins et al., 1988; Gaskins, Ehri, Cress, O'Hara, & Donnelly, 1996–1997) are designed to be taught in no more than 15–20 minutes per day.

Brisk lessons, such as those of Eldredge and Butterfield (1986) and Gaskins et al. (1988, 1996–1997), need not be boring. Of course, boring is in the eye of the beholder, but we have observed high rates of engagement and interest in direct instruction lessons (Stahl, Osborn, & Pearson, 1994). A survey of exemplary primary-grade teachers found that these teachers were highly effective in teaching decoding and also maintained high levels of class engagement (Pressley et al., 1996). Our point is that phonics instruction need not be boring, especially if the instruction is kept brisk, to the point, and does not take an excessive amount of time each day.

Good Phonics Instruction Provides Sufficient Practice in Reading Words

There are three types of practice that might be provided in a phonics program—reading words in isolation, reading words in stories (i.e., expository and narrative texts), and writing words. The ultimate purpose of phonics instruction is for children to learn to read words. Many researchers (see Adams, 1990, for a review) conclude that people identify words by using spelling patterns. These patterns are learned through continued practice in reading words containing those patterns. In addition, all successful phonics programs provide a great deal of practice in reading words containing the letter–sound relationships that are taught. Therefore, the practice given in reading words is extremely important.

Reading Words in Isolation

Phonics programs differ in how much practice they provide in reading words in isolation. Some programs will provide only two or three words as examples of each letter–sound relationship. Others will provide 50 or more examples. Although we do not know what is an optimal number of examples, the more practice that children have in reading words with various patterns, such as silent *e* or short *o* pattern words, the better they will be at reading words with those patterns. It is important for children to look at words in isolation at times so that they can examine the patterns in words without the distractions of context. (Of course, such practice should be minimal and never should dominate instruction.) Good phonics instruction might contain a moderate amount of word practice in isolation, enough to get children to recognize words automatically but not enough to drive them to boredom.

Reading Words in Stories

It is important that children read words in stories or short pieces of expository text. The purpose of reading is comprehension. Reading words in stories may allow children to apply their phonics knowledge to tasks that allow for comprehension of a message as well as to sounding out words. One study found that children who read stories with a high percentage of words that contained letter–sound correspondences that they were taught had significantly higher word recognition than children who read texts that did not contain words that matched their phonics lessons (Juel & Roper/Schneider, 1985). Our informal analyses of texts suggest that many texts do not match what is being taught. We suggest that children read at least some texts that contain a high percentage of words with patterns taught in phonics lessons.

These texts may be contrived, such as *Nat the Rat*, but need not be. There are interesting texts that contain a reasonable percentage of regular words that can be used to reinforce phonics instruction. For example, the classic books *Angus and the Cat* (Flack, 1931) or *The Cat in the Hat* (Geisel, 1957) could be used to reinforce the short *a* sound. (Trachtenburg, 1990, has a list of books that contain high percentages of various vowel patterns.) These texts should not be all that children read. Instead, we recommend that children read a mixture of books containing a high percentage of taught patterns and books ranging more widely in vocabulary. One study found that having children read widely seemed to enhance the performance of a successful phonics-oriented beginning reading program (Meyer, 1983).

Therefore, teachers should have stories for children to read in which they can practice using phonics knowledge in reading for comprehension. Stories (and other prose) should be comprehensible, that is, they should not just be a series of unrelated sentences, although these stories do not have to be elaborate (and cannot be in the beginning of instruction). These stories should be discussed for comprehension, as part of the reading lesson, so that the child will remember that the purpose of reading is getting meaning. We recommend that children read these stories as well as other material at an appropriate, instructional level.

Writing Words

Practice in writing words is usually of two types—either writing words from dictation or using invented spellings. Both of these approaches have their place in beginning reading instruction, and both are valuable ways of practicing letter–sound correspondences.

Dictation is used in many successful phonics programs. In these programs, after a letter–sound correspondence is taught, children practice that correspondence by writing words from dictation. For example, for the short *a* sound, children may write words such as *pat, hand,* and *cap*. This seems to be a reasonably useful practice, one that could be easily added to any program that does not provide for it.

Invented spelling is more controversial. Invented spelling refers to the practice of having children invent their own spellings in their writings, using what they know about letters and sounds. At the early stages of learning to read, a teacher encouraging students to use invented spellings need not correct these spellings, as invented spelling allows children to focus on their developing knowledge of letters and sounds. This development seems to mirror a child's development in both phoneme awareness and letter–sound knowledge (Bear & Barone, 1989; Stahl & Murray, 1998). One study found that having children write using invented spelling greatly improved their phonics knowledge and other word recognition skills (Clarke, 1989).

As children develop letter–sound knowledge, teachers should expect greater control of conventional spelling, at least in final drafts. Invented spelling, as discussed above, has its greatest effect on children's phoneme awareness and knowledge of letter–sound correspondences. Too often teachers have let children continue inventing spellings beyond the point where the practice is useful to fulfill these instructional goals. The result is that some children do not learn to spell conventionally, and the practice of invented spelling in the early grades, where it is particularly useful, has come under attack.

Good Phonics Instruction Leads to Automatic Word Recognition

In order to read books, children need to be able to read words quickly and automatically. If a child stumbles over or has to decode slowly too many words, comprehension will suffer (Samuels, Schermer, & Reinking, 1992). Although we want children to have a strategy for decoding words they do not know, we also want children to recognize many words automatically and be able to read them in context.

The practice activities discussed above—reading words in isolation, reading words in stories, and practicing words through writing—are intended to teach children to recognize the large numbers of words that have a regular pattern. Children learn to read automatically through the reading of stories (Fleisher, Jenkins, & Pany, 1979/1980; Rasinski, 1989; Samuels et al., 1992). Sometimes this practice can use repeated reading or the reading of the same story over and over until the child is able to read it fluently (Herman, 1985; Samuels et al., 1992; Stahl, Heubach, & Cramond, 1997). At other times, it may involve applying phonics lessons to reading books that contain taught letters. It is, however, important to see phonics instruction not as an end but as a means to help children read words automatically.

Good Phonics Instruction Is One Part of Reading Instruction

It is necessary to remember that phonics instruction is only one part of a total reading program. Reading instruction has many different goals. We want children to enjoy reading and be motivated to read. We want children to comprehend what they read. We want children to be able to recognize words quickly and automatically. We know that children do not enjoy reading if they cannot comprehend or if they have to struggle to sound out each and every word. Therefore, we want children to have a good background in letter–sound correspondences and be able to apply this knowledge to recognizing words quickly and automatically. But at the same time, children will not enjoy reading if the only reading they do is sounding out words. Good reading instruction contains a balance of activities around these different goals. For enjoyment, children should be able to choose at least some of the books that they read (Morrow & Tracey, 1998; Turner, 1995) and should be read aloud to from a variety of books from different genres (Feitelson, Kita, & Goldstein, 1986). For comprehension, children should engage in discussions and questioning about the content of what they read. Although phonics instruction is an extremely important part of beginning reading, it is only one part.

SPECIFIC APPROACHES TO PHONICS INSTRUCTION

The conditions under which these principles can be met occur in a variety of reading programs. Reviews of research in this area suggest that it is the emphasis on early and systematic phonics instruction that makes a program effective and that differences between approaches are relatively small (Chall, 1996; Dahl & Freppon, 1995). In this section, we will discuss and review phonics instruction, both traditional and contemporary, from a variety of instructional philosophies. What we call traditional approaches are approaches that were in vogue during the 1960s and 1970s but seem to be returning as teachers grapple with how to teach phonics. Contemporary phonics approaches are those that have been used frequently in the past decade.

Traditional Phonics Approaches

Research on traditional phonics approaches includes mammoth federally funded studies (Abt Associates, 1977; Bond & Dykstra, 1967; Dykstra, 1968), large-scale district evaluations (Kean, Summers, Raivetz, & Farber, 1979), and reviews of research such as that of Adams (1990) and Chall (1996). These reviews consistently find that early and systematic phonics instruction is more effective than later and less systematic instruction.

The differences in quality between phonics approaches are small. Generally, reviews have found a slight advantage for synthetic approaches over analytic approaches (e.g., Chall, 1996), but these differences may be due not to differences in method but instead to differences in coverage, practice, or other factors.

Analytic Phonics Approaches

Analytic approaches begin with a word that a child already knows and break this word down into its component parts. For example, a teacher might begin an analytic phonics lesson by writing the word *bed* on the board and saying something like "the sound in the middle of the word *bed* makes an /e/ sound, which we call the short *e*." The teacher might then say some other words aloud, such as *hen, met, bat, run,* and *rest,* and ask students to raise their hands if the middle sound of the word was a short *e* sound. This instruction might be followed by having students read a series of words on the board, each containing a short *e* sound, and then having students complete a worksheet or two. This analytic approach might be typical of a basal reading lesson in the 1970s. Such lessons tend to be confusing to follow, especially since they seem to have largely been used as an introduction to the worksheets, rather than as lessons in themselves (Durkin, 1988).

Linguistic Approaches. Another variety of phonics instruction that might be called analytic is the so-called linguistic method. This method is based on the theories of linguist Leonard Bloomfield (Bloomfield & Barnhart, 1961) who reasoned that one cannot pronounce many of the sounds that consonants make in isolation (that is, the first sound of *cat* is not /kuh/ but the unpronounceable /k/). Because children cannot sound words out, they should learn words in patterns (such as *cat, rat,* and *fat*) and induce the pronunciations of unknown words from known patterns.

The results of this method were easily lampooned texts such as: "Dan is a man. /Nat is a cat./ Nat is fat./ Nat sat on a mat." Adams (1990) called linguistic texts *visual tongue-twisters,* explaining that these texts made little sense and were so loaded with similar words that they were a challenge for anyone, even a proficient reader or a learner, to read aloud. Although texts like these have gone on to well-deserved oblivion, we have seen the demand for decodable texts (e.g., California Department of Education, 1995) lead to the use of some poorly written texts. It is a challenge to write texts that are both decodable and coherent, but it can be done.

Synthetic Phonics Approaches

The other major division of traditional phonics approaches are the synthetic phonics approaches. Such phonics approaches begin with teaching students individual letters or groups of letters and then showing students how to blend these letters together to form words. A synthetic phonics lesson may begin with the teacher writing a letter on the board, such as *a*, and then saying, "This is the letter *a*, and it makes the sound /a/." The teacher might write a word containing that letter, such as *rat*, and pointing at the letters from left to right have the class blend the word together in unison. This might be followed by some group instruction in reading words with the short *a*, such as *bat, ham, fan, and*, and *ran*. Then the students might read a story containing a high percentage of words with the short *a* sound.

When we reviewed supplemental phonics programs (Osborn, Stahl, & Stein, 1997), we found many of the programs we reviewed for home or supplemental use in schools were synthetic phonics programs. These supplemental programs are usually locally produced and appear to be used only in certain regions of the United States. Many are based on Orton–Gillingham principles but without the extensive training that such programs entail (Gillingham, 1956). In addition, Direct Instruction approaches seem to be undergoing a resurgence. These two synthetic phonics approaches will be reviewed below.

Orton–Gillingham Approaches. Approaches based on Orton–Gillingham methods begin with direct teaching of individual letters paired with their sounds through a VAKT (i.e., visual, auditory, kinesthetic, and tactile) procedure that involves tracing the letter while saying its name and sound, blending letters together to read words and sentences, and finally reading short stories constructed to contain only taught sounds. Among those approaches based on Orton and Gillingham's work are the Slingerland approach (Lovitt & DeMier, 1984), the Spaulding approach (Spaulding & Spaulding, 1962), Recipe for Reading (Traub, 1977), and Alphabetic Phonics (Ogden, Hindman, & Turner, 1989). There are differences among these approaches, largely in sequencing or materials, but these approaches all have the general characteristics discussed. Spelling the words from dictation is also part of an Orton–Gillingham lesson. Each letter sound is learned to mastery through repetition. More advanced lessons involve teaching learners to blend syllables together and read more complex texts. Teachers are specially trained to use Orton–Gillingham methods.

An Orton–Gillingham lesson might begin with the teacher showing the child a card with a letter such as *m*. The teacher might say, "This is the letter *m*, and it says /m/." Then the teacher might take the child's finger and trace the letter, saying, "*M* (letter name), /m/ (sound)." This sequence is repeated until the child has mastered the letter and its sound. The child writes the letter in the air and then on paper, while repeating its name and sound. When a group of letters is mastered, the teacher presents some words containing those sounds. Each of the sounds is identified sequentially. The teacher models blending the sounds together to make a word. This process is repeated, with the child increasingly being held responsible for blending the sounds together. Also in the lesson is spelling from dictation. The same words used in reading are dictated, and the child is supposed to write the sounds that he or she hears. If the child cannot spell the word, the teacher stretches the word when pronouncing it so that each sound can be heard individually, and the child then writes those sounds down. In addition, there are simple books containing words with the taught sounds that the child and teacher read for practice.

In spite of the longevity of use of the Orton–Gillingham approach, there is relatively little research on it. There have been numerous case studies attesting to the approach's effectiveness, beginning with Monroe (1932). These case studies do not, however, meet the criteria for rigorous qualitative research. Other studies of the Orton–Gillingham approach have not included control groups (Ogden et al., 1989; Vickery, Reynolds, & Cochran, 1987). Without a control group, it is hard to tell whether the program worked better than any other.

Kline and Kline (1975) reported a clinical retrospective, comparing the reading abilities of children who were diagnosed as dyslexic in their clinic and given either Orton–Gillingham-based instruction or whatever instruction was given in the child's school. They found that nearly all of the Orton–Gillingham-trained subjects made significant progress while only half of the school-treated subjects did. Again, since the study did not employ typical controls, the differences could have related to reasons the different subjects got different treatments or some other extraneous variables.

Other studies have used single-subject designs, with replications. Lovitt and Hurlburt (1974) and Lovitt and DeMier (1984) compared the Slingerland approach with a linguistic approach that did not include direct instruction in letter–sound correspondences. They found both approaches equally effective. Silberberg, Iversen, and Goins (1973) found that a conventional phonics approach produced the strongest results, significantly greater than those from the Orton–Gillingham approach on 6 of the 10 measures employed.

Given that the Orton–Gillingham approach and its variations have been in use for more than 60 years, this is a disappointing amount of research. When Orton–Gillingham was compared to conventional instruction for children with reading problems (Kline & Kline, 1975), it seemed to be more effective. When compared to with other approaches that were new to the student, the Orton–Gillingham approach did not seem any more effective than any other approach. Given the small number of studies, however, it is difficult to draw any conclusions.

Direct Instruction Approaches. The Direct Instruction approach of Englemann was first published under the name of Distar (Englemann & Bruner, 1969), later Reading Mastery. The Distar approach is a synthetic phonics approach based on a behavioral analysis of decoding (Kame'enui, Simmons, Chard, & Dickson, 1997). Students are taught letter sounds (not letter names, at least in the beginning stages of the program) through highly structured instruction using cuing and reinforcement procedures derived from behavioral analyses of instruction. The task of decoding is broken down into its component parts, and each of these parts is taught carefully and deliberately (see Kame'enui et al., 1997).

Instruction proceeds from letter sounds to blending to reading words in context. Instruction is scripted, with the teacher using a flipbook containing both the stimuli for children's responses and a script of what the teacher is to say. The lessons are fast-paced, with high student involvement. The text for the first-year program is written in a script that, although it preserves English spelling, cues the reader to silent letters (by making the letters relatively small) and different vowel sounds (placing a macron over long vowels). Children practice in specially constructed books containing taught sounds, although children may be encouraged to read widely in children's literature as well (e.g., Meyer, 1983).

Early research with Distar found strong effects (Adams & Englemann, 1996), but in this research Direct Instruction programs have been compared to programs that differed from it on many dimensions. The major study of the effects of Distar is the study of Project Follow Through classes (Abt Associates, 1977). This was a national project, involving hundreds of classes. Distar was the only program that produced achievement in poor students that was near the national average. In this study, and in many of the early studies, Distar was compared to approaches that had radically different goals than Distar and did not stress phonics as strongly as it did.

Adams and Englemann (1996) performed a meta-analysis on the effects of Direct Instruction (in areas including comprehension and mathematics) on student achievement and found that Direct Instruction approaches produced large effect sizes on achievement measures. Although these results are impressive, they need to be viewed critically. First, both Adams and Englemann are associated with Reading Mastery, and their review has not been peer reviewed, so this is not an independent review. Second, we have, in a cursory survey using ERIC, found a number of relevant studies not included in the Adams and Englemann review, including some studies that did not find salutary effects for Distar in beginning reading. Thus, further research investigating the success of Reading Mastery seems warranted.

Contemporary Phonics Approaches

In this section, we discuss three contemporary phonics approaches: (a) spelling-based approaches, (b) analogy-based approaches, and (c) embedded phonics approaches. All of these approaches are usually described in the literature as components of larger reading instruction programs. For example, spelling-based approaches are implemented in programs such as the Multimethod, Multilevel Instruction Program (e.g., Cunningham & Hall, 1997), the Charlottesville Volunteer Tutorial or Book Buddies Project (e.g., Invernizzi, Juel, & Rosemary, 1996–1997; Johnston, Juel, & Invernizzi, 1995), and the Howard Street Tutoring Program (e.g., Morris, 1992). Analogy-based approaches are one aspect of the Benchmark Word Identification Program (e.g., Gaskins et al., 1996–1997), and embedded phonics approaches are utilized in programs such as Reading Recovery (Clay, 1993) or in whole language classrooms (e.g., Dahl & Freppon, 1995; Freppon & Headings, 1996). Thus, it is important to consider the instructional context in which these contemporary phonics approaches often occur.

Spelling-Based Approaches

Three contemporary approaches to phonics instruction, Word Study (e.g., Bear, Invernizzi, Templeton, & Johnston, 1996), Making Words (e.g., Cunningham & Cunningham, 1992; Cunningham & Hall, 1994), and Meta-Phonics (Calfee, 1998; Calfee & Henry, 1996), are based on spelling principles.

Word Study. In Word Study, students examine words and word patterns through strategies such as sorting, in which students categorize words and pictures according to their common orthographic features. Word Study instruction is based on students' developmental levels of orthographic knowledge and is an approach to teaching phonics, vocabulary, spelling, and word recognition. In Word Study, the teacher bases instruction on word features that students are writing but are confusing (e.g., Bear et al., 1996). For example, when a child spells *rane* for *rain* and makes similar errors in other aspects of his or her writing, the teacher may begin instruction with the child on long *a* word patterns.

Word Study is based on research on how orthographic knowledge develops (e.g., Templeton & Bear, 1992) and is included in this section on contemporary approaches to phonics instruction because of recent, published descriptions of Word Study in widely read texts and journals. For example, Word Study has been described in teacher resources (e.g., Bear et al., 1996) and in journal articles (e.g., Barnes, 1989; Bloodgood, 1991; Gill, 1992; Invernizzi, Abouzeid, & Gill, 1994; Invernizzi et al., 1996–1997; Morris, Ervin, & Conrad, 1996; Schlagal & Schlagal, 1992; Templeton, 1989, 1991, 1992).

Much of the Word Study research is described in the contexts in which this approach occurs. For example, Invernizzi et al. (1996–1997) described the use of Word Study in the Charlottesville Volunteer Tutorial program over a 3-year time period. In this program, low-achieving first- and second-grade students are tutored in reading by trained community volunteers. During the third year of program implementation, tutored students' pre- to posttest gain scores increased statistically significantly on measures of alphabet knowledge, phonemic awareness, and word recognition, and 86% of all students read with 90% accuracy a benchmark first-grade level trade book during the third year of the implementation of the tutoring program.

Additionally, Morris et al. (1996) provided a case study of a sixth-grade student with severe reading difficulties in a university-based reading clinic. A reading tutor worked with this student once a week for 2 years in a clinic tutoring program in which Word Study was included, and the student made 2 years' growth in reading and spelling as measured by informal reading assessments.

The effectiveness of the Word Study approach to phonics instruction has been documented in conjunction with other aspects of teaching and supporting reading (e.g., writing, reading of instructional level texts, and rereading independent texts). Thus, it is difficult to document in an empirical sense the effects of word study instruction per se, although this type of phonics instruction seems to be effective as one component in reading interventions and programs.

Making Words. In Making Words (e.g., Cunningham & Cunningham, 1992; Cunningham & Hall, 1994), students are given six to eight different letters on letter cards. Then, the teacher calls out words with two, three, four, and more letters that can be formed using the students' letters, with the teacher and students first making the words and then sorting words based on their common spelling patterns or other orthographic features. At the end of this activity, the teacher challenges the students to use all of their letters to make a big word. The big word is related to something the children are reading.

Making Words is one component of the Working With Words block in the Multimethod, Multilevel Instruction Program (e.g., Cunningham & Hall, 1997). As was the case with Word Study, the effectiveness of this approach to phonics instruction is described in the context of overall reading program effects. In a recent description of program results, Hall and Cunningham (1996) documented that 85%

of students in the Multimethod, Multilevel Instruction Program were reading at or above grade level by the end of their first-grade year, and 94% of students were reading on grade level by the end of their second-grade year as measured by informal reading inventory data.

Objectively, it is not as easy to determine the success of Word Study and Making Words in isolation in improving students' word identification abilities as compared to some of the described traditional phonics approaches. However, both of these approaches seem to be effective as part of overall approaches to teaching reading.

Meta-Phonics. In this approach, reading and spelling are taught simultaneously through social interaction and group problem solving. Sounds are introduced through phonemic awareness instruction. This instruction stresses articulation as a key to learning sounds (Calfee, 1998; Calfee et al., 1973). Thus, /p/ /t/ and /k/ are *popping sounds*. Vowels are taught as *glue letters*. After these are established, students are given letters and sounds and asked to make a make a word, through adding consonants to vowels. Students begin with short consonant–vowel–consonant words but progress to longer words such as *discombobulate* or *sassafras*.

This component has been embedded in a larger program, Project READ (Calfee, 1998). Preliminary results suggest that the program has been successful in three school settings. Students who have used this program were at or above district or national averages in reading comprehension, fluency, word recognition, spelling, and writing. These evaluations were informal, without a true control group, and also were conducted as part of a redesign of reading instruction, making it difficult to ascertain how important this component was to overall achievement gains. This approach awaits a fuller, more controlled evaluation.

Analogy-Based Approaches

In analogy-based approaches to phonics instruction, students learn how to decode words they do not know by using words or word parts they do know. For example, students learn that if they can read the words *he*, *send*, and *table*, they can compare and contrast these words with the word parts in the unknown word *de/pend/able* to help them decode this word. Decades ago, the research of Patricia Cunningham (e.g., Cunningham, 1975–1976, 1978, 1979, 1980) focused on using analogy-based approaches to help students decode unknown words.

Analogy-based approaches are currently used as one instructional component in the Benchmark Word Identification Program (e.g., Gaskins, Gaskins, & Gaskins, 1991; 1992). Current versions of this decoding program include phonics approaches other than analogy-based approaches (see Gaskins et al., 1996–1997), such as teaching students ways to analyze all sounds in a word. In the analogy-based phonics component, students learn 120 key words with common phonogram patterns and word parts. Five to six new words are introduced to students every week, with the teacher providing explicit instruction to students on how to use these key words to decode other words.

There are three different types of research support for analogy-based approaches, all of which suggest using some caution in implementing those approaches. First are basic research studies. Goswami's work (1993, 1998) suggests that young children can use analogies before they can use other phonological information to read words. Bruck and Treiman (1992) and Ehri and Robbins (1992), however, found that children need to be able to use phonetic cue reading, or initial letter–sound relationships, in order to take advantage of analogies in reading. The differences between Goswami's work and Bruck and Treiman's and Ehri and Robbins's studies lie in experimental design. (In Goswami's studies, the analogue word is always available for the child; in the other studies, the child has to rely on memory.) In practice, analogies should be used after children can recognize initial sound cues, which is how they are used in Cunningham's (1995) and Gaskins et al.'s (1996–1997) approaches.

The second line of research on analogies comes from directed studies. Haskell, Foorman, and Swank (1992) and Sullivan, Okada, and Niedermeyer (1971) found that an analogy approach and a synthetic approach performed equally well, and both were more effective than whole-word approaches. Fayne and Bryant (1981) found that a rime-based strategy was not as effective as teaching children initial bigrams (e.g., *co-g*). These were short-term studies. White and Cunningham (1990), in a year-long study, found that analogy training produced statistically significant effects on measures of both word recognition and comprehension.

Finally, analogy approaches are part of successful reading programs, including the approach used at the Benchmark School (Gaskins et al., 1988; see also Cunningham, 1995). The experience at Benchmark is illustrative of both the strengths and limits of an analogy-based approach. The program began as a direct adaptation of analogies with metacognitive strategy training to help children transfer the use of analogy-based decoding in their reading (Gaskins et al., 1992). This program seemed to be successful with many of the children with reading problems at Benchmark, but there were a number of children who did not succeed. In an attempt to reach more children, the program was modified to include a more thorough analysis of the words taught as anchor words (Gaskins et al., 1996–1997), thus teaching more phonological information along with the analogy words. Our conclusion is that analogies can be a very powerful teaching approach but need to be taught after a child has reached the phonetic cue level and in conjunction with other decoding approaches.

Embedded Phonics Approaches

In embedded phonics approaches, phonics instruction occurs in the context of authentic reading and writing experiences. The phonics instruction in Reading Recovery and in many whole language classrooms are examples of embedded approaches to phonics instruction.

Phonics in Reading Recovery. Reading Recovery (Clay, 1993) is a one-on-one tutorial program intended for the lowest 20% of first-grade children in a school. Although lessons are based on daily individual diagnosis of children's needs, there is a common lesson structure (Clay, 1993). First, lessons begin with a rereading of two or more books of the student's choice. The purpose of this rereading is to develop fluency. Next, the student rereads the book that was introduced the previous day. The teacher makes a running record of this reading and addresses one or two teaching points immediately following the running record. Following the running record, there is *making and breaking* with magnetic letters. Next, the child writes a sentence-length story with the help of the teacher. This help may include hearing and recording sounds in words using Elkonin boxes (Elkonin, 1973). After that, the story is cut up and reassembled. Finally, the teacher introduces a new book, using Clay's (1991) procedures, and the child attempts an independent first reading of the book.

Lessons are based on Goodman's (1976) model, suggesting that readers use three cuing systems to recognize words in context. Clay (1993) called these systems visual, structural, and meaning cues. One study found that most of the children referred to Reading Recovery needed work on the visual system (Center, Wheldall, Freeman, Outhred, & McNaught, 1995), especially phonological processes (Iversen & Tunmer, 1993). Within the lesson structure, the teacher has a number of options to teach children to better use visual cues. The individual nature of a Reading Recovery lesson enables the teacher to direct the child's attention to aspects of words relevant to their development. Work with magnetic letters, cut-up sentences, and carefully selected gradient texts gently nudge the Reading Recovery student to the next level of visual sensitivity, balancing the child's reading work through the utilization of and reliance on multiple cuing systems. Thus, phonics instruction is woven throughout the lessons.

Letter sprees are activities that involve the direct teaching of letter names, learned to the point of automaticity (Adams, 1990; Clay, 1993). In their writing, children use invented spellings to approximate words, although the final product always is spelled conventionally. Also, teachers integrate work with Elkonin boxes into spelling work, having children use the boxes to reflect on each sound in a word.

In making and breaking words, the teacher uses magnetic letters to give children practice in reading phonetically controlled words. This component has been part of Reading Recovery from the beginning, but recently it has received more emphasis. Iversen and Tunmer (1993) found that they were able to help children discontinue the program earlier by adding a phonological recoding component to the Reading Recovery lesson.

Reading Recovery teachers can also choose texts that reflect children's increasing mastery of phonics. A teacher might choose a text that requires the child to direct attention to particular visual features of words. If a child is, for example, noticing initial-sound relationships, the teacher would choose a book in which the child must use these relationships to read the book successfully. In the beginning Reading Recovery lessons, texts are highly predictable, and the pattern provides a scaffold for children's reading. As texts become less predictable over the course of the lessons, teachers decrease the amount of scaffolding they provide, encouraging children to use more visual features of words. The result of these cumulative decisions, in text reading and through other aspects of the lessons, is that children advance in their word recognition abilities and phonological awareness (Stahl, Stahl, & McKenna, 1997).

Reading Recovery has been cited by Adams (1990) as an excellent example of what good phonics instruction can be. Although children do receive a great deal of work with letters and sounds, the instruction is always integrated into the reading and writing of texts. Teachers keep track of students' increasing mastery of the visual cuing system in conjunction with the other two systems. Children spend the majority of their lesson time reading and writing connected text, with very little time spent on phonics.

Reading Recovery has been found to be effective, at least for the children in the program (Center et al., 1995; Shanahan & Barr, 1995, Wasik & Slavin, 1993). In their conservative analysis, Center et al. (1995) found that Reading Recovery was able to accelerate the reading progress of 35% of the children who would not, under other programs, reach the level of their successful peers. Although there is some controversy about the cost effectiveness of Reading Recovery, the instruction given seems to be highly effective. Reading Recovery has been adapted to programs in group settings, and these programs seem to be effective in increasing children's reading achievement as well (e.g., Fountas & Pinnell, 1996; Hiebert, 1994; Taylor, Short, & Shearer, 1990).

Phonics in Whole Language Classrooms. As we noted at the beginning of this article, whole language teachers do teach phonics. However, this instruction is often embedded in the context of teaching reading and is sensitive to the child's needs. Letter–sound instruction can occur as one of the cuing systems that children use to recognize words in reading (e.g., Weaver, 1994) and can also occur as part of writing instruction.

Whole language instruction varies considerably from teacher to teacher and from class to class (Watson, 1989). It may resemble the instruction in the Reading Recovery lessons described previously (although Reading Recovery is not a whole language approach; see Church, 1996). Some whole language teachers may provide less organized phonics instruction than occurs in Reading Recovery. An example of whole language phonics instruction comes from first-grade teacher Linda Headings's class:

> I focus on using children's names a lot, especially in the beginning months, because of the significance of names in their lives. Names carry power in giving us identity, and I can gather information by doing this, too. I can see who is unsure and who is not, who is trying to figure out not only his or her own name but also the names of others. Over the next month, I use names to do language play, poetry, games and songs, and to engage with environmental print. That name immersion will be pulled back out and used when children have questions about invented spelling. "It starts like Bobby," I'll say. "Go find his name tag and see what letter his name starts with." I can use this with children who are poor risktakers or developmentally lagging. It also gives them the avenue to monitor their own learning. I teach and guide, and the child acts on his [sic] own and completes the process by finding Bobby's name and writing the letter B. (Freppon & Headings, 1996, p. 71)

The instruction is embedded within the classroom framework, as names and name cards are used in a variety of classroom activities. Also, the name instruction is extended to other language activities, and the teacher strives to make the student an independent learner by not giving the child an answer, but instead providing the child a strategy for finding the answer (e.g., "It starts like Bobby").

In the accounts of phonics instruction from the projects of Dahl and Freppon (1995), Freppon and Dahl (1991), and Freppon and Headings (1996), who discuss observations of the same first-grade teacher, and from the work of Mills et al. (1992), we are given no examples of first-grade whole language teachers who teach something other than consonants. The lesson above is typical of what is presented in illustrative vignettes within these studies. Of course, just because lessons involving vowels or lessons involving the full examination of words were not present in vignettes does not mean that these teachers did not teach vowels. But it is still surprising that vowel lessons were not described, since one would expect that instruction in vowels occurs during the first-grade year (Anderson, Hiebert, Scott, & Wilkinson, 1985).

The lack of phonics instruction beyond consonants may be indicative of whole language teachers' reticence to challenge their students. This may be symptomatic of a general lack of challenge in many whole language classes. One study found that children in whole language classrooms did not read as challenging materials as children in traditional classes and that the amount of challenge determined children's achievement at the end of the year (Stahl, Suttles, & Pagnucco, 1996). Church (1994, 1996), a whole language teacher in Nova Scotia, was also concerned that whole language teachers do not sufficiently challenge their students. In short, some reading programs based on the whole language philosophy may not encourage students to read more challenging texts and may not expose children to the types of phonics instruction they need to improve as readers and writers.

Research on Contemporary Approaches to Phonics

Although there are indications that the contemporary approaches discussed in this section were effective, there is a notable lack of controlled research to validate the effectiveness of these approaches. Part of the reason for the lack of research is the newness of these approaches. Another possible reason is the general trend of the field away from comparative research and toward descriptive research (McKenna et al., 1994). Although descriptive research can give us insights, without some sort of comparison it is difficult to tell whether these new approaches are more effective than traditional approaches. Such comparative research need not be a horse race in which different approaches are saddled up to see which one produces the highest scores on a standardized achievement test. Instead, such comparisons may include qualitative aspects, such as in Dahl and Freppon's (1995) study, and should be directed toward what each approach might be effective at rather than toward choosing the most effective.

CONSTRUCTIONS OF KNOWLEDGE ABOUT WORDS

The principles discussed in the beginning of this article all relate to a teacher guiding students' constructions of knowledge about words. From a constructivist perspective, learners are thought to be actively constructing knowledge through their interactions with the world. This, of course, includes interactions with teachers and reading materials. Ordinarily, researchers have used a constructivist perspective to talk about comprehension, especially in conjunction with schema theory (e.g., Anderson & Pearson, 1984). Researchers in decoding rely on other psychological models, such as connectionism (Adams, 1990) and behaviorist models (Carnine, Silbert, & Kame'enui, 1990). Neither of these models explicitly views the learner as actively constructing information about words.

Our observations of children show them very actively trying to make sense of words, in both their writing and their reading. A child who makes two or three attempts at a word in a text before coming up with one that makes sense and accommodates the letter–sound relationships that he or she knows is actively constructing word knowledge, as is the child who stretches out the letters in the word *camel* and produces *caml*.

Viewing decoding through a constructivist lens may be a whole language perspective (e.g., Weaver, 1994), but one need not adopt teaching techniques commonly associated with the whole language philosophy if one takes this perspective. A constructivist perspective is consistent with any of the methods discussed in the second section of this paper. Constructivism is not synonymous with discovery learning, since children can be guided in their constructions more or less explicitly. What constructivism implies is that the child is an active learner.

What children construct is a network of information about letters. They know, for example that *t* is more likely to be followed by *r* or *h* than by *q* or *p*, that *ck* never starts a word, that *q* is nearly always followed by *u* (with the exception of some Arabic and Chinese words) (see Adams, 1990; Venezky, 1970). Much of this information could be directly taught or learned from repeated experiences with print. Children do differ in their need for guidance. Some children will learn much of what they need to know about words from exposure (e.g., Durkin, 1966), but most children need some explicit support. This support might be provided in context, as in the embedded phonics instruction approaches, through analogy- or spelling-based approaches, or through more direct instruction. It could be that some children with reading problems require more direct instruction (Carnine et al., 1990).

The notion that children construct knowledge about words may explain why the differences among programs are small. As long as one provides early and systematic information about the code (Chall, 1996), it may not matter very much how one does it. If each of the programs discussed previously provides similar amounts of coverage with similar amounts of practice reading words in isolation and in context, they might all have similar effects. From a constructivist perspective, children learn by acting upon information; if the information is similar, the learning should be as well. The principles discussed in the first part of this article suggest the information that should be taught in a phonics program. If this information is made available to children, then it may not matter exactly how the instruction occurs.

An effective first-grade reading program, for example, might involve some systematic and direct instruction in decoding, with associated practice in decodable texts (Juel & Roper/Schneider, 1985). These may include some contrived texts, if they are artfully and interestingly done. They also might include authentic literature chosen for repetition of taught patterns (Trachtenburg, 1990). Children also need a variety of engaging but easy texts, both for interest and for practice in reading a variety of materials. Some of these texts might be predictable where the context supports word recognition, at least until the child develops more independent word recognition strategies (Clay, 1993; Fountas & Pinnell, 1996). Predictable texts by themselves, however, may limit children's word learning (Duffy, McKenna, Vancil, Stratton, & Stahl, 1996), unless the teacher draws specific attention to words in those texts (Johnston, 1995). Writing, using invented spelling, is useful for developing word knowledge (Clarke, 1989). As they invent spellings, children need to integrate their developing phoneme awareness with their knowledge of sound–symbol correspondences (Stahl & Murray, 1998).

Because first-grade children are focused on decoding in their text reading (Chall, 1996), children's comprehension growth might best be accommodated by the teacher reading aloud to the children. Studies have found that children can learn new vocabulary words from hearing stories (e.g., Elley, 1989). In addition, teachers can model more advanced comprehension strategies with stories they read out loud to children since these stories are likely to have richer contexts than stories a child can read independently. This is not to say that comprehension should be ignored during children's reading. Basic strategies such as recall (Koskinen, Gambrell, Kapinus, & Heatherington, 1988) or story grammars (Beck & McKeown, 1981) can be profitably taught to children at this age. An extensive reading program would likely improve first graders' motivation toward reading, as would a daily period of choice reading (Morrow & Tracey, 1998).

Thus, an effective first-grade program might involve elements associated with whole language (teacher reading aloud, invented spelling, free reading, extensive use of literature) as well as more direct instructional approaches (direct sound–symbol instruction, limited use of decodable or contrived texts). How these elements might be managed might also depend on the needs of the children. Children who enter first grade with a low literacy background may need more direct instruction to develop concepts that other children may have learned through print-based home experiences with literacy. Children with print-based literacy backgrounds may benefit from more time to choose their reading, with teacher support to read more and more complex materials.

Effective reading instruction requires that a teacher recognize multiple goals for reading instruction, and that different means are required to reach these multiple goals. Juggling these goals will always be a challenge. We are not sure, however, that the alleged balance we are seeing in some classroom reading programs is based on a forward-looking examination of what is needed for effective reading instruction; rather, it may be based, at least in part, on false allegations popularized by the media and accepted by some legislators and administrators describing the limited success of past reading programs.

The balance in some of today's reading programs appears to be an attempt to lay phonics instruction on top of a literature-based curriculum. This is easy. Good reading instruction, however, is difficult. It involves all teachers asking themselves what skills their students have, what their goals are, and how reading instruction can be directed toward all of their goals.

REFERENCES

Abt Associates. (1977). *Education as experimentation: A planned variation model. Volume IV-B, Effects of follow-through models.* Cambridge, MA: Author.

Adams, G. L., & Englemann, S. (1996). *Research on direct instruction: 25 years beyond DISTAR.* Seattle, WA: Educational Achievement Systems.

Adams, M. J. (1990). *Beginning to read: Thinking and learning about print.* Cambridge, MA: MIT Press.

Anderson, R. C., Hiebert, E. F., Scott, J. A., & Wilkinson, I. A.G. (1985). *Becoming a nation of readers.* Champaign, IL: National Academy of Education and Center for the Study of Reading.

Anderson, R. C., & Pearson, P. D. (1984). A schema-theoretic view of basic processes in reading. In P. D. Pearson (Ed.), *Handbook of reading research* (pp. 255–292). White Plains, NY: Longman.

Barnes, G. W. (1989). Word sorting: The cultivation of rules for spelling in English. *Reading Psychology, 10,* 293–307.

Baumann, J. F., Hoffman, J. V., Moon, J., & Duffy-Hester, A. M. (1998). Where are teachers' voices in the phonics/whole language debate? Results from a survey of U.S. elementary classroom teachers. *The Reading Teacher, 51,* 636–650.

Bear, D. R., & Barone, D. (1989). Using children's spellings to group for word study and directed reading in the primary classroom. *Reading Psychology, 10,* 275–292.

Bear, D. R., Invernizzi, M., Templeton, S., & Johnston, F. (1996). *Words their way: Word study for phonics, vocabulary, and spelling instruction.* Upper Saddle River, NJ: Merrill.

Beck, I. L., & McKeown, M. G. (1981). Developing questions that promote comprehension: The story map. *Language Arts, 58,* 913–918.

Bloodgood, J. (1991). A new approach to spelling in language arts programs. *Elementary School Journal, 92,* 203–211.

Bloomfield, L., & Barnhart, C. L. (1961). *Let's read: A linguistic approach.* Detroit, MI: Wayne State University Press.

Bond, G., & Dykstra, R. (1967). The cooperative research program in first grade reading. *Reading Research Quarterly, 2,* 5–142.

Bruck, M., & Treiman, R. (1992). Learning to pronounce words: The limitations of analogies. *Reading Research Quarterly, 27,* 374–388.

Byrne, B., & Fielding-Barnsley, R. (1991). Evaluation of a program to teach phonemic awareness in young children. *Journal of Educational Psychology, 83,* 451–455.

Calfee, R. (1998). Phonics and phonemes: Learning to decode in a literature-based program. In J. Metsala & L. Ehri (Eds.), *Word recognition in beginning literacy* (pp. 315–340). Mahwah, NJ: Erlbaum.

Calfee, R., & Henry, M. (1996). Strategy and skill in early reading acquisition. In J. Shimon (Ed.), *Literacy and education: Essays in memory of Dina Feitelson* (pp. 97–118). Cresskill, NJ: Hampton Press.

Calfee, R. C., Lindamood, P., & Lindamood, C. (1973). Acoustic–phonetic skills and reading: Kindergarten through twelfth grade. *Journal of Educational Psychology, 64,* 293–298.

California Department of Education. (1995). *Every child a reader: The report of the California Reading Task Force.* Sacramento: Author. Available online at: *www.cde.ca.gov/cilbranch/ eltdiv/rdg_init.htm*

Carnine, D., Silbert, J., & Kame'enui, E. (1990). *Direct instruction reading* (2nd ed.). Columbus, OH: Merrill.

Center, Y., Wheldall, K., Freeman, L., Outhred, L., & McNaught, M. (1995). An evaluation of Reading Recovery. *Reading Research Quarterly, 30,* 240–263.

Chall, J. S. (1989). Learning to read: The great debate twenty years later. A response to "Debunking the great phonics myth." *Phi Delta Kappan, 71,* 521–538.

Chall, J. S. (1996). *Learning to read: The great debate* (rev., with a new foreword). New York: McGraw-Hill.

Church, S. M. (1994). Is whole language really warm and fuzzy? *The Reading Teacher, 47,* 362–371.

Church, S. M. (1996). *The future of whole language: Reconstruction or self-destruction.* Portsmouth, NH: Heinemann.

Clarke, L. K. (1989). Encouraging invented spelling in first graders' writing: Effects on learning to spell and read. *Research in the Teaching of English, 22,* 281–309.

Clay, M. M. (1991). Introducing a new storybook to young readers. *The Reading Teacher, 45,* 264–273.

Clay, M. M. (1993). *Reading Recovery: A guidebook for teachers in training.* Portsmouth, NH: Heinemann.

Clymer, T. (1963). The utility of phonic generalizations in the primary grades. *The Reading Teacher, 16,* 252–258.

Clymer, T. (1996). The utility of phonic generalizations in the primary grades. *The Reading Teacher, 50,* 182–187.

Collins, J. (1997, October 27). How Johnny should read. *Time Magazine, 150*(17), 78–81.

Cunningham, P. M. (1975–1976). Investigating a synthesized theory of mediated word identification. *Reading Research Quarterly, 11,* 127–143.

Cunningham, P. M. (1978). Decoding polysyllabic words: An alternative strategy. *Journal of Reading, 21,* 608–614.

Cunningham, P. M. (1979). A compare/contrast theory of mediated word identification. *The Reading Teacher, 32,* 774–778.

Cunningham, P. M. (1980). Applying a compare/contrast process to identifying polysyllabic words. *Journal of Reading Behavior, 12,* 213–223.

Cunningham, P. M. (1995). *Phonics they use* (2nd ed.). New York: HarperCollins.

Cunningham, P. M., & Cunningham, J. W. (1992). Making words: Enhancing the invented spelling-decoding connection. *The Reading Teacher, 46,* 106–115.

Cunningham, P. M., & Hall, D. P. (1994). *Making words.* Carthage, IL: Good Apple.

Cunningham, P. M., & Hall, D. P. (1997, May). *A framework for literacy in primary classrooms that work.* Paper presented at the 42nd annual convention of the International Reading Association, Atlanta, GA.

Dahl, K. L., & Freppon, P. A. (1995). A comparison of innercity children's interpretations of reading and writing instruction in the early grades in skills-based and whole language classrooms. *Reading Research Quarterly, 30,* 50–74.

Deford, D. E. (1985). Validating the construct of theoretical orientation in reading instruction. *Reading Research Quarterly, 20,* 351–367.

Duffy, A. M., McKenna, M., Vancil, S., Stratton, B., & Stahl, S. A. (1996, December). *Tales of Ms. Wishy-Washy: The effects of predictable books on learning to recognize words.* Paper presented at the annual meeting of the National Reading Conference, Charleston, SC.

Durkin, D. (1966). *Children who read early.* New York: Teachers College Press.

Durkin, D. (1978–1979). What classroom observations reveal about reading comprehension instruction. *Reading Research Quarterly, 14,* 481–533.

Durkin, D. (1988). *A classroom observation study of reading instruction in kindergarten* (Tech. Rep. No. 422). Champaign: Center for the Study of Reading, University of Illinois at Urbana–Champaign.

Dykstra, R. (1968). The effectiveness of code- and meaning emphasis beginning reading programs. *The Reading Teacher, 22,* 17–23.

Ehri, L. C. (1992). Reconceptualizing the development of sight word reading and its relationship to recoding. In P. Gough, L. C. Ehri, & R. Treiman (Eds.), *Reading acquisition* (pp. 107–143). Mahwah, NJ: Erlbaum.

Ehri, L. C. (1995). Phases of development in learning to read words by sight. *Journal of Research in Reading, 18,* 116–125.

Ehri, L. C., & Robbins, C. (1992). Beginners need some decoding skill to read words by analogy. *Reading Research Quarterly, 27,* 12–26.

Eldredge, J. L. (1995). *Teaching decoding in holistic classrooms.* Englewood Cliffs, NJ: Merrill.

Eldredge, J. L., & Butterfield, D. (1986). Alternatives to traditional reading instruction. *The Reading Teacher, 48,* 32–37.

Elkonin, D. B. (1973). U.S.S.R. In J. Downing (Ed.), *Comparative reading* (pp. 551–579). New York: Macmillan.

Elley, W. B. (1989). Vocabulary acquisition from listening to stories. *Reading Research Quarterly, 24,* 174–187.

Englemann, S., & Bruner, E. (1969). *Distar reading program.* Chicago: SRA.

Fayne, H. R., & Bryant, N. D. (1981). Relative effects of various word synthesis strategies on the phonics achievement of learning disabled youngsters. *Journal of Educational Psychology, 73,* 616–623.

Feitelson, D., Kita, R., & Goldstein, Z. (1986). Effects of listening to series stories on first grad-ers' comprehension and the use of language. *Research in the Teaching of English, 20*, 339–356.

Flack, M. (1931). *Angus and the cat.* Garden City, NY: Doubleday.

Fleisher, L. S., Jenkins, J. R., & Pany, D. (1979/1980). Effects on poor readers' comprehension of training in rapid decoding. *Reading Research Quarterly, 15*, 30–48.

Fountas, I. C., & Pinnell, G. S. (1996). *Guided reading: Good first teaching for all children.* Portsmouth, NH: Heinemann.

Freppon, P. A., & Dahl, K. L. (1991). Learning about phonics in a whole language classroom. *Language Arts, 68*, 190–197.

Freppon, P. A., & Headings, L. (1996). Keeping it whole in whole language: A first grade teacher's instruction in an urban whole language classroom. In E. McIntyre & M. Pressley (Eds.), *Balanced instruction: Strategies and skills in whole language* (pp. 65–82). Norwood, MA: Christopher-Gordon.

Gambrell, L. B., Wilson, R. M., & Gantt, W. N. (1981). Classroom observations of task-attending behaviors of good and poor readers. *Journal of Educational Research, 74*, 400–404.

Gaskins, I. W., Downer, M. A., Anderson, R. C., Cunningham, P. M., Gaskins, R. W., Schommer, M., et al. (1988). A metacognitive approach to phonics: Using what you know to decode what you don't know. *Remedial and Special Education, 9*, 36–41.

Gaskins, I. W., Ehri, L. C., Cress, C., O'Hara, C., & Donnelly, K. (1996–1997). Procedures for word learning: Making discoveries about words. *The Reading Teacher, 50*, 312–327.

Gaskins, R. W., Gaskins, J. C., & Gaskins, I. (1991). A decoding program for poor readers—And the rest of the class, too! *Language Arts, 68*, 213–225.

Gaskins, R. W., Gaskins, J. C., & Gaskins, I. (1992). Using what you know to figure our what you don't know: An analogy approach to decoding. *Reading and Writing Quarterly: Over-coming Learning Disabilities, 8*, 197–221.

Geisel, T. S. (1957). *The cat in the hat.* Boston: Houghton Mifflin.

Gill, J. T. (1992). Development of word knowledge as it relates to reading, spelling, and in-struction. *Language Arts, 69*, 444–453.

Gillet, J. W., & Temple, C. (1990). *Understanding reading problems* (3rd ed.). Glenview, IL: Scott Foresman.

Gillingham, A. (1956). *Remedial training for children with specific disability in reading, spelling, and penmanship.* Cambridge, MA: Educators Publishing Service.

Goodman, K. S. (1976). Reading: A psycholinguistic guessing game. In H. Singer & R. B. Ruddell (Eds.), *Theoretical models and processes of reading* (2nd ed., pp. 497–508). Newark, DE: International Reading Association.

Goodman, K. S. (1986). *What's whole in whole language? A parent/teacher guide to children's learn-ing.* Portsmouth, NH: Heinemann.

Goodman, K. S. (1993). *Phonics phacts.* Portsmouth, NH: Heinemann.

Goodman, K. S., & Goodman, Y. M. (1977). Learning about psycholinguistic processes by ana-lyzing oral reading. *Harvard Educational Review, 47*, 317–333.

Goswami, U. (1993). Toward an interactive analogy model of reading development: Decoding vowel graphemes in beginning reading. *Journal of Experimental Child Psychology, 56*, 443–475.

Goswami, U. (1998). The role of analogies in the development of word recognition. In J. Metsala & L. Ehri (Eds.), *Word recognition in beginning literacy* (pp. 41–63). Mahwah, NJ: Erlbaum.

Gough, P. B., & Hillinger, M. L. (1980). Learning to read: An unnatural act. *Bulletin of the Orton Society, 30*, 179–196.

Hall, D. P., & Cunningham, P. M. (1996). Becoming literate in first and second grades: Six years of multimethod, multilevel instruction. In D. J. Leu, C. K. Kinzer, & K. A. Hinchman (Eds.), *Literacies for the 21st century. 45th yearbook of the National Reading Conference* (pp. 195–204). Chicago: National Reading Conference.

Harste, J. C., Burke, C. L., & Woodward, V. A. (1982). Children's language and world: Initial encounters with print. In J. A. Langer & M. T. Smith-Burke (Eds.), *Reader meets author/Bridging the gap* (pp. 105–131). Newark, DE: International Reading Association.

Haskell, D. W., Foorman, B. R., & Swank, P. A. (1992). Effects of three orthographic/phonological units on first grade reading. *Remedial and Special Education, 13*, 40–49.

Haynes, M. C., & Jenkins, J. R. (1986). Reading instruction in special education resource rooms. *American Educational Research Journal, 23*, 161–190.

Herman, P. A. (1985). The effect of repeated readings on reading rate, speech pauses, and word recognition accuracy. *Reading Research Quarterly, 20*, 553–565.

Hiebert, E. H. (1994). A small group literacy intervention with Chapter I students. In E. H. Hiebert & B. M. Taylor (Eds.), *Getting reading right from the start* (pp. 85–106). Boston: Allyn & Bacon.

Hoffman, J. V., McCarthey, S. J., Abbott, J., Christian, C., Corman, L., Curry, C., et al. (1994). So what's new in the new basals? A focus on first grade. *Journal of Reading Behavior, 26*, 47–73.

Hohn, W. E., & Ehri, L. C. (1983). Do alphabet letters help prereaders acquire phonemic segmentation skill? *Journal of Educational Psychology, 75*, 752–762.

Invernizzi, M., Abouzeid, M., & Gill, T. (1994). Using students' invented spellings as a guide for spelling instruction that emphasizes word study. *Elementary School Journal, 95*, 155–167.

Invernizzi, M., Juel, C., & Rosemary, C. A. (1996–1997). A community volunteer tutorial that works. *The Reading Teacher, 50*, 304–311.

Iversen, S., & Tunmer, W. E. (1993). Phonological processing skills and the Reading Recovery program. *Journal of Educational Psychology, 85*, 112–126.

Johnston, F. R. (1995, December). *Learning to read with predictable text: What kinds of words do beginning readers remember?* Paper presented at the annual meeting of the National Reading Conference, New Orleans, LA.

Johnston, F., Juel, C., & Invernizzi, M. (1995). *Guidelines for volunteer tutors of emergent and early readers.* Charlottesville: University of Virginia McGuffey Reading Center.

Juel, C., & Roper-Schneider, D. (1985). The influence of basal readers on first grade reading. *Reading Research Quarterly, 20*, 134–152.

Kame'enui, E. J., Simmons, D. C., Chard, D., & Dickson, S. (1997). Direct instruction reading. In S. A. Stahl & D. A. Hayes (Eds.), *Instructional models in reading* (pp. 59–84). Mahwah, NJ: Erlbaum.

Kean, M. H., Summers, A. A., Raivetz, M. J., & Farber, I. J. (1979). *What works in reading? Summary and results of a joint school district/Federal Reserve Bank empirical study in Philadelphia.* Philadelphia: Office of Research and Evaluation. (ERIC Document Reproduction Service ED 176 216)

Kline, C. L., & Kline, C. L. (1975). Follow-up study of 216 dyslexic children. *Bulletin of the Orton Society, 25*, 127–144.

Koskinen, P. S., Gambrell, L. B., Kapinus, B. A., & Heathington, B. S. (1988). Retelling: A strategy for enhancing students' reading comprehension. *The Reading Teacher, 41*, 892–896.

Leinhardt, G., Zigmond, N., & Cooley, W. (1981). Reading instruction and its effects. *American Educational Research Journal, 18*, 343–361.

Levine, A. (1994, December). Education: The great debate revisited. *Atlantic Monthly, 274*(6), 38–44.

Lovitt, T. C., & Demier, D. M. (1984). An evaluation of the Slingerland method with LD youngsters. *Journal of Learning Disabilities, 17,* 267–272.

Lovitt, T. C., & Hurlburt, M. (1974). Using behavior-analysis techniques to assess the relationship between phonics instruction and oral reading. *Journal of Special Education, 8,* 57–72.

McIntyre, E., & Pressley, M. (1996). *Balanced instruction: Strategies and skills in whole language.* Norwood, MA: Christopher-Gordon.

McKenna, M. C., Stahl, S. A., & Reinking, D. (1994). A critical commentary on research, politics, and whole language. *Journal of Reading Behavior, 26,* 211–233.

Meyer, L. A. (1983). Increased student achievement in reading: One district's strategies. *Research in Rural Education, 1,* 47–51.

Mills, H., O'Keefe, T., & Stephens, D. (1992). *Looking closely: Exploring the role of phonics in one whole language classroom.* Urbana, IL: National Council of Teachers of English.

Monroe, M. (1932). *Children who cannot read.* Chicago: University of Chicago Press.

Moorman, G. B., Blanton, W. E., & McLaughlin, T. (1994). The rhetoric of whole language. *Reading Research Quarterly, 29,* 308–329.

Morris, D. (1992). *Case studies in teaching beginning readers: The Howard Street tutoring manual.* Boone, NC: Fieldstream.

Morris, D., Ervin, C., & Conrad, K. (1996). A case study of middle school reading disability. *The Reading Teacher, 49,* 368–377.

Morrow, L. M., & Tracey, D. (1998). Motivating contexts for young children's literacy development: Implications for word recognition development. In J. Metsala & L. Ehri (Eds.), *Word recognition in beginning literacy* (pp. 341–356). Mahwah, NJ: Erlbaum.

Murray, B. A. (1995). *Which better defines phoneme awareness: Segmentation skill or identity knowledge?* Unpublished doctoral dissertation, University of Georgia, Athens.

Murray, B. A., Stahl, S. A., & Ivey, M. G. (1996). Developing phoneme awareness through alphabet books. *Reading and Writing: An Interdisciplinary Journal, 8,* 307–322.

Ogden, S., Hindman, S., & Turner, S. D. (1989). Multisensory programs in the public schools: A brighter future for LD children. *Annals of Dyslexia, 39,* 247–267.

Osborn, J. (1984). The purposes, uses, and contents of workbooks and some guidelines for publishers. In R. C. Anderson, J. Osborn, & R. J. Tierney (Eds.), *Learning to read in American schools: Basal readers and content texts* (pp. 45–112). Hillsdale, NJ: Erlbaum.

Osborn, J., Stahl, S. A., & Stein, M. (1997). *Teachers' guidelines for evaluating commercial phonics packages.* Newark, DE: International Reading Association.

Pearson, P. D. (1989). Reading the whole language movement. *Elementary School Journal, 90,* 231–241.

Pressley, M., Rankin, J., & Yakoi, L. (1996). A survey of instructional practices of primary teachers nominated as effective in promoting literacy. *Elementary School Journal, 96,* 363–384.

Rasinski, T. V. (1989). Fluency for everyone: Incorporating fluency instruction in the classroom. *The Reading Teacher, 42,* 690–693.

Routman, R. (1996). *Literacy at the crossroads.* Portsmouth, NH: Heinemann.

Samuels, S. J., Schermer, N., & Reinking, D. (1992). Reading fluency: Techniques for making decoding automatic. In S. J. Samuels & A. E. Farstrup (Eds.), *What research says about reading instruction* (2nd ed., pp. 124–144). Newark, DE: International Reading Association.

Schlagal, R. C., & Schlagal, J. H. (1992). The integral character of spelling: Teaching strategies for multiple purposes. *Language Arts, 69,* 418–424.

Shanahan, T., & Barr, R. (1995). Reading Recovery: An independent evaluation of the effects of an early instructional intervention for at-risk learners. *Reading Research Quarterly, 30,* 958–996.

Share, D. L. (1995). Phonological recoding and self-teaching: Sine qua non of reading acquisition. *Cognition, 55,* 151–218.

Silberberg, N. E., Iversen, I. A., & Goins, J. T. (1973). Which remedial reading method works best? *Journal of Learning Disabilities, 6*, 547–556.

Spaulding, R., & Spaulding, W. T. (1962). *The writing road to reading*. New York: Morrow.

Stahl, K. A. D., Stahl, S. A., & McKenna, M. (1997). *The development of phonological awareness and orthographic processing in Reading Recovery*. Unpublished manuscript, University of Georgia, Athens.

Stahl, S. A. (1997). Models of reading instruction: An introduction. In S. A. Stahl & D. A. Hayes (Eds.), *Instructional models in reading* (pp. 1–29). Hillsdale, NJ: Erlbaum.

Stahl, S. A., Heubach, K., & Cramond, B. (1997). *Fluency oriented reading instruction* (Research report). Athens, GA: National Reading Research Center.

Stahl, S. A., & Murray, B. A. (1994). Defining phonological awareness and its relationship to early reading. *Journal of Educational Psychology, 86*, 221–234.

Stahl, S. A., & Murray, B. A. (1998). Issues involved in defining phonological awareness and its relation to early reading. In J. Metsala & L. C. Ehri (Eds.), *Word recognition in beginning literacy* (pp. 65–87). Mahwah, NJ: Erlbaum.

Stahl, S. A., Osborn, J., & Pearson, P. D. (1994). *Six teachers in their classrooms: Looking closely at beginning reading* (Tech. Rep. No. 606). Champaign: Center for the Study of Reading, University of Illinois at Urbana-Champaign.

Stahl, S. A., Suttles, C. W., & Pagnucco, J. R. (1996). The effects of traditional and process literacy instruction on first graders' reading and writing achievement and orientation toward reading. *Journal of Educational Research, 89*, 131–144.

Stanovich, K. E. (1991). The psychology of reading: Evolutionary and revolutionary developments. *Annual Review of Applied Linguistics, 12*, 3–30.

Sullivan, H. J., Okada, M., & Niedermeyer, F. C. (1971). Learning and transfer under two methods of word-attack instruction. *American Educational Research Journal, 8*, 227–240.

Tangel, D. M., & Blachman, B. A. (1992). Effect of phoneme awareness instruction on kindergarten children's invented spellings. *Journal of Reading Behavior, 24*, 233–262.

Taylor, B. M., Short, R., & Shearer, B. (1990, December). *Early intervention in reading: Prevention of reading failure by first grade classroom teachers*. Paper presented at the annual meeting of the National Reading Conference, Miami, FL.

Templeton, S. (1989). Tacit and explicit knowledge of derivational morphology: Foundations for a unified approach to spelling and vocabulary development in the intermediate grades and beyond. *Reading Psychology, 10*, 233–253.

Templeton, S. (1991). Teaching and learning the English spelling system: Reconceptualizing method and purpose. *Elementary School Journal, 92*, 185–201.

Templeton, S. (1992). New trends in an historical perspective: Old story, new resolution— Sound and meaning in spelling. *Language Arts, 69*, 454–463.

Templeton, S., & Bear, D. R. (Eds.). (1992). *Development of orthographic knowledge and the foundations of literacy: A memorial Festschrift for Edmund H. Henderson*. Hillsdale, NJ: Erlbaum.

Trachtenburg, P. (1990). Using children's literature to enhance phonics instruction. *The Reading Teacher, 43*, 648–653.

Traub, N. (1977). *Recipe for reading* (2nd ed.). New York: Walker.

Turner, J. C. (1995). The influence of classroom contexts on young children's motivation for literacy. *Reading Research Quarterly, 30*, 410–441.

Venezky, R. L. (1970). *The structure of English orthography*. The Hague, The Netherlands: Mouton.

Vickery, K. S., Reynolds, V. A., & Cochran, S. W. (1987). Multisensory training approach for reading, spelling and handwriting: Orton-Gillingham based curriculum in a public school setting. *Annals of Dyslexia, 37*, 189–200.

Wasik, B. A., & Slavin, R. E. (1993). Preventing early reading failure with one-to-one tutoring: A review of five programs. *Reading Research Quarterly, 28*, 178–200.

Watson, D. J. (1989). Defining and describing whole language. *Elementary School Journal, 90,* 129–142.

Weaver, C. (1994). *Reading process and practice: From socio-psycholinguistics to whole language.* Portsmouth, NH: Heinemann.

White, T. G., & Cunningham, P. M. (1990, April). *Teaching disadvantaged students to decode and spell by analogy.* Paper presented at the annual meeting of the American Educational Research Association, Boston.

Yaden, D. B., Smolkin, L. B., & MacGillivray, L. (1993). A psychogenetic perspective on children's understanding about letter associations during alphabet book readings. *Journal of Reading Behavior, 25,* 43–68.

Zutell, J., & Rasinski, T. (1989). Reading and spelling connections in third and fifth grade students. *Reading Psychology, 10,* 137–155.

10

More about Phonics

Findings and Reflections

LINNEA C. EHRI

In 1997, the U.S. Congress directed that a panel be convened to review and evaluate research on the effectiveness of various approaches for teaching children to read. The National Reading Panel (NRP) was appointed consisting of 14 members who, during the next 2 years, examined research on instruction in alphabetics, fluency, vocabulary, and comprehension. I chaired the alphabetics subgroup to review research on phonemic awareness and phonics instruction. Many experiments had been published on both topics so we elected to conduct formal meta-analyses.

It was the fall of 1999. The NRP was meeting in Bethesda. I arrived feeling overworked and disabled, with a cast on my ankle to repair a broken bone. We had completed the phonemic awareness meta-analysis and were in the final stages of writing up our findings and conclusions. At that point, we had selected and coded most of the studies of systematic phonics instruction but had gone no further. The report needed to be completed early in 2000. We needed *help* with the data analyses. I knew the best person for the job, so I called Steve Stahl, who was highly knowledgeable about phonics instruction as well as meta-analyses. Thankfully, he agreed. The result was a more timely and thorough analysis of our data and a more informative report. The chapter on systematic phonics instruction was included in the NRP (2000) Report of the Subgroups and was subsequently published in *Review of Educational Research* (Ehri, Nunes, Stahl, & Willows, 2001). I will forever be grateful to Steve for his enthusiasm and willingness to help, for his rich knowledge about phonics instruction, for his technical competence, and for his friendship in this effort.

When the report came out, concerns emerged from several quarters. The most vituperative reactions erupted over the chapter on systematic phonics instruction. Why the excessive fuss about phonics? Steve and I puzzled over this as we constructed a rebuttal to criticisms (Ehri & Stahl, 2001). The report made no claim that phonics instruction is the whole show in teaching beginning reading. As the paper by Stahl, Duffy-Hester, and Dougherty Stahl (1998; reprinted as Chapter 9, this volume) explains, good phonics instruction "is only one part of a total reading program."

However, we did assert that systematic phonics is an essential part that cannot be treated casually. If students do not receive instruction that provides them with a solid foundation in alphabetics and decoding, they will stumble and fall short in learning to read and spell. It was this claim that rankled critics.

My view regarding the importance of phonics instruction has been shaped by my research and that of others, including Steve Stahl. Our findings have clarified the role that knowledge of the alphabetic system plays in learning to read and spell and also have shown that systematic phonics instruction is more effective than other forms involving less or no phonics. My commentary here has three parts. First, I review major points in the Stahl et al. (1998) paper. Second, I present findings of the NRP as they bear on Stahl et al.'s conclusions about the impact of phonics instruction. Third, I consider various ways to read words and their course of development in relationship to various forms of phonics instruction.

"EVERYTHING YOU WANTED TO KNOW ABOUT PHONICS . . . "

At the time that the Stahl et al. (1998) paper was published, many educators were realizing that although the whole language approach engaged students in interesting, meaningful reading and writing activities, it fell short as a method of teaching beginners to decode unfamiliar words and to spell words correctly. In reading text, beginners were too dependent on memorizing the words through repeated readings or guessing print from contextual cues, and they lacked skill in processing letters to determine the identities of words. Instruction that was more phonics-based was needed. The Stahl et al. paper was timely in responding to this resurgence of interest in systematic phonics instruction and to educators' need for guidance in understanding its dimensions.

Many educators had become confused about phonics instruction as a result of the whole language movement. In their zeal to reform how reading was taught, whole language proponents adopted polarizing rhetoric that misled people to believe that whole language was the opposite of phonics instruction rather than a specific form of phonics instruction. This led to an avoidance of many phonics practices, and it suppressed any interest in questions about different ways to teach phonics and that might be more effective. The Stahl et al. paper was a most successful effort to clear up confusion and get thinking back on track.

Stahl et al. (1998) make several recommendations for good phonics instruction in order to correct an abundance of misconceptions: that phonics instruction is necessarily boring, that it depends on mindless worksheets, that it requires memorizing lots of rules, that it monopolizes instructional time and thereby limits the time for reading text. Stahl et al. recommend that phonics instruction begin early so that students become self-sufficient word learners and less dependent on teachers. They recommend the use of direct teacher instruction rather than worksheets to help students acquire phonemic awareness and a thorough knowledge of letters and letter–sound associations. They recommend limiting this instruction to relatively brief periods each day. They advocate focusing on application rather than rule memorization. They recommend having students practice using their alphabetic knowledge to read and write words in order to build accuracy and automaticity. They recommend that teachers monitor students' growth in alphabetic knowledge by observing whether their reading and spelling follow expected developmental paths. They recommend that students engage in plenty of practice reading connected text accompanied by comprehension activities. Various types of texts should be read, not only to practice phonics skills and comprehension but also for enjoyment.

Stahl et al. explain and cite evidence for the effectiveness of several alternative approaches for teaching phonics systematically. Synthetic phonics approaches teach students to sound out and blend letters to form words. Analytic approaches teach beginners to break words into their letter–sound constituents or spelling patterns. Spelling-based approaches have students sort words by spelling patterns or have students combine letters in different ways to make words. Analogy-based approaches teach students to use known words to decode new words sharing syllabic or subsyllabic letter parts with the known words. Studies reveal a slight advantage for synthetic phonics over analytic phonics, but in general the differences among systematic phonics programs are small.

In contrast to systematic programs, embedded phonics approaches such as Reading Recovery and whole language teach phonics casually as needed in the context of "authentic" reading and writing experiences. Typically the embedded approach devotes much less time to phonics than do the other approaches and is not systematic in its coverage of the alphabetic system or in teaching students a letter-based strategy for decoding new words. Rather, students are taught to predict words from context cues and partial letters. In whole language classrooms, phonics is taught when the teacher senses that students need it. Stahl et al. note that in observational studies of whole language classrooms, examples of first-grade teachers teaching consonants are given but no examples of vowel lessons, suggesting that coverage is incomplete when phonics is taught casually as needed.

Stahl et al. remind us that the instructional program is only one ingredient explaining the success of beginning reading instruction. Another ingredient is the student. Stahl et al. offer a constructivist perspective of word learning to capture the idea that students are active learners who regulate their own knowledge acquisition by interacting with the spellings, pronunciations, and meanings of words by correcting and making sense of their errors, by incorporating guidance from teachers, and by adding to or adjusting their existing knowledge to take account of these experiences. As long as phonics programs engage students in knowledge construction that covers the ground and advances them as readers, it may matter less which instructional approach is used.

On the other hand, Stahl et al. raise the possibility that the adoption of a single type of phonics program may not be the optimal approach. Because multiple goals are involved in learning to read and because each approach engages students in a limited set of instructional activities that address one or another of these goals, there may be an advantage to combining activities from the various approaches—for example, teaching students not only to sound out and blend letters but also to invent spellings of words, to sort words by spelling pattern, to decode new words by analogy, to use context to verify that newly decoded words make sense, to read and comprehend different types of texts, and so forth. This is Stahl et al.'s view of comprehensive reading instruction. To be fully effective, it needs to be delivered by a teacher who knows how to use a variety of instructional activities to meet multiple goals and who can assess which activities and goals benefit students at different points in their development as readers.

The Stahl et al. paper is rich in ideas and findings about reading acquisition and instruction. In my commentary, I consider evidence from the NRP report and its consistency with the views of Stahl et al. (1998). Then I discuss students as the other factor in the equation and consider how developmental differences influence the impact of phonics instruction.

THE NATIONAL READING PANEL REPORT ON SYSTEMATIC PHONICS INSTRUCTION

The NRP conducted a meta-analysis to assess the effectiveness of systematic phonics instruction (Ehri et al., 2001; National Reading Panel, 2000). Phonics instruction is considered systematic when the major letter–sound associations are taught in a clearly defined sequence, and students are taught to use them to decode unfamiliar words.

A meta-analysis offers a statistical means for quantifying the impact of an instructional treatment on an outcome by contrasting it to a control treatment and compiling effects across several studies. The resulting statistic is an average effect size. In the meta-analysis of phonics instruction, a search of the literature uncovered 38 experimental or quasi-experimental studies that compared phonics treatment groups to control groups receiving unsystematic or no phonics instruction. These studies were published after 1970 in refereed journals. They measured reading as an outcome. The students ranged from kindergarten to sixth grade and included normally achieving readers, beginners at risk for future reading difficulties, older low-achieving readers, and students with a reading disability.

Three categories of systematic phonics instruction were distinguished: synthetic phonics, analogy phonics that taught the use of larger units such as onsets and rimes to read words, and a miscellaneous category. Five categories of control treatments that provided less phonics or no phonics instruction were formed based on authors' descriptions: basal, regular curriculum, whole word, whole language, and a miscellaneous category. Among the 38 studies were some that included more than one type of phonics instruction or more than one grade level. These types and levels were separated to yield 66 treatment–control group comparisons. Effects of phonics treatments were assessed on various reading and spelling outcomes measured at the end of training (i.e., reading words or pseudowords, spelling words, reading text orally, and comprehending text).

Effect sizes (d) were averaged across comparisons and tested statistically. One question was whether effect sizes were significantly greater than zero, indicating that phonics groups outperformed control groups. Another question was whether effect sizes differed significantly from each other, for example, whether synthetic phonics showed larger effects than larger-unit phonics programs. According to Cohen's (1988) rule of thumb, $d = 0.20$ is considered small, $d = 0.50$ is moderate, and $d = 0.80$ is considered a large effect size.

Results supported many of the conclusions reached by Stahl et al. (1998). Students who received systematic phonics instruction were better readers at the end of training than students receiving less or no phonics instruction. The overall effect size was significantly greater than zero and moderate in size, $d = 0.41$. Phonics instruction produced superior performance compared to control instruction, not only in word and nonword decoding but also in spelling words, in reading text orally, and in comprehending text. The ability to decode words and pseudowords showed significantly larger effect sizes than the other outcomes, not surprisingly as the main goal of phonics instruction is to teach students to decode novel words.

When the grade levels of students were considered, the effect of phonics instruction proved significantly larger for beginning readers ($d = 0.55$ for kindergartners through first graders) than for older readers ($d = 0.27$ for second through sixth graders). Moreover, when groups of younger and older good and poor readers were distinguished and compared, effect sizes were greater for younger average and at-risk students (in kindergarten and first grade) than for average and poor readers beyond first grade. This confirms the Stahl et al. recommendation that systematic phonics instruction should begin early to be most effective.

Several different types of phonics programs were distinguished by Stahl et al. However, all these types did not occur in sufficient numbers to draw comparisons in the meta-analysis. We were able to group studies into three categories: synthetic phonics (39 comparisons), larger-unit phonics programs (11 comparisons), and miscellaneous phonics (10 comparisons). Effect sizes for all categories were statistically greater than zero, indicating that all types of phonics programs yielded superior reading performance compared to controls. Although synthetic programs appeared to have an edge over the others, the difference was not statistically significant. These findings are consistent with the conclusions reached by Stahl et al. that systematic phonics programs produce superior readers but that differences between programs are small.

We also examined whether the method of instruction taught to control groups (i.e., basal, regular curriculum, whole language, whole word, and miscellaneous) made any difference in the advantage seen for phonics instruction. No differences were detected. Regardless of the type of instruction received by the control group, the group receiving systematic phonics showed significantly higher reading scores.

Stahl et al. (1998) characterize whole language as a form of embedded phonics in which letter–sound instruction is handled casually rather than thoroughly, and students are not taught a strategy for using letters to decode novel words. In our analysis, groups receiving a whole language approach were treated as control groups receiving "less phonics" unsystematically. Our data set included 12 cases comparing systematic phonics to whole language controls. Results revealed a significant effect size, $d = 0.31$, showing that full systematic phonics programs were more effective than partial "as needed" phonics programs.

Interestingly our data set also included 10 comparisons in which control groups received whole word instruction. This is a "no phonics" approach. Students are taught to recognize whole words instantly without breaking them into letter–sound parts and without any alphabetics instruction. The effect size favoring phonics instruction over whole word instruction was significant, $d = 0.51$, and was somewhat larger than the effect size seen with whole language control groups. Although the difference between effect sizes fell short of statistical significance, it suggests that programs teaching some phonics are better than programs offering no phonics.

In sum, findings of the NRP meta-analysis supported and extended assertions and conclusions reached by Stahl et al. Phonics instruction was found to be more effective when it began early. Systematic programs were more effective than unsystematic programs and programs teaching no phonics. Variations in the type of phonics programs made relatively little difference in their effectiveness. Systematic phonics instruction boosted not just decoding skill, which is directly taught, but all forms of reading and spelling. Its impact was much reduced in older readers beyond first grade, particularly its impact on their spelling and comprehension, and its benefit for low-achieving readers. It may be that once reading habits and strategies are established through other approaches, it is harder to intervene with phonics instruction in order to implant decoding as a central strategy for reading unfamiliar words.

LINKS BETWEEN THE DEVELOPMENT OF WORD READING PROCESSES AND PHONICS INSTRUCTION

Children vary widely in their reading and writing skills and experiences when they enter school. For children who know little about letters or phonemic awareness when they begin formal reading instruction, an effective phonics program must begin from zero and must teach all of the ingredients as well as their integration and application to word and text reading and to spelling. For children at various points beyond this, some of the ingredients have already been acquired so they may not need instructional attention in order to make progress.

Juel and Minden-Cupp (2000) provide some correlational evidence that the effectiveness of beginning reading instruction is related to the entering skills of students. They studied the relationship between various forms of first-grade instruction and students' growth in word reading during the year by observing four teachers and their students. Findings indicated that early and intensive immersion in phonics proved much more beneficial for children who entered first grade with few literacy skills than a program consisting of trade book reading combined with embedded phonics. The latter approach produced only minimal growth for these children. In contrast, first graders who entered with letter knowledge and some word reading skill showed the reverse pattern. They made the most progress in classrooms that emphasized text reading and taught phonics as needed. Connor, Morrison, and Katch (2004) report similar findings.

The impact of phonics instruction on children at different developmental levels can be understood by taking a closer look at how beginners read words and their course of development. Four different ways of reading words can be distinguished (Ehri, 1990, 1998). Three of these ways describe alternative strategies for reading words that are unfamiliar in print, and one way describes how words are read that are familiar in print because they have been read before. Unfamiliar words may be read by sounding out and blending letters to form recognizable words, or by analogizing to known words sharing spelling patterns (e.g., reading *slide* by analogy to *ride*), or by prediction based on partial letters and context. Familiar words are read by "sight," that is, by accessing them in memory directly from their written forms. Studies indicate that *alphabetic* knowledge provides the foundation for learning to read words by sight. Sight words are learned when connections are formed between letters in spellings and phonemes in pronunciations, thereby securing the spellings in memory (Ehri, 1992, 1998; Ehri & Saltmarsh, 1995; Rack, Hulme, Snowling, & Wightman, 1994; Share, 1999).

Although several strategies are useful for reading words that are unfamiliar in print, phonics programs teach only one strategy. Synthetic phonics programs teach sounding out and blending to decode words. Larger-unit phonics programs teach students to analogize by recognizing shared spelling patterns in known and new words. Embedded phonics programs emphasize the use of semantic cues along with graphic cues to predict the identities of words.

In contrast, the process of reading words by sight is neglected in phonics programs. One reason is that sight word learning has been viewed as a way of reading words that does not involve letter–sound knowledge and hence is regarded as the opposite of decoding words. In earlier times, debates among reading experts pitted the two methods against each other (Chall, 1967). However, this view is mistaken. Beginners need the alphabetic skills that are taught systematically in phonics programs to secure sight words in memory. Hence, phonics instruction provides the foundation for acquiring a well-secured sight vocabulary.

To assess the impact of various types of phonics instruction, it is important to consider the developmental level of students. To portray the emergence of word reading processes in beginning readers, I have distinguished four developmental phases in my research (Ehri, 1999, 2005; Ehri & McCormick, 1998). The phases are prealphabetic, partial alphabetic, full alphabetic, and consolidated alphabetic. They are labeled to reflect the *predominant* type of alphabetic knowledge that readers use to read words.

The first prealphabetic phase depicts prereaders before they have learned much about alphabetics. Their knowledge of letters and phonemic awareness is limited or nil. If these children are observed reading text, they do it by pretend-reading stories that they have heard others read and reread. If they recognize individual words, they do it by noting and remembering salient visual cues in or around the word, such as the golden arches to read *McDonald's* or the two posts to read *yellow*. They are essentially nonreaders when it comes to recognizing words from their letters. Children who begin formal reading instruction as prealphabetic readers need thorough immersion in letter name/sound instruction along with phonemic awareness before they can be expected to learn to read or write words.

The partial alphabetic phase characterizes readers once they acquire some phonemic awareness and knowledge of letter names or sounds and can use their knowledge to process partial letter cues in words to read or spell them. Although they lack sufficient knowledge to decode new words by sounding out or analogizing, they can remember how to read words by connecting some of the letters seen in spellings to sounds they detect in pronunciations and storing these connections in memory (e.g., initial and final consonants to remember how to read *kitten*). If they know the names of letters, they can use sounds in the names to form these connections (Treiman, Tincoff, Rodriguez, Mouzaki, & Francis, 1998). For example, the names of K, T, and N contain the sounds that these letters symbolize in *kitten*. It turns out that most letter names contain sounds that are useful for forming connections in at least some words. In fact, all but the letter W. Partial phase readers can use their letter knowledge to invent simplified spellings containing phonetically plausible letters, for example, *seed* spelled CD or *white* spelled YT. However, they have trouble remembering correct spellings of words because they lack knowledge of the conventional alphabetic system, especially vowels.

Children in this phase benefit from systematic phonics instruction in acquiring the grapheme–phoneme relations they have not yet learned, particularly vowels, and learning how to use these to decode new words. Without this knowledge, they will continue to process and remember only partial cues in new words they read, so sight words will not be well secured in memory and will be confused with other similarly spelled words. Lacking decoding skill, they will use context plus partial letters to guess unfamiliar words in text (Stanovich, 1980). As a result, they will read text more slowly and less accurately. These characteristics have been found to portray not only novice beginning readers but also older low-achieving readers and students beyond first grade with a reading disability.

Embedded phonics programs would not be expected to enable readers in the partial alphabetic phase to make much progress, as Juel and Minden-Cupp (2000) found. This approach does not teach the various skills needed to become full phase readers. For example, students are not likely to learn the major grapheme–phoneme correspondences because their needs are assessed on the basis of their text reading. Miscues can arise not only from inadequate letter–sound knowledge but also from context-based predictions, so text reading is not a reliable indicator of the holes in students' alphabetic knowledge. In fact, words that are predicted correctly on the basis of context cues will mislead and cause teachers to overestimate students' letter–sound knowledge. Because an embedded phonics approach does not teach strategies for decoding new words from their written letters without contextual support, students will continue to rely on partial letter cues for reading words by sight and will remain stuck in the partial alphabetic phase.

The full alphabetic phase characterizes beginners who have acquired foundational alphabetic knowledge and can read words in multiple ways. They have learned the major grapheme–phoneme correspondences. They possess phoneme segmentation and blending skills. They can decode novel words. As a result, they are able to build their sight vocabularies by processing the full array of connections to bond spellings to pronunciations and meanings in memory. Possessing fully specified representations enables students to read words very accurately from their letters without any need to depend on context. They utilize context to cross-check and confirm words rather than to identify the words. As students practice reading, their ability to access words in memory speeds up and they can recognize them automatically. They can invent fully phonetic, conventional spellings of words and can remember the correct spellings of words they practice reading or writing. Children in this phase have succeeded in learning and applying the knowledge and skills that systematic phonics instruction aims to teach. Further development is fostered mainly by experiences reading and comprehending text so that readers' sight vocabularies continue to grow. Also spelling instruction and writing practice contribute by enhancing readers' memory for the complete spellings of words. Students who have become full alphabetic readers would be expected to benefit from embedded phonics programs that offer rich text reading and writing experiences, as Juel and Minden-Cupp (2000) found.

The consolidated alphabetic phase characterizes readers who can decode new words by sounding out and blending units larger than individual graphemes. These units include syllabic and subsyllabic spellings such as onsets, rimes, prefixes, suffixes, and common spelling patterns. Also, they include known words appearing in other words (e.g., *at*, *in*, *on*, *up*). Grapheme–phoneme blends become consolidated into larger units as readers accumulate fully secured sight words in memory. Consolidated units emerge from spelling patterns that recur in parts of known words and also from whole sight words that are read as single units. Teaching and giving students practice breaking new words into parts to read them also helps to form consolidated units. Knowing larger units eases the task of decoding new words because it reduces the number of sounds held in short-term memory before blending them. For example, to read *interest*, the number is reduced from eight graphophonemes to three syllabic units (in-ter-est). Readers in this phase use larger units not only to decode and analogize but also to form the connections that secure new sight words in memory.

In analogy phonics programs, the formation and use of larger units to read new words is the focus of instruction (Gaskins et al., 1988; Lovett et al., 2000). Keywords are taught as sight words, typically about four words per week. Their subsyllabic parts, particularly onsets and rimes, are analyzed. Students practice using known words to read new words. For example, to read *interest*, they might use *her* to read *ter* and *nest* to read *est*.

From the perspective of phase theory, analogy phonics programs are more appropriate for moving students from the full to the consolidated phase than from the partial to the full phase. It takes time for readers to accumulate a sufficient number of keywords in memory before analogizing becomes useful for reading a variety of unfamiliar words. Moreover, analogizing is unlikely to work for beginners in the partial alphabetic phase. If only partial spellings of keywords are remembered, accurate matches between known and new words cannot be made. Students need to possess graphophonemic knowledge, especially vowels, so that keywords and their subsyllabic parts can be fully secured in memory. Also, they need some decoding skill to sound out and blend units in the new words (Ehri & Robbins, 1992). They need to be in the full alphabetic phase to *begin* forming and using larger units, and they need to be in the consolidated phase for the use of larger units to *predominate* in reading words.

Teaching students to sound out and blend graphemes in synthetic phonics programs offers a faster way than analogy phonics to get beginners off the ground in reading new words. It also instills the habit of fully processing letters in words to read them. However, as words grow longer, students have a harder time retaining all the sounds of the letters in short-term memory before blending them. As explained previously, the solution is to consolidate grapheme–phoneme units into larger syllabic units to ease the task of blending. However, synthetic phonics approaches typically do not teach students to decode using larger units.

Stahl et al. (1998) offer a solution. They recommend a more comprehensive approach to phonics instruction that combines features from different programs. An example that enriches the analogy approach with grapheme–phoneme instruction, sight word learning, and spelling is offered by Gaskins, Ehri, Cress, O'Hara, and Donnelly (1996–1997). Their Word Detectives program teaches students to read new words by analogy to keywords. Each week three to four keywords are taught as sight words. To secure the keywords in memory, students are taught to segment the words into phonemes and link them to graphemes in spellings. They also practice remembering how to spell the keywords. They learn to form and use larger chunks of letters by detecting common parts shared by keywords and new words. Results of a 4-year longitudinal study comparing a pure analogy approach to the combined approach revealed superior performance by students receiving the combined approach during the first 2 years of instruction (Ehri, Satlow, & Gaskins, 2006).

Phase theory carries implications for the appropriate use of different types of text. Predictable text can be used during the prealphabetic phase to introduce children to the idea of text reading and to provide opportunities to acquire concepts about print (Clay, 1985). As children learn letters and phonemic awareness, they can practice fingerpoint reading by forming 1:1 matches between written and spoken words (Morris, Bloodgood, Lomax, & Perney, 2003). This will help them move into the partial alphabetic phase. Decodable texts can provide intense concentrated practice using letter–sound relations to decode words and will help students move into the full phase. It is important for words in decodable texts to be repeated sufficiently often so that they become sight words. Books that require a larger bank of sight words and stronger decoding ability but that are still relatively short in length, such as the *Clifford* or *Henry and Mudge* series, can provide students with practice using letter chunks as well as letter sounds to read new words. This can help children move from the full to the consolidated phase. Longer, more difficult chapter books that require larger sight vocabularies and automaticity in recognizing words are best delayed until later in the consolidated phase. To expose readers to literature that is more complex than their current phase of development, teachers might guide students reading such texts in a shared setting.

In sum, analyses based on phase theory suggest that each type of phonics program benefits beginning readers. However, the point during development when beginners are ready to benefit differs. Synthetic phonics may work best at the outset of formal reading instruction to ensure that beginners learn the major grapheme–phoneme correspondences, phonemic awareness, and the strategy of sounding out and blending to decode unfamiliar words. As students use this strategy to secure basic sight words in memory through the reading of simple text, they become ready to benefit from analogy phonics, which teaches them to decode using larger spelling units drawn from familiar sight words. Once students gain decoding skills and a sufficient sight vocabulary to read the variety of words in trade books, they can benefit from embedded phonics programs. Practice reading rich "authentic literature" can extend students' sight vocabularies, their fluency, their comprehension, and their enjoyment of reading. Although we have discussed only three types of phonics programs, there are others mentioned by Stahl et al. (1998) that contribute to effective practices as well, such as spelling-based phonics programs. As Stahl et al. suggest, because students stand to gain from all these approaches, a comprehensive approach to phonics instruction is the call of the future.

REFERENCES

Chall, J. (1967). *Learning to read: The great debate*. New York: McGraw-Hill.

Clay, M. (1985). *The early detection of reading difficulties* (3rd ed.). Portsmouth, NH: Heinemann.

Cohen, J. (1988). *Statistical power analysis for the behavioral sciences* (2nd ed.). Hillsdale, NJ: Erlbaum.

Connor, C., Morrison, F., & Katch, E. (2004). Beyond the reading wars: The effect of classroom instruction by child interactions on early reading. *Scientific Studies of Reading, 8,* 305–336.

Ehri, L. (1990). Development of the ability to read words. In R. Barr, M. Kamil, P. Mosenthal, & P. Pearson (Eds.), *Handbook of reading research* (Vol. 2, pp. 383–417). New York: Longman.

Ehri, L. (1992). Reconceptualizing the development of sight word reading and its relationship to recoding. In P. Gough, L. Ehri, & R. Treiman (Eds.), *Reading acquisition* (pp. 107–143). Hillsdale, NJ: Erlbaum.

Ehri, L. (1998). Grapheme–phoneme knowledge is essential for learning to read words in English. In J. Metsala & L. Ehri (Eds.), *Word recognition in beginning literacy* (pp. 3–40). Mahwah, NJ: Erlbaum.

Ehri, L. (1999). Phases of development in learning to read words. In J. Oakhill & R. Beard (Eds.), *Reading development and the teaching of reading: A psychological perspective* (pp. 79–108). Oxford, UK: Blackwell.

Ehri, L. (2005). Development of sight word reading: Phases and findings. In M. Snowling & C. Hulme (Eds.), *The science of reading: A handbook* (pp. 135–154). Oxford, UK: Blackwell.

Ehri, L., & McCormick, S. (1998). Phases of word learning: Implications for instruction with delayed and disabled readers. *Reading and Writing Quarterly, 14*, 135–163.

Ehri, L., Nunes, S., Stahl, S., & Willows, D. (2001). Systematic phonics instruction helps students learn to read: Evidence from the National Reading Panel's meta-analysis. *Review of Educational Research, 71*, 393–447.

Ehri, L., & Robbins, C. (1992). Beginners need some decoding skill to read words by analogy. *Reading Research Quarterly, 27*, 12–26.

Ehri, L., & Saltmarsh, J. (1995) Beginning readers outperform older disabled readers in learning to read words by sight. *Reading and Writing: An Interdisciplinary Journal, 7*, 295–326.

Ehri, L., Satlow, E., & Gaskins, I. (2006). *Word reading instruction: Graphophonemic analysis strengthens the keyword analogy method for struggling readers*. Manuscript submitted for publication.

Ehri, L., & Stahl, S. (2001). Beyond smoke and mirrors: Putting out the fire. *Phi Delta Kappan, 83*, 17–20.

Gaskins, I., Downer, M., Anderson, R., Cunningham, P., Gaskins, R., Schommer, M., et al. (1988). A metacognitive approach to phonics: Using what you know to decode what you don't know. *Remedial and Special Education, 9*, 36–41.

Gaskins, I., Ehri, L., Cress, C., O'Hara, C., & Donnelly, K. (1996–1997). Procedures for word learning: Making discoveries about words. *The Reading Teacher, 50*, 312–327.

Juel, C., & Minden-Cupp, C. (2000). Learning to read words: Linguistic units and instructional strategies. *Reading Research Quarterly, 35*, 458–492.

Lovett, M., Lacerenza, L., Borden, S., Frijters, J., Steinbach, K., & DePalma, M. (2000). Components of effective remediation for developmental reading disabilities: Combining phonological and strategy-based instruction to improve outcomes. *Journal of Educational Psychology, 92*, 263–283.

Morris, D., Bloodgood, J., Lomax, R., & Perney, J. (2003). Developmental steps in learning to read: A longitudinal study in kindergarten and first grade. *Reading Research Quarterly, 38*, 302–328.

National Reading Panel. (2000). *Report of the National Reading Panel: Teaching children to read: An evidence-based assessment of the scientific research literature on reading and its implications for reading instruction: Reports of the subgroups*. Rockville, MD: NICHD Clearinghouse.

Rack, J., Hulme, C., Snowling, M., & Wightman, J. (1994). The role of phonology in young children learning to read words: The direct-mapping hypothesis. *Journal of Experimental Child Psychology, 57*, 42–71.

Share, D. (1999). Phonological recoding and orthographic learning: A direct test of the self-teaching hypothesis. *Journal of Experimental Child Psychology, 72*, 95–129.

Stahl, S., Duffy-Hester, A., & Stahl, K. (1998). Everything you wanted to know about phonics (but were afraid to ask). *Reading Research Quarterly, 33*, 338–355.

Stanovich, K. (1980). Toward an interactive–compensatory model of individual differences in the development of reading fluency. *Reading Research Quarterly, 16*, 32–71.

Treiman, R., Tincoff, R., Rodriguez, K., Mouzaki, A., & Francis, D. (1998). The foundations of literacy: Learning the sounds of letters. *Child Development, 69*, 1524–1540.

III | FLUENCY

11

Seeking Understanding about Reading Fluency

The Contributions of Steven A. Stahl

TIMOTHY RASINSKI
JAMES HOFFMAN

Steven Stahl was one of a handful of literacy scholars in the 1990s who focused their research on the development of decoding abilities in young readers. Clearly, Jeanne Chall, Steve's academic mentor at Harvard, had a profound impact on his thinking and writing. As the field of reading became increasingly politicized and polarized in the late 1990s, Steve's research and writing were often used to build a case for greater attention to code in instruction and, even further, to support a conservative agenda for the development of "scientific" materials and programs. To his credit, Steve never jumped on this bandwagon. Instead, he relied on scholarship and research to guide his position on issues. He embraced complexity as inherent in the teaching and learning of reading and resisted any simplistic assertions regarding learning to read or quick-fix "solutions" regarding the teaching of reading.

The impact of the work of Steven Stahl can be seen across the reading process and the reading curriculum. Steve's work has led to better understandings and improved instruction in phonemic awareness and early reading, phonics and word decoding, vocabulary, comprehension, and assessment. Most recently, Steve's work has focused on what has been called "the neglected goal" (Allington, 1983) of reading curriculum—reading fluency.

Reading fluency is the ability to negotiate the print level of text—that is, the ability to read words accurately, effortlessly (automatically), and with appropriate phrasing and expression when reading orally. The significance of reading fluency in the overall reading process can be found in LaBerge and Samuels's (1974) theory of automatic information processing in reading. They theorize that all readers have a limited amount of attention, or cognitive resources, that can be applied to reading. Two reading tasks require these resources—word decoding and comprehension. If readers have to apply too much of their limited cognitive resources to the decoding task, then comprehension may suffer as they may not have sufficient cognitive resources available to make sense of what they just read. Thus, although fluency may deal with readers' ability to negotiate the surface level of texts, it has implications for reading comprehension and overall proficiency in reading.

Recent research suggests that reading fluency has a strong connection to comprehension. In one analysis of NAEP (National Assessment of Educational Progress) data, fourth-grade students' oral reading fluency scores were significantly related to silent reading comprehension (Pinnell et al., 1995). Students who read with good accuracy, rate, and expression tended to be the best comprehenders while reading silently. Every drop in fluency was marked by a drop in silent reading comprehension. More recently, in their chapter on reading comprehension difficulties, Duke, Pressley, and Hilden (2004) suggest that reading fluency may be at the heart of reading comprehension problems for a substantial number of students.

Fluency was not Steve's first interest in reading. I (TR) recall asking Steve in the early 1990s if in his clinical work with struggling readers at the University of Georgia he looked at reading rate as a diagnostic variable. He indicated that, at that time, word recognition accuracy was all he used to determine whether readers had developed competency with words and the surface level of text. However, after examining the role of phonemic awareness, vocabulary, and phonics in the reading process, Steve turned his attention to reading fluency while at the National Reading Research Center at the University of Georgia. His initial foray into reading fluency was an intervention study with second-grade students (Stahl, Heubach, & Cramond, 1997; Stahl & Heubach, 2005, reprinted as Chapter 12, this volume). Knowing that modeling fluent reading, repeated readings, and assisted reading have been recommended to promote fluency in reading (Rasinski, 1989), Steve and his colleagues worked to develop an instructional model for teaching fluency. I (JH) had numerous conversations during this time period with Steve regarding a procedure we had developed and experimented with (Oral Recitation Lesson, or ORL; Hoffman & Crone, 1985; Hoffman, 1987). Steve developed an integrated fluency lesson called Fluency-Oriented Reading Instruction (FORI), modeled in part after the ORL, that could be employed with a basal reading program and tested over a 2-year period with intact classrooms of second-grade students. The FORI model used texts that were part of a basal reading program and consisted of the following steps:

- The story is read to students by their teacher.
- Teacher and students discuss the content of the story.
- Optional: Students echo read the story with the teacher.
- Students read the story at home.
- Optional: Students practice a segment of the story.
- Optional: Students continue to practice the story at home two or three times.
- In school, students read the story again with a partner.
- Students engage independently in further work with the story through journals and worksheets.

Reading progress was measured using an informal reading inventory. The results of implementing FORI with second graders were positive and impressive. In the initial year of implementation students made, on average, a gain of 1.88 years in their instructional reading level. The gains occurred regardless of the initial reading level of the students—some students began the year reading below a primer level while others were at the fourth-grade reader. Students beginning the year reading below the primer level made, on average, gains of two grade levels in reading. Of the 85 students in the four classes that were part of the study only 3 were unable to read a second-grade passage at the end of the year.

In the second year of FORI implementation students made an average gain of 1.77 years in their reading. Students who began the second year of the study reading below the primer made an average gain of 2.25 years in reading growth. Nine of the 20 students who were unable to read the primer passage at the beginning of the year were reading at a second-grade level or higher. These results for the struggling readers were particularly impressive in light of the fact that during the previous school year they had made considerably less than a year's reading growth.

This study added significantly to our understanding of fluency as an instructional variable in the primary grades. First, the study demonstrated that fluency instruction could be sustained over the course of a school year. Previous instructional interventions in fluency were limited to considerably shorter durations. Teachers in the study indicated that they continued using fluency instruction in the year after the study, even though support from the researchers was not provided, thus indicating that the teachers saw the instructional value of fluency instruction. Second, the study demonstrated that fluency instruction in a regular classroom context could be implemented and could lead to significant gains in accuracy, fluency, comprehension, and overall reading achievement. Third, Steve's work provided the quantitative evidence for effectiveness that was absent from much of the earlier work.

Steve followed up this work on fluency with reflection on the role of reading fluency in the reading process and its place in reading instruction. Along with his colleague Melanie Kuhn, Steve reviewed the literature related to reading fluency in a paper for the Center for the Improvement of Early Reading Achievement (CIERA) (Kuhn & Stahl, 2000). Kuhn and Stahl defined reading fluency, set it within current models and theories of the reading process, and reviewed research related to its impact on student achievement using a variety of instructional approaches in a variety of instructional settings. Their findings set the stage for more direct research into the role of reading fluency in the reading process and reading instruction.

> Fluency instruction seems to be a promising approach to teaching children in the confirmation and fluency stage of reading, especially those in late first and second grades, but also older children with reading problems who are disfluent. Although the basic approaches have been around for over thirty years, there are many unanswered questions. We are still not sure what the role of repetitive reading is, whether increasing the amount of reading would have similar effects, what the effects of reading texts at a range of relative difficulties are, and whether fluency instruction works by improving automatic word recognition or whether it affects perception of phrasal boundaries. These are questions worthy of exploration. . . . We have come to view fluency instruction as successful in improving the reading achievement of children at a certain point in their reading development. However, we have seen relatively little of this instruction in the schools. To help more readers move from labored decoding to the construction of meaning, we consider it to be important that educators integrate these techniques in the classroom more frequently. (Kuhn & Stahl, 2000, pp. 26–27)

At the time of his death, Steve, along with colleagues Melanie Kuhn, Paula Schwanenflugel, and Lesley Morrow, was engaged in a long-term study of reading fluency instruction in second-grade classrooms (see Stahl & Heubach, 2005, reprinted as Chapter 12, this volume). This study will most definitely have a significant impact on our understanding of reading fluency in the reading process and reading acquisition and its appropriate place in the school reading curriculum.

STEVE STAHL'S CONTRIBUTION TO READING FLUENCY

Although Steven Stahl's work in reading fluency has been cut short by his death, there is no doubt that his work will have a profound influence in this important area of reading. In this portion of our chapter we discuss what we feel is Steve's legacy to reading fluency.

Defining Fluency

Although Steve did not invent the notion of reading fluency, he certainly helped to clarify our understanding of it and he helped to anchor it in a theory of reading development. Steve accepted LaBerge and Samuels's idea that reading fluency involved gaining power or automaticity over the surface-level processing of text—most notably word decoding. Before readers can fully marshal their cognitive resources to the task of comprehending the text they must automatize their word decoding. Otherwise, a significant amount of their cognitive resources must be diverted to consciously attending to word decoding.

Steve also recognized, however, that prosody, the embedding of melodic or expressive features of oral language into reading, plays a part in fluency. Fluent readers not only process words in an automatic fashion but also give meaning to the text through their voicing of words while reading orally. Although he was unsure whether prosody was a cause or consequence of comprehension, he certainly felt that it belonged on the table in any discussion of reading fluency.

In addition to solidifying our definition of reading fluency, Steve's work helped situate fluency in theoretical models of reading. In particular, Steve saw fluency as integral to both Chall's (1996) stage model of reading and Ehri's (1995) phases of sight word development. By placing fluency within models of reading development Steve has helped scholars (and practitioners) design instructional programs that optimize appropriate time and method for instruction in reading fluency.

Long-Term Fluency Instruction

Most studies of fluency instruction have taken place over the short term—weeks or months at best. These studies begged the question: Is it possible to sustain the type of reading practice entailed in reading fluency instruction over an extended period of time and have it yield positive results? Steve's studies of fluency instruction in second-grade classrooms have been among the first that have actually examined the effects of long-term instruction in fluency.

Steve's work demonstrated that it is possible to successfully incorporate elements of repeated and assisted reading into second-grade classrooms over an extended period. Students can make significant progress in their overall reading proficiency as a result of long-term fluency instruction. Moreover, Steve's work demonstrated that it is possible to sustain repeated and assisted reading practice for months at a time without students and teachers suffering from instructional fatigue. Indeed,

Steve's work suggests that teachers and students found fluency instruction engaging and worthwhile over the course of the school year.

Integrating Fluency Instruction

Since the National Reading Panel identified fluency as a key component of school reading programs, schools and teachers have struggled with how to fit reading fluency into the school curriculum. Steve's implementation of his model of fluency instruction, FORI, has demonstrated compellingly that fluency can easily be integrated into existing reading programs, from basal-oriented programs to more literature-based approaches. Indeed, Steve's work in fluency has shown that passages that are already employed for reading instruction can be used for fluency development. Clearly, Steve has shown that fluency instruction does not necessarily require a special curriculum, significant amounts of additional instructional time, or additional texts and materials for teaching fluency. Informed teachers and schools can make it work with the resources they already have at their disposal.

FLUENCY INTO THE FUTURE

Steve's work in fluency has had a substantial impact on our understanding of and instruction in fluency—from anchoring our understanding of fluency in the reading process to demonstrating how it can be taught, Steve's work will endure for a long time. Building on Steve's legacy in this area, we see other questions that we think Steve may have asked if he had had the opportunity to continue his scholarly work in this area.

Wide Reading, Repeated Reading, and Assisted Reading

One of the hallmarks of fluency instruction has been Samuels's (1979) method of repeated readings. Students practice one particular passage to a point of fluency before moving on to another. Another type of practice in reading is wide reading, reading one passage and then moving on to another. We think that Steve would have questioned whether one of these methods was superior for building reading fluency and under what conditions might one be more effective. Indeed, Steve's yet to be completed work in fluency may provide us with some insight into this important question.

Along with repeated reading, assisted, paired, or partner reading has been advocated to promote reading fluency. Although Steve recognized the value of this type of reading, he was also interested in why it seemed to work to promote reading progress. Steve had already begun to look at the nature of the pairing of readers and we are certain he would have loved to have teased apart other aspects of assisted reading to determine the nature of its efficacy.

Silent versus Oral Reading

The findings of the National Reading Panel (2000) suggest that oral reading is superior to silent reading for developing fluency in reading. Regardless of the nature of the text or the type of practice, oral reading appears to have the edge. Steve, we think, would have questioned this finding and would have tried to verify the veracity of this conclusion. If oral reading is superior, what is it about oral reading that leads to this advantage? And if oral reading is indeed superior, how does it fit into a reading curriculum that places greater value on silent reading, the type of reading that dominates most adult reading?

Types of Material for Developing Fluency

Conventional wisdom says that students should be given reading material that is at their instructional reading level (material that they can read with approximately 95% accuracy). It could be argued, however, that students who are working on fluency need even easier material in order to gain automaticity and control over less challenging material before moving on to texts that have greater lexical and syntactic sophistication.

Steve, however, suggested that just the opposite may be case—that students who are engaged in fluency instruction may benefit from material that is somewhat above instructional level. Indeed, this makes sense as students who engage in repeated readings will have multiple opportunities to master challenging texts—and texts that present greater challenge should lead to accelerated growth. This question of text difficulty is one that we think needs to be addressed and one that we think Steve would have loved to tackle.

The Nature and Role of Prosody in Fluency Instruction

Steve was sure to include prosody in his definition of reading fluency. But just how does prosody fit into fluency instruction? Does a specific focus on prosodic reading lead to improvements in reading achievement? What elements of prosody are most important? How can prosody best be measured? Is prosodic reading, by itself, a worthy goal of instruction in the reading program? Again, these are fascinating questions for which Steve's unfinished work with Melanie Kuhn, Paula Schwanenflugel, and Lesley Morrow may begin to provide some answers and insight.

Fluency and Technology

Steve noted that close-captioned television, a form of assisted reading, may have the potential to provide improvements in fluency similar to those found in other studies of assisted reading (see Carver & Hoffman, 1981, for an early application of computer-assisted instruction with repeated readings to support the development of fluency). Indeed, technology that can provide assisted and repeated reading experiences for students as well as model read passages and provide cues for textual phrasing seems ideally suited for fluency instruction. We think Steve would have been in the vanguard of scholars recommending greater experimentation in the use of technology to teach fluency.

Fluency Assessment

We know that Steve was always interested in reading assessment and how best to assess reading fluency would have been a question he would love to have seen answered. Commonly used now, reading rate measures (Deno, 1985; Rasinski, 2004) provide an indication of decoding automaticity. However, they fail to capture the prosodic nature of fluency. Moreover, too great a focus on reading rate may lead to the unintended consequence of fluency instruction focusing solely on building students' reading rate and students' developing a metacognitive model of fluency as reading fast. We think Steve would have wanted to explore the nature of reading fluency from an assessment perspective.

Steven Stahl's life was cut much too short. In a sense, he was truly a renaissance person for reading. His inquiring mind covered the full terrain of the reading process. Fortunately, he was able to help us make significant inroads into reading fluency, an area of reading that has been too long passed over by reading scholars. Steve's work in this area, though brief, was substantial. He helped us gain greater insight into this somewhat nebulous area. Perhaps most important, though, Steve's willingness to make reading fluency a part of his scholarly agenda has given fluency a legitimacy that it certainly needs and may not have otherwise so easily obtained.

REFERENCES

Allington, R. L. (1983). Fluency: The neglected reading goal. *The Reading Teacher, 36*, 556–561.

Carver, R., & Hoffman, J. V. (1981). The effect of practice through repeated reading on gain in reading ability using a computer-based instructional system. *Reading Research Quarterly, 16*, 374–390.

Chall, J. S. (1996). *Stages of reading development* (2nd ed.). Fort Worth, TX: Harcourt-Brace.

Deno, S. L. (1985). Curriculum-based measurement: The emerging alternative. *Exceptional Children, 52*, 219–232.

Duke, N. K., Pressley, M., & Hilden, K. (2004). Difficulties with reading comprehension. In C. A. Stone, E. R. Silliman, B. J. Ehren, & K. Apel (Eds.), *Handbook of language and literacy: Development and disorders* (pp. 501–520). New York: Guilford Press.

Ehri, L. C. (1995). Phases of development in learning to read words by sight. *Journal of Research in Reading 18*, 116–125.

Hoffman, J. V. (1987). Rethinking the role of oral reading in basal instruction. *Elementary School Journal, 87*, 367–373.

Hoffman, J. V., & Crone, S. (1985). The oral recitation lesson: A research-derived strategy for reading in basal texts. In J. A. Niles & R. V. Lalik (Eds.), *Issues in literacy: A research perspective. 34th Yearbook of the National Reading Conference* (pp. 76–83). Rockfort, NY: National Reading Conference.

Kuhn, M. R., & Stahl, S. A. (2000). *Fluency: A review of developmental and remedial practices* (CIERA Rep. No. 2-008). Ann Arbor, MI: Center for the Improvement of Early Reading Achievement.

LaBerge, D., & Samuels, S. A. (1974). Toward a theory of automatic information processing in reading. *Cognitive Psychology, 6*, 293–323.

National Reading Panel. (2000). *Report of the National Reading Panel: Teaching children to read. Report of the subgroups.* Washington, DC: U.S. Department of Health and Human Services, National Institutes of Health.

Pinnell, G. S., Pikulski, J. J., Wixson, K. K., Campbell, J. R., Gough, P. B., & Beatty, A. S. (1995). *Listening to children read aloud.* Washington, DC: U.S. Department of Education, Office of Educational Research and Improvement.

Rasinski, T. V. (1989). Fluency for everyone: Incorporating fluency in the classroom. *The Reading Teacher, 42*, 690–693.

Rasinski, T. V. (2004). *Assessing reading fluency*. Honolulu: Pacific Resources for Education and Learning. Available online at: www.prel.org

Samuels, S. J. (1979). The method of repeated readings. *The Reading Teacher, 32*, 403–408.

Stahl, S., & Heubach, K. (2005). Fluency-oriented reading instruction. *Journal of Literacy Research, 37*(1).

Stahl, S. A., Heubach, K., & Cramond, B. (1997). *Fluency-oriented reading instruction* (Reading research report no. 79). Athens, GA, and College Park, MD: National Reading Research Center.

12 | Fluency-Oriented Reading Instruction

Steven A. Stahl
Kathleen Heubach

Fluent and automatic word recognition has traditionally been considered the hallmark of a good reader. Yet, according to Allington (1983a), traditional conceptions of reading have ignored fluency as a goal. Instead, traditional classes have placed greater emphasis on accurate reading of increasingly more difficult material rather than fluent reading.

This article documents an attempt to reorganize second-grade classes around the goal of fluency. We choose second grade because we see this grade as a transition between the simple and predictable material used in first grade to teach children to decode and the more complex stories and expository text used in third grade and above.

STAGES OF READING DEVELOPMENT

Underlying our belief in the importance of fluency development in second grade is our view that reading development is comprised of a series of stages, where development in one stage is dependent on concepts learned in previous stages and a prerequisite for development in subsequent stages. The advantage of a stage model is that it provides a map describing expectations at different levels of development.

Stage models assume that reading is qualitatively different at different stages of development. That is, a child who is at one stage will have different skills, knowledge, and beliefs about reading than a child at a higher or a lower stage. At each stage, the knowledge and skills needed for the next stage are developed. There have been a number of stage models of reading including those of Doerhing and Aulls (1979), Downing (1979), and McCormick and Mason (1986). We will limit our discussion to Chall's (1983) model because this model essentially contains the basic features of the others with greater elaboration.

Chall (1983) described the development of reading ability in six stages, ranging from prereading to the advanced reading typical of graduate students. Her approach is a global one, encompassing the development of decoding, comprehension, and critical evaluation. Because it is global, Chall's model describes broad trends in children's development as readers. Her stages are as follows:

- Emergent Literacy: In this stage, which Chall called "Readiness," the child develops concepts about the forms and functions of literacy. Recent research has suggested that four areas are most important for success in initial reading: (1) phoneme awareness, or the ability to manipulate sounds in spoken words; (2) print concepts, or the awareness of the functions of print, such as directionality, print conventions, and some knowledge of spelling patterns in the language; (3) letter knowledge, or knowledge of the alphabet; and (4) knowledge of the language (vocabulary and syntax) that one is learning to read.
- Decoding: The student begins to learn about sound–symbol correspondences. The student's reading performance here is "glued to the text," in that she or he is trying to carefully reproduce what the text says. It often sounds like "grunting and groaning," because the child is not yet fluent.
- Confirmation and Fluency: In this stage, the student learns to decode words fluently and accurately and to orchestrate the use of syntactic and semantic information in text to confirm word recognition. In this stage, the child moves from the short, simple, and possibly predictable texts of the Decoding stage to more complex texts with complex plots. At the end of this stage, children are viewed as able to decode much of what is in their knowledge base, limited mainly by vocabulary knowledge and world knowledge.
- Learning the New (Single Viewpoint): Here, students learn to use their reading skill to extract information from text. At this point, they are expected to learn from content area textbooks, with increasingly less teacher guidance.
- Multiple Viewpoints: The student synthesizes information from different texts, acknowledging multiple viewpoints, but still keeping them separate from one's own.
- A World View: In this stage, adults develop the selectivity to weigh information and to add information from text to their world view.

Chall's model is useful for examining how literacy develops over time and has important implications for instruction. For example, beginning reading instruction for children who lack phoneme awareness is likely to result in reading difficulty. Juel (1988) found that no child who ranked in the lowest 25% in phoneme awareness at the beginning of first grade ranked higher than the lowest 25% in reading achievement by fourth grade. This finding has been replicated a number of times (see Adams, 1990).

Although each stage builds upon concepts developed in the previous stages, keeping children at a stage for too long can also be detrimental to their growth. Holding children to a standard of word-perfect oral reading, which might be appropriate for a child in the Decoding stage, may retard their use of context cues typical of the next stage. For example, if students are corrected for each deviation from the text whether it makes sense or not, they may not develop the risk-taking abilities needed to use context and may concentrate on saying the words "right" and not on the construction of meaning (Allington, 1984).

A literal reading of Chall's model may slightly distort the actual development of reading at various stages. By concentrating on the development of automatic word recognition during the early stages, Chall may appear to slight the comprehension component that also occurs during the early grades. Although the development of automatic word recognition is the hallmark achievement of these years, children's basic comprehension abilities also are growing at this time. As Adams (1990) points out, given the interactive nature of the reading process, children's word recognition and comprehension abilities are intertwined. Children learn to recognize words quickly and automatically in the process of reading them in connected text for the purpose of comprehension.

TRANSITION FROM DECODING TO AUTOMATICITY

The transitions in Chall's model are extremely important. The transition between Emergent Literacy and Decoding is effected usually with instruction, although there are a number of self-taught readers who make the transition on their own (see Durkin, 1974). The transition between initial decoding and automaticity may come only with practice. Samuels (1985; Samuels, Schermer, & Reinking, 1992) argues that automaticity comes out of children's practice through wide reading of different texts and/or repeated readings of the same texts. Samuels reviews the work done on repeated reading and concludes that ample evidence exists that such practice does improve automaticity.

Although Samuels (1985) allows that wide reading can also improve automaticity, there is some evidence that wide reading is not enough. Carver and Leibert (1995) failed to find that reading library books improved the reading of children in grades 3, 4, and 5. Taylor, Frye, and Maruyama (1990) did find an effect for the amount of reading fifth-grade children did at school (but not at home); however, this effect was small, about 1% of the total variance (see Carver & Leibert, 1995). These studies and others (e.g., Anderson, Wilson, & Fielding, 1988) were done with intermediate-grade children, using reading logs to measure time spent on reading. Chall's theory suggests that reading practice is especially important at the second-grade transition point, so it is possible that wide reading might have a greater effect in that grade than with older children. Intervention studies such as those of Hoffman (1987), Morris and Nelson (1992), and Rasinski, Padak, Linek, and Sturtevant (1994) have found that fluency-oriented instruction has positive effects on second-grade children's reading (see Kuhn & Stahl, 2003, and Rasinski & Hoffman, 2003, for reviews).

Hoffman (1987) describes an oral recitation lesson format to substitute for the traditional basal reader lesson. In this format, the teacher begins by reading the story from the reader aloud and discussing its content. In this way comprehension is dealt with prior to practice in oral reading. The teacher then rereads the story, paragraph by paragraph, with the children following along and echoing back each paragraph. The students then choose or are assigned a portion of the text to master. They practice this text and read it to the group. They then go on to the next story. On their own, children practice the story until they can read it at an adequate rate with no errors. Hoffman reports that the lessons were successful but does not present statistical data. Morris and Nelson (1992) found that a program based on Hoffman's, but including partner reading rather than small-group work, helped children in one class develop word recognition skills. However, they did not use a control group and did not report statistical tests.

Rasinski et al. (1994) used a similar format in their fluency development lesson, but instead of using basal reader stories, they used 50- to 150-word texts. Teachers read each text aloud, students and teachers read the texts chorally, and students practiced reading in pairs. Because of the short texts, teachers were able to do all parts of the lesson in a 15-minute session each day. The only gains attributable to the treatment were in reading rate. There were no significant differences between the experimental treatment and the control in overall reading level as measured by an informal reading inventory.

GOALS FOR OUR FLUENCY-BASED READING PROGRAM

Using the stage model of reading, the purpose of our fluency-oriented reading instruction was to help children move from the accuracy-driven decoding, typical of the Decoding stage, to the fluency and automaticity needed to take advantage of reading to learn. We hypothesized that children move through this fluency stage largely through practice in reading connected text for comprehension, using both repeated readings of the same text and wide readings of different texts. Therefore, we developed five goals for our fluency-based reading program:

• *Lessons will be comprehension oriented, even when smooth and fluent oral reading is being emphasized.* This was important because we wanted students to be aware that the purpose of reading is getting meaning and that the practice they were undertaking would make them better comprehenders, not simply better word callers. In their analysis of oral reading lessons, Anderson, Wilkinson, and Mason (1990) found that maintaining a focus on comprehension during reading lessons improved not only comprehension but also children's word recognition skills.

• *Children will read material at their instructional level.* Traditionally it is thought that reading material that is too difficult or too easy does not improve children's reading as efficiently as reading material that is well matched to the child's ability (Allington, 1984). (As will be discussed later, our findings question this assumption because children read material that was well above their instructional levels, with a great deal of scaffolding, and appeared to benefit greatly.) We originally defined instructional level as the level at which they could read with 95–98% accuracy (Wixson & Lipson, 1991). Previous research (e.g., Gambrell, Wilson, & Gantt, 1981) suggested that children do very little reading of connected text at an appropriate instructional level, as little as 2 to 3 minutes per day. Our initial goal was to increase the amount of material that children read at this level. However, as will be discussed later, district constraints forced us to modify this goal so that we also increased the amount of reading children did above conventional instructional levels.

• *Children will be supported in their reading through repeated readings.* This was the key aspect of the reading program. Children read each story numerous times—through echo reading at school, at home with their parents, with partners, and by themselves. The repeated reading component of the program was intended to provide practice so that children would develop fluent and automatic reading. Samuels et al. (1992) and Rasinski (1989), among others, suggest that students develop automaticity through repeated exposures to words in context. Repeated readings have been found to effectively improve the oral reading and comprehension of normally achieving students (e.g., Martinez, & Roser, 1985; Taylor, Wade, & Yekovich, 1985) and of disabled and developmental readers of various ages (e.g., Dowhower, 1989; Rasinski, 1989).

• *Children will engage in partner reading.* Partner reading provides an opportunity for students to read connected text within a socially supportive context. This context should both motivate children to read well and provide a supportive environment to aid the development of reading skill. For these reasons, partner reading is used by both traditional educators and those who adhere to a more holistic perspective (Routman, 1991; Vacca & Rasinski, 1992). Partner reading was used for two primary reasons. First, it offered an effective alternative to round robin reading for increasing the amount of time that children spend reading orally. In round robin reading, children spend only a small portion of the reading period actually reading text (Gambrell et al., 1981). In partner reading, children spend considerably more time engaged in reading text. A number of studies (e.g., Topping, 1987) have found that such approaches can increase the amount of engaged time spent in reading as well as encourage children to read more difficult material. Second, partner reading allows teachers to monitor children's reading progress by going around the room and listening to them read. In the lower grades, teachers often organize repeated readings as a paired reading activity.

• *Children will increase the amount of reading that they do at home as well as in school.* Because the schoolday is limited in length, we thought that children would gain significantly in reading proficiency with some practice at home. Anderson et al. (1988) found that even small differences in home-reading practice could make large differences in children's reading achievement. Because the home circumstances of our children differed dramatically from school to school and from child to child, we tried a number of approaches. Several teachers connected the home-reading program with Book It™, a commercial reading-incentive program. Other teachers included reading as part of the child's homework. One school was involved with a Reading Millionaires project (Baumann, 1995; O'Masta & Wolf, 1991). In this project, the number of minutes read by students in the school was tabulated, with the goal being 1 million minutes of at-home reading school-wide. The time spent in our project reading at home was added to the number of minutes that the school as a whole read. In addition, as will be discussed below, children were given structured assignments to read portions of their basal reading book at home as part of the lesson structure.

These five components have all been studied individually but not as part of a total reading program. Implementing a total fluency-based program over a full school year creates a unique set of problems. One problem is maintaining interest in a program that involves rereading of the same text. Most evaluations of programs that involved repeated reading were either short term or did repeated reading for only a portion of each day. In our program, we worried that repeated reading both at home and in school would bore students and teachers alike. Another problem is dealing with diverse reading abilities. In our classrooms, for example, children ranged from virtual nonreaders to children who could handle fourth-grade level material comfortably. These classes were in schools representing mixed to lower socioeconomic status children and were probably representative of similar populations in the state. Providing both material and instruction that is appropriate to the different levels requires new organizational modes.

DEVELOPING A READING PROGRAM

During the summer of 1992, two university-based researchers met with four elementary classroom teachers to discuss how these principles could be instantiated into a reading program. Our goal was to develop a plan for teaching reading throughout the year that would be flexible, adaptable to different classes and different stories, and focused on fluency. The plan also needed to have enough variety for both teacher and student so that it would not become tedious. Because of the need to make this instruction practical, we relied heavily on the teachers' experience in developing the program. Certain aspects, most notably monitoring children's reading using running records, were dropped or heavily modified based on teacher input. There were other elements that had to be part of the program. For example, all teachers were committed to using basal reading programs, through both district policy and personal choice. Therefore, we had to design lessons around the basal material. Moreover, a new county school superintendent mandated whole class reading instruction. Therefore, we had to deliver lessons to the whole class. In another county, the classes were organized homogeneously; one class was high achieving and one was low achieving. These different levels had to be taken into account.

Our meetings stressed one principle per week. We read descriptions of other fluency-based programs, such as Hoffman (1987), and discussed how those ideas would fit into the teachers' classrooms and into our overall goals. At the end of the summer we had a general plan for reading instruction. The general plan had three components—a redesigned basal reading lesson, a home reading program, and a daily free-choice reading period. These will be discussed, in turn, below.

A REDESIGNED BASAL READING LESSON

Because all of the students in one school were required to read the same basal reading lesson, the one at their grade placement, and many were reading significantly below grade level, we used repeated reading of the same material to help children be successful with more difficult material. We followed the logic of an Oral Recitation Lesson format, which has been effective in supporting children with reading difficulties (Hoffman, 1987), but made significant modifications.

Each story is different and requires a slightly different approach. Also, teachers and students need variation to maintain interest. We did not want to have a formula lesson; instead, we provided many options for teachers to use. The basic structure of the lesson is shown in Figure 12.1.

Story Introduction

In Hoffman's oral recitation format, the teacher begins by reading the story aloud and discussing it, using a story map. In this way, the teacher deals with comprehension prior to the fluency practice, keeping the lesson focused on comprehension. We

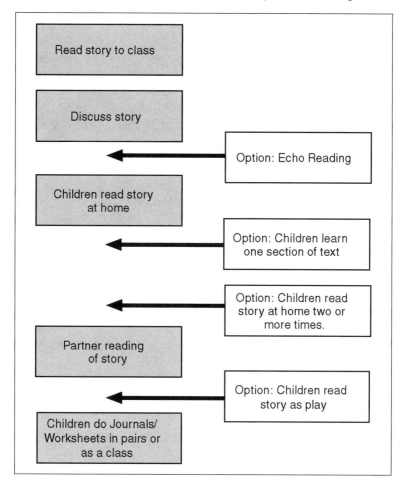

FIGURE 12.1. Fluency-based classroom reading.

followed a similar procedure with the teacher reading the story aloud to begin the lesson. Following this read-aloud, we used a variety of procedures to discuss the story, including traditional questions; student-generated questions; and other graphic organizers, including various types of story maps, plot charts, Venn diagrams, and so on. This usually comprised the first day's lesson.

Children who needed additional help with the story were pulled aside for echo reading. If the story was particularly challenging, echo reading was done with the whole class. In echo reading, the teacher read a paragraph at a time, with the students echoing it back. This was done to scaffold students' recognition of words and to help them successfully read the story.

Partner Reading

The next component was partner reading. Children read the story in pairs, with one member of the pair reading a portion of the story aloud and the other monitoring and providing assistance if needed. The length of the portion was agreed upon by the partners, but most often the students would alternate reading pages.

We tried a number of variations in how partners were assigned. Because of our formative study on partner reading, discussed below, teachers used self-selection for partner reading. One table at a time would choose partners. The pairings varied throughout the year, depending on current friendships. We observed cooperation throughout the year. Students also began to work in pairs on their own during free-choice reading time.

Partner reading was initially difficult to set up. It took several weeks of practice before partner reading jelled and students knew their roles. Odd numbers of students were handled in different ways. Sometimes a group of three was formed. Sometimes the teacher read with the odd child. Generally, however, teachers avoided reading with children because this impaired their own ability to monitor the reading throughout the class.

Additional Instruction

The following day, the teacher worked with the journals that came with the basal reading program. Teachers varied in how they did this. Usually, journal pages were discussed as a whole class as a way of reviewing the story content. Students who were having difficulty were assigned to read the story one more time at home. In addition, teachers sometimes had students reread portions of the story for performance or made the story into a play to provide more practice in reading.

HOME READING

Students did two types of reading at home. They read the basal reading selection at home at least 1 or 2 days a week. The story was sent home the first day with instructions for students to read it to a parent or other person in the household. More able readers read the story to themselves, but most students read it aloud. We met with the parents before school started and talked about reading at home. Often parents sat with the child and followed along. Other times the child read while the parent was doing something else, such as making dinner. In many families, time is often short, so many alternatives were provided. Parents were not able to read with their children every day, as evidenced by the responses to sheets that we sent home with the children, but there seems to have been a general effort to read at home. We also gave parents some guidance in how to correct errors. Because we met during Parent–Teacher Organization meetings, our time was limited. Consequently, we could not provide as extensive parent training as provided by Mudre and McCormick (1989), whose training procedure seemed to improve parents' response to their children's oral reading. Also, the percentage of parents who were able to attend this meeting varied considerably, from two or three parents per class in one school to three-quarters of the parents in another.

Students also were expected to read a book of their choice at home. They brought books from the school, class, or public library or read books that they owned. The object of the home-reading program was to extend the amount of practice that occurred at school.

FREE-CHOICE READING PERIOD

Teachers encouraged students to read a variety of books on their own. The purposes of this reading time were to increase interest in reading as well as to promote reading at the students' own level. The teachers provided periods of time (15–20 minutes) for independent reading, and students were also encouraged to read as they completed assignments throughout the day.

EVALUATION OF THE STUDY

The following questions guided our examination and evaluation of this program:

• *Can a fluency-oriented reading program be sustained over a full year?* Although most of the approaches used in our reorganization have been tested before, these tests have generally been of short durations, usually 1 or 2 months at the most. Because lesson structure involved repeated readings of the same text, some observers thought that either the children or the teachers would tire of the procedures, leading to negative attitudes.

• *Does the program lead to gains in oral reading with comprehension?* Because we stressed oral reading in the program, we wanted to assess the program's effects on oral reading. However, because we did not want to produce word callers who decoded the text without comprehension, we also assessed comprehension.

• *What happens during partner reading?* Partner reading is a prominent feature of this program. The teachers in the program wanted to know the most effective pairings of students; we wanted to know more about why children chose each other and the dynamics of partner reading.

• *What types of books do children choose during choice reading?* If children are to benefit from reading during choice reading, they need to choose books that are at or near their instructional levels. (At least this is the conventional wisdom, but see Carver and Leibert, 1995.) We wanted to examine the relative difficulty of books that children choose and its impact on reading development. We also wanted to see why children chose the books they did.

• *What are the effects of the program on struggling readers?* Given Stanovich's (1986) notion of Matthew effects and Allington's (1983b) observations about the differences in the amount of reading done by struggling and normally achieving readers, we felt that radically increasing the amount of reading would have an especially large effect on struggling readers.

To assess the effectiveness of the program, we conducted a series of evaluations. Because this program is complex and was undertaken over the course of 2 years, the evaluation procedures are complex as well. Some evaluations used the entire population of participating children; others used only a sample of that population. Because the samples differ from substudy to substudy, they will be reported as separate studies, with a description of the sample, methods, results, and discussion.

The studies reported below come from our questions about the program, beginning with whether it could be sustained and whether it affected children's growth in reading to more specific questions about components of the program. Some of these questions were generated by the researchers; others came from concerns of the participating teachers.

STUDY 1—OVERALL PROGRAM EVALUATION

Because of the nature of the program and our theoretical orientation discussed earlier, we used a measure of oral reading with comprehension to evaluate the program. The basic design used was a pretest–posttest design in which children's reading scores in August were compared with their achievement in May. (The first year we also included an interim measure in February.)

Traditionally, program evaluations are conducted with either an experimental or quasi-experimental design (Campbell & Stanley, 1966). In such a design, there is a treatment group and a control group. We had originally planned to use the first year to develop the program, conducting only formative studies and one pretest–posttest evaluation. The second year was intended to be an experimental test of the program developed in the first year. However, the results of the first year were so unexpectedly strong that we felt that denying treatment to a control set of classes was unethical. Therefore, we decided to use all of our classes as treatment classes, and we developed a pretest–posttest design to evaluate the program.

The logic for the analysis is that if the program is more successful than conventional instruction, children then will make greater progress on a standard measure of reading than the 1-year growth expected in 1 year's time. If such growth occurs in a substantial proportion of the treatment classrooms, we then can argue that this growth is due not to chance variations but to the effects of the program itself.

Participants

To assess the overall program effects, we used the entire population of students for both the first and second year. The student population during the first year consisted of 84 students, 49 in Oglethorpe Avenue School in Clarke County, Georgia, and 35 in Greensboro Primary School in Greene County, Georgia. The students at Oglethorpe Avenue were of mixed socioeconomic status. Approximately 60% were African American, the remainder European American. In Greensboro, 85% of the students were African American and were predominantly from homes with a lower socioeconomic status. The student population during the second year was similar except it was considerably larger.

In the first year, all four teachers were female, one was African American and three were European American. One had 2 years' experience, the remainder 9–10 years. During the second year, we added one teacher at Oglethorpe Avenue School and three teachers at Barnett Shoals School in Clarke County. We also added two more teachers at Greensboro. Of the six new teachers, one teacher was male, the remainder female; two teachers were African American, the remainder European American. Two of the new teachers had fewer than 5 years' experience; the remainder had more than 10 years' experience.

The second-grade students who participated from Oglethorpe Avenue and Greensboro were demographically similar to those who participated the first year. The additional students from Barnett Shoals contained a wider variety of parental backgrounds. Approximately 40% of these students were African American. We had an exceptionally high rate of mobility during the second year. At some point, 180 different students participated the second year, but only 125 were present from beginning to end.

Procedure

All students participating in the project were given the Qualitative Reading Inventory (QRI; Leslie & Caldwell, 1988), an individually administered informal reading inventory, during the first month of school and the last month of school. During the first year, the QRI was also administered in February as an interim measure. The QRI was chosen because it gives equal emphasis to oral reading and comprehension, matching our program objectives. According to the material in the manual, alternate form reliability was high. For the eight levels of the test, Leslie and Caldwell (1988) reported that all reliabilities were above 80%, and three-quarters were above 90%. In addition, Leslie and Caldwell reported the concurrent validity of the QRI, as measured by the correlations between instructional level on the QRI and performance on an unnamed standardized achievement test, ranged between .44 and .72 with the majority of correlations above .70.

Year One

Figure 12.2 shows the QRI results for the first year. As shown on that figure, students made an average gain of 1.88 grade levels in their instructional level over the course of the year. This gain was uniform for all four classes. The ordinary assumption is that students will average about 1 year's growth in 1 year's time. We compared the actual growth to this assumed growth through a series of t-tests. For each class, we

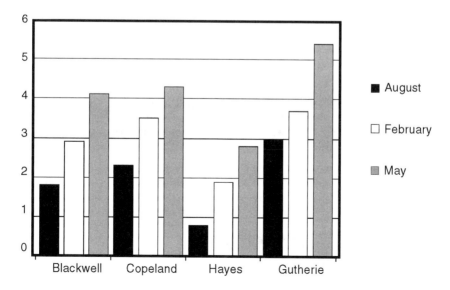

FIGURE 12.2. Gains in instructional level, by class, year one.

tested whether the mean growth was significantly different from 1 year. In all four classes, it was (all $p < .01$).

Furthermore, as shown in Figure 12.3, students entering at different reading levels made gains. That is, the average child entering second grade reading below the primer level made an average of 2 years' progress during the course of the year. The average child reading at the third-reader level in the beginning of the year made a gain of 3 years during the school year. Of the 85 students in the four classes, only 3 were still unable to read the second-grade passage by the end of the year.

Year Two

The second year pretest–posttest evaluations are shown in Figure 12.4. The yearly gains were nearly as high as those for the first years, averaging 1.77 years' growth in instructional level. Again, for each class, we tested whether the mean growth was significantly different from one year. In eight of the nine classes, the growth was significantly ($p < .01$) greater than one. The remaining class made approximately 1 year's gain in 1 year's time.

As shown in Figure 12.5, children at all entering reading levels made gains similar to those made in the first year. Again, these gains were relatively uniform. Children who entered second grade reading below the primer level ended with an average instructional level of 2.25, somewhat below the second-grade level (which we coded 2.5). Of the 20 students who could not read a primer passage at the beginning of the school year, 9 were reading at a second-grade level or higher by the end of the year, and all but one could read at a primer or higher level. This suggests that this program was successful even for children who would ordinarily have a great deal of difficulty learning to read. Of the remaining 105 students who had pretest and posttest data, only 2 failed to read at the second-grade level or higher by the end of the study. Both of these students began reading at the primer level and were able to progress only to the first-reader level.

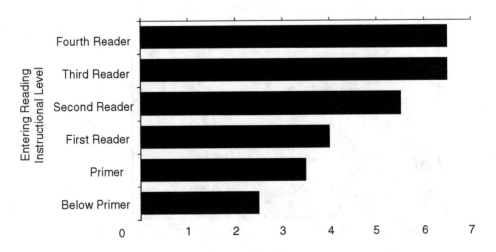

FIGURE 12.3. Median instructional level in spring, by entering level, year one.

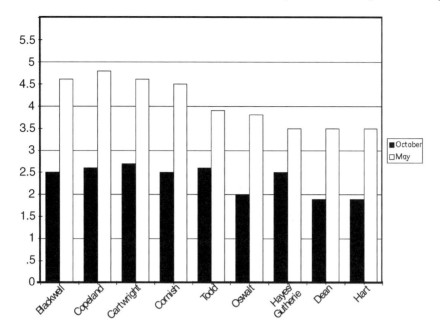

FIGURE 12.4. Gains in reading, by class, year two.

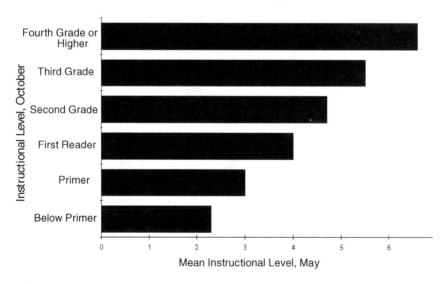

FIGURE 12.5. May instructional level, by entering level, second year of study.

Thus, for all 14 classes over the first 2 years of the project, students made significantly more than 1 year's reading growth in one school year. By the logic discussed earlier, we maintain that this indicates that fluency-oriented reading instruction is more effective than conventional instruction.

STUDY 2—GROWTH OF RATE AND ACCURACY

To examine the development of fluency over the course of the year, we initiated a series of fluency checks during the second year. We operationally defined fluent reading as reading that is both rapid and accurate. Therefore, to examine fluency, we looked at both accuracy and rate. The purpose of these checks was to examine the effects of each lesson on children's accuracy and rate of reading the basal reading selections. We also wanted to see how readers of different entering abilities developed over the course of the year.

Participants

The participants in these sampling studies were the students in the six classes in Barnett Shoals and Oglethorpe Avenue Schools. Because there were different numbers of students in these classes during the year, there were 91 students sampled in November, 87 in January, and 89 in May.

Method

These fluency checks were conducted over a 2-week period. At the end of the first week, after the teacher had finished a story, children read orally two selections of between 150 and 200 words. The first selection was taken from the story just completed; the second selection was from the story not yet read but to be begun the following day. The second week students reread the selection from the story they had just finished. For each story segment, we noted both accuracy of word identification and rate of reading. These checks were given in November, February, and May and allowed us to compare each child's reading of an unread story with one that was just completed as well as with their reading of the same story after a week of treatment. In addition, we could compare children's reading of the previously unread story, which could be considered a baseline, with their reading later in the year, allowing us to assess progress in both accuracy and rate.

All deviations from the text were considered errors for the purpose of this study. We did not distinguish between meaning changing and nonmeaning changing miscues in our analysis for higher interrater reliability.

Results

The results from the checks (see Figure 12.6) suggest that students made significant progress in both rate and accuracy because of the practice (comparing the read story with the unread and reread stories) and made progress over time (comparing the unread stories in November, January, and May). This progress was most pronounced from November to January, suggesting that the bulk of the children's reading growth

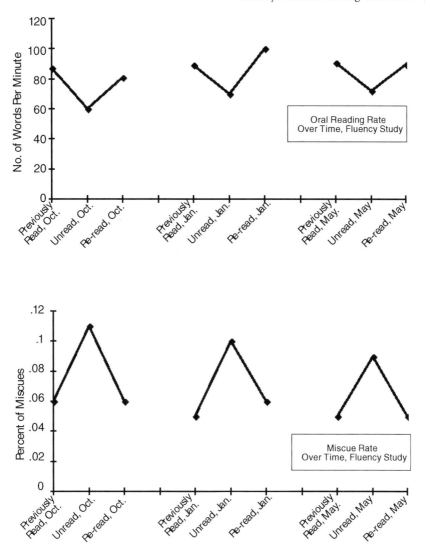

FIGURE 12.6. Oral reading and miscue rates over time.

occurred during that time period. This is similar to the results from the informal reading inventory given during the first year. We found that students made a gain of a full year in the 4 months between September and January and somewhat less than that between January and May.

Looking at growth over time at each level, as presented in Tables 12.1 and 12.2, it seems that there were different patterns of growth in rate and accuracy among children with different entering abilities. Children reading at the highest initial levels, second-grade level or higher, generally made little improvement in rate over the year as suggested by their reading of the unread selection. These students were generally reading the material at or above an instructional level of 95% accuracy (or a 5% or lower error rate). There simply was not much room for them to grow.

TABLE 12.1. Error Rate, by Condition and Entering Level

	October			January			May		
	Previously read	Unread	Re-read	Previously read	Unread	Re-read	Previously read	Unread	Re-read
Below primer	.16 (.09)	.25 (.10)	.15 (.09)	.13 (.08)	.20 (.13)	.12 (.12)	.11 (.05)	.19 (.09)	.13 (.09)
Primer	.08 (.06)	.18 (.06)	.06 (.04)	.06 (.04)	.11 (.04)	.04 (.02)	.07 (.04)	.12 (.04)	.06 (.03)
First reader	.04 (.04)	.09 (.06)	.04 (.03)	.03 (.02)	.06 (.03)	.01 (.01)	.03 (.02)	.06 (.04)	.04 (.02)
Second grade	.03 (.03)	.05 (.03)	.02 (.02)	.02 (.02)	.05 (.02)	.02 (.01)	.03 (.03)	.04 (.03)	.03 (.02)
Third grade	.02 (.02)	.04 (.02)	.02 (.02)	.01 (.01)	.04 (.03)	.01 (.01)	.01 (.01)	.03 (.02)	.01 (.01)
Fourth grade or higher	.01 (.001)	.02 (.02)	.01 (.01)	.01 (.001)	.02 (.02)	.01 (.01)	.01 (.001)	.02 (.01)	.01 (01)

Students who began the year reading below a second-grade instructional level showed different patterns of growth. Again concentrating on the error rates for the unread selection, those children initially reading at the first-reader level dropped their average error rate from 9% in October to 6% in February and May. This improvement suggests that they raised their instructional level to that expected at their grade level. The error rate of children reading at the primer level in October dropped significantly on the unread selection. But the error rate of children who began reading below the primer level remained very low.

TABLE 12.2. Rate, by Condition and Entering Level

	October			January			May		
	Previously read	Unread	Re-read	Previously read	Unread	Re-read	Previously read	Unread	Re-read
Below primer	38.34 (14.12)	28.69 (12.96)	43.36 (20.75)	44.65 (19.42)	37.21 (11.74)	52.25 (21.30)	39.57 (14.25)	32.00 (12.25)	44.39 (16.63)
Primer	60.42 (17.34)	40.60 (13.32)	63.35 (17.48)	70.62 (19.18)	62.17 (23.29)	76.61 (23.11)	69.46 (21.48)	55.94 (21.48)	70.43 (19.16)
First reader	76.70 (32.88)	55.12 (27.86)	74.85 (36.58)	97.98 (30.89)	74.81 (31.10)	111.22 (28.75)	95.37 (35.92)	62.16 (28.80)	78.89 (25.60)
Second grade	92.08 (23.88)	69.92 (14.53)	91.30 (16.98)	103.96 (23.71)	79.92 (15.78)	114.37 (23.34)	108.92 (28.60)	84.68 (22.49)	108.64 (30.02)
Third grade	111.02 (22.09)	78.29 (16.65)	106.21 (21.01)	114.05 (21.01)	93.67 (26.76)	131.27 (22.68)	122.88 (20.93)	90.95 (21.51)	120.50 (21.89)
Fourth grade or higher	143.38 (34.44)	104.18 (32.16)	128.36 (35.47)	138.15 (26.38)	124.78 (37.78)	153.86 (28.04)	149.24 (38.31)	119.06 (36.48)	144.37 (41.05)

The results on the growth of accuracy mirror the pretest–posttest results. This program seems to be highly successful for children who begin the second-grade year with a reading level at or above the primer level; that is, for children who can recognize a simple corps of words. In Chall's (1983) stage model, discussed above, these would be children who are at the Decoding stage or higher.

Although children reading initially at a second-grade level or higher did not make gains in accuracy, they did make gains in rate, especially between the October and February sampling. Children at all levels at or above the primer made average gains of at least 10 words per minute from October to February. Between February and May, gains were inconsistent. Some groups of students read at somewhat lower rates in May than in February. The fall-off of those children who initially read at a first-reader level was dramatic, from 75 to 62 words per minute from February to May. An even larger fall-off occurred on their reading of the reread selection. This may be nothing more than a problem with a particular passage or a somewhat different selection of students at different times due to absences. This was the smallest group (nine or ten) and most susceptible to attrition effects. However, the average reading rate of even our most able readers, those initially reading at a fourth-grade level or higher, grew from 104 words per minute in October to 119 words per minute in May, suggesting that even these able students made palpable gains.

STUDY 3—PARTNER READING

Because partner reading was an important aspect of our program, both in the redesigned basal reading lesson and during the free-choice reading period, we wanted to find out what went on during partner reading. Our interest began with the teachers' questions about how best to organize partner reading, whether teachers should assign children to work in heterogeneous groups, as had been done in one class, or whether students should select their own partners, as had been done in another class. However, our interests were somewhat more complex. We wanted to capture, qualitatively, some aspects of what made partnerships function in our reading lessons.

To understand these questions, we conducted a qualitative and a quantitative analysis of data collected in two second-grade classrooms where partner reading was an integral part of reading instruction. We were interested in (a) the relative efficiency of different pairings of students, (b) the types of interaction taking place while children read in pairs, (c) the factors that influence decision making within the pairs, and (d) the factors that influence smooth and fluent reading.

We viewed partner reading as an example of a closed social circle embedded within a larger classroom context. We examined the functions of literacy within this smaller context and how these functions related to the goals of the classroom at large. In this study, literacy learning and paired reading were examined in relationship to the larger social fabric of the classroom.

Subjects

This study was conducted the first year, using the two second-grade classrooms from Oglethorpe Avenue School, with a total of 42 children. The children were largely from middle-class families of diverse ethnicity and represented a range of reading abilities. In both classrooms a newly adopted basal was the foundation for reading instruction. The students read in pairs after the basal story had been introduced and either read orally to the class or individually by each student. The children also read in pairs during DEAR (Drop Everything And Read) time, which provided an opportunity for reading self-selected books. In these classes, during the 15–20 minutes per day allotted to DEAR, children could choose to read alone or with partners.

Method

During each data-collection cycle, children were assigned to partners in each of three ways: (1) pairs heterogeneous in ability assigned by the teacher, (2) pairs homogeneous in ability assigned by the teacher, and (3) student-chosen pairs. This cycle lasted 3 weeks. Each child participated in each of the three selection conditions and thus served as his or her own control. Following each partner reading session, each child was given a segment of the basal reader text that was read during that session and asked to read it orally. A running record (Clay, 1985) was taken of this reading. The error rate following each reading was used to examine the relative efficacy of the different types of pairings.

During observations, data were collected from multiple sources, including (a) audio recordings of six target students (three from each class) as they read with a partner, (b) video recordings of pairs of students, (c) field notes taken as the students participated in paired readings, (d) interviews with the students and the teachers (see Appendix 12.1), and (e) running records of samples of material read using the partner reading sessions. We collected data from October to March, revisiting each class every 4 weeks. There were a total of six data-collection cycles, one 3-week cycle in which both the quantitative and qualitative data were collected, and five 1-day observations in which only qualitative information was gathered.

Analysis

The qualitative data collection and analysis were done simultaneously using the constant comparative method (Glaser & Strauss, 1967). The analysis began with the collection of data through observation and taping of partner reading sessions. Immediately following the partner reading, one researcher administered a structured interview with individual students on their perceptions of partner reading and the reasons for their choices in partners. The interviews and tapes were transcribed and reviewed. After transcribing, the researcher examined the data for patterns as initial categories and relationships emerged. Subsequent collection cycles were used to confirm or disconfirm initial assertions about the social interactions taking place during paired reading.

The running records were used as a dynamic measure of reading level to note whether student partners were working on the same level. They were also used to compare the effectiveness of the three different partnering situations.

Quantitative Results

The running records were analyzed to examine directly the effects of different partnerings on student reading. We did not find a significant difference between types of pairings. However, the level of performance (accuracy scores ranging from

91% for the homogeneous grouping to 94% for the self-selected grouping) was so high that a ceiling effect may have obscured real differences. All children who initially read at a level of primer or higher could read second-grade material at an instructional level (approximately 95% or higher) or close to it. Of those who read below the primer level, half could read second-grade material at an instructional level. This finding suggests that the support discussed above is useful in helping nearly every child read successfully in grade-level materials. Confirming the qualitative analysis, students selecting their partners seem to produce better results, especially with lower-achieving readers.

Qualitative Results

The major assertion generated from the data analysis was that the relationship the children shared before they paired for partner reading not only helped to determine their choice of a partner but guided their actions during reading as well. This relationship seems to be the most important factor in determining how effectively students worked together in completing the partner reading task. Findings indicate that a positive and established relationship between the partners is important for effective partner reading.

Friendship was the most important relationship for the students. When asked how a certain person became a partner, the majority of students responded with remarks that were categorized as "friendship." For example, when asked how Peter became his partner, one student responded "I play kickball with him everyday." With only one exception, children accepted the partner who had chosen them even if that person was not someone they would have chosen themselves. Data from the teacher interviews confirmed that children tended to pick partners with whom they were getting along at the moment.

Although friendship was the main property of the relationship category, other factors were involved as well. Students were likely to work with others who had the same working style as their own. For example, a no-nonsense-type reader who wanted to get started immediately tended to choose another no-nonsense type. Gender did not play much of a role in determining who was chosen for partner reading. Although same-gender pairs were the norm, it was not uncommon to find boys and girls working together by choice.

Each new pair of students had to work out procedures for reading the story. Decisions were necessary about where to go in the room for reading, whether to read sitting or lying on the floor, who would go first, and how turns would be taken. This decision making was greatly affected by the nature of the relationship already established. If there were disagreements about procedure, the self-selected pairs worked these out without including the teacher or wasting time. Often there was no need to discuss procedures. For example, one pair was so in tune that when one child rolled over on his stomach, the other followed.

One of the key features of paired reading is the assistance that one child gives another when fluent reading breaks down. The most frequent form of assistance took place when a child could not read a word. The reader would stop, wait for the partner to provide the word, and then continue reading. Assistance appears to be connected to the relationship that was established before a partner reading session began. Children who already have a working relationship are more likely to ask for help when it is needed, and assistance is given in a more efficient manner.

When off-task behaviors were noted, they often did not interrupt the reading of self-selected pairs. This is because the pairs had already established routines and ways of relating to one another. These behaviors became more frequent and were more likely to hinder smooth sailing when the partners were not self-chosen.

STUDY 4—CHOICE READING

One of the assumptions in developing this program was that children would have ample time devoted to reading material at their instructional level. To develop fluency, it is important that children read material at or near their instructional level, which we defined initially as roughly 95% accuracy. Because we were required to provide whole class instruction using the basal reader, most children read material at or above their instructional levels during that time. Relatively few second-graders actually read at a second-grade level. For example, only 42 of the 152 students assessed at the beginning of the second year actually scored at a second-grade instructional level.

We assumed that during the period of choice reading, children, both gifted and struggling, would choose to read material at their instructional levels. This assumption has not, to our knowledge, been previously tested. One purpose of this study, then, was to check whether students actually chose books that were instructionally appropriate. A second purpose was to develop a theory of children's book selection.

Method

We asked children in two classes to fill out logs of the books they read during DEAR time for 2 weeks. Subjects in this study were 43 students in the two Greensboro School classes during the first year of the program. After 2 weeks, we interviewed children individually about why they chose these particular books and what criteria they used for choosing books in general. We also did a running record on a small section of one of the books that the child had read during the preceding week to find out its relative level of difficulty for the child. We used oral reading error rate as a measure of relative difficulty.

Results

In the running records, all children except one chose books that were at or near their instructional level. With one exception, students were able to read their chosen book with 92% accuracy or higher; the average was 95.5% accuracy. This rate suggests that students chose material near their instructional level but considerably more difficult than their independent level, which has traditionally been thought of as 98% accuracy (Wixson & Lipson, 1991). As noted below, we have reason to reassess this traditional notion.

The one student whose accuracy was considerably below this level (62%) had been placed in a homogeneous above-average reading class for reasons unrelated to his reading, but read significantly below the class average. He chose books that looked like those his classmates were reading, even though they were too difficult for him. We feel, bolstered by his interview, that this student had chosen books for social reasons, to appear as if he were competitive with his peers. If these results can be replicated, it suggests that Sustained Silent Reading (SSR) is a valid way of increasing children's fluency, because they will most likely choose books that are instructionally appropriate. It also suggests that social pressures need to be taken into account in implementing SSR.

The students were also interviewed about their reasons for their choices. The teachers were a major influence. Books that teachers had read to the class were chosen often. In addition, one teacher encouraged her students to read chapter books that challenged their ability in reading. Her students often mentioned these exhortations. Students did not mention their peers as influences on their reading choice.

DISCUSSION

As noted earlier, the studies used to evaluate this program were driven by a series of questions we had about the program. Some of the questions arose prior to planning the program; other questions arose during the implementation and came either from the researchers or from the participating teachers.

CAN A FLUENCY-ORIENTED READING PROGRAM BE SUSTAINED OVER A FULL YEAR?

As noted above, four teachers developed and implemented the program during the first year of this study. Three of the four teachers were highly experienced, each with more than 10 years of teaching experience, mostly at second grade. The fourth teacher, in her fourth year of teaching, had spent the previous year teaching in a supplemental program aimed at low-income children. All of these teachers would consider themselves traditional. They all had experience using basal reading programs and preferred to use such programs.

The second year we expanded our group to 10 teachers. Our intention was to determine whether the success of the program could be replicated with teachers who did not participate in its creation. All of the teachers participating during the first year also continued during the second year.

At the end of the first year, the four teachers reported that they were very happy with the procedures involved and would enthusiastically continue them into the second year. Of the 10 teachers who participated the second year, all have reported that they used the procedures in the following year, even though we were no longer providing direct support. These results suggest that the program was sustainable over the course of the school year and that teachers maintained their enthusiasm about the instruction.

DOES THE PROGRAM LEAD TO GAINS IN ORAL READING WITH COMPREHENSION?

The results of our 2-year study of fluency-oriented reading instruction suggest that reorganizing instruction so as to stress fluency had positive effects on second-grade children's growth as readers. These effects were most pronounced on children entering the second-grade year reading at a primer level or higher. Over the 2 years of the program, all such children but two were reading at grade level or higher by the end of the year. As might be expected, this program had its largest effects on measures of rate and accuracy in reading. Its effects on comprehension were significant because we used a measure of oral reading and comprehension as a pretest and posttest. We do not report results from standardized comprehension measures because of the difficulty of accessing such results without a treatment control group. However, according to the teachers, the effects on standardized reading comprehension tests were less pronounced and did not seem to differ from those of previous years.

WHAT HAPPENS DURING PARTNER READING?

Partner reading was the only aspect of the program students mentioned when asked what they liked about the reading program. We found that having children choose their partners rather than having them assigned on the basis of reading ability was the most efficacious approach. In our study, such an arrangement did not lead to significantly higher achievement. Instead, the oral reading levels after repeated readings were very high for all arrangements. However, the management aspects of partner reading seemed most efficient when there was a friendship between partners. There were fewer disturbances, and off-task behaviors were more easily handled.

We found, in two separate sets of interviews, that friendship was the primary reason for partner choice. Help with reading was a secondary reason and, as might be expected, this reason was given most often by struggling readers. The social aspect of partner reading appears to have mitigated the effects of children reading at levels well above or well below their instructional levels. As noted above, only about a quarter of the students in the second year of the program were reading at a second-grade instructional level at the beginning of the year. Those who were reading above grade level enjoyed partner reading as a way of sharing interesting stories with a friend. For those reading below grade level, the social aspect of partner reading made it easier to ask for and receive help.

WHAT ARE THE EFFECTS OF READING AT HOME?

This question could not be answered with our data. Although students perceived the process of reading at home positively, we felt that reading log data was not sufficiently reliable for drawing conclusions. Students reported reading the story at home from the basal, with a median of one reading per week and a range of 0 to 5. We did find that students enjoyed reading at home and believed that it made them better readers. Some students enjoyed the opportunity to read by themselves; others enjoyed the interaction with their family. When asked whether reading at home made them more interested in reading, nearly all children said "Yes" but generally did not elaborate on their responses.

WHAT TYPES OF BOOKS DO CHILDREN CHOOSE DURING CHOICE READING?

We had two concerns about the books children chose. First, we wanted students to choose books at an appropriate level. For a fluency-oriented program to work, children need to practice material at an appropriate level. Initially, we defined instructional level in the conventional manner, 95% accuracy with acceptable comprehension (Wixson & Lipson, 1991). We did find that children chose books that they could read at an appropriate level, although our view of what such a level might be in a program like this has changed. Children chose books that they could read with an average accuracy level of 95%, ranging, with one exception, from 92% to 100%. This level of material seems to be appropriate for practice in reading connected text. The one exception, as discussed above, chose his books for social reasons, because he was reading at a considerably lower level than the rest of his group.

We also wanted to know what influenced children's book choice. Here we found that the predominant influence was the teacher, not other students. A book was more likely to be chosen if the teacher had read it aloud, if the teacher had specifically recommended it, or if the teacher had stressed the importance of reading more difficult material, as was the case in the two classes we studied. Where the teacher does not make such a recommendation, as in the classes studied by Heubach and Ivey (1994), children tend to read easier material. The influence of the teacher may be more pronounced at the second-grade level, and similar results may not be found in older grades. Moreover, these were all teacher-centered classes, where children had not been explicitly prepared for making choices. Where children are more accustomed to making choices, peers may have more influence.

WHAT LEVEL OF MATERIAL SHOULD CHILDREN BE READING INDEPENDENTLY?

Because students generally choose books at a 92% accuracy rate or higher, rather than the traditionally accepted 98%, we feel that this somewhat more difficult rate should be thought of as the child's instructional level, at least in a program similar to this. This somewhat more difficult level has also been suggested by Clay (1985) and Powell (cited in Wixson & Lipson, 1991) and adopted by Wixson and Lipson as well. We also have some evidence that children are able to gain instructionally from somewhat more difficult material than is traditionally assumed. This evidence comes from our observations of the effects of repeated reading on oral reading accuracy and rate.

WHAT LEVEL OF MATERIAL IS APPROPRIATE FOR INSTRUCTION?

The results of this study suggest that children can benefit from reading material well below the 95% accuracy rate traditionally recommended for instruction (Wixson & Lipson, 1991). In fact, students appeared to benefit from reading stories in the first sampling even though they were reading them with an average accuracy rate of 85%, which would be considered frustration level. Students were able to benefit from reading material at these lower levels of accuracy because the higher support they were given for the reading through the routines of the program. In this program, students were supported in their reading by having multiple exposures to the same material, by having the stories read to them, by exposure to the vocabulary prior to their own reading, by reading the story at home one or more times, possibly by echo reading, and by partner reading. This high level of support is considerably greater than what is typically provided in a traditional Directed Reading Activity.

We argue that the instructional reading level for a given child is inversely related to the degree of support given to the reader. That is, the more support given, the lower the accuracy level needed for a child to benefit from instruction. In classroom organizations such as our fluency-oriented instruction, students benefited from reading material of greater relative difficulty because they were given greater amounts of support for that reading.

Another source of word recognition support is pictures. Pictures in texts can improve children's word recognition (Denburg, 1976–1977), at least while the picture is present (although pictures can retard the development of context-free word recognition, since readers may overrely on illustrations for cues [e.g., Singer, Samuels, & Spiroff, 1973–1974]). Pictures can also aid in comprehension (see Schallert, 1980, for review). The use of picture books in early grades may support children's ability to read material with fewer words correctly recognized. This may account for the lower criteria for instructional level observed by Clay (1985) and Powell (cited in Wixson & Lipson, 1991) for primary-grade readers. Such readers tend to read more heavily illustrated material, which indicates they are less reliant on knowing the words to read the text competently.

WHAT ARE THE EFFECTS OF THE PROGRAM ON STRUGGLING READERS?

The most pronounced effects of this program were on children who were struggling; that is, those reading above the primer but below the second-grade level. As noted earlier (see Figures 12.3 and 12.5), all children reading at a primer level or higher at the beginning of the year were reading at the second-grade level by the end of the year. In ordinary classroom situations, these children tend to fall progressively further behind the average for their grade (Juel, 1988; Stanovich, 1986). Programs that have successfully accelerated the growth of these readers have been both fairly expensive and difficult to implement, like Reading Recovery (Clay, 1985) or Success for All (Madden, Slavin, Karweit, Donlan, & Wasik, 1997), or designed for first graders. The approach taken here is easy to implement, involves only classroom teachers, and works with second-grade children.

The effects of this program on children who initially read below the primer level were mixed. About half of these children made adequate progress; the remainder did not. For these children, the teachers made special adaptations, including books with reduced vocabulary, providing extra time for reading, and so on. A program based on repeated readings of grade-level material requires a certain initial level of competence. For those without such competence, more intensive remediation is required.

Since our struggling readers had more exposure to the materials, through additional readings at home and through some additional work in class, they were able to read materials of much greater than expected difficulty. In turn, the reading of more difficult material aided their growth as readers, allowing them to read second-grade material with more ease. This seems to be the inverse process to that involved in Matthew effects (Stanovich, 1986). Stanovich suggests that struggling readers, because they read relatively easy material and read less of it than proficient readers, fall further and further behind their higher-achieving peers. Instead, we suggest that our classroom organization provides a mechanism for at least some children to catch up with their peers.

WHAT HAVE WE LEARNED?

This paper has presented a complex evaluation of a complex program, an attempt to reorganize second-grade reading instruction around a set of theory-derived principles. For the most part, this reorganization was successful in achieving its goals. The program was sustainable over 2 years, teachers and children perceived it and its various components positively, and it led to gains in achievement. These gains were found for all children reading at a primer level or higher initially and for about half of those who could not initially read a primer passage.

We also learned about the reciprocal nature of instruction and text difficulty. The traditional notion of instructional level, based as it was on a traditional notion of instruction, seems not to be relevant to this type of classroom setting. Instead, with the greater support given to readers through repeated readings of instructional text in various venues and with various procedures, children are able to learn from material that they initially read with significant difficulty. This program provides that structure in a form easily usable by teachers and responded to by students.

APPENDIX 12.1. INTERVIEW QUESTIONS

Name _____   Class _____

I want to talk to you about the reading program in your class this year. We need to know about what you think about your reading program and the parts of it.

1. How do you like reading in your class?

2. What do you like best about reading in your class?

3. What do you like least about reading in your class?

4. Do you think that you have learned to read better this year?

5. What do you think about when the teacher reads to you from your reading book?

   a. Do you think that this helps you read?

   b. Do you think that this makes you more interested in reading?

6. What does the teacher usually do afterwards?

   a. What do you think about this?

   b. Do you think that this helps you read?

   c. Do you think that this makes you more interested in reading?

7. Do you practice reading the story at home?

   a. About how many times? (If yes, above)

   b. What do you think about this?

   c. Do you think that this helps you read?

   d. Do you think that this makes you more interested in reading?

8. What do you think about partner reading?

   a. Do you think that this helps you read?

   b. Do you think that this makes you more interested in reading?

   c. Who do you read with most often?

   d. Why did you choose that person?

   e. Do you enjoy reading with _____?

   f. How well does _____ read?

9. How often do you have DEAR time?

   a. What do you think about this?

   b. Do you think that this helps you read?

   c. Do you think that this makes you more interested in reading?

REFERENCES

Adams, M. J. (1990). *Beginning to read: Thinking and learning about print.* Cambridge, MA: MIT Press.

Allington, R. L. (1983a). Fluency: The neglected reading goal. *The Reading Teacher, 37,* 556–561.

Allington, R. L. (1983b). The reading instruction provided readers of differing reading abilities. *Elementary School Journal, 83,* 549–559.

Allington, R. L. (1984). Oral reading. In P. D. Pearson, R. Barr, M. L. Kamil, & P. Mosenthal (Eds.), *Handbook of reading research* (pp. 829–864). White Plains, NY: Longman.

Anderson, R. C., Wilkinson, I. A. G., & Mason, J. M. (1990). *A microanalysis of the small-group guided reading lesson: Effects of an emphasis on global story meaning.* Unpublished paper, University of Illinois at Urbana Champaign.

Anderson, R. C., Wilson, P. T., & Fielding, L. G. (1988). Growth in reading and how children spend their time outside of school. *Reading Research Quarterly, 23,* 285–303.

Baumann, N. (1995). Reading Millionaires: It works! *The Reading Teacher, 48,* 730–738.

Campbell, D. T., & Stanley, J. C. (1966). *Experimental and quasi-experimental designs for research.* Chicago: Rand-McNally.

Carver, R. P., & Leibert, R. E. (1995). The effect of reading library books at differing levels of difficulty upon gain in reading ability. *Reading Research Quarterly, 30,* 26–48.

Chall, J. S. (1983). *Stages of reading development.* New York: McGraw-Hill.

Clay, M. M. (1985). *The early detection of reading difficulties.* Portsmouth, NH: Heinemann.

Denburg, S. D. (1976–1977). The interaction of pictures and print in reading instruction. *Reading Research Quarterly, 12,* 176–189.

Doehring, D. G., & Aulls, M. W. (1979). The interactive nature of reading acquisition. *Journal of Reading Behavior, 11,* 27–40.

Dowhower, S. L. (1989). Repeated reading: Research into practice. *The Reading Teacher, 42,* 582–587.

Downing, J. (1979). *Reading and reasoning.* Edinburgh, UK: W. & C. Black.

Durkin, D. (1974). A six-year study of children who learned to read in school at the age of four. *Reading Research Quarterly, 10,* 9–61.

Gambrell, L. B., Wilson, R. M., & Gantt, W. N. (1981). Classroom observations of task-attending behaviors of good and poor readers. *Journal of Educational Research, 74,* 400–404.

Glaser, B. G., & Strauss. A. L. (1967). *The discovery of grounded theory: Strategies for qualitative research.* Chicago: Aldine.

Heubach, K., & Ivey, M. G. (1994, December). *Self-selection in free reading: Examining book difficulty and factors influencing choice in Grade 2.* Paper presented at the annual meeting of the National Reading Conference, San Diego, CA.

Hoffman, J. (1987). Rethinking the role of oral reading. *Elementary School Journal, 87,* 367–373.

Juel, C. (1988). Learning to read and write: A longitudinal study of fifty-four children from first through fourth grade. *Journal of Educational Psychology, 80,* 437–447.

Kuhn, M. R., & Stahl, S. A. (2003). Fluency: A review of developmental and remedial practices. *Journal of Educational Psychology, 95,* 3–22.

Leslie, L., & Caldwell, J. (1988). *Qualitative reading inventory.* New York: HarperCollins.

Madden, N., Slavin, R. E., Karweit, N. L., Dolan, L. J., & Wasik, B. A. (1997). Reading, writing, and tutoring in success for all. In S. A. Stahl & D. A. Hayes (Eds.), *Instructional models in reading* (pp. 109–130). Hillsdale, NJ: Erlbaum.

Martinez, M., & Roser, N. (1985). Read it again: The value of repeated readings during storytime. *The Reading Teacher, 38,* 782–786.

McCormick, C. E., & Mason, J. M. (1986). Intervention procedures for increasing preschool children's interest in and knowledge about reading. In W. H. Teale & E. Sulzby (Eds.), *Emergent literacy: Writing and reading* (pp. 90–115). Norwood, NJ: Ablex.

Morris, D., & Nelson, L. (1992). Supported oral reading with low achieving second graders. *Reading Research and Instruction, 32,* 49–63.

Mudre, L. H., & McCormick, S. (1989). Effects of meaning-focused cues on underachieving readers' context use, self-corrections, and literal comprehension. *Reading Research Quarterly, 24,* 89–113.

O'Masta, G., & Wolf, J. (1991). Encouraging independent reading through the Reading Millionaires club. *The Reading Teacher, 44,* 656–662.

Rasinski, T. V. (1989). *The effects of repeated reading and repeated listening while reading on reading fluency.* (ERIC Document Reproduction Service No. ED 384 666)

Rasinski, T. V. (1989). Fluency for everyone: Incorporating fluency instruction in the classroom. *The Reading Teacher, 42,* 690–693.

Rasinski, T. V., & Hoffman, J. V. (2003). Oral reading in the school literacy curriculum. *Reading Research Quarterly, 38,* 510–523.

Rasinski, T. V., Padak, N., Linek, W., & Sturtevant, E. (1994). Effects of fluency development on urban second grade readers. *Journal of Educational Research, 87,* 158–165.

Routman, R. (1991). *Transitions.* Portsmouth, NH: Heinemann.

Samuels, S. J. (1985). Automaticity and repeated reading. In J. Osborn, P. T. Wilson, & R. C.

Anderson (Eds.), *Reading education: Foundations for a literate America* (pp. 215–230). Lexington, MA: Lexington Books.

Samuels, S. J., Schermer, N., & Reinking, D. (1992). Reading fluency: Techniques for making decoding automatic. In S. J. Samuels & A. E. Farstrup (Eds.), *What research says about reading instruction* (2nd ed., pp. 124–144). Newark, DE: International Reading Association.

Schallert, D. L. (1980). The role of illustrations in reading comprehension. In R. J. Spiro, B. C. Bruce, & W. F. Brewer (Eds.), *Theoretical issues in reading comprehension* (pp. 503–524). Hillsdale, NJ: Erlbaum.

Singer, H., Samuels, S. J., & Spiroff, J. (1973–1974). The effects of pictures and contextual conditions on learning responses to printed words. *Reading Research Quarterly, 9,* 555–567.

Stanovich, K. E. (1986). Matthew effects in reading: Some consequences of individual differences in the acquisition of literacy. *Reading Research Quarterly, 21,* 360–407.

Taylor, B. M., Frye, B. J., & Maruyama, G. M. (1990). Time spent reading and reading growth. *American Educational Research Journal, 27,* 351–362.

Taylor, N. E., Wade, M. R., & Yekovich, F. R. (1985). The effects of text manipulation and multiple reading strategies on the reading performance of good and poor readers. *Reading Research Quarterly, 20,* 566–585.

Topping, K. (1987). Paired reading: A powerful technique for parent use. *The Reading Teacher 40,* 608–614.

Vacca, R., & Rasinski, T. (1992). *Case studies in whole language.* New York: HarperCollins.

Wixson, K. K., & Lipson, M. Y. (1991). *Reading disability.* New York: HarperCollins.

13 Fluency-Oriented Reading Instruction

A Merging of Theory and Practice

Melanie R. Kuhn
Paula J. Schwanenflugel

When Steven Stahl and his colleague Kathleen Heubach first described Fluency-Oriented Reading Instruction (FORI) in a Technical Report for the National Reading Research Center (Stahl, Heubach, & Cramond, 1997), fluency was a largely neglected component of reading development (Allington, 1983; National Reading Panel, 2000). Since then, fluency has become a focus of interest in the reading community, at least in part, as a result of Steve's own work (e.g., Kuhn & Stahl, 2003; Stahl, 2001, 2002). As was often the case with Steve, his work straddled the research–practice divide. He took seriously the question that his mentor, Jeanne Chall, often asked of her students as part of their consideration of research, "What does it mean for teaching?" (J. S. Chall, personal communication, February 24, 1988). In terms of fluency, the answer to this question involves identifying its role in the reading process as well as the way in which literacy instruction can assist learners in becoming fluent readers.

FLUENCY-ORIENTED READING INSTRUCTION

Steve's development of FORI (Stahl et al., 1997; Stahl & Heubach, in press, reprinted as Chapter 12, this volume) is an example of this desire to integrate research and practice. This instructional approach was designed in response to a specific need in a local school district. The school board had mandated that, rather than reading at their instructional level, students must read exclusively from grade-level texts. This was considered to be particularly problematic by the teachers as the district served a large percentage of students of low socioeconomic status (SES) (nearly 80% free and reduced-price lunch), many of whom were reading well below grade level. As a result, Steve met with several second-grade teachers from the district in an attempt to identify an instructional approach that would allow students to access text that would normally be considered beyond their reading ability. Developing such a program seemed particularly crucial if the children were to experience success with their reading over the course of the school year.

The resulting approach was based on the Oral Recitation Lesson (ORL), a program designed by Hoffman (1987) to create meaningful instruction using basal readers. As with the ORL, FORI used repetition, a strategy that underlies numerous fluency-oriented approaches, as one of its mainstays. It also integrated several other principles of effective fluency instruction, including modeling, direct instruction and feedback, support or assistance, and practice with phrasing (see Rasinski, 1989). However, because it had been mandated that the students read from grade-level text, there was one principle, the use of easy and appropriate text, that was, by necessity, violated. Rasinski suggested this principle as disfluent readers often find themselves reading from text that is at their frustration level. If these learners are to develop comfort with print, the argument continues, they need to have the opportunity to practice reading from texts that are at their independent level.

Because the literacy curriculum devised for the FORI study used material that was challenging for the majority of the students, it was unclear how students would do either on a daily basis or over the course of the school year. However, it was hoped that the support provided through the use of repetition and the scaffolded reading strategies would counter some of the difficulties resulting from the texts. Despite the concerns that accompanied this factor, the results from the research were impressive. In the first year, 84 students in four classrooms participated in the study. Using the Qualitative Reading Inventory–II (QRI-II; Leslie & Caldwell, 1995) as the pre–posttest measure, the students made 1.88 years average growth. Given these results, rather than create a control condition as had been envisioned originally, 10 classrooms were asked to participate in a scale-up during the second year. One hundred and twenty-five students completed the pre–posttesting in the second year with results on the QRI-II indicating 1.77 years average growth.

While the decision not to use a control group in the second year was reasonable given the first year's results, it is also the case that the findings would have been strengthened further by the inclusion of a control group and standardized measures (Stahl & Kuhn, 2003). As a result of this understanding, Steve, along with several colleagues, decided to further evaluate the approach through a large-scale research study titled "The Development of Fluent and Automatic Reading: Precursor to Learning from Text," which was funded by the Interagency Educational Research Initiative (IERI) for a 5-year period. The grant is designed to explore a number of questions relating to fluency development, making it much broader than the original study in a number of ways. To begin with, the study looks at developmental factors that are concomitant with fluent reading. Next, it evaluates two potential approaches to literacy instruction with special attention being paid to their role in fluency development. Third, it explores strategies designed to assist students who have not established emergent or early literacy behaviors despite their second-grade standing. Fourth, it incorporates a number of substudies designed to look at a range of questions, from home–school connections to classroom observations to partner reading. Finally, a scale-up component has been included that will determine the success of the primary interventions in situations in which teachers receive a minimal amount of support and feedback. However, because we are focusing on the work of Stahl and

Heubach (Stahl et al., 1997; Stahl & Heubach, 2005), we emphasize our work on the effects of classroom practices designed to promote the development of reading fluency.

AUTOMATICITY THEORY

The original FORI (Stahl et al., 1997; Stahl & Heubach, 2005) implemented repetition as a key component in its approach to fluency development. The use of repetition is a common element across much research on reading fluency. Its use in fluency instruction was derived from research relating to automaticity theory (LaBerge & Samuels, 1974) and is based on the notion that in order to become skilled readers, learners need to be not only accurate in their word recognition but automatic as well. Such automatic word recognition is essential if students are to move beyond word-by-word decoding to fluent reading. Because individuals have only a limited amount of attention available for any complex task, including that of reading, any attention expended on word recognition is attention that is unavailable for comprehension. One question for researchers involves the way in which readers make this transition from purposeful decoding to automatic word recognition.

According to many automaticity theorists (LaBerge & Samuels, 1974; Perfetti, 1985; Stanovich, 1980), the best way for readers to develop automatic word recognition is through extensive practice, such as that which occurs when learners read extensively. Such practice allows learners to develop familiarity with the orthographic patterns of written language by providing successive exposures to print. For example, because of their familiarity with text, skilled readers realize, albeit subconsciously, that the letter *t* is over 50 times more likely to be followed by *h* than it is by the next most likely letter, which is *o* (Adams, 1990). As learners become increasingly familiar with print, they need to spend less attention on word identification; therefore, more can be directed toward the construction of meaning. Given this, the development of automatic word recognition contributes not only to students becoming fluent readers but to their comprehension of text as well.

Traditionally, this exposure to print was developed in the classroom through the daily reading of text that students were encountering for the first time. In other words, children were expected to develop automaticity by reading ever-changing material. When considering the typical literacy lesson, Samuels (1979, 2006) raised concerns about the requirement that learners read previously unpracticed text on a daily basis. If practice was the key to automaticity, he conjectured, it might be more effective for them to practice a given text repeatedly in order to gain familiarity with it. The repeated reading approach was designed to test this theory with readers who were experiencing difficulty making the transition to fluency and has been an effective means of assisting these learners (see Dowhower, 1989, for a review of the repeated readings literature). Furthermore, a number of variations based on the notion of repetition (paired repeated reading, tape-assisted reading, cross-aged reading) have also proven to be highly successful (see, Kuhn & Stahl, 2003, and National Reading Panel, 2000, for a broader look at fluency instruction).

However, a recent review of fluency research (Kuhn & Stahl, 2003) indicated that it may not be the repetition per se that assists learners in their acquisition of fluency but the support that it provides. When comparing repeated reading approaches with those that provided scaffolded, or supported, approaches to reading, such as echo or choral reading, the results indicated that both approaches led to equivalent gains. As such, when designing the FORI study, it was decided that the issue of repetition in comparison to an increase in scaffolded exposure to text should be explored as well. Therefore, the research was designed to answer two primary questions: How effective is the FORI approach in terms of fluency development when compared to other approaches of literacy instruction? And, is it the use of repetition, specifically, that leads to growth in fluency or can the supported reading of a broader range of texts produce equivalent gains?

THE DEVELOPMENT OF FLUENT AND AUTOMATIC READING: PRECURSOR TO LEARNING FROM TEXT

To effectively evaluate the FORI approach while simultaneously taking into account the differences between repetition and supported text, it was decided to use three literacy curricula: FORI, a wide-reading approach, and a control condition. The FORI condition involved the rereading of a single grade-equivalent text, usually a selection from the basal or literature anthology but occasionally a trade book, over the course of a week (see Figure 13.1). On the first day, this involved preteaching activities and a read-aloud, with the students following along in their own copy, followed by a discussion of the text to ensure a focus on comprehension from the outset. The second and third day involved an echo and choral reading of the text, which was followed by a partner reading of the text on day 4. There was also an expectation that the students would read the story at home for extra practice. On the final day, children completed extension activities related to the text. Depending on how many times students read the selection at home, repetitions ranged between four and seven times over the course of the week.

The wide-reading component was based on a modification of the FORI in which the students read three grade-equivalent texts over the course of the week rather than a single text (see Figure 13.2). The first day paralleled that of the FORI lesson with the teacher reading the text aloud and the students following along and then discussing it. On the second day, the children echo read the story and, depending on the text, may have partner read the text as well. On the third day, they completed extension activities for the story. On the fourth and fifth days, the children echo read class sets of trade books (levels J to M, according to Fountas & Pinnell, 1999) provided by the researchers. As with the FORI approach, the students were expected to read the texts at home. As a result, the wide reading group read the primary text between two and three times and read the two secondary texts once or twice. Thus, the difference between this intervention and the FORI intervention was both the number of texts read during the week and the number of rereadings per text.

The control classrooms used a variety of approaches as part of their literacy curriculum including guided reading, reading workshop, and the directed reading activity. They also had support in the form of literacy coaches and reading specialists. The coaches provided their students with instruction that is generally considered effective. Furthermore, the controls, the FORI group, and the wide-reading group were provided with books for each of their classroom libraries.

	Monday	Tuesday	Wednesday	Thursday	Friday
Fluency-Oriented Reading Instruction Basal lesson	**Teacher introduces story.** Teacher reads story to class, discusses. Option: Teacher develops graphic organizers. Option: Class does activities from basal.	**Students practice story.** Teacher and students do choral reading.	**Students practice story.** Teacher and students do echo reading.	**Students practice story.** Students do partner reading.	**Students do extension activities.** These may include writing in response to story, etc. Option: Teacher does running records of children's reading (see below).
Choice Reading	Children read a book of their choosing.	Children read a book of their choosing.	Children read a book of their choosing.	Children read a book of their choosing.	Children read a book of their choosing.
Home Reading	Children read 15–30 minutes per day in a book of their choosing.	Students take story home and read to parents (or other).	Students who need more practice take home the basal story—others take book of their choosing.	Students who need more practice take home the basal story—others take book of their choosing.	Children read 15–30 minutes per day in a book of their choosing.
Wide Reading Instruction	**Teacher introduces story.** Class does activities from basal (Story 1).	**Students practice story.** Option: Teacher and students do echo reading. Option: Students do partner reading.	**Students do extension activities.** These may include writing in response to story, etc. Option: Teacher does running records of children's reading (see below).	**Teacher and students choral read new trade book (Story 2).** Option: Students do partner reading on story (2).	**Teacher and students choral read new trade book (Story 3).** Option: Students do partner reading on story (3). Option: Students do extension activities (writing, etc.). Option: Students do activities from basal.
Choice Reading	Children read a book of their choosing.	Children read a book of their choosing.	Children read a book of their choosing.	Children read a book of their choosing.	Children read a book of their choosing.
Home Reading	Children read 15–30 minutes per day in a book of their choosing.	Students take story home and read to parents (or other).	Children read 15–30 minutes per day in a book of their choosing.	Children read 15–30 minutes per day in a book of their choosing.	Children read 15–30 minutes per day in a book of their choosing.

FIGURE 13.1. FORI and wide-reading weekly lesson plans.

209

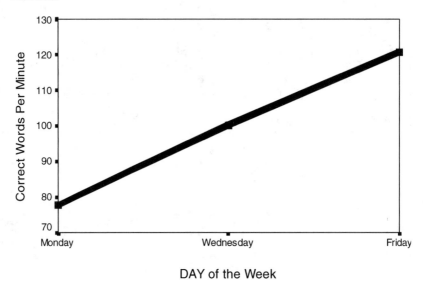

FIGURE 13.2. Weekly progress using the FORI program using a curriculum-based assessment of children's reading fluency.

Nearly 350 second-grade children from 24 southeastern and northeastern U.S. schools participated in the study. All the schools had multiethnic and multiracial populations. The students' word recognition in isolation, rate and accuracy in connected text, and reading comprehension were all assessed using a series of standardized tests. At the end of the school year, the results indicated that the children who received either of the fluency-oriented interventions made greater gains in word reading efficiency and comprehension when compared to controls; however, only the children in the wide reading intervention showed larger gains in text reading rate. Overall, the results for the two variants of fluency-oriented reading instruction were more similar than different. To put these findings into perspective, the word reading efficiency of children receiving both interventions grew at a rate 88% faster than might normally be expected in a similar time frame and the reading comprehension skills grew at a rate 50% faster than might be expected. Furthermore, the study provided tremendous support for the findings of Stahl and Heubach (Stahl et al., 1997; Stahl & Heubach, 2005) and the efficacy of using challenging texts provided there is enough support. The fact that the wide and repeated reading approaches produced nearly identical results helps us to identify what is most important regarding the FORI lesson plan for enhancing the development of fluency in young readers. That is, it is likely that it is not the repetition of text itself that is key to the development of fluency but the use of scaffolded supports and the focus on extensive oral reading of more difficult text that lends to the effectiveness of the methods. Given the structure and simplicity of both approaches, either can be readily integrated into the classroom. Furthermore, because either approach can assist with fluency development, choosing between these approaches may depend on the resources available in the classroom.

A MICROGENETIC STUDY OF FORI

Throughout our work on this intervention, we have been privy to many comments from teachers regarding the enthusiasm that they, the children, and, in some cases, the parents have for the fluency-oriented portions of the literacy curricula. Given the success and enthusiasm that teachers reported with the use of the repeated readings version of the FORI approach, Schwanenflugel and one of her students, Emily Moore, grew curious as to what happened on a weekly basis in children's reading development that was noticeable to all. In the second year of the study, they decided to carry out a microgenetic study of the children's weekly reading fluency growth using a curriculum-based assessment approach similar to that advocated by Hasbrouck and Tindal (1992). Microgenetic approaches involve more continuous sampling of a rapidly changing behavior than is typical in most studies so that cumulative change and variability can be observed (Siegler & Svetina, 2002). This approach has been useful in examining the development of memory (Coyle & Bjorklund, 1997) and attention strategies (Miller & Aloise-Young, 1996) as well as academic topics such as arithmetic (Siegler & Jenkins, 1989) and scientific reasoning (Kuhn & Phelps, 1982).

Because of the intensive nature of the microgenetic approach, they decided to focus on the FORI condition and a relatively small subset of the children participating in the overall intervention. They targeted 18 children randomly selected from five classrooms. Each teacher had selected her own focus passage for the week that the children used for the repeated reading segment of the school day. The tester asked each child to read the first 100 words (or nearest sentence) of the passage being used once on Monday, again on Wednesday, and again on Friday. The tester performed a miscue analysis noting all reading errors using a very stringent criterion that included omissions, repetitions, substitutions, mispronunciations, and so on. Words read correctly per minute were calculated for each child at each testing occasion.

As can be seen in Figure 13.2, children's progress on the weekly passage was remarkable. As a group, children grew in reading fluency on the passage from reading approximately 78 correct words per minute to nearly 120 correct words per minute. Virtually all children made progress in their passage reading fluency. As one of the teachers who have worked with us noted, "By the end of the week, even my worst readers are able to read it! (the weekly passage)." Moreover, when the reading fluency norms of Hasbrouck and Tindal (1992) are used to discern the relative fluency of the passage reading of the children at the beginning of the week, children begin reading the passage at around the level expected of children in the 25th percentile. However, by the end of the week, their reading of the passage falls at a rate more typical of children at the 75th percentile.

This kind of progress is likely to be noticed by teachers and the children themselves. Although the conclusions that can be drawn from this microgenetic study regarding the rate of growth on a weekly basis would be considerably enhanced if control children and more children had been tested, in a very real sense, this type of study provides us with the same sorts of limited information that teachers typically have when deciding to continue, persist, or drop classroom practices that they acquire knowledge of in professional development opportunities. It is our guess that, as teachers and children see real growth weekly, teachers persist and support the use of these practices, and children are motivated to struggle through difficult text to achieve mastery. Moreover, as noted previously, the cumulative effect of such experiences leads to improvement that can later be detected on standardized assessments of reading ability. Taken together, these studies provide considerable support for the classroom practices promoted by Stahl and Heubach (Stahl et al., 1997; Stahl & Heubach, 2005) for fostering the development of reading fluency.

CONCLUSIONS

At the beginning of this chapter, we discussed Steve's commitment to both research and practice. Steve's research on the FORI approach (Stahl et al., 1997; Stahl & Heubach, 2005) allowed him to blend his interest in developing the field's theoretical understanding while simultaneously improving classroom practice. His research confirmed the importance of repetition as a means of developing automaticity and its role in improving students' comprehension. Perhaps more important for struggling readers, however, was his finding that, given extensive support, students can learn from text that would otherwise be considered well above their instructional level. As can be seen in the microgenetic study conducted by Schwanenflugel and Moore, students can move from the 25th to the 75th percentile (based on Hasbrouck & Tindal's, 1992, norms) over the course of four to seven repetitions. Furthermore, in the original research, the students made gains of 1.88 and 1.77 years growth in the first and second years of the study, respectively. For students who are behind their peers in their literacy development, such accelerated gains can be the difference between catching up in their learning or continuing to struggle with their reading.

In addition, the review of fluency instruction conducted by Kuhn and Stahl (2003) has raised additional questions about how learners become fluent readers as well as fluency's role in the reading process. It pondered the role that prosody plays both in fluent reading and in comprehension. It also brought forth the issue of repetition versus scaffolding, which became an underlying focus in the IERI-sponsored research discussed in this chapter. Overall, Steve's work in fluency not only has assisted students in developing their reading but has furthered our understanding of reading itself—a legacy he would be proud of.

ACKNOWLEDGMENTS

This research was supported in part by the Interagency Education Research Initiative, a program of research jointly managed by the National Science Foundation, the Institute of Education Sciences in the U.S. Department of Education, and the National Institute of Child Health and Human Development in the National Institutes of Health (NIH Grant No. 5 R01 HD40746-4).

REFERENCES

Adams, M. J. (1990). *Beginning to read: Thinking and learning about print*. Cambridge, MA: MIT Press.
Allington, R. L. (1983). Fluency: The neglected reading goal. *The Reading Teacher, 37,* 556–561.
Coyle, T. R., & Bjorklund, D. F. (1997). Age differences in, and consequences of, multiple-

and variable-strategy use on a multi-trial sort-recall task. *Developmental Psychology, 33,* 372–380.

Dahl, P. R. (1979). An experimental program for teaching high speed word recognition and comprehension skills. In J. E. Button, T. Loveitt, & T. Rowland (Eds.), *Communications research in learning disabilities and mental retardation* (pp. 33–65). Baltimore: University Park Press.

Dowhower, S. L. (1989). Repeated reading: Theory into practice. *The Reading Teacher, 42,* 502–507.

Fountas, I. C., & Pinnell, G. S. (1999). *Matching books to readers using leveled books in guided reading, K–3.* Portsmouth, MA: Heinemann.

Hasbrouck, J. E., & Tindal, G. (1992). Curriculum-based oral reading fluency norms for students in grades 2 through 5. *Teaching Exceptional Children, 24,* 41–44.

Hoffman, J. V., & Crone, S. (1985). The oral recitation lesson: A research-derived strategy for reading basal texts. In J. A. Niles & R. V. Lalik (Eds.), *Issues in literacy: A research perspective, Thirty-fourth yearbook of the National Reading Conference* (pp. 76–83). Rochester, NY: National Reading Conference.

Kuhn, D., & Phelps, E. (1982). The development of problem-solving strategies. In H. Reese (Ed.), *Advances in child development and behavior* (Vol. 17, pp. 1–44). New York: Academic Press.

Kuhn, M. R., & Stahl, S. (2003). Fluency: A review of developmental and remedial strategies. *The Journal of Educational Psychology, 95,* 1–19.

LaBerge, D., & Samuels, S. J. (1974). Toward a theory of automatic information processing in reading. *Cognitive Psychology, 6,* 293–323.

Leslie, L., & Caldwell, J. (1995). *Qualitative reading inventory–II.* Reading, MA: Addison-Wesley.

Miller, P. H., & Aloise-Young, P. (1996). Preschoolers' strategic behaviors and performance on a same-different task. *Journal of Experimental Child Psychology, 60,* 284–303.

National Reading Panel. (2000). *Report of the Subgroups: National Reading Panel.* Washington, DC: National Institute of Child Health and Development. Available online at: www. nationalreadingpanel.org

Perfetti, C. A. (1985). *Reading ability.* New York: Oxford University Press.

Rasinski, T. V. (1989). Fluency for everyone: Incorporating fluency instruction in the classroom. *The Reading Teacher, 42,* 690–693

Samuels, S. J. (1979). The method of repeated readings. *The Reading Teacher, 32,* 403–408.

Samuels, S. J. (2006). Reading fluency: Its past, present, and future. In T. Rasinski, C. Blachowicz, & K. Lems (Eds.), *Fluency instruction: Research-based best practices* (pp. 7–20). New York: Guilford Press.

Siegler, R. S., & Jenkins, E. A. (1989). *How children discover new strategies.* Hillsdale, NJ: Erlbaum.

Siegler, R. S., & Svetina, M. (2002). A microgenetic/cross-sectional study of matrix completion: Comparing short-term and long-term change. *Child Development, 73,* 793–809.

Stahl, S. A. (2001, August). *Fluency development.* Presentation at CIERA's 2nd summer institute, Ann Arbor, MI.

Stahl. S. A. (2002, June). *Fluency-oriented reading instruction.* Invited paper presented at seminar, Center for Research on Education, Diversity & Excellence, Santa Cruz.

Stahl, S. A., & Heubach, K. (2005). Fluency-oriented reading instruction. *Journal of Literacy Research, 37*(1), 25–60.

Stahl, S. A., Heubach, K., & Cramond, B. (1997). *Fluency-oriented reading instruction* (Reading Research Report No. 79). Athens, GA: National Reading Research Center.

Stahl, S. A., & Kuhn, M. R. (2003, May). *Fluency-oriented reading instruction: Results from the first year.* Paper presented at Reading Research 2003, Orlando, FL.

Stanovich, K. E. (1980). Toward an interactive-compensatory model of individual differences in the development of reading fluency. *Reading Research Quarterly, 16,* 32–71.

I V VOCABULARY

14 | The State of Vocabulary Research in the Mid-1980s

WILLIAM NAGY

JUDITH A. SCOTT

By the mid-1980s, reading research had gained prominence in the field of educational research as a discipline in which linguistic, psychological, sociological, and computer technology converged. The rise of cognitive science in the late 1960s and early 1970s had displaced the behaviorist tradition with information-processing theory (Alexander & Fox, 2004).

Comprehension had become a dominant theme, mentioned in over half of the articles published from 1981 to 1985 in *Reading Research Quarterly* (Gaffney & Anderson, 2000). Whole language was at its peak, and although basals still used controlled vocabulary, this practice would largely disappear in the early 1990s (Gaffney & Anderson, 2000; Hiebert, Martin, & Menon, 2005). The National Academy of Education report *Becoming a Nation of Readers* (Anderson, Hiebert, Scott, & Wilkinson, 1985) summarized the substantial advances made in understanding the process of reading in the previous decade, characterizing reading as a complex skill that requires the active construction of meaning, strategic processes, fluency, and motivation.

The 1980s were also a period of renewed interest in vocabulary research, a field that underwent substantial fluctuations in attention throughout the century. In fact, at the end of the 1980s, Baumann and Kame'enui (1991) described themselves as being "in the midst of a virtual explosion in the research on vocabulary learning and instruction" (p. 604). Graves (1986a) noted several specific indications of this trend: the establishment of a Vocabulary Special Interest Group in the American Educational Research Association in 1986, a special issue of the *Journal of Reading* devoted to vocabulary (1986), and McKeown and Curtis's (1987) book *The Nature of Vocabulary Acquisition.* Several major syntheses of vocabulary research also appeared during this decade (Anderson & Freebody, 1981; Graves, 1986b; Jenkins & Dixon, 1983; Mezynski, 1983; Stahl & Fairbanks, 1986). One of the most influential of these has been the Stahl and Fairbanks (1986) meta-analysis.

In the first half of the 20th century, reading research had documented the strong correlational link between vocabulary knowledge and reading comprehension (e.g., Davis, 1944; see Anderson & Freebody, 1981, for a review) and suggested that vocabulary could be influenced by schooling (Hilliard, 1926, cited in Venezky, 1984). The idea that the ease of understanding what one reads could be attributed primarily to the difficulty of the words found in the text dominated early work in vocabulary research (Venezky, 1984). The 1921 publication of Thorndike's *The Teacher Word Book* with tabulations of word frequency led to an extended period of interest in vocabulary, and the development of readability formulas (Clifford, 1978). In the 1950s, however, interest in vocabulary research began to decline (Calfee & Drum, 1978; Graves, 1986a). In a review of 80 studies on teaching vocabulary, Petty, Herold, and Stoll (1968) despaired that very little was known about teaching vocabulary and that the investigation of the most satisfactory methods for teaching vocabulary remained a "rather wide open area of research" (p. 85). Few researchers rose to the challenge, however, and by the late 1970s, Calfee and Drum (1978) stated that the investigations of reading vocabulary were a "vanishing species" (p. 217).

Several reasons have been suggested for this decline in interest. One was the lack of a guiding theoretical framework for research in vocabulary (Calfee & Drum, 1978; Clifford, 1978; Graves, 1986a). According to Petty et al. (1968), vocabulary research had relied, almost universally, on the "schoolbook grammars of the eighteenth and nineteenth centuries, and on a fuzzy, undeveloped semantics" (p. 61).

The collapse of behaviorism, which had dominated U.S. psychology, also contributed to the declining interest in vocabulary. The behaviorist paradigm had served as the implicit foundation for vocabulary research but had not provided an adequate basis for dealing with word meanings, as was made vividly clear in Chomsky's (1959) review of B. F. Skinner's book *Verbal Behavior* (1957). However, the dramatic advances in linguistics that flowed out of Chomsky's work, which played a seminal role in the cognitive revolution, did not immediately provide a foundation for vocabulary research either, because the initial impact of Chomsky's work (e.g., Chomsky, 1957, 1965) had led to an emphasis on syntax in linguistics and psycholinguistics.

By the 1980s, however, the shift to a cognitive perspective that had undermined the earlier traditions of vocabulary research had begun to provide a new foundation for addressing this area. As Graves (1986a) notes, there was "an increased willingness of psychologists and linguists to deal with semantics" (p. 5). Beck and McKeown (1991) likewise point out that the adoption of an information-processing orientation in psychology provided the theory from which to examine the relationship between words and ideas. Thus, they could define vocabulary acquisition as "a complex process that involves establishing relationships between concepts, organization of concepts, and expansion and refinement of knowledge about individual words" (p. 790).

The cognitive revolution had also made possible a focus on comprehension in reading research. This was evident in particular in the establishment in 1976 of the Center for the Study of Reading, the first federally funded center focused on reading, whose initial charge was to examine reading comprehension, not decoding (Gaffney & Anderson, 2000). The theories of reading comprehension that emerged at the center and elsewhere provided a new framework for reexamining vocabulary knowledge and its role in comprehension.

CHALLENGES TO THE INSTRUMENTALIST HYPOTHESIS

One specific indication of the reawakening of an interest in vocabulary was Anderson and Freebody's (1981) paper on vocabulary knowledge, which first appeared as a technical report of the Center for the Study of Reading in 1978. In addition to synthesizing much of the earlier work on vocabulary, this paper also provided a conceptual framework for much of the later discussion of the role of vocabulary knowledge in reading comprehension.

Though the strong correlational relationship between vocabulary knowledge and reading comprehension had already been thoroughly documented, there was still little known about what type of cause-and-effect relationships might underlie this correlation. Anderson and Freebody (1981) formulated three hypotheses, which could be briefly summarized as follows: The instrumentalist hypothesis is that it is word knowledge per se that promotes comprehension. People with larger vocabularies understand text better because they have larger vocabularies. This might be considered the default or commonsense understanding of the relationship between vocabulary knowledge and reading comprehension. The aptitude hypothesis is that verbal ability underlies both vocabulary growth and reading comprehension. Those who are good at learning words are also good at understanding text. The knowledge hypothesis suggests that one's ability to understand text depends on conceptual knowledge—of which vocabulary knowledge is a highly visible but relatively small part. Anderson and Freebody noted that these hypotheses are not mutually exclusive, and that all are likely to be true to some extent. However, which elements should be used to create the most effective instructional approach to vocabulary, and their relative importance, depends on the veracity of each hypothesis.

Though Anderson and Freebody (1981) left open the question of which of the three hypotheses was most true, one of their purposes was certainly to call into question the instrumentalist hypothesis. They cite two specific types of empirical studies that bear on the truth of the instrumentalist hypothesis: the impact on comprehension of substituting easier or more difficult vocabulary in a text, and the impact of instruction on difficult words in the text.

Anderson and Freebody briefly reviewed two studies (Marks, Doctorow, & Wittrock, 1974; Wittrock, Marks, & Doctorow, 1975) that found that substituting harder or easier synonyms for 15% of the words in a text had a measurable impact on comprehension—findings consistent with the instrumentalist hypothesis. However, they later did their own study (Freebody & Anderson, 1983), comparing comprehension of the original versions of texts with versions modified by substituting more difficult synonyms for one content word in six and one content word in three, respectively. They found that only the higher level of replacement (one content word in three) had a significant impact on comprehension. In another experiment, they found that substituting difficult vocabulary in important propositions, but not in trivial propositions, had a negative impact on vocabulary.

Though these results are not inconsistent with the instrumentalist hypothesis, they do call into question the conditions under which it is relevant. The presence of difficult vocabulary in some of the text, and especially in less important propositions, does not have a consistently negative impact on comprehension. Hence, in such cases it would not be expected that teaching the meanings of these words would have a measurable positive impact.

A second type of evidence Anderson and Freebody (1981) mentioned that called the instrumentalist hypothesis into question was the failure of instruction on difficult words in texts to reliably increase comprehension of those texts. In particular, they cited two studies (Jenkins, Pany, & Schreck, 1978; Tuinman & Brady, 1974) in which vocabulary instruction increased students' knowledge of the instructed words but not their comprehension of text containing those words. Mezynski's (1983) review identified an additional three studies (Jackson & Dizney, 1963; Lieberman, 1967; Pany & Jenkins, 1977) with similar results.

CHARACTERISTICS OF EFFECTIVE VOCABULARY INSTRUCTION

At the time of Anderson and Freebody's (1981) review, then, there was limited empirical support for the instrumentalist hypothesis. There was also evidence that schools were paying limited attention to either comprehension or vocabulary instruction (Durkin, 1978–1979). Partly in response to this situation, Isabel Beck, Margaret McKeown, and their colleagues undertook a series of studies (Beck, Perfetti, & McKeown, 1982; McKeown, Beck, Omanson, & Perfetti, 1983; McKeown, Beck, Omanson, & Pople, 1985) designed to demonstrate the effect that rich vocabulary instruction could have on comprehension.

Their rich vocabulary instruction, which was in fact successful in producing gains in the comprehension of texts containing the instructed words, was different from traditional vocabulary instruction in a number of respects. Perhaps the most important is that it involves a variety of activities that require students to use the words in meaningful ways, rather than just memorizing the pairing between a word and its definition—for example, answering questions about the instructed words ("What would a *hermit* have nightmares about?"). Another characteristic of rich instruction is that students have multiple encounters with the words being taught. In one study (McKeown et al., 1985) it was found that rich instruction was not effective in increasing reading comprehension if it involved only four encounters with each word; 12 was the lowest number of instructional encounters for which a significant effect on comprehension was found. Yet another characteristic of rich instruction was the inclusion of activities that specifically focused on speed of response, aimed at developing fluency as well as accuracy in accessing word meanings.

Mezynski (1983) reviewed eight studies that had examined the effects of vocabulary instruction on reading comprehension, only a few of which had found a significant effect of instruction on comprehension. Mezynski added an additional hypothesis to Anderson and Freebody's (1981) original three, the access hypothesis: Only if words had been learned to the point where their meanings were retrieved automatically would there be a measurable impact on reading comprehension. She suggested this as a reason why the rich vocabulary instruction used by Beck and her colleagues had succeeded in improving comprehension, whereas most other vocabulary interventions had failed.

Though Mezynski's review contributed important additional insight into the relationship between vocabulary and reading comprehension, it did not attempt to provide definitive information about the nature of effective vocabulary instruction. On the contrary, one of the review's main contributions was to clarify conceptual and methodological gaps in the previous research. To confirm her hypotheses about what made some vocabulary interventions such as Beck's successful at improving comprehension, a broader empirical base was necessary. Stahl and Fairbanks's (1986) meta-analysis directly addressed this need.

THE GENERALIZED IMPACT OF VOCABULARY INSTRUCTION

Beck, McKeown, and their colleagues interpreted their findings as validation of the instrumentalist hypothesis: Vocabulary instruction did increase reading comprehension, if the instruction was sufficiently high in quality and intensity. However, some (e.g., Nagy, 1985) challenged this optimism, arguing that even if Beck et al.'s research proved the instrumentalist hypothesis to be true under certain circumstances, the findings did not necessarily establish that vocabulary instruction was an effective means of improving reading comprehension in classrooms. The rationale for the challenge was made on three grounds: the density of unfamiliar words in the text used to measure the effects of vocabulary instruction on comprehension, the time-intensive nature of rich vocabulary instruction, and at a more general level, the gap between the number of words that could be covered in such instruction and the number of words that students actually need to learn.

The stories used by Beck et al. (1982) to assess the impact of vocabulary instruction on reading comprehension had a relatively high proportion of unfamiliar words, about one target word per 11 words of text. Though this might seem to be within a child's "instructional level," these texts were not representative of authentic text, in that all the novel words in the text were substantially more difficult than the unfamiliar words that might be found in grade-level-appropriate text. Hence, one cannot necessarily generalize from the success of the instruction tested by Beck and her colleagues to a situation in which children are reading school texts.

The second objection was that rich vocabulary instruction is too time-intensive to cover very many words. The original study in this line of research (Beck et al., 1982) covered 104 words in a 5-month period. Even allowing for some streamlining, it is unlikely that rich vocabulary instruction could (or should) be attempted for more than 200 words in a school year.

The third, related objection was that the rich vocabulary instruction could not possibly cover the number of words that children actually need to learn. Nagy and Herman (1987), using Nagy and Anderson's (1984) estimate of the number of words in printed school English, estimated that schoolchildren add an average of 3,000 words a year to their reading vocabularies. These estimates have been accepted by some (e.g., Beck & McKeown, 1991), and are consistent with at least some other independent estimates (Anglin, 1993), but have also been challenged by scholars who argued that the true number of root words added to children's reading vocabularies is closer to 1,000 (D'Anna, Zechmeister, & Hall, 1991; Goulden, Nation, & Read, 1990). However, even 1,000 words a year would be a formidable goal to be attained by any kind of vocabulary instruction.

Beck et al.'s response to these objections (e.g., Beck, McKeown, & Kucan, 2002) was to argue that though not all the words children need to learn can be covered, a subset of words can be identified for which such instruction would be appropriate.

"Tier 2" words (Beck et al., 2002) are words infrequent enough that children would not already know them thoroughly yet frequent enough in text to make them worth learning.

The debate on these issues still continues, in part because both the objections and the answers are largely speculative. Whether children add 1,000 or 3,000 words a year to their vocabularies, it still is not known where they learn them, or exactly what these words are for any particular grade levels. Nor have specific sets of Tier 2 words been identified that would, if learned, increase elementary students' reading comprehension. The size and diversity of English vocabulary and of students' vocabularies makes research that would directly answer these questions prohibitively expensive.

These questions can be addressed indirectly, however, by looking at the effects of vocabulary instruction on standardized measures of vocabulary knowledge and reading comprehension. In fact, Beck et al.'s (1982) first study reported an effect of instruction on standardized measures of both vocabulary and reading comprehension. However, the replication (McKeown et al., 1983) failed to find such an effect.

Here again is exactly the sort of case in which meta-analysis is especially likely to be helpful. One would not expect strong effects of vocabulary instruction on standardized measures of vocabulary and reading comprehension, because it is unlikely that many, if any, of the instructed words would actually show up in such tests. On the other hand, there are grounds to expect at least some transfer (Beck et al., 1982; Nagy, in press), even if it is modest in size.

By the mid-1980s, then, there was an increasing body of research on vocabulary, and several excellent narrative reviews had already been published (e.g., Anderson & Freebody, 1981; Jenkins & Dixon, 1983; Mezynski, 1983), or were being written (e.g., Graves, 1986b). However, there were also fundamental issues left unanswered, for which no one study had provided a definitive empirical answer: What kind of vocabulary instruction reliably increases comprehension of text containing the instructed words, and can systematic instruction in vocabulary have a generalized impact on children's vocabulary knowledge and reading comprehension?

Practical advice for effective vocabulary instruction was available, for example, in the form of Johnson and Pearson's excellent book *Teaching Reading Vocabulary* (1978, 1984). However, the suggestions for instruction in this book, though consistent with the developing cognitive paradigm, did not yet have thorough empirical support. Nor were they widely practiced in schools. In the 1980s, as now, asking students to define words constituted much of the vocabulary instruction found in schools (Durkin, 1978–1980; Graves, 1986b; Miller & Gildea, 1987; Scott, Jameson, & Asselin, 2003), with little direct teaching aimed at producing growth in vocabulary knowledge advocated in basal teacher's manuals (Jenkins & Dixon, 1983).

Steve's life work centered on helping teachers become more effective in teaching children to learn to read. It is not surprising that he would take up the challenge of providing guidance to both researchers and teachers regarding best instructional practices for schools. He and Fairbanks seized the opportunity to use meta-analysis, a relatively new technique at the time, to bring a strong theoretical frame to the issue and to assess the effects of vocabulary instruction on learning new word meanings and on the comprehension of passages. The term *meta-analysis* had been introduced by Glass in his 1976 American Educational Research Association Presidential Address (Hedges, 1992). The Stahl and Fairbanks article was one of the first 100 studies to use meta-analysis to consolidate and review an issue of importance to elementary education.[1] In this paper, Stahl and Fairbanks used this relatively new technique to try to shed light on practices that could help teachers in classrooms. Past reviews and studies had mixed results, although Petty et al. (1968) concluded that any instruction in vocabulary was better than no instruction. To determine the components of best instructional practice, Stahl and Fairbanks chose theoretically interesting constructs that reflected current methodology. They also looked at setting factors including the amount of time allocated to instruction, and whether the instruction was within a group or individual setting. It is noteworthy that they did not try to fit instructional studies involving the keyword method into their analysis, as these studies did not fit their theoretical framework. This use of a clear conceptual framework provided the guidance that allowed the meta-analysis to speak strongly in favor of particular guidelines for instruction.

Steve saw the value in looking at various aspects of a problem and did not resort to overly simple dichotomies. His interpretations were nuanced and he recognized the complexity of vocabulary instruction. He looked to the data to point out instructional guidelines, for Steve's primary concern was always improving instruction for children. With this study, he and Fairbanks were able to assert that vocabulary instruction does assist the comprehension of passages containing the instructed words—if the instruction provides both definitional and contextual information, involves students in deeper processing, and provides more than one or two exposures to the words. As for the debate regarding the futility of vocabulary instruction (Nagy & Herman, 1984) versus its fertility (Beck et al., 1982; Beck, McKeown, & Omanson, 1984), Stahl and Fairbanks came down firmly on the side of fertility, claiming that vocabulary instruction is a "useful adjunct to the natural learning from context" (1986, p. 100).

NOTE

1. As determined by an ERIC search, using the terms *meta-analysis*, *education*, and *elementary* as keywords.

REFERENCES

Alexander, P., & Fox, E. (2004). A historical perspective on reading research and practice. In R. Ruddell & N. J. Unrau (Eds.), *Theoretical models and processes of reading* (5th ed., pp. 33–68). Newark, DE: International Reading Association.

Anderson, R. C., & Freebody, P. (1978). *Vocabulary knowledge* (Tech. Rep. No. 136) (ERIC Document Reproduction Service No. ED 177 480). Urbana–Champaign: University of Illinois, Center for the Study of Reading.

Anderson, R. C., & Freebody, P. (1981). Vocabulary knowledge. In J. Guthrie (Ed.), *Comprehension and teaching: Research reviews* (pp. 77–117). Newark, DE: International Reading Association.

Anderson, R. C., Hiebert, E. H., Scott, J. A., & Wilkinson, I. A. G. (1985). *Becoming a nation of readers: The report of the Commission on Reading*. Champaign, IL: Center for the Study of Reading.

Anglin, J. M. (1993). Vocabulary development: A morphological analysis, *Monographs of the Society of Research in Child Development, 58*(Serial No. 238).

Baumann, J. F., & Kame'enui, E. J. (1991). Research on vocabulary instruction: Ode to Voltaire. In J. Flood, J. M. Jensen, D. Lapp, & J. R. Squire (Eds.), *Handbook of research on teaching the English language arts* (pp. 604–632). New York: Macmillan.

Beck, I., & McKeown, M. (1991). Conditions of vocabulary acquisition. In R. Barr, M. Kamil, P. Mosenthal, & P. D. Pearson (Eds.), *Handbook of reading research* (Vol. II, pp. 789–814). New York: Longman.

Beck, I., McKeown, M., & Kucan, L. (2002). *Bringing words to life: Robust vocabulary instruction.* New York: Guilford Press.

Beck, I., McKeown, M. G., & Omanson, R. C. (1984). *The fertility of some types of vocabulary instruction in the role of instruction in learning and using vocabulary.* Symposium conducted at the annual meeting of the American Educational Research Association, New Orleans, LA.

Beck, I., Perfetti, C., & McKeown, M. (1982). Effects of long-term vocabulary instruction on lexical access and reading comprehension. *Journal of Educational Psychology, 74*(4), 506–521.

Calfee, R. C., & Drum, P. A. (1978). Learning to read: Theory, research and practice. *Curriculum Inquiry, 8,* 183–249.

Chomsky, N. (1957). *Syntactic structures.* The Hague, The Netherlands: Mouton.

Chomsky, N. (1959). A review of Skinner's "Verbal Behavior." *Language, 35,* 26–58.

Chomsky, N. (1965). *Aspects of the theory of syntax.* Cambridge, MA: MIT Press.

Clifford, G. J. (1978). Words for schools: The applications in education of the vocabulary researches of Edward L. Thorndike. In P. Suppes (Ed.), *Impact of research on education: Some case studies* (pp. 107–198). Washington, DC: National Academy of Education.

D'Anna, C. A., Zechmeister, E. B., & Hall, J. W. (1991). Toward a meaningful definition of vocabulary size. *Journal of Reading Behavior, 23,* 109–122.

Davis, F. B. (1944). Fundamental factors in reading comprehension. *Psychometrika, 9,* 185–197.

Durkin, D. (1979–1980). What classroom observations reveal about reading comprehension instruction. *Reading Research Quarterly, 14,* 481–533.

Freebody, P., & Anderson, R. C. (1983). Effects on text comprehension of different proportions and locations of difficult vocabulary. *Journal of Reading Behavior, 15,* 19–40.

Gaffney, J., & Anderson, R. C. (2000). Trends in reading research in the United States: Changing intellectual currents over three decades. In M. Kamil, P. Mosenthal, P. D. Pearson, & R. Barr, (Eds.), *Handbook of reading research* (Vol. III, pp. 53–74). Mahwah, NJ: Erlbaum.

Goulden, R., Nation, P., & Read, J. (1990). How large can a receptive vocabulary be? *Applied Linguistics, 11,* 341–363.

Graves, M. F. (1986a). *Vocabulary learning and instruction.* Unpublished manuscript.

Graves, M. F. (1986b). Vocabulary learning and instruction. In E. Z. Rothkopf & L. C. Ehri (Eds.), *Review of research in education* (Vol. 13, pp. 49–89). Washington, DC: American Educational Research Association.

Hedges, L. (1992). Meta-analysis. *Journal of Educational Statistics, 17*(4), 279–296.

Hiebert, E. H., Martin, L. A., & Menon, S. (2005). Are there alternatives in reading textbooks?: An examination of three beginning reading programs. *Reading and Writing Quarterly, 21,* 7–32.

Hilliard, G. H. (1926). Probable types of difficulties underlying low scores in comprehension tests. In C. L. Robbins (Ed.), *University of Iowa studies in education* (Vol. 2). Iowa City: University of Iowa Press.

Jackson, J. R., & Dizney, H. (1963). Intensive vocabulary training. *Journal of Developmental Reading, 6,* 221–229.

Jenkins, J., & Dixon, R. (1983). Vocabulary learning. *Contemporary Educational Psychology, 8*(3), 237–260.

Jenkins, J. R., Pany, D., & Schreck, J. (1978). *Vocabulary and reading comprehension: Instructional effects* (Tech. Rep. No. 100) (ERIC Document Reproduction Service No. 160 999). Urbana–Champaign, IL: University of Illinois, Center for the Study of Reading.

Johnson, D. D., & Pearson, P. D. (1978). *Teaching reading vocabulary*. New York: Holt, Rinehart & Winston.

Johnson, D. D., & Pearson, P. D. (1984). *Teaching reading vocabulary* (2nd ed.). New York: Holt, Rinehart & Winston.

Lieberman, J. E. (1967). *The effects of direct instruction in vocabulary concepts on reading achievement* (ERIC Document Reproduction Service No. ED 010 985).

Marks, C. B., Doctorow, M. J., & Wittrock, M. C. (1974). Word frequency and reading comprehension. *Journal of Educational Research, 67*, 259–262.

McKeown, M., Beck, I., Omanson, R., & Perfetti, C. (1983). The effects of long-term vocabulary instruction on reading comprehension: A replication. *Journal of Reading Behavior, 15*(1), 3–18.

McKeown, M. G., Beck, I. L., Omanson, R. C., & Pople, M. T. (1985). Some effects of the nature and frequency of vocabulary instruction on the knowledge and use of words. *Reading Research Quarterly, 20*, 522–535.

McKeown, M., & Curtis, E. (Eds.). (1987). *The nature of vocabulary acquisition*. Hillsdale, NJ: Erlbaum.

Mezynski, K. (1983). Issues concerning the acquisition of knowledge: Effects of vocabulary training on reading comprehension. *Review of Educational Research, 53*(2), 253–279.

Miller, G. A., & Gildea, P. M. (1987). How children learn words. *Scientific American, 257*, 94–99.

Nagy, W. E. (1985, November). *Vocabulary instruction: Implications of the new research*. Paper presented at the annual meeting of the National Council of Teachers of English, Philadelphia.

Nagy, W. E. (in press). Metalinguistic awareness and the vocabulary–comprehension connection. In R. K. Wagner, A. Muse, & K. R. Tannenbaum (Eds.), *Vocabulary and reading*. New York: Guilford Press.

Nagy, W. E., & Anderson, R. C. (1984). How many words are there in printed school English? *Reading Research Quarterly, 19*, 304–330.

Nagy, W. E., & Herman, P. A. (1984). Limitations *of vocabulary instruction* (Technical Report No. 326). Urbana: University of Illinois, Center for the Study of Reading.

Nagy, W. E., & Herman, P. A. (1987). Breadth and depth of vocabulary knowledge: Implications for acquisition and instruction. In M. McKeown & M. Curtis (Eds.), *The nature of vocabulary acquisition* (pp. 19–35). Hillsdale, NJ: Erlbaum.

Pany, D., & Jenkins, J. R. (1977). *Learning word meanings: A comparison of instructional procedures and effects on measures of reading comprehension with learning disabled students* (Tech. Rep. No. 25) (ERIC Document Reproduction Service No. ED 136 237). Urbana–Champaign: University of Illinois, Center for the Study of Reading.

Petty, W. T., Herold, C. P., & Stoll, E. (1968). *The state of knowledge about the teaching of vocabulary*. Champaign, IL: National Council of Teachers of English.

Skinner, B. F. (1957). *Verbal behavior*. New York: Appleton-Century-Crofts.

Stahl, S., & Fairbanks, M. (1986). The effects of vocabulary instruction: A model-based meta-analysis. *Review of Educational Research, 56*, 72–110.

Sternberg, R., & Powell, J. (1983). Comprehending verbal comprehension. *American Psychologist, 38*, 878–893.

Tuinman, J. J., & Brady, M. E. (1974). How does vocabulary account for variance on reading comprehension tests? A preliminary instructional analysis. In P. L. Nacke (Ed.), *23rd Yearbook of the National Reading Conference*. Clemson, SC: National Reading Conference.

Venezky, R. (1984). The history of reading research. In P. D. Pearson, R. Barr, M. Kamil, & P. Mosenthal (Eds.), *Handbook of reading research* (Vol. I, pp. 3–38). New York: Longman.

Wittrock, M. C., Marks, C. B., & Doctorow, M. J. (1975). Reading as a generative process. *Journal of Educational Psychology, 67*, 484–489.

15 The Effects of Vocabulary Instruction

A Model-Based Meta-Analysis

STEVEN A. STAHL
MARILYN M. FAIRBANKS

Since the earliest investigations of reading comprehension skill (e.g., Thorndike, 1917), researchers in reading have found that knowledge of word meanings has a strong relationship to reading comprehension skill. This relationship has emerged in factor analyses (Davis, 1944, 1972; Spearitt, 1972), in correlations between vocabulary and reading comprehension measures (Farr, 1969), and in readability research (Chall, 1958; Harrison, 1980). Less clear is the nature of the relationship between the teaching of word meanings and growth in reading comprehension skill.

Anderson and Freebody (1981) suggest three hypotheses that might explain the strong relationship between vocabulary and reading comprehension. One, the instrumentalist hypothesis, suggests that vocabulary knowledge has a direct effect on comprehension, or that knowledge of word meanings directly enables one to comprehend text. The other two hypotheses, the general aptitude and general knowledge hypotheses, suggest that vocabulary and reading comprehension are both related to a common third factor, either intelligence or world knowledge.

Of these three, the instrumentalist hypothesis suggests most strongly that vocabulary instruction will directly improve comprehension. The support for this hypothesis has been mixed. On one hand, the studies of vocabulary simplification have indicated that lowering the density of difficult words does appear to make a passage

We would like to thank our research assistants, Sara Hawk and Betty Harmon, and our typist, Irene Dahl.

more readable, but mainly under certain conditions (Chall, 1958; Wittrock, Marks, & Doctorow, 1975), namely, if the manipulations involve large percentages of words and there is some reorganization of the passage (see Freebody & Anderson, 1983). Studies of vocabulary preteaching also have produced mixed results. The often cited studies of Jenkins, Pany, and Schreck (1978), Pany and Jenkins (1977), and Tuinman and Brady (1974) found that no effect on comprehension could be attributed to vocabulary instruction. Some recent studies, such as Beck, Perfetti, and McKeown (1982), Kame'enui, Carnine, and Freschi (1982), and Stahl (1983), found that vocabulary instruction did appear to improve comprehension.

These differences in results also strongly suggest the possibility that some methods of vocabulary instruction may be more effective than others. Petty, Herold, and Stoll (1968) analyzed 80 studies of vocabulary instruction in an attempt to identify the most effective methods of vocabulary instruction. They concluded that the data available at that time did not allow for the choice of a single "best" method of vocabulary instruction, but that any instruction appeared better than no instruction. They also found that methods involving several different techniques seemed more effective than those involving a single technique. In a later review, Mezynski (1983) did find several factors related to the success of vocabulary instructional methods in improving reading comprehension. They were (a) the amount of practice given in learning the words, (b) the breadth of training in the use of the words, and (c) the degree to which active processing is encouraged.

Given the diversity of past findings, meta-analytic procedures, which allow for the synthesis of results of different studies, seem to be a reasonable approach to study the effectiveness of various methods of direct vocabulary instruction and the relationship of such instruction to comprehension. This study reports such a meta-analysis of vocabulary instructional studies designed to examine the effects of vocabulary preinstruction as a way of improving reading comprehension and, further, to examine the components of effective vocabulary instruction.

EFFECTIVE VOCABULARY INSTRUCTION

It could be assumed that different method and setting factors would have different effects on comprehension and word learning. Specifying these factors is difficult, however, because of the lack of a commonly accepted classification system for vocabulary instructional methods. Methods bearing the same label are often vastly different in effect and in execution. For example, the context method studied by Gipe (1979; see also Gipe, 1981, and Gipe & Arnold, 1979) included not only an example of each to-be-learned word in context but also two explicit statements of each word's definition, whereas the context method studied by Johnson and Stratton (1966) contained no such definitional information. Gipe's context method also had each student generate a novel example for each taught word. Margosein, Pascarella, and Pflaum (1982), although ostensibly basing their context method on Gipe's, omitted the generation step. Without some classification system, it is difficult to determine which of these variations is likely to be meaningful and which is likely to be incidental.

Based on recent reviews of vocabulary instructional studies (Fairbanks, 1977; Mezysnki, 1983; Stahl, 1985), three method-specific and two general setting factors that may influence a method's effectiveness were examined. The three method factors examined were (a) whether or not a method gives the student examples of each to-be-learned word in context, (b) the types of activities that are required to learn the word, and (c) the number and type of exposures to information about each word. The setting factors examined were (a) the amount of time allocated to vocabulary instruction and (b) whether the lessons were given to groups or individuals.

METHOD FACTORS

Definitional and Contextual Information

Based on a review of research in various disciplines concerned with word meaning, Stahl (1983, 1985) suggested that a person who "knows" a word has both definitional and contextual information about that word. *Definitional information* was defined as knowledge of the relations between a word and other known words, as in a dictionary definition or in a network model of semantic memory (e.g., Collins & Loftus, 1975). In such a model, a person's knowledge about a word is represented by a network of concept nodes and links between the nodes. A word is understood by activation spreading along the links of the network, first to closely related concepts and later to more distant concepts. Such a model appears adequate to explain some of the laboratory research on semantic memory (e.g., Collins & Quillian, 1969; Meyer & Schvaneveldt, 1975), but not all (see Smith & Medin, 1981). Most important are the findings that people do not ordinarily appear to decompose words into definitional parts during comprehension (Fodor, Garrett, Walker, & Parkes, 1980; Kintsch 1974; Thorndyke, 1975). Another type of information appears to be necessary to account for our knowledge about words. This knowledge will be termed *contextual knowledge*, because it appears to be developed from exposure to words in context.

Contextual knowledge can be defined as knowledge of a core concept and how that knowledge is realized in different contexts. Evidence for the context-sensitivity of word meanings can be obtained from many different areas of research. For example, research by R. C. Anderson and his associates (Anderson & McGaw, 1973; Anderson & Ortony, 1975; Anderson et al., 1976) suggests that people encode words in semantic memory differently when the words are represented in different contexts. There is other evidence that knowledge is first acquired in relation to a particular context and may require contextual support in order for retrieval to occur. Only after a number of exposures in different contexts does a concept become "decontextualized" (Bransford & Nitsch, 1978; Nelson & Nelson, 1978; Werner & Kaplan, 1952).

An earlier review indicated that vocabulary teaching methods that provide contextual information in addition to definitional information about each word's meaning, or "mixed" methods, appear to produce significantly better vocabulary achievement than methods that provide only one type of information (Stahl, 1985). The current review attempts to extend that finding with a larger set of studies and by examining the effects of different emphases on either definitional or contextual information on vocabulary learning. Each method examined was rated on the following scale:

1. *Definitional only*. The only information provided is a definition, synonym, and so forth. There are no examples of the word used in context.
2. *Definitional emphasis*. Some exposure is given to the word in context, but the emphasis is on the child learning the definition.
3. *Balanced*. A balance or near balance between definitional and contextual information is given.
4. *Contextual emphasis*. Although a definition is given, the major emphasis is on learning the word in context.
5. *Context only*. The child is exposed only to each word in context, with no attempt to have the child derive a definition.

Depth of Processing

Another method characteristic that might affect learning is the types of activities students are required to engage in while learning new words. One way to characterize different types of activities might be through an adaptation of the "depth of processing" framework used in short-term memory research (Craik & Tulving, 1975). Studies of list learning have found that subjects who process information more deeply retain that information better than subjects who engage in more "shallow" processing activities. In the original formulations of depth of processing, "depth" was equated with whether semantic information was used (e.g., Hyde & Jenkins, 1973). Later formulations suggested that subjects who used a greater amount of semantic information when learning a list remembered more than subjects who used less information. For example, Johnson-Laird, Gibbs, and deMowbray (1978) asked adults to determine whether items on a list were natural, consumable, solids. On an unexpected recall test, words that had all three of these attributes (e.g., apple) were recalled better than words that had only one or two of the attributes. J. R. Anderson and Reder (1979) suggest that new information is learned more effectively by creating the greatest number of connections to already known information, or by being given the most elaborate processing. Another explanation for this "depth" effect in list learning is that decisions that require more mental effort, or require a greater amount of available cognitive resources, will also be more memorable (Jacoby, Craik, & Begg, 1979; Tyler, Hertel, McCallum, & Ellis, 1979).

Although these two constructs, amount of semantic processing and mental effort, were attempts to more precisely define "depth," its definition is still imprecise. However, Seamon and Virostek (1978) found that intuitive judgments of processing depth (defined here as mental effort) correlated highly with the effectiveness of learning tasks.

The basic principles of depth of processing have been studied mainly in list learning, where the task is the memorization of already known terms. Several authors suggest that depth of processing principles also apply to learning new information, either in studying (T. H. Anderson & Armbruster, 1982) or in vocabulary instruction (Stratton & Nacke, 1974). Stahl (1985) suggested the following intuitive scale, representing different depth of processing demands for vocabulary instructional programs:

1. *Association*, in which a child learns an association between a new word and either a definition or a single context. Learning such an association can be done by rote, as in paired-associate learning.
2. *Comprehension*, in which the child demonstrates the comprehension of a learned association either by showing understanding of a word in a sentence or by doing something with definitional information, such as finding an antonym, classifying words, and so forth.
3. *Generation*, in which the child produces a novel response to the word, such as an original sentence, a restatement of the definition in the child's own words, and so forth. The product could be written or oral. Generative processing seems to involve more of the student's mental resources because it is a more active process (Slamecka & Graf, 1978).

If these represent three successively deeper levels of processing, then it might be suggested that comprehension processing will lead to larger effects than association processing, and generative processing should lead to the largest effects. Stahl (1985) did find such an effect among the method comparison studies he reviewed; this paper attempts to extend those findings using a different methodology and a larger number of studies.

Exposures

A third method factor that might affect children's vocabulary learning is the number and type of exposures a child has to meaningful information about each word. It would be expected, of course, that a method that gives multiple exposures to a word would have a greater effect on vocabulary learning than one that gives the student one or two mentions of the word paired with a definition or used in a sentence.

It is not as clear whether repetitions of the same information, such as drilling a student on the association between a word and its synonym, produce higher effects than multiple exposures to a word in different contexts, using several activities to develop a breadth of knowledge about each word. One of the effects of providing multiple repetitions, or "drill and practice" might be to help students improve their speed of accessing the word's meaning (Beck et al., 1982; see also Mezynski, 1983). Slowness in accessing a word's meaning when a word is encountered in text may cause a "bottleneck" in comprehension, decreasing the student's overall ability to construct a meaningful interpretation of the passage. Increasing the student's speed of access may allow comprehension to proceed more smoothly. Beck et al. do provide such practice as part of a program including a number of diverse vocabulary learning activities.

Multiple exposures to different meaningful information about each word, on the other hand, may be necessary to help a student form a "decontextualized" knowledge of the word's meaning. Nitsch (1977) found that providing examples of concepts in different contexts led to better overall recognition than providing the same number of examples using a single context. This may be the way that young children acquire concepts. Nelson and Nelson (1978) suggest that children learn to form a flexible and decontextualized notion of a word's meaning through successive refinement of the rules of meaning developed through multiple exposures to the word used in different contexts. Thus, multiple exposures to words in different contexts may most nearly replicate natural word learning in a compressed form (Carroll, 1964).

Mnemonic or Keyword Methods

A number of different vocabulary instructional studies have used the mnemonic keyword method to teach word meanings (for reviews, see Levin & Pressley, 1985; Pressley, Levin, & McDaniel, 1987; Pressley, Levin, & Miller, 1982). This method is described as a mnemonic, rather than a semantic, technique for learning new words. In the keyword method, students first learn a concrete keyword that sounds like the target word. This keyword is used to create an interactive image linking the target word to its definition. For example, for the word *angler*, the keyword was *angel*, and the interactive image was that of an angel catching a fish. This is intended to focus on the link between the target word and the definition, rather than only on the isolated definition (Pressley et al., 1987).

The keyword method has been compared to a number of vocabulary teaching methods, with favorable results. For example, Pressley, Levin, and Miller (1981) found that a group given keyword instruction had significantly higher recall of the definitions and comprehension of the target words in sentences than groups asked to study the words without being given a particular strategy. Also, Levin et al. (1984) found that a group given keyword instruction had significantly higher definition learning than groups given contextual analysis and semantic-mapping instruction, two techniques generally found to be effective (see Gipe, 1979; Toms-Bronowski, 1982).

The keyword method would not fit well into the categorical framework developed here, since this framework is best suited for semantic-based vocabulary learning methods. Therefore, the keyword method will not be rated using the categories discussed earlier but will be examined separately.

SETTING FACTORS

Two setting factors assumed to have an effect on vocabulary learning and comprehension are (a) whether instruction is largely individual or done at least partly in a group setting; and (b) the amount of time allocated to instruction.

Group discussion might be expected in this case to produce higher effects than largely individual work. Participation in a discussion, or even anticipation of being called upon to participate, might lead to more active processing of information about a word's meaning, resulting in higher retention. Discussion might also allow the teacher to correct misperceptions, which may otherwise become apparent only after worksheets are graded and the lesson ended. Individualized instruction is largely synonymous with worksheets, and even young children can be very adept at completing worksheets without giving much thought to the content that the teacher intended to cover (L. Anderson, 1984). The main advantage proposed for individualized instruction, allowing children to proceed at their own pace, is not applicable to most of these studies, since the pace was nearly always set by the teacher. Barron and

Melnik (1973), who compared vocabulary instruction with and without discussion, found significantly greater word learning with class discussion.

In classroom research, the amount of time spent on a task has emerged as one of the most powerful predictors of effective instruction. No study reviewed here used observers to determine how much time students actually spent engaged in learning. Twenty-seven studies did give enough information to calculate the average amount of time allocated per word taught. The measurement of time allocated to instruction may not be an accurate measure of the time actually spent on a task (Berliner, 198 1), but it is the best measure available.

Although the method factors were chosen on the basis of a conception of effective vocabulary instruction, the setting factors were chosen on the basis of available information. Certainly many other aspects of setting affect instructional effectiveness (see Rosenshine, 1979), but these were the only two that could be consistently extracted from the information given in the studies.

METHOD

Study Selection

Studies were identified from a computer search of the ERIC document service, past reviews and bibliographies (Dale, Razik, & Petty, 1973; Fairbanks, 1977; Jenkins & Dixon, 1983; Mezynski, 1983; Petty et al., 1968), and cross-checking references. All vocabulary instruction studies suitable for meta-analysis available in April 1985 were used in this study. In order for a study to be included, two criteria had to be met: The study must use one of two types of control groups (described below), and it must provide the statistical information needed to derive an effect size. Effect sizes were calculated from the provided means and standard deviations using the following formula: $ES = (\overline{X}_t - \overline{X}_c)/SD_c$, where $\overline{X}_t$ is the mean of the treatment group, and $\overline{X}_c$ and SD_c are the mean and standard deviations of the control group. If these statistics were not available, effect sizes were derived from t or F statistics, as suggested by Glass, McGaw, and Smith (1981). Also, if SD_c was not available, SD_p was used where SD_p is the square root of the pooled within-group variance. Fifty-two studies were found that met these criteria, making 94 independent method comparisons.

In some studies, the control group appeared unable to perform at all on some measures, producing means and standard deviations of less than one, and producing extremely large effect sizes. Because these would have unduly influenced any conclusions based on calculations including them, the measures where this occurred (Jenkins et al., 1978; Kame'enui et al., 1982; Pany & Jenkins, 1977) were excluded from the analysis. Other measures from those same studies, however, were kept.

Classification

Each teaching method studied was classified by the three method and two setting factors discussed earlier. For the two setting factors, group or individual study and number of minutes allocated per word, information was taken directly from each study. For the three method factors, a description of each method used was written on a 5" × 8" card. These descriptions were rated by the two authors and a graduate student on the three scales described earlier in the paper. Raters were in agreement at least 80% of the time for all scales and were within one category at least 95% of the time. The greatest disagreements occurred with the most vague study descriptions, as will be discussed later. All disagreements were resolved by discussion.

Measurement

Studies reporting effects of vocabulary instruction on comprehension used two types of comprehension measures: (a) global comprehension measures, usually standardized tests, in which the passages did not necessarily contain the taught words; and (b) word-specific measures, in which comprehension assessment was based on passages chosen or constructed to contain the specific words taught. Studies examining the effects of different teaching methods on word knowledge used three types of measures: (a) global vocabulary measures, in which the words tested were not necessarily those that were taught; (b) definitional word-specific measures, such as multiple-choice tests and definition production measures, which measured the knowledge of definitions and synonyms; and (c) contextual word-specific measures, such as sentence anomaly or sentence cloze tests, which measured knowledge of a word's use in context. (Some authors also have used sentence anomaly and sentence cloze measures as measures of sentence comprehension. We believe that both uses are valid, but because these are most usually considered to be vocabulary measures, they will be discussed as such here.)

Effect Sizes

Most research in vocabulary instruction has used one of two types of control groups to gauge the effects of different treatments. To examine the effects of providing or not providing vocabulary content on an outcome such as reading comprehension or for comparing different methods of teaching, a *no-exposure* control group is generally used, in which the control group does not get exposure of any type to the target words prior to the posttests. To measure the effects of a particular or novel strategy for vocabulary learning, a *no-instruction* or *free-study* group is used as a control. In a no-instruction group, students are typically given the target words paired with their definitions and told to study them any way they would like. For this analysis, such a control group is defined as a treatment in which definitional information exclusively was learned with association processing and a single exposure. If a free-study control group appeared to involve more extensive instruction on any dimension, it was not used as a control for this analysis.

Two sets of effect sizes were calculated: one set using no-exposure control groups and one set using no-instruction control groups. Some studies were included in both groups, but the majority of studies fit into only one category or another. The use of two types of comparison groups allowed the use of a larger population of studies than would one type alone. The no-exposure set contained 149 effect sizes; the no-instruction set contained 111 additional effect sizes.

Tables 15.1 and 15.2 list the vocabulary instructional methods used in both sets of studies, divided by type of instrument used, and classified by the method and setting factors identified.

TABLE = 15.1. List of Studies Used in Analysis with Classifications (No-Exposure Control Group)

Study/treatment	Grade	Method factors			General setting factors			Comments
		Emphasis[a]	DOP[b]	Exposures[c]	Group/ ind.	Time per word	Effect size	
Contextual vocabulary measures								
Ahlfors (1979)								
Context	6	4	G	ME	Group	[d]	1.710	Sentence anomaly (delayed)
							1.579	Sentence anomaly (immediate)
Definitions	6	1	A	MR	Ind.	[d]	1.512	Sentence anomaly (delayed)
							1.128	Sentence anomaly (immediate)
Experience	6	3	G	ME	Group	[d]	1.116	Sentence anomaly (delayed)
							.661	Sentence anomaly (immediate)
R. C. Anderson & Kulhavy (1972)								
Context	College	3	G	SE	Ind.	.10	1.980	
Repetition	College	1	A	MR	Ind.	.10	1.230	
Jenkins, Pany, & Schreck (1978)								
Meaning given	[d]	2	A	SE	Ind.	.25	.160	
Meaning practiced	[d]	2	A	MR	Ind.	1.67	2.204	
Johnson & Stratton (1966)								
Classification	College	1	A	SE	Ind.	1.50	.795	
Definitions	College	2	C	ME	Ind.	1.50	.651	
Mixed	College	3	G	ME	Ind.	1.50	1.181	
Sentences	College	5	C	ME	Ind.	1.50	.916	
Synonyms	College	1	A	MR	Ind.	1.50	.807	
Pany & Jenkins (1977)								
Meaning given	[d]	2	A	SE	Ind.	.25	.852	
Meaning practiced	[d]	2	A	MR	Ind.	1.67	3.782	
Stahl (1983)								
Definitional	5	2	G	ME	Group	10.00	1.421	Sentence cloze
							1.347	Sentence anomaly
Mixed	5	3	G	ME	Group	10.00	2.044	Sentence cloze
							1.864	Sentence anomaly
Definitional vocabulary measures								
Ahlfors (1979)								
Context	6	4	G	ME	Group	[d]	2.002	Multiple choice (delayed)

(cont.)

Condition								
Definitions	6	1	A	MR	Ind.	d	2.098	Multiple choice (immediate)
							3.632	Multiple choice (delayed)
Experience	6	3	G	ME	Group	d	4.429	Multiple choice (immediate)
							.958	Multiple choice (delayed)
							1.458	Multiple choice (immediate)
Beck, Perfetti, & McKeown (1982)								
Treatment	4	3	G	ME	Group	21.67	1.360	
Eicholz & Barbe (1961)								
Treatment	7	3	A	MR	Ind.	d	1.642	
Gray & Holmes (1938)								
Treatment	4	3	G	ME	Group	d	1.078	Low ability
							2.020	High ability
Haefner (1932)								
Casual learning	College	3	A	SE	Ind.	5.00	1.490	Group A
							1.780	Group B
Hare (1975)								
Context	2	3	G	ME	Group	5.63	.737	
Definitions	2	1	A	MR	Group	5.63	.638	
Jenkins et al. (1978)								
Meaning given	4	2	A	SE	Ind.	.25	2.419	Immediate
							.478	Delayed
Meaning practiced	4	2	A	MR	Ind.	1.67	3.419	Immediate
							1.115	Delayed
Johnson, Pittelman, Toms-Bronowski, & Levin (1984)								
Semantic Mapping	4	3	G	ME	Group	d	1.826	Posttest moon
							3.513	Posttest prairie
Semantic feature	4	2	G	ME	Group	d	1.559	Posttest moon
							3.338	Posttest prairie
Basal	4	4	C	ME	Group	d	1.855	Posttest moon
							3.484	Posttest prairie
Johnson & Stratton (1966)								
Classification	College	1	A	SE	Ind.	1.50	.600	Synonym
							.613	Classification
							.868	Definitions
Definition	College	2	C	MR	Ind.	1.50	.500	Snyonym
							.563	Classification
							.747	Definitions

TABLE 15.1. *(cont.)*

Study/treatment	Grade	Emphasis[a]	DOP[b]	Exposures[c]	Group/ ind.	Time per word	Effect size	Comments
Definitional vocabulary measures *(cont.)*								
Johnson & Stratton (1966)								
Mixed	College	3	G	ME	Ind.	1.50	.789	Synonym
							.725	Classification
							1.383	Definitions
Sentence	College	5	C	ME	Ind.	1.50	.589	Synonym
							.613	Classification
							1.091	Definitions
Synonym	College	1	A	MR	Ind.	1.50	.467	Synonym
							.325	Classification
							.717	Definitions
McKeown, Beck, Omanson, & Perfetti (1983)								
Treatment	4	3	G	ME	Group	21.63	6.150	
Pany & Jenkins (1977)								
Meaning given	4	2	A	SE	Ind.	.25	.432	Immediate
							.575	Delayed
Meaning practiced	4	2	A	MR	Ind.	1.67	4.867	Immediate
							5.594	Delayed
Schacter (1978)								
Vocabulary	5	2	G	SE	Ind.	2.00	1.124	
Stahl (1983)								
Definitional	5	2	G	ME	Group	10.00	1.934	
Mixed	5	3	G	ME	Group	10.00	1.954	
Toms-Bronowski (1982)								
Semantic mapping	5	3	G	ME	Group	d	1.480	
Semantic feature	5	2	G	ME	Group	d	1.680	
Context	5	3	C	ME	Group	d	1.370	
Tuinman & Brady (1974)								
Treatment	5	3	C	ME	Group	11.43	.903	

(cont.)

Study / Measure								
Wixson (1984)								
Frayer	5	2	G	ME	Group	6.00	.959	Definitions[e]
							.972	Examples[e]
Definition	5	2	C	ME	Group	6.00	.637	Definitions[e]
							.428	Examples[e]
Passage comprehension measures								
Ahlfors (1979)								
Context	6	4	G	ME	Group	*d*	.298	
Definition	6	1	C	MR	Group	*d*	.020	
Experience	6	3	G	ME	Group	*d*	.264	
Beck et al. (1982)								
Treatment	4	3	G	ME	Group	17.31	.461	
Carney, Anderson, Blackburn, & Blessing (1984)	5	2	C	ME	Group	5.00	.547	1 day
							.708	14 days
Jenkins et al. (1978)								
Synonyms	4	2	A	MR	Group	4.00	.699	Free recall
							1.798	Comprehension questions
							.082	Cloze-meaning scoring
Johnson et al. (1984)								
Semantic mapping	4	3	G	ME	Group	*d*	2.267	Moon
							1.826	Prairie
Semantic feature	4	2	G	ME	Group	*d*	1.650	Moon
							1.205	Prairie
Basal	4	4	C	ME	Group	*d*	1.529	Moon
							1.384	Prairie
Kame'enui, Carnine, & Freschi (1982)								
Vocabulary	5	2	C	MR	Ind.	*f*	.846	Literal (study 1)
							d	Inferential (study 1)
							.509	Literal (study 2)
							2.108	Inferential (study 2)
Passage integration	5	3	C	MR	Ind.	*d*	.510	Literal (study 1)
							f	Inferential (study 1)
							1.008	Literal (study 2)
							3.012	Inferential (study 2)

TABLE 15.1. *(cont.)*

Study/treatment	Grade	Emphasis[a]	DOP[b]	Exposures[c]	Group/ind.	Time per word	Effect size	Comments
Passage comprehension measures *(cont.)*								
McKeown et al. (1983)								
Treatment	4	3	G	MR	Group	21.63	2.170	Free recall-central (many)
							2.051	Free recall-central (some)
							1.538	Free recall-noncentral (many)
							.641	Free recall-noncentral (some)
							3.077	Questions (many)
							1.282	(some)
Pany & Jenkins (1977)								
Meaning given	4	2	A	SE	Group	.25	.148	
Meaning practiced	4	2	A	MR	Group	1.67	.445	
Pflaum, Pascarella, Auer, Augustyn, & Boswick (1982)								
Vocabulary	2	1	A	SE	Ind.	4.00	.272	
	3.5	1	A	SE	Ind.	4.00	1.087	
Schacter (1978)								
Vocabulary	5	1	A	SE	Ind.	2.00	.452	
Snouffer & Thistlethwaite (1979)								
Vocabulary	College	1	A	SE	Ind.	3.13	.000	
Stahl (1983)								
Definitional	5	2	G	ME	Group	10.00	.985	
Mixed	5	2	G	ME	Group	10.00	.818	
Tuinman & Brady (1974)								
Treatment	5	3	C	ME	Group	11.43	.622	Group A
							.229	Group B
Wixson (1984)								
Frayer	5	2	G	ME	Group	6.00	.289	Recall[e]
							.432	Questions[e]
Definitions	5	2	C	ME	Group	6.00	-.015	Recall[e]
							.354	Questions[e]

Standardized reading comprehension measures

Baer (1974)							
Treatment	College	2	C	SE	Ind.	*d*	.250
Barrett & Graves (1981)	7–9	2	G	ME	Group	10.00	.342
Beck et al. (1982)							
Treatment	4	3	G	ME	Group	17.31	.421
Blevins (1970)							
Context	*d*	2	A	MR	Ind.	*d*	.850
Wide reading	*d*	4	C	SE	Ind.	*d*	.437
Brown (1965)	*d*	*d*	*d*	*d*	Group	*d*	.314
Draper & Moeller (1971)							
Treatment	4	3	C	ME	Ind.	*d*	.200
	5	3	C	ME	Ind.	2.00	.200
	6	3	C	ME	Ind.	2.00	.100
Gnewuch (1973)							
Treatment	College	4	C	SE	Ind.	4.17	.025
Hogan (1961)							
Part A	10	1	A	SE	Ind.	*d*	.191
Part B	10	1	C	ME	Ind.	*d*	.132
Jackson & Dizney (1963)							
Treatment	12	1	C	ME	Ind.	*d*	.033
Margosein, Pascarella, & Pflaum (1982)							
Context	*d*	4	C	ME	Group	5.41	.309
Semantic mapping	*d*	2	G	ME	Group	5.41	.489
Schacter (1978)							
Treatment	5	2	G	SE	Ind.	2.00	.496

Standardized vocabulary measures

Baer (1974)							
Treatment	College	2	C	SE	Ind.	*d*	.277
Barrett & Graves (1981)	7–9	2	C	ME	Group	10.00	.200
Blevins (1970)							
Context	*d*	2	A	MR	Ind.	*d*	-.610
Wide reading	*d*	4	C	SE	Ind.	*d*	.504

(cont.)

TABLE 15.1. (cont.)

Study/treatment	Grade	Method factors Emphasis[a]	DOP[b]	Exposures[c]	General setting factors Group/ind.	Time per word	Effect size	Comments
Standardized vocabulary measures (cont.)								
Crump (1965)								
Treatment	College	4	A	SE	Ind.	d	.118	
Draper & Moeller (1971)								
Treatment	4	3	C	ME	Ind.	d	.300	
	5	3	C	ME	Ind.	2.00	.500	
	6	3	C	ME	Ind.	2.00	.500	
Gnewuch (1973)								
Treatment	College	4	C	SE	Ind.	d	.027	
Hogan (1961)								
Part A	10	1	A	SE	Ind.	d	.365	
Part B	10	1	C	MR	Ind.	d	.165	
Jackson & Dizney (1963)								
Treatment	12	1	C	-	ME	Ind.	d	.449
Margosein et al. (1982)								
Context	d	4	C	ME	Group	5.41	.097	
Semantic mapping	d	2	G	ME	Group	5.41	.554	
Meyer & Cohen (1975)								
Vocabulary	4	d	d	d	d	d	.256	Stanford
							.164	SRA
Schacter (1978)								
Vocabulary	5	2	G	SE	Ind.	2.00	.607	

Note. Identifications in the Comments column are given only for studies with multiple measures where some confusion might occur. See original reference for full information about each measure.

[a] 1 = definitions only; 2 = definitional emphasis; 3= balanced; 4= contextual emphasis; 5= context only.
[b] A = associative; C = comprehension; G = generation.
[c] SE = one or two exposures; MR = multiple repetitions (same information); ME = multiple exposures (different information).
[d] Not enough information given in study.
[e] Because of large number of comparisons, effect sizes were pooled.
[f] Measurement dropped because mean score of control group was less than 1 (see text).

TABLE 15.2. List of Studies Used in Analysis with Classifications (No-Instruction Control Group)

Study/treatment	Grade	Method factors			General setting factors			
		Emphasis[a]	DOP[b]	Exposures[c]	Group/ind.	Time per word	Effect size	Comments
Contextual vocabulary measures								
Anderson & Kulhavy (1972)	College	4	G	SE	Ind.	.10	3.000	First trial
							1.710	Second trial
Aurentz (1983)	12	K	K	K	Ind.		.704	Immediate
							.368	Delayed
Crist & Petrone (1977)	College	4	C	ME	Ind.	d	.784	
Gipe (1979)								
Context	3	3	G	ME	Ind.	3.75	.897[e]	Ave. sent. Cloze
	5	3	G	ME	Ind.	3.75	1.200[e]	Ave. paraphrase
Jenkins et al. (1978)	d	2	A	MR	Ind.	1.67	.866	LD sent. Cloze
							1.691	LD paraphrase
							1.785	
							2.439	
Johnson & Stratton (1966)								
Classification	College	1	A	SE	Ind.	1.50	-.015	
Definition	College	2	C	ME	Ind.	1.50	-.191	
Mixed	College	3	G	ME	Ind.	1.50	.456	
Levin, Dretzke, Pressley, & McGivern (1985)	College	K	K	K	Ind.	1.50	.311	Cloze I
							.328	Cloze II
Pany & Jenkins (1977)								
Meaning practiced	d	2	A	MR	Ind.	1.67	2.972	
Pressley, Levin, & Miller (1981)	College	K	K	K	Ind.		.724	Experiment 1
							.734	Experiment 2
							1.324	Experiment 3
							.770	Experiment 4
Wixson (1984)								
Frayer	5	2	G	ME	Group	6.00	.621[f]	

(cont.)

TABLE 15.2. *(cont.)*

Study/treatment	Grade	Emphasis[a]	DOP[b]	Exposures[c]	Group/ind.	Time per word	Effect size	Comments
Definitional vocabulary measures								
Bull & Wittrock (1973)								
Imagery given	5	2	C	ME	Ind.	1.50	.625	Ave. immediate
Discovered images	5	2	G	ME	Ind.	1.50	1.250	Ave. delayed
Jenkins et al. (1978)	d	2	A	MR	Ind.	1.67	.900	LD immediate
							.704	LD delayed
							1.934[d]	
Johnson & Noble (1982)								
Standard keyword	College	K	K	K	Ind.		.307	Immediate
							-.689	Delayed
Semantic keyword	College	K	K	K	Ind.		-2.882	Immediate
							-2.506	Delayed
Johnson & Stratton (1966)								
Classification	College	1	A	SE	Ind.	1.50	.183	Definition
							.523	Classification
							.261	Synonym
Definition	College	2	C	ME	Ind.	1.50	.033	Definition
							.432	Classification
							.065	Synonym
Mixed	College	3	G	ME	Ind.	1.50	.717	Definition
							.727	Classification
							.630	Synonym
Levin et al. (1985)	College	K	K	K	Ind.	.25	.414	
Levin, McCormick, Miller, Berry, & Pressley (1982)	4	3	G	ME	Ind.	.25	-.488	
	4	K	K	K	Ind.	.25	.922	
McDaniel & Pressley (1984)								
Keyword	College	K	K	K	Ind.	.33	.604	Exp. 1, liberal
Context	College	5	A	SE	Ind.	.33	-.925	Exp. 1, liberal
Keywords/context	College	4	A	SE	Ind.	.33	-.020	Exp. 1, liberal

McDaniel & Tillman (1985)	College	K	K	K	Ind.	.33	.062	Free recall
						.50	-.439	Free recall
						.33	.670	Cued recall
						.50	.479	Cued recall
McGivern & Levin (1983)								
Structured keyword	5	K	K	K	Ind.		1.482	Hi ability
							2.053	Low ability
Semistructured	5	K	K	K	Ind.		.995	Hi ability
							.937	Low ability
Unstructured	5	K	K	K	Ind.		2.011	Hi ability
							.770	Low ability
Pany & Jenkins (1977)	*d*	2	A	MR	Ind.	1.67	3.876	Immediate
							3.419	Delayed
Pless (1966)	10	1	C	SE	Ind.	*d*	.092	Unit I
							.504	Units II & V
							.239	Final I
							.267	Final II & V
Pressley, Levin, Kuiper, Bryant, & Michener (1982)								
Keyword imagery	College	K	K	K	Ind.	.16	1.100	Experiment 1
Keyword sentence	College	K	K	K	Ind.	.16	1.436	Experiment 1
Imagery	College	2	G	SE	Ind.	.16	-.319	Experiment 1
Synonym	College	1	C	SE	Ind.	.16	-.440	Experiment 1
Read and copy	College	1	A	SE	Ind.	.16	-.440	Experiment 1
Keyword imagery	College	K	K	K	Ind.	.16	1.537	Experiment 2
Keyword familiar	College	K	K	K	Ind.	.16	1.537	Experiment 2
Keyword self	College	K	K	K	Ind.	.16	.640	Experiment 2
Imagery familiar	College	2	G	SE	Ind.	.16	-.635	Experiment 2
Keyword imagery	College	K	K	K	Ind.	.16	1.303	Experiment 2
Imagery	College	2	G	SE	Ind.	.16	.230	Experiment 4, cued recognition
Synonym	College	1	C	SE	Ind.	.16	-.989	Experiment 4, cued recognition
Keyword imagery	College	K	K	K	Ind.	.16	-.111	Experiment 4, cued recognition
Imagery	College	2	G	SE	Ind.	.16	.739	Experiment 5, free recall
Synonym	College	1	C	SE	Ind.	.16	-.096	Experiment 5, free recall
Pressley, Levin, & Miller (1982)								
Imagery keyword	College	K	K	K	Ind.	.16	1.403	Intermediate
Sentence keyword	College	K	K	K	Ind.	.16	.719	Intermediate
Sentence judgement	College	3	C	SE	Ind.	.16	.043	Intermediate

(cont.)

243

TABLE 15.2. (*cont.*)

| Study/treatment | Grade | Method factors | | | General setting factors | | | |
		Emphasis[a]	DOP[b]	Exposures[c]	Group/ind.	Time per word	Effect size	Comments
Definitional vocabulary measures (*cont.*)								
Pressley, Levin, & Miller (1982) (*cont.*)								
Sentence generated	College	3	C	SE	Ind.	.16	-.035	Intermediate
Sentence provided	College	2	C	SE	Ind.	.16	.141	Intermediate
Shaughnessy & Cockrell (1984)	College	2	C	ME	Ind.	[d]	.024	Immediate
							-.238	Delayed
							-.825	Immediate
							-.943	
Wixson (1984)								
Frayer	5	2	G	ME	Group	6.00	.700[f]	
Passage comprehension measures								
Anders, Bos, & Filip (1984)	[d]	2	G	ME	Ind.	4.50	1.125	Vocab. Related
							1.386	Concept related
Johnson (1979)								
Keyword imagery	College	K	K	K	Ind.		.000	Immediate
							.097	Delayed
Keyword verbal	College	K	K	K	Ind.		-.312	Immediate
							-.297	Delayed
Wixson (1984)								
Frayer	5	2	G	ME	Group	6.00	.150	Free recall[f]
							.275	Questions[f]

Note. Identifications in the "comments" column are given only for studies with multiple measures where some confusion might occur. See original reference for full information about each measure.

[a] 1 = definitions only; 2 = definitional emphasis; 3= balanced; 4= contextual emphasis; 5 = context only; K = keyword.

[b] A = associative; C = comprehension; G = generation; K = keyword.

[c] SE = one or two exposures; MR = multiple repetitions (same information); ME = multiple exposures (different information); K = keyword.

[d] Not enough information given in study.

[e] Since three treatments met our criteria for comparison group, effect size was calculated using the combined means of the association, classification, and definition groups.

[f] Because of large number of comparisons, effect sizes were pooled.

244

To test the instrumentalist hypothesis of the vocabulary/comprehension relationship, only the no-exposure set of effect sizes was used, since this hypothesis is concerned with the effects of the presence or absence of vocabulary knowledge on comprehension. For the comparisons of different vocabulary instructional methods, the results from the no-exposure set of effect sizes will be reported first, with the results from the no-instruction set used to confirm and elaborate these results. For the method comparisons, only word-specific measures of vocabulary and comprehension were used, since the variations in effect sizes of the global measure were too small to lend themselves to comparisons.

Analysis

For each of the classified factors (emphasis, depth of processing, exposures, group/individual), the mean effect for each level of each factor was obtained and tested to see if it was statistically different from zero. Because of the small numbers of methods in each cell, comparisons of mean effect sizes using analyses of variance (ANOVAs) or t tests rarely produced significant differences between levels of a factor. Therefore, most of the discussions will be limited to trends, which may not be statistically reliable but represent the best information available.

RESULTS

Vocabulary Instruction and Comprehension

The first question addressed in this meta-analysis was whether vocabulary instruction has a direct effect on reading comprehension. Using only the no-exposure control group set of studies on word-specific comprehension measures, vocabulary instruction produced a mean effect size of .97 ($SD = .81$, $N = 41$), which was significantly different from zero ($p < .01$). Individual effect sizes ranged from 0 to 3.07. This mean effect size of .97 means that, on the average, children at the 50th percentile of groups receiving vocabulary instruction scored as well as children at the 83rd percentile of the control groups on these passage comprehension measures, if both groups were distributed normally. The mean effect for these passage comprehension measures was lower than that for the word-specific contextual vocabulary measures ($\overline{X} = 1.37$, $SD = .76$, $N = 21$, $p < .01$) and definitional measures ($\overline{X} = 1.70$, $SD = 1.42$, $N = 55$, $p < .01$). These are considered large effect sizes.

Vocabulary instruction also appears to have a slight but significant general facilitative effect on reading comprehension of passages in standardized tests not designed to contain taught words. The mean effect size on these measures was .30 ($SD = .22$, $N = 15$), which was significantly different from zero ($p < .01$). This indicates that students at the 50th percentile of the instructed groups scored as well as children at the 62nd percentile of the control groups on the global reading comprehension measures. This also might be considered as an estimate of the long-term effects of vocabulary instruction, since most of these studies involved instruction for 6 weeks or longer. Vocabulary instruction also had a significant effect on global measures of vocabulary knowledge. The mean effect size on these measures was .26 ($SD = .29$, $N = 17$), also significantly different from zero ($p < .01$). Beck et al. (1982) suggested that an effect found on words not specifically taught may indicate that vocabulary-teaching programs may make students aware of learning words they encounter in their reading (see Mezynski, 1983).

Effective Vocabulary Instruction

The second question addressed in the meta-analysis concerned the factors involved in effective vocabulary instruction. For this question, only the effects on the three word-specific measures were considered, first on the no-exposure control group set of effect sizes, later on the no-instruction set.

Method Factors

The three method-specific factors—relative emphasis on definitional or contextual information, depth of processing, and number and type of repetitions—did appear to affect the effectiveness of vocabulary instruction in different ways. Tables 15.3, 15.4, and 15.5 give the mean effect sizes for these factors on the three word-specific measures.

Emphasis

The first factor, emphasis on definitional or contextual information, appeared to produce the most consistent effects. For the word-specific passage comprehension and the two word-specific vocabulary measures, methods providing both definitional and contextual information, or "mixed" methods, appear to be more effective than

TABLE 15.3. Mean Effect Sizes Associated with Different Emphases

Type of measure	No-exposure control			No-instruction control		
	Mean	SD	N	Mean	SD	N
Contextual vocabulary						
Definitional only	1.09**	.30	5	−.02	na	1
Definitional emphasis	1.49*	1.20	7	1.20**	1.08	10
Balanced	1.47**	.56	6	.85*	.37	3
Contextual emphasis	1.64**	.09	2	1.83	1.11	3
Context only	.92	na	1	—	—	0
Definitional vocabulary						
Definitional only	1.37*	1.53	9	.03	.45	11
Definitional emphasis	1.62**	1.52	20	.57*	1.20	24
Balanced	1.72**	1.24	19	.27	.50	6
Contextual emphasis	2.36**	.76	4	−.02	na	1
Context only	.76**	.28	3	−.93	na	1
Passage comprehension						
Definitional only	.37	.44	5	—	—	0
Definitional emphasis	.76**	.60	18	.38*	.51	10
Balanced	1.40**	.97	15	—	—	0
Contextual emphasis	1.07	.67	3	—	—	0
Context only	—	—	0	—	—	0

Probability that mean equals zero:
* $p < .05$.
** $p < .01$.

TABLE 15.4. Mean Effects Sizes Associated with Different Processing Ratings

Type of measure	No-exposure control			No-instruction control		
	Mean	SD	N	Mean	SD	N
Contextual vocabulary						
Association	1.39**	1.06	9	1.62*	1.07	6
Comprehension	.78	.19	2	.30	.69	2
Generative	1.49**	.43	10	1.08**	.95	9
Definitional vocabulary						
Association	1.76**	1.82	20	.96	1.51	11
Comprehension	1.07**	.87	12	.05	.39	15
Generative	1.79**	1.30	23	.19	.77	17
Passage comprehension						
Association	.55*	.58	9	–	–	0
Comprehension	.88**	.82	15	.38*	.51	10
Generative	1.25**	.84	17	–	–	0

Probability that mean equals zero:
* p < .05.
** p < .01.

those providing only definitional information. The category of mixed methods includes those methods classified as definitional emphasis, balanced, and contextual emphasis. For the word in context measures, the combined mean effect size of the mixed methods was 1.50 compared to 1.09 for the purely definitional methods. On the definitional measures, the combined mean effect size for the mixed methods was 1.84 compared to 1.37 for the purely definitional methods. On the passage comprehension measures, the purely definitional methods produced a mean effect size of .37, and the mixed methods produced a mean effect size of 1.05. The mean effect

TABLE 15.5. Mean Effect Sizes Associated with Different Numbers and Types of Exposure to Meaningful Information

Type of measure	No-exposure control			No-instruction control		
	Mean	SD	N	Mean	SD	N
Contextual vocabulary						
One or two exposures	.95	.76	4	1.57	1.51	3
Multiple repetitions	1.78*	1.09	6	1.95*	.80	5
Multiple exposures	1.32**	.46	11	.63*	.61	9
Definitional vocabulary						
One or two exposures	1.04**	.66	10	–.05	.47	21
Multiple repetitions	2.33**	2.05	14	2.17*	1.44	5
Multiple exposures	1.64**	1.17	31	.28	.71	
Passage comprehension						
One or two exposures	.39	.42	5	–	–	0
Multiple repetitions	1.00**	.93	11	.38*	.51	10
Multiple exposures	1.06**	.79	25	–	–	0

Probability that mean equals zero:
* p < .05.
** p < .01.

size of the purely definitional methods on this measure was not significantly different from zero, but this is based on an N of only 5.

Of the three classifications of mixed methods, methods with a contextual emphasis produced the highest mean effect sizes on the two word-specific vocabulary measures, but because these means are based on only a few studies, it is difficult to determine their importance. On the passage comprehension measures, the highest effect sizes were found for the balanced programs. On these measures, the difference between balanced and definitional emphasis methods was relatively large (.64), suggesting an overall difference between the effects of these methods, t (31) = 2.53, $p < .01$.

Looking at the no-instruction control group set, one can again see that the effects of the three combined mixed methods were significantly higher ($p < .01$) than those of definition-only groups (because the comparison group was a definition-only group, significance tests here are based on the difference between the mean effect size for the treatment and zero). Because of the smaller number of studies in this group, drawing conclusions about the relative effectiveness of different mixed methods is even more tenuous than with the other set of studies.

Depth of Processing and Exposure Scales

The depth of processing and exposure factors appeared to have different effects on vocabulary learning and comprehension. For the depth-of-processing factor, it was predicted that methods rated as requiring generative processing would produce the largest effect sizes, and those rated as associative would produce the smallest. For the two word-specific vocabulary measures, this did not turn out to be the case. As noted in Table 15.4, the mean of the methods rated as associative was similar to the mean of those methods rated as generative, both of which were considerably higher than those rated as requiring comprehension processing, at least for the no-exposure set. For the no-instruction set, methods rated as associative produced the highest effect sizes on both definitional and contextual word-specific vocabulary measures. It is only on the passage comprehension measures that the depth-of-processing scale produced the expected results, with a descending ordering of generative, comprehension, and associative processing. The differences on this scale approached but did not reach statistical significance, F (2, 38) = 2.44, $p = .10$.

These results can be best understood when combined with those from the exposures scale (see Table 15.5). For the three word-specific measures on the no-exposure set, multiple repetitions of the same information and multiple exposures to words in different contexts both produced markedly higher effect sizes than one or two exposures, but were similar to each other in effects. When combined with the depth-of-processing scale, however, it seems that two clusters of factors emerge. The mean effect sizes for these two clusters, methods rated associative, which give multiple repetitions of the same information ("drill-and-practice" methods), and methods rated generative, which provide exposure to each word in multiple contexts ("breadth of knowledge" methods), are presented in Table 15.6. These types of programs were also the types most frequently studied. For the no-exposure set, 69 effect sizes concerned either one of these types of methods, compared to 48 for all other possible combinations.

TABLE 15.6. Mean Effect Sizes Associated with Drill-and-Practice and Breadth of Knowledge Instruction

Type of measure	No-exposure control			No-instruction control		
	Mean	SD	N	Mean	SD	N
Contextual vocabulary						
Drill and practice	1.78**	1.08	6	1.95**	.80	5
Breadth of knowledge	1.44**	.42	9	.72**	.61	7
Others	.89*	.60	6	.81**	.81	13
Definitional vocabulary						
Drill and practice	2.80**	1.08	11	2.17*	1.44	5
Breadth of knowledge	1.82**	1.22	22	.35	.86	11
Other	1.05**	.76	22	.31	.91	56
Passage comprehension						
Drill and practice	.76	.74	4	–	–	0
Breadth of knowledge	1.25**	.84	17	.38*	.51	10
Other	.77**	.76	20	–.13	.21	4

Probability that mean equals zero:
* $p < .05$.
** $p < .01$.

Table 15.6 indicates that drill-and-practice methods produced higher effect sizes on both definitional and contextual measures. For the contextual measures, the effects were similar; for the definitional measures the mean effect size for the drill-and-practice methods was nearly a full standard unit above the breadth of knowledge methods. This probably reflects the effect of the massive definition drill used in some studies (Jenkins et al., 1978; Kame'enui et al., 1982; Pany & Jenkins, 1977) on recall of definitions. On the passage comprehension measures, only the breadth of knowledge methods produced a mean effect reliably different from zero. However, the number of effect sizes on passage comprehension measures for the drill-and-practice methods were so small that no firm conclusion should be drawn. The studies not falling into either category also produced effects statistically different from zero.

Keyword Studies

The results of the keyword method studies were somewhat surprising. Keyword research, because it is concerned with validating a *strategy* of vocabulary learning, has used only no-instruction type control groups, and has largely used either definition recall tasks and contextual vocabulary tasks as criterion measures. On the contextual vocabulary measures, keyword methods produced an average effect size of .66 ($SD = .33$, $N = 8$, $p < .01$). For the definitional vocabulary measures, the keyword methods produced an average effect size of .57 ($SD = 1.18$, $N = 26$). This was statistically different from zero ($p < .05$). However, there was a large range of effect sizes. Although the majority of keyword effect sizes were high and positive, obtained effect sizes ranged from 2.011 down to –2.886. This variation was probably due to several factors. First, keyword research has used a planned variation model, with variations in both the criterion task and the execution of the method as a way of defining the effects of the instructional technique. Most of these variations have led to robust and powerful effects; some have not. Some of these differences probably have been due to differences in implementation of the keyword method (see Pressley, Levin, Kuiper, Bryant, & Michener, 1982). Other low or negative effect sizes have been found on measures chosen not to reflect associative vocabulary learning. For example, when the free recall (nonassociative) measures from the McDaniel and Tillman (1985) and Pressley et al. (1982) studies were excluded from the analysis, the mean effect size attributable to the keyword method on the definitional vocabulary measures rose to .70. The meta-analysis procedure used here arithmetically combines all of these effect sizes, without distinguishing studies by these factors, possibly underestimating the overall effects of the keyword method.

Second, keyword studies typically have used relatively short study times, as low as 10 or 20 seconds per word. Semantic-based methods typically use considerably more time. Thus, the average effect for semantic-based methods may be higher simply because of this time factor. When keyword- and semantic-based methods have been equated for time (e.g., Levin et al., 1984), keyword techniques have produced stronger effects than semantic-based programs. For these two reasons, the meta-analysis technique may be less appropriate for addressing this type of research than a conventional review such as that of Pressley et al. (1987).

Setting Factors

Whether instruction was done using group discussion or individual work did not produce very strong differences. As noted in Table 15.7, the effects for group and individual work were extremely similar, with no more than .15 of a standard unit separating the two categories in the no-exposure set, and somewhat higher differences in the no-instruction set. The differences in the second set are based on very small cell *N*s.

The amount of time allocated to vocabulary instruction, on the other hand, had interesting relationships to effect size. For the no-exposure control group set, correlations between the number of minutes allocated to each word and effect size were .28 (*N* = 37) for the definitional tests (*p* < .05), and .22 (*N* = 15) for the word in con-

TABLE 15.7. Mean Effect Sizes Associated with Different Modes of Instruction

	No-exposure control			No-instruction control		
Type of measure	Mean	*SD*	*N*	Mean	*SD*	*N*
Contextual vocabulary						
Individual work	1.32**	.92	13	1.09**	.89	21
Group discussion	1.47**	.44	8	.62	.79	4
Definitional vocabulary						
Individual work	1.64**	1.60	29	.43	1.06	68
Group discussion	1.78**	1.22	26	.70	.80	4
Passage comprehension						
Individual work	.98**	.92	10	.33	.74	6
Group discussion	.96**	.78	31	.16	.23	8

Probability that mean equals zero:
* *p* < .05.
** *p* < .01.

text vocabulary measures (*p* > .05). *Although the first of these correlations is statistically significant, it is only moderate in strength. For the passage comprehension measures, the correlation between time, allocation and effect size was .65 (N = 26), which was not only statistically significant (*p* < .001), but also strong enough to possibly be educationally significant. For the no-instruction set, the corresponding correlations were –.33 for the contextual vocabulary measures (N = 18, *p* > .05), 18 for the definitional vocabulary measures (N = 52, *p* > .05), and –.91 for the passage comprehension measures (N = 10, *p* < .01). Interpretation of this second set of correlations is problematic because of the large number of studies that used short exposure times (see Table 15.2).

SUMMARY AND DISCUSSION

General Effects

From the research reviewed here, it can be concluded that vocabulary instruction does appear to have a significant effect on the comprehension of passages containing taught words. The effect sizes averaged .97 of a standard unit, which is a fairly strong effect and significantly different from zero. This mean effect size would have been larger if the studies in which the control group had means and standard deviations of less than 1 had not been excluded. Vocabulary instruction also appears to have a slight but significant effect on comprehension of passages not necessarily containing taught words. On standardized measures, this effect was .30 of a standard unit. This may indicate that vocabulary instruction generally facilitates growth in reading comprehension, both on measures containing and not containing taught words, possibly by increasing the students' interest in learning new words (Beck et al., 1982; McKeown, Beck, Omanson, & Pople, 1985).

Recently, there has been some discussion of the futility of vocabulary instruction (Nagy & Herman, 1984; Nagy, Herman, & Anderson, 1985) versus its fertility (Beck, McKeown, & Omanson, 1984). Nagy and Herman estimate that the number of distinct words in printed school English is about 88,500, a number too large to instruct. They estimate that children will learn between 1,000 and 5,000 new words from context each year, given normal exposure to printed text. Since a vocabulary teaching program typically teaches 10 to 12 words a week or about 400 a year, of which perhaps 75% or 300 are learned, vocabulary instruction is not adequate to cope with the volume of new words that children need to learn and do learn without instruction.

The results of this meta-analysis suggest that vocabulary instruction is a useful adjunct to the natural learning from context. Accepting Nagy et al.'s (1985) estimates of natural word learning from context, an additional 300 words learned each year would mean vocabulary increments of between 6% and 30%, with the larger amounts coming for the students who are poorest at denying meanings from context.

There is a small but emerging literature on the process involved in learning words from context (e.g., Carnine, Kame'enui, & Coyle, 1984; Jenkins, Stein, & Wysocki, 1984; McKeown, 1984; Nagy et al., 1985; Shefelbine, 1983; van Daalen-Kapteijns & Elshout-Mohr, 1981; Werner & Kaplan, 1952), one that promises to lead to more refined procedures for teaching or encouraging children to develop word meanings from context.

The effect size of .97 found on the passage comprehension measures represents the optimum conditions for word learning, using passages specially constructed to assess the maximum effects of instruction. Because the most usual situation is not going to be optimal, and because the effects of vocabulary instruction may decrease with time (Gipe, 1979), the "real" effects of vocabulary instruction are probably much more modest. The effects found on standardized vocabulary and comprehension measures are probably much closer to the actual effects than those of the study-specific passage comprehension measures. These effects, although smaller, are still significantly different from zero, indicating that vocabulary instruction does appear to have an effect on comprehension.

Method Comparisons

The significant effects of vocabulary instruction on reading comprehension were not found with all teaching methods, however. Methods that provided only definitional information about each to-be-learned word did not produce a reliable effect on comprehension, nor did methods that gave only one or two exposures of meaningful information about each word. Also, drill-and-practice methods, which involve multiple repetitions of the same type of information about a target word using only associative processing, did not appear to have reliable effects on comprehension. Interpretation of these findings should be tempered by the small number of effect sizes involved.

The methods that did appear to produce the highest effects on comprehension and vocabulary measures were methods that included both definitional and contextual information about each to-be-learned word (or "mixed" methods). It was difficult to draw conclusions as to the effects of relative emphases of definitional or contextual information from these data. These effects need to be examined further.

Keyword methods also produced consistently strong effects, at least on measures of definitional and contextual vocabulary knowledge. In studies that compared the keyword method with semantic-based alternatives, the keyword method was found more effective on these measures. Its effect on passage comprehension, however, has not been adequately studied. Pressley et al. (1981) suggest that the keyword method's effect on sentence comprehension measures indicates that it would similarly affect passage comprehension. As noted earlier, the keyword method attempts to strengthen the associative link between a new word and its definition. For other methods that similarly stress the link between word and definition, most usually drill-and-practice methods, little relation has been found between sentence comprehension and passage comprehension measures (see Jenkins et al., 1978; Pany & Jenkins, 1977). There are numerous differences between keyword and drill-and-practice methods. However, whether keyword instruction will improve comprehension of passages should be directly tested.

Confirming the review of Mezynski (1983), methods that provided a "breadth of knowledge" about each to-be-learned word also had strong effect on reading comprehension. On vocabulary measures, breadth of knowledge approaches had effects similar to those of drill-and-practice methods on both definitional and word-in-context measures.

The issue of time allocation is related to these method comparisons. Although the correlations between time allocations and effect size were not educationally significant on either vocabulary measure, they were fairly strong for the passage comprehension measures. This may reflect the large effect sizes found using relatively time-intensive procedures (e.g., McKeown, Beck, Omanson, & Perfetti, 1983) but may also mean that words need to be learned thoroughly in order to contribute to passage comprehension. It may not be possible to accomplish this thorough learning by just mentioning a word's meaning. Time allocation does not totally explain the effects found, however. In studies that controlled for time, Stahl (1983) found that a mixed method produced significantly higher comprehension than a definitional method, and Wixson (1984) found a method classified here as requiring deeper processing generally produced higher comprehension than a method requiring less extensive processing (see Jenkins & Dixon, 1983).

The nature of the passage comprehension tests was not controlled in this analysis, but test factors certainly did influence the results. Since one can get an understanding of a passage without knowing the meaning of a good number of the words in the passage (Freebody & Anderson, 1983; Goodman, 1976), a passage must contain a relatively high density of taught words in order to be sensitive to the effects of vocabulary instruction. Some studies (e.g., Ahlfors, 1979; Schacter, 1978; Tuinman & Brady, 1974) used passages with relatively low concentrations of taught words. Thus, their results might underestimate the effects of vocabulary instruction. Also, whether the words were high or low in the passage structure (see Wixson, 1984) might also influence the overall effect of instruction. One would expect that an unfamiliar word high in importance would affect the processing of information lower in importance, while an unfamiliar word in a less important idea unit would not have as detrimental effects.

It also may be that vocabulary instruction has stronger effects on inferential comprehension, as found by Kame'enui et al. (1982). Therefore, a measure with a higher percentage of inferential questions may also be more sensitive to vocabulary instruction than a measure with more literal questions.

Although differences in measures would be expected to affect results, so might differences in words. In every study reviewed, the words used were chosen on the basis of frequency or other numerical measures of relative difficulty. In no study was there an attempt to make a meaningful classification of properties of words other than difficulty. It may be that certain methods are most effective in teaching words belonging to a constrained area of knowledge, while others are applicable for more general words, such as those that might be found in a variety of contexts (e.g., a technical word such as *proactive interference* vs. a general word such as *discouragement*). When a word is narrowly defined, as a technical term would be, a more associative method, such as keyword or drill and practice, may be the most suitable approach. Some words are also more "definable" than others and may lend themselves to more definitional approaches. The interaction between teaching method and word and passage characteristics has not yet been explored but seems to be a useful direction for vocabulary instructional research.

Limitations and Future Directions

Aside from the limitations endemic to meta-analysis (see Glass et al., 1981), there are other problems that may have affected these results. Most notably, there is the possible lack of reliability of authors' descriptions and some questions about the scales used to classify studies.

There are two problems related to our reliance on the descriptions reported in the study as a basis for our classifications. First, these descriptions varied considerably in their completeness and level of detail. Some studies (e.g., Jenkins et al., 1978; Kame'enui et al., 1982) gave examples of lesson scripts, and others gave only a few sentences. Two studies (Brown, 1965; Meyer & Cohen, 1975) were not classified due to a lack of description, as noted in Table 15.1, but other studies containing only a little more detail were classified. This variation in levels of detail meant that the studies also varied in the amount of inferencing required to make the classifications. A small group of studies with vague or lightly detailed descriptions accounted for the majority of disagreements among raters. Although these were resolved, this is a source of error that needs to be considered.

The second problem with using descriptions is that these descriptions may or may not describe what actually went on in the classroom. One of us (Stahl, 1983) reported that a method that was intended to include only definitional information actually included a great deal of contextual information. This contextual information came from the students and from the dictionaries. The degree to which the actual methods differed from the descriptions reported cannot be determined, but we can assume there were some differences. Again, with studies that used scripted lessons, one would assume that the differences were slight. With studies that used large numbers of classes, not necessarily under experimenter direction, one might expect larger differences. A related problem is that methods described similarly may not have been implemented similarly. For example, the keyword method used by Johnson (1979; Johnson & Noble, 1982) differed in a number of features from that used in other studies (see Pressley et al., 1982). These differences certainly led to differences in effects.

Related to this issue are some problems with the scales themselves. The general setting scales (group/individualized and time allocation) were relatively simple and straightforward. The three method-specific scales required more inference and may be less reliable. A particular problem was noted with the depth-of-processing scale. The three levels of this factor—association, comprehension, and generation—were only an approximation of the concept of processing depth and were used only after several alternatives were tried and discarded. One alternative was a holistic rating of the depth of processing required using procedures similar to those of Seamon and Virostek (1978). The other was a five-section scale that required the ranking of each study on various attributes that might lead to more complete processing. Two parts of this scale, the depth-of-processing and the exposure scales, were retained for this analysis. The other sections were dropped for inability to obtain satisfactory agreement.

The depth-of-processing scale used here was adopted for pragmatic reasons. However, it is only a rough approximation of the construct of depth of processing, as defined by those who have followed Craik and Tulving (1975). The full notion of depth of processing includes aspects such as the amount of mental effort or the amount of available cognitive resources committed to complete a learning task, the amount of elaborative processing, the distinctiveness of the encoding of the learned information, and so forth. These could not be satisfactorily measured using a post hoc analysis such as this, but this does not mean that they may not be important to effective vocabulary instruction. They need to be included, perhaps, in planned experimentation in this area (see Shaughnessy & Cockrell, 1984).

Another problem with the depth-of-processing scale is the possible confounding of depth of processing with increased study time. Certainly, methods that appeared to require deeper processing also took more classroom time. These two factors have been separated in verbal-learning research (see Craik & Tulving, 1975) but need to be separated in vocabulary instructional research as well.

With the use of two types of control groups, most vocabulary-instruction studies could be included in this analysis. However, there were some omissions. Not included were studies that tested commonly suggested techniques such as the instruction of word parts, for example, prefixes, suffixes, and roots (O'Rourke, 1974; Otterman, 1955), and direct instruction in the use of context clues (Camine et al., 1984; Humes, 1978; Quealy, 1969). In addition, studies that compared two methods without either a no-exposure or a no-instruction control could not be included (e.g. Crist, 1981; Mastropieri, Scruggs, Levin, Gaffney, & McLoone, 1985; Scruggs, Mastropieri, & Levin, 1985).

Given these limitations, the general approach taken in this paper can be useful in clarifying some of the issues in vocabulary instruction and in identifying direction for further research. In general, the predictions made by the frameword were borne out in the analysis. The system of classification used appears to be a practical approach to discussing meaningful differences in vocabulary-teaching methods. Such a systematic approach is necessary before one can have a "science" of vocabulary instruction (see O'Rourke, 1974, for a different approach to this problem). It is hoped that future research, designed specifically to investigate some of the hypotheses suggested here, will be more definitive. Some of the problems noted are better dealt with in a planned experiment rather than in a post hoc analysis. For example, the depth-of-processing factor, which was so difficult to extract from authors' descriptions, would be easier to vary systematically in a planned comparison. Similarly, a stronger comparison of the effects of differing emphases on contextual information would be to use the same words with similar groups of students, rather than comparing relative effect sizes. The effects of vocabulary instruction are subtle and complex, but, given their potential effects on comprehension, they are worthy of further investigation.

REFERENCES

Ahlfors, G. (1979). *Learning word meanings: A comparison of three instructional procedures.* Unpublished doctoral dissertation, University of Minnesota, Minneapolis.

Anders, P. L., Bos, C. S., & Filipi, D. (1984). The effect of semantic feature analysis on the reading comprehension of learning disabled students. In J. Niles & L. A. Harris (Eds.), *Changing perspectives on research in reading/language processing and instruction.* Thirty-third yearbook of the National Reading Conference. Rochester, NY: National Reading Conference.

Anderson, J. R., & Reder, L. M. (1979). An elaborative processing explanation of depth of processing. In L. S. Cermak & F. I. M. Craik (Eds.), *Levels of processing in human memory* (pp. 385–404). Hillsdale, NJ: Erlbaum.

Anderson, L. (1984). The environment of instruction: The function of seatwork in a commercially developed curriculum. In G. G. Duffy, L. R. Roehler, & J. Mason (Eds.), *Comprehension instruction: Perspectives and suggestions* (pp. 93–103). New York: Longman.

Anderson, R. C., & Freebody, P. (1981). Vocabulary knowledge. In J. T. Guthrie (Ed.), *Compre-*

hension and teaching: Research reviews (pp. 77–117). Newark, DE: International Reading Association.

Anderson, R. C., & Kulhavy, R. W. (1972). Learning concepts from definitions. *American Educational Research Journal, 9,* 385–390.

Anderson, R. C., & McGaw, G. (1973). On the representation of meaning of general terms. *Journal of Experimental Psychology, 101,* 301–306.

Anderson, R. C., & Ortony, A. (1975). On putting apples into bottles: A problem of polysemy. *Cognitive Psychology, 7,* 167–180.

Anderson, R. C., Pichert, J. W., Goetz, E. T., Schallert, D. L., Stevens, K. V., & Trollip, S. (1976). Instantiation of general terms. *Journal of Verbal Learning and Verbal Behavior, 15,* 667–679.

Anderson, T. H., & Armbruster, B. B. (1982). Reader and text-studying strategies. In W. Otto & S. White (Eds.), *Reading expository material* (pp. 219–242). New York: Academic Press.

Aurentz, J. (1983). *Self-instruction and the keyword method: Effects upon vocabulary usage.* Unpublished manuscript, Florida State University, Tallahassee.

Baer, F. B. (1974). *A comparison of the effects of two methods of teaching vocabulary on the reading vocabulary, comprehension, accuracy and rate of selected students at the George Washington University.* Unpublished doctoral dissertation, George Washington University, Washington, DC.

Barrett, M. T., & Graves, M. F. (1981). A vocabulary program for junior high school remedial readers. *Journal of Reading, 25,* 146–150.

Barron, R. F., & Melnik, R. (1973). The effects of discussion upon learning vocabulary meanings and relationships in tenth grade biology. In H. L. Herber & R. F. Barron (Eds.), *Research in reading in the content areas, second year report* (pp. 46–52). Syracuse, NY: Reading and Language Arts Center, Syracuse University.

Beck, I. L., McKeown, M. G., & Omanson, R. C. (1984, April). *The fertility of some types of vocabulary instruction.* Paper presented at the annual meeting of the American Educational Research Association, New Orleans, LA.

Beck, I. L., Perfetti, C. A., & McKeown, M. G. (1982). Effects of long-term vocabulary instruction on lexical access and reading comprehension. *Journal of Educational Psychology, 74,* 506–521.

Berliner, D. C. (1981). Academic learning time and reading achievement. In J. T. Guthrie (Ed.), *Comprehension and instruction: Research reviews.* Newark, DE: International Reading Association.

Blevins, M. L. (1970). *A comparative study of three methods of instruction in vocabulary achievement of students in the Adult Institute.* Unpublished doctoral dissertation, Oklahoma State University, Stillwater.

Bransford, J. D., & Nitsch, K. E. (1978). Coming to understand things we could not previously understand. In J. F. Kavanaugh & W. Strange (Eds.), *Speech and language in laboratory, school and clinic* (pp. 268–307). Cambridge, MA: MIT Press.

Brown, J. I. (1965). Reading improvement through vocabulary development: The CPD formula. In G. B. Schick & M. M. May (Eds.), *New frontiers in college-adult reading.* 15th annual yearbook of the National Reading Conference. Clemson, SC: National Reading Conference.

Bull, B. L., & Wittrock, M. C. (1973). Imagery in the learning of verbal definitions. *British Journal of Education Psychology, 43,* 289–293.

Carney, J. J., Anderson, D., Blackburn, C., & Blessing, D. (1984). Preteaching vocabulary and the comprehension of social studies material by elementary school children. *Social Education, 48,* 195–196.

Carnine, D., Kame'enui, E. J., & Coyle, G. (1984). Utilization of contextual information in determining the meaning of unfamiliar words. *Reading Research Quarterly, 19,* 188–204.

Carroll, J. (1964). Words, meanings, and concepts. *Harvard Educational Review, 34,* 178–202.

Chall, J. S. (1958). *Readability: An appraisal of research and application*. Columbus: Bureau of Educational Research, Ohio State University.

Collins, A. M., & Loftus, E. E. (1975). A spreading activation theory of semantic processing. *Psychological Review, 82*, 407–428.

Collins, A. M., & Quillian, M. R. (1969). Retrieval time from semantic memory. *Journal of Verbal Learning and Verbal Behavior, 8*, 240–248.

Craik, F. I. M., & Tulving, E. (1975). Depth of processing and the retention of words in episodic memory. *Journal of Experimental Psychology: General, 104*, 268–294.

Crist, R. L. (1981). Learning concepts from contexts and definitions: A single subject replication. *Journal of Reading Behavior, 13*, 271–277.

Crist, R. L., & Petrone, J. M. (1977). Learning concepts from contexts and definitions. *Journal of Reading Behavior, 9*, 301–303.

Crump, B. M. (1965). *Relative merits of teaching vocabulary by a direct and an incidental method*. Unpublished doctoral dissertation, University of Arkansas, Fayetteville.

Dale, E., Razik, T., & Petty, W. (1973). *Bibliography of vocabulary studies*. Columbus: Ohio State University.

Davis, F. B. (1944). Fundamental factors of comprehension in reading. *Psychometrika, 9*, 185–197.

Davis, F. B. (1972). Psychometric research on comprehension in reading. *Reading Research Quarterly, 7*, 628–678.

Draper, A. G., & Moeller, G. H. (1971). We think with words (therefore, to improve thinking, teach vocabulary). *Phi Delta Kappan, 52*, 482–484.

Eichholz, G., & Barbe, R. (1961). An experiment in vocabulary development. *Educational Research Bulletin, 40*, 1–7.

Fairbanks, M. M. (1977, October). *A review of the research on vocabulary instruction*. Paper presented at the annual meeting of the Western College Reading Association, Denver.

Farr, R. (1969). *Reading: What can be measured?* Newark, DE: International Reading Association.

Fodor, J. A., Garrett, M. F., Walker, E. C. T., & Parkes, C. H. (1980). Against definitions. *Cognition, 8*, 263–367.

Freebody, P., & Anderson, R. C. (1983). Effects of vocabulary difficulty, text cohesion, and schema availability on reading comprehension. *Reading Research Quarterly, 18*, 277–294.

Gipe, J. (1979). Investigating techniques for teaching word meanings. *Reading Research Quarterly, 14*, 624–645.

Gipe, J. P. (1981, April). *Investigation of techniques for teaching new word meanings*. Paper presented at the annual meeting of the American Educational Research Association, Los Angeles.

Gipe, J. P., & Arnold, R. D. (1979). Teaching vocabulary through familiar associations and contexts. *Journal of Reading Behavior, 11*, 281–285.

Glass, G. V., McGaw, B., & Smith, M. L. (1981). *Meta-analysis in social research*. Beverly Hills, CA: Sage.

Gnewuch, M. M. (1973). *The effect of vocabulary training upon the development of vocabulary, comprehension, total reading, and rate of reading of college students*. Unpublished doctoral dissertation, Oklahoma State University, Stillwater.

Goodman, K. S. (1976). Behind the eye: What happens in reading. In H. Singer & R. Ruddell (Eds.), *Theoretical models and processes in reading* (2nd ed., pp. 470–496). Newark, DE: International Reading Association.

Gray, W. S., & Holmes, E. (1938). *The development of meaning vocabulary in reading*. Chicago: Laboratory Schools of the University of Chicago.

Haefner, R. (1932). Casual learning of word meanings. *Journal of Educational Research, 25*, 267–277.

Hare, S. Z. (1975). An investigation of the effectiveness of three methods of teaching reading vocabulary (Doctoral dissertation, University of South Carolina, Columbia). *Dissertation Abstracts, 76*(10), 457.

Harrison, C. (1980). *Readability in the classroom*. Cambridge, UK: Cambridge University Press.

Hogan, F. (1961). *Comparison of two methods of teaching word meaning through the use of word parts in grades ten, eleven, and twelve*. Unpublished doctoral dissertation, Boston University.

Humes, A. (1978). Structures, signals, and cognitive processes in context clues. *Research in the Teaching of English, 12*, 321–334.

Hyde, T. S., & Jenkins, J. J. (1973). Recall for words as a function of semantic, graphic, and syntactic orienting tasks. *Journal of Verbal Learning and Verbal Behavior, 12*, 471–480.

Jackson, J. R., & Dizney, H. (1963). Intensive vocabulary training. *Journal of Developmental Reading, 6*, 221–229.

Jacoby, L. L., Craik, F. I. M., & Begg, I. (1979). Effect of decision difficulty on recognition and recall. *Journal of Verbal Learning and Verbal Behavior, 18*, 585–600.

Jenkis, J. R., & Dixon, R. (1983). Vocabulary learning. *Contemporary Educational Psychology, 8*, 237–260.

Jenkins, J. R., Pany, D., & Schreck, J. (1978). *Vocabulary and reading comprehension: Instructional effects* (Tech. Rep. No. 100). Urbana, IL: Center for the Study of Reading, University of Illinois. (ERIC Document Reproduction Service No. ED 160 999)

Jenkins, J. R., Stein, M. L., & Wysocki, K. (1984). Learning vocabulary through reading. *American Educational Research Journal, 21*, 767–788.

Johnson, C. W. (1979). *Effects of imagery, mnemonics, and level of processing in learning definitions upon concept comprehension*. Lincoln: University of Nebraska. (ERIC Document Reproduction Service No. ED 173 426)

Johnson, C. W., & Noble, A. C. (1982, April). *Watch those keywords: Micro-computer assessment of keyword method effectiveness*. Paper presented at the annual meeting of the American Educational Research Association, New York.

Johnson, D. D., Pittelman, S. D., Toms-Bronowski, S., & Levin, K. M. (1984, November). *An investigation of the effects of prior knowledge and vocabulary acquisition on passage comprehension*. (Program Report 84-5). Madison: Wisconsin Center for Education Research, University of Wisconsin.

Johnson, D. D., & Stratton, P. (1966). Evaluation of five methods of teaching concepts. *Journal of Educational Psychology, 57*, 48–53.

Johnson-Laird, P. N., Gibbs, G., & deMowbray, J. (1978). Meaning, amount of processing, and memory for words. *Memory and Cognition, 6*, 372–375.

Kame'enui, E. J., Carnine, D. W., & Freschi, R. (1982). Effects of text construction and instructional procedures for teaching word meanings on comprehension and recall. *Reading Research Quarterly, 17*, 367–388.

Kintsch, W. (1974). *The representation of meaning in memory*. Hillsdale, NJ: Erlbaum.

Levin, J. R., Dretzke, B. J., Pressley, M., & McGivern, J. E. (1985). In search of the keyword method/vocabulary comprehension link. *Contemporary Educational Psychology, 10*, 220–227.

Levin, J. R., Johnson, D. D., Pittelman, S. D., Hayes, B. L., Levin, I. M., Shriberg, L. K., & Toms-Bronowski, S. (1984). A comparison of semantic- and mnemonic-based vocabulary strategies. *Reading Psychology, 5*, 1–15.

Levin, J. R., McCormick, C. B., Miller, G. E., Berry, J. K., & Pressley, M. (1982). Mnemonic versus nonmnemonic vocabulary learning strategies for children. *American Educational Research Journal, 19*, 121–136.

Levin, J. R., & Pressley, M. (1985). Mnemonic vocabulary instruction: What's fact, what's fiction. In R. F. Dillon (Ed.), *Individual differences in cognition* (Vol. 2, pp. 145–172). Hillsdale, NJ: Erlbaum.

Margosein, C. M., Pascarella, E. T., & Pflaum, S. W. (1982, April). *The effects of instruction using semantic mapping on vocabulary and comprehension.* Paper presented at the annual meeting of the American Educational Research Association, New York.

Mastropieri, M. A., Scruggs, T. E., Levin, J. R., Gaffney, J., & McLoone, B. (1985). Mnemonic vocabulary instruction with learning disabled students. *Learning Disability Quarterly, 8,* 57–63.

McDaniel, M. A., & Pressley, M. (1984). Putting the keyword method in context. *Journal of Educational Psychology, 76,* 598–609.

McDaniel, M. A., & Tillman, V. P. (1985). *The keyword method versus learning from context: Where's the link?* Unpublished manuscript, University of Notre Dame, South Bend, IN.

McGivern, J. E., & Levin, J. R. (1983). The keyword method and children's vocabulary learning: An interaction with vocabulary knowledge. *Contemporary Educational Psychology, 8,* 46–54.

McKeown, M. G. (1984, December). *The acquisition of word meaning from context in children of high and low ability.* Paper presented at the annual meeting of the National Reading Conference, St. Petersburg Beach, FL.

McKeown, M. G., Beck, I. L., Omanson, R. C. & Perfetti, C. A. (1983). The effects of long-term vocabulary instruction on reading comprehension: A replication. *Journal of Reading Behavior, 15,* 3–18.

McKeown, M. G., Beck, I. L., Omanson, R. C., & Pople, M. T. (1985, April). *Some effects of the nature and frequency of vocabulary instruction on the knowledge and use of words.* Paper presented at the annual meeting of the American Educational Research Association, Chicago.

Meyer, D. E., & Schvaneveldt, R. W. (1975). Meaning, memory structure, and mental processes. In C. Cofer (Ed.), *The structure of human memory* (pp. 54–89). San Francisco: Freeman.

Meyer, R. E., & Cohen, S. A. (1975). A study of general reading compared to direct instruction to increase vocabulary achievement. *Reading World, 15,* 109–113.

Mezynski, K. (1983). Issues concerning the acquisition of knowledge: Effects of vocabulary training on reading comprehension. *Review of Educational Research, 53,* 253–279.

Nagy, W. E., & Herman, P. A. (I 984). *Limitations of vocabulary instruction* (Tech. Rep. No. 326). Center for the Study of Reading, Champaign: University of Illinois.

Nagy, W. E., Herman, P. A., & Anderson, R. C. (1985, April). *The influence of word and text properties on learning from context.* Paper presented at the annual meeting of the American Educational Research Association, Chicago.

Nelson, K., & Nelson, K. E. (1978). Cognitive pendulums and their linguistic realization. In K. E. Nelson (Ed.), *Children's language* (Vol. 1, pp. 223–286). New York: Gardner.

Nitsch, K. E. (1977). *Structuring decontextualized forms of knowledge.* Unpublished doctoral dissertation, Vanderbilt University, Nashville, TN.

O'Rourke, J. P. (1974). Toward a science of vocabulary development. The Hague: Mouton.

Otterman, L. (1955). The value of teaching prefixes and word-roots. *Journal of Educational Research, 48,* 611–615.

Pany, D., & Jenkins, J. R. (1977). *Learning word meanings: A comparison of instructional procedures and effects on measures of reading comprehension with learning disabled students* (Tech. Rep. No. 25). Urbana: Center for the Study of Reading, University of Illinois. (ERIC Document Reproduction Service No. ED 134 979)

Petty, W., Herold, C., & Stoll, E. (1968). *The state of the knowledge about the teaching of vocabulary* (Cooperative Research Project No. 3128). Champaign, IL: National Council of Teachers of English. (ERIC Document Reproduction Service No. ED 012 395)

Pflaum, S. W., Pascarella, E. T., Auer, C., Augustyn, L., & Boswick, M. (1982). Differential effects of four comprehension facilitating conditions on LD and normal elementary school readers. *Learning Disability Quarterly, 5,* 106–116.

Pless, H. (1966). *The use of structural analysis by high school biology students as a method for learning and retaining the definitions of technical vocabulary terms.* Unpublished doctoral dissertation, Temple University, Philadelphia.

Pressley, M., Levin, J. R., Kuiper, N. A., Bryant, S. L., & Michener, S. (1982). Mnemonic versus nonmnemonic vocabulary learning strategies: Additional comparisons. *Journal of Educational Psychology, 74,* 693–707.

Pressley, M., Levin, J. R., & McDaniel, M. A. (1987). Remembering versus inferring what a word means: Mnemonic and contextual approaches. In M. G. McKeown & M. E. Curtis (Eds.), *The nature of vocabulary acquisition* (pp. 107–127). Hillsdale, NJ: Erlbaum.

Pressley, M., Levin, J. R., & Miller, G. E. (1981). How does the keyword method affect vocabulary comprehension and usage? *Reading Research Quarterly, 16,* 213–226.

Pressley, M., Levin, J. R., & Miller, G. E. (1982). The keyword method compared to alternative vocabulary learning strategies. *Contemporary Educational Psychology, 7,* 50–60.

Quealy, R. J. (1969). Senior high school students' use of contextual aids in reading. *Reading Research Quarterly, 4,* 512–533.

Rosenshine, B. (1979). Content, time, and direct instruction. In P. Peterson & H. Walberg (Eds.), *Research on teaching: Concepts, findings, and implication.* Berkeley, CA: McCutcheon.

Schacter, S. W. (1978). *An investigation of the effects of vocabulary instruction and schema orientation on reading comprehension.* Unpublished doctoral dissertation, University of Minnesota, Minneapolis.

Scruggs, T. E., Mastropieri, M. A., & Levin, J. R. (1985). Vocabulary acquisition by mentally retarded students under direct and mnemonic instruction. *American Journal of Mental Deficiency, 89,* 546–551.

Seamon, J., & Virostek, S. (1978). Memory performance and subject-defined depth of processing. *Memory and Cognition, 6,* 283–287.

Shaughnessy, M. F., & Cockrell, K. (1984, April). *Distinctiveness of encoding and word learning. Forms of "distinctiveness" and retention of vocabulary words.* Paper presented at the annual meeting of the Rocky Mountain Psychological Association, Las Vegas, NV. (ERIC Document Reproduction Service ED 246 666)

Shefelbine, J. L. (1983, April). *Learning word meanings from context.* Paper presented at the annual meeting of the American Educational Research Association, Montreal, Canada.

Slamecka, N. J., & Graf, P. (1978). The generation effects: Delineation of a phenomenon. *Journal of Experimental Psychology: Human Learning and Memory, 4,* 592–604.

Smith, E. E., & Medin, D. L. (1981). *Categories and concepts.* Cambridge, MA: Harvard University Press.

Snouffer, N. K., & Thistlethwaite, L. L. (1979). *The effects of the structured overview and vocabulary pre-teaching upon comprehension levels of college freshmen reading physical science and history materials.* Paper presented at the annual meeting of the National Reading Conference, San Antonio, TX. (ERIC Document Reproduction Service No. ED 182 728)

Spearitt, D. (1972). Identification of sub-skills of reading comprehension by maximum likelihood factor analysis. *Reading Research Quarterly, 8,* 92–111.

Stahl, S. A. (1983). Differential word knowledge and reading comprehension. *Journal of Reading Behavior, 15*(4), 33–50.

Stahl, S. A. (1985). To teach a word well: A framework for vocabulary instruction *Reading World, 24,* 16–27.

Stratton, R. P., & Nacke, P. L. (1974). *The role of vocabulary knowledge in comprehension. Twenty-third yearbook of the National Reading Conference.* Clemson, SC: National Reading Conference.

Thorndike, E. L. (1917). Reading as reasoning. *Journal of Educational Psychology, 8,* 512–518.

Thorndyke, P. (1975). Conceptual complexity and imagery in comprehension and memory. *Journal of Verbal Learning and Verbal Behavior, 14,* 359–369.

Toms-Bronowski, S. (1982). *An investigation of the effectiveness of semantic mapping and semantic feature analysis with intermediate grade children.* Unpublished doctoral dissertation, University of Wisconsin, Madison. (ERIC Document Reproduction Service No. ED 224 000)

Tuinman, J. J., & Brady, M. E. (1974). *How does vocabulary account for variance on reading comprehension tests: A preliminary instructional analysis. Twenty-third yearbook of the National Reading Conference.* Clemson, SC: National Reading Conference.

Tyler, S. W., Hertel, P. T., McCallum, M. C., & Ellis, H. C. (1979). Cognitive effort and memory. *Journal of experimental Psychology: Human Learning and Memory, 5,* 607–617.

van Daalen-Kapteijns, N., & Elshout-Mohr, M. (1981). The acquisition of word meaning as a cognitive learning process. *Journal of Verbal Learning and Verbal Behavior, 20,* 386–399.

Werner, H., & Kaplan, E. (1952). The acquisition of word meanings: A developmental study. *Monographs of the Society for Research in Child Development, 15,* Serial No. 1.

Wittrock, M. C., Marks, C., & Doctorow, M. (1975). Reading as a generative process. *Journal of Educational Psychology, 67,* 481–489.

Wixson, K. (1984). *The effects of two types of vocabulary instruction on reading comprehension.* Paper presented at the annual meeting of the National Reading Conference, St. Petersburg Beach, FL.

16 | Issues in the Advancement of Vocabulary Instruction

Response to Stahl and Fairbanks's Meta-Analysis

Margaret G. McKeown
Isabel L. Beck

Stahl and Fairbanks's (1986) meta-analysis of vocabulary instruction (reprinted as Chapter 15, this volume) has become a classic in the field, and its conclusions are well embedded in understandings of vocabulary learning and teaching: that in order to affect comprehension, more than a couple of exposures to taught words are needed, more than one type of information about words is needed, and deeper processing is called for. The results and conclusions of the meta-analysis are part of a large and consistent picture that has never been contradicted. There was no evidence before nor has there been since that suggests that effective vocabulary learning does not need multiple exposures, could be done simply with definitional information, or needs only surface processing.

The themes are still timely, as demonstrated by a check of current work on vocabulary reviewed by Baumann, Kame'enui, and Ash (2003). Although this may seem like good news for Stahl and Fairbanks's work, it is actually bad news for the vocabulary field, bad in the same way that the International Reading Association's annual survey of hot and not-hot topics perpetually shows vocabulary in the not-hot-but-should-be column. That is, very little is going on instructionally. Despite a strong, consistent picture of what is effective instructionally, classrooms and instructional materials do not reflect it.

Discussion of the research picture since the time of Stahl and Fairbanks's work and of the current status of classroom instruction are major sections of this chapter. However, we begin with a different dimension that we discovered in revisiting the Stahl and Fairbanks work. As we began to reread this work that we thought we knew well, we uncovered, embedded within the framework of the analysis and its conclusions, some important issues that carry explanatory weight for understanding why multiple exposures, varied information, and depth of processing are important to vocabulary learning. Thus we begin by bringing those to light and commenting on them and what we see as their relevance in today's discourse on vocabulary.

IDEAS TO KEEP ON THE FRONT BURNER

Here we consider some issues surrounding the major instructional features that Stahl and Fairbanks identified. The issues we focus on are how multiple exposures may replicate the process of natural vocabulary learning, how instruction may facilitate general comprehension, and the role of word properties in instruction. Our discussion of these issues is intended to deepen understanding of Stahl and Fairbanks's features and the mechanisms of word learning that underlie them. We see these as ideas that should be kept on the front burner in the discourse on vocabulary.

Multiple Exposures May Replicate Natural Learning

Stahl and Fairbanks indicate that multiple exposures to contexts that provide varied and meaningful information may be necessary to forming decontextualized knowledge of a word's meaning. Decontextualization occurs as learners use examples of a word's use in different contexts to refine their concept of what the word means, making it more flexible and less narrowly fitted to a specific context.

Stahl and Fairbanks relate the use of multiple exposures to refine word meaning to natural learning, saying that experiencing multiple exposures in different contexts may most nearly replicate natural word learning in a compressed form (Carroll, 1964). As learners refine aspects of specific words, they also come to refine the "rules of meaning," building an understanding that word knowledge is flexible, that word meanings have "borders" that move and shift depending on the contexts in which the words occur. Perhaps, then, an important part of word learning is learning how to "take" words. That is, how to juggle the meaning elements one thinks a word has in order to come up with a useful but flexible meaning.

Gaining flexibility of word meaning includes the ability to recontextualize words as well as decontextualize them. That is, experiences with various contexts enable a learner not only to separate word meanings from specific contexts but also to integrate the meaning into subsequent contexts and use knowledge of the word to make meaning of those contexts. As Stahl and Fairbanks point out, there is evidence that sophisticated word users encode words differently in different contexts, based on a sense that word knowledge has to be adjusted for each different context met.

The ability to manipulate word meaning for individual contexts is an important aspect of word knowledge that is required for effective comprehension. It is part of that elusive subtlety in the relationship between depth of word knowledge and the type and level of text understanding gained (Baumann et al., 2003).

General Effect on Comprehension

The quest to uncover an effect on general comprehension from teaching vocabulary has been one more of faith than findings. As Baumann et al. (2003) point out most recently, the evidence is still soft. But Stahl and Fairbanks, by producing a meta-analysis, gave us a glimmer of its existence. They found vocabulary instruction to have a slight but significant general facilitative effect on reading comprehension as measured by standardized tests. By examining the distribution of scores for students who received vocabulary instruction compared to uninstructed groups, Stahl and Fairbanks were able to identify that the 50th percentile score for instructed groups was equal to the 62nd percentile score of the control group. Put another way, half of the instructed students had scores as high as roughly the top third of students in the uninstructed group. Stahl and Fairbanks suggested that this might be considered an estimate of the long-term effects of vocabulary instruction. That is, over time as words are added to students' repertoires through instruction, growth in their general comprehension ability can be measured.

But yet to be uncovered are the processes that make such a general effect possible. Is it related to knowledge of specific words or is it development of metalinguistic knowledge? It could be literally that instructed words become numerous enough that they begin to appear on standardized tests in sufficient numbers to enhance students' performance. Or, it may be a "snowball" effect of learning a great number of words such that each word learned helps one learn a few more, and so on. This might allow one's vocabulary to expand enough that the number of unfamiliar words on reading comprehension tests declines enough to allow enhancement in performance. Or is it that students who have been engaged in long-term instruction have developed a greater facility in handling the nuances of words? Thus they might more quickly and accurately assign appropriate meanings to words in context as they read.

The finding that instructed students had an advantage on standardized tests can be likened to the finding from several studies meant to improve vocabulary or reading comprehension that students of high ability or with larger vocabularies often make greater gains (Nagy, Herman, & Anderson, 1985; Shefelbine, 1990). This "rich get richer" finding has been labeled the Matthew effect. Stahl and Fairbanks's finding suggests that students who received instruction became more like high-ability learners in their comprehension test performance, thus in essence creating a Matthew effect by virtue of having received vocabulary instruction. In these cases, however, it was not innate ability or individual characteristics but a program of instruction that gave them the edge.

This suggests that a Matthew effect in the sense of a difference in learning outcomes based on entering characteristics may not be inevitable. It further suggests that a direction for research on vocabulary instruction is to find that "tipping point" when instructional effects become generalized. This may require research scheduled over years of students' lifetimes.

Properties of Words

In discussing factors that might have led to differences in results, Stahl and Fairbanks include the types of words taught. But they had found that no studies "attempted to make a meaningful classification of words other than difficulty." They go on to suggest that certain methods of instruction may be more suited to specific types of words.

The notion that different instruction is appropriate for different words echoes a theme that Graves (1987, 2000) has made prominent in his work. The notion has run through our work as well, in particular in terms of dealing with potentially unfamiliar words that appear in a text used for instruction. That is, a text often contains a mix of words that are unfamiliar to students. Some may pertain very specifically to the context of the story and have only narrow application, such as *spurs* in a story about cowboys. Others may be highlighted because a less familiar sense of a word is used, such as the use of *brave* as a verb. Still others may represent broadly useful words that are refinements of concepts students already know, such as *splurge*, which can be likened to treating yourself to something special. Each of these vocabulary items would require different types of attention to help students understand them, and would provide different benefits to students' vocabulary repertoires. But as we have noted, the differing requirements are barely taken note of in instruction or in research. In fact, Coyne, Simmons, Kame'enui, and Stoolmiller (2004) assert that while knowledge about how to effectively teach vocabulary is accumulating, what to teach remains elusive.

However, a discourse about which words should be taught seems to have begun. We can cite three points of reference on selecting words. One is Biemiller (2005), whose perspective is to focus on words that are partially learned, those that between 20% and 70% of a target group of students know. According to Biemiller's thinking, it is these words where the greatest gains can be made.

Another point of reference for selecting words is word frequency information, with the ubiquitous source being the *American Heritage Word Frequency Book* (Carroll, Davies, & Richman, 1971). Inevitably, discussions of how to select words to teach turn to the notion of printed word frequency. We are not aware of any full-fledged descriptions of how word frequency is to be applied, although references to its use occur in, for example, Nation (2001) and Foorman and Pollard-Durodola (2004). There are clearly some limitations to using frequency, a chief one being that frequency gives no indication of how learnable or usable a word is for a learner. For example, it seems that if learners understand the concept of *sadness*, they could learn and apply the word *forlorn*. But those two words are widely discrepant in frequency (for a fuller discussion of these issues, see Beck & McKeown, in press).

A third point of reference is our position that the words selected as the focus of vocabulary instruction should be sophisticated words of high utility for mature language users (Beck, McKeown, & Kucan, 2002). We have described this set of words as Tier 2 words, juxtaposing them to Tier 1, which comprises the most familiar words commonly found in daily oral conversation, and Tier 3 words, which have a narrow or specialized meaning, often belonging to a specific domain, such as *microscope*, *patina*, or *cantata*. Tier 2 words are domain general words, and are more sophisticated or more refined labels for concepts that young learners are already familiar with. For example, *inseparable* would be a refinement on the concept of wanting to be together all the time; *nuisance* would be a more sophisticated word for something that keeps bothering you. Tier 2 words are more characteristic of written than oral language. Thus in considering words to teach, we favor expending instructional capital in the place least likely to be affected in any other way rather than deliberately selecting words that will be more readily learned, as Biemiller argues for. That is, Tier 2 words are less likely to be learned through everyday oral language and less likely to receive the amount and quality of attention needed through grade-level materials.

INSTRUCTIONAL IMPLICATIONS

Instructional Implications: Taking Them Seriously

The implications of Stahl and Fairbanks's work are rather clear: Provide vocabulary instruction that includes both definitional and contextual information about the words, multiple exposures in context, and activities that require deep processing. But a full understanding of the implications requires a bit more depth. It is not the case that any definition and context will fill the bill. What is called for is a definition that explains and contextual information that reveals how a word is used. Multiple expo-sures, specifically the finding that one or two were not effective, does not mean pro-vide three and you are done! The need is to provide a sufficient number and variety of exposures to allow decontextualization to occur. What Stahl and Fairbanks intended by featuring the need for mixed information and multiple exposures is revealed in their finding that methods that provided multiple exposures by repeating the same type of information did not affect comprehension. The authors also pro-vide more insight into multiple exposures by reporting on the success of time-intensive procedures, specifically suggesting that their success may mean that words need to be learned thoroughly if they are to affect comprehension.

Regarding depth of processing, Stahl and Fairbanks offer a three-level categorization—association, comprehension, and generation. But this does not mean that instruction should provide students one of each and call the job done. Stahl and Fairbanks caution that the concept of depth of processing includes many other aspects as well. Chief among these seem to be creating as many connections as possi-ble between a new word's meaning and prior knowledge—or elaborative processing—and putting forth mental effort in working with word meanings. Thus it seems that beyond asking students to comprehend and generate in instruction, there needs to be as many opportunities as possible for them to relate new words to words and situ-ations they already know, and to work with new words in ways that challenge their thinking. In this way, the newly learned words will become optimally accessible for application in new contextual encounters or productive opportunities.

Instructional Implications: How're We Doin'?

It is at this point in the discussion that the frustration level of every vocabulary researcher rises substantially. The instructional implications are loud and clear. As presented by Stahl and Fairbanks, they have been confirmed and supported by research and by educators. But implementation? That is another story.

Over decades, lack of adequate vocabulary instruction in basal materials and in school classrooms has been documented. And although Baumann et al. (2003) seem to try to put an optimistic face on more recent results, there is not much to rejoice about, especially if we are judging instruction according to the criteria set out by Stahl and Fairbanks. Baumann et al. report as good news results of a study showing that more recent basals have more instruction and that its methods are research-based and students do get definitional and contextual information (Ryder & Graves, 1994). But those same studies report that most of the words targeted for instruction are already known by students and that the definitional and contextual information did not include linking words to students' experiences. Thus it seems that depth of processing was never reached.

Studies by Blachowicz (1987) and Scott, Jamieson-Noel, and Asselin (2003) based on observing intermediate grades reading and language arts instruction found only a small proportion of time devoted to vocabulary (12–15%). Blachowicz found that the bulk of time was spent on figuring out meanings from context and defining and pronouncing words. Scott et al. point to a rather dismal picture in which teach-ers mention and assign but do little teaching in terms of vocabulary. They found a great deal of time devoted to students copying definitions from dictionaries—an activity pretty low on the effective strategies hit parade!

Our own look through a number of current basals suggests that the amount and depth of instruction do not provide for the thorough learning of words that is needed to affect text comprehension. We have gained some sense of what goes on in classrooms from presenting talks and workshops to teachers and coaches over the past several years. From the reactions in those events, it seems that current practice may sometimes provide different types of information and multiple exposures, but at a rather surface level. That is, multiple exposures are likely to offer impoverished information, such as a brief synonym or a perfunctory context. Furthermore, it is our strong conclusion from such encounters that there is very little going on in classrooms that would pass as encouraging depth of processing.

Why aren't we doing better in getting effective implementation in the schools? One contributing factor is likely that "multiple" exposures and "depth" of processing take time, and given all the activities that are squeezed into a schoolday, such recommendations are not allowed the time commitment they require.

But a deeper reason may be that although the recommendations are known, that knowledge is not backed up by true understanding of what multiple exposures do for the learner. The realization may be lacking that what is required is not a rote kind of practice to "get it right." Rather, a wealth of experiences is needed to allow the learner to build a network of meaningful connections that can assist access and production of the word.

One way we have attempted to build understanding of higher-quality instruction is to share with teachers a frame for introducing words that "covers the bases" represented in Stahl and Fairbanks's recommendations. The word introduction frame presents contextual and definitional information and provides for depth of processing. The frame is based on the ways we introduced words in the instructional programs we developed for fourth graders in our research to enhance comprehension through vocabulary (Beck, Perfetti, & McKeown, 1982; McKeown, Beck, Omanson, & Perfetti, 1983; McKeown, Beck, Omanson, & Pople, 1985). When developing instruction more recently for our "text talk" approach, we adjusted the frame to introduce words selected from a text and made it more of a recognizable routine (Beck & McKeown, 2001; Beck et al., 2002).

The frame has four components: (1) contextualizing the word within the text just read, which includes paraphrasing the part of the text containing the word and then restating the context using all familiar words; (2) providing definitional information through a friendly explanation, which presents word meaning in everyday connected language; (3) providing an example beyond the text context so students can immediately begin to decontextualize the word; and (4) presenting a way for students to interact with the word to initiate building connections to their own experiences. The following example of introducing the word *morsel* as used in *Dr. DeSoto* (Steig, 1982) demonstrates the frame:

1. In the story, the fox began thinking about Dr. DeSoto as a tasty *morsel*. That means he thought of him as a little something to eat.
2. A *morsel* is a small piece of food, no bigger than a bite.
3. If you had one little piece of your sandwich left and your friend wants you to go out to the playground, you might say, "Let me finish this one last morsel."
4. When might someone want only a morsel of food (e.g., if you are already full, or if it is a food you don't think you will like)?

WHERE RESEARCH HAS GONE SINCE STAHL AND FAIRBANKS

Just about the time that Stahl and Fairbanks were completing their meta-analysis, we and our colleagues (McKeown et al., 1985) were conducting a study of vocabulary instruction whose target features paralleled to a great extent those features identified by Stahl and Fairbanks. That is, we examined the effects of different numbers of exposures and instruction that included varying types of information and depth of processing.

The number of exposures was manipulated by providing either 12 or 4 encounters with each word. Students received one of three types of instruction: traditional, including only associations between words and their definitions; rich, which presented elaborated information about word meanings and diverse contexts; and extended/rich, which extended use of target words beyond the classroom.

The finding on exposures was much the same as those of Stahl and Fairbanks: 12 encounters yielded better performance on multiple-choice tests of word meanings, although both high (12) and low (4) exposures led to success on that measure compared to control groups. The higher number of exposures was needed to affect comprehension, and then did so only in the rich instructional conditions. This finding mirrored Stahl and Fairbanks's finding that multiple exposures were not effective if based on drill and practice but needed to present different types of information about the word. Rich instruction would seem to encompass depth of processing as it offered students a variety of contexts and called on them to act on information, such as making decisions between examples and nonexamples, selecting appropriate uses, and creating contexts for the words.

Students who were challenged to extend their vocabulary learning beyond the classroom showed advantage in comprehension over the group that got rich instruction alone. In terms of Stahl and Fairbanks, this might be seen as multiplying the number of exposures. So why did it give an extra boost to comprehension? Perhaps experiencing the words in numerous contexts from so many sources provided students a great ease of access to the word's meaning and the ability to integrate the word into new contexts. Our study provides empirical support for the instructional principles that Stahl and Fairbanks identified.

We recently completed vocabulary studies with kindergarten and first-grade children in which they were taught sophisticated words beyond their reading level through read-alouds and rich instruction (Beck & McKeown, 2004). In the first study, we provided an introduction to the words and activities on one day. The results showed learning, but at a rather low rate. In a second study, we either provided instruction on one day or added follow-up activities on subsequent days. We found that children learned the words in each condition but learned twice as many of the words that got the additional instruction. The issue here had been whether the low rate of learning in the first study was a ceiling effect for learning vocabulary, especially the kind of sophisticated words we taught, for children as young as kindergarten and first grade. The second study showed that not to be the case. Again, as in the Stahl and Fairbanks findings, a greater number of exposures provided for better learning results.

The 1980s were a rich and productive period for vocabulary research. In the years since then, vocabulary research has been much less in evidence. But the work that has been done aligns very well with the components of Stahl and Fairbanks. For example, research by Kolich (1991) examined word learning in the context of computer-assisted instruction. The goal was to examine how a computer-assisted learning environment would support vocabulary learning for 11th graders. Results showed that students learned better if both meanings and context information were presented.

Dole, Sloan, and Trathen (1995) embedded vocabulary into literature instruction in 10th-grade English classes. Words for instruction were taken from novels being read in class. The instruction included using the context in which the word appeared and a dictionary followed by discussion to obtain deeper understanding of the words as used in the story context. Students in the experimental group demonstrated greater comprehension of the vocabulary taught and of the novels being read compared to students who experienced a traditional didactic approach. Through the use of a context, the dictionary, and discussion, students received contextual and definitional information and engaged in depth of processing.

Perhaps the most productive area of research in recent years has been work based on stories read aloud to promote vocabulary learning in young children. This research began with investigating the extent of incidental learning from single readings of the story (Biemiller & Boote, 2004; Elley, 1989; Nicholson & Whyte, 1992; Penno, Wilkinson, & Moore, 2002; Robbins & Ehri, 1994; Sénéchal, Thomas, & Monker, 1995). Researchers generally found that there was a learning effect, but a disappointingly small one. Some of these researchers then augmented the read-alouds with direct explanation of word meanings as the story was read (Biemiller, 2004; Elley, 1989; Penno et al., 2002) or repeated readings of the stories (Elley, 1989; Penno et al., 2002). These strategies showed greater effects for acquiring vocabulary. However, Penno et al. (2002) and Biemiller (2004) report concern that children showed boredom with stories read three times, which is the number of repetitions most often recommended as effective. In addition, repeated readings do not expose children to the multiple contexts needed to ensure successful learning. Some of the more recent studies have included following up the read-aloud with additional activities (Beck & McKeown, 2004; Coyne et al., 2004; Wasik & Bond, 2001) or reviewing vocabulary after reading (Biemiller, 2004). These strategies have added to the amount of vocabulary learned, likely because they introduce additional contexts for the words and ask children to interact with word meanings. Thus once again we see that learning effects are meager unless multiple contexts and depth of processing are provided—even when beginning with a fertile, engaging context for word learning, in the form of read-alouds.

WHERE DO WE GO FROM HERE?

There seems to be a new golden opportunity for greater attention to vocabulary instruction and improving the quality of that instruction in classrooms. The opportunity has emerged because reading projects funded by federal money require professional development in vocabulary. And that requirement stems from the National Reading Panel report's (2000) identification of vocabulary as one of five areas of content key to proficient reading.

How can we as researchers best take advantage of such an opportunity to promote widespread use in classrooms of instruction that includes the components needed for successful word learning? Because the components of such instruction have been known for decades, perhaps we should begin by asking what we as researchers have not demonstrated clearly and convincingly enough to make teachers want to take up effective vocabulary instruction. We may need to provide concrete demonstrations of what long-term, effective vocabulary instruction can provide for students' general language and reading achievement. But that will require research activity that extends over several years' time.

REFERENCES

Baumann, J. F., Kame'enui, E. J., & Ash, G. E. (2003). Research on vocabulary instruction: Voltaire Redux. In J. Flood, D. Lapp, J. R. Squire, & J. M. Jensen (Eds.), *Handbook of research on teaching the English language arts* (pp. 752–785). Mahwah, NJ: Erlbaum.

Beck I. L., McKeown, M. G., & Kucan, L. (2002). *Bringing words to life: Robust vocabulary instruction.* New York: Guilford Press.

Beck, I. L., & McKeown, M. G. (in press). Increasing young low income children's oral vocabulary repertoires through rich and focused instruction. *Elementary School Journal.*

Beck, I. L., & McKeown, M. G. (in press). Different ways for different goals, but keep your eye on the higher verbal goals. In R. K. Wagner, A. Muse, & K. Tannenbaum (Eds.), *Vocabulary and reading.* New York: Guilford Press.

Beck, I. L., & McKeown, M. G. (in press). *Different ways for different goals, but keep your eye on the higher verbal goals.*

Beck, I. L., Perfetti, C. A., & McKeown, M. G. (1982). Effects of long-term vocabulary instruction on lexical access and reading comprehension. *Journal of Educational Psychology, 74*(4), 506–521.

Biemiller, A., & Boote, C. (2004). *An effective method for building vocabulary in primary grades.* Manuscript submitted for publication.

Biemiller, A. (2004). Teaching vocabulary in the primary grades: Vocabulary instruction needed. In J. F. Baumann & E. J. Kame'enui (Eds.), *Vocabulary instruction: Research to practice* (pp. 28–40). New York: Guilford Press.

Biemiller, A. (2005). Addressing developmental patterns in vocabulary: Implications for choosing words for primary grade vocabulary instruction. In E. H. Hiebert & M. L. Kamil (Eds.), *Teaching and learning vocabulary: Bringing research to practice.* Hillsdale, NJ: Erlbaum.

Blachowicz, C. L. Z. (1987). Vocabulary instruction: What goes on in the classroom? *The Reading Teacher, 41, 132–137.*

Carroll, J. (1964). Words, meanings, and concepts. *Harvard Educational Review, 34,* 178–202.

Carroll, J. B., Davies, P., & Richman, B. (1971). *Word frequency book.* New York: American Heritage.

Coyne, M. D., Simmons, D. C., Kame'enui, E. J., & Stoolmiller, M. (2004). Teaching vocabulary during shared storybook readings: An examination of differential effects. *Exceptionality, 12,* 145–163.

Dole, J. A., Sloan, C., & Trathen, W. (1995). Teaching vocabulary within the context of literature. *Journal of Reading, 38*(6), 452–460.

Elley, W. B. (1989). Vocabulary acquisition from listening to stories. *Reading Research Quarterly, 24,* 174–186.

Foorman, B. R., & Pollard-Durodola, S. D. (2004, June). *Supplementing implicit vocabulary learning through instruction: Primary-Grade curriculum.* Paper presented at the Society for the Scientific Study of Reading Conference, Amsterdam, The Netherlands.

Graves, M. F. (1987). The roles of instruction in fostering vocabulary development. In M. G.

McKeown & M. E. Curtis (Eds.), *The nature of vocabulary acquisition* (pp. 165–184). Hillsdale, NJ: Erlbaum.

Graves, M. F. (2000). A vocabulary program to complement and bolster a middle-grade comprehension program. In B. M. Taylor, M. F. Graves, & P. van den Broek (Eds.), *Reading for meaning: Fostering comprehension in the middle grades* (pp. 116–135). New York: Teachers College Press.

Kolich, E. M. (1991). Effects of computer-assisted vocabulary training on word knowledge. *Journal of Educational Research, 84*(1), 177–182

McKeown, M. G., Beck, I. L., Omanson, R. C., & Perfetti, C. A. (1983). The effects of long-term vocabulary instruction on reading comprehension: A replication. *Journal of Reading Behavior, 15*(1), 3–18.

McKeown, M. G., Beck, I. L., Omanson, R. C., & Pople, M. T. (1985). Some effects of the nature and frequency of vocabulary instruction on the knowledge and use of words. *Reading Research Quarterly, 20*(5), 522–535.

Nagy, W. E., Herman, P. A., & Anderson, R. C. (1985). Learning words from context. *Reading Research Quarterly, 20*, 233–253.

Nation, I. S. P. (2001). *Learning vocabulary in another language*. Cambridge, UK: Cambridge University Press.

National Reading Panel. (2000). *Teaching children to read: An evidence-based assessment of the scientific literature on reading and its implications for reading instruction* (NIH Pub. No. 00-4754). Washington, DC: National Institutes of Health.

Nicholson, T., & Whyte, B. (1992). Matthew effects in learning new words while listening to stories. In *Literacy research, theory, and practice: Views from many perspectives* (pp. 499–503). Chicago: Forty-first Yearbook, National Reading Conference.

Penno, J. F., Wilkinson, I. A. G., & Moore, D. W. (2002). Vocabulary acquisition from teacher explanation and repeated listening to stories: Do they overcome the Matthew effect? *Journal of Educational Psychology, 94*(1), 23–33.

Robbins, C., & Ehri, L. C. (1994). Reading storybooks to kindergartners helps them learn new vocabulary words. *Journal of Educational Psychology, 86*, 54–64.

Ryder, R. J., & Graves, M. E. (1994). Vocabulary instruction presented prior to reading in two basal readers. *Elementary School Journal, 95*(2), 139–153.

Scott, J. A., Jamieson-Noel, D., & Asselin, M. (2003). Vocabulary instruction throughout the day in twenty-three Canadian upper-elementary classrooms. *Elementary School Journal, 103*(3), 269–312.

Sénéchal, M., Thomas, E., & Monker, J. A. (1995). Individual differences in four-year-olds' ability to learn new vocabulary. *Journal of Educational Psychology, 87*, 218–229.

Shefelbine, J. L. (1990). Student factors related to variability in learning word meanings from context. *Journal of Reading Behavior, 22*(1), 71–97.

Stahl, S. A., & Fairbanks, M. M. (1986). The effects of vocabulary instruction: A model-based meta-analysis. *Review of Educational Research, 56*, 72–110.

Steig, W. (1982). *Doctor DeSoto*. New York: Farrar, Straus and Giroux.

Wasik, B. A., & Bond, M. A. (2001). Beyond the pages of a book: Interactive book reading and language development in preschool classrooms. *Journal of Educational Psychology, 93*(2), 243–250.

V | COMPREHENSION

17 | Comprehension Research over the Past Three Decades

Richard C. Anderson
Qiuying Wang
Janet S. Gaffney

> Both top-down and bottom-up processes are integral parts of perception, problem solving, and comprehension. Without sensory input (bottom-up) we could neither perceive, nor comprehend, nor think. However, perception, comprehension, and thought would be equally impossible without a memory or knowledge component (top-down). It makes no sense to ask whether one is more important than the other: Nothing happens without both. So the question for the theorist is not top-down or bottom-up, but how do these processes interact to produce fluent comprehension?
>
> —WALTER KINTSCH (2005, p. 126)

These have been exciting times. First emerging in the 1960s, blossoming in the 1970s, and coming to full bloom in the 1980s was a new cognitive paradigm, overthrowing a half century of behaviorism. Neglected since Sir Frederic Bartlett's (1932) classic, *Remembering*, schema theory was reinvented (Anderson & Pearson, 1984; Rumelhart, 1980). John Flavell (1979) and Ann Brown (1975) pioneered the concept of metacognition, which according to Brown was about "knowing, knowing about knowing, and knowing how to know" (p. 103). Bonnie Meyer (1975) documented the influence of the structure of text and Nancy Stein (Stein & Glenn, 1979) the influence of the "grammar" of stories on comprehension, learning, and remembering. Walter Kintsch (Kintsch & van Dijk, 1978) led the way in the development of comprehensive models of text comprehension.

The past three decades were a period of intense interest in "top-down" processes in reading but also, it should be emphasized, a period of exceptional vigor in research on "bottom-up" processes. Research on word decoding flourished with new empirical findings about, for instance, automatic processing (LaBerge & Samuels, 1974), phonological awareness (Liberman, Shankweiler, Fischer, & Carter, 1974), and decoding by analogy (Glushko, 1979; Goswami, 1986). Grand theoretical schemes were proposed to account for the development of ability to read words (Ehri, 1991; Frith, 1985) as well as skilled word reading (Seidenberg & McClelland, 1989).

Among the various topics investigated during this period at the Center for the Study of Reading, there was a lively program of research on knowledge of word meanings from the late 1970s into the 1990s and beyond. We tried to answer such basic questions as how many words children know (Nagy & Anderson, 1984), where children learn the words they know (Anderson, Wilson, & Fielding, 1988; Nagy, Anderson, & Herman, 1987; Nagy, Herman, & Anderson, 1985), whether children can use word parts to figure out meanings (Nagy, Anderson, Schommer, Scott, & Stallman, 1989; Nagy, Diakidoy, & Anderson, 1993; Tyler & Nagy, 1990), and the nature of word meanings (Anderson et al., 1976; Anderson & Freebody, 1981; Anderson & Nagy, 1991; Nagy & Gentner, 1990; Nagy & Scott, 1990). Vocabulary researchers at the Center for some or all of this period included William Nagy, Patricia Herman, Peter Freebody, Judith Scott, P. David Pearson, Joseph Jenkins, Angela Tyler, Dedre Gentner, Anne Stallman, Irene-Anna Diakidoy, Hua Shu, and Richard Anderson. Steven Stahl joined the group in the mid-1980s. The research continues to this day under the banner of metalinguistic awareness and with an emphasis on cross-language comparisons (Anderson & Li, 2006; Ku & Anderson, 2003; Kuo & Anderson, in press; Nagy & Anderson, 1999).

During the 1970s and 1980s, many of us thought that there would likely be interactions between top-down and bottom-up processes (Freebody & Anderson, 1983; Stanovich, 1980). This is the theme of the paper on prior knowledge and difficult vocabulary by Steven Stahl and his colleagues (Stahl, Jacobson, Davis, & Davis, 1989; reprinted as Chapter 18, this volume).

Stahl et al. (1989) reasoned that reading involves using several complementary sources of information. A satisfactory understanding of a particular proposition in a text depends not only on knowing the words but also on knowledge of the syntax, the connections between this proposition and other parts of the text, and prior knowledge of the topic. When one source of information is degraded, other sources may provide alternative ways of determining meaning. That is, because reading is an interactive process, readers may be able to compensate for gaps using complementary sources of information.

Stahl et al. (1989) completed three studies in which they created a text with difficult vocabulary by replacing every sixth content word in a grade-appropriate social studies selection with a difficult synonym. As expected, difficult vocabulary interfered with comprehension assessed in a variety of ways. But, contrary to expectation, the interference from difficult vocabulary could not be overcome through preteaching to build up background knowledge.

Thus, the three studies reported by Stahl et al. (1989), as well as earlier studies by Freebody and Anderson (1983) and Stahl and Jacobson (1986), failed to support the idea that when one source of knowledge is degraded, other sources of knowledge may compensate and provide alternate ways of determining meaning.

With the benefit of hindsight, this set of studies was founded on an idea that lacked specificity. Interactive compensation cannot work "in general" but only word by word and proposition by proposition. To be sure, illuminating analyses of some particular cases were provided (e.g., Freebody & Anderson, 1983, pp. 292–293; Stahl et al., 1989, pp. 38–39). However, these analyses were *ad hoc*, when what was needed was a theory that was at once comprehensive and detailed—of the kind that has been worked out for the processing of simple stories (Trabasso & van den Broek, 1985).

Meanwhile, cognitive theory and research have gone beyond the conception of comprehensibility as simply vocabulary difficulty and have begun to make detailed descriptions of text features and reader characters that influence comprehension by considering how readers construct a cognitive representation of incoming information. Theoretical underpinnings of several models of reading comprehension emerges: construction–integration theory (Kintsch, 1988, 1998; Kintsch & van Dijk, 1978), verbal efficiency theory (Perfetti, 1985), a structure-building framework (Gernsbacher, 1996), and capacity-constrained comprehension theory (Just & Carpenter, 1992). Such a cognitive perspective in reading research, with its emphasis on mental activities, has yielded the understanding of reading as a complex process in which a reader constructs meaning by integrating perceptual, linguistic, and conceptual information from the text with his or her own knowledge base.

According to Anderson and Pearson (1984), comprehension is a constructive process that involves building coherent mental representations of information from print. It involves activating or constructing a schema that accounts for the elements in a text, similar to the script for a play (Rumelhart, 1980). As they transact with text, good readers are constantly relating what they are reading to other experiences they have had, other information in the text they have read, and texts previously read. Their interest in the text plays a po2werful role in the web of linkages that they construct. The effect of these connected and accumulated readings is that a reader's understandings and response transcends that of any single passage (Hartman, 1994).

As a text is read, there is a large cognitive load as the reader is decoding the print and incorporating the textual information into his or her knowledge base. Expert and novice readers differ in the knowledge and skill they bring to the task of reading. Those who do not have adequate background knowledge about the subject of a text will have lower comprehension of the text (Spilich, Vesonder, Chiesi, & Voss, 1979; Steffensen, Joag-dev, & Anderson, 1979; Voss, Vesonder, & Spilich, 1980). Schemas representing background knowledge allow the reader to provide coherence to otherwise incoherent texts, permitting better bridging inferences between noncoherent sections and also enabling additional elaborative inferences.

Comprehension is a combination of reader, text, and context. Students who have a richer background can more readily make connections between what they know and what they are reading. In a well-written, very explicit text, the building of necessary background, and instruction in the use of strategies can compensate for weak initial background and a poorly articulated schema (Goldman & Rakestraw, 2000).

Schema theory provides a good description of how familiar situations are understood. Situation model theory provides a more inclusive account of comprehension than the concept of schema alone, because it can handle both schema-based and novel events (McNamara, Miller, & Bransford, 1991). According to Kintsch (e.g., 1994), comprehension involves three levels: surface component, textbase, and situation model. As students read, text is transformed into propositions. Propositions are combined, deleted, and integrated so that a macrostructure is formed. The situation model integrates the reader's schema or background knowledge and information from the text; thus it represents a deeper level of understanding.

Today's students are barraged with an overwhelming amount of information from television, print media, and the Internet. Many Internet sites do not have safeguards to ensure the accuracy or fairness of the information. Children's ability to evaluate what they read has never been more important. Critical reading refers to a type of reading in which the reader evaluates or judges the accuracy and truthfulness of the content based on either internal or external standards (Gunning, 2005). One way to promote this kind of thinking is through the use of multiple conflicting documents.

Stahl, Hynd, Britton, McNish, and Bosquet (1996) extended the boundaries of cognitive theories of text processing in a wide-ranging investigation of high school students' use of multiple sources to comprehend a controversial topic in recent U.S. history. Historical inquiry differs greatly from problem solving in well-structured domains such as algebra, physics, and computer science, in which there is usually a consensus about whether a proposal constitutes a solution to a problem. History is ill structured, problems are open ended, best explanations are controversial (Spiro, Coulson, Feltovich, & Anderson, 1994; Wineburg, 1991). Stahl et al. argue that the study of historical documents poses a challenge for theories of text processing and "calls into question the relevance of . . . psychological models of learning based on the reading of a single text . . . " (p. 433).

Stahl et al. (1996) employed several ingenious methods to exam the influence of multiple texts about an episode in the Vietnam War on the reading of college-bound high school seniors enrolled in an advanced-placement history course. One positive finding was that the "harmony"—or internal consistency—of students' representations increased as they studied additional texts. On a less positive note, only a few of the students engaged in what Wineburg (1991) has called *corroboration*—"Whenever possible, check important details against each other before accepting them as plausible or likely" (p. 77); *sourcing*—"Whenever evaluating historical documents, look first to the source or attribution of the document" (p. 79); and *contextualization*—"When trying to reconstruct historical events, pay close attention to *when* they happened and *where* they took place" (p. 80). Another disappointing finding was that when asked to write a persuasive essay, most students just gave their opinions unsupported with information from the texts they had read.

Stahl et al. (1996) reached the conclusion that simply presenting this elite group of high school seniors with multiple texts "did not encourage them to think like historians. In fact, the greatest growth in knowledge came after the reading of the first text, and the text that had the greatest influence on the growth of 'harmony' was a well-organized history textbook . . . " (p. 448). Stahl et al. explained these disappointing results in terms of the students' lack of background knowledge about the Vietnam War and lack of experience in working with multiple texts. Regarding the shallow essays the students wrote, Stahl et al. said, "it is possible these students did not know they were supposed to provide support for an opinion, even though they clearly learned information that would be appropriate" (p. 448). This interpretation is consistent with the findings of Seixas (1993), who suggests that students in middle and high school are capable of more sophisticated and critical readings of history when they are taught how to read from multiple conflicting sources. Students need to engage in thinking about and discussing the way knowledge is created, shared, and evaluated. They need to modify and deepen their purposes for reading.

Taken together, the two articles by Stahl and his colleagues (1989, 1996) represent the field's attempts to understand the interaction of reader and text variables on students' comprehension. The studies highlight issues that challenge researchers who confront the complex and messy area of students' comprehension of informational text. We can look back on these studies to take stock of the current status of comprehension research a decade out and, then, venture a question or two that may offer avenues for future research.

This "look back" will address text features, comprehension measures, and reader characteristics. Clearly, informational texts offer different challenges to readers than narratives, though the distinction between these categories is not always precise. One series of studies (Stahl et al., 1989) varies the difficulty level of social studies narratives by manipulating the vocabulary. Alternatively, authentic source documents in history are used without revision in the later study (Stahl et al., 1996). Given the robustness of text-driven processes, researchers need to provide detailed descriptions of texts in terms of purpose, genre, content, vocabulary, concepts, structural features, and coherence. A scientific approach to the analysis of informational text that accounts for the interaction of multiple variables that influence difficulty is required. Variations in text features may provide greater clarity in understanding the interaction of readers and texts and explain contradictory results across studies. Menon and Hiebert (2005) have initiated a systematic analysis of the linguistic content and cognitive load of beginning reading materials and may offer a model for undertaking such an analysis of the unique features of informational text. A scientific approach to the interaction of multiple features of content text would heighten awareness to issues of text difficulty.

In terms of assessment, the two studies by Stahl and his colleagues (1989, 1996) provide a virtual catalog of comprehension measures. Free recall, multiple-choice questions including textually explicit and implicit items, sentence verification, cloze procedure, event sequencing, causal relations, importance rating, participants' note taking, text evaluation, open-ended writing, and strength of relationships between key words and phrases comprise the multiple measures of prior knowledge and comprehension used by these researchers. Clearly, our ability to assess students' progress in building knowledge and learning capacity in complex knowledge domains is dependent on making significant advancements in measurement technology. The development of an assessment paradigm that corresponds to complex knowledge building will have to emanate from an integrated theory of coherence (Goldman & Rakestraw, 2000) with tasks that have the sensitivity to tap into the dynamic interplay between the contributions of text and reader in the quest for coherence.

In an interactive model, knowledge-driven processing is determined by characteristics of the reader relative to the text. Two of the social studies experiments (Stahl et al., 1989) used preteaching of relevant versus irrelevant information to vary the prior knowledge that students could contribute while reading multiple texts on a previously unfamiliar topic. The single reader variable, topical knowledge, carries the weight of the intervention. In the study of intertextual processing of historical sources, students' prior knowledge of the topic was measured by an open-ended writing assessment and a task in which the students rated the strength of relationships between 10 concepts on a scale of 1 to 6 (Stahl et al., 1996). Interestingly, the researchers also compared the students' performances on some measures to those of expert historians along three processes: corroboration, sourcing, and contextualization (Wineburg, 1991). Students were also assigned to one of two purposes for the task (i.e., write a description or an opinion). Though the students' performance did not mirror those of historians, the authors suggest that the value that disciplinary knowledge adds to subject-matter knowledge be considered in future research. Of course, the benefits of disciplinary and domain knowledge will vary with the nature of the informational text and task. In innovative research by Palincsar and Magnusson (as described in Palincsar & Duke, 2004), elementary students are guided to read science texts that are written to facilitate knowledge building. The texts are cleverly designed as the notebooks of a fictional scientist to provide students an entrée into the way that scientists think. Use of specially constructed texts that blend elements of narrative and informational text may provide a missing scaffold for knowledge building in complex domains. As students take on the thinking of nascent scientists or historians, we anticipate that knowledge building would be accelerated and that the learners would take on a more interpretive and critical stance to reading of content texts.

On a personal note, the authors of this chapter represent the full range of relationships in academia. At the University of Illinois at Urbana–Champaign, Dick was a mentor, Lydia (Qiuying) a student, and Jan a colleague who cotaught a graduate reading course. Steve would like the fact that we collaborated on this chapter in his honor. If you skim Steve's record of publications, first you might notice the length of the list, then the caliber of the journals. Keep looking and you will be impressed by the array of colleagues with whom he has written. Steve was a consummate collaborator. Whether he was designing a study, writing an article or a book, or teaching a course, he worked from the premise that two would produce a better product than one; that each would learn something new; and that the process would be more fun with colleagues. In addition to his publications, Steve has left us a living legacy—his colleagues.

REFERENCES

Anderson, R. C., & Freebody, P. (1981). Vocabulary knowledge. In J. T. Guthrie (Ed.), *Reading comprehension and education* (pp. 77–117). Newark, DE: International Reading Association.

Anderson, R. C., & Li, W. (2006). A cross-language perspective on learning to read. In A. McKeough, J. L. Lupart, L. Phillips, & V. Timmons (Eds.), *Understanding literacy development: A global view* (pp. 65–91). Mahwah, NJ: Erlbaum.

Anderson, R. C., & Nagy, W. (1991). Word meanings. In R. Barr, M. Kamil, P. Mosenthal, & P. D. Pearson (Eds.), *Handbook of reading research* (Vol. II, pp. 690–724). New York: Longman.

Anderson, R. C., & Pearson, P. D. (1984). A schema-theoretic view of basic processes in reading comprehension. In P. D. Pearson, R. Barr, M. L. Kamil, & P. Mosenthal (Eds.), *Handbook of reading research* (Vol. I, pp. 255–291). New York: Longman.

Anderson, R. C., Pichert, J. W., Goetz, E. T., Schallert, D. L., Stevens, K. V., & Trollip, S. R. (1976). Instantiation of general terms. *Journal of Verbal Learning and Verbal Behavior, 15*, 667–679.

Anderson, R. C., Wilson, P. T., & Fielding, L. G. (1988). Growth in reading and how children spend their time outside school. *Reading Research Quarterly, 23*, 285–303.

Bartlett, F. C. (1932). *Remembering: A study in experimental and social psychology.* New York: Cambridge University Press.

Brown, A. L. (1975). The development of memory: Knowing, knowing about knowing, and knowing how to know. In H. W. Reece (Ed.), *Advances in child development and behavior* (Vol. 10). New York: Academic Press.

Ehri, L. C. (1991). Development of the ability to read words. In R. Barr, M. L. Kamil, P. B. Mosenthal, & P. D. Pearson *(Eds.), Handbook of reading research* (Vol. II, pp. 383–417). New York: Longman.

Flavell, J. H. (1979). Metacognition and cognitive monitoring: A new area of cognitive-developmental inquiry. *American Psychologist, 34,* 906–911.

Freebody, P., & Anderson, R. C. (1983). Effects of vocabulary difficulty, text cohesion and schema availability on reading comprehension. *Reading Research Quarterly, 18,* 277–94.

Frith, U. (1985). Beneath the surface of developmental dyslexia. In K. E. Patterson, J. C. Marshall, & M. Colheart (Eds.), *Surface dyslexia: Neuropsychological and cognitive studies of phonological reading* (pp. 301–330). Hillsdale, NJ: Erlbaum.

Gernsbacher, M. A. (1996). The structure-building framework: What it is, what it might also be, and why. In B. K. Britton & A. C. Graesser (Eds.), *Models of understanding text* (pp. 289–311). Mahwah, NJ: Erlbaum.

Glushko, R. J. (1979). The organization and activation of orthographic knowledge in reading aloud. *Journal of Experimental Psychology: Human Perception and Performance, 5,* 674–691.

Goldman, S. R., & Rakestraw, J. A. (2000). Structural aspects of constructing meaning from text. In M. L. Kamil, P. B. Mosenthal, P. D. Pearson, & R. Barr (Eds.), *Handbook of reading research* (Vol. II, pp. 311–335). Mahwah, NJ: Erlbaum.

Goswami, U. (1986). Children's use of analogy in learning to read: A developmental study. *Journal of Experimental Child Psychology, 42,* 73–83.

Gunning, T. G. (2005). *Creating literacy instruction for all students* (4th ed.). Boston: Allyn & Bacon.

Hartman, D. K. (1994). The intertextual links of eight able readers using multiple passages: A postmodern semiotic/cognitive view of meaning making. In R. B. Ruddell, M. R. Ruddell, & H. Singer (Eds.), *Theoretical models and processes of reading* (4th ed., pp. 616–636). Newark, DE: International Reading Association.

Just, M. A., & Carpenter, P. A. (1992). A capacity theory of comprehension: Individual differences in working memory. *Psychological Review, 98,* 122–149.

Kintsch, W. (1988). The use of knowledge in discourse processing: A construction–integration model. *Psychological Review, 95,* 163–182.

Kintsch, W. (1994). Text comprehension, memory, and learning. *American Psychologist, 49,* 294–303.

Kintsch, W. (1998). *Comprehension: A paradigm for cognition.* Cambridge, UK: Cambridge University Press.

Kintsch, W. (2005). An overview of top-down and bottom-up effects in comprehension. *Discourse Processes, 39,* 125–128.

Kintsch, W., & van Dijk, T. A. (1978).Toward a model of text comprehension and production. *Psychological Review, 85,* 363–394.

Ku, Y.-M., & Anderson, R. C. (2003). Development of morphological awareness in Chinese and English. *Reading and Writing: An Interdisciplinary Journal, 16,* 399–422.

Kuo, L.-J., & Anderson, R. C. (in press). Morphological awareness and learning to read: A cross-language perspective. *Educational Psychologist.*

LaBerge D., & Samuels, S. J. (1974). Toward a theory of automatic information processing in reading. *Cognitive Psychology, 6,* 293–323.

Liberman, I. Y., Shankweiler, D., Fischer, F. W., & Carter, B. (1974). Explicit syllable and phoneme segmentation in the young child. *Journal of Experimental Child Psychology, 18,* 201–212.

McNamara, T. P., Miller, D. L., & Bransford, J. D. (1991). Mental Models and Reading Comprehension. In T. P. McNamara, D. L. Miller, J. D. Bransford, & R. Barr (Eds.), *Handbook of research on reading* (Vol. II, pp. 490–511). Hillsdale, NJ: Erlbaum.

Menon, S., & Hiebert, E. H. (2005). A comparison of first graders' reading with little books or literature-based basal anthologies. *Reading Research Quarterly, 40,* 12–38.

Meyer, B. J. F. (1975) *The organization of prose and its effects on memory.* Amsterdam: North-Holland.

Nagy, W., & Anderson, R. C. (1999). Metalinguistic awareness and literacy acquisition in different languages. In D. Wagner, B. Street, & R. Venezky (Eds.), *Literacy: An international handbook* (pp. 155–160). New York: Garland.

Nagy, W., Anderson, R. C., Schommer, M., Scott, J., & Stallman, A. (1989). Morphological families in the internal lexicon. *Reading Research Quarterly, 24,* 262–282.

Nagy, W., Diakidoy, I., & Anderson, R. C. (1993). The acquisition of morphology: Learning the contribution of suffixes to the meanings of derivatives. *Journal of Reading Behavior, 25,* 155–170.

Nagy, W., & Gentner, D. (1990). Semantic constraints on lexical categories. *Language and Cognitive Processes, 5,* 169–201.

Nagy, W., & Scott, J. (1990). Word schemas: Expectations about the form and meaning of new words. *Cognition and Instruction, 7,* 105–127.

Nagy, W. E., & Anderson, R. C. (1984). How many words are there in printed school English? *Reading Research Quarterly, 19,* 304–30.

Nagy, W. E., Anderson, R. C., & Herman, P. A. (1987). Learning word meanings from context during normal reading. *American Educational Research Journal, 24,* 237–270.

Nagy, W. E., Herman, P. A., & Anderson, R. C. (1985). Learning words from context. *Reading Research Quarterly, 20,* 233–253.

Palincsar, A. S., & Duke, N. K. (2004). The role of text and text-reader interactions in young children's reading development and achievement. *Elementary School Journal, 105,* 184–197.

Perfetti, C. A. (1985). *Reading ability.* New York: Oxford University Press.

Rumelhart, D. E. (1980). Schemata: The building blocks of cognition. In R. J. Spiro, B. C. Bruce, & W. F. Brewer (Eds.), *Theoretical issues in reading comprehension: Perspectives from cognitive psychology, linguistics, artificial intelligence, and education* (pp. 38–58). Hillsdale, NJ: Erlbaum.

Seidenberg, M. S., & McClelland, J. L. (1989). A distributed, developmental model of word recognition and naming. *Psychological Review, 96,* 523–68.

Seixas, P. (1993). Historical understanding among adolescents in a multicultural setting. *Curriculum Inquiry, 23,* 301–325.

Spilich, G. J., Vesonder, D., Chiesi, H. L., & Voss, J. F. (1979). Text processing of domainrelated information for individuals with high and low domain knowledge. *Journal of Verbal Behavior, 18,* 275–291.

Spiro, R., Coulson, R., Feltovich, P., & Anderson, D. (1994). Cognitive flexibility theory: Advanced knowledge acquisition in ill-structured domains. In R. Ruddell, M. Ruddell, & H. Singer (Eds.), *Theoretical models and processes of reading* (4th ed., pp. 602–610). Newark, DE: International Reading Association.

Stahl, S. A., Hynd, C. R., Britton, B. K., McNish, M. M., & Bosquet, D. (1996). What happens when students read multiple source documents in history? *Reading Research Quarterly, 31,* 430–456.

Stahl, S., & Jacobson, M. (1986). Vocabulary difficulty, prior knowledge, and text comprehension. *Journal of Reading Behavior, 18,* 309–324.

Stahl, S., Jacobson, M., Davis, C., & Davis, R. (1989). Prior knowledge and difficult vocabulary in the comprehension of unfamiliar text. *Reading Research Quarterly, 24,* 27–43.

Stanovich, K. E. (1980). Toward an interactive-compensatory model of individual differences in the development of reading fluency. *Reading Research Quarterly, 16,* 32–71.

Steffensen, M. S., Joag-dev, C., & Anderson, R. C. (1979). A cross-cultural perspective on reading comprehension. *Reading Research Quarterly, 15,* 10–29.

Stein, N. L., & Glenn, C. G. (1979). An analysis of story comprehension in elementary school children. In R. O. Freedle (Ed.), *New directions in discourse processing* (pp. 53–120). Norwood, NJ: Ablex.

Trabasso, T., & van den Broek, P. (1985). Causal thinking and the representation of narrative events. *Journal of Memory and Language, 24,* 612–630.

Tyler, A., & Nagy, W. (1990). Use of derivational morphology during reading. *Cognition, 36,* 17–34.

Voss, J. F., Vesonder, G. T., & Spilich, G. J. (1980). Text generation and recall by high-knowledge and low-knowledge subjects. *Journal of Verbal Learning and Verbal Behavior, 19,* 651–667.

Wineburg, S. (1991). On the reading of historical texts: Notes on the breach between school and academy. *American Educational Research Journal, 23,* 495–519.

18 | Prior Knowledge and Difficult Vocabulary in the Comprehension of Unfamiliar Text

Steven A. Stahl
Michael G. Jacobson
Charlotte E. Davis
Robin L. Davis

Of the factors that have been found to affect students' comprehension of expository text, some are intrinsic to the student, such as the student's prior knowledge of the topic (see Schallert, 1982, for a review) and interest in the topic (Asher, 1980), and some are intrinsic to the text, such as the amount of difficult vocabulary in the text (see Graves, 1986, for a review). Many authors suggest that student and text factors function interactively, so that a reader deficient in one area may be able to compensate for that deficiency with a strength in another area (e.g., Stanovich, 1980). For example, a reader who did not know many of the word meanings in a particular text but who had a good knowledge of the topic might be able to use that knowledge to comprehend the text adequately

Such an interactive model appears to work well in describing the processes involved in word recognition (Stanovich, 1980). However, researchers have rarely tested for interactions of higher-level factors, such as those between vocabulary difficulty and more general topic knowledge; and when they have, the expected interactions have not been found. One purpose of the studies reported here is to investigate compensatory interactions between vocabulary difficulty and prior knowledge in text comprehension.

If vocabulary knowledge and prior knowledge do not interact, it may be that they affect comprehension differently. A second purpose of the studies reported here is to examine what such differential effects might be.

PRIOR KNOWLEDGE AND COMPREHENSION

The relations between prior knowledge and comprehension have generally been investigated under the overall framework of schema theory. According to schema theory, the reader's background knowledge serves as scaffolding to aid in encoding information from the text. Thus, a person with more background knowledge is able to comprehend better than a person with less knowledge (Johnston, 1984). The amount of knowledge readers have about a text topic has been found to correlate significantly with their comprehension (Pearson, Hansen, & Gordon, 1979).

In addition, some researchers have suggested that actively building topic knowledge prior to reading will facilitate learning from text. Much of the research on preteaching concerns advance organizers. As described by Ausabel (1980), advance organizers, which are defined as somewhat more abstract previews of the lesson content, serve as "ideational scaffolding" for the students' reading. A meta-analysis of advance organizer studies has suggested that they have only a modest effect on learning (Luiten, Ames, & Ackerson, 1980). However, some studies have found that knowledge-based preteaching aids learning from text when the text is somewhat ambiguous and when the preteaching is closely related to the topic (Beck, Omanson, & McKeown, 1982; Graves, Cooke, & LaBerge, 1983). Beck et al. (1982), for example, found that preteaching that was focused on the central topic of narratives in second- and third-grade basal readers improved comprehension over the relatively unfocused preteaching suggested in the teacher's manual.

However, there are some indications that the relation between prior knowledge and comprehension is not a linear one. Lipson (1983) compared students with Jewish and Catholic backgrounds on their reading of passages concerning Jewish and Catholic topics, as well as on a neutral topic. They found that children from both religious groups comprehended the story relevant to their own background better than the story from the other religious background, as predicted by schema theory. However, they both recalled the most information from the neutral story, about which they had little prior knowledge. Lipson suggested that misunderstandings about the somewhat-known religions interfered with children's comprehension of the text information. Alvermann, Smith, and Readence (1985) similarly found that activating prior knowledge can interfere with students' comprehension if that prior knowledge is incompatible with the information in the text.

PRIOR KNOWLEDGE AND VOCABULARY DIFFICULTY

There is a long history of research showing that vocabulary difficulty affects reading comprehension (see reviews by Anderson & Freebody, 1981; Graves, 1986). For example, the vocabulary factor used in readability formulas appears to be the strongest predictor of text difficulty (Chall, 1958), and substituting easier synonyms for text words appears to make the text easier to read, especially if other changes are made in the text to make the substitutions more natural (Chall, 1958; Wittrock, Marks, & Doctorow, 1975).

Vocabulary knowledge and prior knowledge are also related to each other. A person who knows a great deal about a topic generally knows words specific to that topic (Anderson & Freebody, 1981). A person who knows the meanings of *bunt*, *balk*, and *suicide squeeze* can be assumed to have a good knowledge of baseball, and will probably comprehend a passage written about baseball better than someone without such knowledge (see Chiesi, Spilich, & Voss, 1979). In accordance with this assumption, tests of vocabulary knowledge have been used to assess prior knowledge (e.g., Johnston, 1984; Langer, 1981).

Two studies have examined possible interactions between vocabulary and prior knowledge. In the first, Freebody and Anderson (1983b, Exp. 2) constructed four passages, familiar and unfamiliar versions of passages on two different themes. The unfamiliar versions addressed these themes using information drawn from foreign cultures. These passages were further modified to produce difficult vocabulary versions by substituting rare synonyms for one out of every four content words. They gave one familiar passage and one unfamiliar passage, one on each theme, to their sixth-grade subjects. Some subjects received difficult vocabulary versions of both passages; others received easy versions.

On their posttests, Freebody and Anderson found familiarity produced significant effects on the recall, summarization, and sentence verification measures. Although the scores in the easy vocabulary condition were higher than those in the difficult vocabulary condition, the overall effect for vocabulary difficulty was not statistically significant, and significant differences due to vocabulary difficulty were found only on the sentence verification measure. The interactions between vocabulary difficulty and topic familiarity were not statistically significant on any of the three measures.

In an earlier study (Stahl & Jacobson, 1986), we manipulated the prior knowledge variable differently, but were similarly unable to find an interaction between vocabulary difficulty and prior knowledge. We used a passage taken directly from a fifth-grade social studies textbook (Owen, 1972) concerning an Amazonian tribe, the Yanomamo. The passage is a narrative, describing a ritual feast planned by Koba, the headman of one village, for another village, in order to cement a burgeoning friendship. When the second village comes for the feast, they attack their hosts, leading to a war. This would seem anomalous, given conventional expectations in Western culture, unless students were provided with or inferred additional information about the Yanomamo culture, regarding the ritual of the feast and the extremely violent nature of the tribe.

Before they read the passage, an expository lesson was given to four classes of sixth-grade students, either stressing the distrust and violence of the Yanomamo or discussing an irrelevant topic, Hindu wedding rituals. To manipulate vocabulary difficulty, we created a difficult vocabulary version by substituting a less well-known synonym for every third content word. Each class received a different combination of difficult or easy vocabulary and relevant or irrelevant preteaching.

We found significant overall main effects for both preteaching and vocabulary difficulty, but failed to find a significant interaction. Furthermore, univariate analyses of the vocabulary factor indicated that it had a significant effect on the sentence verification measure, as found by Freebody and Anderson, but not on the multiple-choice measure. Significant preteaching effects were found on both measures.

One reason for the failure to find an interaction may have been that the vocabulary difficulty was so great that students were unable to compensate for it with their prior knowledge. Freebody and Anderson (1983a) found that substituting one difficult word for every third content word, as was done here, was enough to induce comprehension failure. A less extreme vocabulary manipulation might provide better conditions for observing an interaction between these two factors. This possibility was tested in the present set of studies.

RELEVANT VERSUS IRRELEVANT PRETEACHING

Another reason for wishing to attempt a partial replication of our earlier study derived from observations from our graduate classes. Students in a graduate class were given the passage used and were asked to determine what information they felt they needed to preteach so that their students would understand the passage better. Although the majority of students mentioned information about the tribe's violence, a surprising number also suggested teaching about the Yanomamo's marriage practices and the role of women. There was a reference in the passage to "Koba's elder wife," who fixed him breakfast while he planned the major event of the passage, the ritual feast. This was a relatively low-level detail, incidental to the main events of the passage. When this passage was similarly used in a second class, the instructor had the students write down the information that preteaching should provide. Although 15 of 19 students mentioned violence and distrust, 7 mentioned the role of women. (This result has been replicated with other groups of students, both graduate and undergraduate.) When pressed, the class thought that discussing the marriage customs and women's role would interest students in reading about the Yanomamo, and thus help them comprehend. Because 35–40% of our preservice and inservice teachers suggested this topic, we decided to test the effect of such preteaching on passage comprehension.

STUDY 1

Method

Subjects

Subjects were 90 sixth-grade students in four intact classes in a junior high school located in a small college town in the midwestern United States. The school drew students from the entire town, and thus contained children of farm workers as well as children of professors. Nearly all children were Caucasian. These students were administered the comprehension subtest of the Gates–MacGinitie Reading Tests (MacGinitie, 1978) the week before the study began and received a mean score of 28.9 (SD = 7.1), equivalent to the 58th percentile. The four classes were randomly assigned to four conditions; a 2 (preteaching) × (vocabulary) ANOVA (analysis of variance) did not reveal any statistically significant difference or interaction between these groups (p > .05).

Materials

The materials used were adopted from a previous study (Stahl & Jacobson, 1986), described earlier. As in our earlier study, two versions of this passage were developed, a difficult version prepared by substituting words above eighth grade difficulty according to the Dale and O'Rourke (1976) *Living Word Vocabulary*, and an easy version taken directly from the textbook. For this study, approximately every sixth content word was replaced with a difficult synonym, as opposed to every third word in the earlier study (Stahl & Jacobson, 1986). We made every effort to make the modified text sound as natural as possible and to avoid use of stilted language. Excerpts from the original and modified passages are shown in Table 18.1.

TABLE 18.1. Sample Paragraph from Easy and Difficult Vocabulary Texts

Easy vocabulary text

Koba was worried. Two days had passed since he sent his messenger to the Shami village. "Perhaps the Shami have killed him," he thought. That would be very bad. His village already had too many enemies. Now they needed friends. They had traded with the Shami for the whole year, and all had gone well. But, he thought as he lay in his hammock, now they might have to fight another enemy.

Difficult vocabulary text

Koba was worried. Two days had passed since he sent his envoy to the Shami village. "Perhaps the Shami have killed him," he speculated. That would be very bad. His village already had too many adversaries. Now they needed friends. They had bartered with the Shami for the whole year, and all had been satisfactory. But, he thought as he lay in his hammock, now they might have to grapple with another enemy.

Note. Original passage was taken from *Inquiring about cultures* by R. C. Owen, 1972, New York: Holt, Rinehart & Winston. Copyright 1972 by Holt, Rinehart & Winston. Reprinted by permission.

Three tests were prepared to measure comprehension of the material. The first was a free recall measure, in which the students were asked to recall all that they could about what they had read. This measure was not used in the earlier study (Stahl & Jacobson, 1986).

The protocols were scored, using a procedure suggested by Omanson (1982), by the authors and by a graduate student unaware of the grouping and the purpose of the study. First, the easy vocabulary version of the original text was divided into pausal units, at the points where a reader might pause when reading. These pausal units were then rated as *central* to the story, a *supporting* detail, or *distracting*, according to the procedures described by Omanson. This rating was done by all three authors together. Next, the protocols were divided into pausal units, using the same procedure. These pausal units were rated as *central, supporting, distracting, incorrect,* or from the *preteaching*. Each protocol was rated by at least two raters. On trial ratings, 91% agreement was achieved by one pair of raters; 84% by another. All protocols were then rated independently by two raters. All disagreements were resolved by the third rater.

The other two measures were identical to those used in the earlier study. (These measures can be found in Stahl & Jacobson, 1986.) One was a multiple-choice test, consisting of 14 questions. Five were designed to be textually explicit, five textually implicit, and four scriptally implicit (Pearson & Johnson, 1978). A textually explicit question was defined as one for which the answer was explicitly stated in the text, a textually implicit question as one for which the answer needed to be inferred from information presented in the text, and a scriptally implicit question as one for which the answer had to be inferred on the basis of prior knowledge.

The last measure was a sentence verification measure similar to that used by Freebody and Anderson (1983b). This was developed by choosing 23 sentences from the easy version of the text and either reproducing them or changing one or two words so that they would clearly be false. The students were to indicate which sentences "were in the story or mean the same as a sentence in the story."

Procedures

Prior to reading, students were given a 15-minute introductory lesson conducted by one of us, an experienced social studies teacher. This lesson, conducted in an expository format, provided information about the Yanomamo tribe. This information was designed to be either central or incidental to the narrative. In both lessons the teacher discussed where the Yanomamo lived, showing Amazonia on a globe and discussing the general climate, flora, and fauna of the area. The relevant preteaching was given to two of the classes in the study. It stressed the extreme violence of the people, their propensity to break into fights at the slightest provocation, and the need for rituals to overcome the distrust between villages so that they might ally with each other for mutual support. In addition, it detailed the steps leading up to the ritual feast, and described the feast itself. In an analysis of the text, described above, it was found that this information was needed to make inferences concerning the central units of the narrative. The irrelevant preteaching discussed the concept of polygamy and how women were treated in Yanomamo villages. This information related to units judged as distracting in our analysis. This preteaching was used in the remaining two classes. Both lessons were scripted, so that they would be consistent across classes. One of us observed all four classes during preteaching, and, although no formal notes were taken, reported high student engagement and interest in all four classes.

Following the lesson, the students were given either the easy or the difficult vocabulary version of the passages to read. (Vocabulary difficulty and relevance of preteaching were counterbalanced so all four combinations were represented. Classes were randomly assigned to the different treatments.)

The students were given the posttests on the day following the lesson. They were instructed first to recall freely as much information from the text as they could, and then to complete the other two measures, without turning back to their recall. The question posttest was given first, followed by the sentence recognition measure.

Results

The first analysis performed was a 2×2, vocabulary (easy, difficult) by preteaching (relevant, irrelevant) multivariate analysis of covariance (MANCOVA), using the multiple-choice score, sentence verification score, and total number of units recalled as dependent variables and the child's comprehension score from the Gates–MacGinitie as the covariate. The overall main effects were statistically significant for both vocabulary, approximate $F(3, 80) = 4.19$, Wilks's λ (lambda) = 0.86, $p < .01$, and for preteaching, approximate $F(3, 80) = 3.17$, Wilks's $\lambda = 0.89$, $p < .05$. As found in earlier studies (Freebody & Anderson, 1983b; Stahl & Jacobson, 1986), the interaction between vocabulary and preteaching was not statistically significant.

Univariate analyses of the main effect of vocabulary found significant effects on the recall measure, $F(1, 82) = 23.05$, $p < .001$, but not on the sentence verification or multiple-choice measures. Univariate analyses for the main effect of preteaching found similar results: significant effects on the recall measure, $F(1, 82) = 9.27$, $p < .05$, but not on the multiple-choice or verification measures. Means and standard deviations for these measures are listed in Table 18.2.

In our earlier study (Stahl & Jacobson, 1986), we did find significant main effects for vocabulary difficulty on a sentence verification measure identical to the one used

TABLE 18.2. Means (and Standard Deviations) for Multiple-Choice, Sentence Verification, and Recall Measures (Study 1)

Measure	Preteaching Relevant	Preteaching Irrelevant	Total
Multiple-choice			
Easy vocabulary	10.50 (2.10)	9.65 (2.56)	10.11
Difficult vocabulary	10.16 (2.79)	9.18 (3.10)	9.70
Total	10.32	9.23	
Sentence verification			
Easy vocabulary	16.04 (2.95)	14.90 (3.56)	15.52
Difficult vocabulary	14.92 (3.77)	14.40 (3.30)	14.68
Total	15.47	14.55	
Total recall			
Easy vocabulary	11.87 (5.15)	7.79 (6.39)	10.07
Difficult vocabulary	6.44 (5.99)	4.36 (4.50)	5.46
Total	9.10	6.23	

here, and significant main effects for preteaching on both the sentence verification measure and a multiple-choice measure identical to the one here. In the present study, recall was tested after 24 hours; in the earlier study, recall was tested immediately after reading. The delay may have blurred any differences.

To analyze the recall measure further, we looked separately at the types of information recalled. The first analyses involved univariate analyses of the number of central, supporting, and distracting units each child recalled.

For recall of central units, we found significant main effects for both vocabulary, $F(1, 82) = 10.31$, $p < .005$, and preteaching, $F(1, 82) = 10.53$, $p < .005$. The effect of the interaction between vocabulary difficulty and relevance of preteaching on the recall of central units was also statistically significant, $F(1, 82) = 4.91$, $p < .05$. However, because this interaction was not protected by a significant multivariate F, one should be careful in interpreting it.

For the number of supporting units recalled, we found significant main effects for both vocabulary, $F(1, 82) = 7.36$, $p < .005$, and preteaching, $F(1, 82) = 4.93$, $p < .05$. The interaction between the two was not statistically significant. For the number of distracting units recalled, neither the main effects nor the interaction was statistically significant.

The second set of analyses looked for factors which may have interfered with the students' recall of the text. In examining the protocols, we noticed that children given the difficult vocabulary text appeared to recall more information out of order than those given the easy vocabulary text. To confirm this possibility, we examined the number of units that were in the same order as they appeared in the story.[1] An analysis of covariance (ANCOVA), using the percentage of ordered units in the recall as a dependent variable, found the effect for the vocabulary factor was statistically significant, $F(1, 82) = 6.65$, $p < .05$, but the effect for preteaching and the interaction effect were not. Means and standard deviations for these analyses are listed in Table 18.3.

The second factor we examined was the inclusion of information from the preteaching in the protocol. We found two trends. The nine students who did not recall any units from the text tended to include varied amounts of information from the preteaching, possibly to avoid leaving an empty page. These students were distributed across treatments and tended to be those with the lowest reading scores. Of the students who did recall some text units ($n = 81$), those in the relevant preteaching conditions tended to recall more information from the preteaching than those in the irrelevant preteaching conditions, $F(1, 71) = 5.60$, $p < .05$. No other significant main effect was found.

TABLE 18.3. Means (and Standard Deviations) for Recall Analysis (Study 1)

Recall	Preteaching		Total
	Relevant	Irrelevant	
Central units			
Easy	6.62	3.89	5.41
vocabulary	(3.20)	(3.05)	
Difficult	3.52	2.45	3.02
vocabulary	(3.02)	(2.69)	
Total	5.04	3.33	
Supporting units			
Easy	4.75	3.37	4.14
vocabulary	(2.98)	(3.33)	
Difficult	2.64	1.63	2.17
vocabulary	(3.01)	(1.81)	
Total	3.67	2.45	
Distracting units			
Easy	0.50	0.53	0.51
vocabulary	(1.02)	(0.77)	
Difficult	0.28	0.27	0.28
vocabulary	(0.54)	(1.07)	
Total	0.39	0.45	
Units from preteaching			
Easy	1.33	0.62	1.05
vocabulary	(2.16)	(0.72)	
Difficult	1.77	0.44	1.24
vocabulary	(2.39)	(0.89)	
Total	1.54	0.52	
Units in correct order			
Easy	87	78	83
vocabulary	(23)	(36)	
Difficult	61	60	60
vocabulary	(42)	(45)	
Total	74	69	

Children in the irrelevant preteaching conditions might also be expected to focus on incidental details relating to the preteaching. The topic of Koba's wife, which was incidental to the major events of the story but had been highlighted by the preteaching, was mentioned by 9 of the 41 subjects given the irrelevant preteaching (22%), but by only 4 of the 49 subjects given the relevant preteaching (8%).

In order to ensure that the overall lack of effect on the questions did not obscure differential effects for the different question types (textually explicit, textually implicit, and scriptally implicit), separate analyses were conducted for each question type. As in the other analyses, the interaction of vocabulary and preteaching was not significant. The only effect found was a main effect for vocabulary difficulty on answers to textually explicit questions, $F(1, 82) = 4.15$, $p < .05$. Because this result was not protected by a significant overall effect, it may be especially susceptible to a Type I error and should be interpreted with caution.

Discussion

The results of this study confirm past research indicating that prior knowledge and vocabulary difficulty both appear to affect recall from text, but that these effects are independent, not interactive. Giving students relevant information about an unfamiliar topic appeared to facilitate comprehension. Substituting difficult synonyms for text words appeared to impair comprehension, even when only one word out of every six content words was changed. This result contrasts with that of Freebody and Anderson (1983a), who found that a substitution ratio of one out of every six content words did not affect comprehension.

The failure to find a compensatory interaction between vocabulary difficulty and prior knowledge confirms earlier findings (Freebody & Anderson 1983b; Stahl & Jacobson, 1986). Although one should be careful in interpreting null results, taken together, these results strongly suggest that readers do *not* use one higher-level knowledge source (such as prior knowledge) to compensate for difficulty in another higher-level knowledge source (such as vocabulary).

These results also suggest a reason for the failure to find an interaction. The qualitative analysis of the recall protocols suggests that vocabulary difficulty and the preteaching affected comprehension in different ways. Vocabulary difficulty appeared to affect the order in which units were recalled. A disordered recall may result from difficulty in developing a coherent text base from the passage (e.g., Kintsch, 1986). Such a pattern suggests that the reader is recalling bits and pieces, but not a coherent whole. This was the impression given in a number of protocols. It is possible that the effort required to understand difficult vocabulary may have diverted some of the mental resources available to integrate the units into a coherent text base (see Omanson, 1985). Of course, failure to integrate information fully will also impair comprehension in general, leading to a reduction in total information recalled.

If prior knowledge helps one select which information is important, as suggested by schema theory, then the irrelevant preteaching may have biased this selection process, thus impairing comprehension. Children told about polygamy may have looked for this topic in the reading, even though it was incidental to the major events. An analogy might be to a study by Anderson and Pichert (1978), who found that having readers assume the role of either a home buyer or a burglar biased their recall of a neutral passage, and that by switching roles, readers were able to recall different information. They suggested that the reader's schema may suggest which information is important, affecting the reader's allocation of attention. If that attention is misdirected, comprehension may suffer. Such an effect may be evidenced in the number of students who included Koba's wife in the recall.

Thus, it can be hypothesized that vocabulary difficulty and prior knowledge have independent effects, vocabulary difficulty on the connection of propositions into a coherent text base, and prior knowledge on the selection of information to focus on. If these two factors function independently, they might not be able to compensate for each other, suggesting a reason for the failure to find compensatory interactions in the studies cited earlier. We conducted two additional studies with outcome measures more closely tailored to examination of these hypotheses.

STUDY 2

Cloze passages have been found to be sensitive to increases in the difficulty of vocabulary and have been used in numerous readability studies (see Klare, 1984). Although it is widely assumed that prior knowledge also affects cloze performance, we could find no direct evidence that it does so. Erickson and Hansen (1974) and Smith-Burke, Gingrich, and Eagleeye (1978) failed to find that the amount of text preceding a cloze passage affected cloze performance. Presumably, prior context would provide more relevant information about the text, so the amount of prior context would be only an indirect measure of the effects of prior knowledge.

Shanahan, Kamil, and Tobin (1982) suggest that cloze passages measure only sentence comprehension, not intersentential integration. They found that cloze performance was essentially similar whether passages were left intact or sentence order was scrambled. Similarly, Kintsch and Yarbrough (1982) found cloze to measure only local comprehension effects, and not global comprehension processes. If so, cloze might not be sensitive to manipulations which affect macro-level comprehension, as our preteaching was suggested to do. Therefore, we hypothesized that vocabulary but not preteaching would affect cloze comprehension.

Method

Subjects

Subjects were 92 sixth-grade students in five classes located in three small communities in central Illinois. Prior to the study, subjects were given Passage 5A taken from the De Santi Cloze Reading Inventory (De Santi, 1986). This was chosen as a measure of initial ability because the criterion task was a cloze test. No significant difference was found between groups on this measure ($p > .05$).

Materials

The materials used in Study 1 were prepared as cloze materials for this study. Every fifth word was deleted, with the first and last sentences left intact, as is standard. However, two exceptions were made for the difficult vocabulary passage. The few times that this version of the passage had to be reworded (so that it would sound natural), blanks were left for the same word in the easy and difficult vocabulary forms. Also, when the fifth word would have been a substituted word, the blank was placed either before or after the difficult word.

The number of exact replacements was used as a dependent measure. Synonyms were not accepted, because of the difficulty of getting interrater reliability on synonym scoring. Paris and Jacobs (1984), in their study, found a correlation of 0.90 between exact replacement scoring and a system of synonym scoring.

Procedures

The cloze inventory was given the first day. For both the cloze inventory and the experimental cloze passages, the instructions were identical. Students were told to read the entire passage through once before filling in any blanks. Teachers monitored to make sure that this instruction was followed. Then students were told to fill in all the blanks, and were encouraged to guess if they did not know an answer.

The lessons for four of the classes were conducted using the same scripts as in Study 1. As in that study, task engagement appeared to be high during the entire lesson. Following the lesson, students were given the cloze passage, with the above instructions. The fifth class served as an additional control to determine the effects of the preteachings. This class did not receive any preinstruction but completed the cloze passages under the same conditions as the other four classes. Half of the students in this class were randomly chosen to receive the difficult version of the experimental passage, and the other half received the easy version.

Results

Cloze results were analyzed in a two-step process. First, the overall number of exact replacements was examined using a 2 (easy or difficult vocabulary) × 3 (relevant, irrelevant, or no preteaching) ANCOVA, with the raw score from the De Santi Cloze Inventory as covariate. As expected, the main effect for vocabulary difficulty was statistically significant, $F(1, 85) = 7.17$, $p < .01$. Neither the effect for preteaching nor the interaction was statistically significant, although the effect of preteaching approached significance, $F(1, 85) = 2.41$, $p < . 10$.

A second analysis examined function and content words separately. Function words were defined as articles, pronouns, conjunctions, and modal verbs, which have a largely syntactic function within sentences. Content words were defined as nouns, adjectives, adverbs, and transitive verbs, which convey the content of the sentence.

Vocabulary difficulty affected the replacement of function words, $F(1, 85) = 8.73$, $p < .005$; the effects of the preteaching and the interaction were not statistically significant. No significant effect was found on the replacement of content words. The means and standard deviations are presented in Table 18.4.

Discussion

If difficult vocabulary inhibits the formation of a coherent text base, as suggested by the recall data in Study 1, then it should affect the exact replacement of function words, as found here, because function words signal the relations between the ideas in the text. Our informal observations suggest that subjects given the difficult vocab-

TABLE 18.4. Adjusted Means (and Standard Deviations) for
Cloze Passage (Study 2)

Condition	Function words	Content words	Total
Easy vocabulary			
Relevant preteaching	30.8 (5.4)	15.9 (4.5)	46.7
Irrelevant preteaching	30.5 (8.7)	14.3 (6.1)	44.9
No preteaching	28.2 (5.0)	15.0 (4.9)	43.2
Difficult vocabulary			
Relevant preteaching	28.5 (6.1)	14.8 (3.6)	44.3
Irrelevant preteaching	25.9 (6.2)	12.8 (5.1)	38.6
No preteaching	27.3 (5.0)	15.0 (4.9)	42.4

Note. Means were adjusted for covariate. There were 63 function
words and 49 content words deleted.

ulary text generally substituted prepositions for prepositions, modal verbs for modal
verbs, and so on, indicating that they did grasp the syntactic structure of the text.
However, their greater difficulty with the exact replacements suggests that their
knowledge of the relations between ideas was not as precise as those subjects given
the easy vocabulary version.

Neither vocabulary difficulty nor the preteaching affected exact replacement of
content words. We had thought that the preteaching might affect the replacement of
content words. In this text, however, the content words were general terms, not
vocabulary specific to this area. In an expository science text, for example, where the
vocabulary tends to be topic-related, one might find stronger effects of prior knowledge on content vocabulary.

STUDY 3

The results of the cloze comprehension task are supportive of the notion that vocabulary and prior knowledge affect different aspects of the comprehension process.
The purpose of the third study was to examine further the effects found in Study 1,
but using measures more precisely focused on the patterns found in the recall task.
Specifically, we used a measure of recall of the order of events in the narrative, a
measure of children's ability to infer causal relations between ideas in the text, and
an importance rating task measuring children's perception of the relative importance of ideas in the text. Given the findings from the recall measure in Study 1, we
hypothesized that vocabulary difficulty but not preteaching would affect children's
recall of the order of events. On the other hand, the causal relations measure
required the children to make bridging inferences. Because these inferences would
require the child to know or infer information about the Yanomamo, we assumed

that the preteaching should affect performance on this measure. Finally, we hoped the importance rating measure might allow us to examine whether the preteaching affected students' perceptions of the relative importance of ideas in the text, as suggested by the inclusion of Koba's wife in the recalls of subjects given the irrelevant preteaching in Study 1.

Method

Subjects

Subjects were 99 sixth-grade students located in four intact classes in a school serving a suburban community in central Illinois. As part of the study, they were given Passage 5A from the De Santi Cloze Reading Inventory (De Santi, 1986) as a measure of initial ability. There was no significant difference between groups on this measure ($p > .05$).

Materials

In this study, we used the same passages as in the first study, but with three different posttest measures. The first consisted of a set of nine sentences relating to major events in the passage. Subjects were directed to indicate which event happened first, which event happened second, and so on. The accuracy of recall was assessed by calculating a Kendall's τ (tau) between each ranking and the actual order of events in the story. The value of τ can vary between –1 and +1, with 1.0 indicating complete agreement. Actual τ values ranged from 0.167 to 1.0. They used as the dependent variable in the analysis of this measure.

The second measure comprised seven multiple-choice items, developed to assess children's understanding of causal relations in the text. Each item consisted of a sentence stem with four possible completions and a "don't know" option. One such item was the following: "Koba sent his messenger to the Shami (a) to get killed, (b) to invite them to a feast, (c) to get more monkey meat, (d) to attack them, (e) don't know. Although the correct answer was not directly stated in the text, an understanding of the relations between the ideas would lead a reader to infer that "b" is correct. This measure was given to graduate and undergraduate students and refined until they could answer all seven items correctly.

The third measure was an importance rating task, in which subjects were asked to rate each of eight statements as to whether they were "very important," "somewhat important," or "unimportant." It was hypothesized that if the preteaching biased readers' selection of which ideas to focus on, subjects told about the role of women in Yanomamo society would rate items dealing with women higher than subjects told about the Yanomamos' aggressiveness. This measure was developed by giving versions to graduate and undergraduate students who read the passage without preinstruction. The only items retained were those that were rated with 100% agreement. Four of the items were unanimously ranked as "very important"; four were ranked as "unimportant."

In addition, subjects were asked to rate their interest in the presentation and the reading. For both, students were asked whether they were "very interested," "interested," "not very interested," or "bored." These ratings were used as independent variables in a separate analysis.

Procedures

With a few exceptions, procedures were identical to those in the first study. Because the lessons were scripted, they were as close as possible to the lessons used in Study 1. However, instead of making four separate presentations, we combined classes so that only two presentations were made. Easy and difficult vocabulary versions of the text were then randomly distributed to the combined classes. A second difference was that the posttests were given immediately after the reading, rather than the day following.

Results

Vocabulary Difficulty and Prior Knowledge

To examine the effects of preteaching and vocabulary difficulty on our measures, two separate 2 (easy or difficult vocabulary) × 2 (relevant or irrelevant preteaching) MANCOVAs were performed, with the initial cloze score as the covariate. The first used the event ordering and causal relations measures as dependent variables. On these measures, the overall main effect due to vocabulary difficulty was statistically significant, Wilks's $\lambda = 0.92$, approximate $F(2, 91) = 3.76$, $p < .03$. The main effect due to the preteaching was not statistically significant, nor was the interaction. Univariate analyses indicated that vocabulary difficulty had a significant effect on the event-ordering measure, $F(1, 92) = 7.02$, $p < .01$, but not on the causal relations measure. The means and standard deviations for both measures are shown in Table 18.5.

A separate MANCOVA was performed on the importance rating measure, with each of the eight items used as a dependent measure. Overall, the main effect for preteaching was statistically significant, Wilks's $\lambda = 0.81$, approximate $F(8, 84) = 2.53$, $p < .02$, but the main effect for vocabulary difficulty was not significant; nor was the interaction. Univariate analyses showed that the groups differed on only one item, "Koba wanted the Shami's help in attacking other villages," an item our college stu-

TABLE 18.5. Means (and Standard Deviations) for Event Ordering and Causal Relations Measures (Study 3)

Measure	Preteaching		Total
	Relevant	Irrelevant	
Event ordering			
Easy	0.72	0.79	0.75
vocabulary	(0.30)	(0.20)	
Difficult	0.60	0.61	0.60
vocabulary	(0.24)	(0.32)	
Total	0.66	0.70	
Causal relations			
Easy	4.40	4.75	4.57
vocabulary	(1.89)	(1.82)	
Difficult	3.88	3.95	3.91
vocabulary	(2.02)	(1.69)	
Total	4.14	4.36	

Note. Maximum scores: 1.00 for event ordering, 7.00 for causal relations.

dent raters had rated as an important concept in the story.[2] Of the subjects given the preteaching about aggressiveness, 19 rated this point as "very important," 20 rated it as "somewhat important," and 8 rated it as "unimportant." Of the subjects given the preteaching about the role of women, 33 rated it as "very important," 15 rated it as "somewhat important," and only 2 rated it as "unimportant."

It is unclear why subjects would differ on this item. In contrast, there were no significant differences on the items where differences were expected. For example, on the item "Koba had more than one wife," 32 of the students given the "role of women" preteaching rated it as "unimportant," compared to 37 of the students given the "aggressiveness" preteaching. This difference was not statistically significant. Similar results were found with the other items.

Interest

The two multiple-choice items dealing with interest were used to assess possible effects of interest. As we had informally observed of the subjects in Study 1, subjects in this study showed a high degree of interest in the presentations. A total of 92 of 99 subjects rated themselves as "very interested" or "interested" in the presentation. Their interest did not differ significantly between the two presentations. There was a wider range of interest, however, in the reading. Nine subjects rated themselves as "very interested," 63 as "interested" 16 as "not very interested," and 9 as "bored." No significant main effects or interactions were found on a 4×4 MANCOVA, with the two interest ratings as independent variables and the event ordering and causal relations measures as dependent variables.

Discussion

The results of this study partially confirm our hypothesis that vocabulary and preteaching function independently. Vocabulary difficulty appeared to affect children's ability to recall the order of events, but the different preteachings did not. This finding confirms our observations in Study 1.

The preteaching did affect children's overall assignment of importance, but not in the way we had predicted. It is not clear why the two groups of students differed in their assessment of one particular statement. It could be that the importance measure was not sensitive enough to possible biasing effects of the preteaching.

GENERAL DISCUSSION

The results of these studies confirm previous failures to find a compensatory interaction between children's prior knowledge and the relative difficulty of vocabulary used in a text (Freebody & Anderson, 1983b; Stahl & Jacobson, 1986). They also suggest that vocabulary difficulty and prior knowledge affect different aspects of the reading comprehension process.

Although the effects of difficult vocabulary on comprehension have been recognized for a long time (see Chall, 1958; Klare, 1984), the results of these studies begin to suggest *how* vocabulary affects comprehension. Vocabulary difficulty appears to affect recall of both central and supporting information (Study 1), answers to textually explicit questions (Study 1), exact replacement of function words in a cloze task (Study 2), and recall of the order of major events (Studies 1 and 3). In addition, vocabulary difficulty affects recognition of sentences immediately after reading (Anderson & Freebody, 1983b; Stahl & Jacobson, 1986) but not 24 hours later (Study 1). These findings all appear to suggest that vocabulary difficulty affects a very literal comprehension of the text.

Kintsch and van Dijk (1978) suggest two types of processes used in comprehension: *microprocesses* and *macroprocesses*. Microprocesses are concerned with the development of a microstructure, or a text base, which is a coherent and ordered set of propositions representing the ideas in the text. Omanson (1985) found that vocabulary difficulty affected the processing of individual propositions, which may in turn affect the creation of a coherent text representation. Indeed, the tasks that vocabulary difficulty affected all related to the coherence of microstructure representations, suggesting that children given difficult vocabulary passages may develop representations of those texts in memo which are less coherent than those of children given texts containing easier vocabulary. Ryder (1989), using expository text, found that vocabulary difficulty affected recall of the microstructure but not the macrostructure.

If the effects of vocabulary difficulty were on the development of the microstructure, it would be tempting to say that the preteaching affected macroprocessing. Macroprocesses involve selection of propositions as important, and through such selection, the development of a macrostructure, which is similar to a summary. Indeed, Freebody and Anderson (1983b) found that topic familiarity significantly affected text summarization, but vocabulary difficulty did not. In Study 1, subjects given the "role of women" preteaching included more information about women in their recalls, even though such information was of minor importance in the passage. The effects of preteaching on the importance ratings in Study 3 were statistically significant, but these effects were not centered on propositions about women, as we had expected.

One limitation in this series of studies is our operational definition of the prior knowledge factor. Equating prior knowledge with the information provided by the preteaching may not be justifiable. We know little about how prior knowledge functions in "real-life" reading. A different way of manipulating prior knowledge might produce different results, although Freebody and Anderson (1983b), who manipulated prior knowledge in a considerably different manner, found results essentially similar to ours.

Using preteaching as a way of manipulating prior knowledge has other limitations. We do not know how well the students learned the information taught, although according to our observations task engagement was high, and the objectives of the instruction were modest. We also do not know whether students given the irrelevant information inferred the information presented in the relevant preteaching or whether they inferred that the information given in the irrelevant preteaching was tangential to the narrative. The cognitive cost of such inferring might lower the general amount of recall, as in Study 1, but might not have the specific effects looked for in Study 3.

Using a single passage and similar procedures in the three studies allowed full examination of our manipulations without confounding passage effects. However, such effects undoubtedly exist, and the results found here may or may not extend to other passages and manipulations.

Instructional Implications

The studies also have clear instructional implications. As noted earlier, our informal exchanges with teachers suggest that, at least occasionally, they provide students with information tangentially related to the major points in the text, but germane to the general topic, in order to "get them into" the text. Such a sentiment also appears to underlie some of the instructions to teachers in basal readers (Beck et al., 1982). Our results suggest that irrelevant discussion does not improve the learning of text information, extending the findings of Beck et al. to older students and unfamiliar content area text. The relevant information, in contrast, may have directed students to the most important information in the text, thus aiding overall comprehension. Of course, the information was "important" for a literal understanding of the text. If the goal had been for students to read the text in order to learn about male–female relations in that society, then the polygamy preteaching might have been more appropriate.

Vocabulary difficulty also appears to affect comprehension. For the passage used here, its effects seemed most pronounced in the recall of details, in understanding the relations between concepts, and in the recall of the order of events. If we extend this finding, it may be that students can get a rough understanding of a text that contains a higher proportion of unknown words but will have difficulty understanding the precise relations between ideas. This hypothesis suggests that poor readers might be able to learn from texts written "above their level" but would recall main idea information the best.

Interest, on the other hand, had little effect on comprehension. As noted earlier, the teachers in our classes suggested teaching about the role of women in Yanomamo society as a way of interesting the students in the topic. This preteaching produced significantly lower recall than a preteaching that was focused on information directly relevant to the actions in the narrative. Furthermore, the relevant preteaching was rated in Study 3 as being just as interesting as the irrelevant teaching. A better test of the interest hypothesis might be to contrast an interesting but irrelevant preteaching to a boring but relevant one. However, subjects' interest in the text, which varied more than their interest in the preteachings, also did not affect comprehension.

A survey of current practices in the teaching of social studies (Patrick & Hawke, 1982) indicates that over 90% of elementary social studies teachers use a textbook. Our results suggest reasons for the relative difficulty of these texts as well as ways that teachers can overcome some of these difficulties, such as focusing prereading discussions on concepts central to the text and providing instruction in word meanings.

NOTES

1. A unit was considered "in order" if it followed the same order as the analogous units in the original text. Two exceptions were made, for units in the text that were out of natural order. In one case, the text used the passive tense. If subjects reversed the units to change the tense they were considered correctly ordered. In the other case, in the text the unit "Arrows began to fly into the village" preceded the unit stating that the other village was attacking. Recalls including this second unit first were also considered in order.

The percentage of ordered units was calculated by dividing the number of units recalled in order by the total number of units (central, supporting, or distracting only). If a subject recalled zero or one units, they were assigned a score of zero. This was to avoid either dividing by zero or overstating the quality of the recall. (Otherwise, if a person recalled only one unit, this would be considered 100% recall in order.) This measure was used instead of Kendall's τ, as used in Study 3, for efficiency. The results, however, should be analogous.

2. We conducted a similar analysis treating these data as nominal and using contingency tables. The results were identical.

REFERENCES

Alvermann, D. E., Smith, L. C., & Readence, J. E. (1985). Prior knowledge activation and the comprehension of compatible and incompatible text. *Reading Research Quarterly, 20*, 420–436.

Anderson, R. C., & Freebody, P. (1981). Vocabulary knowledge. In J. T. Guthrie (Ed.), *Comprehension and teaching: Research reviews* (pp. 77–110). Newark, DE: International Reading Association.

Anderson, R. C., & Pichert, J. W. (1978). Recall of previously unrecallable information following a shift in perspective. *Journal of Verbal Learning and Verbal Behavior, 17*, 1–17.

Asher, S. R. (1980). Topic interest and children's reading comprehension. In R. J. Spiro, B. C. Bruce, & W. F. Brewer (Eds.), *Theoretical issues in reading comprehension* (pp. 525–534). Hillsdale, NJ: Erlbaum.

Ausabel, D. (1980). Schemata, cognitive structure, and advance organizers: A reply to Anderson, Spiro, and Anderson. *American Educational Research Journal, 17*, 400–404.

Beck, I. L., Omanson, R. C., & McKeown, M. G. (1982). An instructional redesign of reading lessons: Effects on comprehension. *Reading Research Quarterly, 17*, 462–481.

Chall, J. S. (1958). *Readability: An appraisal of research and application.* Columbus: Ohio State University, Bureau of Educational Research.

Chiesi, H. L., Spilich, G. J., & Voss, J. F. (1978). Acquisition of domain-related information in relation to high and low domain knowledge. *Journal of Verbal Learning and Verbal Behavior, 18*, 257–273.

Dale, E., & O'Rourke, J. P. (1976). *The living word vocabulary.* Chicago: Field Enterprises.

De Santi, R. J. (1986). *The De Santi Cloze Reading Inventory.* Boston: Allyn & Bacon.

Erickson, L. G., & Hansen, L. H. (1974). Performance on cloze passages in and out of context. In P. Nacke (Ed.), *Interaction: Research and practice for college-adult reading. Twenty-third yearbook of the National Reading Conference* (pp. 158–162). Clemson, SC: National Reading Conference.

Freebody, P., & Anderson, R. C. (1983a). Effects of differing proportions and locations of difficult vocabulary on text comprehension. *Journal of Reading Behavior, 15*, 19–40.

Freebody, P., & Anderson, R. C. (1983b). Effects of vocabulary difficulty, text cohesion, and schema availability on text comprehension. *Reading Research Quarterly, 18*, 277–294.

Graves, M. F. (1986). Vocabulary learning and instruction. In E. Z. Rothkopf & L. C. Ehri (Eds.), *Review of research in education* (Vol. 13, pp. 49–89). Washington, DC: American Educational Research Association.

Graves, M. F., Cooke, C. L., & LaBerge, M. J. (1983). Effects of previewing difficult short stories on low ability junior high school students' comprehension, recall, and attitudes *Reading Research Quarterly, 18*, 262–276.

Johnston, P. (1984). Prior knowledge and reading comprehension test bias. *Reading Research Quarterly, 19*, 219–239.

Kintsch, W. (1986). Learning from text. *Cognition and Instruction, 3*, 87–108.

Kintsch, W., & van Dijk, T. A. (1978). Toward a model of text comprehension and production. *Psychological Review, 85,* 363–394.

Kintsch, W., & Yarbrough, J. C. (1982). Role of rhetorical structure in text comprehension. *Journal of Educational Psychology, 74,* 828–834.

Klare, G. R. (1984). Readability. In P. D. Pearson (Ed.), *Handbook of reading research* (pp. 681–744). New York: Longman.

Langer, J. A. (1981). Facilitating text processing: The elaboration of prior knowledge. In J. A. Langer & M. T. Smith-Burke (Eds.), *Reader meets author/Bridging the gap* (pp. 149–162). Newark, DE: International Reading Association.

Lipson, M. Y. (1983). The influence of religious affiliation on children's memory for text information. *Reading Research Quarterly, 18,* 448–457.

Luiten, J., Ames, W., & Ackerson, G. (1980). A meta-analysis of the effects of advance organizers on learning and retention. *American Educational Research Journal, 17,* 211–218.

MacGinitie, W. H. (1978). *The Gates–MacGinitie reading tests.* Chicago: Riverside.

Omanson, R. C. (1982). An analysis of narratives: Identifying central, supportive, and distracting content. *Discourse Processes, 5,* 195–224.

Omanson, R. C. (1985). Knowing words and understanding texts. In T. H. Carr (Ed.), *The development of reading skills* (New directions for child development, No. 27, pp. 35–54). San Francisco: Jossey-Bass.

Owen, R. C. (1972). *Inquiring about cultures.* New York: Holt, Rinehart & Winston.

Paris, S. G., & Jacobs, J. E. (1984). The benefits of informed instruction for children's reading awareness and comprehension skills. *Child Development, 55,* 2083–2093.

Patrick, J. J., & Hawke, S. (1982). Social studies curriculum materials. In *The current state of the social studies: A report of Project SPAN.* Boulder, CO: Social Science Education Consortium.

Pearson, P. D., Hansen, J., & Gordon, C. (1979). The effects of background knowledge on young children's comprehension of explicit and implicit information. *Journal of Reading Behavior, 11,* 201–209.

Pearson, P. D., & Johnson, D. D. (1978). *Teaching reading comprehension.* New York: Holt, Rinehart & Winston.

Ryder, R. J. (1989, March). *The effect of word frequency on text comprehension.* Paper presented at the annual meeting of the American Educational Research Association, San Francisco.

Schallert, D. L. (1982). The significance of knowledge: A synthesis of research related to schema theory. In W. Otto & S. White (Eds.), *Reading expository material* (pp. 13–48). New York: Academic Press.

Shanahan, T., Kamil, M. L., & Tobin, A. W. (1982). Cloze as a measure of intersentential comprehension. *Reading Research Quarterly, 17,* 229–255.

Smith-Burke, M. T., Gingrich, P. S., & Eagleeye, D. (1978). Differential effects of prior context, style, and deletion pattern on cloze comprehension. In P. D. Pearson & J. Hansen (Eds.), *Reading: Disciplined inquiry in process and practice. Twenty-seventh yearbook of the National Reading Conference* (pp. 133–137). Clemson, SC: National Reading Conference.

Stahl, S. A., & Jacobson, M. G. (1986). Vocabulary difficulty, prior knowledge, and text comprehension. *Journal of Reading Behavior, 18,* 309–324.

Stanovich, K. E. (1980). Toward an interactive-compensatory model of individual differences in the development of reading fluency. *Reading Research Quarterly, 16,* 32–71.

Wittrock, M. C., Marks, C., & Doctorow, M. (1975). Reading as a generative process. *Journal of Educational Psychology, 67,* 481–489.

19 | Improving Students' Reading Comprehension

BARBARA M. TAYLOR
P. DAVID PEARSON
GEORGIA EARNEST GARCÍA
KATHERINE A. DOUGHERTY STAHL
EURYDICE B. BAUER

In the late 1980s, Stahl, Jacobson, Davis, and Davis (1989, reprinted as Chapter 18, this volume) examined the effects of prior knowledge and vocabulary difficulty on students' reading comprehension in a series of clever experimental studies. As Stahl and his colleagues point out in their article, the independent effects of prior knowledge building and vocabulary difficulty in text on reading comprehension had been well established by the time they engaged in their trio of studies. Some researchers may have thought that enough had been done in both of these areas, but Steve, as always, driven by an ever inquisitive mind, wanted to dig deeper. Based on his earlier finding that there was no interaction between prior knowledge building and vocabulary difficulty on students' reading comprehension, he and his colleagues predicted that prior knowledge and vocabulary difficulty would affect different aspects of the reading comprehension process. Documenting these differential effects was the driving force behind this work.

In the first study, Stahl et al. (1989) had sixth-grade students read a passage on the Yanomamo, an Amazonian tribe. Students either received an easy vocabulary version of the passage or a hard vocabulary version into which less familiar synonyms of key content words had been inserted. Students also were provided with a 15-minute introduction stressing information that was either relevant or incidental to the passage. Stahl et al. found that the difficult vocabulary affected students' ability to recall text, with a particular effect on recalling ideas in the order in which they were presented in the text. This suggested that the difficult vocabulary condition affected students' surface level processing of the text—the ability to connect the ideas in the text into a coherent string. The relevant preteaching condition also positively affected students' recall. However, there was not an interaction between prior knowledge condition and vocabulary difficulty, suggesting that the two factors were independent, not interactive; each made a positive contribution to text recall.

In the second study, Stahl et al. carried out a similar study but used a cloze task to measure comprehension. They found that the preteaching condition did not affect students' ability to replace correct function words, whereas the vocabulary condition did. Students had a harder time replacing function words when they read the difficult passage, suggesting again that difficult vocabulary affects surface level processing. Neither variable affected students' replacement of content words.

In the third study, Stahl et al. again carried out a similar study. This time they found that vocabulary difficulty affected students' ability to recall the order of events in the passage but the preteaching condition did not. However, the preteaching of relevant information had an effect on students' ability to rate the importance of information in the text.

At the end of this important paper, Stahl et al. (1989) concluded that vocabulary difficulty appears to most heavily impact the literal recall of text and that prior knowledge, developed by building background before reading, primarily affects students' understanding of the big ideas in text.

In the early 2000s, Stahl's inquisitive mind led him to his last study on reading comprehension. The National Reading Panel (2000) report had just come out, stressing the importance of comprehension strategies to improve students' reading comprehension. Steve, however, remembered the work of Rosenshine and Meister (1994), who wondered whether comprehension strategies instruction was effective because students actually learned to use reading strategies or whether it was a way to get them more actively engaged in reading a text. They had found little evidence that students who were taught reading comprehension strategies actually demonstrated that they were using them well. As with the prior knowledge/vocabulary difficulty study, Steve was not one to let a well-researched topic lie. Again, he wanted to dig deeper into the topic of comprehension strategies to better understand its impact on students' reading comprehension. Did instruction in reading strategies help students because they learned to use them as they read or did the use of reading strategies help students' reading comprehension because it caused them to process the text more deeply?

This question led Steve to join forces with us (the authors of this chapter). Under Steve's leadership, we submitted a proposal to the U.S. Department of Education's Institute of Education Sciences to further study the impact of reading comprehension strategies instruction on elementary-age students' reading comprehension. Much of the remainder of this chapter was written by Steve after many conversations with the rest of us. It is one of the last pieces he wrote.

As we continue to work on this study, we get together regularly to talk about it—how it is going, what needs to be changed. We think Steve would be pleased with our discussions, especially our ponderings and puzzlements and our endless revision and refinement of the interventions. We are touched to be completing the study in Steve's honor.

IMPORTANCE OF READING COMPREHENSION AND ITS IMPROVEMENT THROUGH EFFECTIVE INSTRUCTION
Written by Steven Stahl with David Pearson, Barbara Taylor, and Georgia García

Throughout the more than 30 years of testing reading, scores on the National Assessment of Educational Progress (NAEP) have, with the exception of minor rises and falls in grade 4, yielded a flat trend. Although we might take some solace in the absence of a decline, the increased literacy demands of today's society and job market mean that the flat profile is really a net decrease in scores. And although there was a steady upward trend for black and Hispanic students over the period 1970–1990, the trends of these groups have flattened out in the 1990s. But the real concern for minority performance is that these slight increases over three decades are trumped by the persistence of an enormous performance gap between their scores and those of white students.

Concurrent with the lack of improvement in NAEP scores is the consistent finding of a lack of comprehension instruction in the elementary grades. Current research (e.g., Pressley, Wharton-McDonald, Mistretta-Hamptston, & Echevarria, 1998; Taylor, Pearson, Clark, & Walpole, 2000) basically confirms the findings of Durkin (1978–1979), who found little comprehension instruction occurring in the fourth through sixth grades she observed. Researchers who have investigated the reading instruction of English-language learners at the elementary level have reported that these students, regardless of the language of instruction, tend to receive passive, whole-class, teacher-directed instruction that emphasizes lower-order skills development (Moss & Puma, 1995; Padrón, 1994; Ramirez, Yuen, & Ramey, 1991). Similar findings have been reported for students in high-poverty schools (Taylor, Pearson, Peterson, & Rodriguez, 2003, 2005). Although we cannot claim that the consistent lack of comprehension instruction observed in the elementary grades underlies the stagnant NAEP scores, it is reasonable to hypothesize that a national effort to improve reading comprehension instruction would improve reading comprehension achievement.

Comprehension Strategy Instruction

Through the "cognitive revolution" in the 1970s and 1980s (see Pearson & Duke, 2002, for review), we have learned a great deal about how to teach children to comprehend. We have developed powerful models of reading comprehension (e.g., Kintsch, 1998), as well as models of teaching comprehension strategies (Pressley & Woloshyn, 1995). We have sufficient research in reading comprehension instruction for the National Reading Panel (2000) to find that the following strategies are effective when taught singly—summarization, self-questioning, story structure instruction (including story maps), graphic and semantic organizers, and comprehension monitoring. The National Reading Panel also found that two multiple-strategy instructional approaches—Reciprocal Teaching (RT; Palincsar & Brown, 1984) and Transactional Strategies Instruction (TSI; Pressley & Woloshyn, 1995)—were effective. RT emphasizes only four strategies—questioning, clarifying, predicting, and summarization; TSI teaches those plus an additional six, including monitoring and remediating comprehension problems, using imagery, and reacting to the text. A larger set of strategies might be more difficult to teach but might be more useful for students to use in a variety of situations.

Some of these strategies have been effective with English-language learners (ELLs) as well. Short-term instructional interventions that have taught ELLs to generate questions while reading (Muñiz-Swicegood, 1994) or to employ the strategies in RT (Padrón, 1992) have had positive results. Given the need for comprehension instruction and the presence of validated methods, it should be a simple matter to take the validated methods to the teachers. Although taking what we know now to teachers would be an improvement over the status quo, there are some significant barriers to such widespread implementation. First, teachers' expertise about reading comprehension needs to be increased (RAND Reading Study Group, 2002). Second, teachers need extended opportunities to try out strategy instruction. Brown and Coy-Ogan (1993) found it took a motivated teacher 3 years to learn how to successfully implement TSI in her classroom. Because many teachers are not even assigned to the same grade level for 3 years, there are practical problems with such an approach.

Third, although we know that teaching strategies can improve reading comprehension, we do not know *why* such instruction is effective. Rosenshine and Meister (1994), in their review of RT instruction, reported that, although RT was effective in improving instruction, there was no evidence that this effectiveness was due to children's increased use of the strategies that were taught.

> . . . there were six studies in which, after the instruction, students were tested on their ability to generate questions. In all six studies, students in reciprocal teaching groups were superior to control students in comprehension skills. . . . However, in five of the same six studies, there was no difference between the reciprocal teaching groups and the control groups in the level of questions generated (Lynsynchuk et al., 1990; Palincsar & Brown, 1984), the number of questions (Taylor & Frye, 1992), or a rating of the quality of the questions (Shortland-Jones, 1986). *In other words, we found no relationship between posttest measures of ability to generate questions and reading comprehension scores.* (p. 509, emphasis added)

Rosenshine and Meister conclude that they could not find evidence that RT affected the *processes* that children used. RT may have been effective because it encouraged children to process the text deeply, or in some more effective way.

> We suggest . . . that in successful studies that taught question generation, what the students learned was not simply to generate questions. Rather as explained by Palincsar and Brown (1984), the new strategies enabled and required students to perform deeper processing of what they read, to engage in making sense of what they read, to be aware of when they did not understand the material, and to engage in additional reading and searching when they encountered comprehension difficulties. (p. 510)

Other studies have similarly suggested that it may be responsive engagement, rather than any taught strategies, that underlie the effectiveness of comprehension instruction. For example, Rinehart, Stahl, and Erickson (1986) found that summarization instruction improved children's social studies learning, but only indirectly. Using path analysis, they found that the summarization instruction led to increased preparation time and improved quality of the notes taken during the study task. The quality of notes, in turn, was the only factor that improved comprehension.

Hacker and Tennant (2002) report a study of RT's implementation in 17 teachers' classrooms. They found that teachers modified RT, often considerably, as they tried to use the principles in teaching children to comprehend. Some teachers changed RT from a small-group to a whole-class activity, at least for part of the lesson. Others included writing as a way of getting at summarization, rather than relying on oral summaries. Although the program appeared to improve children's comprehension as measured both by informal and standardized comprehension measures, both the teachers and researchers were concerned about the shallowness of the questions that the students asked and that clarification was rarely used in the groups, even though there were many words and concepts that the children did not understand. They suggest that "strategies themselves [may] play only a secondary role in improving comprehension" (p. 712).

Thus, although strategy instruction of various types has been found to improve comprehension, we do not know *why* this is the case. Somewhat ironically, strategy instruction may not improve children's use of strategies but may encourage them to look at text in a different manner, possibly increasing their cognitive engagement with text, and, through this increased engagement, become better at comprehending.

Responsive Engagement Instruction

The purpose of responsive engagement instruction is to provide an instructional environment in which children are encouraged to engage deeply with the texts being read and, through that cognitive engagement, develop skill in comprehension. Taylor et al. (2000) and Taylor, Peterson, Pearson, and Rodriguez (2002) found that teachers who used more "higher-level" questions had significantly higher comprehension achievement than those who used lower-level questions. Higher-order questioning may involve children in processing texts deeply. Because Taylor et al. (2000) did not find much evidence of comprehension strategy instruction, it is difficult to compare the effects of higher-level questions to strategy instruction. Also, because their study was naturalistic observation, it is not clear whether it was the higher-level questions that improved comprehension, or that such questions are artifacts of other comprehension-fostering behaviors.

Other studies have found that exemplary or effective teachers, especially in the upper elementary grades, tend to have engaging classrooms but do not embrace much comprehension strategy instruction to any significant extent. Knapp (1995), for example, reported that effective teachers in high-poverty schools promoted higher-level thinking activities to a greater extent than other teachers. Allington and Johnston (2002) similarly found that exemplary teachers spent more time engaging children about text, used more open-ended questions, connected what was being read to children's lives, and otherwise carried out comprehension-fostering activities designed to get children involved in their reading, rather than teaching specific strategies. Turner (1995) found that cognitive engagement instruction increased children's motivation, but because she did not include achievement measures in her work, we do not know if it affected either strategy use or comprehension. Thus, observational studies of "best practices" tend to find that effective teachers, defined in various ways, tend to stress cognitive engagement with text and not comprehension strategies.

There is some experimental evidence that responsive engagement-oriented instruction leads to improved comprehension. Guthrie et al. (1996; Guthrie, Anderson, Alao, & Rinehart, 1999), for example, found that the concept-oriented reading instruction (CORI) framework, which attempted to increase engagement through the use of multiple texts centered on content material using an inquiry approach, significantly improved children's comprehension. Guthrie and his colleagues (1998) found that the improvements were found not only on texts related to the concepts being studied, but transferred to other texts and other topics. Specifically focusing on reading instruction in high-poverty schools, Taylor et al. (2002, 2003) found that teachers who asked more high-level questions (HLQ) about text promoted more growth in their students' reading and writing ability than teachers who asked primarily low-level questions (LLQ). Further examination showed that the HLQ teachers asked about the theme of a story more than LLQ teachers whereas the low-questioning teachers did more talking about the details of a story (Taylor et al., 2003). In an experimental study, Saunders and Goldenberg (1999a, 1999b) found that students, both ELL and non-ELL, in classroom grades 4 and 5 whose teachers used a technique called Instructional Conversations outperformed students in control classrooms. Instructional Conversations focus on story theme, questions relating a story to personal experience, and embedded (as opposed to explicit) strategy instruction. Beck, McKeown, Worthy, Sandora, and Kucan (1996) found that when students engaged in Questioning the Author, in which the discussion focuses on interpreting the author's message, they demonstrated greater higher-level thinking about text than students engaged in a more traditional recitation about a story. Chinn, Anderson, and Wagonner (2001) found that in comparison to recitation, literacy discussions that stressed collaborative reasoning about tensions and conflicts in a text (e.g., Was Jamie right to trust Emily?) fostered greater cognitive engagement and higher-level thinking than a control treatment emphasizing "business as usual."

The focus on higher-level thinking in the techniques described previously are examples of the same general principle that instruction that is cognitively challenging and engaging will encourage children to process text deeply and lead to enhanced comprehension. Guthrie et al. did include explicit strategy instruction in their program and the Instructional Conversations approach includes strategy-like prompts in the repertoire to questioning activities, but the other successful programs have not, suggesting that responsive engagement itself may be sufficient to improve comprehension.

It may also be that responsive engagement is a mechanism by which children learn to apply strategies to written material. That is, if children are engaged in deep processing of information in the text, they are more likely to use cognitive strategies to comprehend the text. A direct comparison of responsive engagement-oriented instruction to strategy-oriented instruction on a variety of measures sensitive to children's strategy use and general comprehension will allow us to tease out these factors.

Developmental Issues

The vast majority of research on comprehension instruction has focused on children in grades 4 and higher (Pearson & Duke, 2002). Older children are assumed to have automatic word recognition (Chall, 1996; Samuels, 1988) and thus have extra cognitive capacity to devote to comprehension strategies. According to this view, children who are still learning to decode (and who therefore devote considerable attention and capacity to unlocking new words) cannot benefit from comprehension strategy instruction. Because strategies, by definition, require the explicit and focused attention of the reader, attention devoted to decoding would interfere with use of strategies during reading. This emphasis on decoding before comprehension is implicit in the lack of use of such strategies before fourth grade in the research we reviewed (Pearson & Duke, 2002).

This assumption, however, has been rarely tested, and, when it has, the results have been inconsistent (Pearson & Duke, 2002). TSI has been used successfully with second graders (Brown & Coy-Ogan, 1993; Schuder, 1993), but few other strategy interventions have been. If we are going to achieve the goal of improving the comprehension of fourth graders, as measured by the NAEP, we may need to begin instruction prior to that grade. The RAND Reading Study Group (2002) noted that many third graders, even those who were reading at grade level, later met difficulties with reading comprehension. To offset this problem, they suggested that comprehension instruction might profitably begin in the primary grades and continue throughout the upper grades. Therefore, it is important to understand whether comprehension instruction works as well with students whose word recognition is neither automatic nor fluent as it does with older students, especially those with adequate fluency.

EFFECTIVE PROFESSIONAL DEVELOPMENT TO IMPROVE COMPREHENSION INSTRUCTION

Researchers studying teacher professional development have reached a strong consensus about what makes it effective (Killion, 2002; Lieberman & Miller, 2002). Teachers who receive quality, ongoing professional development stressing higher-order thinking and concrete learning activities are more likely to use effective classroom practices associated with gains in student achievement (Wenglinski, 2002). Sustained and intensive professional development that is tied to active learning and daily school life is more likely to have an impact than shorter professional development experiences (Garet, Porter, Desimone, Birman, & Yoon, 2001). External sources of support, whether subject-matter collaboratives, reform networks, or school–university partnerships, are also important (Lieberman & Miller, 2002).

The collaborative nature of effective professional development has also been stressed (Killion, 2002; Lieberman & Miller, 2002). In professional learning communities, teachers who share a common purpose for their students and engage in collaborative activities to achieve this purpose see improved student learning (Newmann & Wehlage, 1995) and positive changes in teacher practices (Garet et al., 2001). In the implementation of our professional development for both interventions, we emphasize the principles emanating from this research tradition.

THE CURRENT STUDY: TEACHING TEACHERS ABOUT EFFECTIVE COMPREHENSION INSTRUCTION

It should be clear from the preceding discussion that, although we have several validated approaches to teaching children to comprehend, important theoretical underpinnings are missing, or are assumed but not validated. First is the issue of what processes are affected by comprehension strategy and responsive engagement-oriented instruction. Although strategy instruction purports to teach both specific strategies and work with children in orchestrating these strategies, it is not clear that children actually use the strategies as a result of the instruction. Rosenshine and Meister (1994; Rosenshine, Meister, & Chapman, 1996), Rinehart et al. (1986), and Taylor and Frye (1992) all found that strategy instruction did not necessarily produce children who used the strategies that were taught but instead encouraged children to process text more deeply. If so, then a program that encourages children to become highly engaged with text, such as through higher-level questions, might have the same effect as one emphasizing the use of strategies. As noted earlier, responsive engagement-oriented instruction has been found to improve students' comprehension.

It is therefore important to contrast strategy instruction with instruction that stresses responsive engagement with the text in order to compare the relative advantage of each type of instruction. Both types of instruction should be contrasted with a control using conventional comprehension instruction. It is also important to investigate both the end products of comprehension and the processes used during comprehension to examine whether children are actually using the strategies taught as a result of instruction. Finally, because we suspect that these two approaches will have differential effects on different aspects of comprehension, in the final analysis it is important to also synthesize the two approaches and assess how a combined approach works in contrast to a control condition.

We are examining the following questions:

- Can we develop approaches to comprehension instruction that are sustainable over a full year, or over 2 years, and that can be implemented easily by teachers? Previous research was largely short term or implemented by researchers. Given the difficulty of implementing both strategy instruction and responsive engagement instruction, it is important to develop routines that can be easily carried out by teachers and widely used.
- What are the relative effects of strategy-oriented and responsive engagement-oriented comprehension instruction on a variety of measures, including both measures of text-specific comprehension and transfer to more general comprehension abilities?
- Do strategy-oriented and responsive engagement-oriented instruction transfer from comprehension in English to comprehension of other languages or vice versa?
- What are the effects of different types of instruction on children at different developmental stages (second and fourth graders)? Do children need to be fully fluent to take advantage of comprehension instruction?

The first question is designed to examine whether we can develop a practical approach to comprehension instruction, one that teachers can widely implement and use all year without extensive support. As noted earlier, even exemplary teachers do little strategy instruction but do engage their children in higher-level text comprehension. We want to develop routines for both strategy- and responsive engagement-oriented instruction that can be readily used.

The remaining questions are intended to help us understand *why* and *how* two different types of comprehension instruction work, in two different grade levels. The second question examines how strategy- and responsive engagement-oriented instruction affects students' performance on a variety of measures, both product and process measures. The third question, focusing on bilingual students, gives us another window from which to examine how students internalize comprehension strategies and whether strategy- or responsive engagement-oriented instruction carries over into a different language. The final question is an aptitude by treatment interaction question—examining whether different types of instruction are more appropriate for children at different developmental levels, where development is defined either by age/grade or by proficiency in decoding and fluency.

Participants

Each year this study involves 48 teachers, 12 at each of four sites—Minnesota, northern California, central Illinois, and Chicago, one of which has a large population of Spanish-speaking. ELLs enrolled in bilingual education. All schools serve predominantly low socioeconomic status children, with between 50% and 90% of the children eligible for free/reduced-price lunch. These sites provide different populations with different needs, increasing the likelihood that the treatments that are developed will be widely applicable.

At each site, we are involving three schools, one for strategy instruction, one for responsive engagement instruction, and one for a treated control that is focusing on effective vocabulary instruction. In the first year, we worked with two second-grade and two fourth-grade teachers in each of the three schools at each site to develop and study the routines that would encompass usable strategy and responsive engagement instruction. For the second year, we are using a more conventional quasi-experimental design, randomly assigning treatments to a new set of schools, to examine whether the procedures developed during the first-year transfer to other, similar schools. In the third year, because we anticipate that each type of instruction will produce different desirable outcomes, we want to combine the most effective aspects of strategy and responsive engagement instruction and compare it to a treated control using a quasi-experimental design.

Method

The purposes of the first 2 years are to work with teachers to develop and validate effective instructional routines for both strategic- and responsive engagement-oriented comprehension instruction that can be sustained on a long-term basis. To this end, we have engaged first in formative and then quasi-experimental research with a small cadre of teachers to develop approaches for providing strategy-oriented instruction and responsive engagement-oriented instruction that are feasible to implement. For strategy instruction, we begin with RT as a model, working with teachers to incorporate features of TSI into a strategy instruction routine that is comprehensive and flexible. For the responsive engagement-oriented instruction, we begin with an Instructional Conversations (Saunders & Goldenberg, 1999b) model, but we are expanding our instruction to include features of other responsive engagement-oriented instruction, such as literary discussion techniques and small independent groups in which students are encouraged to take a more central role in the flow of conversation.

Professional development activities are following the recommendations of the National Staff Development Council (2001). In year 2, our current effort, professional development (PD) consists of an initial 3-hour session, eight monthly 90-minute sessions, and monthly drop-in visits. We have developed PD guides for two treatment conditions and a control condition to maximize similarities across conditions and sites. The teachers and the professional development leaders use a common set of instructional principles for each condition to keep instruction focused and similar across sites.

In year 2, the quasi-experiment, we began the initial session with a common approach across sites and conditions:

- Discuss the principles for a particular treatment condition;
- View and discuss a video showing a teacher teaching the treatment condition;
- Read and discuss a relevant research-based article;
- Discuss what teachers were currently doing and not doing;
- Guide teachers in the process of selecting texts appropriate to the condition;
- Discuss ways in which teachers could get started with teaching of treatment condition; and
- Cover teaching and other work to be done prior to next PD session.

In the monthly 90-minute sessions teachers write and share brief reflections about what they have tried since last meeting. Then they discuss an article read since the last meeting and how the article fits with the principles. We engage in activities related to instructional goals for the next month: what/how to teach (e.g., teaching three 30-minute lessons with the teacher leading and modeling, releasing to the students over subsequent weeks, planning lessons with a colleague, selecting appropriate texts, teaching in small groups). Several activities are designed to move forward in the PD sessions (e.g., practicing video sharing prior to someone bringing in a video). In the last 5 minutes of each session teachers receive an article to read before the next session, and someone agrees to bring a video clip or student work to share. Teachers are reminded to keep lesson logs.

In between sessions, the PD provider visits each classroom and completes a feedback form that is tied to the instructional principles. Either in person or on the phone she discusses what worked and suggests possible changes.

Teachers report that they like the time to work together to learn new teaching techniques, to talk about instruction, to view videotapes of one another teaching, to plan and modify lessons, and to look at student work to improve instruction. Teachers like the principles as a guide for their teaching. Teachers report that reading specific research articles and discussing how to implement suggested procedures that fit with the principles have been beneficial.

Cognitive strategies and responsive engagement are hard to teach well. Thus, at this point in the study, we think that teachers may need 2 years of PD, not 1, to be effective. We are investigating this hypothesis in one site by comparing teachers who are in their second year of PD, as pertains to a particular treatment condition, with those who are in their first year.

CONCLUSIONS

While Steve Stahl's legacy to the field of reading research may appear to more prominent in the domains of phonics, vocabulary, or fluency, we think his contributions to comprehension work, particularly work in comprehension instruction, will eventually be regarded on an equal footing with his other work. It is significant that at the time of his death he was heavily involved in administering two federal grants, one in fluency instruction and one in comprehension instruction. Clearly, he had decided that comprehension instruction merited our collective professional attention. As his colleagues, both throughout his career and in the current comprehension research, we share his commitment. When we come to the end of this research project, we think we will have learned more about how to work with teachers to encourage them to implement comprehension instruction than about the efficacy of any particular intervention, strategy, or discussion technique. And this is as it should be, for it is what the field needs. We know a great deal about approaches to discussion that facilitate comprehension and strategies that aid individual problem solving. But we do not have a good track record when it comes to devising professional development and support activities to assist teachers in embedding these approaches into "daily life" in their classrooms. That Steve determined that this was what we, as a field, needed to do at this particular point in time attests to his concern for teachers and students and his wisdom about research and practice. We will be forever grateful that he asked us to join him in this arduous but important journey.

ACKNOWLEDGMENTS

The research described in this chapter was supported by a grant from the U.S. Department of Education, Institute of Education Sciences (No. CDFA 84.305G). The views expressed herein are the authors' and have not been cleared by the grantors.

REFERENCES

Allington, R. L., & Johnston, P. H. (2002). *Reading to learn: Lessons from exemplary fourth-grade classrooms*. New York: Guilford Press.

Beck, I. L., McKeown, M. G., Worthy, J., Sandora, C. A., & Kucan, L. (1996). Questioning the author: A year-long classroom implementation to engage students with texts. *Elementary School Journal, 96*(4), 385–414.

Brown, R., & Coy-Ogan, L. (1993). The evolution of transactional strategies in one teacher's classroom. *Elementary School Journal, 94*, 221–233.

Chall, J. S. (1996). *Stages of reading development* (2nd ed.). Fort Worth, TX: Harcourt-Brace.

Chinn, C. A., Anderson, R. C., & Waggoner, M. A. (2001). Patterns of discourse in two kinds of literature discussion. *Reading Research Quarterly, 36*, 378–411.

Durkin, D. (1978–1979). What classroom observations reveal about reading comprehension instruction. *Reading Research Quarterly, 14*, 481–533.

Garet, M. S., Porter, A. C., Desimone, L., Birman, B. F., & Yoon, K. S. (2001). What makes professional development effective? Results from a national sample of teachers. *American Educational Research Journal, 38*, 915–945.

Guthrie, J. T., Anderson, E., Alao, S., & Rinehart, J. M. (1999) Effects of concept-oriented reading instruction on strategy use and conceptual learning from text. *Elementary School Journal, 99*(4), 343–366.

Guthrie, J. T., Van Meter, P., Hancock, G. R., McCann, A. D., Anderson, E., & Alao, S. (1998). Does concept-oriented reading instruction increase strategy-use and conceptual learning from text? *Journal of Educational Psychology, 90*, 261–278.

Guthrie, J. T., Van Meter, P., McCann, A. D., Wigfield, A., Bennett, L., Poundstone, C., et al.

(1996). Growth of literacy engagement: Changes in motivations and strategies during concept-oriented reading instruction. *Reading Research Quarterly, 31,* 306–332.

Hacker, D. J., & Tenent, A. (2002). Implementing reciprocal teaching in the classroom: Overcoming obstacles and making modifications. *Journal of Educational Psychology, 94,* 699–718.

Killion, J. (2002). *What works in the elementary school: Results-based staff development.* Oxford, OH: National Staff Development Council and NEA.

Kintsch, W. (1998). *Comprehension: A paradigm for cognition.* Cambridge, UK: Cambridge University Press.

Knapp, M. (1995). *Teaching for meaning in high poverty classrooms.* New York: Teachers College Press.

Lieberman, A., & Miller, L. (2002). Transforming professional development: Understanding and organizing learning communities. In W. D. Hawley & D. L. Rollie (Eds.), *The keys to effective schools: Educational reform as continuous improvement* (pp. 74–85). Washington, DC: NEA.

Lysynchuk, L. M., Pressley, M., & Vye, N. (1990). Reciprocal teaching improves standardized reading-comprehension performance in poor comprehenders. *Elementary School Journal, 90,* 469–484.

Moss, M., & Puma, M. (1995). *Prospects: The Congressionally mandated study of educational growth and opportunity. First year report on language minority and limited English proficient students.* Washington, DC: U.S. Department of Education.

Muñiz-Swicegood, M. (1994). The effects of metacognitive reading strategy training on the reading performance and fluent reading analysis strategies of third grade bilingual students. *Bilingual Research Journal, 18,* 83–97.

National Reading Panel. (2000). *Report of the subgroups: National Reading Panel.* Washington, DC: National Institute of Child Health and Human Development.

National Staff Development Council. (2001). *NSCD's standards for staff development, revised.* Oxford, OH: Author.

Newmann, F., & Wehlage, G. (1995). *Successful school restructuring: A report to the public and educators.* Madison, WI: Center on Organization and Restructuring of Schools.

Padrón, Y. (1992). The effect of strategy instruction on bilingual students' cognitive strategy use in reading. *Bilingual Research Journal, 16,* 35–52.

Padrón, Y. (1994). Comparing reading instruction in Hispanic/limited English-proficient schools and other inner-city schools. *Bilingual Research Journal, 18,* 49–66.

Palincsar, A. S., & Brown, A. L. (1984). Reciprocal teaching of comprehension-fostering and comprehension-monitoring activities. *Cognition and Instruction, 2,* 117–175.

Pearson, P. D., & Duke, N. K. (2002). Comprehension instruction in the primary grades. In C. C. Block & M. Pressley (Eds.), *Comprehension instruction: Research-based best practices* (pp. 247–258). New York: Guilford Press.

Pressley, M., Wharton-MacDonald, R., Mistretta, J., & Echevarria, M. (1998). Literacy instruction in 10 fourth- and fifth-grade classrooms in upstate New York. *Scientific Studies in Reading, 2,* 159–194.

Pressley, M., & Woloshyn, V. (1995). *Cognitive strategy instruction that really improves children's academic performance.* Cambridge, MA: Brookline Press.

Ramirez, J. D., Yuen, S. D., & Ramey, D. R. (1991). *Executive summary: Final report: Longitudinal study of structured English immersion strategy, early-exit and late-exit transitional bilingual education programs for language minority children.* San Mateo, CA: Aguirre International.

RAND Reading Study Group. (2002). Reading for understanding: Toward an R & D program for reading comprehension. Santa Monica, CA: Science & Technology Policy Institute, RAND Education.

Rinehart, S. D., Stahl, S. A., & Erickson, L. G. (1986). Some effects of summarization training on reading and studying. *Reading Research Quarterly, 21*(4), 422–438.

Rosenshine, B., & Meister, C. (1994). Reciprocal teaching: A review of the research. *Review of Educational Research, 64*, 479–530.

Rosenshine, B., Meister, C., & Chapman, S. (1996). Teaching students to generate questions: A review of the intervention studies. *Review of Educational Research, 66*, 181–221.

Samuels, S. J. (1988). Decoding and automaticity: Helping poor readers become automatic at word recognition. *The Reading Teacher, 41*, 756–760.

Saunders, W. M., & Goldenberg, C. (1999a). Effects of instructional conversations and literature logs on limited- and fluent-English-proficient students' story comprehension and thematic understanding. *Elementary School Journal, 99*, 279–301.

Saunders, W. M., & Goldenberg, C. (1999b). *The effects of instructional conversations and literature logs on the story comprehension and thematic understandings of English proficient and limited English proficient students.* Santa Cruz, CA: Center for Research on Excellence and Diversity in Education.

Schuder, T. (1993). The genesis of transactional strategies instruction in a reading program for at-risk students. *Elementary School Journal, 94*, 183–200.

Shortland-Jones, B. (1986). The development and testing of an instructional strategy for improving reading comprehension based on schema and metacognitive theories. *Dissertation Abstracts International, 47*(7-A), 2526.

Stahl, S. A., Jacobson, M. G., Davis, C. E., & Davis, R. L. (1989). Prior knowledge and difficult vocabulary in the comprehension of unfamiliar text. *Reading Research Quarterly, 24*(1), 27–43.

Taylor, B. M., & Frye, B. (1992). Comprehension strategy instruction in the intermediate grades. *Reading Research and Instruction, 32*, 39–49.

Taylor, B. M., Pearson, P. D., Clark, K., & Walpole, S. (2000). Effective schools and accomplished teachers: Lessons about primary grade reading instruction in low-income schools. *Elementary School Journal, 101*, 121–166.

Taylor, B. M., Pearson, P. D., Peterson, D. S., & Rodriguez, M. C. (2003). Reading growth in high-poverty classrooms: The influence of teacher practices that encourage cognitive engagement in literacy learning. *Elementary School Journal, 104*, 3–28.

Taylor, B. M., Pearson, P. D., Peterson, D. S., & Rodriguez, M. C. (2005). The CIERA school change framework: An evidenced-based approach to professional development and school reading improvement. *Reading Research Quarterly, 40* 40–69.

Taylor, B. M., Peterson, D. P., Pearson, P. D., & Rodriguez, M. C. (2002). Looking inside classrooms: Reflecting on the "how" as well as the "what" in effective reading instruction. *The Reading Teacher, 56*, 70–79

Turner, J. C. (1995). The influence of classroom contexts on young children's motivation for literacy. *Reading Research Quarterly, 30*, 410–441.

Wenglinski, H. (2002). How schools matter: The link between teacher classroom practices and student academic performance. *Educational Policy Analysis Archives, 10*(12). Retrieved February 26, 2003, from epaa.asu.edu/epaa/v10n12.2002

20 | What Happens When Students Read Multiple Source Documents in History?

STEVEN A. STAHL
CYNTHIA R. HYND
BRUCE K. BRITTON
MARY M. McNISH
DENNIS BOSQUET

After many years of comparative neglect, the study of history has received renewed attention by cognitive psychologists (Wineburg, 1991a, 1991b). Cognitive analyses of history learning have appeared in symposiums presented at major national meetings, as well as in books devoted to the subject (e.g., Leinhardt, Beck, & Stainton, 1994; Perfetti, Britt, & Georgi, 1995) and a special issue of *Educational Psychologist* (Wineburg, 1994).

This renewed attention may presage an interest in new methods of presenting historical content. The traditional means of teaching history was to rely heavily, if not exclusively, on the textbook as a means of conveying information. In 1982, a survey found that roughly 90% of all social studies teachers use a textbook in their class (Patrick & Hawke, 1982). Approximately half of all teachers in that survey reported relying on just one text, with that text being reported as the major determinant of the content of their curriculum.

Currently, the single text approach to history learning and the model of learning upon which it is based are being challenged by those who espouse constructivist views of knowledge acquisition (e.g., Seixas, 1993) as well as those who espouse more traditional views of learning history (e.g., Ravitch, 1992). This article reports on an attempt to examine an alternative approach to learning about historical events, using multiple source materials, and the processes used by students as they negotiate the information in the various documents.

CONSTRUCTION OF MEANING IN HISTORY

The textbook-based teacher can be caricatured as using a *transmission* model of learning, in which the information to be learned is contained in one vessel, the textbook, and transmitted to another vessel, the student's memory, via the teacher's lecture.

Traditionally, many teachers have treated content area knowledge as Hirsch (1987) did, as a *basket of facts*, that must be gathered from text and lecture. These facts are stored in memory, the way information is stored in a computer database. As one history teacher quoted by Wineburg (1991b) put it, "History is the basic facts of what happened. What *did* happen. You don't ask how it happened. You just ask, 'What are the events?' " (p. 513, italics in original).

Such a transmission model is not supported by current views of the nature of knowledge and learning. More recent theories suggest that as information is learned, this information is not merely copied from one source to another but is transformed by the process of learning (Spiro, 1980). In this constructivist view of knowledge acquisition, new information can be retained in short-term memory through rote memorization or rehearsal, but this information is easily forgotten. This is evidenced by the often-experienced phenomenon of a student learning facts for a test and forgetting as soon as the test is through. For information to be learned and retained, it must be actively combined with previously learned information. The new learning is constructed from the new information and the old information into new knowledge, either through *assimilating* the new knowledge into already existing knowledge structures or through *accommodating* the new information by creating new knowledge structures that would account for both the previously known and the new information (Rumelhart, 1980). Because every learner brings somewhat different knowledge and experience to the classroom, the knowledge that each learner retains is going to be somewhat different.

In this constructivist view of knowledge, the conveyance of content is more than merely ensuring that the students devote enough time and attention to memorizing the text or the teacher's lecture. Instead, the teacher must create the conditions that best allow the student to construct a mental model of the knowledge domain, incorporating into this mental model not only the information in the current curriculum but also past knowledge.

The constructivist view of learning not only challenges the transmission model but also calls into question the relevance of those psychological models of learning based on the reading of a single text for examining the processes involved in learning history. Models such as Kintsch and van Dijk's (1978) may accurately describe how readers construct a propositional text base from the reading of a single text. However, texts that we read are understood in relation to other texts that we have previously read and other knowledge that we have acquired (Hartman, 1995). A psychological model of learning from texts, whether a single text or multiple texts, should include not only the text itself but the reader's previous knowledge and how the student uses that knowledge in constructing a new mental model (see Kintsch, 1986).

CONTENT AND DISCIPLINARY KNOWLEDGE

One goal of history instruction, then, should be for the learner to construct a well-articulated mental model of history, understanding the interconnections between various events and actors. Taking the topic of the present study, the origins of the Vietnam War, a student should have an understanding of the relations between the U.S. election of 1964, U.S. views of communism during that era, Lyndon Johnson, the Viet Cong, and the Gulf of Tonkin Resolution. These understandings should be deep enough to understand why a possibly misunderstood incident, involving minor damage to two ships, could trigger a major conflagration. The mental model containing these understandings could be called *content knowledge* or knowledge about a particular domain (Stahl, Hynd, Glynn, & Carr, 1995).

Stahl et al. (1995) argue that, while content knowledge is important, it is not sufficient for the study of history. In addition, a person needs *disciplinary knowledge* or the ability to think like a historian, to evaluate materials and information in relation to their context and their source, and to integrate this information into a historical discourse (e.g., Greene, 1994).

Wineburg (1991a, 1991b) gave eight historians and eight high school seniors a series of historical texts about the Battle of Lexington and had them complete a variety of activities, including thinking aloud as they read, rating the trustworthiness of the documents, and evaluating the historical veracity of three paintings of the Battle. He noted that historians could be distinguished from students by their use of three processes:

- Corroboration, or comparing and contrasting documents with one another;
- Sourcing, or looking first at the source of the document before reading the text itself to consider how the bias of the source might have affected the content of the document; and
- Contextualization, or situating a text in a temporal and spatial context to consider how the time or place in which the document was written might have affected its content or the perspective taken.

The differences were not simply due to differences in content knowledge, since historians who did not know very much about the American Revolution still used the same reasoning processes in their think-alouds. Nor were the differences due to inability to detect bias. The college students in Perfetti, Britt, Rouet, Mason, and Georgi's (1993) study and the high school students in Stahl and Hynd's (1994) study were both able to detect bias in sources.

Instead, the differences between the students and the historians seem to be tied to differences in the way the historians and students viewed text. Wineburg (1991a, 1991b) inferred that students tended to view texts as repositories for facts, as bearers of information, as they might well have, given years of exposure to a transmission model of learning. For example, they tended to rate textbooks as more trustworthy than source documents, a finding replicated by Perfetti et al. (1993) and Stahl and Hynd (1994). Historians tend to view texts as speech acts, produced for a particular purpose by a particular person. To understand historical texts involves understanding both the person and the purpose, and to get at the *truth* hidden within the texts involves comparing various perspectives, with an understanding of who produced the various texts and why. The students in Perfetti et al.'s (1993) study were able to grasp the basic story of the Panama Canal Treaty from documents describing the events leading up to the signing of the Treaty in 1903 but were less able to provide evidence about their stance on whether the treaty should have been signed.

MULTIPLE TEXTS AND HISTORY LEARNING

A number of educators have suggested that the single classroom text be supplemented with or supplanted by multiple original source materials (e.g., Perfetti et al.,

1993; Spoehr & Spoehr, 1994; Wineburg, 1991a). Providing students with multiple perspectives on a particular event can aid them in constructing a richer and more detailed mental model of that event, thus enhancing content knowledge. Spiro, Coulson, Feltovich, and Anderson (1994) likened the use of multiple perspectives to crisscrossing a conceptual landscape and suggested that seeing an event through different perspectives is necessary to create a rich understanding of an event or concept. This use of original material forces students to construct links across information presented in different texts, and this information and the links connecting the different sources are remembered better if students make their own constructions rather than relying on the constructions of a textbook author or teacher (Spoehr & Spoehr, 1994). The links based on this crisscrossing create a rich mental model, or what we are calling content knowledge.

The use of multiple texts can also increase students' disciplinary knowledge. If we consider the tasks that Wineburg (1991a, 1991b) found to distinguish between historians and high school students—corroboration, sourcing, and contextualization—to be at least part of the thought processes used by historians, they can be activated only by providing opportunities to compare and contrast different source materials with different and independent viewpoints. The single, omniscient view of a textbook cannot easily be used to develop disciplinary knowledge, since there is nothing to which the student can compare the information, and thus the student is usually unable to examine the bias of the textbook or the effects of the time and place in which it was written and to compare it to other sources. (However, McKeown, Beck, and Worthy, 1993, have developed procedures to elicit this information from critical examination of a single text.)

If conflicting information is presented in these texts, however, the conflict may impede learning. Perry (1970) examined the development of thought among male college students and found evidence for development from a stance of looking for a single right answer to an understanding that knowledge is relative, depending on one's perspective, to the melding of information from different perspectives. Belenky, Clinchy, Goldberger, and Tarule (1986) replicated Perry's study with a broad range of women. They found that stances of knowledge can move from a belief that knowledge is received, or is transmitted from someone else, to a subjective stance, in which knowledge is seen as subjective and relative, to a procedural stance, in which rational processes are seen as a way to break through the subjectivity, to a stance they call *constructed*, in which knowledge is constructed through both rational processes and the acknowledgment of other perspectives.

It is this last stance that we expect students to take when looking at multiple documents, but it is one that is typically achieved in the later college years or graduate school, after exposure to the more open-ended discussions typical of college classrooms. It may be unreasonable to expect high school students, who tend to be exposed to more lecture and recitation, to think like this, at least not without some greater instruction in how to do it and some expectation that they engage in this kind of thought.

Despite the theoretical sense that multiple sources can enhance learning, there is very little information on *how* readers synthesize information across texts. Crafton (1983) had 11th graders read two science texts, either two on the same topic or two on different topics. She found that those who read two texts on the same topic comprehended significantly more about the topic than those who read texts on the different topics. Further, the students who had prior knowledge (from reading the first, relevant text) were able to focus on larger segments of text during a verbalization task and made more inferences, suggesting that they were better at integrating material in the text.

Spivey and King (1989) examined how 6th-, 8th-, and 10th-grade writers synthesized information across different encyclopedias. They found that older and more able students tended to be more adept at using information that was repeated in all three texts read and was presumed to be more important, better at reorganizing information from the different sources into a coherent whole, and more aware of the needs of their audience.

Greene (1994) gave college juniors and seniors a task either to write a report or to solve a problem in history. He found that students given the problem-based task were more likely to bring their previous knowledge into their essays, to see the task as one of evaluation of the information in the articles, and to draw upon different kinds of information than the students who were given the report writing task. The students who were asked to write a report had difficulty doing so, because they tended not to set their ideas in a context and justify the issues they chose to write about.

The purpose of this study was to examine the processes and outcomes of reading multiple original source materials. The materials relate to the Gulf of Tonkin Incident and the resultant Gulf of Tonkin Resolution passed by the U.S. Congress that eventually began the Vietnam War. We were specifically interested in the following questions: When given multiple historical source documents (a) Could students develop a rich mental model of a historical event? (b) What did students do with the document information? (c) Did the task students were given influence their processing of information? (d) How did students integrate information across texts to form a coherent essay? and (e) Did students engage in corroborating, sourcing, and contextualizing in evaluating historical materials?

The first two questions asked whether students can learn from multiple text documents and how they process these documents to aid their learning. The third question dealt with the effects of task on learning. We used two different tasks, having students write either a description or an opinion of either the incident itself or the events leading up to the Senate resolution. Some studies have found that encoding tasks influence processing (e.g., Reynolds, Trathen, Sawyer, & Shepard, 1993). We hoped to find processes that were used more often in one task than in another, thus illuminating how students process multiple text information. The fourth question dealt with how students put information from multiple documents together. The final question was intended to see whether the multiple text task induced students to use the operations found by Wineberg (1991a) to distinguish historians from high school students in their reading of original source materials.

METHOD

Participants

The participants were 44 students in two classes of 10th-grade advanced placement U.S. history taught by a single teacher. The school was one of two high schools in a small southern U.S. university town, drawing from a wide range of socioeconomic states. Approximately one-quarter of the students participating were African American and the others were of European American origin. These students were enrolled in U.S. history so that they would be exempt from a required course in college. Therefore, only high-achieving students who were expecting to attend college were taking the class. The topics used in this study, the Gulf of Tonkin Incident and the resultant Gulf of Tonkin Resolution, were on the advanced placement exam, but students had not yet studied the incident and resolution in class.

Of these 44 students, 18 students worked in groups. Students were randomly assigned to groups. These groups were used for a study of students' interactions around texts (Hynd, Stahl, Britton, & McNish, 1996). As will be discussed later, these students were included in the analysis of mental models but not in the analysis of note taking, since their note taking was not independent. Six students' notes and final products were not analyzable for a variety of reasons, such as not following instructions. Only 20 of the remaining students produced notes, and these were used in the analysis of note taking. Sixteen students produced analyzable final products; four others produced notes but not analyzable final products. The analyses reflect these differing numbers.

This study was conducted in January, before the students' history teacher began preparing these classes for the document-based question on the advanced placement examination. Thus, these students had not yet had direct instruction in how to integrate information across documents. Instead, the teacher used primarily a lecture mode, believing that "History is a story." The teacher was widely regarded as an excellent history teacher, with high percentages of students passing the advanced placement examination.

Materials

Background Questionnaire

The background questionnaire asked students their political affiliation and their parents' political affiliation. It asked them whether they were liberal, conservative, or moderate on matters of national defense, the economy, and social issues. It also asked them about their stance on certain current affairs and issues debated in public forum, asked them to rate their knowledge of the Vietnam War, and asked them to describe their feelings about what was important to study in history. Finally, the questionnaire asked students to rate the U.S. Congress, U.S. newspapers, the President of the United States, army generals, historians, and history textbooks for their trustworthiness.

Prior Knowledge Writing Task

In addition to the questions on the background questionnaire about students' knowledge of the Vietnam War, we included two additional measures of participants' prior knowledge. The first was an open-ended writing task. We asked the students to "Please write down everything you know about your assigned topic. If you are not sure, then write down what you think you know." This task was scored for number of accurate knowledge statements and expressed as a percentage of accurate to total number of statements. We used this measure only to interpret individual differences in note taking.

Gulf of Tonkin Relationships Task

The final measure of prior knowledge was a relationships task, used by Britton and Gulgoz (1991). In this task, students were asked to rate the strength of the relationship between all possible pairs of 10 key words or phrases—the Gulf of Tonkin Resolution, the Gulf of Tonkin, North Vietnam, South Vietnam, U.S. Congress, President Johnson, Vietnam War, U.S. Forces, Defense, and Aggression. This task was given before any of the reading, as a pretest, and after each reading was completed, as a measure of growth as a result of that reading.

Students rated the pairs on a 1 to 6 scale with 1 being *not very related* and 6 being *strongly related*. The purpose for this task was to determine the coherence (or harmony) of students' mental models before they read texts and as a result of reading. We expected students to have a more coherent way of rating the pairs after having read texts, and we were interested in whether students would evidence steady growth in coherence or whether one or more texts were responsible for more coherent rating than other texts.

The measuring of harmony is described in Britton and Gulgoz (1991) and is expressed in the form of a decimal. For example, a harmony value of 1.00 would mean that an individual had rated the relationships between pairs in such a way that there were no conflicts between ideas. A harmony value of .50, however, would mean that there was a moderate degree of contradiction in the way the pairs were rated. If a student rated the Gulf of Tonkin Resolution and President Johnson as strongly related, and Aggression and President Johnson as strongly related, but Aggression and the Gulf of Tonkin Resolution as not very related, the person's mental model of those three items would be considered inharmonious. As students learn, they sort out internal contradictions between different ideas and begin to generate stable relationships between ideas. A good mental model would have high internal consistency; low internal consistency would indicate some confusion.

Texts

Students read multiple texts presented on Hypercard stacks on Macintosh computers. Computers were used to provide an orderly environment for the exploration of the texts. The computers were also used to provide online help, such as identification of key people and short biographical information about the author.

Before reading any of the texts, students viewed a map showing Vietnam and the Tonkin Gulf and read a one-and-one-half-card background information statement that described in objective terms the Gulf of Tonkin Incidents and resultant resolution. This background text provided an overview of the Vietnam War and the Gulf of Tonkin Incidents' role in that war. It was written to be neutral in terms of the two questions that were posed, providing just the facts that were verified in all selections. The text is reproduced in Appendix 20.1.

After they had read the background information, students were directed to a screen with two buttons, one directing them to documents concerning the incident and one directing them to documents concerning the resolution. They were to refer to their assignment sheets to see which question they were supposed to address. Clicking on a button led to a menu that presented the titles of their assigned readings. Students could browse the readings before deciding which ones to actually read. Because we wanted this task to be as natural as possible, we did not control the order of readings.

Six readings were about the Gulf of Tonkin Incident and five were about the Gulf of Tonkin Resolution. We chose the topics because they have been hotly debated by historians and politicians. Different interpretations of the event and resolution exist, allowing us to choose texts that represented several perspectives. It was the integration of various perspectives that the researchers wished to study. The texts chosen represented a blend of primary to tertiary sources that were as evenly distributed as possible in terms of their stances. The texts are listed in Table 20.1.

Because part of the focus of the study was to see which documents students would choose, we included texts to represent a span of possible documents that might be used to study this incident. About one-half of the texts we judged to be prowar and half antiwar. We included histories (*Vietnam: A History* by Stanley Karnow and *The Pentagon Papers*), newspaper opinion papers, autobiographies of participants (Commander James Stockdale and Dean Rusk), original documents (the text of the Gulf of Tonkin Resolution and the telegram sent from the North Vietnamese protesting the earlier raids in the Gulf), and secondary sources. We wanted to make sure that all viewpoints were represented and that students had a choice of different genres and styles of documents. We also used the information from a pilot study (Stahl & Hynd, 1994), choosing texts students rated as highly believable and those rated less believable.

As students read the texts, they had several options for help. For one, students could find out information about the author of the text. This information was basic, including the source of the document (newspaper, book, etc.) and the author's position (writer, former army colonel, Secretary of State, etc.). Further, if they put the cursor on selected vocabulary (mostly people and organizations), background information appeared on the screen. Students could also search for a keyword by choosing the FIND button and typing in the word for which they were searching. They could take notes on the computer if they wished (although only three tried and all decided against it), and, finally, they could move freely backwards and forwards within and across texts.

Note Taking Option

While students read each text, they could take notes, if they wished, on paper provided in their packet. Although they were not required to take notes, researchers and written directions explained to them that they could use these notes for the final writing task but could not refer to the actual readings.

Evaluation Sheet

We asked students to answer these questions about each text: (a) What do you feel the author's purpose was in writing this? (b) How useful would this be to help you learn about the origins of the Vietnam War? (rated from *Not Very*, 1, to *Very*, 6); (c) How unbiased do you think this account is? (also rated from 1, *Not Very*, to 6, *Very*); (d) How difficult was this text to read? (1 to 6 rating); and (e) How interesting was this text? (1 to 6 rating). Students answered these questions before engaging in the free recall task.

TABLE 20.1. Texts Used in the Study

Name of text	Brief synopsis
Gulf of Tonkin incidents	
Text of telegram written by North Vietnamese to protest the mission of the *U.S.S. Maddox*	North Vietnamese call upon South Vietnamese to stop aggressive raids. Explain that U.S. ships were seen as aiding those raids.
Another Gulf, Another Blip On the Screen	An eyewitness account by James Stockdale, America's highest-ranking prisoner of war during the Vietnam War. He was flying over the Gulf of Tonkin and did not see a torpedo attack.
The Pentagon Papers	The official history of the event written shortly following the incident. It said that the Gulf of Tonkin Incidents were clearly aggressive acts on the part of the North Vietnamese.
Secrets of the Vietnam War	An excerpt from a privately published book written by a retired army colonel, claiming that the North Vietnamese were primarily responsible for the incident and that the U.S. was not overly aggressive.
"The Tonkin Gulf Crisis"	An editorial analysis claiming that the Gulf of Tonkin Incidents were largely trumped up by the United States as a way to widen the Vietnam conflict.
Vietnam: A History by Stanley Karnow	An in-depth historical analysis that explained the events leading up to the U.S.'s interpretation of the Gulf of Tonkin Incidents that resulted in the Gulf of Tonkin Resolution and ultimate widening of the Vietnam conflict.
Gulf of Tonkin resolution	
The Tonkin Gulf Resolution	A copy of the actual resolution as voted on by Congress.
"The Vote that Congress Can't Forget"	A newspaper article that described members of Congress' retrospective thoughts about the Gulf of Tonkin Resolution as they voted to allow the President to attack the Persian Gulf. Most of the congressmen said they regretted voting for the Resolution and that they didn't realize the effect it would have.
The Vietnam Hearings	Text taken from the Congressional Record describing Senator Fulbright's celebrated hearings where U.S. involvement in Vietnam was discredited. Dean Rusk, Senator Fulbright, and others were attempting to decide if spending more money on Vietnam was justified.
As I Saw It	An excerpt from Dean Rusk's autobiography that attempted to exonerate both the President and himself from accusations that they had acted hastily in their decision to escalate the war after the Gulf of Tonkin Incidents.
Vietnam: A History	Same text as for Gulf of Tonkin Incidents.

Free Recall Task

This task directed students to "Write down all the information you can remember from reading this text. Do not refer to your notes or the text before or during writing. Be as complete as possible." Students engaged in this activity after reading each of the texts.

Final Writing Task

We gave students a final writing task that mirrored their assigned purposes for reading. If students had been assigned to read in order to form an opinion about either the Gulf of Tonkin Incident or the Gulf of Tonkin Resolution, they were asked to write about their opinions. If students had been assigned to read in order to describe the Gulf of Tonkin Incident or the Gulf of Tonkin Resolution, they were asked to write a description. We gave students 30 minutes in class to complete this activity. All students finished before the 30 minutes were up.

Procedure

Students who participated in the study met for 3 days in the computer room that was part of their school library. The librarian had equipped the room with 15 Macintosh SE30 desktop computers. As students came into the room on the first day of the study, the researchers handed each one a folder that included questionnaires, written directions for completing the study, and an introduction that assigned them to a topic and a purpose for reading. Researchers distributed these folders in a stratified fashion to students upon entry, resulting in random assignment. Four conditions represented two purposes and two topics. We asked students to read either to (a) form an opinion about the topic or (b) be able to describe the topic. We also told students that they would engage in a writing task related to their purpose for reading at the end of the study. Finally, we asked students to read texts about (a) the Gulf of Tonkin Incidents or (b) the Gulf of Tonkin Resolution. For these topics, students could choose six and five texts, respectively.

Students filled out the background questionnaires, read the introduction that explained their task, wrote down everything they already knew about the topic they were assigned, completed the Gulf of Tonkin relationships task used as a pretest, and read the instructions for accessing the texts from the computer screen while one of us explained those directions out loud and answered questions. All students were familiar with the computers and with using the mouse so that they did not need basic directions for managing the computer. The researcher told students that they could read the texts in any order they wished, and that they could take notes if they wished. After they had completed reading each text they were to write a free recall without looking back to the text they had just read, complete the Gulf of Tonkin relationships task, and fill out a questionnaire about the text.

We did not allow students to look back because we wanted to assess ongoing learning rather than the strategic use of text. After completing those tasks, students could then proceed to their next chosen text. Students started reading on the first day of the experiment, read through the 50-minute period on the second day, and stopped reading on the third day, approximately 30 minutes before the end of the period.

After students stopped reading, we told them to read the directions for their writing task and to follow those directions. The directions asked students to state their opinion about either the Gulf of Tonkin Incident or the Gulf of Tonkin Resolution, or they asked students to describe the Gulf of Tonkin Incident or the Gulf of Tonkin Resolution. We allowed them to consult their notes if they wished but did not allow them to return to the actual texts on the computer screen while they were writing.

Analysis of Notes and Final Products

Because we were interested in identifying processes that students used as they read each text and then formed an essay incorporating some or all of the texts they had read, we developed a format for recording the notes, text, and idea units from the essay so that their correspondences could easily be seen. A sample can be found in Appendix 20.2. We divided pages into three columns, one for the text, one for the notes, and one for the essay. In the middle column, we wrote down the notes (in idea units), in the order in which they were taken. In the left-hand column, we recorded the section of the corresponding text. Although our judgment was sometimes needed to determine the textual basis for the notes, this task was relatively easy to perform because students generally took notes in the same linear order in which they read the text. Further, the majority of their notes were paraphrases or copying of the text. We also recorded idea units from the free recalls in this column, using the same procedures. The free recalls were clearly marked as such so that they would not be analyzed as notes.

In the right-hand column, we recorded idea units from the final essay next to corresponding notes or text. Because the essay was an incorporation of several different texts, sometimes these idea units were recorded in several different places. If no corresponding note or text was found, we placed the idea unit at the end of the third column. Again, we used judgment in deciding whether or not an idea unit represented an idea taken from notes or text. We tried to be inclusive; that is, if there was a possibility that students may have had a certain text in mind when they made the statement, we placed it accordingly.

After each student's notes and essay had been recorded in this manner, three researchers read all protocols. We divided each text into idea units, which were defined as single pieces of information. Usually, there was one idea unit per sentence. However, some sentences contained more than one idea unit, and, of course, students did not always write complete sentences. We had a 95% agreement in breaking protocols into idea units.

We then created a system for categorizing idea units for the notes, free recalls, and essays. The system was not developed with an *a priori* set of categories. Instead, the categories emerged from the data (Glaser & Strauss, 1967). We were also concerned about the reliability of the categories and the replicability of these categories. To develop this system, three of the five authors read through the protocols and discussed what we felt they revealed about what the students were doing as they were taking notes and creating their final products. We attempted to codify these processes into a system that could be reliably used to categorize the processes we found. We went through a number of different systems before we found an approach that we could apply with greater than 90% interrater reliability and that seemed to produce useful interpretations of the data. This categorization system is described below.

We classified each idea unit as (a) copying, (b) paraphrasing, (c) reducing, (d) making a gist, (e) evaluating, or (f) distortion/misreading. We classified an idea unit as *copying* if it was word for word or nearly word for word with close synonym replacement or minimal reordering. An example of copying is when the text said, "Gulf of Tonkin Resolution passed by the Congress on 7 August 1964," and the notes said, "Gulf of Tonkin Resolution—August 7, 1964 passed by Congress."

Paraphrasing was a more radical replacement of words that included within-sentence reduction or elaboration. An example of a paraphrase is when the text said, "Vietnamese coastal targets—this time the Rhon River Estuary and the Vinh Sonh radar installation, which were bombarded on the night of 3 August," and the notes said, "On the night of August 3, Vietnamese coastal targets were bombarded."

We described *reducing* as a summarization process across two or more sentences, so that the writing contained markedly fewer words and details than the original. An example of reducing is when the text said, "At 1940 hours, 4 August 1964 (Tonkin Gulf time) while 'proceeding S.E. at best speed,' Task Group 72.1 (Maddox and Turner Joy) radioed 'RCVD INFO' indicating attack by PGM P-4 imminent," and later "Just before this, one of the PT boats launched a torpedo, which was later reported as seen passing about 300 feet off the port beam, from aft to forward, of the C. Turner Joy." The notes merely said, "On 4 Aug 1964, the Maddox & Turner Joy were attacked by PT boats, who launched a torpedo."

We described *making a gist* as radical reduction in which nouns were replaced with superordinates or more general terms. We noted that gists were often blanket statements that were more topical in nature than reductions, such as, "the text was about the resolution," or made blanket interpretations of details, such as "LBJ uses attack to get control of Congress," when several paragraphs had described the President's dealings with Congress in getting the resolution passed.

We described *evaluating* as stating an opinion about the ideas in the text that were not merely the copied opinion of authors or the opinion of people the authors described. For example, we classified the statement "Johnson was an idiot" as an evaluation.

We described *distortion/misreading* as being either inaccurate textual interpretations or statements that, although not evaluative, were simply not found in the text. An example of a misreading is when the notes said, "South Vietnam mistakes U.S. for South Vietnamese ship," but the text said that the North Vietnamese mistook the Maddox for a South Vietnamese vessel.

As noted earlier, this coding system was developed after much discussion among three of the five authors. After the system was developed, the researchers reached 92% agreement after coding notes on 5 of the 20 protocols. From that point, the researchers coded the remaining notes and free recalls separately.

Analysis of Final Essay

We read the final essays and coded idea units as coming from a single text or two or more texts. If a significant number of statements had come from two or more texts, we assumed that students were either integrating ideas across texts or paying attention to information that was repeated across texts. We also coded each idea unit as being copied, a paraphrase, a reduction, a gist, an evaluation, or a misreading, as we did with the notes and free recalls. The purpose of this categorization process was to analyze what processes students were using to form a coherent essay.

In addition, we noted the order of statements in relation to the order of the texts they read and performed Kendall's Coefficient of Concordance (W) to obtain a measure of the overall agreement in order. This coefficient helped us decide whether students were radically restructuring ideas or merely reporting them in the form in which they were first perceived. A low W indicated that students were reordering from the texts in the final product. A high W indicated that they were generally preserving information in the order that they had read it.

Finally, we calculated a ratio of information found in the text to that which could not be found in the text. This ratio would reveal whether students were sticking to the task of describing or stating their opinions, as they were assigned. It would also reveal whether students who were asked to state opinions would back up these opinions with factual information.

Sourcing, Corroboration, and Contextualization

Wineburg (1991a, 1991b) observed that historians used (a) sourcing (looking first at the source of the document before reading the text itself to consider how the bias of the source might have affected the content of the document), (b) corroboration (comparing and contrasting documents with one another), and (c) contextualization (situating a text in a temporal and spatial context to consider how the time or place in which the document was written might have affected its content or the perspective taken) when thinking about information in the texts they read, while students used these to a lesser degree, if at all.

In this study, we looked for instances of sourcing, corroboration, and contextualization in the notes, in the free recalls, and in the final essays. Sourcing was indicated by an explicit reference to the author or source, corroboration was indicated by a reference to another text in the series, and contextualization was indicated by an explicit reference to the time that the article was written. Because we counted only explicit references in the text, this may have underestimated the amount of sourcing, corroboration, and contextualization that the students were actually doing.

Results and Discussion

Can Students Develop a Rich Mental Model of a Historical Event?

The data from the relationships task were used to track how students developed a mental model of the events surrounding the Gulf of Tonkin Incident and the Gulf of Tonkin Resolution. We took two approaches to examining the development of a mental model. First, we examined the growth of harmony, which we used as a proxy for the internal consistency of the mental model developed by the students. Second, we compared the structures generated by the students to those of experts in order to trace the growth of students' mental models toward those held by experts.

Harmony. The harmony ratings (using Kintsch's 1986 system [cited in Britton & Gulgoz, 1991] of calculating those ratings) are shown in Tables 20.2 and 20.3. This

TABLE 20.2. Harmony Levels

	Read 1 text	Read 2 texts	Read 3 texts
Pretest	.67	.67	.71
Text 1	.70		
Text 2		.76*	
Text 3			.81*

* Probability of difference between last reading and pretest, $p < .05$. Different numbers of subjects read different numbers of texts.

analysis included all 44 students. Some students worked alone and some in groups. We analyzed these two sets of students separately. The results were indistinguishable, so the two sets were combined for the analysis presented here.

As noted on Table 20.2, there was a significant growth in harmony from the pretest to the second reading, and from the pretest to the third reading. The growth in harmony after the first reading was not statistically reliable. Comparing the growth in harmony after each reading, only the difference in harmony between the first and second reading was statistically significant. There was a further small increase in harmony after a third reading. This difference was low (.79 vs..81). This finding suggests that a student needs to read at least two different texts to develop a coherent mental model and that the majority of the growth occurs with two readings, but not much occurs after that.

To examine the effects of individual texts on the growth of harmony, we examined the gains in harmony from their prereading ratings after students read each of the texts (see Table 20.3). Of the 10 texts we used, only the section from the history text, *Vietnam: A History*, produced a significant gain in harmony by itself. This might be expected, since it was the longest and most detailed text we used.

Expert Ratings. Another way to examine mental models is to compare the structures generated by the students with the structures generated by experts. We assume that knowledge consists of knowledge of relations among concepts, and that, as a

TABLE 20.3. Harmony after Reading Specific Texts

Text read	Resulting harmony
Pretest	.67
The Pentagon Papers	.72
Secrets of the Vietnam War	.71
"The Tonkin Gulf Crisis"	.75
Another Gulf	.78
Text of telegram	.71
Vietnam: A History	.81*
The Vietnam Hearings	.77
As I Saw It	.79
"The Vote that Congress Can't Forget"	.75
The Gulf of Tonkin Resolution	.74

* $p < .05$.

person's knowledge grows, his or her knowledge of the relations among concepts will resemble that of experts. We used three expert raters to generate structures, using the same terms and procedures that we used with the students.

The first rater was the students' high school teacher, an experienced history teacher. The second rater was an amateur military history buff who read extensively about the war in Vietnam. The third rater was one of the authors of this study, who had majored in history, taken graduate-level courses, and read the documents thoroughly and responded to the task based on her reading of the texts.

We chose these raters rather than studied experts on the Vietnam War because they represented the expertise that we wanted our students to have. There was not enough information in the texts to allow the students to obtain as full a representation of the events in Vietnam as a scholar would. Because these tasks focused on a small incident embedded in a larger context, it would be unrealistic to compare the knowledge obtained from these readings to that of scholars who were immersed in the larger context. The level of expertise that our raters had was about that which could be reasonably expected on this task.

All three experts tended to cluster the terms around two axes, one separating the terms *Aggression* and *Defense* and the other roughly separating terms into *domestic* (U.S. Congress, U.S. Forces, etc.) and *foreign* (North Vietnam, South Vietnam, Gulf of Tonkin, etc.). Experts tended to have a strong separation between Aggression and Defense and clustered the other terms in the middle, roughly equidistant between these two poles.

A gain in knowledge would be evidenced by an increase in the students' correlation of their mental structure with that of the experts. Examining these correlations, shown in Table 20.4, there was a significant growth in knowledge after the first reading, but no significant gain subsequently. The initial correlations between the students and the individual experts ranged from .15 to .29, and initial correlation between the students and the composite was .26. These are small and not statistically reliable, suggesting that the students' initial knowledge was low and essentially random. The gain to .42, a moderate correlation, suggests that students learned some of the initial relationships after a single reading. Since subsequent readings tended to view the same facts from different perspectives, it is not surprising that there was little gain from these readings. There is also some evidence, as will be discussed below, that students read the first reading more closely than subsequent readings.

In contrast with the experts, students tended to cluster North Vietnam, Gulf of Tonkin, and the Gulf of Tonkin Resolution with Aggression, and South Vietnam,

TABLE 20.4. Correlations with Expert Raters

	Correlation with average of three experts	r with Expert 1	r with Expert 2	r with Expert 3
Pretest	.26	.21	.15	.29
After text 1	.42*	.33*	.26*	.41*
After text 2	.36*	.28	.23*	.37*
After text 3	.43*	.33*	.30*	.41*
After text 4	.38	.33*	.23	.35

* Correlation significantly different from pretest $p < .05$.

U.S. Force, and U.S. Congress with Defense. This may reflect a different world view than that of our experts, who all lived through the Vietnam era. These students tended to see the United States and its allies in a positive light and its enemies in a negative light. In contrast, the experts tended to view both sides in a more balanced regard, as neither side being more defensive or aggressive than the other.

One explanation for the lack of growth after a first reading may be in the nature of the texts and the task. We deliberately chose texts that contradict each other. It could be that students would read a first text to get the basic facts. Beyond these basic facts, which were accepted by all authors, were the different interpretations. Students may have ignored these interpretations and thus did not construct an increasingly complex mental model that might get closer to that of the experts. This supposition needs to be tested in a further study.

Background Information. We gave the students an extensive background questionnaire, asking them information such as their political orientation, their parents' political orientation, their views about current events, their views of the reliability of various people and institutions such as Congress, the President, historians, and so on. We found no relation between any of our background variables and students' responses to these measures or any of the other measures. As will be discussed later, we did find that the students with moderate to high knowledge of the Vietnam War took different types of notes than other students.

What Do Students Do with the Document Information?

As noted previously, we attempted to follow the flow of ideas from each document through the notes to inclusion in the final product. This model suggests that students initially selected ideas from the text as they were reading, deciding which ideas were important and which were not. They may have made a note of a selected idea, copying it, paraphrasing, reducing two or three sentences, or reducing a paragraph or more into a single gist statement. They may also have noted an opinion or reaction to information in the text. In producing the final product, they used similar operations, with ideas from a single text or ideas combined or repeated from multiple texts. These analyses used only those 20 students who worked individually and availed themselves of the notetaking option.

Choosing Texts. The excerpts from two texts—*Vietnam: A History* and *Secrets of the Vietnam War*—were chosen by more students to be read first than any other texts. Each was chosen by about one-third of the subjects; the remaining texts were chosen by the remaining third of the subjects. We speculated that the history was chosen because it seemed to provide an overview, and because students would perceive it as neutral in tone. We do not know why the *Secrets* text was so popular. It seemed to be an important source of information in the students' final products as well.

Selecting Information. When reading a text, students must first select which information is important. Given that these were natural texts, they varied considerably in how well they were constructed. Two texts were especially poorly constructed. *The Pentagon Papers*, for example, is a detailed history of the Vietnam War, written for internal purposes by the Army, and contains many gaps (indicated by a notation reading "Several Paragraphs Missing"). The text was written by and for bureaucrats and is highly inconsiderate of the reader (Anderson & Armbruster, 1984). *The Vietnam Hearings* are a transcript of the hearings, written in a play format. Other texts were written for different purposes than those given to our participants. Commander Stockdale's account used his experiences in the Tonkin Gulf to comment on the unreliability of radar data in a more recent incident. The difficulties of using naturally occurring documents is that the student has to cull through a great deal of irrelevant information to find what is important.

There were differences among documents in how consistent students were in selecting information. We recorded how many students annotated each statement in each of the texts and looked for patterns. In some documents, students tended to select the same idea units in their notes. These tended to be shorter and more focused documents. The statements themselves tended to be clear statements, strongly stating an opinion about the incident or the resolution. For example, seven of the nine students who read "The Tonkin Gulf Crisis" annotated the statement "The accumulated evidence makes it reasonably certain that the alleged North Vietnamese PT boat attack of Aug. 4 was a figment of the U.S. government's imagination." Two other statements were annotated by five students and another by four. In other documents, students diverged widely in terms of what information they selected. In *The Pentagon Papers*, one statement was annotated by four of the six students who read it. ("Upon first report of the PT boats' apparently hostile intent, F-8E aircraft were launched from the aircraft carrier Ticonderoga, many miles to the south, with instructions to provide aid cover but not to fire unless they or the Maddox were fired upon.") Fifty-three statements in total were annotated, but no other statement was noted by more than half of those reading. Few students read *The Vietnam Hearings*, the other text we judged to be poorly structured.

Thus, it appears that the nature of the text affected how students selected information. Students tended to be more consistent in what information they selected from short, well-constructed texts. In these texts, they tended to choose strong, clear statements of a position. In *The Pentagon Papers* excerpt, a longer, less well-structured text, students chose many different statements, with only one statement chosen by more than half of those who read it.

However, students rarely chose irrelevant information. In the Stockdale article, no student mentioned the current incident, annotating only information dealing with the Gulf of Tonkin Incident. In *The Vote that Congress Can't Forget*, which looked back on the Gulf of Tonkin Resolution by contrasting it with the authorization of the Persian Gulf War, only two students annotated information dealing with the Persian Gulf War. Thus, students seemed good at filtering out information they did not need.

Does the Task the Students Are Given, Describing an Event or Forming an Opinion about That Event, Influence their Processing of Information?

Notetaking. We hypothesized that the task, either describing or forming an opinion, would affect processing, as evidenced by the notes they took. Students given a task of describing would concentrate more on details in their notes and might include more copying and paraphrasing. Students asked to form an opinion might reduce larger chunks of text into main idea statements and might include more statements classified as reduction or gist in their notes.

Of the students who took notes, 11 were asked for an opinion and 9 were asked to describe either the incident or the resolution. We examined the differences using discriminant analysis, a fairly sensitive multivariate analysis technique. Neither this analysis nor other appropriate analyses found significant differences between either those given different tasks or those given different topics.

The lack of differences is surprising, because we expected that students asked to form an opinion would concentrate on more global information and construct more gist statements and evaluative statements, and students asked to describe the incident would concentrate on details and copy more information directly or in paraphrase. Even those asked for an opinion included few evaluative statements. Of the 11 students asked for an opinion, 1 student (#43) made nine evaluative statements; 1 other (#21) made four; 2 students made one apiece.

The student who made considerably more evaluation comments than the others, #43, indicated that he had relatively high knowledge of the Vietnam War on the pretest and many of his comments reflect that knowledge. For example, his evaluative comments tended to reflect a strong bias such as "That U.S. was not wrong in firing on the Vietnamese/and that Vietnamese started War./ Johnson's an idiot" and "So it sounds like it's a bunch of idiots playing with their guns." This bias appeared to be based on foreknowledge, rather than developed through reading. This student also read through all six texts in the time allotted for the study, the only student to read this many.

There were strong individual variations in how students approached the task. Some students took copious, detailed notes, no matter which task they were assigned. As noted on Table 20.5, three students asked to write a description (#12, #19 and #28) copied or paraphrased a great deal of information, as did #18, who was asked to form an opinion. Others tended to write gist statements, condensing a great deal of information into brief, even telegraphic, notes, such as #43 (opinion) and #29 (description).

The order of the texts also seemed to affect how many notes were taken. A repeated measures analysis of variance, looking only at the first three text readings, found a statistically significant difference among readings, $F (2, 32) = 9.07$, $p < .001$. Students averaged taking 11 notes for the first text, 5 for the second text read, and 7 for the third. The greater amount of notes taken for the first text may indicate that more effort was expended in reading the first text. Recall that only after the first text was read did students make statistically significant growth toward the experts' knowledge structures. There appeared to be little effect of task or topic on readings of the different texts.

How Do Students Integrate Information across Texts to Form a Coherent Essay?

Free Recall. Students were more likely to reduce and make gist statements in the free recalls than in the notes, regardless of whether they were asked to write a description or form an opinion. This behavior seems reasonable, in that students were relying on memory and were not able to easily paraphrase information in the texts. It also argues for the idea that students processed information in similar ways, regardless of the final task.

TABLE 20.5. Note Taking of Individual Subjects

Task	Topic	Copying	Paraphrasing	Reducing	Making a gist	Evaluating	Distortion/ misreading	Total	Number of texts read
6 Opinion	Incident	1	12	2	2	0	0	17	4
12 Description	Incident	17	20	7	0	0	4	48	3
16 Opinion	Incident	15	4	2	0	1	0	22	4
18 Opinion	Incident	11	17	3	0	0	0	31	4
19 Description	Resolution	17	10	2	0	0	2	31	3
21 Opinion	Incident	10	4	0	3	4	2	23	4
23 Description	Resolution	1	2	0	2	0	0	5	4
26 Opinion	Incident	0	0	0	5	0	1	6	3
27 Description	Resolution	7	12	0	3	1	0	23	2
28 Description	Incident	24	21	2	2	2	1	5	2
29 Description	Incident	11	8	0	21	2	1	43	4
30 Opinion	Resolution	3	21	3	1	0	0	28	4
31 Opinion	Resolution	2	7	3	8	0	0	20	4
33 Description	Resolution	0	1	0	0	0	0	1	4
34 Description	Incident	14	7	3	3	0	0	27	5
37 Description	Resolution	2	10	2	3	0	0	17	2
40 Opinion	Resolution	1	10	1	3	1	4	20	3
41 Opinion	Incident	6	0	0	0	0	0	6	6
42 Opinion	Resolution	12	2	5	3	0	0	22	5
43 Opinion	Incident	7	14	12	18	9	1	61	6

Final Product. On the final product, students tended to stick to the task. As can be seen in Table 20.6, the students who were asked to describe engaged more in paraphrasing, reducing, and making overarching gist statements from a particular text than did students who were asked to form an opinion. Students who were asked to form an opinion rarely paraphrased or reduced. Rather, their final essays were replete with evaluative/gist statements such as, "I believe that the U.S. was too quick to pass the Tonkin Gulf Resolution." These statements can only be seen as conclusions reached from reading more than one text, although evidence backing up these statements was scanty at best. Note the low number of paraphrased statements or reductions relating to either one text or a combination of texts. These types of statements would count as evidence backing up their opinions. Interestingly, student #29, who wrote many gist statements in his notetaking despite the fact that he was asked to write a description, stuck to description when he composed his essay. And many students who mostly copied or paraphrased their notes despite the fact that they were asked to write an opinion, wrote opinion-like statements when they composed their essays.

TABLE 20.6. Processes Used in Final Product

	Paraphrasing (single text)	Reducing (single text)	Making a gist (single text)	Paraphrasing (multiple texts)	Reducing (multiple texts)	Making a gist (multiple texts)
Opinion	.07	.00	.03	.01	.05	.60
	(.07)	(.00)	(.07)	(.04)	(.08)	(.24)
Description	.20	.13	.22	.10	.07	.23
	(.16)	(.13)	(.27)	(.13)	(.08)	(.22)

Note. Numbers are mean percentages. Standard deviations in parentheses.

Students who were asked to write an opinion tended to move away from the text, toward broader generalities and statements without providing much apparent factual grounding from the texts read. Even though they had indicated a depth of reading through their notes, their final products seemed to disregard that depth. For example, student # 6 wrote:

> (1) *My opinion is that the USS Maddox did get attacked by the North Vietnamese the first time (2) but was not attacked in the second "incident."* (3) The reason for the first attack was that the North Vietnamese thought the Maddox was a South Vietnamese ship (4) and since the South had attacked the night before they defended themselves. (5) Later on the South Vietnamese attacked the North Vietnamese again. (6) The Maddox was again patrolling (7) and the US government thought prematurely that the North Vietnamese would once again attack. (8) *The US government reacted. (9) I'm not sure if Johnson lied or what happened. (10) In my opinion, something wrong happened. It sounds like it might have been the US fault. (11) It might be this because several of the texts said the same thing.* (12) That nothing was out there when the Maddox and the Turner Joy were patrolling. (13) *I am not sure exactly why the USA would do this. (14) They might not have.* (italics and numbering added)

This student had taken notes throughout the text, but half of his statements (italics) could not be reconciled directly with any one of the texts that he read. Rather, he appeared to look at the texts in a global fashion. The task of giving his opinion was viewed as being disassociated from obtaining evidence from the text to support that opinion. The first statement is a clear thesis statement; the following statements do support that thesis. However, by the eighth statement ("The US government reacted."), he gets vague and speaks in generalities, ending in confusion. This may be because of lack of experience with writing coherent texts using an argument structure or because he is still confused by the contradictory texts and has not yet examined the evidence to form an opinion.

As might be expected, the description texts tended to stay closer to the readings. Students provided few evaluative statements. An example would be that of student #28:

> (1) The Tonkin gulf incident occurred due to a series of events such as the first battle in which the Maddox was legitimately involved in (due to the attack made by the North Vietnamese). (2) The second battle which some feel never really happened because no one actually saw any PT boats, also had a large effect on the Tonkin gulf situation. (3) It led to Congress passing of the Tonkin gulf Resolution, the retaliatory acts wanted by the Sec. of Def. and other officials that were allowed by President Johnson. (4) These things combined led to the N. Vietnamese feeling that war would occur in the South and moved troops down the Ho Chi Minh trail, resulting in what would possibly be interpreted by US officials as aggression. (Numbers added)

Statements 2 and 3 were supported by three references apiece in the text. The fourth statement was supported by a section in "The Tonkin Gulf Crisis," the last text read. However, this student took copious notes, and very little of the information in his 52 annotations were actually used in this short essay.

Integration. Students did appear to use more than one source of information in forming their final essays, and they engaged in rearranging ideas from single texts as they wrote. To examine how students integrated information across texts, we did two analyses. First, we categorized each statement in the text as to whether it had one source in the readings or whether the idea could be found in multiple readings. (This may have overestimated the number of statements classified as coming from multiple readings, since we categorized an idea as coming from multiple readings whether or not that idea appeared in the students' notes in two places.) We found that students asked to write an opinion tended to use more ideas that came from multiple texts (64% of statements) than students asked to write a description (40% of statements). Students asked to write descriptions used more ideas that could only be found in a single text (55% of statements) than students asked for opinions (10% of statements). (Totals do not add up to 100% due to rounding. Framing and evaluative statements are also not classified here.)

Next, we looked at the ordering of ideas in the texts read and in the final product, using only those ideas that could be identified with a single text. We compared the order of the statements in the final product with the order of those statements in the texts the students read, in the order in which they read them. We used Kendall's Coefficient of Concordance (*W*), a measure of interrater reliability, to compare the different orderings. If students had merely written ideas from the texts in the order in which they were presented, the mean Coefficient of Concordance would have been 1.00. However, the mean of the total final essays was .76, and the range was between .38 and 1.00. Most of the participants made few or moderate changes in how the texts were used in the essay compared to how they were read. Only 2 of the 16 students made drastic reorganizations. There was essentially no difference in the coefficients of the students who were to write descriptions and the students who were to write opinions. The essays from both groups were coherent, in that they had discernable beginnings, middles, and endings.

These results argue for the idea that some students reading multiple texts are able to form a more elaborate network of ideas, in that they seem to be integrating information across multiple sources. For example, Subject #25, whose protocol is reproduced in Appendix 20.2, began his essay with a thesis statement, "President Johnson was definitely justified when he asked Congress to pass the Resolution." His next sentence, "He saw that North Vietnamese were being hostile toward the South Vietnamese, American allies," seemed to draw from two sections of the Resolution as well as two sections of Dean Rusk's autobiographical recollections. The remainder drew from all three sources that he read. The information in the essay was generally not in the same order as the information in the texts, suggesting that he integrated across texts. However, this student was atypical. Most students reproduced ideas nearly in the same order that they read them.

Do Students Engage in Corroborating, Sourcing, and Contextualizing in Evaluating Historical Materials?

As noted on Table 20.7, which contains the number of comments in the notes classified as sourcing, corroboration, or contextualization, few students had comments that could be classified as reflecting the processes used by the historians studied by Wineburg (1991a). What is interesting is that the students who included a great many gist statements also tended to include some sourcing statements. This may reflect the common influence of prior knowledge on both notetaking and critical analysis.

Student #43, who made 18 gist statements, made no references to the source of the documents but made one statement about documents corroborating each other.

TABLE 20.7. Sourcing, Corroboration, and Contextualization, by Subject

ID	Task	Topic	Sourcing	Corroboration	Contextualization
12	Description	Incident	2	0	0
19	Description	Resolution	0	0	0
23	Description	Resolution	1	0	1
27	Description	Resolution	2	0	0
28	Description	Incident	0	0	0
29	Description	Incident	0	2	0
33	Description	Resolution	2	0	0
34	Description	Incident	3	0	0
37	Description	Resolution	0	0	0
6	Opinion	Incident .	0	0	0
16	Opinion	Incident	2	0	0
18	Opinion	Incident	0	0	0
21	Opinion	Incident	4	1	0
26	Opinion	Incident	1	0	0
30	Opinion	Resolution	0	0	0
31	Opinion	Resolution	0	0	1
40	Opinion	Resolution	3	1	0
41	Opinion	Incident	0	0	1
42	Opinion	Resolution	10	0	2
43	Opinion	Incident	0	1	0

Student #29 made 21 gist statements and 2 corroborative statements (but only 2 evaluative statements).

Student #42, who included 10 statements dealing with the source of the documents, wrote short, telegraphic notes, copying a key phrase ("America keeps her word") to stand for a larger idea. These were classified as copying in our system, since he used the same words as the text, but is closer to gist than other students' copying. This student wrote a lot of notes, covering five texts. His notes tended to be telegraphic, using just a few words to cover the main ideas. He began staying closer to the text, mainly paraphrasing in the first two texts he read. In his recall, he produced global statements about the text, such as "This text was basically dialogue that outlined how the Senate felt about the current situation in the Gulf of Tonkin" (notes on *The Vietnam Hearings* excerpt). We also classified this as sourcing, since it makes reference to the text, but this is not sourcing in the same sense that Wineburg suggests. Instead, he refers to the text and the participants, not from foreknowledge of their roles, but instead as placeholders representing sides.

These three students (#29, #42, and #43) indicated that they had at least moderately high knowledge of the Vietnam War prior to the readings and could give a reasonably accurate identification of the Tonkin Gulf incident. It may be that some degree of topic knowledge is required to demonstrate sourcing or corroboration, but we did not have enough subjects with moderate or high knowledge to test this statistically. Wineburg (1991a), however, found that even high school students with high amounts of knowledge about the topic he examined (the American Revolution) did not engage in these behaviors as much as historians did, even historians with less factual knowledge. The differences in our findings may result from the different topics. The vast majority of our subjects knew next to nothing about the Vietnam War; all of

Wineburg's subjects (students and historians) could be assumed to have at least moderate knowledge of the American Revolution.

With the exception of #42, the number of sourcing, corroboration, and contextualization comments were a small percentage of the total number of comments. That students included very few comments that would be considered as sourcing, corroboration, or contextualization, as shown in Table 20.7, suggests that they lack the knowledge of the discourse patterns of historical analysis. There were more comments classified as sourcing, which simply involves noting the source, than those classified as corroboration and contextualization, which involve more complex operations—comparing the information in the text with either information in other texts (corroboration) or knowledge that students have about the time (contextualization). The comments classified as sourcing did not use the source to understand the text, as a historian would, but merely noted it.

As Wineburg (1991a) pointed out, professional historians approach the task of reading documents as members of a discourse community, but high school students do not. This was true even for historians who scored lower than high school students on a test of the factual content. The knowledge of discourse patterns represents the disciplinary knowledge of history, or the ability to think as a historian might, and may need to be directly taught.

CONCLUSION

We studied the processing of students who read multiple historical documents about a controversial event in history—the Gulf of Tonkin Incident and the subsequent Gulf of Tonkin Resolution—that led to heavy U.S. involvement in the Vietnam conflict. We wished to understand what happens to students' mental structures when they read more than one text about an incident, particularly when those texts propose alternate interpretations of the event. We also wanted to see if students would employ different strategies for processing the texts if they were given different purposes for reading.

This study was intended to be exploratory. There were a large number of possible variations in the study—students differed in terms of task and topic and also differed in what texts they read and in what order. From our data, we want to propose a possible model of students' processing of multiple texts, based on our interpretation of our data, and then discuss why studying documents alone might not lead to the disciplinary knowledge, as has been proposed by Wineburg (1991a) and others.

Our basic model suggests that we can break the process down into *Selection* of ideas in each text read, *Processing* of ideas within that text, *Constructing* a mental model of the information, and *Integrating* ideas across texts to produce a final product. These will be discussed in turn.

Selection

Our students tended to be strongly influenced by text features in their selection of ideas. Students consistently chose the same ideas to note from short, well-structured texts. These ideas tended to be clear and strong statements of opinion or topic sentences encompassing a great deal of detail. With long and ill-structured texts, such as

The Pentagon Papers, few students chose the same ideas. With such texts, it was difficult to pick main points, since there was so much detail and little attempt at organizing it. Original source documents, however, tend to be more like *The Pentagon Papers* and *The Vietnam Hearings* than like the shorter, more focused pieces. Students need to learn how to cull information from longer documents if they are going to be used in units such as this.

Students, however, were able to concentrate on relevant information. In two pieces written for a purpose different than the purpose given the students, they consistently ignored irrelevant information, focusing instead on information suited to the purpose.

Processing

We found that task had little effect on how students read the information in the different texts. Students asked for an opinion did not differ from those asked for a description in the types of notes they took. There were few evaluative statements given at all, even by those asked for an opinion. Students tended to take many more notes on the first text than on subsequent texts, suggesting that they were expending more cognitive effort in constructing a mental model of the information in the text.

There were, however, strong individual differences in notetaking. Some students tended to take copious, detailed notes, relying on copying and paraphrasing. Others tended to rely on gist statements, noting only main points, often only telegraphically. These differences in notetaking strategy do not seem to be related to the task or which text was read, but seem to be an individual difference.

Constructing

Our analysis of the students' ratings of relatedness among key terms suggests that students' mental structures tend to grow in two ways while reading multiple texts. Students' structures tend to be more internally consistent after reading a single text, and then still more consistent after reading a second text. The history text tended to produce the greatest gains in harmony or internal consistency. Students' structures also tended to become more similar to those of experts after reading a single text, with no further growth after reading two or more texts.

Since we are using similarity to experts as our metric of the growth of knowledge, this suggests that students did not grow in their knowledge after more than one reading, but they did become more consistent in their understandings. This lack of growth (or failure to move closer to the knowledge structure of experts) may be simply because they did not process the subsequent texts as well. There is evidence of a clear decline in notetaking after the first text read.

Another complementary explanation might lie in the nature of the texts read. Because the texts were chosen to contradict each other, students may have looked for overlap between texts rather than for new knowledge. The overlap would reinforce the basic knowledge acquired by reading the first text but might not add very much to the student's understanding. In fact, to be consistent, some contradictory information would have to be ignored. Because the internal consistency of our students increased, we might posit that students were looking for overlap and ignoring this contradictory new information.

Integrating

The task students were given strongly influenced their final product. Students asked for a description tended to stay close to the texts, with most of their statements coming clearly from information provided, usually in a single text. Students asked for an opinion tended to produce more global statements, not clearly tied to any single text, that could be found either in multiple texts or not in any text.

Limitations

Because the study was intended to be naturalistic, we did not control much that one might ordinarily control. Because we let students make decisions about what they did, we had different numbers of students in different analyses. In future studies, first, we need to systematically vary the texts that students read. We wanted to see what would happen if students were given freedom to choose whatever texts they wanted to. We expected to see if there was a pattern to their choice. We need to vary the texts in a principled manner to see how different types of texts—histories, opinions, source information—affect students' learning.

Second, we need to vary background knowledge of our topic. Students' knowledge was uniformly low. A great deal of effort seemed to be expended on constructing a basic understanding of what went on in the Gulf of Tonkin and in the U.S. Senate during the discussion of the Resolution. This may have hampered students in evaluating the information in the texts as we hoped they would.

Third, the problem of the Tonkin Gulf is a problem of perception—which of two clearly contradictory sides is correct? The processes described here might not be found in a less polarized topic, such as the Panama Canal Treaty as studied by Perfetti and his colleagues (1993). We need to compare different types of historical problems to examine their separate effects on students' learning.

It should be noted that the task used differed in at least one important way from that of professional historians. Students were asked to read each paper and recall the information from it. Although students could go back and forth between documents, we had no data about whether they actually did. Historians, on the other hand, read and reread texts. Also, in a more natural setting, students would have had access to the texts in writing their final product.

Thinking Like a Historian Using Multiple Source Documents

Some students did engage in some of the processes described by Wineburg (1991a) as being typical of professional historians—contextualizing, corroborating, and sourcing. This was also an individual difference, with some students doing this frequently. Most did not evidence these processes at all.

For most of these students, though, simply presenting them with multiple texts did not encourage them to think like historians. In fact, the greatest growth of knowledge came after the reading of the first text, and the text that had the greatest influence on growth of harmony was a well-organized history textbook, albeit a text devoted entirely to Vietnam. Students read the first text to get basic facts and information and read subsequent contradictory texts trying to sort out that information.

One reason that many students did not seem to develop disciplinary knowledge from reading multiple texts was their lack of initial knowledge about the topic. Students' initial reliance on the history text and their tendency to take paraphrase-type notes may have been reflections of their need to gain a literal understanding of the content before attempting to produce an opinion. Alexander and Judy (1988) argued that students become able to use more sophisticated strategies for learning new information when they already have some content knowledge. The students we studied may have initially been taking notes in paraphrase fashion because they lacked background knowledge and were reading to gain this knowledge, regardless of the final task they had been assigned. They may not have been sophisticated enough to develop an opinion, if that was their task, until they had read at least two documents. Students began by paraphrasing the texts closely and were more likely to reduce information as they read subsequent texts. This tendency to move toward reduction may have been a result of their growing background knowledge.

A second reason that students did not seem to benefit from just reading multiple texts is that they may need to be taught what it means to think like a historian, and that, without this teaching, students will be less able to engage in historical analysis. In other words, students who know more about historical analysis may be more able to engage in it. It is possible, for instance, that the four students who exhibited more gisting, evaluating, sourcing, and corroborating may have been more sophisticated readers of historical text, regardless of whether they were familiar with the Gulf of Tonkin Incident. Textbooks in history are written so that the author's background and stance and his or her methodology are hidden (Luke, DeCastell, & Luke, 1983). Therefore, interpretations of events are presented as fact, not analysis, and two or more interpretations to an event are rarely shared. While original documents and argumentative essays positing different interpretations should help students come to the realization that history is interpretation rather than fact, this idea may be less obvious to students who have relied mainly upon history texts for information and who have been taught to think of history as merely a series of chronicled events. The teacher in this study generally presented history as a story, stressing the relations among events, rather than the interpretations.

In this study, students tended to respond to the description task in a transmission mode. That is, they looked at the task as one of getting information from the text and writing it down. In contrast, they looked at the opinion task as a prior knowledge task and did not rely on the information in the texts to support their opinion. In neither task did the students use the texts to respond critically and evaluatively, as intended.

The lack of critical response may suggest that students need to be taught to write persuasive essays, with a warrant and evidence supporting that warrant. Chambliss (1994) found that there are differences in how students evaluate persuasive essays to formulate their own opinions. Our students made many unsupported statements when asked to form an opinion, even though their notes indicated that they had attended closely to the information in the texts and did have that information at hand. It is possible that these students did not know that they were supposed to provide support for an opinion, even though they clearly learned information that would be appropriate. This is another aspect of the disciplinary knowledge of history, and of other disciplines as well.

A final possible reason for the apparent lack of benefit from reading multiple texts may be a lack of experience with the task of working with multiple texts. As noted earlier, their teacher did not provide such experience but planned to do so later in the year. Experience (and teacher guidance) may improve students' ability to integrate information from different original source documents.

APPENDIX 20.1. BACKGROUND INFORMATION

The war in Vietnam has been called the United States' longest war, because, even though the United States was not in combat the entire time, it was involved in the affairs of Vietnam for approximately 25 years, from 1950 to 1975. The United States became involved during the Truman administration, when it supported the French (who controlled the Vietnamese government) against a group of Communist rebels fighting for Vietnamese independence. By the time Lyndon Baines Johnson had taken over the presidency (in 1963), Vietnam had been divided into North and South, with the North being governed by the Communist president Ho Chi Minh, and the South being governed by a U.S.-supported president. In South Vietnam, a civil war had broken out in an attempt to topple the existing government and reunite North and South Vietnam under communism. This movement was led by a group the United States labeled the Viet Cong. The United States sent monetary aid, equipment, and advisors to the South Vietnamese government to support their fight against the Viet Cong and monitored, with concern, North Vietnamese support of the rebels. It was against this backdrop that the Gulf of Tonkin Incident took place.

On August 2, 1964, shots were fired toward the *U.S.S. Maddox* by three PT boats while on patrol off the North Vietnamese coastline in the Gulf of Tonkin. Two days later, while the *Maddox* and a companion ship, the *C. Turner Joy*, were again on patrol, there were reports of another attack. President Johnson ordered a retaliatory strike and asked Congress to pass the Southeast Asia Resolution (also known as the Gulf of Tonkin Resolution) to give him the authority to "take all necessary steps, including the use of armed force, to assist any member or protocol state of the Southeast Asia Collective Defense Treaty requesting assistance in defense of its freedom." This resolution was passed. Johnson used this approval to commit the United States to heavy involvement in the Vietnam War. "Hawks" (those who were supporters of the war) and "Doves" (those who were against the war) disagreed about what actually happened and about President Johnson's motivations in handling the incident.

APPENDIX 20.2. ANALYSIS SHEET FOR NOTES AND FINAL PRODUCT

Text	#25–Take side in a debate (pro resolution) Notes	Final product
		(1) President Johnson was definitely justified when he asked Congress to pass the Resolution.
	1. Gulf of Tonkin Resolution	
Three days after the second incident in the Tonkin Gulf, the Administration submitted a Joint Resolution to Congress which approved in advance the President's taking "all necessary steps" to assist South Vietnam or any other member or protocol state of the Southeast Asia Treaty Organization.	Administration submitted a Joint Resolution to Congress which approved the President's request to assist the Southeast Asia Treaty Organization	

(cont.)

APPENDIX 20.2. *(cont.)*

Text	#25—Take side in a debate (pro resolution) Notes	Final product
It was approved unanimously by the House and by a vote of 88 to 2 in the Senate.		(7) The vote passed unanimously in the House of Representatives and 80 to 2 in the Senate in approval of military action against the North Vietnamese (Viet Cong).
Whereas naval units of the Communist regime in Vietnam, in violation of the principles of the Charter of the United Nations and of international law,	Communist Regime violated the Charter	
have deliberately and repeatedly attacked United States naval vessels lawfully present in international waters, and have thereby created a serious threat to international peace;	attacked UN vessels creating a threat to international peace	(2) He saw that North Vietnamese were being hostile toward the South Vietnamese, American allies (3) and in the process were attacking U.S. ships in the Gulf of Tonkin.
Whereas these attacks are part of a deliberate and systematic campaign of aggression that the Communist regime in North Vietnam has been waging against its neighbors and the nations joined with them in the collective defense of their freedom;	attacks are part of a deliberate and systematic campaign of aggression that the Communist regime has been waging against its neighbors	(2) He saw that North Vietnamese were being hostile toward the South Vietnamese, American allies
Whereas the United States is assisting the peoples of Southeast Asia to protect their freedom and has no territorial, military or political ambitions in that area, but desires only that these peoples should be left in peace to work out their own destinies in their own way:	U.S. protecting the people's freedom	

(cont.)

APPENDIX 20.2. *(cont.)*

Text	#25—Take side in a debate (pro resolution) Notes	Final product
Consonant with the Constitution of the United States and the Charter of the United Nations and in accordance with its obligations under the Southeast Asia Collective Defense Treaty, the United States is, therefore, prepared, as the President determines, to take all necessary steps, including the use of armed force, to assist any member or protocol state of the Southeast Asia Collective Defense Treaty requesting assistance in defense of its freedom.	the U.S. is prepared to take all necessary steps to assist the Southeast Asia Collective Defense Treaty requesting assistance in defense of its freedom	
This resolution shall expire when the President shall determine that the peace and security of the area is reasonably assured by international conditions created by action of the United Nations or otherwise, except that it may be terminated earlier by concurrent resolution of the Congress.	this power of the President will expire when peace has returned to South Vietnam or as Congress sees fit	
	2. "The Vote that Congress Can't Forget"	
For more than two decades, the Congressional vote that lawmakers most often cite as the one they would like to take back is their 1964 vote for the Gulf of Tonkin Resolution, the resolution that was used as authority for the war in Vietnam. Only two Senators and no Representatives voted no.	The vote that lawmakers would most like to take back is the Gulf of Tonkin Resolution in which two Senators and no Representatives noted no.	(7) The vote passed unanimously in the House of Representatives and 80 to 2 in the Senate in approval of military action against the North Vietnamese (Viet Cong).
Twenty-seven of those lawmakers are still in Congress.	27 of these lawmakers are still in Congress	

(cont.)

APPENDIX 20.2. *(cont.)*

Text	#25—Take side in a debate (pro resolution) Notes	Final product
And as they prepared for Saturday's vote on what was even more clearly the equivalent of a declaration of war, the resolution to authorize the use of military force in the Persian Gulf, the memories of that earlier vote weighed heavily on the minds of the seven senators and 20 representatives who served then and still serve now.	They thought about this when making the decision to invade the Persian Gulf.	
He recalled the earlier resolution as one President Johnson had "distorted," and one whose repeal he accomplished as a freshman Senator in 1970.	the resolution was repealed one year after it was passed	
He added, "The Gulf of Tonkin Resolution was used as a declaration of war and plunged this country in 8 or 9 years of really disastrous war in Vietnam."	was used as a declaration of war	
Representative Charles E. Bennett, Democrat of Florida, said; "I am 80 years of age, I have been in this chamber 43 years. Out of the 17,000 votes I have cast, the only one I really regret is the one I cast for the Bay of Tonkin Resolution.	Charles E. Bennett regrets it.	
Representative Dan Rostenkowski, Democrat of Illinois, did not offer second thoughts about his old vote, but said the Persian Gulf decision was even more difficult for him. "Today's situation is clearer," he said in a statement in the Congressional Record, "The possibility of armed conflict, casualties and even death is much more apparent.	Persian Gulf situation is clearer	

(cont.)

APPENDIX 20.2. *(cont.)*

Text	#25—Take side in a debate (pro resolution) Notes	Final product
But few avoided comparisons with Vietnam more generally.	Several lawmakers avoided comparisons of the situations	
When it came time to vote, 12 of the Tonkin veterans voted to authorize force and 14 voted against it.	12 authorized 14 no for the Gulf	(8) Even 20 years after the vote in Congress, 12 Congressmen still believed that the Resolution was justifiable.
The Tonkin Democrats sided against authorizing force.	The Tonkin Democrats sided against authorizing force in the Gulf	
So did Representatives Jack Brooks of Texas, John D. Dingell of Michigan, Dante B. Fascell of Florida, and Jamie L. Whitten of Mississippi, the only current member of Congress who was also on hand in December 1941, to vote the last formal declarations of war, against Japan, Germany and Italy.	James L. Witten of Mississippi, the only current member of Congress who was on hand in December 1941, to vote the last formal declarations of war, against Japan, Germany, & Italy voted Yes.	
	3. *As I Saw It*	
He consistently favored strong American involvement, arguing that "aggression" must be stopped. (from "About the Author")	Dean Rusk favored American involvement	
Dean Rusk was Secretary of State under Presidents Kennedy and Johnson, 1961–68. (from "About the Author")	Dean Rusk was Secretary of State under Kennedy and Johnson	
On August 2 and 3, 1964, we received reports that the USS Maddox and USS C. Turner Joy, American destroyers operating in the Gulf of Tonkin off the coast of North Vietnam, had been attacked by North Vietnamese torpedo boats in two separate incidents.	On August 2 and 3 1964 the USS Maddox and USS C Turner Joy on the coast of North Vietnam had been attacked	(2) He saw that North Vietnamese were being hostile toward the South Vietnamese, American allies (3) and in the process were attacking U.S. ships in the Gulf of Tonkin.

(cont.)

APPENDIX 20.2. *(cont.)*

Text	#25—Take side in a debate (pro resolution) Notes	Final product
The Republic of Vietnam today celebrates August 2—the day of the Tonkin Gulf attacks—as part of its national war effort against the Americans, so whatever happened that night in the Tonkin Gulf, evidently it takes credit for it now.	The Republic of Vietnam takes credit for something happening because they celebrate August 2 as part of its efforts against America	
North Vietnam was using coastal waters to infiltrate men and arms into South Vietnam;	North Vietnam was using the coast to infiltrate men and arms into South Vietnam	(2) He saw that North Vietnamese were being hostile toward the South Vietnamese, American allies
South Vietnam under the doctrine of self-defense was trying to block this infiltration and mount retaliatory raids of its own-a secret operation called 34-A, supported by the American Navy. But the destroyers attacked in the Gulf of Tonkin were on intelligence-gathering missions, not participating in South Vietnamese actions along the coast. It is entirely possible that the North Vietnamese thought that our destroyers were involved in these 34-A raids and in blockading operations along North Vietnam's coast to stop their infiltration of the South by sea. But even if Hanoi thought this, it isn't valid to call the exercise of self-defense a provocation.	North Vietnamese could have thought that Americans were part of a South Vietnamese operation called 34-A	(9) The navy needed to protect the South Vietnamese and American intelligence vessels.
		(4) President Johnson could not allow for the continued meaningless destruction of governmental property by North Vietnamese without doing something about it.

(cont.)

APPENDIX 20.2. (cont.)

Text	#25—Take side in a debate (pro resolution) Notes	Final product
Indeed, the Tonkin Gulf Resolution, in which Congress declared its support for the United States' willingness to come to the assistance of those protected by the SEATO Treaty, including the use of armed force "as the President shall determine," was passed rapidly: 88–2 by the Senate and 416–0 by the House.	The resolution was also unanimously voted	(6) Congress also felt he was justified in his actions. (7) The vote passed unanimously in the House of Representatives and eighty to two in the Senate in approval of military action against the North Vietnamese (Viet Cong).
Some later complained, "We didn't anticipate sending a half million men to South Vietnam," but neither did Lyndon Johnson.		(5) He would not foresee the tragic death and destruction in the future Vietnam War.
	but shortly after people began to change their minds	
I felt the Tonkin Gulf Resolution was not congressional evasion of its war powers responsibility, but an exercise of that responsibility.	Resolution was an exercise of congressional powers not an evasion of them	
		(10) Thus, Lyndon B. Johnson and Congress acted rightly and in good faith regarding the approval of the Gulf of Tonkin Resolution.

AUTHOR NOTE

The work reported herein was funded in part by the National Reading Research Center of the University of Georgia and University of Maryland. It was supported under the Educational Research and Development Centers Program (PR/Award No. 117A20007) as administered by the Office of Educational Research and Improvement, U.S. Department of Education. The findings and opinions expressed here do not necessarily reflect the position or policies of the National Reading Research Center, the Office of Educational Research and Improvement, or the U.S. Department of Education.

REFERENCES

Alexander, P. A. , & Judy, J. (1988). The interaction of domain-specific and strategic knowledge in academic performance. *Review of Educational Research, 58*, 375–404.

Anderson, T. H., & Armbruster, B. B. (1984). Content area textbooks. In R. C. Anderson, J. Osborn, & R. J. Tierney (Eds.), *Learning to read in American schools* (pp. 193–226). Hillsdale, NJ: Erlbaum.

Belenky, M. F., Clinchy, B. M., Goldberger, N. R., & Tarule, J. M. (1986). *Women's ways of knowing.* New York: Basic Books.

Britton, B. K., & Gulgoz, S. (1991). Using Kintsch's computational model to improve instructional text: Effects of repairing inference calls on recall and cognitive structures. *Journal of Educational Psychology, 83*, 329–345.

Chambliss, M. J. (1994). Why do readers fail to change their beliefs after reading persuasive text? In R. Garner & P. A. Alexander (Eds.), *Beliefs about text and instruction with text* (pp. 75–89). Hillsdale, NJ: Erlbaum.

Crafton, L. K. (1983). Learning from reading: What happens when students generate their own background information? *Journal of Reading, 26*, 586–592.

Glaser, B. G., & Strauss, A. L. (1967). *The discovery of grounded theory: Strategies for qualitative research.* Chicago: Aldine.

Greene, S. (1994). The problems of learning to think like a historian: Writing history in the culture of the classroom. *Educational Psychologist, 29*(2), 89–96.

Hartman, D. K. (1995). Eight readers reading: The intertextual links of proficient readers reading multiple passages. *Reading Research Quarterly, 30*, 520–561.

Hirsch, E. D. (1987). *Cultural literacy.* Boston: Houghton Mifflin.

Hynd, C. R., Stahl, S. A., Britton, B., & McNish, M. (1996, April). *Group processes involved in studying multiple documents in history.* Paper presented at the annual meeting of the American Educational Research Association, New York.

Kintsch, W. (1986). Learning from text. *Cognition and Instruction, 3*, 87–108.

Kintsch, W., & van Dijk, T. A. (1978). Toward a model of discourse comprehension and production. *Psychological Review, 85*, 363–394.

Leinhardt, G., Beck, I. L., & Stainton, C. (1994). *Teaching and learning in history.* Hillsdale, NJ: Erlbaum.

Luke, C., Decastell, S., & Luke, A. (1983). Beyond criticism: The authority of the school text. *Curriculum Inquiry, 13*, 111–128.

McKeown, M. G., Beck, I. L., & Worthy, M. J. (1993). Grappling with text ideas: Questioning the author. *The Reading Teacher, 46*, 560–566.

Patrick, J. J., & Hawke, S. (1982). Social studies curriculum materials. In *The current state of social studies: A report of Project Span* (pp. 105–185). Boulder, CO: Social Science Education Consortium.

Perfetti, C. A., Britt, M. A., & Georgi, M. C. (1995). *Text-based learning and reasoning: Studies in history.* Hillsdale, NJ: Erlbaum.

Perfetti, C. A., Britt, M. A., Rouet, J. F., Mason, R. A., & Georgi, M. C. (1993, April). *How students use texts to learn and reason about historical uncertainty.* Paper presented at the annual meeting of the American Educational Research Association, Atlanta, GA.

Perry, W. G. (1970). *Forms of intellectual and ethical development in the college years.* New York: Holt, Rinehart, & Winston.

Ravitch, D. (1992). *The democracy reader.* New York: HarperCollins.

Reynolds, R. E., Trathen, W., Sawyer, M., & Shepard, C. R. (1993). Causal and epiphenomenal use of the selection attention strategy in reading comprehension. *Contemporary Educational Psychology, 18*, 258–278.

Rumelhart, D. E. (1980). Schemata: The building blocks of cognition. In R. Spiro, B. Bruce, &

W. Brewer (Eds.), *Theoretical issues in reading comprehension* (pp. 33–58). Hillsdale, NJ: Erlbaum.

Seixas, P. (1993). The community of inquiry as a basis for knowledge and learning: The case of history. *American Educational Research Journal, 30,* 305–324.

Spiro, R. (1980). Constructive processes in prose comprehension and recall. In R. Spiro, B. Bruce, & W. Brewer (Eds.), *Theoretical issues in reading comprehension* (pp. 245–259). Hillsdale, NJ: Erlbaum.

Spiro, R. J., Coulson, R. L., Feltovich, P. J., & Anderson, D. K. (1994). Cognitive flexibility theory: Advanced knowledge acquisition in ill-structured domains. In R. B. Ruddell, M. R. Ruddell, & H. Singer (Eds.), *Theoretical models and processes of reading* (pp. 602–615). Newark, DE: International Reading Association.

Spivey, N. N., & King, J. (1989). Readers as writers composing from sources. *Reading Research Quarterly, 24,* 7–26.

Spoehr, K. T., & Spoehr, L. W. (1994). Learning to think historically. *Educational Psychologist, 29*(2), 71–78.

Stahl, S. A., & Hynd, C. R. (1994, April). *Selecting historical documents: A study of student reasoning.* Paper presented at the annual meeting of the American Educational Research Association, New Orleans, LA.

Stahl, S. A., Hynd, C. R., Glynn, S., & Carr, M. (1995). Beyond reading to learn: Developing content and disciplinary knowledge through texts. In P. Afflerbach, L. Baker, & D. Reinking (Eds.), *Developing engaged readers in home and school communities* (pp. 139–163). Hillsdale, NJ: Erlbaum.

Wineburg, S. S. (1991a). Historical problem solving: A study of the cognitive processes used in the evaluation of documentary and pictorial evidence. *Journal of Educational Psychology, 83,* 73–77.

Wineburg, S. S. (1991b). On the reading of historical texts: Notes on the breach between school and academy. *American Educational Research Journal, 28,* 495–519.

Wineburg, S. S. (1994). Introduction: Out of our past and into our future—The psychological study of learning and teaching history. *Educational Psychologist 29*(2), 57–60.

21

Reading Multiple Documents in History Class

Evolution of a Teaching Strategy Based on the Reading Processes of Practicing Historians

CYNTHIA HYND SHANAHAN

CONTEXT FOR THE *READING RESEARCH QUARTERLY* STUDY

I had long been interested in the effects of multiple texts with disparate messages on students' thinking, and I had long been intrigued with historical controversies, when I discovered that Steve had similar interests. At the time, I considered him a word knowledge expert only, and I was fascinated to learn that he actually had quite broader intellectual interests. In 1994, in the context of research for the National Reading Research Center, Steve and I began an extended conversation about the work of Samuel Wineburg (Wineburg, 1991a, 1991b). Wineburg had done a study comparing the reading processes of practicing historians with those of high school students as they read multiple historical documents. He found that whereas students seemed to read each document as if it were a "basket of facts," practicing historians, even though they were reading about an unfamiliar topic, used three processes that were unique. They engaged in sourcing, contextualization, and corroboration. That is, they thought about the source of the document (e.g., who wrote it and where it appeared), tried to place the document in a historical/social/political context (e.g., when it was written, for what purpose, and in what setting), and compared and contrasted it with the other documents about the same topic they were reading.

We found his work intriguing, and in line with other studies we had read that pointed to students' difficulties in reading *across* documents and in thinking about them critically (Britt, Rouet, & Perfetti, 1996; Perfetti, Britt, Rouet, Mason, & Georgi, 1993). Wineburg's study was unique, though, in that it provided us with a way to look at online processing—as a comparison with the processing of experts who approached the texts as arguments rather than as truth and who used specific techniques to evaluate the veracity of the arguments. Thus, the germ of our own study was born. We subsequently engaged in an elaborate study of student processes while reading multiple texts, one that included measures of students' understanding of each text, students' note taking, and students' writing after having read. Students responded in writing to two kinds of prompts—one asking for a summary of what they read and one that asked for an opinion about what they read. We did the study using honor's students in Dennis Bosquet's 10th-grade U.S. history classes. These students chose from a series of online documents about the Gulf of Tonkin Incident and subsequent resolution, a topic about which both of us had a rather keen interest because of the surrounding controversy (and the fact that we were both young adults during the Vietnam era). Students all had access to information about each author, where and in what form the text was published, the time frame, and any other information we could gather that might encourage sourcing and contextualization. All students, in addition, preceded their reading with a short, descriptive summary of the event, the resolution, and its significance.

We expected these good students to take advantage of the information we provided, to engage in some cross-textual comparisons and contrasts, and to use the texts to provide evidence for their writing. We were pretty much wrong on all counts. As noted in the *Reading Research Quarterly* article (Stahl, Hynd, Britton, McNish, & Bosquet, 1996), students wrote copious notes without critique. Their mental models did not become more coherent as they read more than two documents. They rarely engaged in sourcing, contextualization, and corroboration. They seemed to learn the information in common across the texts but did not pay attention to the disparate information. Their essays lacked evidence from their reading for both the opinion and summary tasks.

Creating, implementing, and analyzing the results of this study are among some of my fondest memories of Steve. He had a keen grasp of the "big picture" but could also be quite oriented toward detail in terms of the design of the study and the coding of the results. We spent many days creating reliable coding schemes for the students' artifacts, and I learned that he really had a knack for solving some of the problems we faced. His ability to move between macro- and microaspects of the work helped us to think about the implications of what we were finding in a way that I would not have if I had done the study alone.

FOLLOW-UP STUDIES

We did a follow-up study that required students to process historical documents about Christopher Columbus (Stahl, Hynd, Montgomery, & McClain, 1997), finding that, whereas students could perceive bias, mental representations did not change after reading one text (confirming results of the previous study). Again, students read the various documents as if they were not related. We did another in which students worked in groups as they read about Vietnam (Hynd, Stahl, & McNish, 1996). In this study we found that groups had rather idiosyncratic ways of reading and discussing the documents, but that only one group, who read the material out loud to each other, actually engaged in any analysis. Their discussions, corroborating our other work, were constrained to their online comments about each text rather than demonstrating cross-textual critique. Our conclusion: We need to teach students what it means to read like historians.

While Steve became enmeshed in other projects, I pursued this idea further. In a pilot study with college students, my colleagues and I altered the computer presentation to teach students about sourcing, contextualization, and corroboration (Hynd,

Jacobsen, Reinking, Holschuh, & Heron, 1999). We also focused on fewer reading tasks that were more tightly controlled in terms of their stances about the Gulf of Tonkin Incident, and we began to interview the students about what they were thinking. This pilot helped us to think that maybe we were on the right track. When we talked to students, they discussed what they were reading in totally different, much more interesting ways when they took into account the source of the text, the context in which it was published, and its comparison with other texts.

In the meantime, I was also teaching a "Learning to Learn" class at the University of Georgia. We had structured the class to feature three extended units—one in psychology, one in science, and one in history—and we taught students strategies that helped them to learn and think about the information they were reading. We focused the history unit on the Vietnam conflict, and I introduced the task of reading multiple conflicting documents to my students. I taught them about the processes that historians used, and I told them that their task was to read the assigned texts to figure out what to believe, as the historians in Wineburg's study had done. They read the documents on the computer—accompanied by information that dealt with the source of information, the context of the times in which the texts were written, and the way in which the texts agreed or disagreed with each other. One addition was that when we met in groups, we had discussions about the issues of concern to students. What were some of the strengths and drawbacks of firsthand accounts? What was considered a credible newspaper or publisher? What is the drawback to publishing your own book? What is the strength of a peer review? How do historians decide what "story" to tell?

Another addition was that we asked students to engage in comparison–contrast charting. From the conversations (and my prodding) we derived the issues that surfaced across the texts:

1. What really happened on August 4, 1964?
2. Did the United States intentionally provoke the Gulf of Tonkin Incident?
3. Was Johnson duplicitous in his using the Gulf of Tonkin Incident to pass the Gulf of Tonkin Resolution?

Students put these issues on the horizontal axis. Also on the horizontal axis were the three processes that historians use when reading. They put the various readings on the vertical axis, writing the arguments of the authors in the chart's boxes. This allowed students to pay attention to the similarities and differences across texts, to record significant details, and also to consider the veracity of the sources. I wasn't doing an experiment—just trying to engage students in the process of thinking like historians, and thus the data I have in terms of outcomes is only anecdotal. However, the essays students wrote at the culmination of the unit were the best I had read in the years that I had taught college students. Not only did they show that these students could engage in thoughtful critique of historical texts, but they could write using appropriate amounts of textual evidence. These students did appear to be able to back up their arguments. I partly attributed that to the charts they constructed.

Jodi Holschuh and Betty Hubbard took over teaching the courses in subsequent semesters, and we decided to collaborate on a more formal study of the processes that students were using. They taught the unit as they normally would, but this time, we interviewed 13 students—once before they read and once after they read. The data from his study are published in the *Journal of Literacy Research* (Hynd-Shanahan, Holschuh, & Hubbard, 2004). As had happened in the earlier pilots and in my teaching, students expressed a keen interest in the way they were reading and the strategies they used. They also changed their ideas about what it meant to read history and in their beliefs about historiography. We noted that students began the study with the view that historians merely documented truth (a naive view) or, at the very least, synthesized different accounts (a more sophisticated, but still naive view), but ended the study believing that historians arbitrated between conflicting accounts or had biases that determined what documents they chose and what interpretations they made. They also ended the study torn between their original leanings toward texts written by authors who were "there" to a more nuanced view that participants in an event, even though they had firsthand knowledge, might have reasons for not being entirely objective in their account of that event. For example, Dean Rusk, the author of one of the texts (an excerpt from his autobiography), maintained that the Johnson administration was not looking for trouble when they sent ships into waters the North Vietnamese believed were theirs, that, even though there was some dispute about it, the North Vietnamese most likely attacked the two ships on August 4, and that the administration was well within their rights to use that attack to quickly get the Gulf of Tonkin Resolution passed through Congress. These three points were contested in the two historians' texts. In discussing the issues, students mentioned, sometimes reluctantly, that Rusk had a vested interest in maintaining his position because he was in the higher echelons of the Johnson administration. Thus, students ended the study with a complicated, critical view of what they were reading. They began to think about the reasons why the authors wrote what they did, given the context. We were struck by their thoughtfulness and their engagement. We attributed some of their changes not only to the reading but also to the interview process. We asked students open-ended questions (e.g., What do historians do? and How do you decide which account is believable?), and these questions seemed to cause students some perturbation and change. It may be that without our questions, they would not have thought so deeply about the issues. Thus, we reason that the teacher's job is more than skillfully arranging the materials, more than teaching students a strategy. It also involves grounding the learning within a disciplinary framework and making sure that students are addressing critical issues within that framework through questioning and discussion. There is nothing new about that insight, but it did seem to be a factor in their epistemological growth. I will get back to that point later. Note what these students said below.

> ALTHEA: Life isn't like school; there usually isn't a textbook that tells you what to think, so learning how to come to conclusions when presented different sides of the same story will be useful.

> LESLIE: I thought it was a lot different than when I had history before, and I've never been given multiple things before. In some ways I liked it better but in some ways I didn't because I had to decide for myself. I think of the stuff I've been reading, and I don't believe it as much.

> ANNA: I like the way I am thinking as I am reading. I'm reading and analyzing all these things I've read before and comparing them while I'm reading. It's kind of weird, but it's cool. . . . There is no real answer, so you have to analyze everything yourself and come up with your own conclusions. (Hynd-Shanahan et al., 2004, pp. 166–167)

NEXT STEPS

In the future, my colleagues and I plan to engage in experimental (or quasi-experimental) studies of this kind of instruction and will test the efficacy of the instruction with younger students—students in high school and middle school. There is growing evidence that younger students are capable of more sophisticated readings across texts. VanSledright (2002a, 2002b) and VanSledright and Frankes (2002) showed that teaching students as early as fourth and fifth grade to interpret historical documents had similar results as the Hynd-Shanahan et al. (2004) study. After teaching a group of students to make historical interpretations for an entire semester, VanSledright concluded that the approach he used holds promise for teaching fifth graders "how to make sense of historical documents as evidence, identify the nature of the documents as sources, judge the reliability and perspective of those documents, and corroborate details across accounts in order to construct evidenced-based assumptions" (VanSledright, 2002a, p. 131). Wolfe and Goldman (2005) studied middle school students' reading of two contradictory texts explaining the fall of the Roman Empire. These texts were crafted to be short and easy to read, given the low reading achievement of the students in the study. In addition, the researchers structured the tasks to ensure that students made cross-textual connections. They found that students did evidence cross-textual reasoning, and that the number of connections students made to other text information predicted the complexity of that reasoning. Similarly, Stevens, Wineburg, Herrenkohl, and Bell (in press) showed that students in sixth grade could, after undergoing a curriculum that stressed historical thinking and strategy use, form historical arguments using multiple texts (cited in Wineburg & Martin, 2004).

INSIGHTS GAINED

I am grateful to Steve for starting me along this line of research. I am also grateful to him for his insights into the process of critical reading within a discipline, and I would like to share some of the more crucial ones. Early on (Hynd & Stahl, 1998; Stahl, Hynd, Glenn, & Carr, 1996), we had discussed the necessity for students to develop *disciplinary knowledge*. By disciplinary knowledge, we meant knowledge of the task in which historians are engaged. Individuals with high levels of disciplinary knowledge in history know how knowledge is created and reported. They know how power relations are structured to determine "what counts." But in most high school history classes, there is a single textbook, and students learn the "story" of history. They may never realize that there is more than one version of it, and that historians have points of view and use conventions that determine what information is privileged in the writing of history textbooks.

In addition, we contended that *strategy teaching* is important; however, if strategies are not embedded within a disciplinary framework, they are unlikely to be used for the purposes of thinking deeply or critically. Students often do not know what counts as quality within particular disciplines; thus, they cannot evaluate textual information. They do not understand what is entailed in knowledge creation; thus, they cannot analyze evidence within arguments. In the discipline of history, historians engage in creating various interpretations of events based on their analysis, synthesis, and evaluation of multiple historical documents. Often, the documents they gather are contradictory or piecemeal, and they represent various genre, purposes, and biases. Historians synthesize a coherent "story" from disparate sources. Yet, many students do not recognize that historians view these various texts as evidence and view their syntheses of them as arguments. Unlike historians, students view the writing of historians as "Truth." If students were shown how to engage in the strategies that historians use as they process textual information, they would be better equipped to read history texts with a critical eye.

The idea is that rather than merely insisting that students learn general strategies that can be applied to all content areas, teachers serve students better if they also teach them discipline-specific strategies that draw on the real-life tasks of disciplinary experts, using materials such as the ones that these experts would use, thus providing students with the opportunity and challenge of engaging in the practice of reading in the same way that historians do.

In 2003, Steve and I wrote a chapter in which we described the state of knowledge in history reading and its instructional implications (Stahl & Shanahan, 2004). Steve made the distinction between teaching *history* and teaching *historiography*.

> These two perspectives could be labeled *historiography* and *history*, reflecting the difference between history as a discipline of thought and history as a narrative of a people's political and social changes over time. Teaching *history*, then, means teaching a narrative. The field of content area reading has developed a great many techniques for teaching children strategies for learning the narrative of history (Vacca & Vacca, 2001). These include using graphic organizers, time lines (e.g., Armbruster, Anderson, & Meyer, 1991) and summarization (e.g., Rinehart, Stahl, & Erickson, 1989). Teaching historiography means teaching the processes of history, focusing on the critical analysis of the various narratives that exist about any particular event or cluster of events. The field of content area reading has not typically focused its efforts on strategies for historiography. (p. 96)

Historians write *history* when they write textbooks; they always read as *historiographers* (and write that way, too, when they are engaged in academic dialogue). Making this distinction helped me to think about the processes involved in reading as historiographer versus reading as history learner. The elaboration-likelihood model (Chaiken, 1980, 1987; Sinatra & Dole, 1998), from the field of social psychology, suggests that readers process two aspects of texts—their central features and their peripheral features. If readers pay attention to the central features of texts, they are paying attention to what texts say—the arguments, the facts, the descriptions, and so on. Central processing makes it likely that elaborative understanding of the ideas in the text will result.

If readers pay attention to the peripheral features, they are noting information outside the text—the author, the publication format, the structure, and so on—and they are evaluating those features based on a heuristic, or rule. For example, students in the Hynd-Shanahan et al. study (2004) originally evaluated the authors' credibility based on the heuristic that involvement in an event makes it more likely that the author's message is credible, but changed that heuristic as their thinking became more sophisticated.

Historians appear to use both central and peripheral processes. They rely on the central processing of texts primarily for basic comprehension and for an understanding of and the evaluation of the arguments themselves; they rely on the peripheral processing of texts to help them evaluate further the information's credibility. Historians tend to read all history texts as arguments, and this tendency may, in fact, trigger their peripheral processing. In Wineburg's (1991a) study, historians used the peripheral processes of sourcing and contextualization and the central process of corroboration. (However, corroboration across texts is a distinctly more complicated task than the central processing of a single text, as studied by social psychologists.)

Experts in other fields use these two processes as well. In the field of education, for instance, academics are likely to assume that a non-peer-reviewed study described in a chapter should not hold the same evidentiary weight as one that is published in a major peer-reviewed research journal. This peripheral processing of the chapter is based on a heuristic that is bound up in the disciplinary understanding of "what counts." Another key point, then, is that disciplinary knowledge appears to be at the core of a reader's sophisticated movements from central to peripheral processing and, in history, at the core of historiography.

A related crucial insight derived from my work with Steve is the interplay of strategies, processes, and aspects of development such as epistemology as students move from naive readings of single textbook narratives to more critical readings of multiple documents. The simultaneity of movement across variables representing diverse theoretical positions (central/peripheral processing theory, strategy use, theories of epistemology, intertextuality theory, to name a few) suggests that developmental improvements in disciplinary reading are highly multidimensional, and these dimensions seem to be embedded with the discourse of the discipline. Especially important may be the social and intellectual aspects of the discipline: "what it means, for instance, to be a historian, to think like a historian, to grapple with the issues of history" (Hynd-Shanahan et al., 2004, p. 169).

A final, more applied insight is that the field of content literacy and the discipline of history would be better served if they combined their efforts to engage students in history learning through reading. In a field in which discipline experts spend almost 100% of their time reading and writing, it is ironic that history teachers often do not ask their students to read the printed word or even to interpret multimedia messages that include print (see Barton, 1996; Cuban, 1991; Goodlad, 1984; Levstik, 1996; Seixas, 1999; VanSledright, 1995, 1996); rather, history teachers compensate for students' inability to read history by presenting material orally and visually (Schoenbach, Greenleaf, Cziko, & Hurwitz, 1999). The lack of instruction in reading within this discipline can only ultimately be detrimental to students and to the field.

In the Stahl and Shanahan (2004) chapter, we noted, on the other side of the coin, that reading strategies that focused on historiographic reading across texts were notably rare in the content reading literature. The chapter described strategies that could be modified to use for such purposes: I-charts (Hoffman, 1991), Question the Author (Beck, McKeown, Hamilton, & Kucan, 1997; Beck, McKeown, Sandora, Kucan, & Worthy, 1996), Collaborative Reasoning (Anderson, Chinn, & Waggoner, 2001; Chinn & Anderson, 1998), and the Discussion Web (Alvermann, 1991). However, it described only one kind of strategy for the processing of multiple texts, procedural facilitators. Steve and I both believed in the idea that historians and content area reading experts should collaborate to produce strategies that would help students engage in appropriate reading processes given the need to engage in historical thinking across multiple, often conflicting documents.

CONCLUSION

Steve was the epitomy of a big-picture researcher who was grounded in making a difference in the everyday reading instruction of students, young or old. He never lost sight of the necessity for application; yet he could eloquently espouse the theoretical underpinnings of an instructional technique or strategy. For me, he was a provocateur, a synthesizer, a problem-solver, a trusted colleague and friend, a good heart—and student achievement in reading was at the center. Whenever I engage in research and writing, I think about him and his contributions to my understanding and thinking. His work regarding history is embedded in how I think about it.

REFERENCES

Alvermann, D. E. (1991). The Discussion Web: A graphic aid for learning across the curriculum. *Reading Teacher, 45*, 92–99.

Anderson, R. C., Chinn, C. A., & Waggoner, M. A. (2001). Patterns of discourse in two kinds of literature discussion. *Reading Research Quarterly, 36*, 378–411.

Barton, K. (1996). Narrative simplifications in elementary students' historical thinking. In J. Brophy (Ed.), *Advances in research on teaching* (Vol. 6, pp. 51–84). Greenwich, CT: JAI Press.

Beck, I., McKeown, M. G., Hamilton, R. L., & Kucan, L. (1997). *Questioning the Author: An approach for enhancing student engagement with text.* Newark, DE: International Reading Association.

Beck, I. L., McKeown, M. G., Sandora, C., Kucan, L., & Worthy, J. (1996), Questioning the author: A yearlong classroom implementation to engage students with text. *Elementary School Journal, 96*, 385–414.

Britt, M. A., Rouet, J.-F., & Perfetti, C. A. (1996). Using hypertext to study and reason about historical evidence. In J.-F. Rouet, J. T. Levonen, A. Dillon, & R. Spiro (Eds.), *Hypertext and cognition* (pp. 43–72). Mahwah, NJ: Erlbaum.

Chaiken, S. (1980). Heuristic versus systematic information processing and the use of source versus message cues in persuasion. *Journal of Personality and Social Psychology, 39*, 752–766.

Chaiken, S. (1987). The heuristic model of persuasion. In M. P. Zanna, J. J. Olson, & C. P. Herman (Eds.), *Social influence: The Ontario symposium* (Vol. 5, pp. 3–39). Hillsdale, NJ: Erlbaum.

Chinn, C. A., & Anderson, R. C. (1998). The structure of discussions that promote reasoning. *Teachers College Record, 100*(2), 315–368.

Cuban, L. (1991). History of teaching in social studies. In J. Shaver (Ed.), *Handbook of research on social studies teaching and learning* (pp. 197–209). New York: Macmillan.

Goodlad, J. I. (1984). *A place called school: Prospects for the future.* New York: Oxford University Press.

Hoffman, J. V. (1991). Critical reading/thinking across the curriculum: Using I-Charts to support learning. *Language Arts, 64*(2), 121–127.

Hynd, C., Jacobsen, M., Reinking, D., Holschuh, J., & Heron, A. (1999, April). *Students' responses to multiple texts in a hypertext environment.* Paper presented at the annual conference of the American Educational Research Association, Montreal, Canada.

Hynd, C. R., & Stahl, S. A. (1998). What do we mean by knowledge and learning. In C. R. Hynd (Ed.), *Learning from text across conceptual domains* (pp. 15–44). Mahwah, NJ: Erlbaum.

Hynd, C. R., Stahl, S. A., & McNish, M. (1996, April). *Group processes involved in studying multiple documents in history.* Paper presented at the annual meeting of the American Educational Research Association, New York.

Hynd-Shanahan, C., Holschuh, J., & Hubbard, B. (2004). Thinking like a historian: College students' reading of multiple historical documents. *Journal of Literacy Research, 4,* 238–250.

Levstik, L. (1996). NCSS and the teaching of history. In O. L. Davis, Jr. (Ed.), *NCSS in retrospect* (Bulletin No. 92, pp. 21–34). Washington, DC: National Council for the Social Studies.

National Center for Education Statistics. (2003). *The nation's report card.* Washington, DC: Author.

Perfetti, C. A., Britt, M. A., Rouet, J. F., Mason, R. A., & Georgi, M. C. (1993, April). *How students use texts to learn and reason about historical uncertainty.* Paper presented at annual meeting, American Educational Research Association, Atlanta, GA.

Schoenbach, R., Greenleaf, C., Cziko, C., & Hurwitz, L. (1999). *Reading for understanding.* San Francisco: Jossey-Bass.

Seixas, P. (1999). Beyond "content" and "pedagogy": In search of a way to talk about history education. *Journal of Curriculum Studies, 31,* 317–337.

Sinatra, G., & Dole, J. (1998). Case studies in conceptual change: A social psychological perspective. In B. Guzzetti & C. Hynd (Eds.), *Perspectives on conceptual change: Multiple ways to understand knowing and learning in a complex world* (pp. 52–71). Mahwah, NJ: Erlbaum

Stahl, S. Hynd, C., Britton, B., McNish, M., & Bosquet, D. (1996). What happens when students read multiple source documents in history? *Reading Research Quarterly, 31,* 430–457.

Stahl, S. A., Hynd, C. R., Glynn, S. M., & Carr, M. (1996). Beyond reading to learn: Developing content and disciplinary knowledge through texts. In P. Afflerbach, L. Baker, & D. Reinking (Eds.), *Developing engaged readers in school and home communities* (pp. 136–164). Mahwah, NJ: Erlbaum.

Stahl, S. A., Hynd, C. R., Montgomery, T., & McClain, V. (1997). *"In 1492 Columbus sailed the ocean blue": Effects of multiple document reading on student attitudes and prior concepts* (Report No. 82). Athens, GA: National Reading Research Center.

Stahl, S. A., & Shanahan, C. (2004). Learning to think like a historian: Disciplinary knowledge through critical analysis of multiple documents. In T. L. Jetton & J. A. Dole (Eds.), *Adolescent literacy research and practice* (pp. 94–118). New York: Guilford Press.

VanSledright, B. (1995). "I don't remember—The ideas are all jumbled in my head": Eighth graders' reconstructions of colonial American history. *Journal of Curriculum and Supervision, 10,* 317–345.

VanSledright, B. (1996). Closing the gap between disciplinary and school history? Historian as high school history teacher. In J. Brophy (Ed.), *Advances in research on teaching* (Vol. 6, pp. 257–289). Greenwich, CT: JAI Press.

VanSledright, B. (2002a). Confronting history's interpretive paradox while teaching fifth graders to investigate the past. *American Educational Research Journal, 39,* 1089–1115.

VanSledright, B. (2002b). *In search of America's past: Learning to read history in elementary school.* New York: Teachers College Press.

VanSledright, B., & Frankes, L. (2002). Concept-and strategic-knowledge development in historical study: A comparative exploration in two fourth-grade classrooms. *Cognition and Instruction, 18,* 239–283.

Wineburg, S. S. (1991a). Historical problem solving: A study of the cognitive processes used in evaluation of documentary and pictorial evidence. *Journal of Educational Psychology, 83,* 73–87.

Wineburg, S. S. (1991b). On the reading of historical texts: Notes on the breach between school and academy. *American Educational Research Journal, 28,* 495–519.

Wineburg, S., & Martin (2004). Reading and rewriting history. *Educational Leadership, 62*(1), 42–45.

Wolfe, M. B. W., & Goldman, S. R. (2005). Relationships between adolescents' text processing and reasoning. *Cognition and Instruction, 23*(4), 467–502.

VI | ASSESSMENT

22 | Connecting Scientific and Practical Approaches to Reading Assessment

Scott G. Paris

All research on reading, including psychological, educational, and sociopolitical research, is situated in particular contexts that influence the design of studies and the interpretation of data. Steve Stahl understood the multiple contexts that shaped his own research, and he worked hard to avoid insularity in his studies. He addressed different audiences and connected scientific research to problems in classrooms. His firsthand experiences working with struggling readers made him sensitive to the many frustrations elicited by readers' articulation problems, unknown vocabulary, and labored decoding. Steve's experiences made him feel compassion for classroom teachers who every year face higher expectations with a greater variety of students while simultaneously facing declining resources and public support. Moreover, he helped graduate students understand the contexts of their own work and the importance of bridging science and practice in educational research.

On the one hand, Steve's identity as a teacher helped to make his research practical, relevant, and useful. On the other hand, Steve was a widely respected researcher who consolidated his academic experiences at Illinois, Harvard, and Georgia in a variety of innovative research. With these personal experiences and values as a foundation, Steve did an extraordinary job of connecting scientific and practical research on reading so there are reciprocal benefits for both. He was a compassionate researcher and a rigorous humanist, as well as a humorous scholar and great friend to many people. To set the stage for a discussion of his work on reading assessment, I want to examine some of the academic, historical, and collegial contexts that influenced his work.

ACADEMIC CONTEXTS

Steve's early training and research were embedded in an era of volatile changes for the study of reading and training of reading educators. The "cognitive revolution" in psychology and education that began in the 1960s was transformed into sociocultural and sociocognitive approaches by the 1990s. Reading education became a popular field for researchers and educators between 1975 and 2000, and doctoral programs around the country flourished. Many teachers were attracted to academic careers in reading education, and they became the new cadre of reading researchers. Along with the new waves of academics and graduate students came new journals, expanded professional organizations, and new sources of research funding. National reading research centers were established in the 1970s at the University of Illinois and in the 1980s at the Universities of Maryland and Georgia. In the 1990s, the Center for the Improvement of Early Reading Achievement (CIERA), a coalition of researchers at the University of Michigan, Michigan State University, University of Minnesota, and the University of Virginia, was created. Steve Stahl played vital roles at all of these research centers, and he was a prolific researcher in each new national effort. His research contributed directly to the dramatic increase in scientific evidence about reading development and instruction.

Steve's research questions and methods were influenced by his academic journey through these research centers and outstanding universities, and also by his collaborative relationships with faculty and students. From his training at Harvard, Steve developed solid research skills, a developmental approach influenced by Jeanne Chall, and a professional commitment to clinical practices of assessment and instruction. At the Center for the Study of Reading at Illinois, Steve's research focused on vocabulary and comprehension, two prominent emphases at the time, and he started to examine early instruction based on whole language, phonics, and basal reading series. He continued these lines of research at the University of Georgia in the 1990s and was at the forefront of researchers who advocated early and intensive phonics instruction in grades K–3. His more recent focus on fluency-oriented reading instruction combined scientific research on decoding skills with classroom instruction, and those studies continue to yield important data. Steve's interest in assessment can be traced to his experiences as a special education teacher and later as the director of the Reading Clinic at the University of Georgia. Assessment was a peripheral research topic for Steve, but he regarded it as increasingly important in an era of educational accountability. His approach to assessment was oriented more to processes than standards and aimed more at individual diagnostic evaluation than group accountability. His clinical approach is a wonderful example of the bridge between scientific studies of reading and the practical application of the information to help children.

HISTORICAL–POLITICAL CONTEXTS

Steve's research reflects historical changes in the field of reading research in several ways. First, his early work highlighted the limitations of instruction based on whole language and language experience methods, and, correspondingly, his research showed the importance of teaching phonics and decoding strategies in primary grades. Second, his conceptual approach to assessment and remediation, exemplified in the model described by Stahl, Kuhn, and Pickle (1999; reprinted as Chapter 23, this volume), is consistent with recent trends in special education that provide more intensive training on basic skills to children with reading problems. For example, Steve's clinical model is consistent with the three-tier model of intervention advocated by Good, Simmons, and Kame'enui (2001) and the recent emphasis on "response to intervention" as a benchmark of instructional effectiveness. Third, Steve's most recent project involved the design and testing of comprehension assessments, a topic identified by the National Reading Panel (NRP; 2000) as a critical need. For example, he designed methods to assess children's comprehension processes through think-aloud procedures, and he showed how vocabulary knowledge confounds comprehension processes and assessments.

His work on assessment is set in a time of renewed educational accountability and increasing political control of educational practices. Since the 1980s there has been a steady proliferation of standardized tests, and every state except Iowa has implemented high-stakes testing in reading and math to compare students and schools (Heubert & Hauser, 1999). Despite concerns that high-stakes testing can have negative consequences on students' learning and motivation (Paris, Lawton, Turner, & Roth, 1991), can narrow instruction (Smith, 1991), and can be biased against minorities and students with special needs (Sacks, 1999), policymakers have increased the frequency of high-stakes testing and the consequences attached to the outcomes. The public thirst for reassuring measures of educational success, coupled with political desires to make schools accountable to uniform standards, culminated in the No Child Left Behind Act (NCLB; 2002). Part of NCLB established annual standards for schools based on test scores as well as sanctions for failing to meet them, and another part of NCLB emphasized scientifically based approaches to reading instruction and assessment in grades K–3. It is clear that reading achievement in 2006, as indicated by comparative assessment data, is a benchmark of educational success throughout K–12 that has important consequences for teachers and students.

THE COMMUNITY OF CIERA RESEARCHERS

The broad and collaborative research agenda of CIERA was proposed in 1997 in a time of gathering momentum for more rigorous approaches to reading education in K–3. It is important to note that the CIERA research was proposed before the NRP (2000) and the NCLB (2002) and thus did not address the same issues. Nevertheless, the portfolio of research conducted by CIERA researchers included a broad range of "basic" research on discrete reading skills, professional development, instructional studies, community reading programs, and many issues surrounding early reading assessment. Paris and Hoffman (2004) summarized the CIERA studies on classroom assessments, teachers' practices, and new assessments of children, texts, and environments. The initial studies were surveys of the K–3 reading assessments used by teachers or produced commercially. We also surveyed exemplary schools to determine the kinds of reading assessments they used (Paris, Paris, & Carpenter, 2002). The surveys revealed a huge variety of early reading assessments available to teachers, a preponderance of informal and nonstandard measures, and a lack of resources, time, and training to support teachers' implementation of new assessments.

Because of the potpourri of assessments and lack of uniform data in the 1990s, many states (e.g., Texas, Michigan, Virginia, and Illinois) created their own batteries of early reading assessments to diagnose struggling readers and to generate measures of adequate yearly progress in reading. Some researchers devised commercial and psychometric assessments, such as the Comprehensive Test of Phonological Processing (CTOPP; Wagner, Torgeson, & Rashotte, 1999) and the Dynamic Indicators of Basic Early Literacy Skills (DIBELS; Good & Kaminski, 2002), in order to assess young children on critical indicators of early reading. These new assessments have been used widely to assess student progress and to align instruction with the five essential components of reading identified by the NRP (2000) and included in the NCLB, namely, alphabet knowledge, phonemic awareness, oral reading fluency, vocabulary, and comprehension.

Researchers at CIERA gave increased attention to the creation of new measures of these five essential components, and especially comprehension. Steve, who joined CIERA after it was established, contributed to the research on assessment and helped organize the CIERA conference on reading comprehension and assessment. The conference was held in Ann Arbor in October 2002, and in many ways it was a culmination of years of collaboration for many of the participants. The conference included many other nationally respected researchers; it generated lively discussions about diverse issues; and it resulted in an edited volume that breaks new ground in reading comprehension research (Paris & Stahl, 2005). Steve worked on editing the book until he became too ill, and the volume is dedicated to his legacy of reading research.

Steve's research on reading assessment was a work in progress that charted important directions for the future. Clearly his work was influenced by academic emphases on rigorous scientific research, political concerns for educational accountability, practical needs for diagnostic usefulness, and collegial collaborations at CIERA. The representative articles and the responses to them in this section explore these dimensions in depth. To foreshadow these papers, I want to examine three broad issues that Steve confronted in his research on assessment.

HOW CONCEPTUAL VIEWS OF READING INFLUENCE ASSESSMENT

Many critical issues about educational assessment pivot on the definitions of the constructs, knowledge, and skills that are measured, like all other scientific research. Reading skills, and especially reading comprehension, follow the same rule, but academics from different theoretical positions and different eras have defined reading in various ways so some assessments rise and fall in popularity (e.g., readability, cloze procedure, and constructed responses). Cynics might point out that standardized reading tests have not been impeded by the lack of academic consensus on definitions, and when new definitions appear, they often beget new assessments. In the educational enterprise, both knowledge building and profit making have led to a greater variety of reading assessments. Until federal and state policymakers began identifying approved assessments at the turn of the new century, teachers were left to sort among the baffling array of tools and choose their own reading assessments, particularly K–3 teachers. Now the five essential components of reading are the focus of many early assessments. Steve understood how conceptual views of reading might lead to narrow assessments, and he was cautious about the trend to make reading assessments too simple, too quick, and too uniform.

In their chapter (Stahl & Hiebert, 2005), Steve and Freddy examine the "simple view of reading" suggested by Gough and Tunmer (1986). The simple view posits that reading is composed of two main factors: the ability to decode words efficiently and the ability to comprehend language. This view is an extension of a position described by LaBerge and Samuels (1974) that posits sequential and mostly independent relations between decoding and comprehending. Stahl and Hiebert (2005) explain why they believe a more complex model is needed, one that predicates comprehension on automatic word recognition and vocabulary knowledge. They show that many children cannot comprehend text because they do not understand the words readily or fully (i.e., fluency confounds comprehension for beginning and struggling readers). In their view, oral reading fluency, including accuracy, rate, and prosody, should be assessed in order to separate the problems in word recognition from comprehension.

Stahl et al. (1999) also discuss the simple view of reading. They claim that it contradicts their clinical experiences because they have seen young children with adequate language abilities who can decode automatically yet still exhibit problems comprehending text. Their complex model for reading assessment and instruction adds strategic control of reading to the simple view and emphasizes many skills and knowledge that contribute to word recognition and language comprehension. Their clinical model of reading assessment is not a series of formal tests that quantify each skill or result in a label or category for the child. Instead, they advocate probing questions as children engage print and text to determine the source of their difficulties as they try to decode and comprehend. Their approach to assessment leads naturally to instruction and remediation so it can be implemented in a clinical setting or a classroom. It is important to note that the probing questions, the assessed skills, and the prescribed instruction are all based on scientific reading research, but facilitating the child's progress, not the summative data, is the goal of the assessment. In their approach, assessment is recurring and dynamic, administered by a teacher who acts more like a coach than an evaluator.

DEVELOPMENTAL ASPECTS OF LEARNING TO READ

Steve's approach to reading development was influenced by Chall's (1983) model of reading stages, but as stage theories lost favor in psychology after the 1970s, most reading researchers adopted developmental approaches that resembled information processing models. For example, the complex model described by Stahl et al. (1999) emphasizes multiple cognitive components that develop independently. There is little mention of how maturational or experiential factors influence or permit the development of the various components because the model is designed as a basis for intervention. However, there are two important developmental aspects of Steve's research that I want to highlight, partly because they were the topics of many of our conversations and partly because they were directions he might have pursued in his own future research.

The first developmental aspect of reading is described by Stahl and Hiebert (2005) when they discuss the development of fluency. They suggest that fluent reading follows a power curve in which initial acquisition, perhaps in K–2, displays accelerated growth that reaches an eventual asymptote. Although Chall (1983) thought the asymptote was reached by the end of third grade, Stahl and Hiebert suggest it might be a year or more later, especially for struggling readers. If fluency follows such a pattern, then correlations between fluency scores and comprehension (or any other skill) would diminish as fluency reaches asymptote. That is exactly what we have found in our research (e.g., Paris, Carpenter, Paris, & Hamilton, 2005) on fluency and alphabet knowledge, two skills that show nonlinear growth and reach an asymptote. Other researchers have also observed the pattern of decreasing correlations between comprehension and skills that are learned to a high asymptote (e.g., Adams, 1990; Walsh, Price, & Gillingham, 1988).

This developmental pattern suggests that two reading skills, such as fluency and comprehension, may be dependent during initial acquisition, but they become independent after one skill is mastered. The dependent relation would be evident among first graders who struggle to decode words but understand little of the text whereas the independent relation would be evident among fifth graders who read fluently but have poor comprehension (i.e., word callers). Stahl et al. (1999) describe exactly such children in their clinical cases. Steve and I discussed this developmental pattern because it has profound implications for reading research. For example, no current models of reading development describe how reading skills might be codependent only at some points during development. Extant models of component reading skills, including the current focus on the five essential components, assume that all reading skills can be analyzed as developmentally stable, normally distributed variables with parametric statistics in multivariate research designs, but that may be false if some skills exhibit nonlinear growth, reach asymptotic levels, and display temporary codependent relations.

In one of our last conversations, Steve and I discussed the possibility that fluency might operate as a threshold variable in which readers must attain a minimum level of rapid and accurate word recognition in order to comprehend text, but beyond that threshold, fluency may not influence comprehension. The same kind of conditional relation may operate between other reading skills. For example, young children may need to know some threshold number of letter names and sounds before they can begin to decode words, and they may need to understand some minimum concepts about print before they can read words on a page. I have elaborated a developmental view of conditional relations among reading skills (Paris, in press) because it has provocative implications for the analysis and interpretation of data on developing reading skills. I suggest that some reading skills, such as alphabet knowledge, concepts of print, and oral reading fluency, are developmentally constrained by nonlinear growth patterns that resemble sigmoid curves (i.e., slow initial learning followed by rapid growth followed by decelerating growth as the asymptote is approached). These constrained patterns yield variable and transitory correlations with other skills that must be interpreted cautiously. For example, our data show that predictive validity correlations may depend on the relative degree of mastery of a constrained skill, and that some correlations between skills that are mastered early and later reading achievement are spurious (Paris et al., 2005). I think Steve's recent view of fluency was compatible with this interpretation.

"Constraints" may seem like a vague term to distinguish various skills, but it indicates that the developmental trajectories can be limited by different factors. The three strands of skills identified in the Stahl et al. (1999) model illuminate differences in type and degree of developmental constraints. Skills in the first strand include print concepts, awareness, purpose, and strategic knowledge. These are generally the same metacognitive aspects of reading that are learned by skilled readers to a high level of mastery and consistency. Skills in the second strand include phonemic awareness, decoding knowledge, sight word knowledge, fluency, and word recognition. These skills vary most during acquisition (between and within subjects), but they reach personal asymptotes of mastery by 10–12 years of age. Thus, they are constrained with skill mastery, but the duration of learning is longer and the variation among asymptotes is greater than for skills in the first strand. The skills in the third strand, background knowledge, vocabulary, language knowledge, and comprehension, are the least constrained because they develop continuously over the lifespan and vary widely in asymptotes among people.

The second important developmental aspect of Steve's approach to reading was his emphasis on strategic control. He used that term to signify children's emerging awareness of their own reading skills and purposes, the metacognition they develop about the task of reading as well as the instruction they receive. Stahl et al. (1999) describe how children can be confused about the purposes of reading and become unmotivated to read. Teachers can help children acquire better metacognition about strategic reading through modeling and instruction (Almasi, 2003), and strategic control of reading fosters self-regulated learning (Paris & Paris, 2001). Thus, an important developmental accomplishment, along with automatic word recognition and language comprehension, is children's cognitive orchestration of their own reading skills.

A less obvious manifestation of Steve's emphasis on strategic control of reading is in his work on educational materials. We both worked on a team of researchers and publishers for a commercial reading program, and Steve was a strong advocate for teaching children reading strategies explicitly. We shared the view that deliberately applied reading strategies could become automatic reading skills with appropriate practice and awareness. Consequently, we encouraged publishers to provide detailed information for teachers so they could explain strategies such as decoding by analogy and identifying main ideas to young children. We also tried to ensure that instructed strategies would be assessed in the program so that strategic control of reading was a valued outcome for both teachers and students. We had similar discussions with colleagues in CIERA when we created publications for teachers such as *Teaching Every Child to Read* (Neuman, 2001). The translation and dissemination of scientific information in materials for teachers were another way that Steve built bridges between his research and educational practices.

ASSESSING COMPREHENSION

Since 2000, a recent trend in reading research has been a renewed focus on reading comprehension and, in particular, how to assess it. Traditional approaches, motivated by the simple view of reading, regarded comprehension as the outcome of decoding, a by-product of successful word recognition and interpretation of language. In that view, comprehension difficulties were usually due to inefficient decoding processes that used excessive cognitive resources and thus did not permit adequate time or processes for understanding. Steve's approach to assessing comprehension elaborates the simple view with attention to both word meanings and strategic control.

Stahl and Hiebert (2005) describe how lack of automatic word recognition and inadequate vocabulary skills can impede comprehension, especially for beginning readers. Several solutions to that problem are possible. One possibility is to ensure that children can read 90–95% of the words accurately and quickly on any passage used to assess comprehension. A second solution might be to use statistical procedures to make comprehension scores conditional on fluency scores. A third option might be to allow repeated reading on a test passage to build fluency before assessing comprehension. A fourth solution might be to preteach key vocabulary words before reading. A fifth possibility might be to compare a child's comprehension scores on increasingly difficult passages (defined by declining fluency scores) to examine within-subject changes in comprehension. All these options are consistent with the use of informal reading inventories, classroom practices of guided reading, and clinical practices of dynamic assessment.

The emphasis on strategic control of reading is part of the complex view of reading, but it has always been troublesome to assess. Paris and Flukes (2005) identified three general methods that researchers have used to assess children's emerging use and understanding of reading strategies. One method is to use self-reports, such as asking readers to think aloud as they process text. The method has an extensive research base (Pressley & Afflerbach, 1995), and Steve's recent work showed how think-aloud protocols could be used as classroom assessments of comprehension and strategic control. The second method of assessment is interviews before, during, or after reading that query readers about the processes they will or did use to monitor and repair comprehension. Less work has been done on this method because the data are difficult to quantify. The third method is the use of surveys that can be administered independently of reading a specific text. Surveys can be given to groups of subjects with Likert responses that are readily quantified, but the method is decontextualized and open to distortion (e.g., subjects giving desired responses rather than accurate reports). The first two assessment methods that are administered individually as children read text may provide more valid indicators of strategic control and comprehension.

There are many possible future directions for assessing reading comprehension. For example, CIERA researchers showed that children's comprehension of televised stories (van den Broek et al., 2005) and their understanding of wordless narrative picture books (Paris & Paris, 2003) are strongly related to children's reading comprehension. A second direction charted by CIERA researchers is the design of better ways to measure text difficulty and readability (e.g., Hoffman, 2002; Menon & Hiebert, 2003). A third direction is the assessment of the literacy environment that supports frequent, engaging, and interactive reading (e.g., DeBruin-Parecki, 1999; Dickinson, McCabe, & Anastasopoulos, 2001). These new directions are promising and continue to be explored even though CIERA has closed. Steve's work on comprehension assessment will also be continued by his colleagues, and we can expect it to be as useful, rigorous, and compelling as his other research.

CONCLUSION

As you explore Steve's papers on reading assessment and consider his colleagues' elaborations of his work in this section of the volume, remember the contexts and purposes that influenced his work. You may find it easy to imagine Steve lecturing an International Reading Association audience or exhorting his graduate students to dig deeper into the data. He was a dynamic teacher who believed in the value of research with a rare combination of personal and professional dedication. His legacy will last a long time because his ideas about children's reading were both rigorous and practical, and his influence on people was deep and genuine.

REFERENCES

Adams, M. J. (1990). *Beginning to read: Thinking and learning about print*. Cambridge, MA: MIT Press.

Almasi, J. F. (2003). *Teaching strategic processes in reading*. New York: Guilford Press.

Chall, J.S. (1983). *Stages of reading development*. New York: McGraw-Hill.

DeBruin-Parecki, A. (1999). *Assessing adult/child storybook reading practices* (Technical Report #2–004). Ann Arbor: University of Michigan, Center for the Improvement of Early Reading Achievement.

Dickinson, D. K., McCabe, A., & Anastasopoulos, L. (2001). *A framework for examining book reading in early childhood classrooms* (Technical Report #1-014). Ann Arbor: University of Michigan, Center for the Improvement of Early Reading Achievement.

Good, R. H., & Kaminski, R. A. (Eds.). (2002). *Dynamic indicators of basic early literacy skills* (6th ed.). Eugene, OR: Institute for the Development of Educational Achievement.

Good, R. H., Simmons, D. C., & Kame'enui, E. J. (2001). The importance and decision-making utility of a continuum of fluency-based indicators of foundational reading skills for third-grade high-stakes outcomes. *Scientific Studies of Reading*, 5(3), 257–288.

Gough, P. B., & Tunmer, W. E. (1986). Decoding, reading, and reading disability. *Remedial and Special Education*, 7, 6–10.

Heubert, J. P., & Hauser, R. M. (1999). *High stakes: Testing for tracking, promotion, and graduation*. Washington, DC: National Academy Press.

Hoffman, J. V. (2002). Words on words in leveled texts for beginning readers. In D. Schallert, C. Fairbanks, J. Worthy, B. Maloch, & J. V. Hoffman (Eds.), *Fifty-first Yearbook of the National Reading Conference* (pp. 59–81). Oak Creek, WI: National Reading Conference.

LaBerge, D., & Samuels, S. J. (1974). Toward a theory of automatic information processing in reading. *Cognitive Psychology*, 6, 293–323.

Menon, S., & Hiebert, E. H. (2003). *A comparison of first graders' reading acquisition with little books and literature anthologies* (Technical Report #1-009). Ann Arbor: University of Michigan, Center for the Improvement of Early Reading Achievement.

National Reading Panel. (2000). *Teaching children to read: An evidence-based assessment of the scientific research literature on reading and its implications for reading instruction: Reports of the subgroups*. Bethesda, MD: National Institute of Child Health and Human Development.

Neuman, S. (Ed.). (2001). *Teaching every child to read*. Ann Arbor, MI: Center for the Improvement of Reading Achievement.

No Child Left Behind Act of 2001, Public Law No 107-110, 115 Stat. 1425 (2002).

Paris, S.G. (in press). Re-interpreting the development of reading skills. *Reading Research Quarterly*.

Paris, S. G., Carpenter, R. D., Paris, A. H., & Hamilton, E. E. (2005). Spurious and genuine correlates of children's reading comprehension. In S. G. Paris & S. A. Stahl (Eds.), *Children's reading comprehension and assessment* (pp. 131–160). Mahwah, NJ: Erlbaum.

Paris, S. G., & Flukes, J. (2005). Assessing children's metacognition about strategic reading. In S. E. Israel, C. C. Block, K. L. Bauserman, & K. Kinnucan-Welsch (Eds.), *Metacognition in literacy learning: Theory, assessment, instruction, and professional development* (pp. 121–139). Mahwah, NJ: Erlbaum.

Paris, S. G., & Hoffman, J. V. (2004). Early reading assessments in kindergarten through third grade: Findings from the Center for the Improvement of Early Reading Achievement, *Elementary School Journal*, 105(2), 199–217.

Paris, S. G., Lawton, T. A., Turner, J. C., & Roth, J. L. (1991). A developmental perspective on standardized achievement testing. *Educational Researcher, 20,* 12–20.

Paris, S. G., & Paris, A. H. (2001). Classroom applications of research on self-regulated learning. *Educational Psychologist, 36*(2), 89–101.

Paris, A. H., & Paris, S. G. (2003). Assessing narrative comprehension in young children. *Reading Research Quarterly, 38*(1), 36–76.

Paris, S. G., Paris, A. H., & Carpenter, R. D. (2002). Effective practices for assessing young readers. In B. Taylor & P. D. Pearson (Eds.), *Teaching reading: Effective schools, accomplished teachers* (pp. 141–160). Mahwah, NJ: Erlbaum.

Paris, S. G., & Stahl, S. (2005). *Children's reading comprehension and assessment.* Mahwah, NJ: Erlbaum.

Pressley, M., & Afflerbach, P. (1995). *Verbal protocols of reading: The nature of constructively responsive reading.* Hillsdale, NJ: Erlbaum.

Sacks, P. (1999). *Standardized minds.* Cambridge, MA: Perseus Boks.

Smith, M. L. (1991). Put to the test: The effects of external testing on teachers. *Educational Researcher, 20*(5), 8–11.

Stahl, S. A., & Hiebert, E. H. (2005). The "word factors": A problem for reading comprehension assessments. In S. G. Paris & S. A. Stahl (Eds.), *Current issues in reading comprehension and assessment* (pp. 161–186). Mahwah, NJ: Erlbaum.

Stahl, S. A., Kuhn, M. R., & Pickle, J. M. (1999). An educational model of assessment and targeted instruction for children with reading problems. In D. Evenson & P. Mosenthal (Eds.), *Reconsidering the role of the reading clinic in a new age of literacy* (pp. 249–272). Stamford, CT: JAI Press.

van den Broek, P., Kendeou, P., Kremer, K., Lynch, J., Butler, J., White, M. J., et al. (2005). Assessment of comprehension abilities in young children. In S. G. Paris & S. A. Stahl (Eds.), *Current issues in reading comprehension and assessment* (pp. 107–130). Mahwah, NJ: Erlbaum.

Wagner, R. K., Torgeson, J. K., & Rashotte, C. A. (1999). *Comprehensive test of phonological processing.* Austin, TX: Pro-Ed.

Walsh, D. J., Price, G. G., & Gillingham, M. G. (1988). The critical but transitory importance of letter naming. *Reading Research Quarterly, 23*(1), 108–122.

23

An Educational Model of Assessment and Targeted Instruction for Children with Reading Problems

STEVEN A. STAHL
MELANIE R. KUHN
J. MICHAEL PICKLE

Over the past several years, there has been a change in the way educators view reading difficulties and the type of work that is undertaken to help learners struggling to become literate. In the past, learners experiencing reading difficulties were diagnosed at a reading clinic. A plan of remediation was then devised to help correct any areas of difficulty. Since the causes of reading difficulties were primarily viewed as having a neurological basis, the underlying model for this perspective was a medical one.

In contrast to the medical model which emphasizes descriptions based upon pathologies or what is wrong with the reader, we, along with many other educational specialists, have come to advocate an educational model based upon both learning theory and a cognitive analysis of what the reading process entails. This model is based upon theories of reading development and processes. The focus of such a model emphasizes what the learner is able to do, and points to instruction that will allow for further conventional reading. This chapter presents this educational model, explains how it can be used to assess children experiencing difficulties in learning to read, and specifies how to target instruction in order to meet these learners' needs.

A "SIMPLE VIEW" OF READING

In 1986, Gough and Tunmer proposed their "simple view" of reading, namely, that reading comprehension could be accounted for by the combination of two factors: a decoding factor (D) and a language comprehension factor (C). Reading comprehension skill (RC) could be thought of as the product of these two ($D \times C$). If a child could not decode ($D = 0$) but could comprehend language well, that child would be unable to read (RC = 0). Similarly, if a child could not comprehend the language of the text ($C = 0$), he or she would not be able to comprehend the text, even if he or she could pronounce each of the words in the text correctly. Gough and Tunmer used this model to provide functional definitions of dyslexia and hyperlexia. Dyslexia was defined as decoding difficulties in spite of adequate language comprehension; that is, the first case of the two cases described above. Hyperlexia, demonstrated by the second of these examples, was defined as inadequate language comprehension in spite of adequate decoding ability.

Yet, in our clinical work, we have encountered many children who can decode automatically and fluently and have adequate language abilities but who still experience difficulty coordinating the processes needed to comprehend text. They appear to be unable to adjust their reading to meet their specific purposes or they simply fail to understand why they are engaged in reading. This observation led Stahl (1992) to propose that "Reading" is a bit more complex. To begin with, the reading task differs in relation to the reader's purpose. "Reading to Do," or reading to accomplish a task by following directions, for example, differs both from "Reading to Enjoy," or reading for aesthetic purposes, and from "Reading to Learn." Still, despite the variations in purpose, certain basic processes underlie each of these types of "Reading." By adding one additional component, that of Strategic Control, Gough and Tunmer's "simple view" seems to provide an adequate description of what readers need to do to read in specific contexts. Strategic Control is a necessary addition since our notion of Strategic Control encompasses much of what has been labeled "metacognition" (e.g., Garner, 1987; Paris, Wasik, & van der Westhuizen, 1989). It incorporates the awareness of the purposes of reading, both why reading is done in general and ways of adjusting reading under specific conditions. It further involves developing a variety of strategies for achieving those goals.

A MODEL FOR READING ASSESSMENT AND INSTRUCTION

One of the major assumptions underlying our view is that each of the basic reading processes—decoding, language comprehension and strategic control—develops independently (see Stanovich, 1992). We therefore make the assumption that children's word identification skills develop independently from their language ability and that these, in turn, develop independently from their ability to strategically control the entire process. We also make the assumption that it is possible to assess each of these processes in order to establish an understanding of a child's level of word identification skill, their language comprehension, and their knowledge and strategic control of the reading process. It should be noted that these assumptions stand in contrast to those that constitute the basis of other models (e.g., Goodman, 1986).

The general development of these basic processes forms the underlying structure for the assessment and instructional model used at the University of Georgia Reading Clinic, presented in Figure 23.1. This model assumes both that the three "strands" of abilities underlie a child's reading skill, and that each area can be either a strength or a weakness for a particular learner. This model can best be understood when read from right to left, beginning with the most advanced area and working backwards.

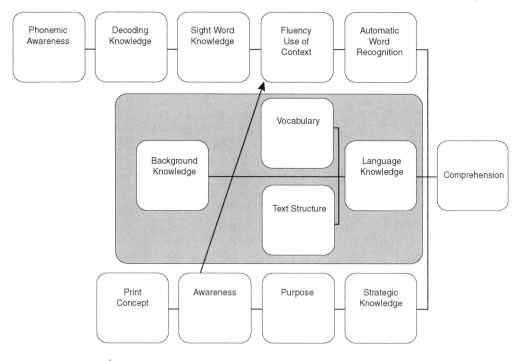

FIGURE 23.1. Abilities that underlie a child's reading skill.

Developing Word Recognition

The first strand within this model consists of word recognition. Given that many children attending the clinic demonstrate a specific difficulty in the area of word recognition, we consider this area as one that can have a negative impact on a child's comprehension. Correspondingly, as children's sight word vocabulary and decoding skills develop, they find themselves able to comprehend increasingly complex texts.

A number of authors have suggested that word recognition skill develops in three stages:

- An emergent literacy stage, in which children build the concepts necessary for learning about print, including basic print concepts such as directionality and the concept of "word," and phoneme awareness (Yopp, 1992) or the ability to reflect upon sounds in spoken words.
- An accuracy stage, in which students learn some basic sound–symbol correspondences and some basic sight word knowledge. Chall (1983) refers to this stage as "grunting and groaning," since a child's word recognition is often labored. Our work (Stahl & Heubach, 2005) suggests that this stage is attained around the time a child is able to read a primer-level passage.
- An automaticity stage, in which students learn to read words fluently, without having to strategically decode a word. At the end of this stage, with the attainment of about a beginning fourth-grade reading level, word recognition is transparent and is no longer a source of difficulty.

We will talk about these stages in turn.

Emergent Literacy

It is a truism that children's reading begins well before they start formal instruction in school. Indeed, their reading occurs from the time they begin to notice words that exist in their environment, as they begin to make up rhymes, and as they begin to recognize individual letters. In fact, their later success in formal reading instruction is often built upon those experiences involving language and print that occur outside the school setting (Lomax & McGee, 1987). These include a child's familiarity with print and written language conventions as well as his or her ability to manipulate sounds in spoken words. Recent research suggests that an awareness of the form and functions of print, phoneme awareness, and knowledge of letter names are all strongly related to a successful beginning reading experience (e.g., Lomax & McGee, 1987).

When children do not have access to such experiences with print, it is likely that they will experience difficulty with formal instruction. However, many of the students assessed at our clinic have had a great deal of exposure to such experiences outside their school environment yet still face difficulties in learning to read texts independently. It is our sense that such children have developed a basic misconception about reading at some point in the learning process, and that other misunderstandings have been built upon the initial misconception. Because their basic concepts about print are so confused, reading appears to be a muddle to them.

An example of such a child is Jocelyn,[1] a first grader with whom we worked in the clinic. She was the only child of a single parent who had the highest expectations for Jocelyn's reading. Jocelyn's mother bought many books for her daughter and read "four or five" of them aloud every night. Despite this, Jocelyn was able to read only a few words presented on a pre-primer list. When then given the Concepts about Print test (Clay, 1993a) and asked to push two index cards together until one word was showing, Jocelyn pushed the cards together so that the "hed" of the word "splashed" showed. Further, when asked for two words, Jocelyn showed two letters. When asked to write out all the words she knew, she spelled "Fish" with an initial "f" and continued by adding an additional six letters, stating that "words that begin with 'f' have a lot of letters in them." When writing connected text in school, it was noted that Jocelyn did not use spaces between words, but rather wrote strings of letters to represent sentences. Additionally, she often began words on the right, rather than the left, spelling "to," "go," and "me" as "ot," "og" (with the g reversed), and "em." For each of these examples, she wrote the correct initial letter, but then proceeded in the wrong direction.

Jocelyn's confusions about the nature of words could not help but interfere with her learning to read. After talking to her mother, we felt that some of these confusions may have arisen out of her mother's work with Jocelyn. While her mother did positive things such as extensive reading aloud and discussing books, her mother's expectations were excessively high. Jocelyn's mother had introduced an extensive vocabulary and had attempted to have Jocelyn sound out words before her daughter was ready for it. From "too much, too soon," Jocelyn became confused, and her confusions built upon themselves until she was turned off to reading entirely.

Print Concepts

Part of Jocelyn's confusion could be located in her concept of print. She was confused about what a "word" was, as evidenced both by her inability to identify one when asked to do so and by the lack of spaces found in her writing. For other children, it is possible to note other confusions regarding print. For example, they may not have learned that written language communicates meaning or how "storybook" language differs from regular speaking. It is also possible that they have failed to distinguish that the "writing," rather than the "pictures," carries the meaning.

For Jocelyn, the confusion extended to the directionality of print, and evidenced itself in her reversals of both words and letters in her writing. At one point, these reversals would have been considered the result of a neurological deficit. As a result of the writings of Samuel Orton and others, reversals came to be viewed as a symptom of "hemispheric imbalance," "visual perceptual difficulties," and the like. These explanations for reading difficulty, however, have gradually been disproved (see Coles, 1987, for review). The current view of reversals is that they are a result of children's low reading knowledge, rather than a cause (see Adams, 1990). As children become better readers, these reversals disappear.

We would argue that for a child like Jocelyn who had little or no print concept, instruction that concentrates on the mechanics of reading, such as phonics, is simply an abstract and artificial task. Until the child has additional meaningful encounters with print, he or she will be unable to make sense of such instruction. For this reason, it is important to develop a concept of the wholeness and meaningfulness of reading. This can be done by providing numerous experiences with written text prior to the start of formal reading instruction. By presenting Jocelyn with instruction in the mechanics of reading before she had the foundation to support it, confusions regarding the nature of reading took hold. It was necessary, therefore, to straighten out these confusions if she was to be able to make sense of further instruction.

Developing Print Concepts

In order to develop such a base of experience for a child, one might begin targeted reading instruction with activities such as sharing books, writing down dictated stories, and engaging the learner in authentic reading and writing tasks. For example, predictable books, or books with consistent language patterns, work especially well for beginning word recognition (Bridge, Winograd, & Haley, 1983); however, it is important that an early reading program include a wide range of books, including expository texts. Stahl and Miller (1989) found that whole language programs are effective in developing these basic print concepts. Such programs include a great deal of work with predictable materials, child-dictated experience stories, and teacher storybook reading.

With Jocelyn, we jointly read a number of highly predictable books, including Eric Carle's *Is this your cat?* and Donald Crew's *Blue Sea*. (Lists of other predictable books can be found in sources such as Barr & Johnson [1990], Bridge et al. [1983], and Tierney, Readence, & Dishner [1995].) As part of this shared reading, we had Jocelyn point to each word as we said it together. Such print to speech matching is extremely important in establishing the concept of word, as well as directionality. As she became more proficient at reading, this word pointing disappeared. Additionally, we had Jocelyn dictate stories as part of a language experience approach (Tierney et al., 1995), in order to help her develop an understanding of the relation between print and speech. These stories and nursery rhymes were put on charts and Jocelyn could then point to her own words as we read along.

Jocelyn also developed print concepts through her experiences in writing text. She began to use spaces, and she started to use the correct initial consonants in connected text, whereas she previously used them only when asked to spell words in isolation.

We consider writing to be a useful way to reinforce the learning that goes on in targeted instruction. For one thing, it provides children with a concrete place to work out their difficulties with written language. As they struggle with the problem of how to represent language in written form, they are able to work through many of the concepts we want them to establish regarding written language. However, it is important to stress that children experiencing reading problems need direct guidance in writing. We have found that by monitoring their writing, through guided questions (such as "What does that say?" or "Where does this word begin?"), for example, we see greater progress than when children are left alone to experiment with print.

Phonemic Awareness

In addition to an adequate print concept, children need to develop phonemic awareness or the awareness of the sounds in spoken words. Phonemic awareness incorporates a child's ability to rhyme, to recognize the number of phonemes in a spoken word, and to manipulate phonemes through word play. This is a difficult task for many children since spoken words do not naturally divide into readily identifiable phonemes. For example, the word "fish" consists of one speech sound represented by three phonemes (and four letters). In English, as well as other alphabetic languages, letters, or in some cases several letters, represent these phonemes in print. For children to make meaningful sense of the correspondence that exists between letters and phonemes, they must first be aware of the existence of phonemes in the spoken word.

This was another area of difficulty for Jocelyn. When asked to delete phonemes from the beginning of words, she could not say "take" without the /t/ or "meat" without the /m/. She would either say she did not understand what was being asked or she would provide us with a rhyming word. However, she was able to remove a syllable from a given word (e.g., "cucumber" without the "cu"). When spelling in isolation, her writing reflected the beginning of phoneme awareness, since she generally included the correct initial consonants (e.g., "wibshn" for when," or "binwas" for "bump").

Phoneme awareness is also important in seeing how speech relates to written language. For most communication, focusing on meaning is the primary goal. But when learning to read, especially in regard to sound–symbol correspondence, it is essential to view words in terms of the sounds they contain. A child told that the "first sound in 'dog' is /d/" needs to understand that we are talking about the spoken word "dog," rather than the animal. We have had children tell us that the first sound in "dog" is the nose! It is only by recognizing that spoken words are comprised of phonemes that the further letter–sound relationship can be established.

The importance of phonemic awareness as a prerequisite for success in beginning reading comes from a variety of sources. To begin with, a series of correlational studies indicate that a strong relationship exists between phoneme awareness and success in reading. One study assessed students in the first and fourth grades; they found that children experiencing difficulty with phoneme awareness tasks in their first year of formal schooling remained in the bottom quarter of their class 4 years later (Juel, 1988). Similarly, MacLean, Bryant, and Bradley (1987) determined that children's knowledge of nursery rhymes at 3 years old is a strong predictor of both their later phonological knowledge and their early reading ability.

In fact, Stanovich (1986) suggests that a great deal of children's reading difficulties may develop as the result of poor phonemic awareness. Most children develop phonemic awareness without difficulty, but some children fail to intuit the notion that words can be thought of as consisting of phonemes. He argues that children who lack phonemic awareness early on have a greater amount of difficulty making sense of the concepts involved in word identification. As a result, they read less, read texts that are less challenging, and receive qualitatively different reading instruction as a result (see Allington, 1983). It is often the case that these children fall further behind their classmates, and what begins as a lack of phonemic awareness develops into a more global reading difficulty. Stanovich calls this the "Matthew effect" from a passage in the Bible discussing how the rich get richer and the poor get poorer. Indeed, children with these initial confusions fall further and further behind their peers.

Teaching Phonemic Awareness

While phonemic awareness does not develop automatically for every child, several instructional techniques can be used to teach children an awareness of the spoken sounds in words. These range from formal programs including those by Lindamood and Lindamood (1975), Rosner (1974), and Wallach and Wallach (1979) to series of informal activities, such as those found in Griffith and Olson (1992), Yopp (1992), and Eldredge (1995). Some activities we have found particularly helpful and enjoyable involve teaching nursery rhymes (especially if written out on charts), tongue twisters (especially when stretching the onset, as in P-eter p-iper p-icked a p-eck of p-ickled p-eppers), deletion tasks (say "hear" without the /h/), sound adding tasks (Say "ache." Add a /k/ to the beginning and what does it say? Change the /k/ to a /b/."), and stretching out the sounds in a word so that each phoneme can be identified (e.g., "dog" could be stretched to "d-d-d-o-g-g-g"). Such stretch sounding provides a natural lead-in to invented spelling, since the process helps children identify individual phonemes which then can be written down. Conversely, invented spelling appears to improve phonemic awareness in children.

Invented Spelling

Invented spelling further allows children to establish the link between oral and written language. It, like many other aspects of reading acquisition, appears to move through a series of stages. At first, children's spellings do not seem to bear any resemblance to the sounds in spoken words. However, consonants, and later vowels, soon come to be represented in their writing. To help children move the former non-phonemic spelling to the later phonemic stage, it is useful to begin by helping the children stretch out those words they want to spell. They should be encouraged to write down all the sounds they hear. Initially, this may consist of only the initial and final consonant, but as the child gains familiarity with the letter–sound correspondences, his or her spellings will come to more closely resemble the conventional spellings.

Knowledge of Letters and Their Names

In research conducted in the United States, a child's knowledge of letter names in kindergarten has traditionally had the strongest correlation with a child's reading success. Not only does this relationship exist for beginning reading, but it continues to be a significant predictor of success even at the fourth-grade level (Chall, 1983). However, it is a complicated issue since research further indicates that knowledge of letter names, in and of itself, is not sufficient for reading success. Indeed, children do not need to have knowledge of all the letter names before beginning to learn how to read. We have found that letter knowledge is best developed alongside other concepts about print.

We worked with Jocelyn for 2 years in the clinic. We began with very simple, predictable books, which we used as means of developing a "book sense," including basic print concepts such as directionality and the concept of "word." We also used the books as a means of introducing words. We gradually introduced more difficult and less predictable books, with more varied vocabulary, similar to the approach used by Reading Recovery™ (Clay, 1993b). By the end of that 2-year period, she was in third grade, reading materials appropriate for that level. Her program did not stay at the emergent level, but moved on to teach automatic word recognition, using activities similar to those described below.

Accuracy of Word Identification

We see that accuracy and automaticity of word recognition are separate but related parts of learning to read. There are children who read accurately but not automatically. Traditionally, approaches for teaching children with reading problems have focused on accuracy. Several traditional methods have been designed to remediate this difficulty including the Fernald approach (Fernald, 1943), the Orton–Gillingham approaches (Gillingham & Stillman, 1966) and the Hegge–Kirk–Kirk drills (1955). Although these methods are often slow and laborious, they are highly successful. These methods have recently been joined by newer approaches such as those designed at the Benchmark School (Gaskins et al., 1988).

Overall, as educators, we can be reasonably successful at teaching decoding or accurate word recognition to those children who have established an adequate conceptual base.[2] One child with difficulties in accurate word recognition is Thomas. Thomas was first seen by us as a third grader and was followed through the beginning of fourth grade. He was the child of two highly educated professionals. His scores on the Wechsler Intelligence Scale for Children–Revised (WISC-R) were 136 verbal, 95 nonverbal, and 118 for the Full Scale. However, these scores underestimate his potential, since he was reported to respond impulsively to the test items, especially on the performance items. He further tended to be easily distracted, especially when not interested in what he was doing.

Thus, we felt that Thomas is a child with a great deal of intellectual ability. However, he was not able to decode very well upon our first seeing him. For example, on an informal phonics survey developed for the clinic, Thomas was able to read only 7 out of 10 CVC (consonant–vowel–consonant) words containing a short vowel sound, 5 out of 10 words with a vowel digraph, and 4 of 6 with a vowel diphthong. Performance at this level is typical of first or second graders. On a list of words from the Durrell Analysis of Reading Difficulty (Durrell & Catterson, 1980), Thomas correctly identified 21 out of 30 words presented, equivalent to a low-second-grade level. His spelling also reflected his lack of awareness of sound–symbol relationships, as is evidenced by his performance on the following list, taken from Gillet and Temple (1990):

1. late
2. wind
3. shed
4. geese   geus
5. jumped   jomped (j reversed)
6. yell   uaill
7. chirped   chrppt
8. learned   lrned
9. shove   shved
10. trained   traned
11. year   yere
12. shock   shoce
13. stained   sand
14. chick   cike
15. drive

In this spelling sample, letters stand for the syllable. Such spellings are typical of children in kindergarten or first grade. Other spellings made use of correct vowels, but random substitutions (jomped) as well as long vowels for short or vice versa (cike, shoce) were also apparent.

All of these tasks involved reading or spelling words presented in isolation. When given a context, Thomas's word recognition dramatically improved. On an information reading inventory (IRI), he read a third-grade passage adequately. His reading, however, was slow, and he read the passage in twice the amount of time customary for a third grader. An analysis of his oral reading miscues suggested that he relied heavily on context along with the initial sounds, often trying two or three words before finding one that fit the context or giving up. Relying excessively on context is very time-consuming, more time-consuming than is the rapid word identification typical of good readers. Stanovich (1992) found that using the context to guess at a word took considerably longer than the rapid word identification that is the hallmark of good reading. Contrary to common belief, he also found that it is the struggling reader who relies most heavily upon context, whereas the proficient reader recognizes words automatically. Thus, Thomas's reliance on context not only slowed him down, it interfered with his comprehension.

Even with his difficulty in recognizing words, Thomas's comprehension was adequate. For example, on the fourth-grade passage, he read with 17 miscues in 109 words, few of which made sense within the passage. Despite this, he was able to answer six out of eight literal questions about the passage content. In spite of what appeared to be adequate comprehension, his parents and teachers reported that

Thomas did not like to read independently, probably because it was so difficult for him.

At the time of testing, Thomas was able to use his strengths, his ability to construct meaning from minimal cues in the text and thus comprehend what he was reading, to overcome his weaknesses in word identification. By using his prior knowledge, he was able to ignore words as much as possible. But it was his difficulty in recognizing words that made reading a laborious and unpleasant task and limited the progress he was able to make.

Our instructional emphasis was on teaching Thomas to focus on the internal structure of words. We felt that this would be a temporary strategy until he developed automatic word identification skill. (We discussed the importance of the temporary focus on word identification with Thomas, explaining why we were doing it.) We used a variety of activities designed to meet this goal. A basic approach was a compare–contrast approach to word identification (see Cunningham, 1995), in which Thomas was taught to look at unknown words and compare them to words that he already knew. In support of this basic approach, we used word sorts (Gillet & Temple, 1990), in which children are given groups of words and asked to sort them by features, and various word recognition drills, including a set of word cards developed from words that Thomas missed during oral reading and practiced until he could read them on three separate occasions. We also used, the Hegge et al. (1955) drills to automatize his word recognition.

Decoding instruction, although key for Thomas, never took more than a fourth of our hour-long sessions. Most of the time was spent on oral and silent reading of material that was interesting to Thomas. It is important that even when the major goal is to improve decoding, most of the time is spent reading connected text at the child's instructional level. There are several reasons for this. First, reading connected text gives the child an application for the decoding and word recognition skills that are being learned so that they seem relevant. Second, it is only practice in reading connected text that leads to automatic word recognition, and thus to permanent gains in comprehension (Fleisher, Pany, & Jenkins, 1979–1980). Third, and perhaps most importantly, it is important to keep the focus on reading for comprehension and enjoyment, so that children will know the purpose of reading. Thus, even if one has to focus on individual words, it is important that the child understand that this focus is a means to the end of comprehending more and more complex texts. One type of text which worked well with Thomas was the Choose Your Own Adventure series, at least in the beginning. The reason this worked so well was that the text was presented in discrete, one-page sections, giving Thomas small units that, together, amounted to an entire story. Thomas's lack of automaticity prevented him from dealing with large amounts of text, although he was mentally capable of understanding complex texts and eager to read them. The Choose Your Own Adventure Series was an effective compromise. Later, Thomas began reading science fiction novels appropriate for his grade level.

At the end of about 1 year of tutoring (three academic quarters), Thomas had progressed from a middle second-grade level, overall, in third grade to a fourth-grade instructional level in oral reading and a fifth-grade instructional reading level in silent reading. Perhaps more importantly, Thomas had begun to read avidly at home, and reading became an activity that he would choose to do. His reading ceased to be a problem in school. Thomas's father reported to me a few years later that he was getting A's in language arts in middle school and kept reading avidly.

Automaticity of Word Recognition

As mentioned earlier, schools are generally successful in teaching children accurate word recognition skills. However, a large proportion of the children are referred to our clinic because their word recognition has failed to become automatic.

In order for children to focus on the meaning of the text, as opposed to the words, it is necessary for them to develop automatic word recognition skills. These skills are usually in place by the end of the fourth grade and should make decoding transparent. In other words, the reader should be able to concentrate on making sense of the text rather than on the print itself. Should a child have to work through even a small percentage of the words in a text, he or she will be sacrificing attention that could otherwise be focused on meaning.

Greg came to the clinic demonstrating accurate, but effortful reading. A fourth grader, Greg's reading was halting even when engaged with a basic text. As a result of the effort Greg expended in his decoding, there was virtually no attention left over for his comprehension. Greg could recognize words in third-grade lists, but his oral reading (with comprehension) level on an IRI was at the primer level. Because his reading was so effortful, he could not comprehend what he was reading. Because he was not comprehending, he could not take advantage of context.

Developing Fluency

The one essential element in moving learners from accurate to automatic word recognition is that of practice. The majority of children make this transition in the normal course of their learning to read. In general, they encounter a reasonable amount of text, either at their instructional level, that is material which they can read with at least 95% accuracy, or at their independent level material in which they achieve 99% accuracy. As they read more text, they become more fluent and automatic. The importance of having children read widely at an appropriate reading level cannot be overstated. Fortunately, there are several special techniques designed to assist learners experiencing reading difficulties develop fluent and automatic reading more efficiently. It is important to note that these techniques, which include variations of repeated readings and computer programs, are meant only as one component of a broader reading program that emphasizes reading for meaning and learning.

The basic method of repeated readings (Samuels, 1985) is just that, having children read the same material repeatedly, until they reach a desired level of fluency and accuracy. In our clinic, we take a section of text of about 100 words and have the child practice it repeatedly until the student can read it at a rate of 100 words per minute with 99% accuracy.[3] Often, the first reading is taped, and the child and tutor listen to the tape, reviewing the accuracy of the reading together. At other times, we will use longer sections of text, and adhere to the same standard. Other variations of this basic techniques include the impress approach (Tierney et al., 1995) in which the student and tutor read the same section together, repeatedly, with the tutor gradually phasing his or her voice out as the student takes over, taped readings (Chomsky, 1978) in which the student practices a longer story along with a tape, and echo reading in which the teacher reads a portion of the text (a paragraph or even a sentence) and the student echoes it.

We found a variation of repeated readings, Supported Contextual Reading, to be effective with Greg. First, we chose material that was considerably above his instructional level. Books were chosen at the second- or third-grade reading level and passages were selected from the text for practice both in the tutoring session and at home. This was done partially for motivational purposes. Because be had to read the same material repeatedly, it was important that he knew that he would be able to master material at the end of this effort. In fact, he enjoyed both the comfort of revisiting a familiar text and the sense of mastery in improving his speed and accuracy with practice. In addition, the lesson structures provided a scaffold so that he could read more difficult material. By using more difficult material, we were able to "pull him up," rather than work gradually up from his "level." We find that children like Greg often have had a great deal of instruction but can't put it together. They are able to sound words out when words are presented in isolations, like Greg could, but cannot deal with connected text. The use of more difficult material allowed Greg to implement what he already knew to use.

In Supported Contextual Reading, children are given material which is considerably above their instructional reading level and supported as they learn to read that material orally. Typically, we use selections that are 1 or 2 years above the child's instructional level, depending on our judgment of how much effort the child is willing to put forth and how much frustration the child can handle. The first day's lesson usually begins by having the tutor read the selection out loud to the child. The tutor and student discuss the selection, using questions, a story map, or any other technique deemed appropriate. The purpose of this discussion is to make sure that the student understands, before repeated readings, that the purpose of reading is to comprehend the text. Handling comprehension first allows the student to concentrate on word recognition.

The next step is typically echo reading, in which the teacher reads a paragraph and the child echoes it back, pointing to each word with his or her finger as it is read. Echo reading introduces new words.

After this lesson, we send the book home with the child to be read with his or her parents. The reading is assisted; that is, as the child has a problem with a word, the word is given immediately and written down to be worked with later. The parent and tutor are instructed not to provide any cueing (such as "What does this word begin with?") for fear of having the child use confusing cues. This procedure is used both when the tutor and the parent read with the child.

The child reads the same materials over the course of several lessons until the material is mastered. Sometimes the tutor reads along with the child, using impress reading techniques (Tierney et al., 1995). Sometimes, we use tapes to support a child's reading. There was one child who traveled an hour and a half to the clinic. We had the child listen to the tape and read along, pointing to each word as it was read in the car using the cassette player. We use material that is long and complex, suitable for the child's maturity. We do not use predictable materials, since the content provides so much support that the child may not be using information from the words at all (see Johnston, 1995). The material used is so complex and long (usually our selections are at least 1,000 words in length) that it cannot be memorized. Instead, we hypothesize that children are using cues from their memory of the stories, along with cues from the words in the text, to successfully master each story. Using the word-level information requires the students to put together previously learned phonics information, supported by context. Thus, they can move from strategic decoding to the automatic recognition of orthographic patterns which is the hallmark of proficient reading (Adams, 1990).

This supported contextual reading procedure has produced fairly dramatic results. Greg's reading improved to a third-grade level at the end of a 6-week intensive summer program using these procedures. The second child we tried this with, a third-grade girl whose reading level was at the pre-primer stage, is currently reading at the early fourth-grade level in this, her fourth-grade year. We also began this approach with another child, a fourth-grade boy, with promising results.

Language Comprehension

The second component of our reading model is language comprehension. There are three aspects of language that are, in turn, incorporated into this component: vocabulary, general knowledge and knowledge of text structure. These were deliberatively selected since they are areas in which children with reading problems often experience deficiencies. Again, each aspect is discussed below, in turn.

One important distinction that needs to be established is the difference between language difficulties which hinder reading progress and language difficulties which result from reading difficulties. For example, some suggest that children with reading problems have subtle deficiencies in the area of syntactic development (e.g., Wiig & Simel, 1976). However, we found it difficult to distinguish these from dialect differences or a lack of familiarity with literate language. As children become more proficient readers or as they are exposed to more literature, they gain familiarity with literate language and the syntactic patterns found in written texts.

Stanovich (1986) suggests that many of the differences between competent and struggling readers in regard to language knowledge result from differences in their amount of exposure to written language. At a certain point, the primary means children have for learning new word meanings is texts, rather than oral language. Children learn new word meanings either from their own reading or by being read to by others. It therefore follows that children who are exposed to a greater amount of text, learn more words as a result. This increased vocabulary allows them to read more complex texts, which, in turn, exposes them to even more new words, enabling them to increase their vocabulary even further. Even if a struggling reader did not have a vocabulary deficit when he or she started formal schooling, one may have developed as a result of his or her lack of exposure to text. A similar pattern may occur with other aspects of language, including the subtler forms of syntactic development.

However, at the clinic, we do not attempt to "remediate" language per se. To begin with, it is not possible to directly teach the thousands of vocabulary words that might be learned, nor is it reasonable to provide all the necessary background knowledge that is required to comprehend every possible text. Instead, we concentrate on teaching what a child needs to know in order to comprehend a particular passage with the assumption that this knowledge will prove useful in the future as well. Further, we try to stress the general processes of learning, rather than just the learning of specific information. Whenever there is discrete information that can be taught within a session, the structure of a narrative text, for example, we try to teach it. But, in the majority of cases, we attempt to facilitate a student's reading of a specific text, rather than attempt to remediate a general language problem.

Vocabulary

Whereas word recognition develops in a series of stages, vocabulary knowledge grows continually throughout a person's life. Our store of word meanings, along with our knowledge of the world, is constantly increasing. According to some estimates, children learn, on average, 3,000 new words each year with approximately 45,000 words known by the end of the 12th grade (Nagy & Anderson, 1984). This extensive degree of word knowledge cannot be accounted for by vocabulary instruction. Even under the most intensive vocabulary instruction children can learn only 800–1,000 new words in a school year. The only reasonable alternative is that children learn most words from context. And, in fact, it appears children learn in the region of 5% of the words they are exposed to through their reading.

While we have stated that children learn 3,000 new words, on average, each year, this represents quite a significant range. White, Graves, and Slater (1990) found that this growth can fall between 1,000 and 5,000 words per year. This means children experiencing high growth are learning as many as five new words for every word learned by low-growth children.

There are three channels of remediation available for students experiencing slower vocabulary development. The first involves improving the students' overall reading skills, so that they will be able to equal the same pace of reading as those who had formerly been more skilled. Second, it is helpful to supplement the students' own reading by reading aloud to them. Reading literature to children aids in developing their knowledge of word meanings and this effect is especially pronounced for children with reading difficulties (Stahl, Richek, & Vandevier, 1991). Third, direct vocabulary instruction is particularly important for struggling readers. Whereas such instruction does not have a significant impact on the vocabulary growth of a competent reader, the 800–1,000 words that can be taught over the course of a school year could nearly double the number of words that a struggling reader gains from context.

Stahl and Shiel (1992) propose such vocabulary instruction be designed so that each word taught generates more words and, as such, is productive. This involves a three-pronged approach. To begin with, children should be taught to notice unknown words and to reflect on how that word works within the surrounding context. This seems to help them use context more efficiently, although, it is unclear whether this approach transfers to learners' independent reading (see Herman & Weaver, 1988; Jenkins, Matlock, & Slocum, 1989). The second strategy involves teaching word parts, such as common prefixes and root words, to children. White, Sowell, and Yanagihara (1989) have a list of common prefixes that occur frequently enough to aid in determining the meanings of a great many words. Third, vocabulary instruction should incorporate semantic fields so that when a word is taught, other words related to the first are presented simultaneously. An example of such an approach is that of semantic mapping (Heimlich & Pittelman, 1986) in which each word is graphed in relation to other words and these are taught as a unit. Other examples of semantic field vocabulary instruction include Semantic Feature Analysis and Possible Sentences (see Tierney et al., 1995).

General Knowledge

A number of studies have demonstrated the effect of general knowledge upon reading comprehension. It is readily apparent, however, that all of the knowledge useful to children cannot be taught in a clinic setting. Instead, we have found it most effective to provide the information necessary for children to understand specific passages. This involves first establishing what a child knows about a given subject. This can be done using a preassessment strategy such as PreP (Langer, 1984), a structured, free association task. Langer suggests that one use a term such as *carpetbagger* for a history passage about the post-Civil War era, or a picture of a courtroom for a story about justice, and have children tell you the first thing they think of when they hear the term or see the picture. Or, one could simply ask the student what he or she knows about a given topic.

Many students do not spontaneously tie in the information they are getting from the text with their own knowledge. Often struggling readers do not know that they can do that. Raphael (1984) reports that children often do not realize that some questions require them to use their own information. One technique that we find useful is the K–W–L lesson (Ogle, 1986), which we used with Steven, a student described below. Another technique which we find useful, and which is similar to the K–W–L in many respects, is the DR-TA (Stauffer, 1976), which involves having children make predictions about what is going to be in a text, based on their knowledge and the information available in titles, headings, and pictures.

Text Structure

Another strategy that can help children with reading difficulties is developing their understanding of text structure. Struggling readers often fail to use the structures of narrative or expository texts as an aid to comprehension. While Dreher and Singer (1980), among others, found that teaching story grammars to competent readers did not lead to an improvement in their comprehension (since such readers already made use of this knowledge), others (e.g., Fitzgerald & Spiegel, 1983; Short & Ryan, 1984) found that instruction in story grammar elements does improve comprehension for those readers experiencing difficulties in this area.

It is possible to model the use of story grammar to fill out a story map in collaboration with our students (see Beck & McKeown, 1981). Using a scaffolding model, we might initially work with students as they fill in the story map, while gradually releasing control as they gain competency with this technique. We also directly teach the story grammar categories, as well as how information fits into one of three categories, as a further aid to these children.

Students often encounter a different set of problems with expository texts since its structure is not usually as clear as is that of a narrative. For example, expository texts may have mixed or embedded structures making the use of a text structure diagram too difficult for most struggling readers. Instead, we rely on maps that highlight compare/contrast structures, problem/solution structures, or time-line structures to assist students understanding of specific texts.

Strategic Control

A child's strategic control of the reading process develops first through an increasingly sophisticated awareness of the uses and purposes of reading, and then through the application of a wide range of strategies to achieve those purposes. At first, children develop a general concept of what print is used for and how it works. This print concept is gradually refined to understand that the purpose of reading is to comprehend text and then to be able to set specific purposes for specific texts and situations.

We presented Jocelyn as an example of a child who did not understand the basic forms of print. We do run into a number of children who do not understand that the purpose of reading is comprehension. Often they are receiving instruction which stresses accurate, "word perfect" reading, that does not hold them responsible for comprehending, or, when comprehension questions are asked, these questions stress trivial details, rather than main points or inferences. Allington (1983) suggests that many struggling readers get a qualitatively different program than that given to more proficient readers, a program which stresses decoding, interrupts sustained reading more often, and stresses literal comprehension and accurate reading over comprehension and contextually acceptable miscues. He suggests that this type of program leads many struggling readers to view reading in a qualitatively different manner. One such child is Steven.

When we first saw Steven, he was in fourth grade. As part of our evaluation, we asked Steven about his perceptions of reading and literacy instruction. His responses suggested that misconceptions about reading were slowing his academic progress. When asked "If I gave you something to read, how would you know if you were reading it well?" Steven responded that he would be "saying all the words right." When asked what makes something difficult to read, he replied "words that [he] couldn't pronounce." In his oral reading, he read slowly, but very accurately, making very few miscues. Often he would make a contextually appropriate miscue, even as common as "a" for "the," and go back and correct it. His comprehension was poor, even on passages he read at an independent level. He would make up answers for questions, seeming to construct answers out of his prior knowledge rather than from the text information.

When asked about his reading program, Steven described a literacy curriculum rooted in drill and practice exercises. He viewed these activities as independent tasks and did not understand that the exercises were interrelated. Completing a letter recognition worksheet was distinct from a class discussion about the sounds associated with letters; comprehension was separate from decoding. Steven perceived reading not as an act of communication, but rather as a muddled morass of memorization tasks with little use outside of school.

Conventionally, Steven would be considered a "word caller." He had a history of poor decoding skills, but, at this point in time, his decoding skills were adequate. His listening comprehension was slightly above his grade placement. Steven needed to shift his emphasis from a mastery of word recognition skills to text comprehension. Because of his instruction, he developed a misunderstanding of the purpose of reading.

We have been successful in teaching children like Steven to shift their focus by making them responsible for their comprehension (and also easing up on the demands for word-perfect reading). Steven's instruction began with his teacher's modeling the processes. During a lesson, his teachers would as such questions as: Is this like other things I already know? What would be the best way to do this lesson? What do I already know about this topic? What do I think will happen next? With practice, Steven began to internalize these questions and ask them to himself. He became partially responsible for his own learning. We also did more explicit modeling by talking through the processes we used during reading.

Another form of modeling involved questioning. We began by using ReQuest (Manzo, 1969). ReQuest involves having the teacher and the student alternate asking questions of each other about a text. In general, students' first questions are extremely literal, since most of our students see the questioning process as a game of "Can I Catch You?" During a simulated content area lesson, Steven was asked to complete a set of adjunct questions. Although he had read and understood the text, answering the questions became a seek-and-destroy activity. He began his search on the first page and proceeded serially through the text until he came across a word that appeared in the question. Steven then copied the sentence. The strategy was repeated for each question.

We find that teaching Question–Answer Relationships or QARs at the same time allows us to have a vocabulary to talk about questions, as well as giving us a vocabulary to talk about comprehension in general. Raphael (1984) suggests three different types of QARS: Right There, when the answer to the question is in the same sentence as the question stem or in an adjoining sentence; Think and Search, in which the student has to construct the answer to the question by synthesizing from different parts of the passage; and On my Own, in which the student has to combine prior knowledge with text information to come up with an answer. We used QARs in two ways with Steven. First, we suggested it as a strategy to answer questions, to supplant his previous one. He was taught to ask whether he knew the answer to a question prior to reading. If so, he was to skim through the text to confirm that the answer he knew was the one talked about in the passage. If he didn't think he knew the answer, he was to see if the answer was "Right There," by skimming to find the question stem in the text. If this didn't work, he knew he had to think and search to come up with the answer. Second, we used QARs as a way of talking about questions. In reciprocal questioning, we could prompt Steven by asking him to come up with a Think and Search or an On My Own question, to supplement his literal questions.

We also found the K–W–L strategy to work well with Steven. The K–W–L lesson (Ogle, 1986) involves first asking students what they Know about a particular topic, then what they Want to know about the topic, putting questions that the text might address in the second column of the K–W–L chart. The students then read the text, and finally discuss whether their questions were answered. They also brainstorm about what they have Learned about the topic, putting that information in the final column of the K–W–L chart. This use of the chart scaffolds the process of using one's prior knowledge to anticipate information in the text, and then tying text information to one's prior knowledge.

Provided with daily opportunities for literacy activities and with conceptually integrated instruction, Steven began to understand the purposes of reading and reading instruction.

EDUCATIONAL MODEL

The four cases highlighted in this chapter, those of Jocelyn, Thomas, Greg, and Steven, help to demonstrate how a model built upon current research, in psychology and incorporating effective educational practices can be used to assess children experiencing reading difficulties and help to devise effective remediation programs. We have found that a view of reading that evaluates children's development in the areas of word recognition, language, and strategic control of the reading process provides valuable insight for reading instruction. This model can be used both to assess children and to determine appropriate instruction for the learner.

Many aspects of the model are assessed through interviews, others through formal or informal tests. We do not see assessment as the giving of tests, but instead the asking of questions. Our three general questions are: (1) Can the child decode text fluently and automatically? (2) Can the child understand oral language? and (3) Does the child understand the strategies involved in the comprehension of written text? If the answer to any one of these questions is "Yes," then no more exploration is needed. If the answer is "No," then we work backwards, looking for an explanation of why the child is having problems with this particular area. We use that explanation to guide our instruction.

Notice that we did not label these children. It would be possible to label Jocelyn as "learning disabled" or to label Thomas as having an "attention deficit disorder." But Jocelyn's "learning disability" began to disappear as she learned to read. To label her is to make excuses for our own failure to teach her. Similarly, Thomas can now settle down and read for long periods of time, although he still squirms a bit and still does not like doing assignments he finds "boring." We do not generally find these labels to be helpful, except as they serve to help a child through the educational bureaucracy to a position where they can receive appropriate instruction. But, generally, labels serve to excuse our failures to teach by blaming the students for their failure. Rather, we should accept that some children are harder to teach, and we need to work harder to reach those children.

A child with the confusions about the nature of print that Jocelyn had internalized is difficult to teach, since instruction involves the unlearning of many things that she feels are true. Because much of her subsequent learning was based on this faulty knowledge, there was much that was needed to be unlearned. She required a great deal of interaction with a knowledgeable tutor to straighten out her conceptions and put her on the right track. But instruction can be successful. Thomas needed to be convinced of the utility of learning to decode, and once given a relatively conventional program stressing accuracy and automaticity of decoding, he was able to read quite well. Steven's reading problem stemmed from the success of previous reading interventions. He needed to shift his focus, from decoding accuracy to a broader view of reading, but he was able to do this with relative ease through assistance.

We have found very few children who could not be taught to read, with some effort. For the children, their parents and their teachers, the effort is worthwhile.

NOTES

1. All case studies are pseudonyms and, in some cases, are composites.
2. Although we are seeing more and more children in our clinic who have difficulties in this area, suggesting that current programs may not be as successful as those in the past (see Stahl, 1998).
3. I "borrowed" this technique from Gene Cramer at the University of Illinois at Chicago.

REFERENCES

Adams, M. J. (1990). *Beginning to read: Thinking and learning about print.* Cambridge, MA: MIT Press.

Allington, R. L. (1983). The reading instruction provided readers of differing reading abilities. *Elementary School Journal, 83,* 549–559.

Barr, R., & Johnson, B. (1990). *Teaching reading in elementary classrooms: Developing independent readers.* New York: Longman.

Beck, I. L., & McKeown, M. G. (1981). Developing questions that promote comprehension: The story map. *Language Arts, 58,* 913–918.

Bridge, C. A., Winograd, P. N., & Haley, D. (1983). Using predictable materials vs. preprimers to teach beginning sight words. *The Reading Teacher, 36,* 884–891.

Chall, J. S. (1983). *Stages of reading development.* New York: McGraw-Hill.

Chomsky, C. (1978). When you still can't read in third grade? After decoding, what? In S. J. Samuels (Ed.), *What research has to say about reading instruction* (pp. 13–30). Newark, DE: International Reading Association.

Clay, M. M. (1993a). *An observation survey of early literacy achievement.* Portsmouth, NH: Heinemann.

Clay, M. M. (1993b). *Reading Recovery: A guidebook for teachers in training.* Portsmouth, NH: Heinemann.

Coles, G. S. (1987). *The learning mystique: A critical look at "learning disabilities."* New York: Pantheon.

Cunningham, P. M. (1995). *Phonics they use.* New York: HarperCollins.

Dreher, M. J., & Singer, H. (1980). Story grammar instruction unnecessary for intermediate grade students. *The Reading Teacher, 34,* 261–268.

Durrell, D., & Catterson, J. (1980). *Durrell Analysis of Reading Difficulty.* New York: Psychological Corporation.

Eldredge, J. L. (1995). *Teaching decoding in holistic classrooms.* New York: Merrill.

Englemann, S., & Bruner, E. (1969). *Distar Reading Program.* Chicago: SRA.

Fernald, G. (1943). *Remedial techniques in basic school subjects.* New York: McGraw-Hill.

Fitzgerald, J., & Spiegel, D. L. (1983). Enhancing children's reading comprehension through instruction in narrative structure. *Journal of Reading Behavior, 15,* 1–17.

Fleisher, L. S., Pany, D., & Jenkins, J. R. (1979–1980). Effects on poor readers' comprehension of training in rapid decoding. *Reading Research Quarterly, 15,* 30–48.

Garner, R. (1987). *Metacognition and reading comprehension.* Norwood, NJ: Ablex.

Gaskins, I. W., Downer, M. A., Anderson, R. C., Cunningham, P. M., Gaskins, R. W., Schommer, M., et al. (1988). A metacognitive approach to phonics: Using what you know to decode what you don't know. *Remedial and Special Education, 9,* 36–41.

Gillet, J., & Temple, C. (1990). *Understanding reading problems.* Glenview, IL: Scott Foresman/ Little, Brown.

Gillingham, A. O., & Stillman, B., W. (1966). *Remedial training for children with specific difficulty in reading, spelling, and penmanship* (7th ed.). Cambridge, MA: Educators Publishing Service.

Goodman, K. S. (1986). *What's whole in whole language.* Portsmouth, NH: Heinemann.

Gough, P. B., & Tunmer, W. E. (1986). Decoding, reading, and reading disability. *Remedial and Special Education, 7,* 6–10.

Griffin, P., & Olson, M. (1992). Phonemic awareness helps beginning readers break the code. *The Reading Teacher,* 516–523.

Hegge, T., Kirk, S., & Kirk, W. (1955). *Remedial reading drills.* Ann Arbor, MI: George Wehr.

Heimlich, J. E., & Pittelman, S. D. (1986). *Semantic mapping: Classroom applications.* Newark, DE: International Reading Association.

Herman, P. A., & Weaver, R. (1988). *Contextual strategies for learning word meanings: Middle grade students look in, look out.* Paper presented at the annual meeting of the National Reading Conference, Tucson, AZ.

Jenkins, J. R., Matlock, B., & Slocum, T. A. (1989). Two approaches to vocabulary instruction: The teaching of individual word meanings and practice in deriving word meaning from context. *Reading Research Quarterly, 24,* 215–235.

Johnston, F. R. (1995, December). *Learning to read with predictable text: What kinds of words do beginning readers remember?* Paper presented at the annual meeting of the National Reading Conference, New Orleans, LA.

Juel, C. (1988). Learning to read and write: A longitudinal study of fifty-four children from first through fourth grade. *Journal of Educational Psychology, 80,* 437–447.

Langer, J. A. (1984). Examining background knowledge and text comprehension. *Reading Research Quarterly, 19,* 468–481.

Lindamood, C., & Lindamood, A. (1975). *Auditory discrimination in depth.* New York: Teaching Resources.

Lomax, R. G., & McGee, L. M. (1987). Young children's concepts about print and reading: Toward a model of reading acquisition. *Reading Research Quarterly, 22,* 237–256.

Maclean, M., Bryant, P., & Bradley, L. (1987). Rhymes, nursery rhymes, and reading in early childhood. *Merrill-Palmer Quarterly, 33,* 255–281.

Manzo, A. V. (1969). The ReQuest procedure. *Journal of Reading, 13*(2), 23–26.

Nagy, W. E., & Anderson, R. C. (1984). How many words are there in printed school English? *Reading Research Quarterly, 19,* 304–330.

Ogle, D. (1986). K–W–L: A teaching model that develops active reading of expository text. *The Reading Teacher, 39,* 564–570.

Paris, S. G., Wasik, B., & van der Westhuizen, G. (1989). Meta-metacognition: A review of research on metacognition and reading. In J. Readence & S. Baldwin (Eds.), *Dialogues in literacy research. Yearbook of the National Reading Conference* (pp. 143–166). Chicago: National Reading Conference.

Raphael, T. (1984). Teaching learners about sources of information for answering comprehension questions. *Journal of Reading, 27,* 303–311.

Rosner, J. (1974). Auditory analysis training with prereaders. *The Reading Teacher, 27,* 379–384.

Samuels, S. J. (1985). Automaticity and repeated reading. In J. Osborn, P. T. Wilson, & R. C. Anderson (Ed.), *Reading education: Foundations for a literate America* (pp. 215–230). Lexington, MA: Lexington Books.

Short, E. J., & Ryan, E. B. (1984). Metacognitive differences between skilled and less skilled readers: Remediating deficits through story grammar and attribution training. *Journal of Educational Psychology, 76,* 225–235.

Stahl, S. A. (1992). *The state of the art of reading instruction in the USA* (IIEP Research Report No. 97). International Institute for Educational Planning.

Stahl, S. A. (1998). Teaching children with reading problems to decode: Phonics and "not-phonics" instruction. *Reading and Writing Quarterly: Overcoming Learning Difficulties, 14,* 165–188.

Stahl, S. A., & Heubach, K. (2005). Fluency-oriented reading instruction. *Journal of Literacy Research, 37,* 25–60.

Stahl, S. A., & Miller, P. D. (1989). Whole language and language experience approaches for beginning reading: A quantitative research synthesis. *Review of Educational Research, 59,* 87–116.

Stahl, S. A., Richek, M. G., & Vandevier, R. (1991). Learning word meanings through listening: A, sixth grade replication. In J. Zutell & S. McCormick (Ed.), *Learner factors/teacher factors: Issues in literacy research and instruction. Fortieth yearbook of the National Reading Conference* (pp. 185–192). Chicago: National Reading Conference.

Stahl, S. A., & Shiel, T. G. (1992). Teaching meaning vocabulary: Productive approaches for poor readers. *Reading and Writing Quarterly, 8,* 233–241.

Stanovich, K. E. (1986). Matthew effects in reading: Some consequences of individual differences in the acquisition of literacy. *Reading Research Quarterly, 21,* 360–407.

Stanovich, K. E. (1992). The psychology of reading: Evolutionary and revolutionary developments. *Annual Review of Applied Linguistics, 12,* 3–30.

Stauffer, R. G. (1976). *Action research in L.E.A. instructional procedures.* Newark: University of Delaware.

Tierney, R. J., Readence, J., & Dishner, E. (1995). *Reading strategies and practices.* Boston: Allyn & Bacon.

Wallach, M. A., & Wallach, L. (1979). Helping disadvantaged children learn to read by teaching them phoneme identification skills. In L. B. Resnick & P. A. Weaver (Ed.), *Theory and practice of early reading* (pp. 197–216). Hillsdale, NJ: Erlbaum.

White, T. G., Graves, M. F., & Slater, W. H. (1990). Growth of reading vocabulary in diverse elementary schools: Decoding and word meaning. *Journal of Educational Psychology, 82,* 281–290.

White, T. G., Sowell, J., & Yanagihara, A. (1989). Teaching elementary students to use word-part clues. *The Reading Teacher, 42,* 302–309.

Wiig, E., & Semel, E. (1976). *Language disabilities in children and adolescents.* Columbus, OH: Charles Merrill.

Yopp, H. K. (1992). Developing phonemic awareness in young children. *The Reading Teacher, 49,* 696–703.

24 | Intelligent Action as the Basis for Literacy Instruction in Classroom and Clinical Settings

MARJORIE Y. LIPSON

Lucky for us that Steve Stahl did not see the world as a simple place, nor reading as a simple matter. In pursuing a more complete understanding of reading, he helped us work more effectively with children—all children—including those who find learning to read quite difficult. In the chapter "An Educational Model of Assessment and Targeted Instruction for Children with Reading Problems" (1999; reprinted as Chapter 23, this volume), Steve and his colleagues Melanie Kuhn and Michael Pickle move beyond a "simple view of reading" and "complexify" it for us. Characteristically, Stahl does not seek to build his own reputation with flamboyant rejection of earlier scholarship. Rather, he builds on it—drawing from the very best of earlier thinking and using newer ideas to flesh out the model.

In their chapter, Stahl, Kuhn, and Pickle discuss remedial reading within a comprehensive model noting that, until quite recently, the so-called medical model of reading had dominated the field of reading disability. They note, in particular, that educators and physicians alike had thought that struggling readers' problems were caused by weaknesses in visual discrimination and/or visual perception. While these, and other, presumed deficits have been largely discredited as an explanation for reading difficulties, the residual influence of these models can still be observed today in the form of recommendations for such things as colored lenses and optometric visual training for poor readers (Iovino, Fletcher, Breitmeyer, & Foorman, 1998). As Snow, Burns, and Griffin (1998) note, these are "controversial therapies" for which "there are no confirmed or replicated research findings" (p. 271).

Today, most researchers and educators understand that linguistic, not visual, factors are implicated in reading difficulties (Catts & Kamhi, 2005). This insight is clearly one of the major contributions of Gough and Tunmer's (1986) "simple view" of reading, since it placed both phonology and language comprehension at the center of the reading process, a development that ultimately led Stahl and his colleagues to develop what they call an "educational model" in contrast to the "medical model." The model they describe focused less on identifying deficits and more on describing "what the learner is able to do" so that teachers can "target instruction."

While embracing a linguistically based model, Stahl et al. (1999) concluded that an additional element—what they call "Strategic Control" and others call "executive function" (Brown, 1987; Denckla, 1991)—was missing from the earlier "simple view." Consequently, the educational model includes attention to three clusters of underlying processes that, when working together, result in meaning construction, or comprehension.

> *Cluster 1.* Elements having to do with Purpose, Function, and Control of reading. The authors include "print concepts," "awareness," "purpose," and "strategic knowledge" in these cluster.
>
> *Cluster 2.* Knowledge and skill related to reading words in print. In this cluster are "Phonemic Awareness," "Decoding and Sight Word Knowledge," "Fluency," and "Automaticity."
>
> *Cluster 3.* Language Comprehension, which according to Stahl and his colleagues includes "vocabulary," "general knowledge," and "knowledge of text structure."

This more complex view of reading and reading difficulty is important because it offers the opportunity to seek more comprehensive and powerful interventions and programs and to provide more focused instruction to individual students. In their article, Stahl and his colleagues use a series of four mini-case discussions to illuminate the various components of the educational model. These case discussions "bring to life" the ways in which these difficulties appear in actual school and clinic settings and the ways that the three "clusters" of reading knowledge and skill can and do hamper reading development.

AN INTERACTIVE MODEL FOR ASSESSMENT AND INSTRUCTION

Like Steve, Melanie, and Michael, my colleague, Karen Wixson, and I have been working to understand reading difficulties for a long time. In 1985 and 1986 (just as Gough and Tunmer were publishing their article), we made our first attempt at applying new, emerging concepts about the nature of reading to the arena of reading (dis)abilities (see Lipson & Wixson, 1986; Wixson & Lipson, 1985). In those early pieces, we were attempting to apply an interactive model of general reading ability to our work with struggling readers.

Our work rested on Rumelhart's (1977) interactive model but specifically argued that reading was the result of an interaction among the learner, the text, and the context. This interactive view of reading and reading disability was inspired by Jenkins's (1979) discussion of research in the area of memory. He proposed that experimental results could only be useful if four elements were considered and described. He argued that the types of people who participated, the types of materials used, the types of test(s) used, and the research setting itself (including orienting activities, instructions, subject strategies, etc.) all affected the results of research studies. This model, called the *tetrahedral* model, is still recognized today as the way to describe the complexity of reading (see RAND Reading Study Group, 2002). Importantly, it recognizes that linguistic components and other learner factors such as motivation are central to readers' performance. By themselves, however, language-based differences do not account for the very large number of students who fail to learn to read with competence. Other factors also influence student performance.

At the time, this view contrasted strongly with the deficit model of reading, which had a stranglehold on thinking about reading difficulties. Indeed, Sarason and Doris (1979) called the work related to reading difficulties a "search for pathology." Using this view, a wide array of deficits or weaknesses was posited as the source of reading difficulty (see Poplin, 1984). No matter what deficit was hypothesized, these models shared a common orientation that led teachers to believe that what was needed was to "fix" what was wrong; hence, "remedial reading." The problem was always conceived as inherent to the learner (often with an organic base) and the idea was to return the student to the "regular" reading program once the problem was "fixed." The model did not invite a complex of component difficulties, nor did it entertain the thought that instruction itself might contribute to the difficulties.

Like Steve and his colleagues, we were more interested in helping struggling readers to learn how to read than we were in labeling their "deficits." We noted that "an interactive view is well-suited to the understanding of reading (dis)ability because it predicts variability in performance within individuals across texts, tasks, and settings. This perspective moves discussions of reading disability away from simply specifying deficits and toward the specification of the conditions under which a child can and will learn" (Lipson & Wixson, 1991, p. 40).

Evaluating the Context

In the intervening years, we continued to apply this model to our discussions of both assessment and instruction in the area of reading ability and disability (Lipson & Wixson, 1991, 1997, 2003; Wixson & Lipson, 1991). An important contribution of this work was a focus on the importance of evaluating not only the learner but also the materials, tasks, and settings. We argued, for example:

> Because readers' performance is the result of a complex set of interactions between the reader and the reading context, no assessment will be complete until we have assessed the reading context. . . . The assessment of the reading context has additional importance because it is through changing or controlling contextual factors that we are most likely to bring about improved learning and/or performance in the reader. (Lipson & Wixson, 1991, p. 57)

In other words, an interactive model of reading difficulties includes the various components of the reading process as described in the three clusters by Stahl, Kuhn, and Pickle, but also acknowledges that changing the reading materials, methods, or tasks can actually cause students to be more or less successful (Lipson, Cox, Iwankowski, & Simon, 1984). Although Steve and his colleagues do not describe these aspects within their Educational Model, it is clear that they were understood. Note, for example, that they describe how Thomas, a third grader with weak word analysis/word recognition skill, performed very much better *"when given a context,"* They also note that Thomas could read and comprehend grade-appropriate texts. Certainly, Thomas needed to improve his automatic word recognition skills, but observing that he was able to read and comprehend grade-appropriate texts adds significantly to the assessment picture and distinguishes Thomas's difficulties from those of others who do not demonstrate those abilities.

Evaluating the context is important in order to generate appropriate alternative interventions, but it is also important because some students are experiencing difficulties precisely because the materials, methods, or tasks that have been used are not suitable for them. Many (perhaps most) children will learn to read by a variety of methods. Some students, however, require quite specific approaches or materials. Cultural and linguistic factors interact here as well as interest, learning style preferences, and background experiences/readiness (Tomlinson, 2001). Some students simply will not thrive in a particular program/approach.

In addition, as Stahl, Kuhn, and Pickle (1999) note, the instructional program(s) for struggling readers too often keep them from developing appropriate ideas about the goals of reading:

> . . . many struggling readers get a qualitatively different program than that given to more proficient readers, a program which stresses decoding, interrupts sustained silent reading more often, and stresses literal comprehension and accurate reading over comprehension and contextually acceptable miscues . . . this type of program leads many struggling readers to view reading in a qualitatively different manner. (p. 267)

In cases like this, students will probably not improve their reading performance until/unless the context for instruction is altered.

Despite a much clearer idea about the linguistic and phonological underpinnings of reading acquisition and despite the acceptance of a complex, interactive model of reading, many researchers and teachers still operate from a surprisingly simple view of reading difficulties. Too many still think that reading problems result from a "single factor" and recommend the same specific program for all struggling readers.

A recent study by Buly and Valencia (2002, 2004) highlights the dangers of assuming that all students who are struggling to read need the same response from teachers and schools. They conducted in-depth assessments of students who had failed to pass the reading tests administered by Washington State. The profiles they constructed of these students revealed six distinct subgroups of reading difficulty. Fewer than half the students had problems located in word recognition. While that in itself is a bit startling, what is even more interesting is that within that group, there were three distinct subtypes. Approximately 9% of the students were what Buly and Valencia called "disabled readers," students who were struggling in all aspects of reading (word recognition, fluency, and comprehension). Another 17% were students like Thomas, "word stumblers," who could comprehend but were not fluent or accurate in isolation. Another 15% were not accurate but they did maintain a good rate and pace of reading (the beginnings of fluency). Three other groups of struggling readers had good accuracy but were either not fluent or unable to comprehend despite good word recognition skills. Imagine prescribing the same program to all of these students! Not surprisingly, Buly and Valencia conclude that "reading failure is multifaceted and it is individual." They go on to argue that instruction cannot be focused exclusively on a set of "standards" but must be focused on "teaching the students."

One-size-fits-all instruction will not do when working with struggling readers. Intelligent action on the part of teachers requires a firm understanding of the complexities of assessment and instruction and a willingness to solve problems creatively while making decisions based on particular students and contexts (see Lipson, Mosenthal, Mekkelsen, & Ross, 2004).

GUIDELINES FOR WORKING WITH STUDENTS IN CLASSROOMS AND CLINICS

The guidelines provided here for effective and intelligent action are drawn from multiple sources: from Stahl and his colleagues, from my work with Karen Wixson, and from the work of others who believe as Steve did that, we need to acknowledge that some children are harder to teach and we need to figure out how to do that.

• *Work from a complex and comprehensive model.* The Educational Model proposed by Stahl, Kuhn, and Pickle is still a good comprehensive one. As noted earlier, I would make a strong recommendation for assessing and using contextual factors as well as learner factors. "The variability within and across individuals means that reading and writing performance are a function of what learners can and will do at any given moment. Appropriate instruction requires that we understand the variability that exists *within* individual learners" (Lipson & Wixson, 2003, p. 10).

Although working from a complex model can be difficult, it is much more likely to yield educationally meaningful responses than a model that is too simple. Importantly, the simple model does not acknowledge that the behaviors we are observing may be *the result* of a set of interactions rather than the cause of the reading failure. Recently, for example, a large number of Bantu children have arrived in my city. These children cannot read or write (or speak) English. Traditional English as a second language courses are not likely to be effective, however, unless other factors are considered. First, none of these children and none of their parents is literate in their first language. Second, they represent an oppressed group within an otherwise well-educated country. In other words, they are not literate in any language because of a complex combination of socioeconomic and political reasons. They lack not only vocabulary and sound–symbol knowledge but also the *idea* of reading and the *idea* of school. Importantly, they also lack many concepts that underlie everyday life in the United States. Clearly, a literacy program for these children must be different than the one for other immigrant children who come with literate families and some schooling.

This case provides a strong example of how complex literacy instruction can be, but the more subtle differences between and among children born in the United States from many different backgrounds is also important. Far too many children in this country do not learn to read very well. Far too many, but not all, are from poor families. A simple model of reading has not served them well.

• *Engage in high-quality assessment that identifies how students read across multiple contexts and under different task conditions.* Stahl, Kuhn, and Pickle argue strongly that good assessment involves using a variety of tools (not just tests) and has, as its purpose, a focus on teaching: "we [are] . . . looking for an explanation of why the child is having problems with this particular area. We use that explanation to guide our instruction" (p. 269). This is strikingly similar to my own view. In our first text, Karen Wixson and I argued that "the purpose of assessment is to find patterns of interactions that allow us to make relatively good decisions about instruction. Few standardized tests provide this kind of information" (Lipson & Wixson, 1991, p. 41).

Using the components framework of the educational model coupled with an assessment–instruction process developed by Lipson and Wixson (see Figure 24.1) should ensure a comprehensive student assessment. Gathering information is extremely important in both models. We identify a more elaborated series of steps designed to promote teacher reflection and decision making (Steps 4–6). An especially important aspect of the Lipson and Wixson framework is Step 6, Diagnostic Teaching. In this step, teachers explore alternate instructional responses to generate the best possible instructional response for the individual student. Clearly, this model is more appropriate for a clinic setting than a classroom because it entails a very close examination of the individual student's needs and strengths. We believe, however, that this is a better use of clinic time and resources than the routinized and mechanistic use and implementation of preestablished programs.

  • *Ask good questions.* In providing advice to practitioners, Stahl et al. (1999) say, "We do not see assessment as the giving of tests, but instead the asking of questions"

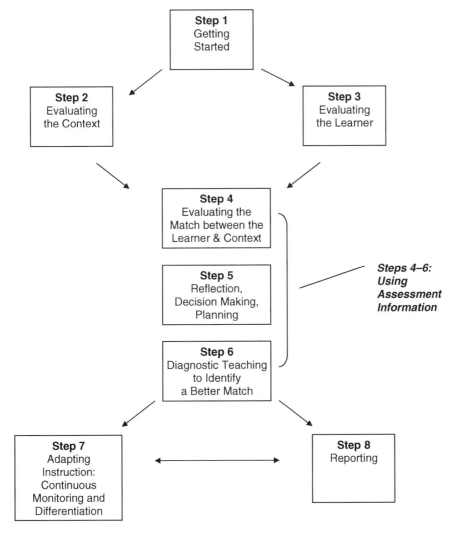

FIGURE 24.1. Assessment–instruction process model. From Lipson and Wixson (2003). Copyright 2003 by Allyn & Bacon. Adapted by permission.

(p. 269). We too, have made heavy use of a questioning approach to shape a complex assessment/instruction plan. The following, although not exhaustive, should provide good guidance to educators as they work with struggling readers.

Three questions (Stahl et al., p. 269):
1. Can the child decode text fluently and automatically?
2. Can the child understand oral language?
3. Does the child understand the strategies involved in the comprehension of written text?

Additional questions (see Lipson & Wixson, 2003):
4. What impact do the program and teacher have on student learning?
   a. What are the priorities of the classroom literacy instructional program?
   b. What materials/tasks are used to teach children in this room?
5. Does Instruction help all students?
   a. What does the teacher believe is important to teach and how does he/she view struggling readers?
   b. What is the overall quality of literacy instruction: focus on higher-order thinking, depth of knowledge, substantive conversation and support for learning (see Newmann & Wehlage, 1995).
6. How does the classroom organization impact student learning?
   a. Do the routines help teachers address individual differences?
   b. How do students spend their time? How much reading/writing of connected text occur?
   c. Do routines and grouping increase instructional time?
7. (For struggling readers in particular) What is the nature of the support/ remedial programming?
   a. What level of congruence is there between the classroom and clinic instructional programs, materials, tasks?
   b. How knowledgeable are the tutors for the most struggling learners?
   c. For older struggling readers, is there appropriate provision for both well-conceived remedial instruction and grade/age-appropriate content?

Although this series of questions can guide the knowledgeable teacher to explore a wide range of assessment possibilities, it does not, of course, provide all the tools necessary.

FURTHER CHALLENGES

Working with struggling readers requires our very best—best teachers, best thinking, best tools. And, even then, it will take time. Becoming an effective reader does take time. Because it does, one further area needs to be considered. Evidence suggests that vulnerable students need multiple years of high-quality instruction in order to become capable readers (see Mosenthal, Lipson, Torncello, Ross, & Mekkelsen, 2004; Snow, Barnes, Chandler, Goodman, & Hemphill, 1991).

The very last question in my list asks whether there is appropriate provision for both well-conceived remedial instruction and *also* for grade/age-appropriate content.

Like others, we are finding that struggling readers continue to struggle even after they have acquired appropriate decoding abilities—sometimes even after they have become fluent. The problem appears to be that too many of these students have spent so much time learning how to read that they have not acquired the vocabulary and concepts that would have been introduced during content instruction or acquired during wide reading (see Hirsch, 2003).

For teachers who work in clinical settings this is an especially difficult issue. Generally, there is little time allocated for anything but the specific instruction of component aspects of reading. Yet, much more is needed. As a first step, clinicians can work as closely as possible with classroom teachers to limit the impact of pullout remediation on struggling readers' overall development. As a next step, all professionals must work together to provide more opportunities for struggling readers to be remain in the classroom receiving appropriate support.

Finally, more powerful but also differentiated content instruction is essential (see Tomlinson, 2001). This type of instruction, what Stahl, Kuhn, and Pickle call "conceptually integrated instruction," must include opportunities to learn both content and vocabulary but also to engage in literate activity that is supported and accounts for individual differences in reading and writing ability. This is the next generation agenda—one that would clearly be supported by Steve given his deep commitment to teaching *all* students. As he said, we cannot use "labels to excuse our failures to teach by blaming the students for their failure" (Stahl et al., 1999, p. 269). We must help our struggling students learn not only how to read but how to learn.

Today, even more than when the article was written, we know that we can teach all but a very few children to read—and read well. It appears that this will require not only our own, individual, intelligent action but also the coordinated efforts of school faculty over the course of several years.

REFERENCES

Brown, A. L. (1987). Metacognition, executive control, self-regulation, and other more mysterious mechanisms. In F. E. Weinert & R. H. Kluwe (Eds.), *Metacognition, motivation, and understanding* (pp. 65–116). Hillsdale, NJ: Erlbaum.

Buly, M. R., & Valencia, S. W. (2002). Below the bar: Profiles of students who fail the state reading assessments. *Educational Evaluation and Policy Analysis, 24*(3), 219–239.

Buly, M. R., & Valencia, S. W. (2004). Behind test scores: What struggling readers REALLY need. *The Reading Teacher, 57*(6), 520–531.

Catts, H. W., & Kamhi, A. G. (2005). *The connections between language and reading.* Mahwah, NJ: Erlbaum.

Denckla, M. (1991). Biological correlates of learning and attention: What is relevant to learning disabilities and ADHD? *Journal of Developmental and Behavioral Pediatrics, 17*(2), 114–119.

Gough, P. B., & Tunmer, W. E. (1986). Decoding, reading, and reading disability. *Remedial and Special Education, 7,* 6–10.

Hirsch, E. D. (2003). Reading comprehension requires knowledge—of words and the world, *American Educator, 27,* 10–22, 28.

Iovino, I., Fletcher, J. M., Breitmeyer, B. G., & Foorman, B. R. (1998). Colored overlays for visual perceptual deficits in children with reading disability and attention deficit/hyperactivity disorder: Are they differentially effective? *Journal of Clinical and Experimental Neuropsychology, 20*(6), 791–806.

Jenkins, J. J. (1979). Four points to remember: A tetrahedral model of memory experiments. In L. S. Cermak & F. I. M. Craik (Eds.), *Levels of processing in human memory*. Hillsdale, NJ: Erlbaum.

Lipson, M. Y., Cox, C., Iwankowski, S., & Simon, M. (1984). Explorations of the interactive nature of reading: Using commercial IRIs to gain insights. *Reading Psychology, 5*(3), 209–218.

Lipson, M. Y., Mosenthal, J. H., Mekkelsen, J., & Russ, B. (2004). Building knowledge and fashioning success one school at a time. *The Reading Teacher, 57*(6), 534–542.

Lipson, M. Y., & Wixson, K. K. (1986). Reading disability research: An interactionist perspective. *Review of Educational Research, 56*(1), 111–136.

Lipson, M. Y., & Wixson, K. K. (1991). *Assessment and instruction of reading disability: An interactive approach*. New York: HarperCollins.

Lipson, M. Y., & Wixson, K. K. (1997). *Assessment and instruction of reading and writing disability: An interactive approach* (2nd ed.). New York: Addison Wesley-Longman.

Lipson, M. Y., & Wixson, K. K. (2003). *Assessment and instruction of reading and writing difficulties* (3rd ed.). Boston: Allyn & Bacon.

Mosenthal, J. H., Lipson, M. Y., Torncello, S., Russ, B., & Mekkelsen, J., (2004). Contexts and practices in six schools successful in obtaining reading achievement. *Elementary School Journal, 104*(5), 361–385.

Newmann, F., & Wehlage, G. (1995). *Successful school restructuring*. Madison: Center on Organization and Restructuring of Schools, University of Wisconsin.

Poplin, M. (1984). Summary rationalizations, apologies, and farewell: What we don't know about the learning disabled. *Learning Disabilities Quarterly, 7*, 130–134.

RAND Reading Study Group. (2002). *Reading for understanding: Toward an R&D program in reading comprehension*. Washington, DC: RAND Education.

Rumelhart, D. (1977). Toward an interactive model of reading. In S. Dornic (Ed.), *Attention and performance, VI* (pp. 573–603). Hillsdale, NJ: Erlbaum.

Sarason, S. B., & Doris, J. (1979). *Educational handicap, public policy, and social history*. New York: Free Press.

Snow, C. E., Barnes, W. S., Chandler, J., Goodman, I. R., & Hemphill, L. (1991). *Unfulfilled expectations: Home and school influences on literacy*. Cambridge, MA: Harvard University Press

Snow, C. E., Burns, M. S., & Griffin, P. (Eds.). (1998). *Preventing reading difficulties in young children*. Washington, DC: National Academy Press.

Stahl, S. A., Kuhn, M. R., & Pickle, J. M. (1999). An educational model of assessment and targeted instruction for children with reading problems. In D. Evenson & P. Mosenthal (Eds.), *Advances in reading/language research* (Vol. 6, pp. 249–272). Stamford, CT: JAI Press.

Tomlinson, C. A. (2001). *How to differentiate instruction in mixed ability classrooms* (2nd ed.). Washington, DC: ASCD.

Wixson, K. K., & Lipson, M. Y. (1985). Reading (dis)ability: An interactionist perspective. In T. E. Raphael & R. Reynolds (Eds.), *Contexts of school-based literacy* (pp. 131–148). New York: Random House.

Wixson, K. K., & Lipson, M. Y. (1991). Perspectives on reading disability research. In P. D. Pearson (Ed.), *Handbook of reading research* (Vol. 2, pp. 539–570). New York: Longman.

25

The "Word Factors"

A Problem for Reading Comprehension Assessment

STEVEN A. STAHL

ELFRIEDA H. HIEBERT

If we were to ask experts on reading comprehension, such as the contributors to this volume, on how they define "reading comprehension," answers might range from making meaning from text to thinking critically about the text. Our guess would be that none of these scholars would mention word recognition, even in elaborated definitions. Many models of reading comprehension, such as those of Kintsch (1998) and Anderson and Pearson (1984), begin once words are recognized, as in "supposing the reader recognizes the words in the text, here is how comprehension proceeds. . . ."

Yet, from a psychometric perspective, word recognition plays an important role in reading comprehension. Studies that include both measures of word recognition and reading comprehension (which were surprisingly difficult to find) find strong correlations between the two variables, not only in the primary grades, but also through the grades (e.g., Carver, 2000). This was found for word recognition both in and out of context, in paragraphs, and in lists.

Word meaning also plays an important role both in word recognition and in reading comprehension. Some (e.g., Carver, 2000; Thorndike, 1972), in fact, have suggested that a person's knowledge of word meanings is so closely correlated to his or her ability to comprehend text that the two constructs are almost identical. We do not want to make as strong a claim here, but the consistently high correlations between vocabulary and reading comprehension need to be taken into account in any theory of comprehension assessment. Word meaning is also related to word recognition. Words that are meaningful to a reader are recognized faster and more accurately than words whose meaning is unknown, including nonwords (e.g., Adams, 1990).

We present this as a problem to theories of reading comprehension assessment. If these word factors account for significant proportions of variance in reading comprehension, as they seem to do, then this leaves less variance that can be accounted for by differences in higher-order processes. It becomes increasingly possible to suggest, as some have, that comprehension will take care of itself after accounting for fluent and automatic word recognition. This position has profound implications for both assessment and instruction. The strong position of this relationship is not just a "straw man" argument. This argument has been used to make a number of claims including calls for more phonics instruction, even in the middle grades. We believe that the strong version of this position is wrong. However, to understand why is it wrong, one must understand *how* fluent word recognition, vocabulary, and reading comprehension relate to each other. Instead, we suggest that words do matter in reading comprehension, but that word knowledge, both word recognition and knowledge of word meanings, interact with other sources of knowledge to affect reading comprehension.

ASSUMPTIONS, SPOKEN AND UNSPOKEN

A Simple View of Reading

There is an assumption about the nature of reading that supports this strong view of the relationship between fluent word recognition and comprehension. This assumption is exemplified by the "Simple View of Reading" (Gough & Tunmer, 1986). Gough and Tunmer suggested that Reading (or reading comprehension, R) can be discussed in terms of two factors—the ability of children to decode words quickly (D) and efficiently and their language comprehension (C). This view can be expressed in the equation:

$$R = D \times C$$

If we think of these variables as ranging from 0 (or complete inability) to 1 (or complete ability), Reading comprehension skill can be thought of as the product of a person's Decoding and Language Comprehension. People who cannot decode a text will not be able to comprehend a written version, regardless of their knowledge of the language of the text. Similarly, people with perfect decoding ability will not comprehend a text if they do not understand the language of the text. This is true of hyperlexics reading in their native language or people reading phonetically regular foreign languages without knowledge of that language. The simple view has been tested by Carver (1993, 2000) and Hoover and Gough (1990), who found that, as a metaphor if not as an equation, it captures quite well the importance of both word recognition and language comprehension. Both studies found that once word recognition and language variables were entered into a regression equation, the only remaining variance was test error. In this view, once a child can read fluently (or that $D = 1$), then any variation in comprehension is due to their language understanding. That is, once the written text is transparent, the reader can look through the words to the meaning of the language contained within.

The simple view is an extension of LaBerge and Samuels's (1974) classic model of reading. In this theory, the mind is seen as a limited capacity information processor, capable of paying attention to only a limited number of operations at any given time. LaBerge and Samuels suggested that some operations are nonautomatic or demand attention and others are automatic or do not demand attention. Processes involved in comprehension, especially those involving certain inferences or critical judgment, will always demand attention. If word recognition is automatic, then the reader can devote a larger proportion of cognitive resources to comprehension, especially the attention-demanding aspects of comprehension. If word recognition is nonautomatic, as in younger children who have to concentrate on decoding, then less attention is available for comprehension.

That this theory is still cited in discussions of fluency is a testament to its classic nature. We know of only one theorist who has extended LaBerge and Samuels's (1974) model—Logan, Taylor, and Etherton (1999). Logan et al. (1999) suggest that automaticity can be thought of in terms of speed, obligatoriness, and availability of resources. As a response moves toward automaticity, it follows a power curve. That is, increases in speed will be greater at the beginning of learning than they will be as the response becomes close to automatic, or that gains in speed will move toward an asymptote. Once a response is automatic, a person cannot not perform it. An example would be the Stroop task, in which the child is asked to identify a particular color or picture while ignoring a printed label as when word "green" is presented in blue ink. Identification of the color ("blue") would be hampered by obligatory processing of the word ("green"). Thus, automatic responses are also obligatory. Similar to the LaBerge and Samuels model, the result of automatic processing in Logan et al.'s model means that the reader has more resources available for nonautomatic or thoughtful processes.

Being Fluent Is More Than Being Fast

One problem with the "simple view" is that word recognition is not independent of a person's language knowledge. Gough and Tunmer (1986) seem to imply that their decoding factor is a measure of the reader's automaticity of word recognition. First, word recognition is affected by the word's semantic properties. When the recognition of words in isolation has been studied, it has been found that known words are recognized more quickly and accurately than unknown words and nonsense words (Adams, 1990). Further, semantic properties of words, such as their concreteness and abstractness (Schwanenflugel & Akin, 1994), affect both children's and adult's recognition of words. A model such as that of Adams posits that word knowledge is connected to lexical knowledge, so that semantic factors will affect readers' recognition of words. Recognizing words is more than a function of quickly executing decoding algorithms. Knowledge of the word's meaning affects even activities such as finding a letter embedded in a word, as unsemantic a task as one could find (Gibson & Levin, 1975).

Second, and more important, recognizing words in context is more than simply serial recognition of words in isolation. We prefer to discuss "fluent reading" rather than automatic word recognition. Fluent reading occurs when a reader's recognition of words in context is so transparent that readers are able to move from the text to comprehension without conscious attention to words. When we hear such a reader read orally, it seems natural and "language-like." Of course, fluent reading does not have to be oral. In fact, fluent readers spend more of their time reading silently. This involves more than just recognizing words quickly in isolation. It also involves prosody (Kuhn & Stahl, 2003; Schwanenflugel, Hamilton, Kuhn, Wisenbaker, & Stahl, 2004). Prosody refers to the language-like quality of the reading, including the preservation of supra-segmental features that signal syntactic relations (Schwanenflugel, Hamilton, et al., 2004). This includes the drop in pitch at the end of a declarative sentence and the rise in pitch at the end of a question.

We will discuss these three components of fluent reading—accuracy, rate, and prosody—and their contributions to comprehension in turn.

ACCURACY AND COMPREHENSION

The relationships between reading accuracy, usually oral, and comprehension have traditionally been studied through informal reading inventories and the use of oral reading accuracy to establish appropriate levels for instruction. This body of research dates back at least to the work of Betts (1946), and probably before that. We examine first evidence for the word recognition levels established for instructional, independent, and frustration designations on informal reading inventories (IRIs), oral reading measures.

Word Recognition Levels and Comprehension on Informal Reading Inventories

Traditionally, an "instructional level," or the level at which a child can benefit from instruction is that level at which the child can read with 95–98% accuracy (Betts, 1946). This level is used in most informal reading inventories (IRIs) (Johns, 1997, pp. 87–96). There are other views of the appropriate level of accuracy. Clay (1993) suggests that first graders in Reading Recovery programs read material that they can read with 90% accuracy. Stahl, Heubach, and Cramond (1997) found that children could benefit from instruction in texts that they could originally read with an 85% accuracy level in a program—Fluency-Oriented-Reading Instruction (FORI)—that involved repeated reading and other instructional support. In programs such as Reading Recovery or FORI where substantial support is provided to readers, children might be able to benefit from more difficult texts. Taft and Leslie (1985) found no difference in comprehension as measured by free recall or questions whether students read with 95–99% accuracy or with 90–94% accuracy.

Using standardized measures of word recognition and comprehension, Kendall and Hood (1979) identified struggling readers with good comprehension but poor word recognition and those with poor comprehension but adequate word recognition. Those students with good comprehension but poor word recognition were found to make more use of contextual information in oral reading of two short stories. In addition, their rate was significantly slower than that of the children with adequate word recognition, suggesting that their gains in comprehension came at a cost of slower reading.

Carpenter and Paris (2004) found similar groupings with both struggling and normally achieving readers. They found a greater tendency for older (fourth, fifth, and sixth graders in their study) to have low comprehension/high accuracy, suggesting that there is a separation between comprehension and accuracy, especially as children get past third grade. Carpenter and Paris presented two studies, each with a different set of children given a different informal reading inventories at two different time points apiece. They found the same pattern of correlations across each replication. Basically, accuracy on the IRI correlated significantly with passage comprehension only at the achievement levels below third grade. Above third grade, the correlations were nonsignificant and some were even negative. Figure 25.1 shows the most dramatic of four graphs, but all show a similar pattern.

A similar developmental trend was found by Willson and Rupley (1997). Using structural equation modeling, they found that phonemic knowledge (the ability to decode words) appeared to drive comprehension in grades 2 and 3, but its effects diminished in the upper grades. By third grade, background knowledge and strategy knowledge became more important (see also Rupley & Willson, 1997).

Similarly, the Oral Reading Special Study, conducted as part of the National Assessment of Educational Progress (NAEP) (Pinnell et al., 1995) found no significant relations between oral reading accuracy of the fourth graders they examined and their fluency rating scale. Fluency, in turn, was significantly related to comprehension. In their sample, the majority of children read the test passage at an accuracy rate above 94%, possibly restricting the range of possible correlations. However, similar to Kendall and Hood (1979) and Paris and Carpenter (2003), Pinnell et al. (1995) found sizable numbers of children who were accurate, but nonfluent, as shown in Tables 25.1 and 25.2.

These numbers can be a bit misleading. The 7% of the 7% who got a fluency rating of 1 with 99% accurate reading is only about 5 children out of the 955 children tested, for example. However, it is clear that there are sizable numbers of children in the NAEP data set who were rated nonfluent but who read relatively accurately. In addition, 18% of the children in this set, nearly a fifth, could read fluently with less than 94% accuracy. Since Pinnell et al. (1995) do not simultaneously present the data for rate and accuracy, it is not possible to determine whether these fourth graders had the same rate/accuracy trade-off as in the Kendall and Hood (1979) study, but it is possible to speculate that they did.

Thus, it appears that accuracy alone (at least in grades 3 and higher) does not seem to be sufficient for comprehension, at least within a certain band. Children

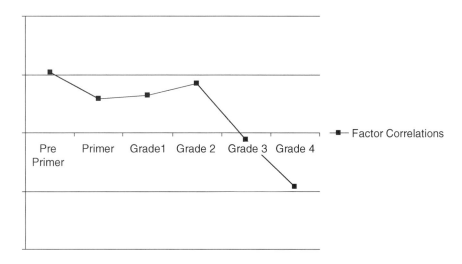

FIGURE 25.1. T1 factor correlations by passage.

TABLE 25.1. Percent Accuracy and Words per Minute by Grade 4 Reading Fluency

Fluency levels	1	2	3	4
Percent accuracy	94	94	96	97
Words per minute	65	89	126	162

Note. Data from Pinnell et al. (1995, p. 44).

seem to be able to comprehend well, even if they can read no more than 1 word in 10 accurately.

Miscue Analysis

A widely held view in the field of reading suggests that oral reading accuracy reflects children's construction of meaning during reading, as much as it reflects their word recognition skill. Goodman (1968) suggested that readers use a variety of types of knowledge when reading words in context, including knowledge of syntax, prior knowledge of the topic of the text, ongoing information gained from context, as well as knowledge of grapheme–phoneme relations (see Clay, 1993). When confronted with challenging texts, readers' ongoing construction of meaning is evidenced by miscues that reflect the meaning of the text, as evidenced by both semantic and syntactic similarity, and, when a miscue does not make sense, that miscue is corrected.

Goodman and Goodman (1977; Goodman, Watson, & Burke, 1987) have developed an extensive system of miscue analysis in which miscues, or deviations from the text in oral reading, are analyzed by asking a series of questions about the miscues and self-corrections. The question areas include syntactic acceptability (presence of miscue in same grammatical form class as the text word); semantic acceptability (whether the miscue makes sense in the passage or sentence or part of the sentence); meaning change (the degree of meaning change related to what the teacher/ researcher); correction (whether the reader self-corrected); and graphic similarity and sound similarity (the degree to which the graphophonic system is being used during reading). Questions about the type of acceptability can be asked at the passage, sentence, partial sentence, and word levels.

TABLE 25.2. Percentage of Students at Each Fluency Level by Five Levels of Accuracy (Grade 4)

	0–4 deviations; 99% accurate	5–9 deviations; 97% accurate	10–14 deviations; 96% accurate	15–19 deviations; 94% accurate	> 20 deviations; less than 94% accurate
Fluent					
4 (13%)	25	39	20	13	3
3 (42%)	8	28	28	18	18
Nonfluent					
2 (37%)	2	12	19	29	38
1 (7%)	7	15	13	26	39

Note. Data from Pinnell et al. (1995, p. 45).

Goodman (1968; Goodman & Goodman, 1977) considered grapheme–phoneme knowledge the least important of these knowledge sources, arguing that efficient reading requires the reader to orchestrate the knowledge of the topic and ongoing context with knowledge of the syntactic structure of the language to predict possible meanings for each word encountered, using a minimal amount of visual information to confirm the predictions. There is ample evidence to disconfirm the strong version of his theory, that readers proceed through text actively predicting the identity of each word in turn relying heavily on context (see Stanovich, 2000; Nicholson, 1991). However, there is also ample evidence that readers are somewhat better at reading words in context than they are in isolation, although this effect is smaller than Goodman suggested (Nicholson, 1991) and may be more important for struggling readers than for proficient readers (e.g., Stanovich, 2000). For example, Adams (1998) found that children read irregularly spelled words better in sentences than in lists.

There have been a number of criticisms of this model (see Allington, 1984, for review), but its influence is undeniable. The presence of meaning-acceptable miscues suggests that if proficient readers perceive miscues as semantically acceptable, they will proceed through the text, believing that they are understanding the text. If the miscue is not acceptable, they will correct it. Clay (1991) has taken this pattern as evidence that beginning readers have developed a "self-extending system." That is, they are able to orchestrate the various cues in the text in order to learn words. From this model, the pattern of miscues described by Goodman and Clay has been used as evidence that beginning readers are comprehending the text. Consequently, for some educators (e.g., Fountas & Pinnell, 1996), the pattern of miscues is used as a measure of comprehension, in addition to oral reading.

Within the extensive research on readers' miscues (see Allington, 1984, for review), researchers have found the most variation in behavior among beginning readers, usually first graders, but also with older, struggling readers. For example, Biemiller (1970) found three stages in children's miscues. The miscues of very beginning readers, produced words that made sense in the story but had little graphical relation to the text word. After this emergent phase, Biemiller found that children would not respond to words they did not know. After this period of nonresponse, children would produce miscues that were both semantically acceptable and graphically similar to the text word. Similar developmental patterns were found by Sulzby (1985) in her observations of young children's attempts at storybook reading.

The children Biemiller studied were in "meaning-oriented" programs, in which the emphasis was on constructing meaning during reading. Barr (1974–1975) found different patterns in the initial miscues of children in meaning-emphasis and code-emphasis programs (see also Cohen, 1974–1975). Barr found that children generally adhered to the approach they were taught, with phonics-taught children sounding words out more often and sight-word-taught children used more visual strategies. Barr (1974–1975) and Cohen (1974–1975) both found that children in code-emphasis programs gave nonsense words for between 15 and 28% of their substitutions in oral reading. Connelly, Johnston, and Thompson (1999) found that 38% of the oral reading errors made by children involved in intensive phonics instruction were nonsense words. Similarly, in Cohen's study of children in phonics instruction, 30% of all substitutions made by good readers and 2% of those made by poor readers were self-corrected. Similar patterns were found more recently by Johnston and Watson (1997), who examined reading instruction in Scotland in which strong phonic emphasis programs were contrasted with whole language programs. This suggests that, in these older programs, children taught with a phonics emphasis were not viewing reading as a meaningful act.

However, in current reading instruction, even the most explicit phonics instruction stresses the importance of meaning, Stahl, McCartney, and Montero (2004) found that children's miscues did not vary as a result of programs which all emphasized decoding and some degree of comprehension. Children in that study self-corrected a high percentage of miscues and rarely produced nonsense words. Even these program differences seem to wash out by the time students' proficiency reaches late first-grade or second-grade levels (Allington, 1984). The vast majority of children who have reached that proficiency make semantically acceptable miscues and self correct those which are not. While this brief review necessarily oversimplifies a rich literature, a conclusion that can be drawn is that children's reading miscues seem to be due to initial differences in instruction and to lack of proficiency at the initial stages of reading in orchestrating various cues to maintain ongoing meaning during reading.

What Do We Mean by "Comprehension"?

The preceding discussion assumes that comprehension is unitary; that is, one can comprehend more or less. Instead, we feel that it is important that we think about comprehension as a set of interacting processes, and that word recognition difficulties will impact comprehension in different ways.

Kintsch's (1998, 2005) construction–integration (CI) model suggests that representational models, or the mental models of the information learned from the text, are mediated in interactions with written texts. Kintsch's model supports the notion that representation of texts is cyclical and ongoing and that lower and higher systems inform and extend each other. All of Kintsch's work has been done with adults and "developed" readers. Basically, CI is a bottom-up constraint-satisfaction theory. It addresses two stages of psychological processing that occur during reading. During *construction*, concepts from the text are activated to produce a network of activated mental concepts. This may be represented as a set of propositions in a hierarchy, with some propositions being higher (more important) in the hierarchy and others lower (Kintsch & van Dijk, 1978) or as a network of propositions. In the second stage, *integration*, the network concepts that are compatible with the context enhance the activation of one another, while concepts that are not compatible with the context lose activation. "Thus, comprehension arises from an interaction and fusion between text information and knowledge activated by the comprehender" (McNamara & Kintsch, 1996, p. 251). The product of the CI process is a unitary mental representation structured from the text-based and situation model. The textbase consists of elements directly derived from the text. According to Kintsch (2005; McNamara & Kintsch, 1996), this is a propositional network that would yield an impoverished and incoherent network without the addition of the links brought by the reader based on her prior knowledge and experience.

Without adequate background knowledge, the textbase will predominate in the comprehension process. That is, the representation might appear fragmented or as a list of "facts" without much coherence. Without an adequate textbase, the representation would rely more heavily on the reader's knowledge and experience. The readers' previous knowledge might intrude into their representation for the text, even when that information was not in the text or was contradicted by text information. The more knowledge and experience brought to the text, the greater the influence of the situation model. This influence can take the form of elaborations and cognitive integration of the text or a disregard for the text. Ideally, we are striving for a balance of text-derived and situation model contributions to comprehension.

Miscues and Microprocesses

Even if substantial variations in miscues occurred after the initial stages of reading, what would they tell us about the relation between oral reading and comprehension? If we were to analyze the original sentence in terms of propositional analysis (Kintsch, 1974), we would have two propositions, the second subordinate to the first:

(ISA, DAY, WARM)
  (DAY, SUMMER)

Consider the following sets of miscues for the text line:

Text: It was a warm summer day.
Child₁: It was a warm *spring* day.
Child₂: It was a warm *winter* day.
Child₃: It was a warm *simmer* day.

The first of these miscues, "spring" for "summer," would be considered acceptable, since the substituted word is of the same semantic class, "seasons," as the text word and is similarly a warm season, so it does not violate the constraints of context. Further, it contains the same initial sound as the text word. This would suggest that the reader is integrating context, semantic, and graphophonemic cues. However, "spring" is not "summer." In most ordinary situations, this difference would not impair comprehension, but it is possible to think of scenarios where it would. The second miscue, "winter" for "summer," is less acceptable, because it would seem to violate the constraint, "warm." It is, however, a season, and may not represent a serious problem with comprehension. In both cases, the reader has correctly parsed the sentence, so that it read that it was a "warm day," regardless of what season it was.

The last miscue, "simmer" for "summer," is more problematic, since it violates all constraints, except some phonics elements. Even with the anomalous word included, the basic parts of the sentence are intact. The reader still produced that it was a warm day, the major part of the sentence.

In all cases, the reader correctly identified the first proposition. Since we would not expect readers to remember all the propositions, especially those lower in the text hierarchy (Kintsch, 1974), we might not expect proposition 2 to be remembered, unless some subsequent information highlighted its importance. Thus, even a miscue that would be judged as in violation of the semantic cues in the text might preserve enough of the meaning so that the reader can get a main point. In fact, the reader making this miscue might remember as much as a reader who did not, because it is likely that the subordinate proposition would not be remembered anyway. (It also may be that the reader may process miscue 3 as a typo.)

A miscue such as *It was a warm summer dog.* creates a different problem, since this involves a misunderstanding of the key proposition, that it was a "day" that is being described. Such a major change might impact comprehension. In our experience, we see such miscues rarely, usually when there is a picture, which distracts a child. In other words, if there was a picture of a dog with this sentence, the child might say "dog" in place of the "d word" by overrelying on the picture.

In the first three miscues, the violation would have impaired the child's ability to develop a fully realized textbase. However, even if such a textbase were developed, the detail of "season" would have been forgotten, unless it tied to something else in the text, such as fireworks on July 4. Thus, the miscue would impact the child's comprehension of a detail, which might have been forgotten in ordinary comprehension. In the fourth case, the violation was at the macrolevel. This would not integrate well with prior knowledge and with information from the rest of the text, thus impairing the development of the situation model. In our experience, a child making such a miscue would either (a) make other changes in the text compatible with the "dog" idea, or (b) have their comprehension fall apart. As predicted above, such a reader might be able to remember facts or fragments but have difficulty putting together a coherent account of the text. In practice, most of the miscues we see are at the microlevel, especially with children beyond the initial stages, but we know of no study that has made that distinction.

Our experience is that children's miscues overwhelmingly preserve the syntactic functions of the text. Schlieper (1977) found a developmental pattern in the oral reading of first, second, and third graders with third graders making a significantly higher proportion of syntactically acceptable miscues (70.4%) than first (42.3%) or second graders (49.4%). This echoes still earlier work by Goodman (1965) and Ilg and Ames (1950).

Meaning changing miscues, such as "dog" for "day," are related to comprehension. Pinnell et al. (1995) found that the number of meaning-changing miscues was significantly related to children's overall comprehension level. One explanation for this finding is that meaning-changing miscues disrupted the comprehension of the passage. However, since this data is correlational, it is possible that impairments in children's ongoing comprehension may have led to a higher proportion of meaning-changing miscues. Taft and Leslie (1985) found that children who had high knowledge of the text topic made significantly fewer meaning-changing miscues than children who had low topic knowledge. This suggests that their topic knowledge influenced their ongoing processing of the words in the text. The influence may be at the word recognition level or at a somewhat higher level (Adams, 1990).

Our reading of the research leads us to conclude that most miscues will disrupt the development of a textbase, forcing children to overrely on background knowledge. A less than coherent textbase would impair the development of an integrated representation of the information in the text, Thus, when a reader misses a sizeable proportion of words, comprehension will suffer. A critical question for instruction as well as assessment pertains to the size of the corpus of words that are recognized incorrectly, before comprehension breaks down.

RATE AND COMPREHENSION

Since this research shows that conventional word recognition levels do not predict comprehension particularly well at all grades, we need to examine the aspect that

Gray (1919) suggested as part of his original oral reading assessment but has often not been part of the designation of reading levels from IRIs in decades since—rate of reading. In the NAEP study (Pinnell et al., 1995), accuracy was not related to comprehension but rate was. Similarly, Rasinski (1999; Rasinski & Padak, 1998) examined the oral reading accuracy and rate of fifth graders involved in remedial reading programs. He found that the average accuracy of his remedial readers was near the instructional level, as was their general comprehension, similar to the findings of the NAEP study (Pinnell et al., 1995). However, the remedial readers in his studies had significantly lower reading rates. This suggests that, at least for children receiving instruction in decoding, accuracy levels may be generally high, since children are using decoding skills to compensate for a lack of automatic word recognition. However, this involves a trade-off, which would be reflected in a slow reading rate. If the rate is too slow, it is likely that comprehension might be very difficult.

The relations between rate and comprehension, then, reflect a trade-off between word identification and comprehension. If word recognition is not automatic, as reflected in slower rates, then the reader is presumed to be devoting resources to decoding. Under LaBerge and Samuels's (1974) and Logan et al.'s (1999) models, this would mean that there are fewer resources available for comprehension. This does not mean that comprehension cannot occur; only that it is more difficult. This trade-off would also explain the success of curriculum-based measurements (CBMs) in measuring comprehension. CBMs are short passages, either taken from children's texts (Deno, 1985; Shinn, 1988) or from standard passages (Good, Wallin, Simmons, Kame'enui, & Kaminski, 2003), which children read aloud. Scoring is based on the number of correct words read in one minute. Typically, a child will read three passages at a level in order to get a score. These CBM-based scores also have high concurrent validity when compared to reading comprehension measures. Hintze, Shapiro, Conte, and Basile (1997) found correlations between 0.64 and 0.69 for CBM and the Degrees of Reading Power test in grades 1–5. Shinn, Good, Knutson, Tilly, and Collins (1992) found correlations between CBMs and the Stanford Diagnostic Reading Test Literal and Inferential comprehension subtests of 0.55 for fifth graders, and correlations between CBMs and cloze measures of 0.75 for third graders and 0.62 for fifth graders.

One would expect that word recognition accuracy would have a strong effect in first grade, tapering off as children develop decoding skills that would enable them to read reasonably accurately. One would expect rate to affect reading comprehension strongly at first. As children improve as readers, rate should hit an asymptote, following the power curve (Logan et al., 1999), where possible improvements in rate are slight.

We have found some indication of this developmental effect in our data. Schwanenflugel, Strauss, et al. (2004) examined 195 first, second, and third graders on a variety of measures of single word reading, text reading, orthographic knowledge, obligatory processing (as evidenced by variations of the Stroop test), and reading comprehension. Using LISREL modeling, they found that the measures of isolated word recognition, including phonemic decoding and orthographic knowledge as well as recognition of irregular words, loaded on the same factor as a measure of text reading (the Gray Oral Reading Test) and that this factor was strongly related to the comprehension measure (from the Wechsler Individual Achievement Test) at all three grades tested. However, this relationship diminished between first and second and between second and third, suggesting that, as children become more automatic in their decoding abilities, other factors account for more variance in comprehension than word recognition factors.

The Schwanenflugel, Strauss, et al. (2004) study also established that single word decoding and recognition loaded on the same factor as text reading. Although studies have differed in the size of the effect, children have been found to read words better in context than in isolation (e.g. Goodman, 1965; Adams & Huggins, 1985; Nicholson, 1991). Regardless of the size of the effect, measures of children's reading words in isolation and in context are bound to be highly correlated with each other. Koolstra, van der Voort, and van der Kamp (1997) reported correlations between measures of decoding and comprehension in Dutch as part of a 3-year study of the effects of television on reading comprehension and decoding. For third graders, they reported correlations of 0.53, 0.49, and 0.41 for each of the three years of the study. For fifth graders, the corresponding correlations are 0.32, 0.33, and 0.27, a sizable drop.

The preponderance of research presented so far is correlational. The results of the instructional research is mixed. On one hand, Fleisher, Jenkins, and Pany (1979), working with fourth and fifth graders, found that speeded practice in reading words did not significantly improve comprehension. On the other hand, Blanchard (1980) working with sixth graders and Tan and Nicholson (1997) working with 7- to 10-year-olds found that training in automatic word recognition did improve comprehension. It is unclear why there were such differences between studies. Tan and Nicholson taught 20 difficult words from a 200-word story. Both Blanchard and Fleisher et al. taught all the words in the to-be-read passages. Blanchard found that only "very poor" readers and not the "poor" readers in his study benefited from the training. The poor readers were from a half-year to 2 years below grade placement. The very poor readers were students who more than 3 years behind grade placement on a standardized test—some as much as 4 years. Thus, the children with whom Tan and Nicholson and Blanchard worked with may have had lower reading abilities than those in Fleisher et al.'s study.

The general picture from these studies is that, as children become more automatic in word recognition, the relationship between word recognition and comprehension drops. As the process of word recognition demands fewer resources, comprehension of written language would become more like comprehension of oral language. This would confirm the predictions of both the "simple view" (Gough & Tunmer, 1986; Hoover & Gough, 1990) and Chall's (1996) stage model. Chall's model assumes that automatic word recognition is achieved by the end of grade 3. Our data (Schwanenflugel et al., 2003) as well as that of others suggest that automaticity is not attained by the end of that grade.

PROSODY AND COMPREHENSION

The third aspect of fluency, prosody, has not been as well researched as accuracy and rate. It is commonly observed that children who are not fluent read choppily, or in ways that diverge from naturally sounding language (e.g., Clay & Imlach, 1971). Dowhower (1987) found good and poor reader differences on several measures of prosody. Such differences could reflect that differences in prosody are caused by differences in reading ability or that differences in reading ability and prosody are caused by common factors, such as differences in comprehension or word recognition. Schreiber (1991) suggests that prosody is related to syntactic processing. In oral language, children seem to rely more heavily on prosody in syntactic processing (Read & Schreiber, 1982). However, it is not clear whether the use of prosody reflects children's understanding of the syntax of what they read or whether the understanding of syntax comes from the ability to assign prosodic cues.

Our data (Schwanenflugel, Hamilton, et al., 2004) suggests that prosody's link to comprehension goes indirectly through automatic word recognition. Digitized recordings of second- and third-grade children reading a passage from the Gray Oral Reading Test–3 were made as part of a larger study on the development of reading fluency. The children were assessed on reading comprehension. In LISREL models, we found that differences in automatic word recognition accounted for significantly more variance than nearly all the prosody variable. The exception was the overall resemblance of the child's reading to that of adults from the child's community. In addition, based on the features we have sampled from the recordings, we found that poor readers have longer and more variable intersentential pause lengths than good readers. The drop in pitch of poor readers showed smaller declinations at the end of declarative sentences than that of good readers, and poor readers were somewhat less likely to drop in pitch consistently.

In this study, we used simple declarative and question structures, These are prosody features which emerge early in children's language development. Prosody–comprehension relationships may be seen in more complex constructions. We are currently testing these relations using other syntactic patterns.

FLUENCY AND COMPREHENSION

Reviewing the research concerning all three aspects of fluent reading behavior–rate, accuracy, and prosody–it seems that at least two (accuracy and prosody) seem directly connected to the ability of the reader to create a textbase or an ordered list of propositions (Kintsch, 1998). A fragmented textbase would entail a reader over relying on prior knowledge to construct a representation of the meaning of the text.

When we measure comprehension in broad forms, we might be missing the specific knowledge used to develop a textbase. There is a trend toward including "response" questions, for example, such as "How do you think [a character] felt about [an action]?" Such questions may be important, not only because they measure an important aspect of reading but also because they encourage teachers to include response to literature in their teaching. However, an overreliance on such questions may inflate the measurement of comprehension, since they would allow a reader who has not developed a textbase representation to appear to have understood. The answers to these questions could be derived largely from the readers' prior knowledge and general world knowledge, rather than specific items from the text. Other items vary in terms of their text dependency (Tuinman, 1974).

The relationship between comprehension and fluency appears to be developmental. There seems to be a stronger relationship between word recognition accuracy, rate, and prosody and comprehension in the first and second grades. This relationship appears to diminish in the third and fourth grades (Carpenter & Paris,

2004). There are several possible explanations for this. First, as word recognition becomes more automatic, there is less variation in word recognition itself, so that there is less potential correlation. Although we (Schwanenflugel et al., 2003; see also Pinnell et al., 1995) have been finding that children do not seem to reach automaticity by the end of third grade as assumed by Chall (1996), there certainly is less variation in fluent reading behaviors by third grade. Second, as the texts children read become more complex, higher-level factors, such as those involved in reasoning and inference, become more important. The simple texts used in first and second grade, if the words are recognized, may present few higher-level comprehension problems. The more complex texts read in later grades, however, may require both more involved background knowledge and more involved reasoning about the text in order to understand them.

A third explanation for the diminishing relationship between word recognition and comprehension may be that another word factor, vocabulary knowledge, becomes more important by third grade and that variations in children's store of word meanings becomes more important as children progress through school. Vocabulary knowledge is an important correlate with reading comprehension throughout the grades (Anderson & Freebody, 1981). Tests of knowledge of word meaning correlate so highly with measures of reading comprehension that some have suggested that they are close to 1.0, given the error inherent in both measures (Carver, 2000; Thorndike, 1972). Evidence from correlational studies, readability research, and experimental studies all found strong and reliable relationships between the difficulty in a text and text comprehension (Anderson & Freebody, 1981).

But why is there such a relationship? The most obvious notion is that knowing word meanings *causes* comprehension of a text containing those words. The cause of this correlational relationship is unclear, however. Anderson and Freebody (1981) suggest three hypotheses that might explain these strong correlations. The instrumentalist hypothesis suggests that knowledge of word meanings directly causes comprehension. Although Stahl and Fairbanks (1986) found that teaching word meanings directly improved comprehension, there might be more to the relationship than this hypothesis predicts. Two other of Anderson and Freebody's hypotheses, a general knowledge hypothesis and a general aptitude hypothesis, suggest that vocabulary knowledge's relationship to a third factor, either a person's overall knowledge store or their general cognitive abilities, underlies the correlations between vocabulary knowledge and comprehension. Knowledge of certain words certainly does imply that a person has knowledge of a general cognitive domain, such as knowledge of the meaning of *jib* implies that a person knows about sailing or knowledge of the word *dharma* suggests a familiarity with Hinduism. For this reason, vocabulary tests have been used as tests of domain knowledge (Johnston, 1984). Vocabulary knowledge is also strongly related to a person's overall cognitive aptitude, as evidenced by high correlations between vocabulary tests and overall intelligence tests.

It is important to make a distinction between recognition of written words that a person knows the meaning of (the child learning to decode a word like "sun") and knowledge of word meanings themselves (words like "corona," solar flare," etc.). It is not unreasonable to suggest that there is a shift in the "word factor" in comprehension from a recognition factor to a word-meaning factor. Observing common reading measures such as the Wide Range Achievement Test (Jastak & Wilkenson, 1995), for example, shows high correlations between the Reading subtest, which is mostly a list of words to be read aloud, and passage comprehension measures. In the technical manual, correlations between the Wide Range Achievement Test and the Comprehensive Tests of Basic Skills, California Achievement Test, and Stanford Achievement Tests, all respected passage comprehension measures, are reported as between 0.69 and 0.87. They do not present the correlations broken down by grade level, but, assuming that they are consistent across grade, these are substantial correlations, suggesting a strong relation between word knowledge and passage comprehension. The nature of the words, however, changes on the measure. The first three words on one form of the WRAT are "see," "red," and "milk," which most English-speaking first graders will know. Items 10–12 are "cliff," "stalk," and "grunt," words of moderate difficulty. Items 20–22 are "rancid," "conspiracy," and "deny," which are difficult words and have somewhat irregular spelling–sound correspondences that probably have to be known in order to be pronounced. The test goes up to "epithalamium," "inefficacious," and "synecdoche," which are not known by many college-educated adults and are difficult to pronounce for those who know them.

Although we have been talking about accuracy of word recognition, it is impossible to separate this factor from word knowledge. Words are easier to pronounce if one knows their meaning, even words whose pronunciations can be derived from basic decoding rules (Adams, 1990).

Richness of Language

Related to the issue of vocabulary and word recognition is the issue of richness of language. In recent years, under the influence of "Guided Reading" (Fountas & Pinnell, 1996), there has been a growth in the use of leveled texts, or primary grade texts designed to be readable for early readers. These texts are designed to become increasingly less predictable in terms in syntactic patterns, to be less reliant on picture information, to be more complex in topic, to have longer and more complex page layouts, and to depend more on children's increasing capabilities in knowledge of the alphabetic system (Peterson, 1991). Decodable texts, or texts tightly controlled for use of taught sound–symbol correspondence, may create similar problems. The result is texts useful for supporting children in knowledge of decoding (e.g., Stahl, Stahl, & McKenna, 1999). However, the richness of the language that children read suffers.

Consider the following three texts—the first a leveled text, the second a decodable, and the third a literary text—all intended for the early second-grade level.

Example 1: *Wet Grass*
Ned and Lottie were playing inside. Mom looked out of the window. "The rain's stopped," she said. "Come for a walk." They walked down the road. Lottie climbed over a fence. "Come and walk in the wet grass," she said. Mom climbed over the fence. "Come on, Ned, " she said. (Wright Group, 1996)

Example 2: *Big Hog's House Hunt*
Big Hog was looking for a new home when he met Hot Dog. "It's my job to help pals look for new homes," Said Hot Dog. "It just so happens that at the present time, I have seven homes for sale. I bet I can sell you a home!" (Cooper et al., 2003)

Example 3: *Julius*

Maya's granddaddy lived in Alabama, but wintered in Alaska. He told Maya that was the reason he liked ice cubes in his coffee. On one of Granddaddy's visits from Alaska, he brought a crate. A surprise for Maya! "Something that will teach you fun and sharing." Granddaddy smiled. "Something for my special you." (Johnson, 1993)

While similar in their word recognition demands, texts of these three types may create different expectations about the nature of texts. Such expectations may affect children's processing of text on comprehension assessments. With excessive exposure to leveled or decodable texts, children may attend to decoding the texts, not devoting attention to comprehension (LaBerge & Samuels, 1974). We are not saying that texts used in instruction should be of one type or another, but that there be a "balanced diet" of texts, so that children will develop varied expectations and flexible processing of texts.

WORDS AND COMPREHENSION ASSESSMENT

Although, as we suggested at the beginning of this chapter, the majority of attention in comprehension assessment research is devoted to "higher level" aspects of comprehension, including meta-cognition, the use of cognitive strategies, and inferencing, the arguments in this paper suggest that one ignores word-level factors, both fluent reading and vocabulary knowledge, at one's risk. Children whose reading is not fluent tend to either fail to create a coherent textbase or read slowly to compensate for their difficulties. Either of these strategies would impact comprehension assessment.

Our observations of comprehension testing suggest that developers do ignore word level factors. Consider the following excerpt from the 2000 NAEP (Donahue, Finnegan, Lutkus, Allen, & Campbell, 2001), a measure used to develop the "Report Card for the Nation":

Excerpt 1: The meeting houses had no heat of their own until the 1800s. At home, colonial families huddled close to the fireplace, or hearth. The fireplace was wide and high enough to hold a large fire, but its chimney was large, too. That caused a problem: Gusts of cold air blew into the house. (Donahue et al., 2001)

Then peruse an excerpt of similar length from the Basic Reading Inventory (BRI; Johns, 1997), a typical IRI:

Excerpt 2: Martha and Johnny traveled in a covered wagon pulled by horses. As time passed, the weather became colder. One night when they stopped to sleep, it was six degrees below zero. The next night they were caught in a blizzard. Martha and Johnny stopped at a house to ask for directions. (Johns, 1997)

Both passages are intended for fourth graders. If a criterion for a word that could challenge a fourth grader who is not reading with rapidity is one that is infrequent and multisyllabic, about 6 unique words in every 100 running words of text in the Johns's text will be difficult. In the NAEP text, approximately 9 unique words out of every 100 running words of text will be difficult. If these words give students the greatest difficulty, we might expect students to read with approximately 94–95% accuracy on the Johns and at 90–91% accuracy on the NAEP. The 95% accuracy level would conventionally be considered a child's instructional level; the 90–91% level would be considered a "frustration" level, especially without any instructional preparation (Betts, 1946).

While it is unlikely that all challenged students will struggle with precisely the words that we would predict to be difficult, a consideration of some of the words in the two excerpts illustrate the task that confronts them. The NAEP passage contains words like "hearth" or "meeting house" that, even if they do not represent decoding problems (and "hearth" probably does), represent concepts that may not be known by fourth graders. The BRI passage contains fewer difficult concepts, although the general topic (olden times) is similar. Among the group of difficult words in the NAEP passage, 45% had a standard frequency index on Zeno's word list (Zeno, Ivens, Millard, & Duvvuri, 1995) that indicates that frequency of appearance less than once per 1 million words. None of the difficult words on the Johns's passage had frequency levels below three appearances per 1 million words. For students who do not read much, such differences may not seem great but the difference between words such as *huddled* and *hearth* when attempting to make sense of text on an assessment and words such as *degrees*, *zero*, and *blizzard* (on the Johns assessment) is a substantial one. This is not to say that passages such as the one on the NAEP are not appropriate for learning and instruction. Questions of whether passages with a substantial number of rare words are appropriate for a national assessment or for large-scale state assessments need to be addressed in light of policies and perceptions that follow such assessments.

This review has shown that word recognition is central in defining the reading performances of beginning readers. For challenged readers, word recognition accounts for a significant portion of the variance in student performance beyond the beginning levels as well. While an empirical and theoretical foundation exists for identifying the end of third grade as the point where processes other than speed and accuracy in identifying words should dominate, this is not the case for many children. A substantial portion of a grade-level cohort has developed a grasp of the alphabetic principle but this knowledge has not moved to an automatic level (Schwanenflugel et al., 2003).

These findings call for the inclusion of fluency as a task that is part of reading assessment at least through the third grade and possibly through the elementary grades. We are certain that this proposal will meet with less argument for beginning reading batteries than with students in the middle grades. However, we think it is as critical for the middle-grade students who are not attaining standards. We hasten to emphasize that we are not suggesting more assessment of word recognition. What we are arguing for is attention to fluency.

As well as assessment of fluency, attention is required to the difficulty of the words within texts. For beginning readers, texts in which high-frequency and phonetically regular words dominate are read with more speed than texts where a sizable number of the words fall into the category of rare words (Hiebert & Fisher, 2002). We expect that that is also the case with challenged readers in the middle grades. At the macrolevel of selecting grade-appropriate texts, consideration is given to texts on assessments. For example, a selection from *Charlotte's Web* (White, 1952) does not appear in an assessment for first graders, just as excerpts from Minarik's (1957) *Little*

Bear do not appear in an assessment for fifth graders. But we are arguing for more than attention to genre and the cohesiveness of ideas within texts. We are suggesting that, in selecting beginning and challenged readers, the words in texts matter.

Strong and Weak Views of Fluency and Comprehension

Thus, the strong view, that automaticity of word recognition enables children to comprehend text at the ability predicted by their level of language development, is clearly inadequate. First of all, children's ability to recognize words is related to their knowledge of word meanings, so that language knowledge and word recognition are not independent. This is true for words in isolation (e.g., Adams, 1990; Schwanenflugel & Akins, 1994) and in context (Goodman, 1965; Nicholson, 1991). Second, word recognition in context reflects children's perceptions of the syntax and meaning of the text they are reading. This has been found in studies of miscue analysis as well as studies of the relations of prosody to comprehension. Third, the relationship between word recognition and comprehension seems to be developmental, in that the relationships seem stronger in first and second grade than in third grade and beyond. As children develop as readers, the variations in their word recognition ability diminish since they are moving toward automaticity, and other aspects of reading such as text complexity and reasoning skills become more important, both of which may reduce the correlations.

The strong view that word recognition causes children to be able to comprehend would suggest that older children need more intense instruction in word recognition in order to be better readers. In fact, the report of the National Reading Panel (Ehri, Nunes, Stahl, & Willow, 2001) found that phonics instruction was not effective for children in grades 2–6 for improving comprehension, although it was significantly effective in grade 1.

There are important entanglements between word recognition, vocabulary, and reading comprehension. Misreading of individual words can have an impact on ongoing comprehension. This impact might show up in measures of a coherent representation, but might be missed on questions that ask for a literary response or for which the reader can use prior knowledge to infer an answer. Further, vocabulary knowledge impacts children's text reading, a factor that may influence scores of children on measures such as the NAEP, which require a great deal of specialized knowledge. In short, comprehension is built on a foundation of words.

REFERENCES

Adams, M. J. (1990). *Beginning to read: Thinking and learning about print.* Cambridge, MA: MIT. Press.
Adams, M. J. (1998). The three-cuing system. In J. Osborn & F. Lehr (Eds.), *Literacy for all: Issues in teaching and learning* (pp. 73–99). New York: Guilford Press.
Adams, M. J., & Huggins, A. W. F. (1985). The growth of children's sight vocabulary: A quick test with educational and theoretical implications. *Reading Research Quarterly, 20,* 262–281.
Allington, R. L. (1984). Oral reading. In P. D. Pearson, R. Barr, M. L. Kamil, & P. Mosenthal (Eds.), *Handbook of reading research* (Vol. 1, pp. 829–864). White Plains, NY: Longman.

Anderson, R. C., & Freebody, P. (1981). Vocabulary knowledge. In J. T. Guthrie (Ed.), *Comprehension and teaching: Research reviews* (pp. 77–117). Newark, DE: International Reading Association.

Anderson, R. C., & Pearson, P. D. (1984). A schema-theoretic view of basic processes in reading comprehension. In P. D. Pearson, R. Barr, M. L. Kamil, & P. Mosenthal (Eds.), *Handbook of reading research* (Vol. 1, pp. 255–291). White Plains, NY: Longman.

Barr, R. (1974–1975). The effect of instruction on pupil reading strategies. *Reading Research Quarterly, 10,* 555–582.

Betts, E. (1946). *Foundations of reading instruction.* New York: American Book.

Biemiller, A. (1970). The development of the use of graphic and contextual information as children learn to read. *Reading Research Quarterly, 6,* 75–96.

Blanchard, J. (1980). A preliminary investigation of the transfer effect between single word decoding ability and contextual reading comprehension in poor reading sixth graders. *Perceptual and Motor Skills, 51,* 1271–1281.

Carpenter, R. D., & Paris, S. G. (year). *Developmental disjunction between oral reading fluency and reading comprehension.* Manuscript submitted for publication.

Carver, R. P. (1993). Merging the simple view of reading with rauding theory. *Journal of Reading Behavior, 25,* 439–455.

Carver, R. P. (2000). *The causes of high and low reading achievement.* Mahwah, NJ: Erlbaum.

Chall, J. S. (1996). *Stages of reading development* (2nd ed.). Fort Worth, TX: Harcourt-Brace.

Clay, M. M. (1991). *Becoming literate: The construction of inner control.* Portsmouth, NH: Heinemann.

Clay, M. M. (1993). *Reading Recovery: A guidebook for teachers in training.* Portsmouth, NH: Heinemann.

Clay, M. M., & Imlach, R. H. (1971). Juncture, pitch, and stress as reading behavior variables. *Journal of Verbal Behavior and Verbal Learning, 10,* 133–139.

Cohen, A. S. (1974–1975). Oral reading errors of first grade children taught by a code emphasis approach. *Reading Research Quarterly, 10,* 616–650.

Connelly, V., Johnston, R. S., & Thompson, G. B. (1999). The influence of instructional approach on reading procedure. In G. B. Thompson & T. Nicholson (Eds.), *Learning to read: Beyond phonics and whole language* (pp. 103–123). New York: Teachers College Press.

Cooper, J. D., et al. (2003). *Houghton Mifflin reading: The nation's choice.* Boston: Houghton Mifflin.

Deno, S. L. (1985). Curriculum-based measurement: The emerging alternative. *Exceptional Children, 52,* 219–232.

Donahue, P. L., Finnegan, R. J., Lutkus, A. D., Allen, N. L., & Campbell, J. R. (2001). *The nation's report card for reading: Fourth grade.* Washington, DC: National Center for Education Statistics.

Dowhower, S. L. (1987). Effects of repeated reading on second-grade transitional readers' fluency and comprehension. *Reading Research Quarterly, 22,* 389–406.

Ehri, L., Nunes, S., Stahl, S. A., & Willows, D. M. (2001). Systematic phonics instruction helps students learn to read: Evidence from the National Reading Panel's meta-analysis. *Review of Educational Research, 71,* 393–447.

Fleisher, L. S., Jenkins, J. R., & Pany, D. (1979). Effects on poor readers' comprehension of training in rapid decoding. *Reading Research Quarterly, 15,* 30–48.

Fountas, I. C., & Pinnell, G. S. (1996). *Guided reading: Good first teaching for all children.* Portsmouth, NH: Heinemann.

Gibson, E. J., & Levin, H. (1975). *The psychology of reading.* Cambridge, MA: MIT Press.

Good, R. H., Wallin, J. U., Simmons, D. C., Kame'enui, E. J., & Kaminski, R. A. (2003). *System-wide percentile ranks for DIBELS Benchmark Assessment* (Technical Report 9). Eugene: University of Oregon Press.

Goodman, K. S. (1965). A linguistic study of cues and miscues in reading. *Elementary English*, *42*, 853–860.

Goodman, K. S. (1968). The psycholinguistic nature of the reading process. In K. S. Goodman (Ed.), *The psycholinguistic nature of the reading process* (pp. 13–26). Detroit, MI: Wayne State University.

Goodman, K. S. (1983). A linguistic study of cues and miscues in reading. In L. M. Gentile, M. L. Kamil, & J. S. Blanchard (Eds.), *Reading research revisited* (pp. 187–192). Columbus, OH: Charles E. Merrill.

Goodman, K. S., & & Goodman, Y. M. (1977). Learning about psycholinguistic processes by analyzing oral reading. *Harvard Educational Review*, *47*, 317–333.

Goodman, Y. M., Watson, D., & Burke, C. (1987). *Reading miscue inventory: Alternative procedures.* New York: Owen.

Gough, P. B., & Tunmer, W. E. (1986). Decoding, reading, and reading disability. *Remedial and Special Education*, *7*, 6–10.

Gray, W. S. (1919). *Standard passages for oral reading.* Bloomington, IN: Public School Publishing.

Hiebert, E., & Fisher, C. W. (2002, April). *Describing the difficulty of texts for beginning readers: A curriculum-based measure.* Paper presented at the annual meeting of the American Educational Research Association, New Orleans, LA.

Hintze, J. M., Shapiro, E. S, Conte, K. L., & Basile, I. M. (1997). Oral reading fluency and authentic reading material: Criterion validity of the technical features of CBM survey-level assessment. *School Psychology Review*, *26*, 535–553.

Hoover, W. A., & Gough, P. B. (1990). The simple view of reading. *Reading and Writing: An Interdisciplinary Journal*, *2*, 127–160.

Ilg, F. L., & Ames, L. B. (1950). Developmental trends in reading behavior. *Journal of Genetic Psychology*, *76*, 291–312.

Jastask, J., & Wilkinson, G. (1995). *Wide Range Achievement Test–3.* Wilmington, DE: Wide Range.

Johns, J. (1997). *Basic Reading Inventory.* Dubuque, IA: Kendall-Hunt.

Johnson, A. (1993). *Julius.* New York: Orchard Books.

Johnston, P. (1984). Prior knowledge and reading comprehension test bias. *Reading Research Quarterly*, *19*, 219–239.

Johnston, R. S., & Watson, J. (1997). Developing reading, spelling, and phonemic awareness skills in primary school children. *Reading*, *31*, 37–40.

Kendall, J. R., & Hood, J. (1979). Investigating the relationship between comprehension and word recognition: Oral reading analysis of children with comprehension or word recognition disabilities. *Journal of Reading Behavior*, *11*, 41–48.

Kintsch, W. (1974). *The representation of meaning in memory.* Hillsdale, NJ: Erlbaum.

Kintsch, W. (1998). *Comprehension: A paradigm for cognition.* Cambridge, UK: Cambridge University Press.

Kintsch, W. (2005). Comprehension. In S. G. Paris & S. A. Stahl (Eds.), *Children's reading comprehension and assessment* (pp. 71–92). Mahwah, NJ: Erlbaum.

Kintsch, W., & van Dijk,, T. (1978). Toward a model of text comprehension and production. *Psychological Review*, *85*, 363–394.

Koolstra, C. M., van der Voort, T. H. A., & van der Kamp, L. J. (1997). Television's impact on children's reading comprehension and decoding skills: A 3-year panel study. *Reading Research Quarterly*, *32*, 128–152.

Kuhn, M. R., & Stahl, S. A. (2003). Fluency: A review of developmental and remedial practices. *Journal of Educational Psychology*, *95*, 3–21.

LaBerge, D., & Samuels, S. J. (1974). Toward a theory of automatic information processing in reading. *Cognitive Psychology*, *6*, 293–323.

Logan, G. D., Taylor, S. E., & Etherton, J. L. (1999). Attention and automaticity: Toward a theoretical integration. *Psychological Research*, *62*, 165–181.

McNamara, D. S., & Kintsch, W. (1996). Learning from text: Effects of prior knowledge and text coherence. *Discourse Processes*, *22*, 247–287.

Minarik, E. (1957). *Little Bear*. New York: Harper.

National Reading Panel. (2000). *Report of the subgroups: National Reading Panel*. Washington, DC: National Institute of Child Health and Development.

Nicholson, T. (1991). Do children read words better in context or in lists: A classic study revisited. *Journal of Educational Psychology*, *83*(4), 444–450.

Paris, S. G., & Carpenter, R. D. (2003). FAQs about IRIs. *The Reading Teacher*, *56*(6), 578–580.

Peterson, B. (1991). Children's literature in Reading Recovery. In D. E. DeFord, C. A. Lyons, & G. S. Pinnell (Eds.), *Bridges to literacy: Learning from Reading Recovery*. Portsmouth, NH: Heinemann.

Pinnell, G. S., Pikulski, J. J., Wixson, K. K., Campbell, J. R., Gough, P. B., & Beatty, A. S. (1995). *Listening to children read aloud: Data from NAEP's integrated reading performance record (IRPR) at grade 4*. Washington, DC: National Center for Education Statistics.

Rasinski, T. V. (1999). Exploring a method for estimating independent, instructional, and frustration reading rates. *Reading Psychology*, *20*, 61–69.

Rasinski, T. V., & Padak, N. (1998). How elementary students referred for compensatory reading instruction perform on school-based measures of word recognition, fluency, and comprehension. *Reading Psychology: An International Quarterly*, *19*, 185–216.

Read, C., & Schreiber, P. A. (1982). Why short subjects are harder to find than long ones. In E. Wanner & L. Gleitman (Eds.), *Language acquisition: The state of the art* (pp. 78–101). Cambridge, UK: Cambridge, University Press.

Rupley, W. H., & Willson, V. L. (1997). Relationship between reading comprehension and components of word recognition: Support for developmental shifts. *Journal of Research and Development in Education*, *30*, 255–260.

Schlieper, A. (1977). Oral reading errors in relation to grade and level of skill. *The Reading Teacher*, *31*, 283–287.

Schreiber, P. A. (1987). Prosody and structure in children's syntactic processing. In R. Horowitz & S. J. Samuels (Eds.), *Comprehending oral and written language* (pp. 243–270). New York: Academic Press.

Schreiber, P. A. (1991). Understanding prosody's role in reading acquisition. *Theory into Practice*, *30*(3), 158–164.

Schwanenflugel, P. J., & Akin, C. E. (1994). Developmental trends in lexical decisions for abstract and concrete words. *Reading Research Quarterly*, *29*, 96–104.

Schwanenflugel, P. J., Hamilton, A. M., Kuhn, M. R., Wisenbaker, J., & Stahl, S. A. (2004). Becoming a fluent reader: Reading skill and prosodic features in the oral reading of young readers. *Journal of Educational Psychology*, *96*, 119–129.

Schwanenflugel, P. J., Kuhn, M., Meisinger, E., Bradley, B., Stahl, S., & Wisenbaker, J. (2003, April). *An examination of the attentional resource model and the development of reading fluency*. Paper presented at the biennial meeting of the Society for Research in Child Development, Tampa, FL.

Schwanenflugel, P. J., Strauss, G., Morris, R. K., Sieczko, J., Kuhn, M. R., & Stahl, S. A. (2004). *The influence of word unit size on the development of Stroop interference in early word decoding*. Athens: University of Georgia Press.

Shinn, M. R. (1988). Development of curriculum-based local norms for use in special education decision making. *School Psychology Review*, *17*, 61–80.

Shinn, M. R., Good, I. R. H., Knutson, N., Tilley, W. D., & Collins, V. L. (1992). Curriculum based measure of oral reading fluency: A confirmatory analysis of its relation to reading. *School Psychology Review*, *21*(3), 459–478.

Stahl, K. A. D., Stahl, S. A., & McKenna, M. C. (1999). The development of phonological awareness and orthographic processing in Reading Recovery. *Literacy, Teaching and Learning, 4*(3), 27–42.

Stahl, S. A., & Fairbanks, M. M. (1986). The effects of vocabulary instruction: A model-based meta-analysis. *Review of Educational Research, 56*(1), 72–110.

Stahl, S., Heubach, K., & Cramond, B. (1997). *Fluency-oriented reading instruction.* Athens, GA: National Reading Research Center, U.S. Department of Education Office of Educational Research and Improvement Educational Resources Information Center.

Stahl, S. A., McCartney, A. A., & Montero, M. K. (2004). *Reading first: An extensive investigation of intensive phonics instruction.* (CIERA technical report). Ann Arbor: Center for the Improvement of Early Reading Achievement/University of Michigan.

Stanovich, K. E. (2000). *Progress in understanding reading: Scientific foundations and new frontiers.* New York: Guilford Press.

Sulzby, E. (1985). Children's emergent reading of favorite storybooks: A developmental study. *Reading Research Quarterly, 20,* 458–481.

Taft, M. L., & Leslie, L. (1985). The effects of prior knowledge and oral reading accuracy on miscues and comprehension. *Journal of Reading Behavior, 17,* 163–179.

Tan, A., & Nicholson, T. (1997). Flashcards revisited: Training poor readers to read words faster improves their comprehension of text. *Journal of Educational Psychology, 89,* 276–288.

Thorndike, R. L. (1972). Reading as reasoning. *Reading Research Quarterly, 9,* 135–147.

Tuinman, J. J. (1974). Determining the passage-dependency of comprehension questions in five major tests. *Reading Research Quarterly, 9,* 207–223.

White, E. B. (1952). *Charlotte's web.* New York: Harper.

Willson, V. L., & Rupley, W. H. (1997). A structural equation model for reading comprehension based on background, phonemic, and strategy knowledge. *Scientific Studies in Reading, 1*(1), 45–63.

Wright Group. (1996). *Sunshine reading program.* Bothell, WA: Wright Group/McGraw-Hill. Rigby Education.

Zeno, S. M., Ivens, S. H., Millard, R. T., & Duvvuri, R. (1995). *The educator's word frequency guide.* Brewster, NY: Touchstone Applied Science Associates.

26 | Making the Invisible Visible

The Development of a
Comprehension Assessment System

KATHERINE A. DOUGHERTY STAHL
GEORGIA EARNEST GARCÍA
EURYDICE B. BAUER
P. DAVID PEARSON
BARBARA M. TAYLOR

Throughout Steve's life, he relied on data to evaluate the success of instructional practices and interventions. Steve and Freddy wrote " 'The Word Factors': A Problem for Reading Comprehension Assessment" (Stahl & Hiebert, 2005; reprinted as Chapter 25, this volume) after Steve had spent 4 years investigating Fluency-Oriented Reading Instruction and the interaction among word recognition, fluency, and comprehension. At about the same time, Steve was having conversations with us about the important aspects of reading comprehension instruction in elementary classrooms. Steve used these conversations to shape a proposal to the U.S. Department of Education, Institute of Education Sciences, to study the impact of specific types of reading instruction on elementary students' reading comprehension (see Taylor, Pearson, García, Stahl, & Bauer, Chapter 19, this volume). One of the challenges facing the research team was deciding what kinds of evidence would meet the criteria of the Department of Education and the criteria of our research group. We wanted reading comprehension measures that would be sensitive to developmental and instructional influences and that would reflect students' ability to apply what they had learned about reading comprehension through classroom instruction to new texts, not previously taught.

We knew that it would not be an easy task to assess students' internalization of comprehension strategies because the processes that students use to comprehend text can only be measured indirectly (Pearson & Johnson, 1978). In addition to the "word factors" addressed by Stahl and Hiebert (2005), we were cognizant of the challenges identified in the RAND Report (RAND Reading Study Group, 2002; Snow, 2003). In particular, Snow (2003) notes that it is difficult for assessment measures:

- To adequately reflect the complexity of reading comprehension;
- To identify why comprehension breaks down, separating "comprehension processes (inferencing, integrating new with existent knowledge) from lack of vocabulary, of domain-specific knowledge, of word reading ability, or of other reader capacities involved in comprehension";
- To capture the "developmental nature of comprehension" and teachers' instructional emphases and effectiveness;
- To focus on "comprehension for engagement, for aesthetic response, for purposes of critiquing an argument or disagreeing with a position";
- To capture instruction and to be psychometrically reliable and valid. (pp. 193–195)

Our purpose in this chapter is to discuss how we, as a research team, addressed various assessment challenges in our development of an assessment system for an instructional investigation of reading comprehension in grades 2 and 4. As the original principal investigator, Steve played a key role in the development of this line of research. In his last study, it is easy to see the culmination of his earlier research reflected in the theoretical foundation of this study on comprehension. There is a move away from looking at isolated aspects of comprehension, such as prior knowledge and vocabulary, to a broader instructional perspective that incorporates what he learned over the years about the role of decoding and fluency, stretching comprehension instruction to include novice readers and varied forms of scaffolding and instructional interactions. We designed the instructional study to answer the following research questions:

- Can we develop approaches to comprehension instruction that are sustainable over 1 or 2 years and implemented easily by teachers?
- What are the relative effects of cognitive strategy and responsive engagement instruction on a variety of measures, including measures of text specific comprehension and transfer to more general comprehension abilities?
- Do cognitive strategy and responsive engagement instruction transfer from comprehension in English to comprehension of other languages or vice versa?
- What are the effects of different types of instruction on children at different developmental stages (second and fourth graders)? Do children need to be fully fluent to take advantage of comprehension instruction?

In the discussion that follows, we briefly present the theoretical framework of the research study and discuss the theoretical connections that we wanted to make between instruction and assessment. Then we review several of the assessment measures that we developed or used. Throughout our discussion, we reflect on Steve's earlier work and its link with our current work. We conclude the chapter by briefly summarizing what we have learned about the assessments and by identifying several of the challenges that we still face.

THEORETICAL RATIONALE FOR THE STUDY AND ASSESSMENTS

As we write this chapter, we are in the second year of a research study that is comparing cognitive strategy instruction with responsive engagement instruction and a treated control (see Taylor et al., Chapter 19, this volume, for a more extensive discussion of the study). The two instructional interventions (cognitive strategy and responsive engagement instruction) and the system of assessment measures that we have developed and utilized reflect our theory of comprehension. The underpinnings of this theory are represented by the following points:

- Comprehension is developmental. Changes over time in children's biosociocultural development and ever-increasing bank of experiences result in changes in reading comprehension capabilities (Kintsch, 1998; Nelson, 1996).
- Reading comprehension demands capable decoding, language processes, vocabulary, and prior knowledge (Kintsch, 1998; Stahl & Hiebert, 2005).
- Proficient readers tend to engage in some common strategies during the initiation of reading, during the act of reading, and after reading that enable them to integrate the material from the text with prior knowledge and experience. Strategies enable the reader to monitor, repair, and enhance comprehension (Kintsch, 1998; Paris, Lipson, & Wixson, 1983).
- Reading comprehension is enhanced by reader transactions that facilitate inter- and intratextual connections, lively discussions of personal perspectives, and diverse reactions to text (Pressley, 2002; Rosenblatt, 1978; Saunders & Goldenberg, 1999; Schuder, 1993).
- Instruction influences reading comprehension outcome measures (Brown & Coy-Ogan, 1993; Taylor, Pearson, Clark, & Walpole, 2000).

Stahl and Hiebert (2005) discuss the influence that word recognition and fluency are likely to have on comprehension and comprehension measures. Historically, instruction before grade 3 has focused on decoding and learning how to read the words, rather than taking an aggressive approach to comprehension and text interpretation (Pearson & Duke, 2002; K. Stahl, 2004). We suspected that comprehension instruction might be advantageous in the primary grades, especially when students with decoding difficulties were aided with fluency instruction. Accordingly, with our emphasis on reading comprehension instruction in second grade as well as fourth grade, we wanted measures that would capture developmental differences in comprehension at different ages. We specifically needed measures that would allow us to test the relationship among decoding ability, fluency, and students' comprehension.

We also wanted assessment measures that would tap into each of our instructional interventions and the treated control. Cognitive strategy instruction required that teachers explicitly teach cognitive strategies (prediction, questioning, clarification, summarization, and visualization) and gradually release responsibility until the students were leading discussions about the text. Our goal was for the students to assume the teacher role established in Reciprocal Teaching (Palincsar, 1991; Palincsar & Brown, 1984; Palincsar, David, & Brown, 1992), but for the participants in the discussion to use multiple strategies in flexible ways in response to the text, more along the lines of Transactional Strategy Instruction (Brown & Coy-Ogan, 1992; Pressley et al., 1992; Schuder, 1993). In terms of assessment, we wanted measures that would tap how students were using cognitive strategies to help them make meaning of text and eliminate roadblocks to comprehension.

The responsive engagement intervention required that teachers engage students in high-level discussions about themes and make personal connections to the big ideas in complex texts. The responsive engagement intervention was based on research that showed the benefits of asking students high-level questions (Taylor et al., 2000) and getting them involved with reading rather than teaching them specific comprehension skills or strategies (Allington & Johnston, 2002). It drew on aspects of Saunders and Goldenberg's (1999) Instructional Conversations, in which students learned how to participate in student-oriented discussions of complex text. We wanted measures that specifically captured the type of thinking that would be generated by responsive engagement instruction, such as students' identification of themes, their ability to make personal connections, and their ability to ask and answer high-level questions.

The treated control group worked on prior knowledge and vocabulary instruction in association with text comprehension. It drew from the work of Stahl (1999) and Beck, McKeown, and Kucan (2002). Teachers provided instruction during and after the reading of a specific text to facilitate students' integration of prior knowledge with new information in the text and to provide repeated exposures of vocabulary in multiple contexts. We needed an assessment that took into account the specific vocabulary and prior knowledge instruction that students received within the treated control group.

ASSESSMENT MEASURES

See Table 26.1 for a list and brief description of all components of the assessment system that we developed. Given the length constraints of this chapter, we discuss the assessments that offer some solutions to the concerns addressed by Stahl and Hiebert (2005). These measures are the maze, the common instructional passage assessment, and the think-aloud.

Maze

The maze is a timed multiple-choice cloze task. We selected it as a measure of students' reading fluency and comprehension because it can be group administered to an entire class and takes no more than 5–10 minutes to administer. Fuchs and Fuchs (1992) evaluated oral and written recalls, oral and written cloze tasks, oral questioning, and maze. In terms of validity, reliability, correlation with a standard measure, teacher satisfaction, capacity to demonstrate student abilities and progress, the timed maze task showed the most promise. Stahl and Hiebert (2005) address the high concurrent validity that exists between maze measures and other comprehension measures (Hintze, Shapiro, Conte, & Basile, 1997; Shinn, Good, Knutson, Tilly, & Collins, 1992). Evidence suggests that maze tasks are sensitive to the reading comprehension development of novice readers (Francis, 1999; Shin, Deno, & Espin, 2000).

We chose to use the maze passages and scoring protocol developed by Shin et al. (2000). Shin et al.'s maze assessment consists of three 100-word passages, in which after the first sentence in each passage, every seventh word has been deleted and students must choose the correct word from three word choices. The passages, of similar readability, deal with everyday topics that are familiar to second or fourth graders (e.g., television and class meetings). Students are given 1 minute to read and complete each passage. Following Shin, et al.'s scoring procedures, we counted every correct word circled in a passage until a student made three consecutive errors, either

TABLE 26.1. Student Assessments

Test	Description	What it measures
	Product	
Gates–MacGinitie Reading Test (MacGinitie, MacGinitie, Maria, & Dreyer, 2000)	Standardized comprehension test—pictures or passage followed by multiple-choice questions	General comprehension; transfer
Maze (Shin, Deno, & Espin, 2000)	Timed, multiple choice cloze task	Fluency; microlevel comprehension
	Process	
Common instructional passage	All teachers in a grade level taught a common research team selected story according to the principles of their respective treatments.	
1. Narrative retelling	Reconstruction of common story that was read by all participants. Grade 2 assessment was administered verbally to nine students/classroom; grade 4 assessment was administered to all students using written format.	Summarization or reconstruction of information in story; open format allows for observation of thought processes, what is valued as important and sociocultural influences
2. Constructed response	12 short-answer questions; administered immediately after retelling, using a common format.	Targeted behaviors associated with each intervention (4 questions each)
Think-aloud	Prompted student think-aloud of a novel text provided to a sample of students in grades 2 and 4.	Transfer measure; provides evidence of cognitive processes and affective aspects of reading; developmental differences

by choosing incorrect words or by skipping the word choices. At the three-error point, we stopped counting correct answers and subtracted half of the incorrect answers from the total correct answers. We then used the median score of the three passages for our analysis. We administered the maze three times across the study so that we could assess students' gains in fluency and comprehension.

Common Instructional Passage Assessment

Across all of the sites and treatments, we had all of the teachers at the same grade level use the same book for 3 days of their experimental instruction. We requested three 30-minute sessions of instruction. The utilization of a common instructional passage allowed us to overcome several challenges in comprehension assessment research, including those addressed by Stahl and Hiebert (2005). For example, we were able to use authentic literature in an authentic instructional setting. We also could select texts that were fairly lengthy and complex in content because the teacher provided a scaffolded instructional experience. We observed and took field notes on how the teachers used the book in their instruction, providing us with a measure of their instruction and fidelity to the treatment.

We required that the first instructional passage for second grade, *The Lazy Lion* (Hadithi & Kennaway, 1990), be conducted as a teacher read-aloud. We required that the second instructional passage for second grade, *Mushroom in the Rain* (Ginsburg, 1978/1990), and both fourth-grade texts, *The Big Orange Splot* (Pinkwater, 1977) and *The Honest-to Goodness Truth* (McKissack, 2003), be conducted as shared reading. Steve's influence was noticeable in the second-grade classrooms as the teachers and students used Fluency-Oriented Reading Instruction (Stahl & Heubach, 2005) to make the texts accessible to the students. This helped us to avoid the decoding obstacles that often hinder the comprehension of novice or struggling readers.

We followed the 3 days of instruction with a curriculum-linked assessment. Students engaged in a retelling and constructed response on day 4.

Retelling

Our retelling task required the child to orally retell the story in grade 2 or to provide a written retelling in grade 4. We viewed the retelling as a process measure because it required the child to reconstruct the information from the text with varying degrees of integration with prior knowledge and links to other texts (Gambrell, Koskinen, & Kapinus, 1991). The openness of the retelling task allows room for the observation of the thought processes, what is valued as important, and sociocultural influences in story interpretation (Narvaez, 2002). Since story retellings have been used successfully with children in kindergarten and first grade, we judged them to be appropriate measures of comprehension for the second-grade participants (Geva & Olson, 1983; Morrow, 1985).

We used a 4-point rubric to score the retellings. We scaled the rubric based on the degree of elaboration, coherence, and the ability of the student to infer beyond the text. Interrater reliability was .86 (Fall, second grade), .87 (Fall, fourth grade) and .90 (Spring, second and fourth grade).

Although retellings can provide us with valuable information about what the reader perceives as important and the ability of the child to put together a sequence of events that is causally and logically propelled, research indicates that children understand much more than they are likely to include in a retelling (Mandler & Johnson, 1977; Stein & Glenn, 1979). Information relating to the goals, motives, and feelings of the characters is commonly omitted from the retellings of young children (Geva & Olson, 1983; Mandler & Johnson, 1977; Stein & Glenn, 1979). However, when asked questions about these areas, children have demonstrated insight and awarenesses that were not displayed in their retelling (Mandler & Johnson, 1977; Stein & Glenn, 1979). Therefore, we chose to develop a set of questions that would prompt a constructed response related to the text, as opposed to cued recall of the text.

Constructed Response

Answering questions reduces cognitive demands for children. The specificity of a question makes it clear to the child what information the adult is seeking, finds important, and is interested in hearing (Goldman, Varma, Sharp, & Cognition and Technology Group at Vanderbilt, 1999). In developing the questions for the constructed response, we wanted to tap the knowledge and comprehension processes emphasized in the two instructional interventions and targeted control. We developed four questions for each of the instructional interventions and the targeted control, resulting in a constructed response of 12 questions for each passage. An example of a question targeting each intervention and the targeted control for the *Lazy Lion* is listed below:

> *Responsive engagement*: If Lion were a person, is he the kind of person you would like for a friend? Why or why not?
> *Cognitive strategy*: Suppose the lion had asked a hippopotamus to build him a house. What do you predict would happen?
> *Vocabulary/prior knowledge*: Besides lazy, what other words would you use to describe the lion?

The constructed response was individually administered to a sample of nine second graders in each of the classrooms. Research assistants read the questions aloud to the students and wrote down the students' answers, as well as audiorecording them. All of the fourth graders in each classroom were given the written questions and asked to write their answers. Scoring was conducted on a 3-point scale, with students receiving 0 points for an answer that did not fit the question, 1 point for an answer that addressed one issue in the question, and 2 points for a complete answer that elaborated on the 1-point answer. The interrater reliability was consistently above .90.

Think-Aloud

Inherent in the theoretical frame of our study was the role that instruction plays in teaching and facilitating the use of strategies and engagement that enables the integration of material from the text with prior knowledge and experience. We used the think-aloud as a transfer measure to investigate the processes that students used to monitor their reading, extend their interpretations, and make sense of a text not previously taught. The think-aloud gave us an opportunity to compare how students in the cognitive strategy group approached, monitored, and made sense of a new text as compared to the students in the responsive engagement group and in the treated control group.

Think-alouds have a number of advantages as measures of student comprehension (Afflerbach & Johnston, 1984). Their validity is based on a different set of assumptions than most data sources. Pressley and Afflerbach (1995) found that the verbal protocols in the 38 studies of reading that they reviewed centered on getting meaning from text, monitoring behaviors, and evaluative comments. They reported that think-alouds provide a window for developmental analysis of mental processes and insights into cognitive processes and affective aspects of reading that may not be fully represented by product measures. However, think-alouds were rarely used with novice readers.

Given that we wanted to use the think-aloud with second graders, we thought that it was especially important to introduce them and the fourth graders to the think-aloud process prior to using it as an assessment. Training participants to engage in verbal reporting needs to be thorough enough that they understand the task, but not so rehearsed that it influences the validity of the student think-aloud. We used the cover and first three pages of the story, *Wednesday Surprise* (Bunting, 1990), to introduce the students to the think-aloud. We first piloted the training and the think-aloud protocol with a small group of children, making modifications to the training and protocol.

In the training that we used in the study, the assessor explicitly told a small group of students that they would be asked to share their thinking about another story a little later. However, they first would practice doing a think-aloud together. Our training consisted of the assessor thinking aloud about the cover and page 1 of the story *Wednesday Surprise* (Bunting, 1990). The assessor then invited the group of students to think aloud about sections of text on pages 2 and 3. The training took between 10 and 15 minutes.

We selected two below-average readers, two average readers, and two above-average readers from each classroom to participate in the think-aloud. We wanted to study how age differences, instructional differences, and ability differences might affect children's text processing as reflected in the think-aloud.

We were able to use the same think-aloud protocol and text (about 250 words), with a few modifications in the text's vocabulary and syntax, for the second and fourth graders. The second graders read the text aloud and stopped at predetermined points in the text to answer set questions about their thinking, whereas the fourth graders silently read the text until they reached the same predetermined points and were asked the same questions. The assessors took notes on the students' responses as well as audiorecorded their answers.

In the pilot, some of the second graders had difficulty decoding the text, so when the second graders missed decoding 30% of the words in the first three paragraphs, the assessor alternated reading the paragraphs aloud with the child. In this way, we were able to observe how second graders, who could not decode the text completely on their own, approached, monitored, and made sense of the text.

We currently are in the process of designing a scoring protocol for the think-alouds. However, preliminary findings for this measure are intriguing. First, the student-training model was extremely effective. Despite minimal or no prior experience with the think-aloud format, almost without exception the students were able to engage in thinking out loud about the text in a small group. Second, by alternating the oral reading of the text for those students with decoding difficulty, we were able to address Stahl and Hiebert's (2005) concerns about separating decoding, fluency, and comprehension.

CONCLUSIONS

What We Have Learned

Over the course of a year, we developed and piloted an assessment system to provide us with key information related to the reading comprehension development of second and fourth graders enrolled in an instructional study. We tried to be deliberate in developing an assessment system that was faithful to our theory of comprehension and also addressed the concerns expressed by the RAND Reading Study Group

(2002) and Stahl and Hiebert (2005). We wanted an assessment system that would provide us with key information about developmental issues, the complexity of comprehension, and the role of the instructional context. In the discussion that follows, we briefly note how well we did with each goal and some of the "new" challenges that we encountered.

Developmental Issues

Our selection of participants in second grade and fourth grade provided an opportunity for us to compare the processing of young novice readers with older more experienced readers. Recent research convinced us that word recognition and fluency were contributing factors to reading comprehension in varying degrees throughout the elementary years (see discussions by Paris, Carpenter, Paris, & Hamilton, 2005, and Stahl & Hiebert, 2005). Our inclusion of the maze task, a fluency measure on familiar topics, enabled us to quantify the variance of reading comprehension attributable to reading fluency. Our think-aloud was a transfer measure that provided a window for viewing a wider range of cognitive processes. The use of a common, complex text for the think-aloud for grades 2 and 4 provided us with the opportunity to assess developmental differences in strategy use, reasoning, and text interpretation. However, we have to acknowledge that some of the below-level second-grade readers, some of whom had histories of other more complex learning difficulties, found the think-aloud to be challenging and often did not verbalize much of their thinking.

Except for the maze, we also missed the opportunity to assess the role of decoding and fluency in the reading of the fourth graders. Although we accommodated the second graders' status as beginning readers by orally reading the constructed response questions to them and alternating the oral reading of the think-aloud passage when students had problems with decoding, we provided no such accommodations for the fourth graders.

Comprehension as a Complex Process

The complex interplay between word recognition, fluency, and conceptual difficulty makes it challenging to capture the nature of comprehension. Again, the think-aloud provided a window for viewing the ways that children handled the "simple" challenges, such as decoding an unknown word, as well as the more complex processes of applying prior knowledge during reading, synthesizing story information, generating inferences, and responding to text with personal connections and critique. However, due to the individual administration of the think-aloud assessment, we could only administer it to six students in each classroom.

In choosing texts for the instructional passage, we also looked for authentic texts that had sophisticated vocabulary and that required application of background knowledge and reasoning to gain understanding of the big ideas. For the constructed responses, we generated high-level questions that tapped the themes and big ideas in the texts and that showed some evidence of students' thinking, vocabulary, and background knowledge. Although the constructed responses provide us with additional information on how students interpreted complex text, the only way that we could include large numbers of fourth graders in the constructed responses was to have them write their answers, adding yet another factor that needs to be differentiated.

The Role of Instruction

Today, most theories of comprehension address the importance of the instructional or social context in comprehension. However, few comprehension assessment procedures incorporate consideration of these factors. Our use of the instructional passage, which teachers taught using their assigned treatment, enabled all students, even novice and below-grade-level readers, to interact with complex texts in a realistic, social, instructional setting. In a sense, it provided a type of scaffolded instruction.

Although we designed the constructed response so that it targeted each of the interventions, we also are aware of the fact that our study was not the only influence on the teachers' instruction. Similarly, the teachers and their instruction were not the only influences on the students' reading comprehension. We still are working on how to capture influences outside the assigned treatment.

Final Thoughts

We offer the foregoing observations in the hope of aiding others who are involved in the difficult task of assessing students' reading comprehension, or making the invisible visible. The Stahl and Hiebert (2005) piece, in particular, showed the importance of examining developmental factors and differences in reading comprehension. We thank Steve for getting us started on this journey.

ACKNOWLEDGMENTS

The research described in this chapter was supported by a grant from the U.S. Department of Education, Institute of Education Sciences (No. CDFA 84.305G). The views expressed herein are the authors' and have not been cleared by the grantors.

REFERENCES

Afflerbach, P., & Johnston, P. (1984). Research methodology: On the use of verbal reports in reading research. *Journal of Reading Behavior, 16*, 307–322.

Allington, R. L., & Johnston, P. H. (2002). *Reading to learn: Lessons from exemplary fourth-grade classrooms.* New York: Guilford Press.

Beck I., McKeown, M. G., & Kucan, L. (2002). *Bringing words to life: Robust vocabulary instruction.* New York: Guilford Press.

Brown, R., & Coy-Ogan, L. (1993). The evolution of transactional strategies instruction in one teacher's classroom. *Elementary School Journal, 94*, 221–233.

Bunting, E. (1990). *Wednesday surprise.* New York: Houghton Mifflin.

Francis, N. (1999). Applications of cloze procedure to reading assessment in special circumstances of literacy development. *Reading Horizons, 40*, 23–44.

Fuchs, L. S., & Fuchs, D. (1992). Identifying a measure for monitoring student reading progress. *School Psychology Review, 21*, 45–58.

Gambrell, L. B., Koskinen, P. S., & Kapinus, B. A. (1991). Retelling and the reading comprehension of proficient and less-proficient readers. *Journal of Educational Research, 84*, 356–362.

Geva, E., & Olson, D. (1983). Children's story retelling. *First Language, 4*, 85–109.

Ginsburg, M. (1990). *Mushroom in the rain.* New York: Aladdin Paperbacks. (Original work published 1978)

Goldman, S. R., Varma, K. O., Sharp, D., & Cognition and Technology Group at Vanderbilt

(1999). Children's understanding of complex stories: Issues of representation and assessment. In S. R. Goldman, A. C. Graesser, & P. V. d. Broek (Eds.), *Narrative comprehension, causality, and coherence: Essays in honor of Tom Trabaso*. Mahwah, NJ: Erlbaum.

Hadithi, M., & Kennaway, A. (1990). *Lazy lion*. Sevenoaks, Kent, UK: Hodder & Stoughton.

Hintze, J. M., Shapiro, E. S., Conte, K. L., & Basile, I. M. (1997). Oral reading fluency and authentic reading material: Criterion validity of the technical features of CBM survey level assessment. *School Psychology Review, 26*, 535–553.

Kintsch, W. (1998). *Comprehension: A paradigm for cognition*. Cambridge, UK: Cambridge University Press.

MacGinitie, W. H., MacGinitie, R. K., Maria, K., & Dreyer, L. G. (2000). *Gates-MacGinitie Reading Test* (4th ed.). Itasca, IL: Riverside.

Mandler, J. M., & Johnson, N. S. (1977). Remembrance of things parsed: Story structure and recall. *Cognitive Psychology, 9*, 111–151.

McKissack, P. C. (2003). *The honest-to-goodness truth*. New York: Aladdin Paperback.

Morrow, L. M. (1985). Retelling stories: A strategy for improving young children's comprehension concept of story structure, and oral language complexity. *Elementary School Journal, 85*, 646–660.

Narvaez, D. (2002). Individual differences that influence reading comprehension. In C. C. Block & M. Pressley (Eds.), *Comprehension instruction: Research-based best practices* (pp. 158–175). New York: Guilford Press.

Nelson, K. (1996). *Language in cognitive development: Emergence of the mediated mind*. New York: Cambridge University Press.

Palincsar, A. S. (1991). Scaffolded instruction of listening comprehension with first graders at risk for academic difficulty. In A. M. McKeough & J. L. Lupart (Eds.), *Toward the practice of theory-based instruction* (pp. 50–65). Mahwah, NJ: Erlbaum.

Palincsar, A. S., & Brown, A. L. (1984). Reciprocal teaching of comprehension-fostering and comprehension-monitoring activities. *Cognition and Instruction, 2*, 117–175.

Palincsar, A. S., David, Y., & Brown, A. L. (1992). *Using reciprocal teaching in the classroom: A guide for teachers*. Ann Arbor: University of Michigan Press.

Paris, S. G., Carpenter, R. D., Paris, A. H., & Hamilton, E. E. (2005). Spurious and genuine correlates of children's reading comprehension. In S. G. Paris & S. A. Stahl (Eds.), *Children's reading comprehension and assessment* (pp. 131–160). Mahwah, NJ: Erlbaum.

Paris, S. G., Lipson, M. Y., & Wixson, K. K. (1983). Becoming a strategic reader. *Contemporary Educational Psychology, 8*, 293–316.

Pearson, P. D., & Duke, N. K. (2002). Comprehension instruction in the primary grades. In C. C. Block & M. Pressley (Eds.), *Comprehension instruction: Research-based best practices* (pp. 247–258). New York: Guilford Press.

Pearson, P. D., & Johnson, D. D. (1978). *Teaching reading comprehension*. Orlando, FL: Holt, Rinehart & Winston.

Pinkwater, D. M. (1977). *The big orange splot*. New York: Scholastic.

Pressley, M. (2002). Comprehension strategies instruction: A turn of the century status report. In C. C. Block & M. Pressley (Eds.), *Comprehension instruction: Research-based best practices* (pp. 11–27). New York: Guilford Press.

Pressley, M., & Afflerbach, P. (1995). *Verbal protocols of reading: The nature of constructively responsive reading*. Mahwah, NJ: Erlbaum.

Pressley, M., El-Dinary, P. B., Gaskins, I., Schuder, T., Bergman, J. L., Almasi, J., et al. (1992). Beyond direct explanation: Transactional instruction of reading comprehension strategies. *Elementary School Journal, 92*, 513–555.

RAND Reading Study Group. (2002). *Reading for understanding: Toward an R & D program in reading comprehension*. Santa Monica, CA: RAND Corporation.

Rosenblatt, L. (1978). *The reader, the text, the poem: The transactional theory of the literary work*. Carbondale: Southern Illinois University Press.

Samuels, S. J. (1988). Decoding and automaticity: Helping poor readers become automatic at word recognition. *The Reading Teacher, 41,* 756–760.

Saunders, W. M., & Goldenberg, C. (1999). Effects of instructional conversations and literature logs on limited- and fluent-English-proficient students' story comprehension and thematic understanding. *Elementary School Journal, 99,* 279–301.

Schuder, T. (1993). The genesis of transactional strategies instruction in a reading program for at-risk students. *Elementary School Journal, 94,* 183–200.

Shin, J., Deno, S. L., & Espin, C. (2000). Technical adequacy of the maze task for curriculum-based measurement of reading growth. *Journal of Special Education, 34,* 164–172.

Shinn, M. R., Good, R. H., Knutson, N., Tilly, W. D., & Collins, V. L. (1992). Curriculum-based measurement of oral reading fluency: A confirmatory analysis of its relation to reading. *School Psychology Review, 21,* 459–479.

Snow, C. E. (2003). Assessment of reading comprehension: Researchers and practitioners helping themselves and each other. In A. P. Sweet & C. E. Snow (Eds.), *Rethinking reading comprehension* (pp. 192–206). New York: Guilford Press.

Stahl, K. A. D. (2004). Proof, practice, and promise: Comprehension strategy instruction in the primary grades. *The Reading Teacher, 57,* 598–609.

Stahl, S. A. (1999). *Vocabulary development.* Newton Upper Falls, MA: Brookline.

Stahl, S. A., & Hiebert, E. H. (2005). The "word factors": A problem for reading comprehension assessments. In S. G. Paris & S. A. Stahl (Eds.), *Children's reading comprehension and assessment* (pp. 161–186). Mahwah, NJ: Erlbaum.

Stahl, S. A., & Heubach, K. (2005). Fluency-oriented reading instruction. *Journal of Literacy Research, 37,* 25–60.

Stein, N. L., & Glenn, C. G. (1979). An analysis of story comprehension in elementary school children. In R. O. Freedle (Ed.), *New directions in discourse processing* (Vol. 2, pp. 53–120). Norwood, NJ: Ablex.

Taylor, B. M., Pearson, P. D., Clark, K., & Walpole, S. (2000). Effective schools and accomplished teachers: Lessons about primary grade reading instruction in low-income schools. *Elementary School Journal, 101,* 121–166.

Epilogue

Michael C. McKenna

The chapters in this volume illuminate the professional contributions of a rare and influential scholar, and the result has not been without surprises. The chapters written by Steve's colleagues to contextualize and extend his contributions convey important lessons that go well beyond the findings Steve produced and interpreted. Many of these lessons are about the issues he investigated, but there are less obvious lessons as well. By considering his key writings in the context of insightful commentary, we distill the essence of what exceptional scholarship requires. To be sure, teachers who have read this volume with care have been able to judge their classroom practice against a host of empirical insights. But researchers have been afforded a similar opportunity (perhaps an uncomfortable one), that of weighing their own approach to scholarship in a telling balance.

BREADTH AND DEPTH

Steve set a famously high standard in conducting investigations, but reading any specific study, or thread of studies, is unlikely to result in an appreciation of his overarching philosophy—that the conduct of research requires multiple areas of expertise. This collection is a testament to that philosophy.

After the death of Jeanne Chall, Steve's esteemed mentor, he wrote that her greatness derived from "her ability to situate the problem she was working on in a larger picture, and to use as broad a lens as possible, across a variety of disciplines, on that problem" (Stahl, 2000, p. 41). Steve shared this perspective, even though its rigors are considerable. A conventional view of scholarship holds that the depth of one's knowledge should be inversely proportional to the scope of the domain one claims. This view calls to mind the adage that specialists are individuals who know more and more about less and less until they know everything about nothing. This unfortunate trajectory is one that Steve scrupulously sought to avoid. He did not view it as the inevitable consequence of specialization because he saw such a goal as self-defeating. There is, he believed, a myopia inherent in too narrow a focus. Rather, he recognized the components of reading as a seamless web. Understanding one component requires an appreciation of others so that findings can be properly contextualized as part of a "larger picture." It is only in this way that fundamental errors of interpretation can be avoided. To extend Steve's own metaphor, the reading researcher needs not only a microscope but a wide-angle lens to view circumstances as they truly are.

This guiding principle, which he inherited from Chall, is part of a scholarly lineage that can be traced to Chall's own mentor, Edgar Dale. Dale advised Chall to conduct research in more than one area so that relationships across domains could be better understood. This advice may have been reasonable in the 1940s, when the body of educational research was modest. To adopt it today, amid the superabundance of available evidence, seems unthinkable. And yet for Steve, the question was never between breadth and depth. The question was how to attain both. To have a deep knowledge of any aspect of reading requires a thorough grounding in other dimensions as well. Otherwise, the specialist risks being blind to important interplay, and to contexts that may be explanatory. This is a rigorous epistemology, but Steve insisted that it was attainable if one is willing to devote the time and energy needed to realize it.

The benefits of framing research from a multidimensional perspective go beyond the ability to contextualize findings. They include the ability to combine in productive ways concepts from various domains. Examples abound in Steve's work, and several have been pointed out by the contributors to the present volume.

Scott G. Paris (see Chapter 22) points out that Steve's breadth permitted him to construct a model of assessment that integrated multiple domains in a logical manner. Steve and I used this model to ground our assessment text (McKenna & Stahl, 2003), and the result has permitted practitioners to analyze complex cases in a straightforward manner. Paris also reminds us that the model makes clear how the "simple view" of reading is in fact too simple—first in omitting the reader's strategic knowledge, and second by assuming that word recognition and comprehension are independent components when in fact their interrelationship is complex.

Linnea C. Ehri (see Chapter 10) observes that Steve's knowledge of stage (and phase) theory prompted him to suggest that various approaches to phonics instruction, long thought to constitute alternatives, should in reality be seen as complementary techniques. Thus, the letter-by-letter blending associated with synthetic phonics is appropriate near the beginning of the decoding stage, while onset-rime decoding is appropriate later on. Keith E. Stanovich and Paula J. Stanovich (see Chapter 3) conclude that Steve's knowledge of stage theory also permitted the nuanced interpretation of effect sizes in the Stahl–Miller meta-analysis.

Additional examples reveal an astonishing variety of combinations. They include vocabulary and comprehension (Nagy & Scott, Chapter 14), stage theory and comprehension (Hynd Shanahan, Chapter 21), phonological awareness and phonics (Murray, Chapter 8), comprehension and professional development (Taylor, Pearson, García, Stahl, & Bauer, Chapter 19), achievement and policy (Shanahan, Chapter 5), phonics and technology (Kuhn & Stahl, 2006), comprehension and fluency (Stahl & Heubach, 2005), fluency and phonics (Stahl, 2004), and vocabulary and fluency (Stahl & Nagy, 2005). Clearly Steve had reached the point at which knowledge of one area synergistically enriched his knowledge of others. Put differently, he had attained critical mass as a researcher, a condition that multiplied his insights (and his influence) exponentially.

METHODOLOGICAL VERSATILITY

Steve did not typically team with researchers who specialize in experimental design and statistical analysis. He preferred to master these skills himself so that he would be better situated to match questions of interest with appropriate designs and analyses. His work, including the cornerstone pieces collected in this volume, applies a variety of quantitative and qualitative approaches, though he much preferred the former. (He once quipped that as a Jew, he preferred the Book of Numbers to the Book of Revelations.)

While Steve insisted on methodological rigor, it was his versatility that defined his work. He was conversant with established approaches but enthusiastically applied new ones. He contributed to the early popularity of meta-analyses and vote-counting approaches, which he preferred to best-evidence syntheses, and he often explored relatively arcane statistics (e.g., McNemar's Test) if he believed they would lead him to the answers he sought. This versatility was enabled by a willingness to extend his knowledge, the same willingness that defined his broadly based approach to reading.

LINKS TO PRACTICE

Steve very much enjoyed working with children, especially in clinical settings, and he regarded doing so as key to becoming an insightful researcher. As Scott G. Paris has observed (see Chapter 22), his clinical work helped him refine his approach to assessment and to enrich his appreciation of stage theory. It also reinforced, firsthand, the efficacy of the methods he championed. No doubt it sharpened his cognizance of the human consequences of research when its results inform practice.

Steve questioned the appropriateness of investigations without a clear link to practice. Studies holding little or no promise for improving the lot of struggling readers raised his eyebrows and sometimes his ire. He likewise scolded those who used ill-conceived research to defend ineffective practice. Though politically liberal, he was critical of colleagues whom he believed had strayed too far from an achievement connection in the name of "liberating" disadvantaged children and of forwarding political agendas at the expense of learning. "My idea of a gender issue," he once remarked, "is why girls read better than boys."

For Steve, linkage to practice meant far more than investigating the effects of methods on achievement. It entailed a connection with practitioners as well. Steve's gift for clear and poignant writing allowed him to become not only a producer but an interpreter of research. He helped teachers make sense of confusing and sometimes conflicting findings by distilling the lessons that bear most reasonably on the matter of best practice. Both teachers and researchers can name important titles by Steve, but these two groups are unlikely to choose the *same* titles.

A LASTING LEGACY

Steve's legacy has many dimensions. His research has made reading instruction more effective. His critical commentaries have helped curb the excesses of ideology. His philosophy and methods have made him an exemplar of what a great researcher must be. But it is perhaps a rare combination of head and heart that makes his contributions indelible. To a person, the contributors to this volume acknowledge our debt to his insights and cherish the good fortune that made him our colleague, but we have created this book not only out of respect but out of love. Teachers who will never meet him owe Steve Stahl a debt of gratitude for enhancing their proficiency, and legions of children are better readers because he was their friend.

REFERENCES

Kuhn, M. R., & Stahl, S. A. (2006). More than skill and drill: Exploring the potential of computers in decoding and fluency instruction. In M. C. McKenna, L. D. Labbo, R. Kieffer, & D. Reinking (Eds.), *International handbook of literacy and technology* (Vol. 2, pp. 295–301). Mahwah, NJ: Erlbaum.

McKenna, M. C., & Stahl, S. A. (2003). *Assessment for reading instruction*. New York: Guilford Press.

Stahl, S. A. (2000). Jeanne S. Chall (1921–1999): An appreciation. *Educational Researcher, 29*(5), 41–43.

Stahl, S. A. (2004). What do we know about fluency? Findings of the National Reading Panel. In P. McCardle & V. Chhabra (Eds.), *The voice of evidence in reading research* (pp. 187–211). Baltimore: Brookes.

Stahl, S. A., & Heubach, K. M. (2005). Fluency-oriented reading instruction. *Journal of Literacy Research, 37,* 25–60.

Stahl, S. A., & Nagy, W. E. (2005). *Teaching word meanings*. Mahwah, NJ: Erlbaum.

Index

Page numbers followed by f indicate figure; t indicate table